The Business of
Events Management

The Business of Events Management

Edited by

John Beech
Sebastian Kaiser
Robert Kaspar

Harlow, England • London • New York • Boston • San Francisco • Toronto • Sydney • Auckland • Singapore • Hong Kong
Tokyo • Seoul • Taipei • New Delhi • Cape Town • São Paulo • Mexico City • Madrid • Amsterdam • Munich • Paris • Milan

PEARSON EDUCATION LIMITED
Edinburgh Gate
Harlow CM20 2JE
United Kingdom
Tel: +44 (0)1279 623623

Web: www.pearson.com/uk

First published 2014 (print)

© Pearson Education Limited 2014 (print and electronic)

ISBN: 978-0-273-75862-4 (print)
     978-0-273-75864-8 (PDF)
     978-0-273-78103-5 (eText)

British Library Cataloguing-in-Publication Data
A catalogue record for the print edition is available from the British Library

Library of Congress Cataloguing-in-Publication Data

The business of events management/edited by John Beech, Sebastian Kaiser and Robert Kaspar.
     p. cm.
   Includes index.
   ISBN 978-0-273-75862-4 – ISBN 978-0-273-75864-8 (PDF) –
ISBN 978-0-273-78103-5 (eText)
   1. Special events – Planning.   2. Special events – Management.   I. Beech, John G., 1947–, editor of compilation.
   GT3405.B87 2014
   394.2–dc23

                                        2013048292

10 9 8 7 6 5 4 3 2 1
16 15 14

Cover design by Alina Eckert
Cover photo: Spinning at the Calgary Stampede © James Boud, Flickr Vision

Print edition typeset in [10/12.5 pt and Sabon LT Std] by 75
Print edition printed and bound in Gosport by Ashford Colour Press Ltd

NOTE THAT ANY PAGE CROSS REFERENCES REFER TO THE PRINT EDITION

Brief contents

Contents

Part 2

Business functions applied to events 71

Part 3

Management issues specific to the events sector 163

Lecturer Resources

For password-protected online resources tailored to support the use of this textbook in teaching, please visit **www.pearsoned.co.uk/beech**

ON THE WEBSITE

Case studies

Preface

The world of events has changed significantly in recent years. Whether one considers the sports events sector, the cultural events sector or the business meetings and conferences sector, the sheer number of events taking place every year has grown, and the level of professionalism among practitioners has developed significantly.

Courses in Events Management are now offered in a wide number of universities throughout the world. They have proved to be particularly popular in both the English-speaking world and the German-speaking world.

Emerging in business schools, these courses have faced the difficult challenge of blending, on the one hand, the familiar studies of marketing, human resource management, finance and strategy with the very distinctive real world of events practitioners. For the first time, this text draws together the skills and knowledge of both academics and events practitioners, based in North America, the UK, Germany and Austria, as chapters on a range of specialist topics.

The editors themselves have between them considerable experience as academics in the events management field and in the practice of managing events.

Each of the chapters in this book contains the following elements:

- a statement of learning outcomes;
- a chapter overview;
- case studies;
- a conclusion;
- guided reading;
- recommended websites;
- key words;
- a bibliography.

Chapter 1 provides a guide to the rest of the book.

At the time of writing, all recommended websites were live. However, it may be the case that sites become inaccessible. In the event of this happening, readers are asked to contact the publisher with details of any problems.

The editors would like to thank all the Pearson Education staff who have been involved in the preparation of the book, and to acknowledge the support of their respective partners, Sue, Jasmina and Karoline. Robert would also like to acknowledge the inspiration of his daughter, Leonie.

Acknowledgements

We are grateful to the following for permission to reproduce copyright material:

Figures

Figure 6.4 from *Exploring Corporate Strategy: Text and Cases*, 6th edn, Prentice Hall (Johnson, G. & Scholes, K., 2002); Figure 8.1 adapted from 'Lessons Learned. Review of the 2002 Commonwealth Games in Manchester for DCMS, Sport England and Manchester City Council', Final report December 2002; Figure 8.3 adapted from *The Economics of Staging the Olympics. A Comparison of the Games 1972–2008*, Edward Elgar (Preuss, H., 2004), reproduced by permission of Edward Elgar Publishing Ltd and Dr H. Preuss; Figure 9.1 from *Event Management and Event Tourism*, 2nd edn, Cognizant (Getz, D. 2005) p. 7; Figure 9.2 from *Event Management and Event Tourism*, 2nd edn, Cognizant (Getz, D., 2005) p. 113; Figure 12.7 from *Eventmanagement – Veranstaltungen professionell zum Erfolg führen*, Springer (Holzbauer, U., Jettinger, E., Knauss, B., Moser, R. and Zeller, M., 2005), with kind permission of Springer Science+Business Media; Figure 12.9 from http://www.lautstark .at/, by permission of lautstark communications; Figure 14.2 from *The Tourism Area Life Cycle: Applications and Modifications* (Vol. 1), Channel View Publications (R. Butler (ed.), 2006) p. 5; Figure 17.1 from *Corporate Hospitality bei Sportevents – Konzeption eines Wirkungsmodells*, Gabler (Walzel, S., 2011) p. 11, with kind permission of Springer Science+Business Media; Figure 17.2 from *The International Sports Hospitality Market: unpublished research report* (Digel, H. & Fahrner, M. (2008).) p. 19.

Tables

Table 1.2 from *Statistical Bulletin: Marriages in England and Wales, 2010*, ONS (2012), source: Office for National Statistics licensed under the Open Government Licence v.1.0; Table 2.1 from *Megaevents and Modernity: Olympics and Expos in the Growth of Global Culture*, Routledge (Roche, M., 2000) Table 1.3, p .4, adapted from Hall 1989; IOC 1996a, p. 50; Table 5.1 adapted from 'Towards a typology of events venues', *International Journal of Event and Festival Management*, vol. 2(2), pp. 106–116 (Hassanien, A. and Dale, C., 2011); Table 5.2 from 'The Future of Meetings: The Case for Face-to-Face', *Cornell Hospitality Industry Perspectives* p. 13 (Duffy, C. and McEuen. M.B., 2010); Table 8.1 adapted from *The Sport Event Management and Marketing Playbook*, John Wiley & Sons (Supovitz, F., 2005); Table 14.1 from A Model of Destination Image Formation, *Annals of Tourism Research*, vol. 26(4), pp. 868–97 (Baloglu, S. and McCleary, K., 2011).

Text

Case study 6.2 from http://www.towerseyfestival.com/; Case study 8.1 adapted from www.cortina2019.it; Case study 12.1 from MK Marketing GmbH 2011, by permission of lautstark communications; Case study 12.2 from DMG Marketing GmbH 2009; Case study 17.2 from *Sales prospect: Official Hospitality Programme for the 2010 FIFA World Cup South Africa™*, Match Hospitality.

In some instances we have been unable to trace the owners of copyright material, and we would appreciate any information that would enable us to do so.

About the authors

John Beech (co-editor)

John is an Honorary Research Fellow at Coventry University, UK, where he was formerly the Head of Sport and Tourism. His other roles have included Visiting Professor at FH Kufstein Tirol, and the IE Business School, Madrid, Spain. He is an International Professor at the Russian International Olympic University, Sochi. With Simon Chadwick he is the co-editor of Pearson Education's *The Business of Sports Management, The Business of Tourism Management* and *The Marketing of Sports*. He is the author of Sage's *Doing Your Business Research Project,* and he has written numerous articles for both academic and professional journals. He broadcasts regularly on football finance and governance, and is an award-winning blogger on the (mis)management of football clubs.

Sebastian Kaiser (co-editor)

Sebastian is a Professor at SRH University Heidelberg, Germany. He is editor (Social Sciences) of the German *Journal of Sports Science* and (co-)author and editor of a range of books, book chapters and journal articles. Sebastian is an International Professor at the Russian International Olympic University, Sochi, and taught on various international study programmes, including Vrije Universiteit Brussel, German Sport University, Cologne, University of Florence and Charles University Prague. He headed the organising committee of the German Congress for Sport Economics and Sport Management (2006–8).

Robert Kaspar (co-editor)

Robert is Professor for Sports and Events Management at FH Kufstein Tirol. He has been Director of Studies for the Bachelor and Master degree programmes in Sports, Culture and Events Management since 2008; is an International Professor at the Russian International Olympic University, Sochi, and has been a guest lecturer in places as diverse as Croatia, Finland, France, New Zealand and Russia. Since 1994, he has served in a number of mega-event companies, ranging from Expos to World Championships, and acted as managing director for the Salzburg 2010 Olympic Winter Games bid. He has published widely in the field of mega events. (*www.robertkaspar.com*)

Ariane Bagusat

Ariane is a Professor of Sponsoring and Event Management at the Institute of Sport Management at the Ostfalia University of Applied Sciences, Germany, and course leader of the BA programme in Sport Management. Her main research interests are sponsoring, event management, customer relationship management and market research. She also works as a consultant in the field of market research, marketing consulting and customer relationship management for several national and international companies. (*www.drbagusatconsult.de*)

Louise Bielzer

Louise holds a Chair in Communication and Strategic Management at Karlshochschule International University, Karlsruhe, Germany. She is Head of Studies in the MEEC Management (Meetings, Exhibitions, Events and Conventions) programme, and an elected member of Karlshochschule's Senate. As Full Professor since 2007 at Karlshochschule, she is a regularly invited guest lecturer at universities in Italy, England and Austria.

Claire Burnill

Claire studied English and Drama Education at the University of Exeter and, following an extended period living, working and travelling throughout South and South East Asia, returned to the UK to complete her MSc in Development Studies at the University of Bath. During the course of studies at Bath she developed her interest in Cultural Studies. With articles published by Routledge and Springer, her research interests include audience development and cultural policy. Now living in Germany she lectures in Cultural Studies and English in Austria.

Rick Burton

Rick is the David B. Falk Professor of Sport Management at Syracuse University, USA. Prior to that, he served as the US Olympic Committee's chief marketing officer for the 2008 Beijing Summer Olympics, and was the Commissioner of the Australian National Basketball League in Sydney from 2003 to 2007. Rick is a frequent contributor to *Sports Business Journal* and *Sport Business International* and his first novel, a spy thriller entitled *The Darkest Mission,* was published by Long Reef Press in 2011.

Terri Byers

Terri is a Principal Lecturer in Sport Management at Coventry Business School and the Centre for the International Business of Sport (CIBS). She is an experienced researcher and consultant, with many publications on the structure and function of sport organisations. Terri provides strategic leadership for research in her department and is responsible for managing multiple research projects, research staff and students. Her latest project is an EU-funded trans-continental initiative called CARNIVAL, examining why mega events fail to deliver sustainable legacies. Her experience in event management is vast, ranging across small community-run events, fundraising for events, regional and national sporting events, volunteering and managing impacts of mega events.

Hilary S. Carty

Hilary is an independent consultant specialising in leadership development, management and organisational change. Former roles include Director, Cultural Leadership Programme UK; Director, London (Arts) at Arts Council England; and Director, Culture and Education at London 2012. A Visiting Professor at FH Kufstein Tirol, lecturing in Leadership and the Creative Industries, Hilary's work has been recognised with Honorary Doctorates from De Montfort and Middlesex Universities, and an Honorary Fellowship of Goldsmith's University of London.

Chris Chard

Chris is an Assistant Professor in the Department of Sport Management at Brock University in Ontario, Canada. Chris teaches classes related to financial and business management practices in the sport sector. His research interests focus on the sustainable management of sport, including environmental, financial and operational initiatives. Chris has published articles in journals such as the *Journal of Management and Sustainability, Sport Management Review, Case Studies in Sport Management,* and *The International Journal of Sustainability Policy and Practice.*

Rob Davidson

Rob is a Senior Lecturer in Events Management at the University of Greenwich in London, where he teaches in the London Centre for Events Management, within the Business School. His main areas of expertise are conferences and business events, and over the last ten years he has written widely on these themes in academic and professional publications. He also runs his own consultancy business, and has carried out research for a number of major conference organisations in the UK and overseas. For the past five years, he has been included in *Conference and Incentive Travel* magazine's 'Power 50' – the 50 most influential people in the UK conference industry.

Martin Egger

Martin has worked in the events management business since 1992, organising regional and international sport and corporate events in the DACH region. He is a part-time lecturer at FH Kufstein Tirol, New Design University, St Pölten, and the Russian International Olympic University Sochi with a special focus on events management, event marketing and finance. With a partner he runs an advertising agency in Vienna.

Samantha Gorse

Samantha holds a full-time research post at Coventry Business School in the Department of Sport and Event Management and the Centre for the International Business of Sport (CIBS). Her research interest for the past four years has focused specifically on the subject of corruption in sport. Her interest in events management concerns the commercialisation and ethical management of sports events and the relationship between sponsorship, corruption and impacts on the event product. She has published her work in academic journals and in a commercial consultancy report, commissioned by the RGA (Remote Gambling Association) and has attracted interest from media and other organisations across the globe including Danish-based 'Play the Game' and Transparency International.

Dominik Kocholl

Dominik is a Rechtsanwalt (attorney-at-law) specialising in business and sports law and Assistant Professor for Private Law, European Private Law, Private International Law and Sports Law at the University of Innsbruck. He lectures in Event Law at FH Kufstein Tirol – University of Applied Sciences in Austria/Tyrol. He has published books and over 60 articles/book chapters on Austrian and international law. He counsels event managers, speaks at international conferences and is an editor of the 'Causa Sport'. As a former World Cup athlete in Olympic sailing classes, he acts as a race official/manager/ judge and advises the Austrian Sailing Federation and other event-hosting sports organisations, e.g. in the field of mountaineering and skiing. (*www.kocholl.com*)

Martina Lettner

Martina is director of studies of the Marketing and Communication Management programme at FH Kufstein Tirol. Prior to joining the staff in Kufstein she worked as a journalist for the weekly news magazine *profil* in Vienna, winning the national award posted by the EU Parliament, together with her colleague Otmar Lahodynsky, in 2010. Media and political communications have fascinated her ever since. First, Martina studied Multi-media Arts in Salzburg, Austria (1999–2003), then she completed the Master's programme in Journalism and Mass Media at the European Academy of Journalism Vienna (2003–2005) and afterwards joined the International Photojournalism Class of Denmark's Journalism University in Aarhus (2005). After returning to Austria, she started working for *profil* and on her dissertation. In 2011, she completed her PhD in Communication Science at the University of Vienna.

Helmut Lux

Helmut is a sport scientist and sport manager by education, hence his special focuses on event organisation and tourism are on sport events. He is a part-time Lecturer at the IMC in Krems, where he teaches Project Management. His core themes are innovation as well as service quality. He works as a business consultant in Lower Austria.

Cheryl Mallen

Cheryl is an Associate Professor in the Department of Sport Management at Brock University in Ontario, Canada. Cheryl teaches classes related to sport facility management, sport events management and social sustainability. Cheryl has published articles focusing on sports facilities and event environmental sustainability in journals such as the *Journal of Sport Management, European Sport Management Quarterly, Sport Management Review* and the *Journal of Management and Sustainability*.

Scott McRoberts

Scott is the Director of Athletics and Recreation at the University of Toronto, Scarborough, Canada. He has served as an adjunct faculty member with university institutions in Austria, Canada and the USA. He has advised in several municipalities on the development of sport councils, and his published material has concentrated on events management and examining the relationship between sport and the environment.

Andreas Reiter

Andreas is Future Researcher and Consultant in Corporate Foresight. He is author of various books (*Mayflower Strategy, Forever Young*), and speaker at congresses and company meetings. Andreas is founder and Director of ZTB Zukunftsbüro, a company located in Vienna, Austria, focusing on strategic future issues and product development.

Lukas Rössler

Lukas is the founder of the Austrian New Media Agency Fosbury, where he follows the convergent philosophy of 'Events 2.0'. He combines real events with virtual worlds such as social media and mobile apps. He is a Lecturer at several Austrian and Swiss institutes, being known for his practical approach and cross-media thinking.

Martin Schnitzer

Martin is a Researcher and Lecturer at the Department of Sport Science at the University of Innsbruck, Austria. He has served in various positions in major sports events. He acted as CEO of the Innsbruck 2012 bid campaign for the Youth Olympic Games. Previously he held the position of Secretary General of the UEFA EURO 2008™ Host City Innsbruck, and is currently serving as Bid Director of the FIS Alpine Ski World Championship Candidate City of Cortina d'Ampezzo in Italy.

Norbert Schütte

Norbert is a Lecturer in Sport Management and Sport Sociology at the Johannes Gutenberg University, Mainz, Germany. The main area of his activity is the realisation of research projects on sociological and economic topics. He works mainly on the cost–benefit analysis of sport events, occupational field analysis of sport managers, professionalisation tendencies in the third sector and other themes of organisational change.

Stefan Walzel

Stefan works as a Senior Lecturer at the Institute of Sport Economics and Sport Management of the German Sport University, Cologne. His major research interests lie in sport marketing communications, corporate social responsibility in sport and sport event marketing.

Gernot Wolfram

Gernot is Professor of Arts Management at the MHMK University for Media and Communication in Berlin, and a Lecturer in Cultural Studies at FH Kufstein Tirol. He also works as an expert in cultural affairs within the Europe team of the European Commission in Germany. His research interests include synergetic cultural projects in the international field, and integration through cultural projects.

3G	'Third generation' of mobile telecommunications technology
AAA	American Accounting Association
AG	*Aktiengesellschaft*; roughly the equivalent in Germany, Austria and Switzerland of the UK's plc (*qv*)
ASA	Amateur Sports Association
ATM	Automated teller machine; a card-driven cash dispenser
B2B	Business-to-business
BBC	British Broadcasting Corporation; UK's public service broadcasting organisation
BCCI	Board of Control for Cricket in India
BEA	Break-even analysis
BEP	Break-even point
BGB	*Bürgerliches Gesetzbuch*; the German civil code of law, used as a template in a number of other countries
BGH	*Bundesgerichtshof*; German Federal Court of Justice (Germany's highest court)
BSC	Balanced scorecard
CAS	Court of Arbitration for Sports
CBE	Competency-based education
CBM	Cross-Border Marathon
CBS	Major US commercial broadcasting system; derived from its earlier (full) name of Colombia Broadcasting System
CEM	Corporate environmental management model
CEO	Chief Executive Officer
CFEE	Certified Festival and Events Executive
CIC	Convention Industry Council
CLM	Contract lifecycle management
CMP	Certified meeting professional
CNBC	Major US news broadcasting channel; derived from its earlier (full) name of Consumer News and Business Channel
CO_2	Carbon dioxide
COLF	City of London Festival
COMPEVENT	A Leonardo da Vinci-funded partnership project
CRM	Customer relationship management
CSEP	Certified Special Events Professional
CSR	Corporate social responsibility
CTHRC	Canadian Tourism Human Resource Council
DMC	Destination management company
DMO	Destination management organisation
e.V.	*eingetragener Verein*; legal status of a registered voluntary association in Germany
ECB	England and Wales Cricket Board
ECHR	European Convention on Human Rights
EIA	Events Industry Alliance
EMBOK	Event Management Body of Knowledge
EMICS	Event Management International Competency Standards
ESPN	A US-based global television network which specialises in sports broadcasting; derived from its full name of Entertainment and Sports Programming Network
EU	European Union

EUR	Abbreviation for the euro currency unit; alternatively designated as €
FASPO	*Fachverband der Sponsoring-Agenturen und -Dienstleiste*; German Sponsorship Association
FEI	*Fédération Equestre Internationale*; the international governing body for all Olympic equestrian disciplines
FIFA	*Fédération Internationale de Football Association*; association football's international governing body
FINA	*Fédération Internationale de Natation*; in English, International Swimming Federation
FIS	*Fédération Internationale de Ski*; the international body for snow sports
FRA	Financial ratio analysis
FSA	Financial statement analysis
GEO	Global Environment Outlook
GPS	Global positioning system
GSC	General service contractors
HR	Human resource(s); also used as an alternative for HRM
HRM	Human resource management
HSBC	Hong Kong and Shanghai Banking Corporation
IAAF	The International Association of Athletics Federations; the international governing body for the sport of athletics
ICC	International Chamber of Commerce
ICC	International Cricket Council
ICG	International Children's Games
ICL	Indian Cricket League
IEF	International Equestrian Federation
IEG	International Events Group
IF	International (Sport) Federation
IFEA	International Festivals and Events Association
IIHF	International Ice Hockey Federation
IOC	International Olympic Committee; the international governing body of the Olympic Games
IP	Intellectual property
IPCC	Intergovernmental Panel on Climate Change
IPL	Indian Premier League (cricket)
ISES	International Special Events Society
ISU	International Skating Union
IYOGOC	Innsbruck (2012) Youth Olympic Games Organising Committee
KPI	Key performance indicator
LCA	Life-cycle assessment
LEED	Leadership in Energy and Environmental Design
LEST	Local Employment Skills and Training programme
LTE	'Long-term evolution' – a standard for telecommunications devices
MBO	Management by objectives
MICE	Popular abbreviation of 'meetings, incentives, conferences, and exhibitions'
MMS	Multimedia messaging service
MOS	Margin of safety
NADA	Nationale Anti Doping Agentur (Deutschland); National Anti-Doping Agency (of Germany)
NFC	Near-field communication; a wireless communication technology
NFL	National Football League; the governing body for American football
NGO	Non-governmental organisation
NOC	National Olympic Committee
NPO	Non-profit organisation (also termed not-for-profit organisation)
OBE	Officer of the Most Excellent Order of the British Empire (a decoration for public service)

OC	Organising committee
OECD	Organisation for Economic Co-operation and Development
p.u.	per unit
PC	Personal computer
PCO	Professional conference organiser
PEST	Abbreviation for 'political, economic, social and technological'
PESTEL	Abbreviation for 'political, economic, social, technological, environmental and legal' (also Pestle)
PGA	Professional Golf Association
PLC	Product life cycle; in the UK, Public Limited Company, although frequently in lower case as 'plc'
QR	Stands for 'quick response; a QR code is a two-dimensional version of a bar code associated with mobile phone technology
RBV	Resource-based view
RFID	Radio-frequency identification
RFP	Request for a proposal
RIOL	Abbreviation for 'requirements, input, output and legacies'
ROE	Return on equity
ROI	Return on investment
SARS	Severe acute respiratory syndrome; often referred to in the media as 'bird flu'
SE-EPM	Sport Event Environmental Performance Measure
SHNC	Summer Hockey National Championships
SME	A small- or medium-sized enterprise
SMS	Short message service, widely used for texting with mobile phones
SO	Sports organisation
SOCOG	Sydney Organising Committee for the (2000) Olympic Games
SPC	Service profit chain
StGB	*Strafgesetzbuch*; the German criminal code of law
SWOT	Abbreviation for 'strengths, weaknesses, opportunities and threats'
TALC	Tourism area life cycle
TBL	Triple bottom line
TTL	Triple top line
UEFA	Union of European Football Associations
UK	United Kingdom
UNEP	United Nations Environment Programme
UNESCO	United Nations Educational, Scientific and Cultural Organisation
URL	Uniform resource locator
USA	United States of America
USP	Unique selling proposition
VANOC	Vancouver Organising Committee for the 2010 Olympic and Paralympic Winter Games
VIK	Value in kind; the payment for goods or more frequently services through goods or services rather than in money; used as a form of sponsorship
VIP	A 'very important person'
WADA	World Anti-Doping Agency
WBS	Work breakdown structure
WiFi	A system for exchanging data through radio waves
WTA	Women's Tennis Association

Chapter 1

Events management – an introduction

John Beech, Coventry University UK

Learning outcomes

Upon completion of this chapter the reader should be able to:

- understand how the study of events management has emerged from a number of different academic disciplines;
- identify the more common terms applied to particular **events**;
- explain the common characteristics of events;
- appreciate the wide range of events;
- understand the structure and rationale of the book.

Overview

This chapter fulfils two purposes. In the first part we begin by exploring the differing academic disciplines that the study of events management has emerged from. Next we investigate the different shades of meaning in the various terms that are used to identify particular types of events. In doing this, we begin to identify the characteristics of those events we would normally count as 'events' for the purpose of studying events management. This in turn leads us to consider how some of the largest events ever do not fit in the pattern normally ascribed to them.

The second part provides an outline of the structure and rationale of the rest of the book. In particular, the following sections of the remainder of the book are identified and briefly introduced:

- The events management context
- Business functions applied to events
- Management issues specific to events
- Trends in events management

Introduction

The study of events management in universities – study in the senses of both research and teaching – is a relatively new topic. While Leisure has a long history of academic study, its origins lay in a sociological approach, and it was only as recently as 1991 that the first taught course in Leisure Management in the UK was introduced at Coventry University.

As interest grew, more academics became involved in teaching the modules which were generally seen to be the appropriate ones to include in a Leisure Management programme. As this was a new degree programme, they came from different backgrounds, typically including Management, Sociology, (Town and Country) Planning, Human Geography and Anthropology. This proved both a help and a hindrance to the new topic – the variety of backgrounds provided a richness to the course content, but it also led to a weakness in the overall coherence. Over time, graduates from Leisure Management degrees started to progress to being lecturers, and the coherence of the topic began to grow.

At the same time, however, demand was growing for more specialised forms of Leisure Management, and courses began to appear in Tourism Management and Sports Management, and in yet more specialised areas such as Spa Management, Applied Golf Management and even Surf Management.

It soon became apparent that, even with seemingly different topics such as Tourism Management and Sports Management, there were areas of overlap – students shared modules in Sports Tourism and in Events Management. This conceptualisation is shown in Figure 1.1.

The emergence of Events Management saw the drawing in of lecturers with a previous background in either Tourism Management or Sports Management, together with a third stream, whose background was in Arts and Cultural Management, arguably yet another spin-off from the earlier Leisure Management.

This general pattern of development was repeated in other English-speaking countries such as Australia and New Zealand. In German-speaking countries such as Germany and Austria there was a similar evolution of Events Management, except that the two key drivers were Sports Management and Cultural Management rather than Sports Management and Tourism Management.

In most countries Creative Industries Management, which has obvious connections with Events Management, has evolved from Arts/Cultural Management.

Again this has been both a help and a hindrance. One particular hindrance has been the tendency to see Events Management through filters of either Sports Events Management or Cultural Events Management. There were also lecturers coming from another

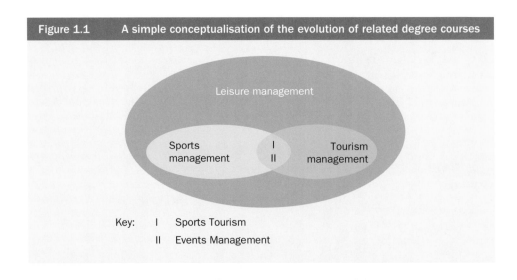

| Figure 1.1 | A simple conceptualisation of the evolution of related degree courses |

Leisure management

Sports management   I   Tourism management
                    II

Key: I   Sports Tourism
      II Events Management

subdivision of Tourism Management – Business Tourism Management. It is worth noting that ATLAS, an international organisation of universities engaged in teaching tourism, has special interest groups in Cultural Tourism, Business Tourism and Events. Because boundaries remain blurred and can change over time, it is common for individual lecturers to be members of more than one of these groups.

Does this blurring of subjects actually matter to you, the student? The short answer is a straightforward 'No, it doesn't!', yet it is important that you recognise the complex background from which Events Management has emerged and is continuing to move forward from. It is this complexity which explains why:

- Courses in Events Management in different universities often have different emphases on the types of event which they focus on.
- Individual lecturers who teach you may be more drawn towards one type of event than another.
- Case studies tend to be embedded in one area rather than focus on one overall generic kind of event, which in any case doesn't exist.

In briefing authors what kind of case studies they should write in their chapters, we suggested they should find cases across the following classifications:

1. Sports events;
2. Cultural events;
3. Business events (including conferences and trade fairs);
4. Other events.

The last of these, other events, might, in theory, cover an enormous and varied range of events. The range or scope which Events Management is generally seen to cover is limited. In the next section we will consider the characteristics of events which are generally included in Events Management, and why some other events are not normally included.

The scope of events management

At the simplest level, an **event** is simply something which happens. An event can thus range from a friend dropping round unexpectedly for coffee to a major sporting event such as the Summer Olympics, a major cultural event such as the Edinburgh or Salzburg Festivals, or a major conference such as the annual Davos Economic Summit or an annual political party conference.

In this book we have used the word 'event' generically. Language is rich, and a number of other terms are commonly used. These include:

- *Carnival*: a term often used to suggest public participation in creating the event. Examples include the Notting Hill Carnival and the Rio Carnival. A carnival is a celebratory event centred on public participation.
- *Conference*: a term which generally implies that the primary function of the event is the exchange of ideas, so commonly found in the academic and political worlds.
- *Convention*: very similar to conference, but with more emphasis on informal, rather than formal, interaction. Often used for gatherings of fans, as, for example, in Star Trek Convention, or of those of a particular sect or faith.
- *Exhibition*: an event which signifies a display of artefacts around a common theme, and hence related to the notion of a collection of artefacts. A term frequently used by museums and art galleries; the exhibition is thus a special event set in an appropriate and permanent venue of relevance to the nature of the contents being exhibited. The event celebrates the achievements of the artist or culture which is the focus of the event.

- *Expo*: a rather vague term that suggests that the event has a global content. Typically the event is built around pavilions representing the participating nations.
- *Fair*: often of mediaeval origins, the central theme is the trading of goods, now frequently with overtones of leisure activities. A trade fair carries forward the central feature of trading, within the restriction of a particular industry or sub-sector, but with very little emphasis on leisure side-shows.
- *Festival*: a term frequently used for an arts or cultural event; often applied to an umbrella event incorporating a series of related mini events.
- *Fête* (English): a small-scale event, typically at village level and usually held in the spring or summer, which normally has as its raison d'être fund-raising for a nominated charity.
- *Messe* (German): again often of mediaeval origin, a *messe* is essentially a trade fair. In its modern form, it has a permanent fully serviced venue.
- *Show*: A very difficult term to pin down! Events which use this term include the following: the Chelsea Flower Show, which provides an interface between amateur gardeners and the horticultural industry, and a series of prestigious competitions for amateur and professional gardeners; Crufts, where dog owners compete for prestigious best-of-breed and best-in-show awards; and the Geneva Motor Show, which goes beyond being a conventional trade fair as it showcases new cars to the public as well as journalists and other motor manufacturers. While the emphasis of a show is ostensibly on displaying, often it is the associated competitions which give the show its status among cognoscenti.

The last term, show, in particular demonstrates the difficulty as defining these terms in mutually exclusive ways. Rather than attempting to define prescriptive definitions of them, each group tends to define itself descriptively, and the event's choice of term to describe itself is what matters. Some events have evolved with either no descriptive term, such as the New Orleans Mardi Gras (which is French for Fat Tuesday, an allusion to the fact that it celebrates the last day before the restrictions of Lent) or Preston Guild (a unique civic celebration held in Preston, Lancashire, once every 20 years, most recently in 2012 – see Case 1.1).

By comparing the extreme forms of events, a number of critical differences appear. As we will be looking at events which are large-scale and which have a commercial dimension rather than having an in-depth look at your friend's unexpected arrival for coffee, let us set out the crucial characteristics which distinguish the former group. For us, an event can be characterised in the following ways:

Events need managing

By adopting this parameter we exclude the spontaneous event of a friend calling round, but we still include events like a children's birthday party, or a street party to celebrate Queen Elizabeth II's Diamond Jubilee.

Events occur on a scale where lack of management might lead to chaos

At some point, as an event grows in size, the need to manage it – to use the classical definition of management formulated by Fayol (1916), the processes of planning, leading, organising and controlling – becomes essential. Because it is essential, it does not always follow that it actually happens, as Case 1.2 shows.

Although the larger events listed in Table 1.1 in Case 1.2 do not lend themselves to the tight management practices of a sporting World Cup or an arts festival such as the Salzburg festival, they have some management functions embedded in them, specifically those that surround the need for security and other emergency services to be

THE SCOPE OF EVENTS MANAGEMENT

| Case 1.1 | 'Once every Preston Guild' |

The expression 'once every Preston Guild' used to be widely used to mean very infrequently, as in once in a blue moon. It refers to an event which has been held in the northern English city of Preston every 20 years since 1542 (with a single exception during the Second World War) and irregularly before that since at least 1328.

The website for the event notes: 'Held only once every twenty years, the Guild plays an important role in the development of Preston as a thriving and important Lancashire city. The changing times mean that each Guild has its own identity but shares a heritage of over 800 years.' Its origins lie in the time when each trade guild held and protected a monopoly on the right to trade. The event thus was in part a trade fair, but also in part a celebration. Today's event has a wider remit, and, because of its infrequency, it plays a part in retaining links with the diaspora of erstwhile Preston citizens.

Preston Guild 2012 retained key elements that have characterised previous Guilds, such as the formal proclamations, the holding of a Guild Court, formal processions and church services, and a Mayoral Ball. For the first time, in 2012, ceremonies included the admission of Honorary Burgesses to the Guilds. Nominations for this title were sought from those who have contributed to life in Preston. Perhaps surprisingly in the 21st century, those who are elected will pass their status as a burgess on to their sons and daughters.

Throughout the summer of 2012 a series of less formal events took place. These included cultural events, such as a Mela (a festival celebrating South East Asian culture) and a Caribbean Festival, and more traditional events such as a carnival King and Queen competition and the Annual Whit Fair. Sports-related events had a prominence in 2012, including an Olympic Torch Relay event, and were related to the fact that Preston was the designated UK European City of Sport in 2012. There was also an emphasis on encouraging the people of Preston to organise their own community events and street parties, an event planning toolkit being available from the organisers of the Guild. Preston citizens could volunteer as Guilders, and participate in the four major processions: the Trades Procession, the Churches Procession, the Community Procession and the Torchlight Procession.

The organisers were a team called the Guild 2012 Team who operated within Preston City Council.

Sources: various including *http://www.prestonguild2012.com*

Discussion questions

1 What challenges does managing an event which takes place on a 20-year fixed cycle pose?
2 What challenges does managing an 800-year old event pose?

---

involved. This separation between external management as opposed to internal management by the event organiser can be seen at all levels of events management – at football matches in the UK, for example, policing is left to volunteer stewards within the stadium and the police everywhere else, and First Aid is contracted out to the St John Ambulance Brigade, a registered charity.

■ Events operate in a commercial environment requiring a budget

Unless the organiser has an infinitely deep pocket, any kind of event is going to be financially constrained within a budget. Consider, for example, the case of arranging a wedding and its associated reception. Traditionally, in most societies, this has been within the remit of the bride's parents. They will lay down limits on spending. They will interact with external organisations such as caterers and florists, but crucially they will retain direct control of the development of the event.

■ Events require the event organiser to engage with the consumers of the event

As, to continue with the same example, weddings have grown in size, in terms of the number of guests, and budget, so their complexity has grown, and a new profession has emerged – the professional wedding organiser. While the family will agree a budget with

Case 1.2 The world's largest events

Which are the world's largest events? If we count the number of people participating in an event, Table 1.1 shows the all-time Top Ten.

The figures in Table 1.1 are of course estimates, and subject to a high level of uncertainty. The more recent events probably have more accurate estimates since the development of the use of aerial photography. A precise head-count is made of a measurable area within the photograph, and then this is scaled up for the total area.

Some readers may find this list surprising. Among the characteristics of the events listed are:

- They tend to be religious events and include many funerals.
- Ownership of the event lies with a non-commercial organisation, and there is an absence of any profit imperative.
- They generally have taken place in Asia rather Europe or North America.
- There is only limited evidence that big events are getting even bigger.
- What we more normally think of as big events, such as the Summer Olympic Games and the FIFA World Cup, do not feature in the Top Ten.

One obvious reason that sports mega events do not feature in this list is that their size is attributable not to **spectators** at the event but to the numbers of people who watch the event live on television.

Nielsen Media (2008) estimated that 4.7 billion **viewers** (70% of the world's population) tuned in to watch the Beijing Summer Olympics. This is an increase on the 3.9 billion who watched the 2004 Athens Games, and the 3.6 billion who watched the 2000 Sydney Games on television. Estimates for London 2012 were that the Beijing viewing figures had been exceeded.

Estimating viewing figures is an even more inexact science than estimating the numbers in crowds, which with aerial photography can be reasonably accurate. FIFA's claim of a billion viewers for the 2006 FIFA World Cup was challenged as wildly inflated (Harris, 2007), and FIFA was forced 'to admit yesterday that numbers up to now have been massively exaggerated in some cases, and simply guessed in others.' FIFA responded saying that they would only use verifiable data in future and 'We are going to steer clear of estimating, and publish data from audited measurement systems only'.

More recently, Sreenivasan (2011) rejected projections of 2 billion viewers for the Prince William–Kate Middleton wedding as decidedly unrealistic.

Even allowing for exaggerated estimates, it is clear that the world's largest events are unarguably large in comparison with the events we are more likely to experience normally.

Table 1.1 Top ten events by participation

Rank	Event	Year	Country	Participants
1.	Ardh Kumbh Mela	2007	India	70m Hindus
2. =	Simhastha Kumbh Mela	2004	India	30m Hindus
2. =	Maha Kumbh Mela	2013	India	30m Hindus
4.	C.N. Annadurai Funeral	1969	India	15m
5.	Mass Gatherings of Red Guards	1966	China	11m
6.	Arbaeen Anniversary	2009	Iraq	9m Shiite Muslims
7.	Sabarimala Pilgrimage	2007	India	5m Hindus
8.	World Youth Day	1995	Manila	4m Catholics
9.	Ayatollah Khomeini Funeral	1989	Iran	2m to 9m
10.	Pope John Paul II Funeral	2005	Vatican City	2m to 4m

Notes: Ardh Kumbh Mela occurs every six years; Simhastha Kumbh Mela occurs every 12 years; the Sabarimala Pilgrimage occurs annually (other sources give much higher numbers of participants). Mela is a Sanskrit word meaning gathering, often of a celebratory nature.

Sources: various, including http://www.siena.org/October-2010/what-are-the-ten-largest-gatherings-of-people-ever

Discussion questions

3 What vested interests are there in over-estimating numbers? Are there vested interests in under-estimating at times?

4 What particular issues are there with estimating viewers globally?

the wedding organiser, the wedding organiser takes overall control of the day-to-day planning and organisation. For this to work, there will need to be continuous liaison and consultation between the parents and the wedding organiser.

While the arrangements remain a labour of love for the parents, for the wedding organiser they are part and parcel of the mainstream of their business. However, perhaps more than in most businesses, the organisers need to be sensitive to the needs of their customers if they wish to develop and grow their business – a badly organised wedding would destroy their reputation very quickly through bad word-of-mouth advertising. Their business, as is the case with all events, is especially challenging in that they have only one opportunity to get their product right. Note that we have moved considerably away from the scenario of a friend dropping in for coffee, where there will be many other opportunities to get it right, and in any case there is little chance of getting it badly wrong.

The example of wedding organisers is explored in Case 1.3.

Case 1.3   The wedding event market in the UK

The number of marriages in 2010, the most recent year for which records are available, was almost a quarter of a million. For the first time, the number of civil ceremonies topped two-thirds of all marriages. The peak age range in which people got married was from 25 to 29. The largest percentage increase in numbers from 2009 to 2010 was for men aged 45 to 49 and women aged 30 to 34, both rising by 6%.

Following the passing of the Marriage Act 1994, there was a fundamental change in where marriages were allowed to take place. Until then, they could only take place in churches or in Registry Offices, the local state outlet for civil ceremonies. The Act allowed weddings to take place in premises which had been given official approval. Unsurprisingly, the number of locations which sought and gained approval has grown rapidly as weddings offer the venue an additional revenue stream. A searchable index at http://www.weddingvenues.com/ gives an idea of the number and range of approved venues. At the time of writing there were 429 in the Greater London area alone.

Table 1.2 gives some basic annual data on weddings at five-year intervals from 1989 for England and Wales.

The data in Table 1.2 shows a number of trends:

1. the number of weddings each year is tending to decrease slowly but

2. there is a distinct move towards holding weddings in approved premises, and away from Christian churches in particular and

3. the number of ceremonies which are religious but non-Christian is growing steadily.

Table 1.2   Numbers of weddings in England and Wales

England and Wales		Numbers						
		With civil ceremonies		With religious ceremonies				
Selected years	All marriages	All	Approved premises	All	Church of England and Church in Wales	Roman Catholic	Other Christian denominations	Other
2009	232,443	155,950	111,313	76,493	56,236	8,426	8,973	2,858
2004	273,069	184,913	85,154	88,156	62,006	9,850	13,578	2,722
1999	263,515	162,679	37,709	100,836	67,219	12,399	18,690	2,528
1994	291,069	152,113	..	138,956	90,703	16,429	29,807	2,017
1989	346,697	166,651	..	180,046	118,956	23,737	35,551	1,802

Source: http://www.ons.gov.uk/ons/rel/vsob1/marriages-in-england-and-wales-provisional-/2010/rtd-area-of-occurrence-type-of-ceremony-and-denomination.xls

Case 1.3 *(continued)*

While the overall decrease in numbers is not good news for professional wedding organisers, the second and third trends present opportunities for them. Religious but non-Christian ceremonies, which are often considerably larger in terms of the number of invited guests, have become the focus of specialist wedding organisers (see, as examples, *http://www.redhotcurry.com/weddings/wedding_planner.htm* and *http://www.occasianz.com/asian-wedding-planning-coordination*).

Another specialist market which is being developed is the organisation of weddings abroad (see *http://www.confetti.co.uk/article/view/4964-8185-0-How_to_plan_a_wedding_abroad_Getting_Married_Abroad.do* as a UK example, and *http://www.globalweddings.com.au/* as an Australian example). Even mainstream tour operators like TUI Thomson and Thomas Cook are engaging with this market (see *http://www.thomson.co.uk/editorial/weddings/weddings-abroad.html* and *http://www.thomascook.com/holidays/weddings/*).

One further specialist market which is growing has evolved since changes in the law in many countries – Denmark (1989), the Netherlands (2001), Belgium (2003), Spain (2005), the UK (2005), Norway (2009) and Sweden (2009), for example – have allowed same-sex civil partnerships (Ross, Gask and Berrington, 2011). An example of a professional wedding organiser specialising in this segment is the Gay Wedding Organiser (see *http://www.gayweddingorganizer.co.uk/*).

Reasons why there has been a growth in the number of professional organisers, a profession which is a relatively recently founded one, include the general growth in the scale of weddings and the number of guests invited, and thus in the amount of money that is spent on each wedding. Table 1.3 gives two broadly similar sets of estimates of the cost of an average wedding.

Table 1.3   Wedding costs

Item	Weddingsday.com	WeddingGuideUK.com
Insurance	£110	£50
The service	£520	£200
Reception (venue, food and drinks)	£4,000	£2,750
Evening reception (venue, food and drinks, entertainment, decorations)	£3,050	£2,000
Flowers	£685	£275
The bride's outfit	£1,590	£975
Hair and beauty	£170	£75
The groom's outfit	£200	£150
Attendants' outfits	£575	£500
Photography	£905	£400
Videography	£905	£400
Transport	£480	£300
Stationery	£465	£300
The wedding cake	£370	£200
Wedding rings	£630	£350
The bride's going away outfit		£150
Stag and hen nights	£280	
Honeymoon and first night hotel	£3,400	£1,625
Other expenses	£205	£300
TOTAL	£18,540	£11,000

Discussion questions

5 What are the advantages and disadvantages to the family of a couple who are planning their wedding in engaging a professional wedding organiser?

6 How might a professional wedding organiser expand their business by covering other events?

■ **Events involve external stakeholders beyond the event producer and the event visitor**

We have already noted in our developing example of the wedding as an event the presence of external **stakeholders**. At an immediate level there are the caterers and the florist. At another level there may be a professional wedding organiser, to whom the management of the event has, in effect, been subcontracted.

As we move up the scale of events in terms of their size, we see the emergence of more external stakeholders. Let us compare our wedding plans with those who organised the wedding of Prince William and Kate Middleton. The plans will certainly have included caterers and florists. Obviously the police have a vested interest in the organisation of the event. The media need to be allowed for, both those from the press and those from broadcasters. Negotiations will have taken place with both local councils and, for such a significant event, the government. Souvenir producers will have been preparing their goods for some considerable time before the event, and will be selling them at the event. The only stakeholder group that has not yet become involved is sponsors.

While this exploration of the pragmatic limits which determine whether an event falls inside or outside a descriptive definition of an event has been developed around the wedding event, this is a far from typical event, even though it coincides with the generally accepted view within the events industry and the world of Events Management academia.

We have advanced a long way from our initial definition of an event as something which happens. The main characteristics of the events with which we will concern ourselves can be summarised as:

■ built around a clear and distinct theme, which has the potential to develop into a brand, which has an underpinning rationale associated with it;
■ large enough to be impossible without management (both the process and the people);
■ having a planning phase and an operational phase;
■ having a requirement to make a profit, or at least to break even after all subsidies have been accounted for;
■ the participation of spectators, and, in the case of larger events, viewers of broadcasts;
■ happening in a commercial environment involving external stakeholders;
■ requiring proactive interaction between the organiser(s) and other stakeholders.

For the purposes of this book, and to follow the conventional focus in universities offering Events Management courses, we will classify events into three main categories:

1. sports events;
2. cultural and arts events;
3. business events, including trade fairs and conferences.

To these must be added a fourth category of miscellaneous events to allow for the inclusion of religious ceremonies and political events, for example.

All these events share many common characteristics, especially with respect to the way they are organised and managed. These we will now review in setting out the format of this book and its underpinning rationale.

The rationale and format of this book

The main part of this book is divided into four sections, which cover a variety of topics relevant to the business of events management. The first three are:

1. the events management context;
2. business functions applied to events;
3. management issues specific to the events sector.

A concluding section provides a view of the directions in which events and events management are moving from a practitioner's perspective.

The events management context

This section begins with a chapter on the **dimensions of events management** (Chapter 2). In particular, the various ways of classifying events are investigated. Next there is a chapter on the basic **theories and models** (Chapter 3) used in events management. This explores the ways in which different academic disciplines have been used in approaching events management, and discusses the extent to which events management might be considered a discipline in its own right. It also looks at the requirements for training suitable managers in terms of the skills and competences they actually need. There follows a pair of chapters which outline two particular types of event. The first of these is on **sports and cultural events** (Chapter 4), and the second covers **corporate events** (Chapter 5). As well as the more obvious differences between these types of events, the similarities and commonalities are discussed.

Business functions applied to events

This section takes a systematic tour of events management from the different perspectives of the functions which together make up the study and practice of management. We begin with a chapter on **human resource management** (Chapter 6) both in general and with particular reference to **volunteers,** upon whom so many events depend. Next we turn our attention to **marketing** (Chapter 7) and the more specialist form of marketing that is particularly important in the context of events, **destination branding**. In many cases events and the city in which they take place have become almost synonymous. It is difficult, for example, to think of Rio de Janeiro without thinking of the Rio Carnival. Much the same is true of New Orleans and Mardi Gras, or Edinburgh and its eponymous Festival. In the case of cultural events this close connection is because the city was the birthplace of the person the event celebrates. A classic example here is the Bayreuth Festival, held in the birthplace of Richard Wagner. From marketing we turn to the world of **finance** (Chapter 8). The chapter looks at both the softer issues of context as well as the more specific tools available for financial management. Finally in this section we investigate **events planning and strategy** (Chapter 9). Here the various business functions are woven together and a broader overview of both the event's internal operation and its operation in the external business environment are considered.

Management issues specific to the events sector

In the last section the emphasis was on the similarities between management in general and management in the events sector. In this third section, we explore how management in the events sector is arguably different to general management. In some cases, events management needs a shift in emphasis within the particular business function, and in others events management has its own special topics within a business function. There is thus a shift away from the mainstream management theories explored in the second section, and a move towards topics that, while essentially still management topics, might seem out of place in a general business management textbook.

We begin with a look at the topic of **sustainable events management** (Chapter 10). The key theoretical aspects of sustainability are set out, together with the practical tools necessary for measuring and controlling sustainable practices. From sustainability we move on to **the law and risk management** (Chapter 11). This topic is of particular importance in the management of events because of the high concentration of members of the public at an event, a phenomenon which is rather more unusual in other business sectors. We turn next to **event operations and project management** (Chapter 12). Here the heart of an event is explored from a practical perspective, and the various tools necessary for successful planning of operations are discussed. **New media technologies** (Chapter 13) present both an opportunity and a challenge to managers in the events sector. The reader is left in no doubt as to how exactly the internet age has impacted so significantly on events management. The limited life of an event, even when both the pre-event and post-event phases are considered along with the event itself, leads us to a look at the **event life cycle** (Chapter 14) and its relevance to the various **stakeholders** in an event. Next we turn our attention to one of those stakeholders – the **venue** (Chapter 15). Increasingly events are being justified because of their intended legacy, and the impacts – economic, socio-cultural and environmental – they have, so a particularly significant feature of the events management landscape is the process of **impact evaluation** (Chapter 16). The difficult prospect of fair and neutral evaluation techniques is explored through practical case examples. The events sector has an intractable link with the **hospitality industry** (Chapter 17) and this is naturally included in our coverage.

Next we turn in Chapter 18 to perhaps the key to any successful event – its **creation and design**. A systematic approach is presented, using the principles of a creative lens to develop the events theme and a design lens to develop the event concept. In Chapter 19 the relatively new topic of **events in public spaces** is explained. Finally in this section Chapter 20 covers the increasingly important topic of **sponsorship,** both as a necessary source of funding for the event organiser and as an investment for the sponsor.

▪ Conclusion section

The single chapter in this section (Chapter 21) provides an overview and commentary on current **trends in events management** from a practitioner's perspective.

Conclusion

As the study and practice of events management continue to develop, it has become clear that certain conventions have evolved, in particular regarding what actually constitutes an event that falls within our field of study. The focus of most current courses is with sports, cultural and business events. While this textbook sees no reason to shift from that focus, it aims to be more embracing in what forms of event are worthy of study and practical management. It is, in that sense, both traditional in its scope, yet more embracing in its coverage of events.

Guided reading

Throughout the book, each chapter contains recommendations for guided reading, and it makes more sense for readers and students to consult the guided reading for each chapter.

That said, there are academic journals which should be read and consulted. It is good practice to monitor their regular new issues in terms of the specific articles published in them. These include:

Event Management

International Journal of Event and Festival Management

International Journal of Hospitality and Event Management

Journal of Convention and Event Tourism

Journals outside the narrow confines of events management frequently publish articles of obvious relevance to events management, and may even publish entire special issues devoted to events. Good examples of such journals are:

Cultural Trends

European Sport Management Quarterly

International Journal of Arts Management

Managing Leisure

Recommended websites

Again the reader is referred to the more focused recommendations in the corresponding section of each of the following chapters.

An events management blog associated with this book is being developed at **http://eventmanagement.blog.com/**. It includes a webpage of useful links.

A regularly updated news portal to support users of this book is available free of charge at **http://www.scoop.it/t/the-business-of-events-management**.

Key words

event; spectator; stakeholder; viewer

Bibliography

Fayol, H. (1916) *Administration Industrielle et Générale*. Paris: Dunod.

Harris, N. (2007) Why FIFA's claim of one billion TV viewers was a quarter right. *The Independent* [London], 1 March.

Nielsen Media (2008) Beijing Olympics draw largest ever global TV audience. 5 September. **http://blog.nielsen.com/nielsenwire/media_entertainment/beijing-olympics-draw-largest-ever-global-tv-audience**

Ross, H., Gask, K. and Berrington, A. (2011) *Civil Partnerships Five Years On*. London: Office for National Statistics.

Sreenivasan, Hari (2011) 2 billion Royal Wedding viewers? Was it or wasn't it? *PBS Newshour*, 29 April. **www.pbs.org/newshour/rundown/2011/04/2-billion-royal-wedding-viewers-really.html**

Part 1
The events management context

Chapter 2

The dimensions of events management

Robert Kaspar, FH Kufstein Tirol – University of Applied Sciences, Austria

Learning outcomes

Upon completion of this chapter the reader should be able to:

■ describe the new school of differentiation of **place events** versus **mobile events**;

■ understand the financial dimensions of mega, macro and micro events;

■ differentiate between creative and standardised events;

■ outline the categories of events (sports, culture, business and society);

■ explain the role of the stakeholders and shareholders in designing event strategies.

Overview

The chapter starts with a discussion of the author's suggested new school of differentiation between place and mobile events.

Place events are events that happen again and again in the same place and thus the place is associated with the event. It may have historic origins or have developed as a result of a clever strategy to host the same event in the same place on a very regular basis (most often annually). Naturally many events that fall in this category also take place elsewhere around the world.

A very special dimension of place events is events that have formed joint brands with the destination, such as the New York Marathon, the Geneva Motor Show, the Holmenkollen Ski Jumping Event or the Monte Carlo Formula 1 Grand Prix.

On the exclusive side, some place events are even unique to a place (such as the Rio Carnival, the Munich Oktoberfest, the Vienna Opera Ball), occur on an annual or very regular basis, and contribute to the place making and the unique selling proposition (USP) of the destination; they can even become franchised around the world.

Mobile events move from destination to destination in a national, international or global context. In today's competitive world, cities, regions and nations compete in attracting mobile events whose rights are usually held by stakeholders such as international sports federations, political institutions (e.g. the European Commission) or other important stakeholders such as the Bureau Internationale des Expositions or the European Broadcasting Corporation.

Nevertheless, there is an ongoing debate on finding event dimensions in order to distinguish between micro, macro and mega events. This chapter focuses on the organising committee's core budget for the event as the key criterion.

The Big Five mega events have a major impact on the host nation from the infrastructure as well as from the budget point of view. It is suggested that only these five – the Olympic Summer Games, the FIFA World Cup and the UEFA European Football Championships, the World EXPO and the Eurovision Song Contest – legitimise this attribute by their wide impact on the host nation and their truly international reach.

A further important factor is whether the event is standardised and defined by key stakeholders (for example, most sports events are guided by their national or international federation's rule books), or whether it can be created and designed without any restrictions (for example, cultural festivals).

Naturally, events are distinguished by category. While sports events dominate the global television arena, cultural events have a significant impact on the identity of a destination. Society events have a major impact on society, are large in number, and can be staged even in the smallest country villages in the 'back of beyond'. Business events, ranging from world congresses to small company events, are either revenue-driven or designed to impact on customers, the media or other stakeholders.

The chapter concludes with a short discussion on the fit between events and the destination brand, and how important it is to bring all stakeholders on board when designing an integrated local/regional/national events strategy.

Introduction to event dimensions – the old school approach

Events have always had a smaller or larger impact on local residents or even on nations. Smaller society events have had a major role in rites and traditions whereas the more organised forms of, in particular, sports events have grown in size and number with the availability of live television coverage in the last few decades.

The scientific debate on event dimensions and event impacts has seen many interpretations over the past decades. The range of different terms, e.g. hallmark events, special events and major events, proves this divergence. The following section gives an overview of the discussions and the terms used to date.

Hallmark tourist events are major fairs, expositions, cultural and sporting events of international status which are held on either a regular or a one-off basis. A primary function of the hallmark event is to provide the host community with an opportunity to secure high prominence in the tourism market place.

(Hall, 1989: 263)

A definition which is used not only in academic contexts but also by practitioners is that of Ritchie (1984). He defines hallmark events as

major one-time or recurring events of limited duration, developed primarily to enhance the awareness, appeal and profitability of a tourist destination in the short and/or long term. Such events rely for their success on uniqueness, status, or timely significance to create interest and attract attention.

(Ritchie, 1984: 2)

Getz (2005) defines the uniqueness of an event by its duration, setting, management and people. An event is described as being temporary, either one-time or periodic. Although an event can be recurring it is still specified as a unique experience for all stakeholders due to the fact of its changing characteristics. Getz segments events into the categories of mega, hallmark, major and minor according to their economic impact on the host community and destination, their coverage in the media, the level of indicated tourism appearance and number of visitors (Getz, 2005: 1ff.).

In line with the characteristics of the previous definition is that of Roche. He specifies mega events as 'large-scale cultural (including commercial and sporting) events, which have a dramatic character, mass popular appeal and international significance' (Roche, 2000: 1). On the basis of these characteristics he further divides events into special, hallmark and community events. Table 2.1 gives a detailed overview.

Table 2.1	Event types		
Event type	Example	Target market	Media coverage
Mega event	Expos, Olympic Games, FIFA World Cup	Global	Global TV
Special event	Grand Prix (F1), Pan American Games (international sport event)	Global, national	International and/or national TV
Hallmark event	Australian Games (national sport event), large-scale sport festivals	National, regional	National TV, local TV
Community event	Local events	Regional, local	Local TV, press, local press

Source: Roche, 2000: 4

Whereas those definitions focus on the term mega event, Burns and Mules (1986) coined the term 'special events' for those with the following four characteristics:

1. The major demand generated by the special event is, for the most part, not the demand for the event itself, but the demand for a range of related services – typically accommodation, food, transport and entertainment.
2. This demand is condensed into a relatively short period of time, from a single day to a few weeks, and, as services cannot be produced ahead of time and stored, this leads to the typical 'peaking' problems experienced in the main service industries mentioned.
3. 'Peaking' influences both the level and the distribution of benefits received.
4. The net impact of redirecting local funds towards Special Events is relatively small; the major benefits arise from the attraction of new funds from outside the regions by way of goods and services, especially services.

As can be seen from the above literature review, there is a major controversy on which factors legitimise an event as being ranked in a smaller or larger category. Some authors include the number of participants as a key issue, thus depriving two of the Big Five mega events, namely the football competitions, of their mega event status (because their number of participants is limited to the number of players in each team times the number of qualifying nations). Also, any small city marathon will have a great many more active participants compared to the football events and number of participants should thus not be considered a valid factor in categorising events.

New perspectives of event dimensions – the new school approach

Definitions of segmenting events as discussed above have their limitations in complexity when using statistical data. On the basis of the debate on current variations in the literature, the author suggests some new perspectives of event dimensions.

■ Mobile vs. place events

As a new perspective the author suggests the differentiation between place and mobile events.

Mobile events take place in different host cities at each edition of the event and are mobile in nature. They are normally regulated and standardised in the event format by the event property owner and leave only a certain amount of autonomy to the local organising committee.

Place events happen in the same place on a regular basis and thus become increasingly associated with the place after each edition of the event.

In a best case scenario the event and the place have built a joint brand. Examples of jointly branded events range from sport events (e.g. the New York City Marathon), to cultural events (e.g. the Cannes Film Festival, Berlinale), to business (e.g. the Detroit Auto Show) and to society events. In a very few cases, the event is unique to a place and is franchised to other places or copied. Famous examples are the Rio de Janeiro Carnival, the Munich Oktoberfest and the Vienna Opera Ball.

Mobile events can be found in all categories from sports to cultural, business and society events. The Olympic Summer Games have rotated ever since their rebirth in 1896. While every city and National Olympic Committees is free to bid for any given edition, there is a very general rotation between the continents; however, the majority of the Olympic Summer Games have taken place in Europe. The last decade has seen the rising importance of the BRIC countries (Brazil, Russia, India and China) with only India lagging behind in its international sports presence (an exception being the Commonwealth Games held in Delhi in 2010). One of the assets of Rio de Janeiro's campaign to host the Olympic Summer Games was the issue of the Games being held for the first time in South America, as is shown by Figure 2.1.

Figure 2.1   Map of new Olympic world order (2016)

So far, Africa is the only continent that has never hosted an Olympic Summer Games. The Olympic Winter Games also rotate between the continents, but fewer countries are capable of hosting them given the mountain ranges and cold climate required for snow sports events.

World championships are awarded by the respective international sports federation, and are also mobile by nature, with every edition of the event taking place in a different city, country or continent every edition of the event. The same applies to continental events, from European to Pan American or African.

The two major European cultural events are mobile under different circumstances. Since 2001, the European Capital of Culture has been regularly extended to two cities each year from different European Union member countries. With the current (2014) total of member states being 28, each member country can expect to receive this prestigious nomination every 14 years. The Eurovision Song Contest, on the other hand, is mobile, but the event is automatically hosted in the country of the winner of the past edition. While this is logical in a sense, it may present challenges for cities as was the case of Baku in Azerbaijan in 2012 which had to build a brand new event venue in order to fulfil the requirements of the event owner, the European Broadcasting Corporation. Even the smallest sports or cultural events may be mobile, rotating between cities or regions of a country.

Mobile business events are, for instance, the World's Fair Expo (Exposition Universelle Internationale, Exposition Mondiale), the showcase of countries and the world audience's perception. While held under the one roof of the specially built Crystal Palace during its premiere in London in 1851, it was only in Paris in 1867 that the concept of countries showcasing their talents in their own pavilions was introduced. Several well-known monuments still exist today that were built for an Expo (e.g. the Atomium in Bruxelles, the Eiffel Tower in Paris).

Society events tend to be more locally rooted and less mobile by nature. Non-profit educational events also may follow mobile patterns, as do events by international associations such as those in the medical profession as they tend to prefer having their annual general meeting in different locations on each occasion.

Certain society events are mobile – from political events (such as the G8 and G20 summit meetings of world leaders) to garden shows that take place in different cities for each edition.

Place events are hosted by the same place very regularly and have developed a number of strengths. First of all, the place is associated with the brand value of the event and may implement it within its overall destination strategy. Ideally the image fit between the event and the destination is strong, building on a concise event strategy. Secondly, the venues are used on a regular basis allowing the organising committees to keep a core staff and to transfer the event knowledge from one edition of the event to the next.

Sports place events are to be found in nearly all sports that have a World Cup calendar type of championship. From snow sports (e.g. Oslo and Nordic Skiing, Kitzbühel in Alpine Skiing) to Formula 1 (e.g. in Monte Carlo), many world championships or world cups are staged annually with a number of fixed places hosting the event. Certain world sports federations have even branded the top places and formed leagues (e.g. the tennis 'grand slam' major tournaments held in Wimbledon, Paris, New York and Melbourne) or developed sports sub-brands such as the IAAF Diamond League (formerly known as Golden League), which in 2014 consists of 14 meetings in 14 different cities, 11 countries and 3 continents (Asia, North America and Europe).

Tourism is the major business sector benefiting enormously from place events as they keep enforcing the destination image, and, most often, the sports infrastructure may be utilised by both elite athletes and the wider sports tourist.

In the field of culture, place events are of paramount importance, being on a local, regional, national or international dimension. Cultural place events include festivals, concerts, indoor and outdoor performances, and may be attached to a season, as in a summer open-air theatre festival, or a winter mountain concert.

Business events, especially by international associations, are very often place events. Hosting an international motor show (e.g. Detroit, Frankfurt, Geneva) or a telecommunications summit (e.g. Barcelona) annually in the off-peak tourist season provides hotels, restaurants and congress centres with additional revenue from industry representatives, the public and the media. An important example is the Davos Business Summit, which assembles world economic and business leaders each year.

Society events, especially religious events, are naturally rooted in a place of pilgrimage, and range from the smallest local event to the largest international events. The Hajj to Mecca and the Kumbh Mela in India are very important events for the Muslim and Hindu religious communities, respectively. Those events require sophisticated events management covering issues such as security, accommodation, catering, transport and waste management.

Many places create their own events, fitted to their brand values. Food and wine festivals or fashion shows are typical examples of local place events.

Place-branded events are the premium version of place events, integrating the place's name with the event. Sports events range from marathons (e.g. the New York City Marathon) to ski races (e.g. Austria's Kitzbühel Hahnenkamm Downhill). In the field of culture, a series of events has developed as place brands, especially in the domain of film (e.g. the Cannes Film Festival, the Berlinale, the Viennale) and music festivals (the Montreux Jazz Festival, the Salzburg Festival). Society events range from the Vienna Opera Ball to the Munich Oktoberfest, attracting either elite society or an international event crowd. The Rio de Janeiro carnival is another example of these place-branded events. Later events have developed a 'certificate of origin', being either officially franchised (the Vienna Opera Ball in Washington and Moscow) or copied in many places around the world.

Micro, macro and mega events

As discussed in the introduction to this chapter, various categories have been used to put events into a certain dimension using one or more categories. Certainly, the number of event visitors who watch the event live at the venues or at least in the host city fan zones generates an important direct economic impact for both the host city/nation and related suppliers in the tourism service chain. For local/national stakeholders this is credibly perceived as a key criterion for hosting an event as it directly impacts on tax revenues and generates business in hotels, restaurants, shops and in a variety of companies.

The global television audience has developed into an important consideration for a number of stakeholders. For the host city/nation, the global viewership can prove to be a very cost-efficient way of promoting a destination. Nevertheless it is debatable how and when the improved image leads to an increased number of city tourists or even businesses interested in locating their headquarters or subsidiaries to the city. For sponsors the global television coverage is of paramount importance and a key issue in deciding which event is targeted within the sponsoring portfolio to fit the company's positioning, image and desired target marketing reach. Certainly, sponsors are also looking into the options of inviting key people to the event in order to best activate the sponsorship investment.

The unique website visits and other social media channels generating impressive numbers are a further quantitative factor in ranking the events and their impacts. While very important in the younger target markets, it is still seen as complementary to the global live (or time-delayed) television coverage.

Events can be further classified into micro, macro and mega events according to the size of the organising committee's budget. Whereas other authors have suggested including a set of different criteria such as live event visitors, participants and TV coverage, we consider that the budget is the strongest and clearest criterion for differentiation in this dimension.

The event budget is a clear indicator of how much is invested in organising an event, and we argue here is the most important indicator in ranking events from a micro to a macro then to a mega scale. The only limit is with the larger events where it has to be carefully split between the core event budget, being essential for the staging of the event, and the wider event budget (often called the non-organising committee budget (see Figure 2.2)). The wider event budget may include investments by the host city/nation in traffic infrastructure (airports, roads, railways, traffic management systems), public infrastructure (water, power and sewage systems), city infrastructure, and the tourism and leisure infrastructure (hotels, entertainment complexes).

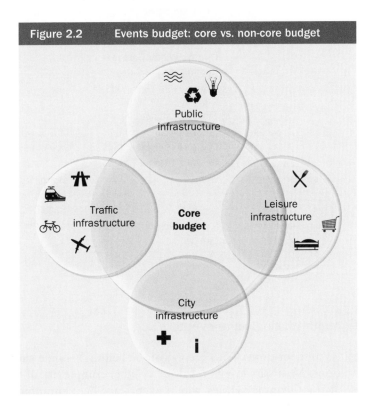

Figure 2.2   Events budget: core vs. non-core budget

Additionally, security costs, most often borne by the police or military forces, have escalated dramatically over the past decade.

In Chapter 16, event impact evaluation – the respective impacts before, during and after the event – will be discussed. Readers should also see Chapter 14 on the event life cycle.

The differentiation between the core (typically the organising committee) and non-core (typically the non-organising committee) budget is quite straightforward. The core event budget includes all budget items that are central to the hosting of the event operations and strictly associated with the event. Human resources management, including the management of volunteers and paid staff, reflects a major budget item in any kind of event. The business functions such as marketing are also a major part of most events, whether sports, culture, business or society. The venue needs to be prepared, operated and cleaned and sometimes enlarged in order to fulfil the event requirements. If the venue is a temporary one, it may be included in the core budget. The venue in its permanent nature, if newly built, is to be associated with the non-core budget. It may be built and operated by governmental or private stakeholders. If a destination is hosting a mega event, it is often a stimulus to advance city/regional governmental projects that, without the event, would have happened at a later stage, or even not have happened at all. Typical examples of projects are power plants, waste management and water facilities, railway schemes and airports, as well as city beautification projects. Table 2.2 gives examples of event classification.

Table 2.2	Indicators for the classification of events dimensions		
Dimensions indicators	**Mega events**	**Macro events**	**Micro events**
Core budget	> €10 million and major impact on host city/nation	€10,000 to €10 million	Up to €10,000
Examples sport	Olympic Summer Games, FIFA Football World Cup, UEFA European Soccer Championships, Olympic Winter Games, Commonwealth Games, Asian Games, Pan American Games, Larger World Championships	Smaller world championships, national or continental events	Any small sports event
Examples culture	Eurovision Song Contest, European Capital of Culture, Salzburg Festival	Any larger cultural event and festival	Any smaller cultural event and festival
Examples business	World Expo	Detroit Auto Show, Mobile World Congress Barcelona	Any smaller conference or congress
Examples society	Munich Oktoberfest, Rio Carnival		Balls, weddings

Multi- vs. single-site events

As another dimension, events can be held in a single site or be spread over various locations. Multi-site events result in a higher complexity of event operations as, for example, at the Olympic Games where events are held simultaneously in various sites, and the broadcast of the individual events, as well as any risk management, has to be centrally managed, most often from a main operations centre.

Local, regional, national and international events

As a further dimension, events can be easily differentiated into regional, national or international events by the origin of the majority of active participants. On an international perspective, many continents have developed their own events, such as the Pan American Games for the American continents, and the Africa Cup as a pan-African football tournament. Special geographical categories are events built on specific regions, such as the Mediterranean Games for all countries bordering the Mediterranean Sea. Language, heritage and historical relations still form the basis of events such as the Commonwealth Games and the Jeux Francophones events, with a wider international significance. Europe hosts many of the sports championships with the European Games (Baku in Azerbeijan 2015) being the first attempt for a multi-sports event such as seen in the Asian Games.

Creative vs. standardised events

The emphasis here is on whether the event follows a standardised pattern and is driven by a strict set of rules under the governance of an international or national institution, or whether an event is created independently.

Nearly all sports events are standardised events as there is a strict need for competition rules as well as for the sports venue. Sports rules are governed by either the national or international sports federation in order to guarantee fair and equal sports events. Within the cultural mega events, events may be standardised in format (e.g. the Eurovision Song Contest) or created with a very light set of rules (the European Capital of Culture). Business events may be developed with a highly standardised framework (e.g. trade fair participation) or very creatively from the perspectives of both the location and the whole event design. Society events, from weddings to religious events, tend to be standardised events with a certain flexibility for creative elements.

Live vs. virtual events

As an event, by nature, is a live event, many event visitors are following the event either live at the site, live in an adjacent fan park or live via broadcast social media channels (or at any later stage).

Live streaming of events is now common practice, ranging from free to paid formats, thus extending the target audience and enlarging the market for key stakeholders such as sponsors. Due to the uncertainty of outcome in sports, people tend to favour the live consumption of events, whereas concerts are most often watched at a later stage on formats such as YouTube.

On-demand content is made available by either television stations or international event owners, and ranges from being free to any kind of subscription rate. **Chapter 13 on events and new media technologies further elaborates this discussion.**

Synergies of event formats

Over the past decade synergies have developed further between event formats. The Olympic Games have from very early times had opening and closing ceremonies with a strong focus on the representation of the host city and host country's culture. Since the Barcelona Olympic Games of 1992, a cultural programme, the Cultural Olympiad, running over the four years before the event, has become an integral part of the mega event. The football mega events, on a global as well as at the European level, have seen the integration of small opening ceremonies in the event format as well as a cultural programme for those visiting the host cities.

The European Capitals of Culture, conversely, have sometimes developed a focus on sports as part of the wider cultural picture.

Event match to destination

Cities around the world are sharpening and refining their destination brand. Events may be a major tool for re-launching or re-enforcing a destination brand. In event tourism, events have 'specific roles in attracting tourists, fostering a positive destination image, acting as animators and catalysts' (Getz, 2012: 11). Hallmann and Breuer (2010: 234) suggest that, 'knowing that image fit favours future visits to the destination, destination marketers should use the positive connotations of sport events'. A challenge lies within the diverse nature of events and their multiple ownership. While local/regional sports federations may bid for and host sports events in accordance with the appropriate sports council, cultural associations may organise festivals and events in close cooperation with the cultural department, whereas the local/regional tourism organisation or convention association will also strive to host events. In a few places event commissions are implemented to coordinate the events of a destination. While cultural departments will make their support dependent on the programme, sports federations will have their elite athletes or wider general public in mind. Whatever the case, all events should fit the desired image of a destination in order to achieve the optimum benefits. Additionally, Xing and Chalip's study (2006: 72) suggests that 'priming, rather than match, should guide event choice. In other words, what seems to be important is not which characteristics of the event match with the destination; what matters is how an event can be used to prime particular schemata to then be associated with the destination brand'.

Event strategy success factors

In general, Thompson and Martin (2005) define the significant elements for strategic success as the following:

- tracking events in the market and the environment, choosing responses (both proactively and reactively) and monitoring the outcomes of the actions which follow. Competitor initiatives must be dealt with; benchmarking best practices and general awareness can suggest new ideas;
- making sure that the important information from the questioning and learning from these emergent changes is disseminated effectively;
- reflecting upon outcomes in the context of E–V–R (environment–values–resources) congruence to ensure that the organisation can sustain an effective match with its environment;
- where appropriate, adapting policies and procedures to better guide future decisions (Thompson and Martin, 2005: 241).

Concerning events management, Anderson (2010: 12) suggests that strategy be employed 'in all phases of events management. This includes the initial planning process, recruitment of chair persons and committee members, development of the budget, venue selection, solicitation of sponsors, obtaining donations, food and beverage, invitations to guests, and more'.

An event strategy for a destination only has a potential for success if a thorough analysis is followed by a commitment of all key stakeholders involved.

> The meanings attached to planned events and event tourism experiences are both an integral part of the experience and are antecedents to future event tourism behaviour. To the extent that event tourism experiences are transforming, that is they change beliefs, values or attitudes, then individuals will likely adopt new behaviours in the future. It may be that multiple event experiences are required for transformation, or it might occur as part of a social bonding.
>
> (Getz, 2008: 414)

Once all stakeholders agree on the strategic focus of an events strategy and its milestones, the implementation needs to be managed by an events commission/events board that oversees the funding as well as the image-fit and the transfer of know-how amongst the organising committees.

Conclusion

In recent years, numerous ways of classifying events have emerged out of a growing amount of events management literature. Consistent with the growing number and ongoing differentiation in characteristics of events, the chapter has suggested only using the current classification of mega, macro and micro for describing the core budget of an event, but differentiating according to whether an event is a mobile or a place event. Then the event can be classified by further qualities and features, e.g. creative or standardised, live or virtual, multi- or single-sited. Thus, numerous possibilities arise for strategically planning an event, and can be considered in order to develop the one event that perfectly matches the destination where it will be held. The better this match, the more likely it is that the event itself will be successful and sustainable. In order to reach this goal, it is essential always to keep key stakeholders and their interests in the event in mind as their satisfaction and commitment are critical to an event's success too.

Case 2.1 **Event Nation Russia – hosting mobile events**

Russia was formed in 1992 from the former Soviet Union. The last mega event hosted before the dissolution of the Soviet Union was the partly boycotted Moscow Olympic Summer Games in 1980. With the breakaway of many now-independent countries such as Kazakhstan, Kirgizstan and Georgia, Russia lost many of its winter sports hubs and training centres.

President Vladimir Putin, being a passionate skier and sportsman himself, has put a strong emphasis on developing Russia into a leading sports nation. The first strategic goal was to create and develop a prime international winter sports destination and training centre in Sochi and the nearby Krasnaya Polyana mountain range. Sochi won the right to host the Olympic Winter Games in 2014, and thus created infrastructure for ice and snow sports events in all disciplines. While an estimated amount of more than €30 billion was apparently spent in order to create the sports, hotel and transport infrastructure, other regions of Russia were soon demanding part of the sports event business market.

In its first bid for the particular event, defeating countries such as Belgium and the Netherlands, England, Portugal and Spain, Russia won the right to host the FIFA Football World Cup in 2018. The intra-Russian competition to host matches was large as Russia will invest massively in its railway and road infrastructure connecting the host cities.

Having secured those two mega events, Russia has meanwhile attracted the annual Formula 1 Grand Prix to Sochi, as well as the leading world sports congress to St Petersburg, amongst other major events including the FINA World Swimming Championships and the IAAF World Athletics Championships.

Discussion questions

1 What were the reasons to host major sports events in Russia?
2 What will be the legacy of the Sochi 2014 Olympic Winter Games?
3 Which other events would suit Russia's event strategy?

Case 2.2 **The global rotation of mobile sports events – a myth?**

The International Olympic Committee as the rights holder for the Olympic Games, as well as FIFA as the one for the football World Cup, sees their events rotate between the continents. The IOC leaves each host city election process for the Olympic Summer Games open, and any city nominated by its National Olympic Committee (NOC) may bid. While the mega event has most often been awarded to Europe, for the first time in 2016 it will be held in a South American city (Rio de Janeiro); it has to date never been awarded to a city on the African continent. A certain pattern of rotation between the continents may be observed since the first modern Olympic Games in 1896.

The Olympic Winter Games are different in the sense that they require snow-covered mountains with a minimum altitude difference for the alpine events. While also having taken place more often in Europe, the latest trend has been to open up new markets for snow sports and its related industries, with the Olympic Winter Games of 2014 being held in Sochi (Russia) and those of 2018 in Pyeongchang (South Korea), both nations with relatively little experience in hosting winter sports events so far.

FIFA has taken different views over the past decade. Having had a selection procedure similar to the IOC's until that for the 2006 World Cup, an enforced continental rotation was implemented for the editions of the 2010 until the 2014 World Cup; this policy was subsequently cancelled for future World Cups, however.

▶

Case 2.2　　　*(continued)*

In 2010 the event was given to the African continent, with bidders from Morocco, Nigeria and South Africa; the event was successfully staged in South Africa. For 2014, the event was moved to South America, with Brazil being the only candidate and consequently the host country. For the 2018 and 2022 editions the choice was more complex, with the 2018 edition prescribed for Europe and 2022 for non-European countries. Thus the event was again awarded to nations with limited experience in hosting sports mega events, but again opening up new and relevant markets and regions for the sport.

Discussion questions

4　Why do mobile events rotate between the continents?

5　Why are new markets (Brazil, India, China, Russia, South Africa) so important for mega event rights holders?

Case 2.3　　　The Vienna Life Ball – rigidity, steadiness or a smart move?

The public society AIDS LIFE, which was founded by Mr Gery Keszler and Dr Torgom Petrosian in 1992, held the Vienna Life Ball for the first time in 1993. The first aim was to generate as much financial revenue as possible for projects that support people affected with HIV or AIDS. The second, even more important, purpose of the Vienna Life Ball was to sensitise the public to the problems of HIV and AIDS. In order to send out the strongest possible sign of solidarity with those affected with the illnesses, Mr Keszler, together with Vienna's former mayor, Helmut Zilk, managed an extraordinary achievement: the Vienna Life Ball was the first AIDS charity event ever to be held in a city's town hall. This is where the Life Ball has taken place ever since, celebrating life in all its facets.

The Life Ball Event does not simply start in the evening when guests arrive; the real starting point is when the year's motto is revealed, months before the actual event. The actual Life Ball weekend itself is all for the good cause. The night before the Life Ball the Red Ribbon Celebration Concert takes place, where internationally known musicians and actors perform. The following morning there is an international press conference meant as a platform for organisations and celebrities to present their commitment to the fight against HIV and AIDS. While everybody who was lucky enough to get hold of tickets to the Life Ball prepares themselves for the big party, some even luckier ones are invited to the AIDS Solidarity Gala which is hosted by Austria's President. In the evening the official celebration finally begins: in front of the Vienna Town Hall the great opening ceremony, including a famous' designer's fashion show and the calling-in of the best costumes, takes place before the party inside and outside the town hall reaches its peak.

Discussion questions

6　Why did the Vienna Life Ball never change its location? Would it have been a good idea to change locations?

7　Have Vienna and the Life Ball already built a joint brand? Give your reasons.

General discussion questions

8　Why is there a need to develop new classifications of event dimensions?

9　What are the differences between the old and the new school approach of event dimensions?

10　Which categories do the above–mentioned events (e.g. Olympic Games, Vienna Life Ball, Expositions Mondiales) belong to when you think of already discussed characteristics like passive vs active, place vs mobile, creative vs standardised, life vs virtual?

11　What other qualities, features or characteristics that are not mentioned could be used in order to classify events?

Guided reading

Getz, D. (2012) *Event Studies: Theory, Research and Policy for Planned Events* (2nd edn). London: Taylor and Francis.

Masterman, G. (2009) *Strategic Sports Event Management: Olympic Edition* (2nd edn). Oxford: Butterworth-Heinemann.

Preston, C.A. (2012) *Event Marketing: How to Successfully Promote Events, Festivals, Conventions and Expositions* (2nd edn). Hoboken, NJ: Wiley.

Schaumann, P. (2005) *The Guide to Successful Destination Management*. Hoboken, NJ: Wiley.

Recommended websites

Official website of European Capitals of Culture: **http://ec.europa.eu/culture/our-programmes-and-actions/capitals/european-capitals-of-culture_en.htm**

Official website of Expo 2015 in Milano: **http://en.expo2015.org**

Official website of the Eurovision Song Contest: **www.eurovision.tv**

Official website of the Fédération Internationale de Football Association (FIFA): **www.fifa.com/**

Official website of the Olympic Movement: **www.olympic.org/**

Official website of the Pan American Games 2015 in Toronto: **www.panam2015.gov.on.ca/en/**

Official website of UEFA: **www.uefa.com/**

Official website of Vienna's Life Ball: **www.lifeball.org**

Key words

mobile events; place events

Bibliography

Anderson, J.L. (2010) *Event Management Simplified*. Bloomington, IN: AuthorHouse.

Burns, J.P.A. and Mules, T.J. (1986) A framework for the analysis of major special events. In J.P.A. Burns et al. (eds) *The Adelaide Grand Prix: The Impact of a Special Event*. Adelaide: Centre for South Australian Economic Studies.

GamesBids.com (2009) **www.gamesbids.com/eng/olympic_bids/2016_bid_news/rio_2016//1216134745.html**

Getz, D. (2005) *Event Management and Event Tourism* (2nd edn). New York: Cognizant Communications Corporation.

Getz, D. (2008) Event tourism: definition, evolution and research. *Tourism Management*, 29, 403–28.

Getz, D. (2012) *Event Studies: Theory, Research and Policy for Planned Events* (2nd edn). London: Taylor & Francis.

Hall, C.M. (1989) The definition and analysis of hallmark tourist events. *GeoJournal*, 19(3), 263–8.

Hallmann, K. and Breuer, C. (2010) Image fit between sport events and their hosting destinations from an active sport tourist perspective and its impact on future behaviour. *Journal of Sportand Tourism,* 15(3), 215–37.

Roche, M. (2000) *Mega-Events and Modernity: Olympics and Expos in the Growth of Global Culture.* Abingdon: Taylor & Francis.

Ritchie, B. (1984) Assessing the impact of hallmark events: conceptual and research issues. *Journal of Travel Research,* 22(1), 2–11.

Thompson, J.L. and Martin, F. (2005) *Strategic Management: Awareness and Change* (5th edn). London: Cengage Learning EMEA.

Xing, X. and Chalip, L. (2006) Effects of hosting a sport event on destination brand: a test of co-branding and match-up models. *Sport Management Review,* 9(1), 49–78.

Chapter 3

Theories and models in events management

Sebastian Kaiser, SRH University Heidelberg, Germany

Learning outcomes

Upon completion of this chapter the reader should be able to:

■ describe events management as an academic field as well as outline relevant contributions from several disciplines to the body of knowledge;

■ critically reflect on the development of events management as a **profession** as well as appraise the status of professionalisation;

■ describe the competences needed to plan, organise and control events successfully against the backdrop of empirically as well as analytically derived models.

Overview

This chapter examines the development of events management as a profession and as an academic field. Empirically as well as analytically derived models specifying and categorising the competences needed are introduced. Furthermore, in addition to existing enumerations of scientific approaches to the field, theories and bodies of knowledge are presented and discussed that seem to be particularly helpful, opening the doors to a wider range of specific approaches:

1. the theory of services management, which looks at the specifics of the production and consumption of services;
2. the perception of event destinations being value-added chains and **virtual companies**; and
3. resource-based theory, which sees the level of an organisation's access to resources as the foundation of entrepreneurial success and the generation of long-term competitive advantages.

Having so far not taken into account the background of the development of the market as well as current trends, those perspectives are of high and rising importance. Finally, the status of professionalisation of events management is evaluated referring to functionalist theories of Anglo-American sociology. According to these, professions can be understood as a crucial structural development in 20th-century society. Under the terms of this conceptual framework it has to be stated that events management does not entirely fulfil the requirements for being a profession yet. Against the backdrop of the aforementioned situation, analysing the relevant framework conditions is an important task if one wants to predict and affect the further consolidation of the field.

Introduction

One of the basic problems regarding theory construction and modelling in events management is the ambiguity in the use of the term 'event'; there is little agreement on standardised categories so far. This lack of conceptual clarity is due to the mere fact that its perception contains diverse contextualisations and implications from several disciplines (sociology, economics, psychology, cultural studies, communications science, etc.). Moreover, events occur 'throughout all sections of society and across all different types of organisations' (Berridge, 2007: 5). The event sector is thus not one coherent but many sectors (Goldblatt, 2000: 3), including a wide range of different types of events, like conferences/meetings, exhibitions, incentive travel, festivals, corporate hospitality and associated organisations, such as events management companies, events industry suppliers, venues, industry associations, etc. Not least, events are embedded in and subject to social change; they are, in this regard, modern forms of social representation, and hence constitute new ways of social interaction and communication.

Following a very basic definition, events are a 'unique moment in time' distinguishing them from routine activities such as daily work (Berridge, 2007: 7; see also Goldblatt, 1990; Getz, 2005). Beyond that there are a lot of common features regarding which different events and event settings resemble each other and overlap.

> Festivals typically include a large program of events, including sports, concerts, participatory recreation, consumer shows and sales, hospitality places for sponsors, and educational events. Major sport competitions encompass other types of event. For example, organisers of the Olympics are required to include a cultural festival, and many other sport event organisers have learnt that they can broaden their appeal by turning a competition into a festival.
>
> (Getz, 2000: 11)

Common approaches to the categorisation of events mainly refer to three dimensions:

1. their form or content (sports events, cultural events, business events, etc.);
2. their particular size; as well as
3. their scale of impacts.

In the academic discussion; a multitude of definitions and distinctions between different event types like major/mega events, hallmark events and local/community events has emerged over the past decades (see, for example, Bowdin et al., 2011; Kaspar and Kaiser, 2013). As large events bring with them an additional range of effects, such as positive external effects which take on the character of public goods (for instance, national pride, image or sports and/or cultural participation), the assessment of their various impacts as well as of the socio-cultural relevance is of high importance. Roche, for example, defines mega events as 'large-scale cultural (including commercial and sporting) events, which have a dramatic character, mass popular appeal and international significance' (Roche, 2000: 1). For Roberts (2004), what defines certain sports events as 'mega' is that they are 'discontinuous', out of the ordinary, international, and simply big in composition. 'In fact in recent years one could reasonably argue that the term "event" has been used to define that which is extraordinary in popular culture' (Goldblatt, 2000: 3).

Hallmark events are major events with a limited duration. They usually rotate between different host cities and/or countries that are selected according to a bidding process, faced with an international audience, usually have high media coverage and impacts of different nature (economic, social, ecological, infrastructural, political, etc.). Recurring events occur on a regular basis (for example each year), may also rotate between host cities/countries, but are regularly staged in the same host cities as part of a circuit. Many characteristics of recurring events are similar to those of hallmark events. However, their particular impacts might be smaller, but they may be more efficient from a long-term perspective (Kaspar and Kaiser, 2013; **for a critical discussion and an overview of terms and definitions, see Chapter 2**).

In the following, events management as an academic field will be described. Based on this, the questions of which theoretical perspectives and approaches contribute to the field and to what extent there is (or can be) a genuine theory of events management will be addressed.

Events management as an academic field

In the editorial of the journal *Events Management* (formerly *Festival Management and Event Tourism*) Getz (1999) asked if there is 'an identifiable body of knowledge and skills that defines events management as a separate field of study'.

> The events industry, if we can call it that, is well established in many forms such as expositions, sport marketing, or concert productions, but as an academic field of study and a research topic it is quite new and immature.
>
> (Getz, 2000: 10)

In event-related literature, issues concerning the academic status of events management are raised time and again, questioning, for example, the relevance of empirical approaches and research into events management practice. Furthermore, a relatively low credibility in comparison to the so-called 'home disciplines' (economics, management, sociology, etc.) is often stated, similar to perceptions of the status and progress of various other young and emerging academic disciplines, such as, for example, sports management:

> In fact, the kinds of malaise we have experienced regarding our status, our work, and our place in academic institutions is typical of young disciplines. A century ago, medicine . . ., business . . . and public administration . . . were each concerned about their poor academic status, their seemingly derivative paradigms, and their appropriate place in tertiary education. The malaise in our field is neither a flaw nor a drawback; it is a necessary process for our maturation.
>
> (Chalip, 2006: 2)

Against the background of a dynamically evolving education and training sector with more and more universities and colleges as well as industry associations offering dedicated courses in events management, some authors argue that events management has come to be a discrete discipline (for example, Bowdin et al., 2011: 33); the answer, however, to the question above (still) has to be 'no'. The main reason lies in the nature of the subject area itself, namely the heterogeneity of the field.

There are clearly some basic commonalities: all planned events have a particular agenda and are of limited duration (Getz, 2000: 12). Similar to other economic sectors and businesses, successful events management is subject to professional pursuance of general managerial functions such as strategic planning, budgeting and accounting, controlling, etc., as well as certain specific tasks related to event operations and project management.

Beyond those basic commonalities, however, there is a high variance in events with regard to their blend of management, programme, setting and stakeholders or customers, and it is due to this singularity that managers are faced with particular challenges (see Getz, 2000: 12; Tum et al., 2006: 11). According to Getz, 'an examination of the basic common elements and the specific way they interact should be the logical starting point' trying to define the academic field. However, a scientific discussion of the particular skill requirements of the event industry is still in its infancy, being a major driving force for the consolidation of events management as an academic discipline. Literature is still dominated by practitioner, 'how-to-do-it' guidelines, dealing with the processes for planning, organising and managing of an event, assuming that one only has to adhere closely to such guidelines and then the event itself will be a success (Berridge, 2007).

The described status is reflected in the heterogeneity of curricula and, not least, the great variety of subjects that are addressed from the scientific community. An analysis of articles published in the journal *Events Management* (formerly *Festival Management and Event Tourism*) up to vol. 14, no. 4, 2011, underlines this picture. The articles can be assigned to 15 different categories with several singular ones that cannot be associated. The comparison to an earlier breakdown of articles of the same journal conducted by Getz (2000) reveals the importance of particular subjects and the increasing importance of certain others. The most important topics were and are:

1. economic development and economic impacts of events (2011: 47 articles; 2000: 26 articles); and
2. sponsorship and event marketing from the corporate perspective (2011: 33 articles; 2000: 14 articles).

The categories that have developed most dynamically in this regard are:

1. visitor or participant motives (2011: 32 articles; 2000: 7 articles);
2. education, training, accreditation, research, professionalism (2011: 29 articles; 2000: 7 articles); and
3. community impacts, resident attitudes and perceptions of event impacts (2011: 24 articles; 2000: 6 articles).

Theories in events management

In the introduction to their book on festivals and events management, Yeoman et al. (2004) state that the characteristics of festivals and events are unique, and, as such, no one standard model of management fits all. As has been shown in the previous chapters, there is hardly and can hardly be such a thing as a generic and comprehensive theory of events management. To summarise, it can be said that events management is not a coherent academic field of research and study. The description of the professional field as well as the literature review show that it draws on, and has to draw on, various other disciplines. It also becomes clear that, against the backdrop of the peculiarities mentioned, simply transferring methods and approaches from other disciplines such as economics or sociology is not adequate in order to deal successfully with the challenges of the business (see Kaiser and Schütte, 2012). The progress of events management towards a distinctive academic discipline in this regard requires two complementary approaches: one that critically reflects on the relevance of classical theories and models from the 'home disciplines' and the degree to which they can be applied successfully, and a second one that takes into consideration specific event phenomena as well as industry trends.

According to Getz (2000: 13) 'a top priority should be to attract contributions from other fields . . . or to get their contributions exposed to those in the event field'. Having a look at the particular research topics it becomes clear that the emerging scientific discussion is strongly dominated by the various perspectives on evaluating event impacts, still with a strong focus on economic impacts. Which other contributions and theoretical approaches are needed? After having enumerated major components of events management education as well as of current research practice, Getz (2000: 14) lists the following relevant perspectives on events and related disciplines:

- an environmental perspective (natural and environmental sciences, physical geography, environmental design and psychology);
- a community perspective (anthropology, sociology, community planning);
- an economic perspective (economics, finance, tourism, economic development);
- a perspective of event programming (recreation and sport, arts and entertainment);
- a legal perspective (impact on the regulatory environment, risk management, incorporation or charitable status, protection of name, logo, designs, etc.);
- a management perspective (business, public administration, not-for-profit);
- a psychological perspective (psychology, social psychology);
- a political perspective (political science).

Added to this general enumeration, theories and bodies of knowledge from three fields seem to be particularly helpful, each of which opens the doors to a wider range of specific approaches (see Kaiser et al., 2013). Not having been taken into account so far against the background of the development of the market, as well as current trends, those perspectives are of high and rising importance. Their consideration may thus also lead to a further professionalisation of the field. These perspectives are:

- the theory of services management, which looks at the specifics of the production and consumption of services (e.g. Bleuel and Patton, 1978; Fitzsimmons, 2011);
- the perception of event destinations being service and value added chains or virtual companies (e.g. Sydow, 2006);
- resource-based theory, which sees the level of an organisation's access to resources as the foundation of entrepreneurial success and the generation of long-term competitive advantages (e.g. Barney and Clark, 2007).

In contrast to material goods, services are of an intangible nature. They can only be provided in close spatial and timely contact with the customer (the 'uno actu principle'). Being the so-called 'external factor', the consumers are integrated into the production process; spectators of a soccer game, for example, may contribute to the overall quality of the match by supporting their team and enhancing the atmosphere of the game. As a consequence, important and quality-affecting aspects can only be controlled in a limited way by the event organiser, since aspects like timing, quality and quantity of the demand can hardly be estimated ahead of time. This also results in a high degree of decisional uncertainty on the demand side. Initially, services are only performance promises; the utility impact is difficult or impossible for the consumer to ascertain (credence goods). A high level of experiential and confidential characteristics is typical (see Fitzsimmons and Fitzsimmons, 2008; Maleri, 1973). The necessity of co-production by the demanders and the suppliers, as well as mutual uncertainty about the motivation and the performance of the parties involved, creates special challenges for the management and the marketing of events. A second important feature which is under-represented in the scientific discussion so far, also separating the event-related production process from those in other economic sectors, is the fact that the individual suppliers are connected in a compound structure consisting of various competing suppliers. Event tourists typically have demands for a variety of goods and services which can only be provided by a number of different suppliers. This is an important characteristic because whereas in other economic sectors the collaboration of competing suppliers is an exception, in event tourism especially it is a characteristic element of service production and an important element of the successful marketing of the product (this is commonly referred to as '**co-opetition**'; see Brandenburger and Nalebuff, 1998).

In this context, tourism and event destinations can also be seen as 'virtual companies' (Sydow, 2006; Siller, 2010). This term describes a dynamic network of companies that, without the customer knowing about it, (have to) cooperate to produce the product. Virtual companies are, according to Bieger (2008), company networks that operate very closely together on the basis of shared resources and keep up a very close cooperation, subsequently needing a common strategic plan to build up and develop the shared resources like core competencies. The connection between service quality, customer satisfaction, customer loyalty and economic success can be analysed in service value-added chains. According to the **service profit chain** (SPC), there is a direct economic connection between extraordinary service experiences, customer loyalty and economic success in terms of profit and growth (Heskett et al., 1997). In the SPC it is generally argued that employee satisfaction positively affects service quality, and that a high level of service quality leads to customer satisfaction. A high level of customer satisfaction is a prerequisite for customer loyalty and leads to a higher likelihood that the customers will recommend the supplier to other potential customers. The connection between customer satisfaction and customer loyalty generally depends on the number of choices a customer has. In low-competition markets, a higher level of customer loyalty is generally achieved, even though customer satisfaction is lower. The competition in the events industry is high and rising. Further, regarding event tourism, it is not regionally confined, since tourism destinations are competing for guests worldwide (Kaiser et al., 2013).

In contrast to an industrial organisation, which tries to explain a company's economic success based on the structure of the market, the degree of supplier concentration, the level of product differentiation and the size of entry barriers into the industry or the market (e.g. de Jong and Shepherd 2007), the **resource-based view** (RBV) sees the organisation's configuration of resources as the basis for entrepreneurial success and the creation of a long-term competitive edge (e.g. Mahoney and Pandian, 1992). Regarding the event industry and its great variety of stakeholders, individual and collective resource knowledge, as well as network resources, seem to be of particular relevance (see Penrose, 1959; Wernerfelt, 1984).

Events management as a profession

According to a common attribution, events management can be seen as an industry that has undergone 'phenomenal growth, coupled with increased consumer awareness and choice' (Yeoman et al., 2004: ix). Bowdin et al. (2011: 29–33) argue that the rapid growth of events in the past decade has resulted in the formation of an identifiable event industry. As evidence for the development as well as the industry's consolidation, the authors list a number of institutions such as events organisations, events management companies, events industry suppliers, venues and industry associations. From a labour market perspective, events management is also considered as an emerging profession, transitioning from growth into maturity (Goldblatt, 2000: 2). Bowdin et al. (2011: 37) highlight the development of a particular events methodology with the recognition and description of the processes used to create an event – the 'eureka' moment when events management progressed from being a skill to becoming a profession. The perception of events management being a profession is not least supported by the fact that the event industry increasingly offers long-term career opportunities. 'The need for management and education has become more important as people make life-long careers in this area' (Yeoman et al., 2004: ix).

However, Goldblatt (2000: 2) identifies several skills gaps that hinder or defer the evolutionary progress of the discipline. He states that the organisations still operate 'from a reactionary mode that is ironic given the central skill of strategic planning that is required for most events'. He continues:

> the profession lacks the standardisation tools and reporting procedures needed to provide empirical data to enable event stakeholders to make informed decisions. . . . The absence of this standardisation promotes speciousness, distrust, and lack of credibility on the part of governments, the private sector, and others whose support is critical to the long term health of the profession.
>
> (Goldblatt, 2000: 2)

Particularly if one takes as a basis the term 'profession' in the proper meaning of the word, one has to state that the level of professionalisation is still rather low. Most of the approaches according to which the status of professionalisation of an occupation can be evaluated refer to functionalist theories of Anglo-American sociology (for example Parsons, 1939). According to these, professions can be understood as a crucial structural development in 20th-century society. The definition of professions, as well as their distinction from common occupations, is done by means of a list of characteristic features which are applicable, for example, to the legal and medical profession.

Those are:

1. the existence of a self-governing professional association;
2. a code of ethics;
3. a theory-based academic formation;
4. the perception of the occupation as a service for the public good; and, last but not least,
5. social prestige and reputation.

Under the terms of this conceptual framework, it has to be stated that events management does not entirely fulfil the requirements for being a profession yet. Looking at the organisational environment, for example, there are indeed lobbying groups representing and advocating the interests of various stakeholders, but the overall situation is characterised by partitioning rather than consolidation. Bowdin et al. (2011: 31) lists 40 associations, each of them representing different sectors of the industry, such as conference/meetings, exhibitions, incentive travel, festivals, corporate hospitality, venues and suppliers. Against the backdrop of the aforementioned situation, analysing the relevant framework conditions is an important task if one wants to predict and affect the further consolidation of the field. Taking into consideration the development of established professions such as medicine, law, accounting, etc. might be a useful approach for this purpose. 'The challenges these professions faced and overcame may be used as a model for the emerging profession of events management' (Goldblatt, 2000: 2).

Events management models

Taking the low level of professionalisation into consideration, and regarding the fact that events management is still a young and evolving discipline, important questions are (and will increasingly be) which competences are needed for successful management, and how far those competences differ from the ones needed in other fields of business. Bratton (1998) as quoted by Ratmawati (2007: 557) defines competence as 'any knowledge, skill, trait, motive, attitude, value or other personal characteristic essential to perform a job'. The term 'model' in this regard will be understood as a coherent description of the body of knowledge – including competences and skills – needed to successfully plan, organise and control events, which may be derived either theoretically or empirically. Generalising events management includes any combination of skills related to planning, organising, leading and controlling within the context of an event. However, few studies have been conducted within the events industry so far to identify the skills requirements and attributes of successful event managers (Bowdin et al., 2011: 35). Frequently events management programmes have been set up with little empirical evidence regarding their appropriateness. Particularly in view of the rising economic significance of the event industry, there is a growing demand for scientific-based, professional educational offers, and professionalisation of the events management sector presupposes professional training and recruiting.

The fit of educational offer and educational needs is the central focus of curriculum theory and research. In comparison to a traditional scheme of work, a curriculum is defined as the result of scientific research and a development process which contains guidelines for learning goals, learning content, learning material, learning organisation and assessment. The particular courses and the relevant competences developed should reflect the aim of mastering real-life situations (see Kaiser and Schütte, 2012). The implementation of empirically obtained qualification requirements in the process of designing curricula is known as Competency-Based Education (CBE). 'The method involves identifying competencies or composite skills in practice and then relating them to the training and educational needs of students and personnel' (Jamieson, 1987: 49). As opposed to analytical/deductive approaches that derive competences and skill requirements from the logic of the job assignment (for example, Fayol, 1916), simplifying research into managerial work can be structured as shown in Table 3.1.

Table 3.1	Research into managerial work	
Work activity research		**Function-based research**
Structured observation to study the work activities of managers		Assessment of the importance of several managerial activities
Typical methods		
(Self-)observation of frequency of activities, diary method	Observation of frequency of activities, verbal contacts, mail, etc.	Standardised questionnaires Qualitative interviews

Source: Kaiser and Schütte 2012; see also Kaiser 2004

Indeed, as Mahoney et al. (1965: 106) state 'there seems to be a basic core of management performance common to most managerial assignments'. However, as the Work Activity School introduced by Henry Mintzberg (1973) demonstrated, the activities of a manager cannot be limited to Fayol's (1916) generic management functions of planning, analysing, leading and controlling. Various other activities are also of particular importance and constitute central tasks; these include communicating, cultivating social contacts and external representation. In order to identify the competences and qualification requirements of managers, it is therefore not sufficient to proceed analytically from the logic of the job assignment, since there is the risk of falling prey to 'myths of management' (Mintzberg, 1973).

If you ask managers what they do, they will most likely tell you that they plan, organise, coordinate, and control. Then watch what they do. Don't be surprised if you can't relate what you see to these words.

(Mintzberg, 1990: 163)

There have been numerous attempts during the last decades to conceptualise empiri-cally managerial tasks and leadership skill requirements (for example, Carlson, 1951; Mahoney et al., 1965; Mintzberg, 1973; Katz, 1974; Lau et al., 1980; Kanungo and Misra, 1992; Connelly et al., 2000). Having reviewed these studies, Mumford et al. (2007) suggest that leadership skill requirements can be understood in terms of four general categories:

1. cognitive skills;
2. interpersonal skills;
3. business skills; and
4. strategic skills.

Furthermore, leadership research in general has recognised that managerial compe-tencies and skill requirements manifest themselves in different ways at various organi-sational levels. Leadership scholars have called for additional research on leadership skill requirements and how those requirements vary by organisational level (Kaiser and Schütte, 2012).

Against the backdrop of the above-mentioned findings as well as the current state of research, an empirical assessment of the specific qualification requirements of event managers is particularly important; the more so since it concerns products, organisa-tions and cultures, general economics and business management only being dealt with on the side. In contrast to the (prescriptive) Classical School of Management of Fayol, one important research method is the questioning of managers' individual assessment of the relevance of various competencies needed in the practice of their profession.

Perry et al. (1996) asked 105 managers attending the 1996 Australian Events Conference to indicate the importance of several knowledge areas on a five-point Likert scale from 1 = 'strongly disagree' to 5 = 'strongly agree'. The most important were reported as project management, budgeting, time management, media relations, business planning, human resource management and marketing (cited in Bowdin et al., 2011: 35).

Hovemann et al. (2003) asked 76 managers representing German sport event agencies to indicate the importance of several activities for their daily work routine. Most impor-tant (on a five-point Likert scale from 1 = 'unimportant' to 5 = 'very important') were establishing and cultivating external contacts, managing organisational structure and workflow, leading, motivating and controlling employees as well as initiating projects.

Since professional training and education have become necessary, the major event industry associations offer qualification and credentialing/certification programmes such as the Certified Festival and Events Executive certification programme (CFEE), offered since 1983 by the International Festivals and Events Association (IFEA), the Certified Special Events Professional designation (CSEP), offered by the International Special Events Society (ISES), and the Certified Meeting Professional designation (CMP), the credential programme offered by the Convention Industry Council (CIC).

Events Management International Competency Standards (EMICS, formerly known as IEMS) have been developed by the Canadian Tourism Human Resource Council (CTHRC). They are categorised into 12 domains, 34 tasks, 145 subtasks and 985 skill statements (abilities). The domains are: strategic planning, project management, risk management, financial management, administration, human resources, stakeholder man-agement, event design, site management, marketing, professionalism and communication.

A recent attempt to establish the competencies required when organising and mana-ging events is the Leonardo da Vinci funded partnership project COMPEVENT which was started in 2010 as a European research project bringing together partner institutions from Germany, Austria, France, Hungary and Great Britain (see *www.compevent.eu*). It aims to examine the full range and scope of skills required in events management, with a special focus on small and medium-sized enterprises (SMEs), considering also whether the competencies identified are generic to all events, or whether some are specific to par-ticular activities. From January to March 2011, a questionnaire was sent out to over

1,600 SMEs via email in France, Germany and Hungary. The five most important knowledge areas (on a four-point scale from 'very important' to 'not important at all') were organisational and planning skills, the ability to work autonomously, customer orientation, problem solving and team working.

The Events Management Body of Knowledge (EMBOK) project is an international approach to establish global process standards for the event industry. The aim of the EMBOK executive is 'To create a framework of the knowledge and processes used in events management that may be customised to meet the needs of various cultures, governments, education programs, and organisations' (*www.embok.org*). The EMBOK model is a three-dimensional description of the knowledge and skills essential to create, develop and deliver an event. The term 'event' includes conferences, exhibitions, festivals, special events, civic events, sports events and the like. According to the model, events management is made up of the following five areas of management: design, administration, marketing, operations and risk. The EMBOK term for these areas is 'knowledge domains'. 'Every event manager, from festival organisers to conference planners, must manage each of these areas. They represent the temporary departments or divisions of the events management' (*www.embok.org/html/domains.htm*).

Conclusion

In this chapter the development of events management as a profession and as an academic field has been examined. Applying functionalist theories of Anglo-American sociology, it has to be stated that events management does not yet entirely fulfil the requirements for being a profession. The academic field of study and research is still quite immature. Theories have been presented that are helpful in dealing with the very typical managerial challenges of the field. Furthermore, empirically as well as analytically derived models specifying and categorising the competences need to be introduced. However, a comprehensive documentation of existing models is not possible and was not intended. In conclusion it can be said that theoretical and empirical approaches reveal some particular competences needed for successful events management. As opposed to analytical approaches from the perspective of Fayol, an empirical assessment of the skill requirements in the field is of high relevance. Against the backdrop of the heterogeneity of the still young and emerging event industry, it is not appropriate to simply proceed from the logic of the job assignment – one also has to look closely at the already existing practice. In general within the process of defining curricula and models, it is important to draw on the knowledge and experience of current managers. An overview of different international guidelines and models that have been developed for events management so far can be found in Bowdin et al. (2011: 38–39).

Case 3.1	Skiing world championships

The characteristics of events are unique, and, as such, no one standard model of management fits all (Yeoman et al., 2004). Thus a critical reflection on the relevance of theories and models from the so-called 'home disciplines', as well as the consideration of specific event phenomena, are crucial to deal successfully with the particular requirements. When skiing emerged in the 20th century in Alpine countries the emphasis was on downhill (Alpine) skiing. It was seen by its developers as a way of promoting activity in what was otherwise an 'off-season' period of tourism. Previously Alpine ski resorts had focused on richer tourists who came to the destinations for either health reasons or for the nascent sport of climbing. By the 1970s Alpine skiing had developed into a major element of tourism, and, because of these developments, its image has changed significantly from being an elitist sport into being more accessible to everybody, even though the associated costs still make it more exclusive than most other sports (Kaiser et al., 2013).

Case 3.1 *(continued)*

The Fédération Internationale de Ski (FIS) Alpine World Ski Championships in 2001 took place in St Anton, Austria. The place is a very traditional Alpine ski resort. Its famous Arlberg Ski Club was founded in 1901. The resort has positioned itself as a sport tourism destination, having hosted major events not only in skiing, but also in various other sports such as cycling, triathlon and volleyball. It is thus a well-established destination, seeking to grow tourism, not least with the help of events (Kaiser et al., 2013). In contrast to St Anton, Ramsau am Dachstein, host of the FIS Nordic World Ski Championships in 1999, is not a typical Alpine ski resort. The place is located on a plateau, it thus seems natural that it has been developed as a Nordic rather than Alpine skiing destination. St Anton and Ramsau, very much in common with other winter sport tourism destinations, both face a number of broad challenges, including the general economic climate, climate change, changing consumer demand patterns and pressure on innovations for tourism development, as well as specific market conditions. However, they face these challenges at quite different stages in their respective destination life cycles, St Anton having been at a mature stage for many years while Ramsau is still in a growth phase (Kaiser et al., 2013).

Discussion questions

Please answer the following questions with a special regard to the particular differences between the two events as well as the surrounding conditions described:

1 What managerial competences would the head of the destination marketing organisation require? How far would they differ between the two examples?
2 Comparing both cases, would you argue that staging the events has been an efficient way of investing scarce public resources?

General discussion questions

3 Identify and explain the main challenges regarding theory construction and modelling in events management.
4 What are the basic dimensions of common approaches to the categorisation of events?
5 Discuss the academic status of the field. Do you think it is justifiable to establish events management as a separate field of study?
6 Are there any specific managerial challenges caused by the very typical integration of the 'external factors' (customers, spectators) in the production process of events?
7 Would you say that events management fulfils the requirements for being a profession?

Guided reading

The following two journals are useful sources of articles on events management:

Event Management (formerly *Festival Management and Event Tourism*)

International Journal of Hospitality and Event Management

Recommended websites

Convention Industry Council (CIC): **www.conventionindustry.org**

Events Industry Alliance (EIA): **www.eventsindustryalliance.com**

International Festivals and Events Association (IFEA): **www.ifea.com**

International Special Events Society (ISES): **www.ises.com**

Leonardo da Vinci funded partnership project COMPEVENT: **www.compevent.eu**

The Event Management Body of Knowledge (EMBOK): **www.embok.org**

Key words

co-opetition; profession(s); resource-based view; service profit chain; virtual companies

Bibliography

Barney, J.B. and Clark, D.N. (2007) *Resource-based Theory: Creating and Sustaining Competitive Advantage*. Oxford/New York: Oxford University Press.

Berridge, G. (2007) *Events Design and Experience*. Oxford: Butterworth-Heinemann.

Bieger, T. (2008) *Management von Destinationen*. Munich: Oldenbourg.

Bleuel, W.H. and Patton, J.D. (1978) *Service Management, Principles and Practices*. Pittsburgh, PA: Instrument Society of America.

Bowdin, G., Allen, J., O'Toole, W., Harris, R. and McDonnell, I. (2011) *Events Management*. Oxford: Elsevier Butterworth-Heinemann.

Brandenburger, A.M. and Nalebuff, B.J. (1998) *Co-opetition: A Revolutionary Mindset that Combines Competition and Co-operation*. New York: Doubleday.

Carlson, S. (1951) *Executive Behaviour: A Study of the Work Load and the Working Methods of Managing Directors*. Stockholm: Strömberg.

Chalip, L. (2006) Toward a distinctive sport management discipline. *Journal of Sport Management*, 20, 1–21.

Connelly, M.S.C., Gilbert, J.A., Zaccaro, S.J., Threlfall, K.V., Marks, M.A. and Mumford, M.D. (2000) Exploring the relationship of leadership skills and knowledge to leader performance. *Leadership Quarterly*, 11, 65–8.

De Jong, H.W. and Shepherd, W.G. (2007) *Pioneers of Industrial Organisation*. Cheltenham: Elgar.

Fayol, H. (1916) *Administration industrielle et générale*. Paris: Dunod.

Fitzsimmons, J.A. (2011) *Service Management: Operations, strategy, information technology*, Boston, MA: McGraw-Hill/Irwin.

Fitzsimmons, J.A. and Fitzsimmons, M.J. (2008) *Service Management: Operations, Strategy, and Information Technology* (6th edn). New York: McGraw-Hill Publishing.

Getz, D. (1999) Editorial. *Event Management: An International Journal*, 6(1).

Getz, D. (2000) Developing a research agenda for the event management field. Events Beyond 2000: Setting the Agenda, Proceedings of Conference on Event Evaluation, Research and Education, Sydney, 10–21 July.

Getz, D. (2005) *Event Management and Event Tourism* (2nd edn). New York: Cognizant Communications Corporation.

Goldblatt, J. (1990) *Special Events: The Art and Science of Celebration:* New York: Wiley.

Goldblatt, J. (2000) A future for event management: the analysis of major trends impacting the emerging profession. Events Beyond 2000: Setting the Agenda, Proceedings of Conference on Event Evaluation, Research and Education, Sydney, 10–21 July.

Heskett, J.L., Sasser, W.E. and Schlesinger, L.A. (1997) *The Service Profit Chain. How Leading Companies Link Profit and Growth to Loyalty, Satisfaction, and Value*. New York: Free Press.

Hovemann, G., Kaiser, S. and Schütte, N. (2003) *Der Eventmanager*. Düsseldorf: IST.

Jamieson, L.-M. (1987) Competency-based approaches to sport management. *Journal of Sport Management*, 1, 48–56.

Kaiser, S. (2004) Competence research in sport management – the German case. In G.T. Papanikos (ed.), *The Economics and Management of Mega Athletic Events: Olympic Games, Professional Sports, and Other Essays*. Athens: Athens Institute for Education and Research, 253–65.

Kaiser, S. and Schütte, N. (2012) Patterns of managerial action – an empirical analysis of German sport managers. *International Journal Management in Education*, 6(1/2), 174–89.

Kaiser, S., Alfs, C., Beech, J. and Kaspar, R. (2013) Challenges of tourism development in winter sports destinations and for post-event tourism marketing – the cases of the Ramsau Nordic Ski World Championships 1999 and the St Anton Alpine Ski World Championships 2001. *Journal of Sport and Tourism*, 18(1), 33–48.

Kanungo, R.N. and Misra, S. (1992) Managerial resourcefulness: a reconceptualization of management skills. *Human Relations*, 45, 1311–32.

Kaspar, R. and Kaiser, S. (2013) The impacts of sport. In J. Beech and S. Chadwick (eds), *The Business of Sport Management* (2nd edn). Harlow: Pearson Education.

Katz, R.L. (1974) Skills of an effective administrator. *Harvard Business Review*, 52(5), 90–102.

Lau, A.W., Newman, A.R. and Broedling, L.A. (1980) The nature of managerial work in the public sector. *Public Management Forum*, 19, 513–21.

Mahoney, J. T. and Pandian, R.J. (1992) The resource-based view within the conversation of strategic management. *Strategic Management Journal*, 13(5), 363–80.

Mahoney, T.A., Jerdee, T.H. and Carroll Jr, S.J. (1965) The jobs of management. *Industrial Relations*, 4, 97–110.

Maleri, R. (1973) *Grundzüge der Dienstleistungsproduktion*. Berlin/Heidelberg: Springer-Verlag.

Mintzberg, H. (1973) *The Nature of Managerial Work*. New York: Harper and Row.

Mintzberg, H. (1990) The Manager's Job: Folklore and Fact. *Harvard Business Review*, 68(2), 163–76.

Mumford, T.V., Campion, M.A. and Morgeson, F.P. (2007) The leadership skills strataplex: Leadership skill requirements across organisational levels. *The Leadership Quarterly*, 18, 154–66.

Parsons, T. (1939) The professions and social structure. *Social Forces*, 17, 457–67.

Penrose, E.T. (1959) *The Theory of Growth of the Firm*. Oxford: Basil Blackwell.

Perry, M., Foley, P. and Rumpf, P. (1996) Event management: an emerging challenge in Australian education. *Festival Management and Event Tourism*, 4(1), 85–93.

Ratmawati, D. (2007) Managerial competency commitment to employee empowerment: banking companies case. In Proceedings of the 13th Asia Pacific Management Conference, Melbourne, Australia, 556–62.

Roberts, K. (2004) *The Leisure Industries*. Basingstoke: Palgrave Macmillan.

Roche, M. (2000) *Mega-Events and Modernity: Olympics and Expos in the Growth of Global Culture*. London/New York: Routledge.

Siller, L. (2010) *Strategisches Management alpiner Destinationen. Kultur als Wettbewerbsvorteil für nachhaltigen Erfolg*. Berlin: Schmidt.

Sydow, J., ed. (2006) *Management von Netzwerkorganisationen. Beiträge aus der 'Managementforschung'*. Wiesbaden: Betriebswirtschaftlicher Verlag Dr Th. Gabler/GWV Fachverlage GmbH Wiesbaden.

Tum, J., Norton, P. and Wright, N. (2006) *Managing Event Operations*. Oxford: Elsevier Butterworth-Heinemann.

Wernerfelt, B. (1984) A resource-based view of the firm. *Strategic Management Journal*, 5(2), 171–80.

Yeoman, I., Robertson, M., Ali-Knight, J., Drummond, S. and McMahon-Beattie, U., eds (2004) *Festival and Events Management: An International Arts and Cultural Perspective*. Oxford: Elsevier Butterworth-Heinemann.

Chapter 4

The business of sports and cultural events

Gernot Wolfram, MHMK Berlin, Germany, and **Sebastian Kaiser**, SRH University Heidelberg, Germany

Learning outcomes

Upon completion of this chapter the reader should be able to:

- differentiate between the different approaches of management in the field of sports and culture;

- understand the complex history and significance of the term 'games' in both fields;

- reflect the gaps between the for-profit and non-profit sectors in both fields;

- recognise the differences between the expectations of the Creative Industries vs. the new approaches of the Arts Management;

- explain different economic prospects in the sport and culture business sectors.

Overview

Sports and cultural events feature various similarities with regard to their goals and organisational principles and thus to the basic managerial competences needed. They both express specific cultural knowledge as well as a deep understanding of rituals and symbols within the space of games. However, events in both fields also differ to an important extent, as for example in the understanding of the term 'management' as well as basic managerial principles and, not least, the predictors and determinants of success. Therefore events management in the fields of both sport and culture can benefit to a great extent not only from a dialogue between science and practice but particularly from an interdisciplinary perspective integrating theories and approaches from the relevant disciplines of sports and cultural management. In this chapter cultural and sports events are pictured as being embedded in their particular home disciplines (such as **arts management**, sports management) as well as their common socio-cultural background. Furthermore, similarities and differences regarding the **business models** of cultural and sports events are discussed, with a special focus on goals, and demand, as well as on resources.

Introduction

Sport and culture are at first sight two different worlds. But in times of postmodern discourses and a huge variety of new combinations between different areas in the field of events management, it becomes more and more obvious that sport events and cultural events are *both* expressions of certain social experiences which are grounded in cultural developments of the past and of current times. Sport events and cultural events express special cultural knowledge and a deep understanding of rituals and symbols within the space of games. The term 'game' therefore constitutes a common basis for the fields of sport and culture. In both fields people use games as an expression for their emotions, for their longings for spaces and social constructions which don't belong to their daily life experiences. In both fields there are certain rules, rituals and a special knowledge which are important in sharing the event. And in both fields massive differences are to be seen between active and passive participation. Richard Sennett (1996) made clear that, since the time of Ancient Greece, sport events were not simply an act of entertainment or competitive shows. The bodies of the athletes were representations of the values, ideas and self-concepts in the Greek *polis* (city state). Culture was expressed through bodies which were presented in 'contests' like the Olympic Games (Stuttard, 2012). Sport was, according to Richard Sennett, not first of all an event in itself – it was a symbolic representation of political, social and cultural ideas. The perfect body of the Greek athlete was a mirror for the proclaimed strength and power of the city that the sportsmen came from. A similar development happened with Greek theatre, which had in its original meaning shades of a religious and socially determined spectacle. The actors reflected essential questions of life, like sorrows about the destiny of human beings or love and hate. Later, especially with the plays of Aristophanes, political and social references became an important part of theatre events (Ley, 1991). Very often fantastic elements were included to make clear that the spectators weren't experiencing real life; rather, they were seeing a symbolic show which gave the opportunity to reflect on the issues of their political and social existence. Interestingly, in the times of the great 'theatre contests', structures of representation were implemented which were near to sports events. There was a competition between different plays and at the end a winner was announced. These historical links are important in understanding that sports and culture have a common tradition in the sense of their use of symbols and certain rituals to draw a clear line between the experience of daily life and the extraordinary experience of games. Not only in the European tradition is this bridging development between sports and culture visible. Games and fictional approaches to express ideas about the body and the mind are found in almost every cultural tradition in the world. In the 19th and 20th centuries cultural historians like Johan Huizinga (1971) stated the deep significance of the term 'game' as a key word to see the connecting links between sports and culture. The philosophy of sport as a science is still strongly defined by this approach (see Estes and Mechikoff, 2009). The German philosopher Hans Georg Gadamer (1986) made clear in the 20th century that the symbolic values of games are also closely connected to the question of aesthetics which are also present in the field of sports and culture.

Common features of sports and cultural events

As is evident today, sports and cultural events are increasingly converging. One can look at the FIFA World Cup, the Olympic Games or other mega events in the field of sport and see that there is a framing cultural programme involved. This development has consequences in the fields of both sports and culture management. Both kinds of planning processes use similar strategies to attract the attention of spectators (see Kennedy, 2011). Both sport and arts management call for a certain kind of knowledge from their spectators to make the event functional. The spectators have to know the rules to a certain level, and the goals and the symbolic power of the 'game' they see. Neither a sports event nor a cultural one would be attractive without a proper resonance of the spectators. Knowledge and resonance are two key terms for sport and cultural events in matters of planning the attractiveness of events for spectators. Both fields, moreover, share a high acceptance in society. Sports and cultural events are used as symbolic representations of nations, cities and regions. Their common use is therefore an innovative approach to refer to the integrative power of events which combine physical and psychological performances to open the space of games to different target groups. Arts managers and sports managers are, in their respective areas, experts of innovative event formats because they can prove that both fields have the strength to activate, stimulate and connect spectators with different cultural and social backgrounds (see Byrnes, 2008; Chong, 2009).

Cultural events are very often seen today as an important part of the **creative industries** in different countries. The symbolic and economic impact of the term 'culture' leads to new strategies of representation. For example, the new orientation of the official funding programme of the European Union is deeply connected with this development. The title of the 2014–2020 programme is 'Creative Europe'. That means that projects must not only prove their artistically innovative approach, but also present a concept for their economic goals and structures. This is a tremendous change towards a completely different understanding of cultural projects in Europe. The orientation towards economic success will probably change the perception of events within artistic scenes and their audiences. On the other hand, this change reveals a new potential for artists to prove their broad knowledge and their ability to present their work in a more comprehensive way. Likewise, in the USA different art scenes change into complex areas of new economic activity. That also has consequences for arts management.

> We are used to imagining music, dance, theatre, literature, crafts and the visual arts as the most significant aspects of our cultural experience. Around them we visualise those newer forms of artistic expression that include things like performance art, video art, installations, computer and multimedia creations . . . Underlying this way of looking at culture is the romantic assumption that the activities at the centre are somehow worthier than those at the circumference because they are less tainted by commercial ambition . . . The trend is clear. The high-end cultural stuff that survives only through the beneficence of state or municipal subsidies – the opera, ballet, national theatres, public galleries and museums . . . – has had to make way as the products of the creative economy claim centre stage.
>
> (Torr, 2008: 134)

This critical approach towards traditional structures of so-called 'high-culture' is, at first sight, very convincing, because there is undoubtedly a growing problem of acceptance and resonance for these cultural events, especially in the younger generation. On the other hand, it is part of the task of Arts Management not to change, in a general perspective, the cultural sector in a profit-orientated business of creativity. It is necessary to find solutions for managing the special needs of exploring new aesthetic values, innovative art formats, or new kinds of personal interactions with the audiences. Otherwise, for example, every theatre could simply offer musicals – one of the most successful formats of the last 20 years. But would a theatre represent cultural developments properly by just fulfilling the current wishes of a dominant majority of visitors? With a conventional management approach, one would agree. Simply following the needs of the market would lead to a pure customer-orientated perspective which wouldn't meet the self-understanding of arts management (see Chong, 2009). Innovative artistic formats need a smart concept for funding opportunities, marketing activities, media presence and a proper time schedule – and a complex reflection of how new approaches to **audience development** measures can be implemented (see Sims, 2011). Within the non-profit-sector sub-cultural and cultural developments grow under completely different circumstances as in the field of the creative industries where conventional management approaches are seen as a generally accepted base of all issues of the management process around creative products and services. This gap between the for-profit-sector and the non-profit-sector is very often not properly reflected when it comes to questions of how to organise cultural events. There is also a huge gap between arts and sports management because of different traditions of understanding how to create a stable economic base for the different event formats.

Arts management and cultural events

Organising cultural events needs a special understanding of management which is focused on planning events with links to artistic and cultural expressions:

> Arts Management is anything but a mere amalgamation of the world of the arts and the world of business management; it is the confrontation of two opposing methodologies, one being a field of human creativity that produces something new that did not exist before, the other one diving into the existing world of business practices, in order to improve their efficiency. Some references to (cultural) philosophy, (economic and arts) history and other important subjects are indispensable or at least helpful in understanding the chances and risks of arts management practices. This is the aim of this book, which is based on more than twenty years of teaching, researching, and consulting in the field of cultural administration and arts management.
>
> (Bendixen, 2009: 1)

In this definition arts management is closely linked to historical references, to current discourses of the arts and to business practices. The concepts of artists have to be reflected, especially the formulation of their goals and aims. The clear goal of sports events – that there is ultimately a winner – doesn't generally exist in these concepts. Although arts are competitive within distributional processes, they do not focus on this fact as an essential part of their self-understanding. Looking at concrete organisational processes in the field of cultural events, one can formulate some important elements which determine this area of management:

- management theory and its changes and transfers to arts management;
- organisational hierarchies;
- marketing;
- audience development;
- accounting and budgeting;
- admission and box office;
- donors, sponsors, fundraising and grants;
- career development;
- **cultural policies;**
- media management and cross-over cooperation;
- evaluation.

Moreover arts managers have to be able to differentiate between several kinds of organisations facilitating the day-to-day operation of artistic projects. Arts organisations can be professional for-profit (galleries, auction houses, music presenting companies, arts agencies, projects in the creative industries, etc.) or not-for-profit (independent art projects, socio-cultural projects, etc.) There are also arts-related businesses like theatres, museums or exhibitions halls which have their focus on the functioning relationship between artistic approaches and the management of the institution. Arts managers are also important mediators in the field of socio-cultural events. They organise funding, donors and grants to stimulate cultural and intercultural discourses (for example, within the context of migration developments, cultural expressions of minority groups, etc.).

One of the basic problems regarding theory construction and modelling in events management is the ambiguity in the use of the term 'event' – there is little agreement on standardised categories so far (**see Chapter 3**). This particularly applies to the field of cultural events. Many books about events management prefer, for example, a definition that defines events as 'marketing events' (Schäfer-Mehdi, 2006: 9). This is a difficult term for the field of cultural events because it reduces events to a tool which serves economic reasons and goals. Due to references to cultural history and arts sciences, the term 'event' is used in the field of culture, but very often it is also an example for new discoveries and experiments. That might be one of the reasons that the relations between arts management and events management are very often problematic although the connections are obvious. Therefore it is necessary to stress the fact that events in the field of arts management do not generally follow the strategies used by mainstream companies to support a product or special services. The event in itself and its performances and aesthetic strategies form the goals and targets of the artistic representations. Here an important dividing line is to be seen which has, of course, strong relations to discourses about the freedom of the arts which are, in many countries, part of the constitution (Wolfram, 2012).

Similarities are to be found between arts management and events management in the way that both fields understand the terms 'creativity', 'marketing', 'fundraising', 'budgeting' and 'accounting'. A proper knowledge of business practices, organisational transparency and sustainable research in matters of relevance, resonance and audience development is a central base for successful events. One can say that the approach to sustainable measurement of the proclaimed goals of the event before, during and after the performance unites both fields.

A special difference is to be seen in the contacts with the political areas and surroundings of cultural events. As already mentioned, culture is a term with a high symbolic significance. Cultural events mostly do not offer just a relevant show, they also express meta-discourses such as about identity, integration, aesthetical preferences, etc. That leads to a certain kind of reception which can stimulate not only cultural but also political participation. The famous example of Bob Geldof's Live Aid concerts shows that these concerts were not only cultural highlights. They have also put important political issues like reflection about the situation in Africa and in other emergent countries at the centre of international (media) attention. Cultural events use performances as a mirror for issues and topics which are widely present in society, but which often lack a proper language or form of expression. Cultural events present an aesthetic and fictional space which reflects longings for events (Schulze, 2005) within society instead of just fulfilling them. Similar to the area of sport, they are used for tasks and aims which do not always come from their genuine self-understanding. The symbolic values of cultural events are provable also by the support of the European Union, which has increased the budget for the new funding programme 'Europe 2014–2020' to €1.8 billion. If one reads the text of the publication of the new programme it is obvious that the events and projects which can get support are closely connected to the expectation of expressing certain values – not necessarily artistic ones – which recalls that the Culture Programme is the only EU instrument exclusively dedicated to support arts and culture. Over the past 10 years the EU Culture Programme has supported a vast number of cultural co-operations across borders that have contributed to the development of the cultural sector across Europe. Investing in a unique instrument that nourishes a vision of societies that values arts and culture as factors that strengthen solidarity between communities, is particularly important in the context of uncertainty due to the financial crisis and to the delivery of the EU2020 objectives on inclusive growth.

(www.wearemore.eu/wp-content/uploads/2010÷12/
Creative-Europe-statement_EN.pdf)

Sport management and sports events

Sport management has seen dramatic changes in recent years. Both as an occupation and as an academic discipline, the field has experienced exceptional growth. Starting in 1927, courses in organisation and administration of physical education and sport were generally included in all university physical education curricula in the USA (Soucie, 1998). The first formal sport management graduate programme was instituted by Ohio State University in 1966 (Parks and Quain, 1986). In Australia, the first dedicated degree programme was introduced in 1991 (Smith and Westerbeek, 2004). In Germany, the first chair of sport economics and sport management was at the German Sport University Cologne in 1995 (Kaiser and Schütte, 2012). Commercialisation of sport institutions and changes in the demand for sport have led to the increasing necessity for an efficient management of resources, and to an increase in the demands on the management of sport organisations (Kaiser, 2004; Kaiser and Schütte, 2012).

Clubs and sporting organisations must perform well financially, or at the least remain viable, if they want to survive in the highly competitive world of commercialised sport . . . Sport has devolved into a business that demands nothing less than specific, professional preparation. Subsequently, a more systematic and serious approach to the management of sport has emerged, which has culminated in an inexorable slide towards the implementation of business practices in the management of sporting organisations, and has led many sport management practitioners and educators to talk about increasing the level of 'professionalism' amongst graduates.

(Smith and Westerbeek, 2004: 39–40)

The economic prospects of sports are of special interest within the framework of sports economics research. As a result of the traditional and distinctive distance between the role of economists and sports scientists, the academic study of the subject was restricted for a long time. The main focus of economists was, and remains, the analysis of organisation and professional asset production within companies, for markets. The leisure/voluntary nature of the production of (sports) services from members of non-profit organisations on which, up until now, the sports system in Europe has been based has been of little interest to economists and has not fitted within their economic models. From the opposing perspective, the particular distance of sport to the economy should be mentioned. Traditionally, sport was perceived as part of leisure time. Therefore, in view of club-based sports' own perception of being a counterpart to the job market and wage-earning, for a long time there was no cause for economic research. Not least, as a result of the unique resource structure whereby clubs are mainly financed by club members, donations as well as high public subsidies minimised the need for economic expertise. Amateur status, as well as restrictive advertising regulations for sports organisations, additionally limited/slowed the economic exploitation of sport (see Horch, 1994).

In the course of the process of commercialisation and professionalisation this framework has changed fundamentally over recent years. The economic significance of sports is high and increasing and there is an even greater integration between sport and the economy. Against the backdrop of these developments and the high and rising economic importance of sport, the understanding of its impacts, as well as the discussion of appropriate assessment methods, are emerging as more relevant. Not least the political dimension of this debate has to be considered. Among other factors, reliable information about the actual effects of sport is of particular interest for decision making in the process of the awarding of public funds, in the course of institutional funding, or in the discussion regarding the construction of sports facilities. A special concern is given to the aspect of sustainability, a subject which is becoming more and more significant, not least due to the increasing social value of sports and cultural events.

When deciding about whether or not to bid for and organise a sports and/or cultural event, it is essential – in advance – to thoroughly assess the potential direct and indirect effects. To this end, economic feasibility and impact studies are carried out. However, sober *ex post* (i.e. after the event) investigations usually show that the fantastic predictions about the outcomes made prior to the event could not be achieved. On the contrary, it has been demonstrated that temporary, large events are not a rational instrument for stimulating short- or medium-term economic growth (e.g. Preuß, 2010). Furthermore, the economic effects that can be seriously considered are, in fact, too insignificant to influence regional or national economies. Does this mean that a sports event with a negative net benefit for the country should not be organised, or should not be supported by the government? In fact, one should not draw this conclusion too quickly, because sports and cultural events bring with them an additional range of impacts such as positive external effects which take on the character of public goods, for instance national pride, image or sports participation. Not least, sustainable events management is also important – in addition to the economic aspects, a series of other aspects such as ecology and society must be considered. This shift in perspective from short-term to long-term, and from tangible to intangible effects, gives rise to a new set of methodological challenges.

Of course the discussion about the effects of large sports and cultural events is not only interesting from a scientific point of view; it also has immense value for practice because it delivers the foundations upon which informed decisions can be made.

The business models: similarities and differences

If the organisation of sports or culture events were, per se, a profitable business, the private sector could organise and manage such events without any taxpayer subsidy. But since large sporting and cultural events can generally only be achieved with substantial public support and subsidies, it is crucial that the funds are allocated selectively. Therefore, a government must be provided with good arguments for supporting an event, which also means examining the opportunity costs in consideration of alternative uses. The main questions in this respect are under which conditions such investments are justifiable and how the viewpoints of different stakeholders can be properly integrated on the path to successful realisation.

The business models in the respective fields feature more parallels than one may at first have thought (see Schellenberg and Hedderich, 2011: 2). However, there are differences within the process as well as the understanding of management in both fields. First of all, in both fields goals with regard to content (athletic/artistic success) are of much greater importance than a focus on corporate profits. However, a central focus of sports management research is to assess the various measurable results and effects of events in the respective field. The involvement of sponsors, media channels and other stakeholders in particular produces a certain kind of expectation towards the event. In the field of the arts this is also a common approach, but with different basic assumptions: the success of a concert, an art exhibition, a play, etc. would not be measurable in a proper way if the effects could be described in a similar way to those in the world of sports. Every real artistic approach has the character of an experiment. The rules of cultural games are not fixed in the same way as within the games of sports. Therefore the organisational frame of cultural events always has to deal with the unpredictable character of the arts, which are, in contrast to sports, not focused on clear results, as in the dichotomy of winning or losing.

On the other hand, as studies on the demand factors have shown, the drawing potential of a sporting competition can be explained to a great extent just by the fact of the unpredictability of the outcome (see the 'uncertainty of outcome hypothesis', Rottenberg, 1956). There are two basic elements that make a sport event interesting for the spectators and the media: first the aesthetics of sports movement and secondly its specific competition logic. Both these aspects are typically combined and connected by the special drama associated with sport. Elias expresses it thus:

> The exquisiteness of sport consists of the fact that the aesthetics of body and body movement . . . is a part of a drama. The beauty belongs to a competition with which a tension curve is generated as well as is closed again – it is closed with the victory of one and the defeat of the other.
>
> (Elias, 1992, cited in Neidhardt, 2007: 2)

This 'drama' in particular creates the special charm or attraction of sport. Added to this is the fact that results of sports competitions are transient in a particular way: sport continually produces new events and, with that, continually gives new raw material to the media. These characteristics have various economic and managerial implications. First of all, one of the main goals of sport events management is to ensure competitive balance between the teams/ opponents. Secondly, as, in sports, only one sportsman or one team can win the competition, it is impossible to increase the branch output: if a sportsman or a team win more often, other sportsmen or teams must, by necessity, lose more often. In contrast to that, the whole branch output can be increased in any other branch. The markets in top-class sports show the special character of so-called 'winner-takes-all' markets. George Akerlof (1976) describes this fact using the so-called 'rat-race' metaphor. This metaphor describes a situation where several rats have a race to get a piece of cheese. The special idea of the rat race is that it leads to an increase of the input of the racing participants, while the prize remains the same. Corresponding to this, the specific remuneration structures in competitive sports become clear too. In contrast to other markets where the remuneration of a worker is dependent on his or her productivity, regardless of the achievement of the remaining workers, the remuneration in 'winner-takes-all' markets depends on the relative and not the absolute achievement. Even marginally better achievements can thus lead to disproportionately better remuneration. Under these market terms, for a 1% higher achievement an actor gets not 1% but 1,000% more wage. This explains the immense sums that are invested in sports.

Important parallels between the two fields can also be seen by looking at the income as well as expenditure structure. Compared to other businesses, both cultural and sports events feature a heterogeneous revenue structure consisting of public funding, visitors, sponsorship, TV rights and so on. As a consequence, this first of all reduces the economic pressure as they are not subject to just sales revenue. On the other hand, the high amount of public funding in particular causes a high dependency; both cultural and sports event organisers have only a very limited influence over a large part of their income. Regarding the expenditure structure in culture and sports, personnel expenses play an important role.

> Athletes and artists are a decisive productive factor and the fees for 'employees with star qualities' have in the course of internationalisation grown steadily in the past few years.
>
> (Schellenberg and Hedderich, 2011: 4)

The above differences have to be reflected when an arts manager and a sport manager are working together. One of the main challenges is that they very often use the same language of general management, but the meaning of these terms in the practical field shows tremendous differences. Therefore a synergistic approach between sports and culture needs first of all a clear description of what these two fields mean when we speak about terms of management.

Conclusion

As we have shown, there are a lot of similarities between sport and cultural events with regard to their organisational principles and thus to the basic managerial competences needed. However, events in both fields also differ to an important extent, as for example in the understanding of the term 'management', as well as in basic managerial principles, and, not least, in the predictors and determinants of success. Therefore events management in both the fields of sport and culture can benefit to a great extent not only from a dialogue between theory and practice, but particularly from an interdisciplinary perspective, integrating theories and approaches from the disciplines relevant to sports and cultural management. In examining how themes from the cultural sciences and the sports sciences may be combined in an integrative rather than a simply additive sense, one has only to look at the various European capitals of culture with their numerous projects whose objective is to integrate sports and culture. This combination of approaches, as well as the re-evaluating of commonplace concepts against this background, may open further perspectives, giving a new impetus to a practically orientated, interdisciplinary form of event research.

Case 4.1	Changing cricket – the Indian Premier League (IPL)

The official national sport of India is field hockey, but cricket is the most popular one. Indian cricket has a long and rich history but recently it went through significant changes. Cricket was first played in India in the early 17th century. The first clubs had been founded by the end of the 18th century (1792: Calcutta Cricket and Football Club). Due to its popularity cricket today plays an important role in Indian society. Not least, it has been considered to be a catalyst for social transformation. Indian cricket is managed by the Board of Control for Cricket in India (BCCI) which is known to be the richest Cricket Board worldwide. The most popular domestic competitions are the Ranji Trophy, founded in 1934 as the Cricket Championship of India, the NKP Salve Challenger Trophy, which started as the Challenger Series in 1994, and the Indian

Case 4.1   *(continued)*

Premier League (IPL), started in 2008 after the downfall of the Indian Cricket League (ICL), a private cricket league which has been funded by Zee Entertainment Enterprises. With the emergence of the Indian Premier League, cricket has undergone a major transformation. Since it was launched by the BCCI it has gained immense popularity and has made huge profits. Its brand value is estimated to be more than US$2 billion and it has become the most watched TV programme (Ryder and Madhavan, 2009: 210).

How can this success be explained? First of all, managed by Lalit Kumar Modi, Chairman and Commissioner of the Indian Premier League and Vice President of the BCCI, and following the example of US major leagues, the organisational and the event-related frameworks have been changed, with the main aim being to appeal to an international mass audience. The League consists of city-based franchises, and international players can be drafted. Not least the commercialisation of the IPL has opened up many business opportunities for the franchises. The eight franchise teams are owned by well-known film actors, industrialists and media magnates, among them the 'King of Bollywood' Shahrukh Khan. Secondly, the game itself has been changed, and crowd participation has been encouraged more strongly than in other forms of the game, in order to raise the attractiveness of the events. It has particularly been adapted to follow the model of baseball. The players' outfits have been altered, and the events have been enriched with laser-shows, live music and cheerleading to add some glamour-appeal. The mode of play has been changed to the Twenty20 system: eight teams play a 20 overs cricket match against each other, over a period of 45 days, in different venues across India. This system was first introduced by the England and Wales Cricket Board (ECB) in 2003 in England (Twenty20 Cup). When the Twenty20 Cup was launched it was described as the most revolutionary step since the invention of one-day cricket. Critics state that Twenty20 is not cricket, as entertainment is the primary objective, and the main aim is commercialisation via satisfying spectators' demands. Especially remarkable is the fact that these major changes described above took place under the auspices of the International Cricket Council (ICC), the international governing body for cricket, one of whose main aims is to protect the game and its unique spirit.

Sources

Ryder, R.D. and Madhavan, A. (2009) 'Intellectual Property League': the importance of IP in the Indian Premier League. *Journal of Intellectual Property Law and Practice*, 4(12), 901–3.

Internet sources

www.iplt20.com/

www.ecb.co.uk/

http://icc-cricket.yahoo.net/

Discussion questions

1 Which are key success factors for the commercialisation of the Indian Premier League?

2 Do you think the organisational and game-related changes described would automatically lead to commercial success, even in other sports and/or countries?

Case 4.2   Paphos (Cyprus): European Capital of Culture 2017

Paphos, situated on the south-western coast of the island of Cyprus, the only divided country in Europe, is a natural gateway and timeless bridge between three continents, Europe, Asia and Africa. Today, this city, with its long history of 2,300 years, aspires to become the first European Capital of Culture in the south-eastern extremity of Europe. The big challenge for Paphos is to bring together these different elements in its history and to show how it can a living example of the contribution of Cyprus in shaping the cultural identity of modern Europe. The tragic experiences of the continuing division of Cyprus, the mosaic of people from different nationalities and cultures representing the society of a small town of 50,000 inhabitants, and the island's distance from the heart of Europe have all strongly influenced the city, which has suffered over the years from foreign invaders. The diverse influences have affected tourism development in recent decades, and the search for a balance between the development and preservation of cultural and environmental character has determined the parameters of the project to be undertaken.

Paphos and the wider district have had a significant role in shaping European culture and civilisation throughout the years. In these areas ideas and principles were fertilised, contributing to the enrichment of European culture. Ideas and principles such as love and beauty are recognised elements of

▶

Case 4.2 *(continued)*

the common European cultural heritage. To this direction, monuments, texts, ideas, art, crafts and the vast amount of myths and traditions have made a significant contribution. A universal recognition of this contribution is the declaration of the new Paphos area (the ancient city of Paphos) as a World Heritage site by UNESCO in 1981.

Paphos's relationship with European culture is not limited to the past. Over the last 25 years or so, the area of Paphos, spearheaded by the city of Paphos itself, has developed a wide network of contacts and relationships with local and regional authorities, organisations and individuals in Europe. Examples include the twinning of Paphos with six towns in Greece, and also the twining of Paphos with Anzio in Italy, Sofia in Bulgaria and Sefton (Merseyside) in Great Britain, and through organisations like Europa Nostra and Les Rencontres. The effect of such a relationship in European cultural activities and events covers a wide range such as arts, cultural heritage, environment, sports, youth, etc. Notable examples in the field of culture are the internationally recognised annual opera event 'Paphos Aphrodite Festival' and also the annual 'International Festival of Ancient Greek Drama.'

These relationships, contacts and experiences are a good basis for developing a multi-layered network of relations and exchanges between Paphos and other cities, artistic and spiritual bodies (academic), non-governmental organisations active in the broader field of culture, institutions (museums, research centres, libraries, galleries), media, etc. Through the Institution of the European Capital of Culture the stated ambition of Paphos is to transform itself into a factory of European culture. Using the essential characteristics of modern European cultural creativity and prominent elements of local cultural tradition, it aims to produce an authentic cultural product, capable of enriching and enhancing European cultural identity for a long time. Understandably, such a project will promote and highlight the cultural diversity of modern Europe, while highlighting the common aspects of the culture of Europe.

The concept of Paphos 2017 includes different projects which use approaches of the creative industries as well as concepts from arts management. This example can help the understanding of how cultural events can lead to a new stimulation of citizenship, political sensitivity and economic effects on cities and regions.

Sources

Patel, K.K. (2012) *The Cultural Politics of Europe: European Capitals of Culture and European Union since the 1980s.* Abingdon: Routledge.

Richards, G. (2007) *Eventful Cities. Cultural Management and Urban Revitalisation.* Abingdon: Taylor & Francis.

www.pafos2017.com/

Discussion questions

3 What are the political dimensions of this concept and how is it linked with specific approaches to a sustainable arts management?

4 Explain the idea of 'revitalisation of cities through culture'.

5 Why include within the concept strong cooperation with other cities on the island?

6 Which aspects of the concept are transferable to other cultural events in bigger cities?

General discussion questions

7 Describe the importance of the term 'game' for the historical understanding of the significance of both sport and cultural events. What are the connecting symbolic values in both fields?

8 Explain the differences between 'stimulating' and 'activating' the awareness of different audiences in the fields of sport and culture events.

9 What are new approaches developed by the creative industries in comparison to other events in the non-profit sector of culture events?

10 Which important phenomenon can be explained with the so-called 'rat-race metaphor'? What are the consequences for the management of sports and/or sports events?

11 Name and explain major similarities and differences between the business models of cultural and sports events.

Guided reading

The following books are helpful sources to understand new approaches in the respective fields:

Chong, D. (2009) *Arts Management*. Abingdon: Routledge.

This book offers new case studies and several chapters with the focus on central questions of arts management. Derrick Chong takes an interdisciplinary approach in examining some of the main impulses informing discussions on the management of arts and cultural organisations.

Anheier, H. et al. (2010) *Cultural Expression, Creativity and Innovation*. London: Sage.

This book reflects the interactions between globalisation and different forms of artistic practice and cultural expression. Bringing together over 25 high-profile authors from around the world, this volume offers a complex variety of insights into the international field of culture events.

Torr, G. (2008) *Managing Creative People. Lessons in Leadership for the Ideas Economy*. Hoboken, NJ: Wiley & Sons.

This book reflects the new opportunities of creative management processes within different areas of cities and their development potentials. The student can also reflect here on the differences between arts management approaches and the ideas of the creative industries.

Richards, G. et al. (2013) *The Routledge Handbook of Cultural Tourism*. Abingdon: Routledge.

The Routledge Handbook of Cultural Tourism explores and critically evaluates the debates and controversies in this field of tourism. It brings together leading specialists from a range of disciplinary backgrounds and geographical regions, to provide state-of-the-art theoretical reflection and empirical research on this significant stream of tourism and its future direction. This book can help in the understanding of the meaning of cultural events in different areas of economies, such as tourism being one of the most important factors for cultural events.

Razaq, R. and Musgrave, J. (2009) *Events Management and Sustainability*. Wallingford CAB International.

This book discusses concepts of sustainable management and how it relates to various sectors within the events industry. It illustrates the fundamental importance of local communities, businesses and interested stakeholders in relation to future events in regional, national and international locations. Historical and documented reports supplement this area. The book focuses on international governing bodies and national government strategic objectives as the cornerstone for sustainable development in the events sector. The relationship between these strategic objectives and on-the-ground operational responsibilities is presented using research by contributing authors and accredited organisations.

Masterman, G. (2009) *Strategic Sports Events Management: Olympic Edition*. Oxford: Elsevier.

The hosting of sports events – whether large international events or smaller niche interest events – has huge and long-lasting impacts on the local environment, economy and industry. *Strategic Sports Events Management: Olympic Edition* provides students and event managers with an insight into the strategic management of sports events of all scales and types. The framework offers a planning process that can be used to understand the importance of a strategic approach, and shows how to implement strategies that can achieve successful sports events over the short and long term.

Recommended websites

European Network of Cultural Administration Training Centres: **www.encatc.org/pages/index.php**

International Festivals and Events Association (IFEA): **www.ifea.com**

International Platform for Arts, Policy and Creative Industries: **www.cultureaction europe.org/think/creative-industries**

International Special Events Society (ISES): **www.ises.com**

International Website for Arts Management: **www.artsmanagement.net**

The Commonwealth Games Federation: **www.thecgf.com**

Youth Olympic Games: **www.olympic.org/youth-olympic-games**

Key words

arts management; audience development; business models; creative industries; cultural policies; demand determinants; philosophy of games

Bibliography

Akerlof, G. (1976) The economics of caste and of the rat race and other woeful tales. *The Quarterly Journal of Economics,* 90(4), 599–617.

Bendixen, P. (2009) *Managing Arts. An Introduction to Principles and Conceptions.* Berlin/Münster: Lit-Verlag.

Byrnes, W.J. (2008) *Management and the Arts.* Oxford: Butterworth Heinemann.

Chong, D. (2009) *Arts Management.* Abingdon: Taylor & Francis.

Elias, N. (1992) *Über den Prozeß der Zivilisation. Soziogenetische und psychogenetische Untersuchungen* (17 edn). Frankfurt am Main: Suhrkamp.

Estes, S.G. and Mechikoff, R.A. (2009) *A History and Philosophy of Sport and Physical Education.* New York: McGraw Hill.

Gadamer, H.G. (1986) *Die Aktualität des Schönen.* Stuttgart: Reclam.

Horch, H.-D. (1994) Besonderheiten einer Sport-Ökonomie – ein neuer bedeutender Zweig der Freizeitökonomie. *Freizeitpädagogik,* 16, 243–47.

Huizinga, J. (1971) *Homo Ludens. A Study of the Play-Element in Culture.* Boston, MA: Beacon Press.

Kaiser, S. (2004) Competence research in sport management – the German case. In G.T. Papanikos (ed.), *The Economics and Management of Mega Athletic Events: Olympic Games, Professional Sports, and Other Essays.* Athens: Athens Institute for Education and Research, 253–65.

Kaiser, S. and Schütte, N. (2012) Patterns of managerial action – an empirical analysis of German sport managers. *International Journal Management in Education,* 6(1–2), 174–89.

Kennedy, D. (2011) *The Spectator and the Spectacle. Audiences in Modernity and Postmodernity.* Cambridge: Cambridge University Press.

Ley, G. (1991) *A Short Introduction to Ancient Greek Theatre*. Chicago, IL: Chicago University Press.

Neidhardt, F. (2007) Sport und Medien. In Deutsche Sporthochschule Köln (ed.), *Universitätsreden*, 13, 2–13.

Parks, J.B. and Quain, R.J. (1986) Curriculum perspectives. *Journal of Physical Education, Recreation and Dance,* 57(4), 22–6.

Preuss, H. (2010) Olympic economics. *Olympic Review* (2010), 64–7.

Rottenberg, S. (1956) The baseball player's labour market. *Journal of Political Economy,* 64, 242–58.

Ryder, R.D. and Madhavan, A. (2009) 'Intellectual Property League': the importance of IP in the Indian Premier League. *Journal of Intellectual Property Law and Practice,* 4(12), 901–3.

Schäfer-Mehdi, S. (2006) *Event-Marketing* (2nd edn). Stuttgart: Cornelsen.

Schellenberg, F. and Hedderich, F. (2011) Sports and culture – different worlds with parallels. *Arts Management Newsletter,* 106, 2–6.

Schulze, G. (2005) *Die Erlebnisgesellschaft: Kultursoziologie der Gegenwart.* Frankfurt am Main: Campus.

Sennett, R. (1996) *Flesh and Stone. The Body and the City in Western Civilization.* New York: Norton & Co.

Sims, W.S. (2011) *Creative Change. Audience Development and Cultural Engagement in the Non-Profit-Arts.* Umi Dissertation Publishing.

Soucie, D. (1998) Sport management: a new discipline in the sport sciences. In *Sport Science Studies,* 9, Special Issue: *Research in Sport Management: Implications for Sport Administrators,* 14–22.

Smith, A.C.T. and Westerbeek, H.M. (2004) Professional sport management education and practice in Australia. *Journal of Hospitality, Leisure, Sport and Tourism Education,* 3(2), 38–45.

Stuttard, D. (2012) *Power Games. The Olympics of Ancient Greece.* London: British Museum Press.

Torr, G. (2008) *Managing Creative People. Lessons in Leadership for the Ideas Economy.* Hoboken, NJ: Wiley & Sons.

Wolfram, G. (ed.) (2012) Kulturmanagement und Europäische Kulturarbeit. Bielefeld: Transcript.

Chapter 5

The business of corporate events

Rob Davidson, University of Greenwich, UK

Learning outcomes

Upon completion of this chapter the reader should be able to:

- differentiate between the principal types of corporate events and the various ways in which these may be categorised;

- recognise the key stakeholders in the corporate events market;

- evaluate how different types of corporate events help companies reach their business goals;

- understand the impacts that economic, technological and demographic trends are having on the corporate events sector.

Overview

Meetings run on behalf of, and for the benefit of, private sector companies are commonly referred to as business events or corporate events. They may also be categorised under the collective term 'MICE' – Meetings, Incentives, Conferences and Exhibitions – although this term is increasingly being avoided by meetings professionals on account of its negative associations and general lack of intelligibility to those outside this sector of the events industry.

Ranging from a half-day training seminar for six managers in a local hotel's seminar room to an international trade show for tens of thousands of attendees, corporate events have been widely recognised as one of the most effective ways in which companies can use face-to-face events in order to achieve their business objectives. And even in a world rich in electronic and virtual channels of communication, face-to-face meetings between colleagues and between company employees and their potential or actual clients continue to demonstrate their resilience as drivers of business success.

This chapter examines the wide range of events that are used by companies, large and small, to achieve their business goals. The principal stakeholders in the corporate events sector are reviewed; and the main trends currently shaping the ways in which corporate events are designed and run are discussed.

Types of corporate events

Although meetings are held by a wide range of organisations, including professional and trade associations, governments and trade unions as well as collectors' clubs and other common-interest groups, corporate events are generally agreed to constitute the largest single market segment – estimated by Lawson (2000), for example, to constitute over 65% of all meetings. Zeller (2006) estimates that 0.5% to 1% of company expenditure is on meetings and that this proportion is potentially higher in the pharmaceutical, technology and financial services industries. Companies have a number of important motives for holding meetings, and their face-to-face events therefore represent a key segment within the meetings market. Occasionally, company meetings are held on companies' own premises and are organised in-house, with little or no commercial significance for any stakeholders beyond the companies themselves. However, most companies recognise that in the main there are many compelling reasons for holding their meetings off-site. These include:

- a lack of capacity in their own premises (few company offices have facilities and the necessary audio-visual equipment for large meetings);
- the need to give staff a break from their normal working environment (to free them from day-to-day work-related distractions; to help them think more creatively, in a different setting);
- the wish to motivate staff by holding the meeting in an attractive location, possibly with leisure elements, such as golf or a spa, added;
- the need to keep proceedings confidential, when, for example, sensitive topics, such as redundancies, are under discussion;
- the need to meet on 'neutral' ground, as, for instance, when representatives from two companies are meeting to discuss a merger.

Corporate events may take a number of different forms. Davidson and Rogers (2006) list the principal types as follows:

- *Annual general meetings*: Publicly owned companies invite their shareholders (or stockholders) to these events, at which the company's annual results are presented. Shareholders are usually asked to approve the dividend and to endorse a certain number of resolutions, which will determine the company's activities in the year ahead. Every shareholder who wants to take part in the decision-making process of his or her company can attend such meetings and vote personally.
- *Sales meetings*: A sales meeting is a regular forum used by management to impart information, enthusiasm and team spirit to those selling their products and services 'out in the field'. Sales figures for a particular period are generally reviewed, and the achievements of particularly high-performing sales staff are recognised and praised. The type of information imparted generally concerns the company's market share, competitors' activities or new legislation that affects the selling process. Such meetings also give those present the opportunity to share their experiences, positive and negative, of selling.
- *Staff training*: It is generally recognised that, in order to keep their skills and knowledge up to date, employees at all levels must regularly attend training sessions in subjects such as information technology, customer relations skills and employment law. Staff training sessions therefore represent a key channel of **knowledge transfer** for companies. Frequently, these events are held in seminar rooms that are situated off-site, bringing business to suppliers such as hotels and management training centres. Occasionally they are combined with an element of team-building, when the participants learn how better to work together on physical and/or intellectual challenges presented to them by the organisers of the event.

- *Product launches*: Introducing a new product or service to the market is an important stage in the marketing process. A new car, perfume, laptop computer, type of medical insurance policy – whatever the product, companies often use an off-site event as a way of presenting it and explaining its properties and features to those who will be selling it, who may be buying it and to journalists in the specialist press who may write about it for their readers. Such events are usually short but with high production levels, using special effects, sound and vision, in order to make the maximum impact on the audience.
- *Incentive trips*: It is widely recognised that an extremely effective way of motivating and rewarding staff is by offering them the opportunity to compete in order to participate in an incentive trip, as the prize for exceptional achievement in their work. This exceptional achievement may take the form, for example, of selling more of the company's products than other colleagues during a particular period. These trips, often held in exotic and lavish locations, may look like holidays, and indeed they are designed to be highly enjoyable and memorable; but they are firmly considered to be business events, since they are in essence a management tool, designed to elicit higher levels of performance from the company's employees.

To these types of business event may be added *exhibitions,* also known as trade shows or trade fairs. According to Davidson and Cope (2003: 193), the purposes of exhibitions are 'to generate sales, promote new products, maintain or create industry contacts and to act as places that facilitate the exchange of ideas and information between exhibitors, industry experts and visitors'. Thus, from the point of view of those companies exhibiting at trade/consumer shows, these events are a key component of their communications and marketing mix.

Corporate events may also be categorised according to who the participants are: internal, external or mixed.

- *Internal* events are organised solely for the company's own employees. Such events include strategy meetings, team-building days, staff training sessions and incentive trips.
- *External* events are attended largely by people who are not directly employed by the company funding the event. These include shareholders' meetings and product presentations.
- *Mixed* events include both employees and non-employees of the company funding the event. These include product launches and corporate hospitality days.

An alternative method of classifying corporate events is to categorise them according to the primary objective for which the event is being held. Accordingly, the three principal categories are:

- *Legal/constitutional*: internal or external meetings held for the purpose of, for instance, electing company directors or voting on business strategies.
- *Commercial*: events designed directly to boost sales of the company's products or services – for example, new product presentations to clients or potential clients; or training sessions for members of the company's sales force.
- *Social*: events held with the aim of strengthening bonds between staff members or between representatives of the company and its key clients – for example, management retreats, team-building events and corporate hospitality days.

In whichever way they are classified, however, corporate events generally have three principal objectives: to educate, to inspire and to provide the participants with opportunities for **networking** with each other. The proportions of these elements will vary according to the type of corporate event in question. For example, in incentive trips, inspiration and networking will be the dominant features; and in training sessions, the educational aspect will be prominent. But commentators generally agree that any organised gathering of colleagues and associates ought to feature each of these three characteristics in some measure.

Stakeholders in the corporate events sector

The corporate events sector encompasses a variety of players. Davidson and Rogers (2006), Rogers (2008), Davidson and Cope (2003) and McCabe et al. (2000) divide the main stakeholders into three broad categories: demand, supply and intermediaries.

Demand

Demand in this market originates from those private sector companies that make use of destinations and venues for their corporate events. In order to justify the outlay in terms of time and financial resources in such events, companies expect a return on their investment. This may come in a variety of tangible or intangible forms – for example, increased levels of sales of the company's products, as a consequence of sales staff training sessions or an incentive trip; or a boost in staff morale and a fall in staff turnover, arising from a team-building event, for instance. Individual participants at corporate events, also known as attendees, delegates or guests, may be considered as the end consumers of the corporate event product, and they too seek a return on their personal participation in meetings of the various types listed above. This may be new skills, increased levels of product knowledge, or a closer working relationship with fellow-workers, for example.

Supply

Suppliers in the corporate events sector are those businesses and organisations that provide the wide range of goods and services that are required for meetings of all types to take place. Venues, the key suppliers in this market, come in a variety of forms, from hotels and universities to purpose-built conference centres and tourist attractions such as museums and theme parks. Hassanien and Dale (2011) present a number of criteria that can be used to classify the events venues sector, according to specific themes, as shown in Table 5.1.

Other suppliers in the corporate events sector include accommodation providers (for residential events), transport companies and destination management companies (DMCs) – specialist agencies that operate in the event destination, providing on-site assistance and expertise to corporate events organisers. To these may be added numerous other goods and services providers, ranging from florists and interpreters to caterers and (for exhibitions) stand contractors.

Intermediaries

The final sub-division of stakeholders in the corporate events sector comprises the intermediaries operating in this market in order to bring buyers and suppliers together. Intermediaries can act on behalf of either buyers or suppliers. Those in the former category include corporate events organisers, who work on behalf of companies and play a pivotal role in the design and management of meetings. They generally have a wide range of responsibilities including site selection, contract negotiation, registration management, event promotion and marketing, invitations, transportation planning and speaker selection and management (Beaulieu and Love, 2004; Toh et al., 2005).

Table 5.1	Criteria that can be used to classify the events venues sector
Theme	**Criteria**
Strategic	Core business activity (i.e. primary or secondary)
	Ownership (i.e. public, private and charitable trust)
	Management (i.e. independent, franchised and multinational)
	Competitive strategy (i.e. cost leadership, differentiation, focus, hybrid, etc.)
	Industry context (i.e. hospitality, tourism, leisure, sport, educational or religious)
	Product life cycle (e.g. birth, growth, maturity and decline)
Market	Buyer type (i.e. individual, corporate, association and government)
	Market place/space (i.e. regional, national and international)
	Benefits sought (i.e. leisure, business, entertainment, training, marketing, study, etc.)
Physical	Age (i.e. historic or modern)
	Location (i.e. city or town centre or rural)
	Size of the venue (i.e. large, medium sized or small)
	Site (i.e. natural or purpose built)
	Space (i.e. indoor, outdoor or a combination)
Service	Provision of services (i.e. in-house, outsourced or contracted)
	Class, grade or service quality
	Facilities and services provided (i.e. full service, self-catering or residential and non-residential venues)
	Licensed and unlicensed
Activity	Type (i.e. conferences, exhibition, congress and/or conventions, etc.)
	Duration (i.e. short or long)
	Admission (i.e. fee paying or free entry)

Source: Adapted from Hassanien and Dale (2011)

Those intermediaries working on behalf of suppliers include a broad range of agencies that aim to connect suppliers with the clients who need their products and services in order to run their corporate events. These include venue finding agencies, professional speakers' bureaux and convention bureaux – organisations that market the destinations they represent in order to help the venues operating within those destinations gain more business.

It is clear from the above list of stakeholders that the corporate events sector is a complex system of individuals and companies, each working to achieve their individual and organisational goals. All of their best efforts are necessary to ensure that the events that they are organising or hosting or servicing in some way are a success. Large budgets are often at stake, and the highest standards of professionalism are required of all stakeholders, to ensure that such investment brings real benefits to the companies funding corporate events.

In a recent discussion of competitive advantage in the corporate events sector, professionalism, flexibility, partnership, communication and trust between stakeholders were highlighted as being crucial qualities for all stakeholders. One participant in the discussion, an events planner, said:

I would like to add 'respect' to that list. We have to accept that in all sectors of the industry we all want the event to be a success; we are all working to that common end goal. Recognising the expertise of others, respecting their view and knowledge, and applying due courtesy will inevitably lead to a more successful event.'

(Anon, 2009: 4)

These qualities are in demand now more than ever, as the corporate events sector is undergoing a period of upheaval, produced by changes in society as a whole. The next section examines those changes and their consequences for corporate events.

Trends in corporate events

The corporate events sector, in common with all industries, is influenced by trends in the wider marketing environment. At a basic level, the volume and value of corporate events are affected by the changing fortunes of those sectors that are major users of such events, including the pharmaceutical, technology, financial services and automotive industries. But there are a number of deeper transformations in society that are changing the face of the corporate events sector. Three of these will now be reviewed.

■ Procurement and return on investment

Even before the economic crisis of 2008 made it crucial for companies worldwide to closely monitor the value that their suppliers were providing them, **procurement** departments were already taking responsibility for strategic sourcing initiatives on the purchasing of materials, supplies and services required for the effective running of their firms, from office furniture and computer hardware to cafeteria and consulting services. Given companies' high levels of outlay on meetings, it was inevitable that procurement departments' attention would come to focus on that particular item of expenditure.

Now most companies' procurement departments have extended their range of responsibility to include the purchasing of corporate events services, and buying decisions in that field of corporate activity are increasingly influenced by those responsible for sourcing and obtaining items for their companies' use. Companies' events procurement strategies are generally designed to create savings by bringing meetings and other events purchasing processes under more effective control. In order to reach this objective, such strategies focus on two aspects: the efficiency of expenditure and the return on investment from the company's spending on corporate events.

The impact of procurement on the process of purchasing event services has been significant, as indicated by Rogers (2007: 9):

> This has translated into a much greater emphasis on the need for transparency with programme costings and a clear requirement to identify added value as well as providing effective and quantifiable measures to gauge return on investment (ROI). As part of this process, companies are looking to establish preferred supplier lists to give them greater control over the quality of delivery as well as additional leverage through increased buying power and, importantly, to track their event spend more accurately. Attractive destinations and facilities are no longer enough – business results are what count.

This new procurement approach to purchasing goods and services for corporate events initially constituted a source of anxiety for those meeting planners with responsibility for choosing the venues, accommodation, transport, speakers, entertainment, etc. that make such events possible. The concern of many was that the events planning function would be reduced to a mere cost-based purchasing decision made by procurement departments intent on insisting that the suppliers offering the lowest prices should be those used by their companies. A moment's thought tells anyone with even a basic knowledge of how corporate events work that cheapest is not always best in this field of company spending, particularly if a meeting, for example, is supposed to motivate employees by making them feel valued by their firm.

But in most reported cases, the involvement of procurement departments in corporate events has proved to be more of an opportunity than a threat. According to Zeller (2006: 6)

> There is a real opportunity for meeting planners to collaborate with procurement to achieve a goal of aligning marketing, sales, sourcing strategies, technology solutions, account management/reporting and meetings effectiveness . . . By having a mission and following the new procurement approach, meeting planners can change the value proposition of their department and strategically assist the corporation in achieving success through their meetings and events.

Accordingly, it is widely held that the involvement of procurement departments in companies' events buying decisions has boosted the trend for events planners' roles to progress from being merely logistical to being strategic in nature, a development noted by commentators such as Lenhart (2006). By, for example, demonstrating how the events they organise help their companies reach their business goals, corporate events planners are increasingly playing central roles in their organisations and, in many cases, raising the status and expectations associated with their jobs.

■ Technology

Most of those working in the corporate events sector today have only the dimmest of memories of a time without the internet and all the ways its powers can be harnessed to improve how events are organised and run. From online registration to venue websites offering 360-degree tours, the World Wide Web has revolutionised the corporate events world. But the same technology has also brought to market a range of virtual conferencing and online collaboration services that in certain circumstances provide a viable alternative to face-to-face corporate events. With the advent of virtual meeting technology, the question of how to format corporate meetings and events has become increasingly complex. Meetings can now be completely virtual, completely face-to-face or hybrid – a combination of the two.

The advantages of virtual meetings are many: reduced carbon footprint, removal of the risks and inconveniences incurred through travel, reduction of the amount of work-time lost through participation in the event, as well as the immediate savings incurred through not having to pay for travel, accommodation and meeting space.

Nevertheless, the future of face-to-face corporate events seems secure – for now, at least. Forbes Insights' (2009) survey of 760 business executives measured perceptions of face-to-face versus virtual meetings. More than eight out of ten of those surveyed claimed a preference for in-person meetings. The most frequently cited reasons given for this preference were 'Building stronger, more meaningful business relationships' (85%); 'Ability to read body language and facial expressions' (77%); and 'More social interaction and an ability to bond with co-workers and clients' (75%).

The challenge now facing corporate events planners is to decide which format is most likely to enable the meeting to reach the objectives that have been set for it. This decision is a strategic one that ought to be based on specific, scientific criteria, as opposed to, for example, the planner's personal preferences or the longstanding tradition within the company. As the cost of face-to-face events is generally higher than that of virtual meetings, expectations of an adequate return on investment tend to be higher. Duffy and McEuen

(2010: 8) have suggested that face-to-face meetings are more effective than **virtual events** when the objective is:

1. *To capture attention*: People's full attention is needed when you want to initiate something new or different. When you want to initiate a new or different relationship, culture, strategy or product, face-to-face is best.
2. *To inspire a positive emotional climate*: Do not under-estimate the power of inspiration and positive emotional climate as a currency of business. When you want to energise and inspire, face-to-face is best.
3. *To build human networks and relationships*: Information and resources are not the only things needed for work to get done. Increasingly, information is being commoditised, while there is much greater value in 'people networks and relationships'. To power up human networks and relationships, face-to-face is best.

Table 5.2 provides examples of corporate events for which face-to-face meetings are most likely to reach the funding company's objectives.

Table 5.2	Examples of face-to-face corporate events classified by needs
Broad business need	**Examples of specific business needs**
Capture attention for change	■ Initiate a new strategic direction for the organisation ■ Launch a new product or suite of products ■ Merge two cultures into a new culture ■ Renew focus and attention on an existing strategy
Inspire a positive emotional climate	■ Annual or semi-annual meetings to energise people around company goals, values and priorities ■ Inspirational events to build community and cohesion towards a shared interest or goal ■ Recognition events to celebrate top performing individuals and teams ■ Celebration events that mark important milestones
Building human networks and relationships	■ Annual or semi-annual meetings to enable cultural cohesion and relationship building ■ For dispersed workforces, a regular rhythm of face-to-face meetings to build trust and effective working relationships ■ Practitioner, user group and professional community conferences ■ Dynamic knowledge-sharing and innovation summits

Source: Duffy and McEuen (2010: 13)

■ Demographics

Given that the end users of corporate events are almost exclusively people in work, this sector is directly and profoundly affected by changes in the profile of the global workforce. In terms of demographics, the most significant change currently underway is the rise in importance and influence of that category of employees drawn from '**Generation Y**' – people in their 20s and early 30s. Currently the fastest growing cohort in the working population, Generation Y is rapidly replacing the '**Baby Boomers**' generation (born between 1946 and 1964) that has dominated business life, as well as politics and the arts, for the past 30–40 years. As growing numbers of Baby Boomers enter the retirement phase of their lives, their values, attitudes and preferences are gradually being replaced by those of Generation Y, in all aspects of personal and professional life, including the way in which corporate events are organised and run.

Perhaps the clearest difference between Generation Y and previous generations lies in their attitude towards, and competency with, technology. This generation grew up with the internet, and regard applications of technology as integral and indispensable features of their personal and professional lives, including the events they attend. Ramsborg and Tinnish (2008: 32), discussing the attitude of this generation towards training events in particular, state that:

> The full capabilities of technology must be exploited before, during, and after a meeting. Blogs, mobile phones, YouTube, Facebook, MySpace, podcasts, virtual meeting environments, RSS feeds, videos, widgets, mashups, wikis, moblogs, and social networking sites . . . Learners who use these technologies every day expect technology to be seamlessly interwoven into learning situations, i.e., meetings.

Technology also facilitates another preference of Generation Y: higher levels of participation and interaction with speakers and with other attendees at corporate events. This is a generation that has already demonstrated their lack of interest in the old 'declamatory' style of meetings, characterised by one-way communication from speakers to participants, the passive recipients of their discourses. Generation Y have also expressed a clear preference for shorter presentations at such events, calling into question the time-honoured tendency to allocate speakers hour-long sessions. Davidson (2010: 122) believes that:

> The drive towards shorter, more interactive sessions will intensify as Y-ers account for an increasingly large proportion of participants in business events. Generation Y participants expect interaction, in real time, with each other and with speakers, through having the opportunity, for example, to text-message their questions to a big screen on the conference stage, during sessions.

Above all, speakers at corporate events need to deliver their material in a way that combines education and information with entertainment – 'infotainment' is what Generation Y participants expect from the corporate events they attend. According to Ramsborg and Tinnish (2008: 34):

> The adult learners of today expect 'infotainment', the delivery of information in an entertaining format. Even the most serious programming on television, the news, is created now with graphics, music, lighting, and special effects. There aren't many places that people go where they are not treated to a 'show' – and meetings are no exception.

A final impact of this generation on the corporate events they attend has arisen as a consequence of their concern for environmental issues and corporate social responsibility. Many commentators agree that Generation Y represents the most socially conscious and civic-minded generation yet, and their progressive environmental and social awareness are changing the way in which corporate events are planned and run. The ongoing endeavours to create and publish agreed standards for 'green' meetings by bodies such as the Green Meeting Industry Council are just one indication of the growing wish of those planning and those attending corporate events that those events should have the least possible negative impact upon the natural environment. And Generation Y events planners and participants have been instrumental in driving the green meeting agenda forward.

But there is also evidence that this generation's collective social and ethical conscience is re-shaping corporate events. Much has been written about their wish to 'make a difference' or 'leave something behind' in the destinations where such events take place. This has come to be known as the 'social legacy' of events. Social legacy relates to the people aspect of the triple bottom line of corporate social responsibility – people, planet and profit – and, as such, goes far beyond the simple greening of corporate events. While the planet-centred greening of events involves practices such as recycling materials, hosting paperless meetings, choosing meetings destinations served by public transport and building green clauses into contracts with suppliers, social legacy also takes into account how a meeting or incentive trip impacts upon the people and economy of the local community.

Social legacy elements encompass community initiatives and the raising of social awareness among meetings and incentive travel participants. This aspect of corporate events is closely linked to the growing interest, especially among members of Generation Y, in volunteerism (or 'volun-tourism') as a form of community service that promotes goodwill and provides personal fulfilment. For many attendees, social legacy has also become an essential part of the experiential dimension of a meeting or incentive trip. It can take various forms, from a simple donation to a local charity to attendees taking time out from their events to participate in renovation or environmental projects such as painting a local school playground or planting trees; or it can be participating in outreach activities, which give the attendees the opportunity to meet and interact directly with local people. This approach works particularly well when part of the objective is to raise participants' awareness of social issues impinging on the local community.

An example of this was seen in the 2008 'Greening the Hospitality Industry' conference, held in Vancouver, where the organisers made a commitment to do something that would directly benefit the community. In addition to selecting a carbon offset programme, they partnered with the Vancouver Food Bank and participated in their volunteer programme. Attendee volunteers toured the food bank and learnt about the various local groups that benefit from its work. They then sorted and separated food and household items, weighed and measured items, and arranged goods into boxes for disbursement. In one hour, 31 attendee volunteers from around the globe assisted 1,600 people with meals in the Vancouver Metro area.

Conclusion

Corporate events are an integral element in the business world of today. They are instrumental in forging links between a company and its clients and between colleagues, and they are an essential channel of knowledge transfer within and between companies. The wide range of events that can be used to inform, to motivate and to provide opportunities for networking are only made possible thanks to the professionalism of all of the stakeholders involved in organising events and providing the services and facilities that are required to make them successful.

Nevertheless, at no other time in history has the corporate events sector been under such pressure to justify the resources invested in such events in these times of growing competition and corporate cost-cutting. This challenge has been exacerbated by the increase in availability of virtual alternatives to face-to-face meetings. But man is a sociable animal, with an irrepressible drive to communicate for all purposes, including business. This simple biological fact, combined with the knowledge that much communication is non-verbal – the strength of a handshake, for example – will ensure that face-to-face events remain an essential part of business life in the future.

Case 5.1	RSA Group incentive trip to Vietnam

The client

The RSA Group is one of the world's leading multinational insurance groups, employing around 22,000 people and serving 17 million customers in 130 countries. Each year, senior members of RSA staff are nominated for their achievements within the company, and the top 15 'Platinum Club' winners earn a place on the company's overseas incentive trip.

The agency

The intermediary responsible for the planning and design of the 2011 trip was marketing communications agency *dmbt,* based in Essex, England.

The brief

A straightforward brief was given to *dmbt*: organise a trip that delivers the 'wow' factor and a memorable experience for a group of well-travelled executives. The accommodation had to be in the five-star category; there had to be a balance between group activities and leisure time; and the destination had to be accessible to all of the different members of the group, who would be travelling there from locations all across the globe.

The company's incentive trip to Rio de Janeiro and Iguaçu Falls in Brazil the previous year had been a great success. So it was vital that the 2011 incentive trip should be at least as outstanding.

The planning

Out of a shortlist of four possible destinations submitted to the RSA Group by *dmbt,* Vietnam was selected as being the most suitable for their purposes. Arrangements were then underway for a five-night trip to take place in March 2011, with the help of a destination management company, Destination Asia.

This was the second year that *dmbt* had run this event for RSA Group, and *dmbt* Senior Account Manager Jaclyn Sammells noted that the meticulous planning required for such an event begins about 10 months in advance of the actual trip:

> This year we had people travelling from places including Buenos Aires, Columbia and Scandinavia – and many had business meetings before and after the event, so it was a question of liaising with their PAs as much as possible, because they really could be coming from and travelling to anywhere in the world, before and after the incentive trip.

During the lead-up to the event, *dmbt* set up a dedicated website containing all of the trip information and the itineraries. Post-event, all of the photographs were uploaded to the website for the participants to download, and each winner was sent a coffee-table book of the best photographs.

The Park Hyatt Hotel in Ho Chi Minh City was chosen for the first two nights, due to its being the best hotel in the city and therefore the most capable of offering the required standard of service and accommodation. This was followed by three nights at the Nam Hai resort in Hoi An, which again offered the highest standard of accommodation and facilities and was able to cater for the group's dinners and events.

The Platinum Club guests were treated to a welcome dinner at the Botanical Gardens in Ho Chi Minh City. The magical setting for this occasion featured hanging lanterns and a red carpet up the steps of the pagoda. As the guests arrived, children greeted them with flower garlands and they watched a traditional Dragon Dance. The evening's entertainment included drummers, dancers and a jazz band. According to Sammells,

> This venue offered the beauty of a botanical garden as well as the ability to light and dress the area with corporate colours – and provided out-of-doors dining right in the heart of the city. The sounds of the city and the open-air dining provided the perfect backdrop to immerse the group in Vietnam.

While there was ample leisure time available to the group during the trip, there were also a number of organised tours including a trip to the Cu Chi Tunnels – an intricate network of over 200 miles of underground tunnels that were dug and used during the Vietnam War. Other activities included a cycling tour of Da Nang and a walking tour of bustling Hoi An.

A gala dinner at the Nam Hai resort was also planned for the final night, during which the group was treated to the sounds of a saxophonist. The venue was dressed with floating boat-shaped lanterns in the infinity pool, and flowers and candles adorned the tables. Twelve traditional dancers performed between courses and, as a finale, there was a surprise 'dessert dance', when dancers entered with various desserts and presented them to the guests.

Case 5.1 *(continued)*

The challenges

Sammells noted that a few challenges were encountered during the planning of this event:

> The weather became a challenge due to unforeseen, and extremely unusual, weather fronts coming into Vietnam. The average temperature at the time of travel should have been 28–34C, but it dropped to as low as 15C during the trip and the threat of heavy rain was a challenge to our welcome dinner in the Botanical Gardens. We assessed the weather every day and had back-up plans as necessary.

A beach barbecue at Nam Hai had to be altered to an 'outdoor club', due to the threat of bad weather. But the club was dressed in the RSA Group's corporate colours, and the evening was a success after all.

David Weymouth, RSA Group Director Operations and Risk, who was one of the trip hosts added:

> The guests on these trips are well-travelled people, many of whom are used to staying in top hotels and receiving five-star treatment. However, the quality of the accommodation, the cuisine, the range of activities plus those all-important 'extra touches' added by *dmbt* were simply outstanding.

RSA Group commissioned *dmbt* to organise the following year's Platinum Club event.

Discussion questions

1 A specific website was created for this event. What are the features that a website can offer those who are participating in an event such as this?
2 Incentive trips can be expensive to run, but they are often said to be 'self-liquidating'. What does this mean, and how might it have transpired that this specific incentive trip was self-liquidating?
3 What tools might be used to measure the success of this incentive trip?

Case 5.2   **Cisco Systems' One Africa Partner Summit in Cape Town**

The client

Cisco Systems is an American multinational corporation, headquartered in San Jose, California, that designs and sells consumer electronics, networking, voice and communications technology and services. Cisco has more than 70,000 employees and an annual revenue of US$40.0 billion as of 2010.

The planning

Cisco Systems devised the One Africa Partner Summit as a platform to bring 260 of its partners together, to discuss recent developments and encourage loyalty and networking. The event was held from 21 to 23 June 2011 at the five-star deluxe Crystal Towers Hotel in Cape Town, South Africa.

Cape Town was chosen for its relaxed atmosphere, excellent food, facilities and accessibility. According to Cisco's regional marketing manager and in-house event organiser Jade Penfold, the venue was chosen on recommendation from a South African colleague: 'I wanted a hotel in the business district that was a short drive from the Waterfront for evening entertainment'. The Summit's theme and content were influenced by delegates, who contributed ideas via blogs and webinars.

The challenges

Technology infrastructure was the primary concern prior to the event. Live video footage is regularly used at Cisco's events, which can be problematic to manage. But the Cisco team worked closely with event sponsor Vodacom to ensure that all modes of communication were thoroughly tested.

The programme

The event included a welcome plenary session, keynote presentations from internal experts and a live demonstration by Den Sullivan, Head of Architectures and Enterprise, Emerging Markets, who was linked from a regional office to the main audience for a two-way live video stream. The programme also included an awards dinner at Restaurant 221 in the harbour area.

▶

Case 5.2   (*continued*)

Post-event analysis

Cisco was satisfied that the event met its objectives – cementing relationships between partners, colleagues and vendors. Penfold said that the conference ran smoothly due to careful planning, helpful hotel staff and efficient transport links. Using the Phillips ROI Methodology, which focuses on measuring satisfaction, learning, behaviour and results, the company was able to gather comprehensive feedback on the event and, three months later, to quantify learning application and business impact in order to estimate the return on investment for this event.

Discussion questions

4 In this context, who are Cisco's 'partners', and why was it important for them to network and stay loyal to the company?

5 Discuss the role played by technology in this corporate event.

6 Discuss the Phillips ROI Methodology and make a case for using it in the context of this Summit.

General discussion questions

7 Identify a specific example of a recent face-to-face corporate event, from an online search, and discuss the extent to which it might have been replaced by a virtual meeting, using a technological solution. Give (a) the advantages that might have been gained from running the event as a virtual meeting, and (b) the advantages of the face-to-face event that would have been lost if the meeting had been run on a virtual basis.

8 This chapter has contained numerous references to the importance of networking and colleagues bonding with each other. Find evidence from the human resources literature for the significance of these activities for efficiency in the workplace. And discuss how corporate events can be organised in such a way as to maximise opportunities for networking and bonding between participants.

9 Identify a local venue and analyse it according to the various themes and criteria used by Hassanien and Dale in their venue classification system (Table 5.1).

10 Discuss the various ways in which a corporate event planner can save money for their employer without compromising the quality of the events he/she organises. Use as a starting point the quotation above from Rogers (2007: 9):

> **As part of this process, companies are looking to establish preferred supplier lists to give them greater control over the quality of delivery as well as additional leverage through increased buying power and, importantly, to track their event spend more accurately.**

Guided reading

The following two journals are useful sources of articles on corporate events:

International Journal of Event and Festival Management

Journal of Convention and Event Tourism

Recommended websites

Global Meetings Industry Portal: **www.smiportal.com**

The professional associations for the meetings industry are also a valuable source of information. Here are three of the most useful:

Professional Convention Management Association – particularly for archived editions of the association's *Convene* magazine: **www.pcma.org**

Meeting Professionals International – particularly for archived editions of the association's *One+* magazine: **www.mpiweb.org**

Society of Incentive and Travel Executives: **www.siteglobal.com**

Key words

baby boomers; generation Y; knowledge transfer; networking; procurement; virtual events

Bibliography

Anon (2009) Making your destination more competitive in the eyes of buyers. *Odyssey,* Odyssey Media Group, 22 October.

Beaulieu, A.F. and Love, C. (2004) Characteristics of a meeting planner: attributes of an emerging profession. *Journal of Convention and Event Tourism,* 6(4), 95–124.

Davidson, R. (2010) What does Generation Y want from conferences and incentive programmes? Implications for the tourism industry. In I. Yeoman et al. (eds), *Tourism and Demography*. London: Goodfellow.

Davidson, R. and Cope, B. (2003) *Business Travel: Conferences, Incentive Travel, Exhibitions, Corporate Hospitality and Corporate Travel*. Harlow: Pearson Education.

Davidson, R. and Rogers, T. (2006) *Marketing Destinations and Venues for Conferences, Conventions and Business Events*. Oxford: Butterworth Heinemann.

Duffy, C. and McEuen, M.B. (2010) *The Future of Meetings: The Case for Face-to-Face*. Ithaca, NY: Cornell Hospitality Industry Perspectives.

Forbes Insights (2009) Business meetings – the case for face-to-face. **http://images.forbes. com/forbesinsights/StudyPDFs/Business_ Meetings_FaceTo-Face.pdf**

Hassanien, A. and Dale, C. (2011) Towards a typology of events venues. *International Journal of Event and Festival Management,* 2(2), 106–16.

Lawson, F. (2000) *Congress, Convention and Exhibition Facilities: Planning, Design and Management*. Oxford: Architectural Press.

Lenhart, M. (2006) In the driver's seat. *The Meeting Professional,* 6(4).

McCabe, V., Poole, B. and Leiper, N. (2000) *The Business and Management of Conventions*. Milton, QLD: John Wiley & Sons.

Ramsborg, G. and Tinnish, S. (2008) How adults learn, Part 2. *Convene* (PCMA), February.

Rogers, T. (2007) *Business Tourism Briefing*. London: Business Tourism Partnership.

Rogers, T. (2008) *Conferences and Conventions: A Global Industry*. Oxford: Butterworth Heinemann.

Toh, R., DeKay, F. and Yates, B. (2005) Independent meeting planners: roles, compensation, and potential conflicts. *Cornell Hotel and Restaurant Administration Quarterly,* 46(4), 431–43.

Zeller, D. (2006) Understanding procurement. *The Meeting Planner's Handbook,* supplement to *Meeting News,* July.

Part 2
Business functions applied to events

Chapter 6

Managing people and the role of volunteers

Terri Byers and **Samantha Gorse**, Coventry University, UK

Learning outcomes

Upon completion of this chapter the reader should be able to:

- explain the main theories of **motivation** and discuss examples from events management scenarios;

- discuss the key components of organisations that influence the management of people;

- discuss the importance of managing people as human resources (HR) to the overall strategic position of an organisation;

- explain the role of **volunteers** in an event and understand the challenges that managing them involves;

- discuss strategies and methods of managing people (volunteers and paid employees) in different scenarios within the events management context.

Overview

This chapter focuses on developing a broad and comprehensive understanding of the management of people within the context of events organisations. We do this through examining the individual (motivation theories), the organisation (factors that influence how we manage) and the context of managing within the events industry. The result of this chapter is to provide readers with practical strategies and tools for effectively managing people that take into consideration the individual, organisational and context of events management situations. We use theories from psychology, sociology, organisation theory and general management to provide the reader with appropriate knowledge and tools to understand the complexity of managing people in different organisational settings and to analyse situations which require 'people management' solutions. The chapter is about managing people in an events management organisation, but we limit the focus to people working or volunteering to make events successful and not to the management of crowds and the general public who attend events. Many textbooks, chapters and research articles focus on issues related to organising a single event or they focus on aspects of the events management process such as sponsorship, logistics and impacts of the event concept. This chapter differs from most in that it focuses on key issues to consider when creating an event organisation that seeks to successfully manage a portfolio of events, create a strategic advantage and provide consistent and high-quality events management services to clients.

The chapter begins with a case study to briefly show many of the issues we will cover in the chapter. We then move from the broad issues to the more specific. The organisation and its components are discussed, followed by key theories of individual motivation, the role of volunteers as a human resource and how they differ from other human resources. Finally, we focus our attention on strategies and techniques to manage people, taking into consideration what we have covered about individuals and organisations.

Case 6.1	Free Spirit Events company

The new owner of Free Spirit Events took control of the business in 2006. He quickly realised that there are many problems with running an event company. Profits were falling and he had no idea how to motivate the staff. The events were taking up too much of his time and interfering with his personal life (a young family). The new owner, although only 27, had a strong background in corporate events working for some major brands and delivering very high-profile events to both the public and private sectors. He had graduated with a good degree and was very hands-on in his approach to management. He was confident that with his youth, enthusiasm and experience in the cut-throat world of corporate events he could take Free Spirit Events and turn it into a formidable force in the industry.

The business model was simple – the company rented the land surrounding a stately home, rented space to exhibitors, who sold various products to the public. The public were then charged a nominal fee of between £3 and £6 to patronise the event. (Visit *www.livecraftslimited.co.uk* for an example of the type of organisation.) The Craft and Food events were extremely popular for some years, but were now becoming very old-fashioned. The visitors had simply grown old and nothing had been offered to younger generations to attract them to the events. The company's portfolio of events included two royal venues, which were the 'flagship' events in the eyes of the customers and exhibitors. However, the two key events were running at a loss and serious questions had to be asked about the future viability of these shows. In general all of the other events were still profitable; however, the business was steeply in decline and a shift in direction was required urgently. Many of the shows had a 30-year pedigree and had a number of owners over the years. Some of the staff had worked for the company over the period of about 30 years and often reminisced about the 'old days' and how wonderful they were. In the 1990s each event would expect to attract in the region of 10,000 visitors and have about 150 exhibitors. The business model was solid and extremely profitable. In 2005 these figures had halved.

The new owner was convinced that with his event experience, contacts and keen eye for reducing costs that the decline could be arrested and a business model developed that would offer some longevity and profitability to all of the people involved. The new owner spent some time working on the events to see if he could highlight areas where cost savings could be made and how the company could became more efficient. It became very apparent that the staff were instrumental in the success of the organisation; however, the lack of direction that they'd had under the previous owner had left them all feeling very insecure and unsure what to do for the best to help save the business.

Essentially they all started doing their 'own thing' and directing their team in terms of what they thought was right. The result was power struggles between key members of staff and a state of unrest.

While at the shows, the new owner approached each of the key managers one by one and had an informal chat about what their thoughts were and why they were involved in the events. He was horrified to discover how different all of the team leaders were in their management approach. There was also considerable mistrust between managers. Many of these people had worked together for a decade and from the outside it appeared that they worked well together. However, it was evident that the problems within management were beginning to affect customer perceptions of the event. This simply could not be allowed to happen, yet the new owner was still unsure how to deal with the problem or even what potential solutions existed. He knew something needed to change but struggled to identify what it was, and how to manage that change. He worried that he risked losing key members of staff and he didn't have the knowledge to instantly replace them. He could also lose his exhibitors if he didn't take their needs into account and this was unsatisfactory.

Case 6.1   *(continued)*

The new owner was starting to question just what he had taken on. He knew very little about the Craft Show industry and had probably been slightly arrogant in his thinking when he thought he would be able to turn the company around quickly and easily. His knowledge of organisational structure and culture was not as good as it could be, but he remembered from his time at university that two of the key factors that impact on all areas of business success are the formal structures (or lack of them) and the informal culture (and the managers' influence on this). He was wishing he had listened to his lectures on this more carefully!

Not knowing exactly where to start he reflected on the many conversations that he'd had with his senior management team and was wondering how to interpret them to make sure that he got the best out of them. He kept wondering if he was going to need to adopt one style of management for all of the varying groups or if he was going to need to spend a lot of time with each individual team leader.

Observations

Each team leader gets paid on an event by event basis. They get paid a fixed fee for working on an event (the more events they do the more they earn). They also get a free trade stand (normally worth £400) to sell anything they want on the day.

Each team leader seems to be an expert on running the events and does not believe that their team needs to change. Essentially they have spent most of their time telling the new owner how everyone else is doing it wrong.

Discussion questions

1 What do you see as the key problems in this case?

2 What are your proposed solutions to resolving these problems and ensuring a successful event?

3 What should you do to be sure you are making the right decisions?

Case 6.1 demonstrates that managing organisations and the people within them is a difficult task and there are not often easy answers to the problems that managers face. There is not often one solution to a problem but several alternatives that you must choose from. The case study focuses on one particular problem, but there are also other issues/problems that can been seen in the example. This chapter cannot tell you what to do in every situation, but we can give you the tools to think critically about a situation, analyse that situation and make an informed decision about what action to take. Of course, managing people is not all about problem solving and part of the people management function is proactive planning to provide a clear structure to enable people to operate within an organisation. This chapter also discusses theories and examples which are relevant to taking a proactive approach to managing people.

The management of people involves some degree of uncertainty. Managers should attempt to limit that uncertainty in order to reduce the risk involved in making decisions. To do this, we need to understand:

- individual motivation (people) and
- the structural components of organisations and how they influence individual behaviour.

Understanding organisations

All organisations, regardless of size, age or purpose, have two broad components that significantly influence their operation, development and ability to function effectively. These components are structure and culture. This section defines organisational structure and culture before moving on to discuss how these two basic components can influence how people behave in organisations.

■ Structure

Organisational structure is often thought of as the 'hierarchy' of an organisation, ideally providing a clear chain of command from the top of the organisation, such as a director, owner or CEO (Chief Executive Officer), down to front-line staff, who deal directly with customers. Mintzberg (1979) suggests that organisational structure is 'the sum total of the ways in which it [the organisation] divides its labour into distinct tasks and then achieves coordination between them' (cited in Cole, 2004: 184). Sherratt et al. (2009: 5) provide an even more insightful view, stating that organisational structures 'describe and determine the way work is arranged, how authority is exercised and the channels of communication that prevail, up, down and across the various divisions'. Slack and Parent (2006) explained these mechanisms in the context of sport organisations, but these mechanisms of structure are applicable to all types of organisations across all industries. 'Hierarchy' is only one of the three components of structure, which are:

1. *complexity*: the number of 'levels' in an organisation;
2. *formalisation*: the extent to which there are formal rules, policies and procedures;
3. *centralisation*: the extent to which decisions are made at the 'top' of the organisation.

Complexity

Organisations can be seen as tall, flat, wide or thin in structure or even adopt a matrix-like design. This structure depicts the complexity of management within that organisation. A small event company is likely to be less complex in structure, and thus less differentiated, than a large organisation employing many people. The immediate effect of structure can be seen when considering a small event company where the owner/manager would perform all tasks including administration, marketing, day-to-day functioning, etc. In a large organisation, these roles would be delegated to specific members of staff or even departments, requiring greater communication and integration of tasks. Complexity can therefore be seen in the many job descriptions, levels of management and different departments created to accomplish the work of a large company.

Differentiation can occur in three ways:

1. horizontal differentiation;
2. vertical differentiation;
3. spatial differentiation.

There are two 'types of *horizontal differentiation* – through specialisation of tasks or departmentalisation. Specialisation can occur through the breakdown of work into simple, repetitive tasks or through employing trained specialists. Within a large event company, a team working on producing and distributing promotional material may create an assembly line production resulting in a promotions pack that is then ready to be posted to a mailing list. Alternatively, a small events company may outsource their promotions to a specialist company if they do not have the staff or expertise to do this themselves.

Departmentalisation can occur by product, function or geographic location. Product differentiation in an event company would involve separate departments for the different 'event products' on offer, such as separate departments for weddings, corporate events and sport events (see Figure 6.1). This allows the event company to be product orientated but requires considerable resources to be duplicated across the organisation. For example, 'marketing' would still need to be embedded into each of the product departments, as would consideration for finances, human resources, etc.

If an event company were to departmentalise based on function, they would create different departments such as Public Relations, Finance, Operations and Marketing. This would allow the company to focus on the key business tasks across a range of products (see Figure 6.2).

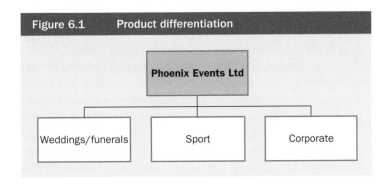

Figure 6.1 Product differentiation

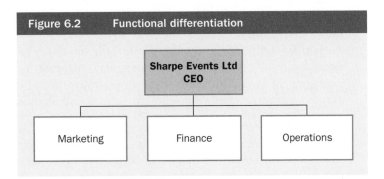

Figure 6.2 Functional differentiation

An event company differentiated by geographic location would see tasks duplicated across different regions (within countries, across countries) but would allow the organisation to recognise cultural differences relevant to their business (see Figure 6.3).

Vertical differentiation refers to the number of 'levels' within an organisation. The more levels of authority, the taller the structure – for example, a large events management company such as Rushmans (*www.rushmans.com/index.html*), that has several levels of hierarchy including founder, directors (safety, security, communications, accounts), managers (general, finance, Africa and Middle East), assistants and administrative support, would be more vertically differentiated than a small event company that consists of a sole proprietor and casual staff employed on a project/event basis. There are advantages and disadvantages associated with having more or fewer levels, relating to issues such as control, communication and coordination. Span of control of managers at all levels in an organisation (the number of staff reporting to any one manager) will be determined by the organisational structure (greater vertical differentiation means a narrower span of control).

Spatial differentiation can be either vertical or horizontal to create tall or flat structures, respectively.

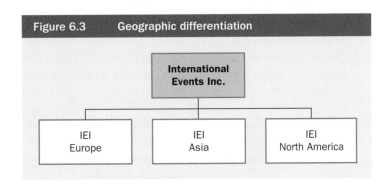

Figure 6.3 Geographic differentiation

Formalisation

Formalisation is the extent to which an organisation adopts formal rules, policies and procedures to guide employee action. Highly formalised organisations have comprehensive documents for operating policies, strategy, procedure manuals and suchlike. Many event companies may wish to have policies on sustainability in event planning/management, legacy, environmental practices (carbon footprint targets).

Formalisation, or rules, policies and procedures, is often essential in organisations as it provides an indication to employees as to appropriate behaviour. Formalisation can also take the form of job descriptions, used in recruitment and selection to ensure managers are getting the 'right' employee. Too much formalisation is often referred to as bureaucracy and can be frustrating to employees if the rules are not helpful in facilitating work. Managers sometimes make the mistake of creating too many rules in an attempt to control their workforce. This can have the opposite effect as employees find ways around the excessive rules.

Too much formalisation also means little flexibility in a job role. This needs to be considered carefully as creativity and personal customer focus are often required by events management companies and if the operating procedures do not allow this, employees may be prevented from responding to customer demands or business opportunities.

Centralisation

Centralisation refers to the amount of 'control', or decision-making 'power', held centrally in an organisation. In a small company, it is to be expected that the CEO will make decisions for the organisation as a whole, given that they will have a clear understanding of what is occurring across the company at all stages of product or service deliverance. However, in a large, potentially multinational, company, is it feasible for a CEO based in the UK or in the USA to have this same level of understanding about issues affecting customers and employees in a subsidiary in the Far East or in Africa?

The geographic departmentalisation (as seen in Figure 6.3) may lead to a vital need for a more decentralised approach to decision making.

There are also potential issues with a more centralised group of authority holders/decision makers in that employees further down in the power chain may feel that their ideas or suggestions are being ignored, thus negatively impacting on motivation, which will be highlighted later in this chapter.

All of the components together (formalisation, centralisation, complexity) indicate an organisation's structure and are important in guiding employees' and volunteers' behaviour as the structure indicates hierarchy, communication channels, job duties/responsibility and serves to provide formal control of the organisation's function. Structure alone, however, does not fully explain how organisations operate. We need to understand the informal side of organisations – culture.

■ Culture

Where structure is the 'formal' element of an organisation, culture is the informal, intangible aspect of an organisation. This area of management has received a lot of attention from researchers around the world, with many suggesting definitions, impacts and strategies for managing culture in an organisation. Schein (1992, cited in Johnson and Scholes, 2002: 45) defines **organisational culture** as the 'basic assumptions and beliefs that are shared by members of an organisation, that operate unconsciously and define in a basic taken-for-granted fashion an organisation's view of itself and its environment'.

There are a number of key issues to be discussed based on this definition. First, Schein (1992) argues that assumptions and beliefs are shared by members of an organisation (primarily employees) – it is important for any organisation that all employees understand and 'buy in' to this culture. If they don't, it can develop into a serious problem for managers and may lead to organisational change, which will be highlighted later in this chapter. Customers, whether they are attendees at an event or organisations seeking events management expertise, need to see a consistent message and approach to business and, ultimately, this consistency is determined by culture.

Secondly, culture becomes ingrained in an organisation, meaning that it becomes part of everyday life. If new employees join the organisation or new customers are being targeted, there may be an impact on the culture of the organisation – new views, new expertise, new ways of doing things. These new employees or customers need to be 'educated' in the ways of doing business without imposing a culture on them. It is also important to consider the potential impact the introduction of volunteers can have on an organisation's culture. The same level of training, motivation and assimilation into the organisation needs to be given to volunteers and paid employees – volunteers need to provide the same consistency of message to customers. If there is a constant turnover of volunteers over the course of a given time period (i.e. if there is no real commitment between organisation, event and volunteer), this can be a very time- and labour-intensive activity.

Thirdly, an organisation's external environment can impact on its internal culture. Johnson and Scholes (2002) discuss cultural frames of reference, elements of both the internal and external environments that impact on the behaviour of an individual employee (Figure 6.4 – taken from Johnson and Scholes, 2002: 46). Just as in wider society, organisational culture can be influenced by history, religion, gender, race and many other factors which can lead to problems in managing that culture and the impact it can have on the success or failure of an organisation.

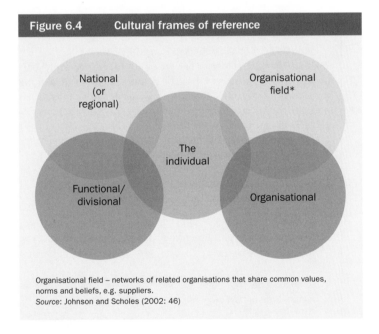

Figure 6.4   Cultural frames of reference

National (or regional)

Organisational field*

The individual

Functional/ divisional

Organisational

Organisational field – networks of related organisations that share common values, norms and beliefs, e.g. suppliers.
Source: Johnson and Scholes (2002: 46)

It is clear from Figure 6.4 that while these frames overlap, indicating a level of commonality in beliefs, norms and values of these groups, it would be expected that there are also significant differences between the cultural nature of these elements of an organisation. This is further exacerbated by the international environment.

The work of Hofstede (1980) analyses the differences between national and international cultures and how these differences impact on how organisations operate. Hofstede (1980) identified four dimensions of culture:

- *Power distance*: the perceived inequality of the manager–employee relationship (the differences between levels of power).

■ *Uncertainty avoidance*: how societies use technology, religion and the law to cope with uncertainty about the future (e.g. what are contingency plans based on?).

■ *Individualism v. collectivism*: the extent to which individual goals are pursued over the needs of the collective.

■ *Masculinity v. femininity*: cultural values, gender roles and power relations.

In an events management organisation, cultural awareness is vital to the success or failure of the organisation, particularly in today's society. Many countries are multicultural, meaning that while an organisation's culture might meet the needs of the employees within it, it may not be acceptable to the market or markets in which the business is operating. In addition, events may attract international audiences – employees and volunteers need to be aware of how to deal with people from different backgrounds and cultures different from their own. As events like the Towersey Festival (see Case 6.2) continue to grow, cultural awareness becomes even more important!

Case 6.2   Towersey Festival

Towersey Festival is 'a celebration, a gathering of friends, family and neighbours to meet others and relax, eat, drink and party in a common and friendly atmosphere' (*www.towerseyfestival.com*). In 2012, its 48th year of operation, this festival has a long history of success. With reports of a decline in British music festivals (Bainbridge, 2012) and the lure of cheaper alternatives throughout Europe (Bowes, 2012), the Towersey Festival seems to have the right formula for a successful event in difficult economic times.

According to its website, Towersey is all about great music, dance, spoken word, street theatre, visual art, film and song. Add to that great campsites, beautiful surroundings and the very special feeling you get when you Festival at Towersey. With five nights and four days of music 'there is no better way to bring your summer holidays to a close'.

Started as a one-day festival in 1965, Towersey Festival aims to celebrate a thousand years of Towersey village. The festival has grown in size and popularity year on year. In 1966, due to the immense popularity of the festival, it became a three-day event. Now a five-day event, the festival aims to have something for everyone. There is storytelling, poetry, theatre, arts, crafts, workshops and, of course, music! The festival is for all the family, with The Rainbow (Children's festival) dedicated to children of all ages. There are special workshops and activities for younger children (under 6 years old) and an extensive programme of singing, crafts and activities for all children.

The festival is organised by a small village committee and six full-time staff who all have a passion for festivals and for Towersey Festival in particular. Add to this over 240 volunteers and you have a better picture of how this event happens. Integral to the financial viability of the festival is the registered charity, Friends of Towersey, whose purpose is:

● to support the education of people in music, dance, song, theatre, arts and crafts;

● to encourage the young to encompass performing and visual arts at an early age;

● to support the careers of people, developing their skills and even taking them on to a fully professional level;

● to support people in later life who decide perhaps they missed out and now turn to the arts in their leisure time or new careers.

Sponsorship plays a big role in supporting the festival, with 15 official sponsors listed on the Towersey Festival website.

Source: *www.towerseyfestival.com*

Discussion questions

4 Discuss different ways to structure the organisation of Towersey Festival and compare the advantages and disadvantages of each structure.

5 Discuss the management implications for how to educate new and existing volunteers on the culture of the organisation.

6 What do you think is the key to success of Towersey Festival – efficient management structures and clear responsibilities or the culture of the organisation?

Change

There are many different reasons why an organisation might change – planned or unplanned, forced or unforced, immediate or incremental, internal or external pressures. In most cases, if an organisation doesn't change, it will have to deal with serious issues in remaining competitive.

External drivers for change

External drivers may require a more immediate response by the organisation to changes in the environment:

- Changes in the external environment may force an organisation to change: for example, government instability, international economic downturns or volatility, new or additional legislation governing business practices (a PESTEL analysis would allow an organisation to potentially identify areas where these changes might be influenced).
- Changes in customer needs may lead to an organisation having to offer new or improved products or services in order to remain competitive.
- Competitors may change how or where they do business which could make them more appealing to potential customers (e.g. outsourcing production or moving facilities or staff to more cost-effective places).

Internal need for change

As a company grows (or shrinks), the structure must change to accommodate the increase (or decrease) in the number of employees and/or volunteers and to decide how the work of the organisation will be divided between people, commonly known as division of labour. The culture of the organisation *will* inevitably change as a result of any structural alterations, due to greater management control, more employees to accommodate, etc.

For events management companies, a planned short-term structural change may occur at a number of points during a year – for example, a company arranging a number of high-profile events over the course of a year will have varying levels of human resource requirement (employees, volunteers or, more usually, a combination of both) to run these events effectively. The increase in the number of staff leads to a taller management structure (i.e. more 'layers' of management).

Organisational change can also occur due to changes in the products or services offered by a company, utilisation of new and/or improved technologies or production techniques, or a change in ownership or leadership of the company.

With change comes uncertainty – how will employees, volunteers and customers be affected by change, whether caused by internal or external environmental factors? Will everyone in the organisation accept change? Does everyone understand why change has occurred?

Managers must choose the pace at which change is implemented: fast or slow. In slow, incremental change, the reasons for change can be disclosed to employees – the benefits to the organisation can be communicated as necessary and 'not change for change's sake'. Ultimately, change needs to be part of an organisation's strategy. There may be times when change must be fast in order to respond to, for example, customer demands or environmental changes. Recently, there has been a significant decrease in economic activity and much uncertainty in political and economic conditions. Events companies may find this requires a fast response by downsizing their structures to provide events at more competitive prices. In this case, the financial viability of the business is at stake and it would be perilous not to react quickly to the external economic/political situation.

Event industry context: managing sustainability

If an events management company is to be successful, the manager needs to consider how the events and portfolio of events can be sustainable over time. Of course customer service and providing a 'memorable' event is an important factor to consider. Ralston et al. (2007) built on the work of Pine and Gilmore (1999), who explored how successful companies have moved beyond service delivery by designing memorable experiences, to investigate the integration of service factors with experience factors to advance a model for delivery of unique experiences which will ensure that events are memorable and increase consumer inclination to return.

Another factor to consider is working towards 'institutionalisation' of your event. Getz and Andersson (2009) discuss how festivals and other recurring events can become institutionalised to the extent that they are considered tourist attractions, used in place marketing and destination image-making strategies of local governments. Their research is based on 14 live musical festivals in Sweden and found that institutional status and a niche in the community, sustaining committed stakeholders and constant innovation are deemed essential by practising event managers.

Ensor et al. (2011) examined the concept of sustainability further by focusing on festival leaders' attitudes towards the dynamics of creating and directing sustainable festivals. Of the constructs identified, the most significant relate to four areas: the event subject focus; the leadership; the funding; and the organisational culture. The research also revealed that festival leaders conceive sustainability not as an environmental concern, but as a matter of festival survival.

Strategy

Johnson and Scholes (2002: 4) state that strategy provides 'long term direction' for an organisation – a long-term plan, usually looking five to ten years into the future.

By conducting a strategic analysis, including a SWOT analysis (strengths, weaknesses, opportunities and threats of the organisation), along with an external environment analysis (e.g. Porter's Five Forces Analysis examining competition, suppliers, buyers, threat of new entrants and of substitute products, as well as the broader external environment (political, social, economic, technological and legal situation), managers need to understand:

1. Where the organisation 'is' – in terms of revenue, market share, market position, product or service portfolio, etc.
2. Where the organisation 'wants to be' – e.g. bigger market share.
3. How does the organisation 'get there' – how does the organisation maximise its competitive advantage to grow?

By understanding customers and competitors, an organisation can establish what it does better than rivals in the market place. It could be that the costs involved in manufacturing a product or running an event may be lower than those of a competitor (meaning that customers are charged a lower price). Alternatively, an organisation, and the products and services it offers, may derive competitive advantage through the history or status of an event giving it a high profile in the eyes of customers.

Ultimately, the events management industry is a very competitive one, with small or local companies competing with large, sometimes multinational, organisations for clients and customers being able to attend a vast array of events every year. It is crucial that managers understand what they do better than their competitors whilst maximising the skills of employees and volunteers to run the best event possible.

Motivation

Theories of motivation attempt to explain individual and group behaviour. We can draw on psychology and sociology to explain the behaviour of staff, managers and groups of people in organisations. As a manager, it is essential to appreciate what motivates people in your organisation in order to effectively manage their time and efforts, to coordinate those efforts and to recognise when there may be problems with staff (or volunteer) motivation. Where there are problems, theories of motivation may be able to provide solutions and we will look at these options in this section. However, as we have discussed in the previous section, the structure and culture can have an impact on motivation so managers need to look to these aspects of their organisation as well as theories of motivation to understand behaviour in their organisation.

Understanding what motivates a person to do or not to do something is a complicated task – there are many factors which can be considered, and theories of motivation reflect this. Relying on an individual theory to explain all behaviour is not advisable, but considering the theories as possible explanations in a given context (e.g. small event company or established large events management company) can help managers perform more effectively and understand motivation as a whole.

Drummond (2000) discussed several different theories of motivation, illustrating that there are different ways to conceptualise the concept. We now discuss some of these categories of motivation theory in the context of event organisations:

- needs;
- goals;
- expectancies;
- self-efficacy;
- job design;
- dispositional factors.

Theories related to individual needs and goals assume motivation is linked to what we *want* to do or become. Theories of self-efficacy link motivation to what we *believe* we can do or become. Expectancy theory suggests motivation is the outcome of three factors:

- expected outcome;
- assessment of the value of that outcome;
- perceived probability of attaining the outcome.

■ Needs

Each of the categories above assumes a slightly different definition of motivation. This is an important point because as we change the definition for motivation, we also change how we would 'apply' or motivate a person/group. We will discuss each of these applied to an events management context and highlight some of the limitations of theories in each category.

Theories which assume motivation is based upon human needs suggest that individuals act to satisfy their perceived needs. The best known of these theories is Maslow's (1943) hierarchy of needs, as depicted in Figure 6.5.

According to the theory, basic physical needs are the most important factor in motivation and must be met before a person feels motivated by the next level, physical and psychological safety. Next, people are motivated by a sense of belonging, needs for emotional connections, affection, friendship and the like. Once these needs are met, motivation is driven by esteem needs including recognition, power, achievement or status. Finally, once all the previous needs are met, Maslow suggests that individuals seek self-actualisation or

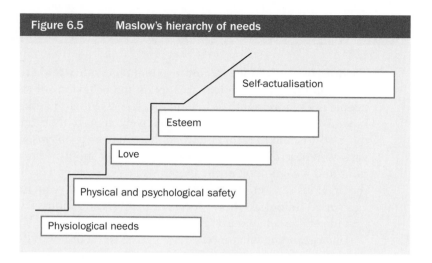

Figure 6.5   Maslow's hierarchy of needs

the realisation of one's potential. If we are to apply this to managing staff and volunteers in an event organisation, the theory suggests that we need to provide suitable physical premises and conditions in which to work, then appropriate physical and psychological conditions that facilitate a safe working environment.

Individuals can then be motivated by provision of social programmes that allow them to 'belong' to the organisation. Next we can provide opportunities for achievement, advancement in the company, promotion or recognition of their achievements. Self-actualisation is more difficult to provide for every member of an organisation as it requires the fulfilment of an individual's perceived potential. The key to the theory is that once a level of need is satisfied, it ceases to be a motivational factor. If you provide good physical working conditions, a physically and psychologically stimulating environment, then you must provide the next level of need to motivate someone to work.

There are some difficulties and limitations in applying this theory in practice. Firstly, it is difficult to know what level of physical and psychological comfort and safety is appropriate and levels will vary from individual to individual. Managers can address this through managing expectations of new employees and volunteers in the recruitment and training processes. For example, working and volunteering at an outdoor event may mean exposure to inclement weather and as a manager you can make sure people understand this before agreeing to work/volunteer. You may also look at advising on or even providing suitable facilities, clothing or nourishment given the weather conditions.

Another limitation of Maslow's theory is that it does little to explain individual differences. It may be that some people have little desire for affection or companionship at work and their needs are more focused on progression, advancement and other esteem factors. If an individual will only be motivated by the next level of needs, there would be a stage where it is impossible to motivate, if we accept Maslow's theory in its entirety.

Maslow's theory was not developed specifically for understanding organisations or the workplace. Herzberg et al.'s two-factor theory (1959) was developed based on primary research in the workplace. According to the theory, there are what Herzberg calls 'hygiene factors' (e.g. policies, physical space, salary and quality of management) which 'satisfy' individuals in the workplace, but we can only motivate people through 'motivational factors' such as achievement, recognition, the work itself, responsibility and advancement.

Goals

Goal-setting theory suggests that people are motivated by setting goals they wish to achieve, to give a sense of purpose and accomplishment. Drucker (1954) popularised the term 'management by objectives' (MBO), a process of participative goal setting and decision making that assumes by involving employees in setting their own goals (in line with strategic direction of the organisation) they will be more motivated to achieve those goals. Part of this system requires management to assess actual performance against goals set to identify where individuals have or have not met their targets.

Goals are useful to help motivate and provide direction for behaviour in organisations. For example, if part-time staff are employed to promote an event and sell tickets to the event, they need some sales targets to know how many tickets they need to sell. Their sales targets would be based on organisational needs for break-even or profits, but it would be beneficial to involve the employees in setting those targets. Goals can be de-motivating if they are unrealistic or cannot be easily measured, or indeed if there are too many goals/targets set, leaving little flexibility in the job. Thinking back to the previous discussion of structure, too many goals means over-formalisation and therefore people can become resistant to adapting to demands outside of their goals. Considering our example above of selling/promoting an event, if we used only goals theory to motivate our staff and they were not meeting targets, despite following the rules and direction set by management, simply setting more goals would not help the situation. Managers need to be 'reflective thinkers' and recognise when there may be problems with the systems they have designed and work to identify where change could improve the organisation's performance.

Expectancies

Expectancy theory suggests individuals are motivated by considering the perceived consequences of their actions. This assumes that individuals rationally assess the consequences of their actions and make choices based on a complex array of factors. Motivation is strongest when a person assesses that their actions can or will yield some positive result for them personally. For example, if you employ 'casual' event staff to work on a commission basis, expectancy theory suggests that individuals will assess whether this commission is sufficient to motivate them to work harder or to a certain standard in order to achieve the targets and rewards set out by the commission. But they will also assess their other options for employment, work experience and so on (and alter their motivation to work for you), depending on why they engaged with your organisation in the first place.

One criticism of this theory is the assumed rationality – this means people consider all their options before deciding on what will motivate them the most. This simply isn't practical and is unlikely because people have time restrictions, emotional/intellectual restrictions and cultural norms which 'bound' their decision-making processes. These prevent us from considering all the options and so a rational approach to motivation is inherently flawed. Think about a time when you were searching for a job – did you consider *all* job adverts from every possible source or did you locate a few jobs you were interested in and apply for those? You may have chosen based on location, salary, benefits or opportunity for advancement, but it is unlikely you considered every possible job in existence; you filtered your search based on available information, time and your knowledge/perception of your needs.

While the above factors may have played an important role in your motivation for applying for certain jobs, you probably also considered advice from friends, family or lecturers as to what is the best option for you. And so it is limiting to think people are motivated purely on their expectancies of the implications of their choices.

■ Self-efficacy

Theories of self-efficacy suggest that individuals achieve what they believe they can achieve. If a person has a positive impression of their abilities then they are more likely to pursue challenging tasks and goals. High self-efficacy also means that a person is more likely to commit to a task and work hard to achieve their goals. For a manager, it is useful to think about how to encourage positive self-perceptions of workers' abilities so that they perform their duties with confidence and determination.

Some examples of self-efficacy theories include social cognitive theory, social learning theory, self-concept theory and attribution theory. We will not cover each theory here but have listed them to make readers aware of the different theories and suggested further reading to provide direction to learn more about their differences. Important to understanding self-efficacy as an event manager is also understanding what factors affect a person's self-efficacy. Broadly there are four ways in which a manager can influence self-efficacy:

- *Experience*: success increases and failure decreases self-efficacy. If a manager sets targets too high or goals are not achievable, you risk decreasing individuals' self-beliefs and efficacy.
- *Modelling*: when a person identifies with another person who is succeeding and performing effectively, they can consider that if that person is able to perform, then they are also able to achieve similar results.
- *Social instances*: periods of social interaction in a person's life where they consider the event a catalyst for significant change.
- *Physiological reactions*: physical responses to stressful situations (e.g. sweating, upset stomach, stuttering) may signal to a person that they are not competent at a task and they doubt their ability to perform the task effectively, decreasing their self-efficacy further. Someone with high self-efficacy would interpret these physiological responses as normal and unrelated to their ability.

■ Job design

Job design involves identifying tasks required by individuals and how they will be performed in the context of other individuals/job roles within an organisation. Typical components of job design which are thought to be important to motivation include (Taylor et al., 2008):

- *autonomy*: degree of independence in performing duties;
- *intrinsic job feedback*: actual task is motivating;
- *extrinsic job feedback*: external feedback is motivating;
- *social interaction*: opportunity to be part of a team or group;
- *task/goal clarity*: job description is clear;
- *task variety*: a good variety of activities in the job role;
- *task identity*: a specific and clear output is produced (i.e. an event, a brochure);
- *ability/skill level requirements*: requirements are high skilled;
- *ability/skill variety*: different skills/knowledge required;
- *task significance*: job important to others' work as well;
- *growth/learning*: opportunity to learn within the job;
- *promotion*: clear opportunity to advance in career;
- *communication*: receiving and disseminating information clearly;
- *recognition*: good work acknowledged and rewarded.

Motivational theories related to job design assume that people's motivation is linked to the pleasure and satisfaction they obtain through their work. Herzberg (1968) coined the term 'job enrichment' and suggested that work should be organised to facilitate individual achievement, recognition for effort and responsibility. According to this, we can motivate people by giving them the chance to utilise their skills and knowledge to their maximum ability. And if we do not provide these opportunities, employees become bored and stagnant in their work. Practically, this means a task or tasks must be meaningful and challenging but achievable.

Job design as a motivational tool can be applied to paid staff or volunteers as it relies on intrinsic, non-financial factors and incentives. Applying Taylor et al.'s (2008) list of factors to the events management organisation wishing to motivate volunteers, we can see similarities to the principles of structures talked about earlier. We also need to be careful in designing jobs that we don't lose sight of how structure can influence behaviour and cause motivational problems as well as incentives to work.

Of course, workers' and volunteers' perceptions of the various elements of job design are heavily influenced by social norms and by organisational cultures.

■ Dispositional factors

Dispositional theory focuses on the link between the person (their 'world views', self-efficacy, self-esteem, etc.) and job satisfaction as indicative of their motivational tendencies in the workplace (or as a volunteer, in the case of events management). Judge et al. (1998) suggested that people with a positive outlook and attitude are more likely to be satisfied in their jobs/roles than people who have negative/sceptical or overly critical views of life and the nature of the world. This may have implications in recruiting and selecting for your events management company.

Case 6.3   **Pause for thought . . .**

Think of important successes and achievements in your life to date (getting a job, attaining a place at university, etc.). Make a list of reasons why you think you achieved those things, such as 'prepared well for interview', 'knew the boss', 'achieved good grades' and so on.

Thinking of the different categories of motivation we have discussed, which do you think explains your motivation to achieve the success you have achieved?

The role of volunteers

Events of all sizes need volunteers. Small community events are particularly reliant on volunteer labour. Managing volunteers can be a complex task as they do not have the same motivation as a person would have for paid employment, namely economic necessity. Events are organised in a wide variety of contexts – tourism events, corporate, religious, sports, music, cultural and community are just some examples. The role of volunteers in events management and in organisations which provide events or event services is varied. Some volunteers are members of a committee with decision-making power; other volunteers may be 'temporary' and available to the organisation/event for a short period of time.

Some research has produced 'classifications' of volunteers which indicate different types of volunteer. Broadly, there are 'formal' and 'informal' volunteers. Informal volunteering includes unpaid work done for friends and family or neighbours, such as running errands or performing odd jobs. Formal volunteering is where an individual volunteers their time and skills to organisations or programmes/ initiatives. As volunteers may be with an organisation for a short (i.e. one event) or extended period of time (i.e. volunteer committee member), and the skills required of the volunteer may also vary, the recruitment and training (including motivating) are very important. A variety of organisations have produced guidance on good governance of volunteers which relates to the recruitment and training of volunteers generally and in sport specifically. In Table 6.1 some of the key points from a selection of these guides are summarised.

▶

Case 6.3	*(continued)*

Table 6.1   Good governance of volunteers: implications for recruiting and training

Organisation	Publication	Guidance best practice
Sport England	Voluntary Code of Good Governance for the Sport and Recreation Sector	■ clarify volunteer roles and functions ■ do not over-complicate or put unnecessary pressure on volunteers ■ clear distinction should be made between volunteers in strategic and operational functions ■ appreciate and acknowledge volunteer contribution ■ consider length of service, offer exit routes for formal volunteers to remain a member and contribute ■ recognise diversity in volunteer motivations and needs
Volunteering England	The Recruitment Guide www.volunteering. org.uk/resources/ goodpracticebank/ Core+Themes/recruitment/ therecruitmentguide- overview.htm	■ consider why you want volunteers and what they will do ■ consider formal or informal selection processes ■ consider creating a volunteer policy ■ prepare to offer induction of some kind for the volunteer (e.g. taster session, experience of the organisation)
Gaskin (2008) Media Trust	*Inspiring Volunteers: A Guide to Recruitment and Communications*	■ use a variety of methods to communicate with volunteers (e.g. email, social networks, Facebook, etc.) ■ be inclusive and sensitive to diverse populations who may volunteer, considering how you will engage with their needs (e.g. disabled persons) ■ social media is most effective when you are an active participant amongst the potential volunteers ■ identify your target audience and understand their needs ■ develop a recruitment campaign designed with your target audience in mind ■ evaluate your policy and achievements to continuously improve

Academic research has also identified effective strategies in the recruitment and training of volunteers in sport. Table 6.2 summarises the key points from a selection of current research.

Table 6.2   Research evidence of best practice in sport volunteer recruitment and training

Author/date	Best practice evidence
Misener et al. (2010)	■ Older volunteers require sport organisations to work towards meeting their needs for social and well-being motivations rather than being managed as a resource
Barnes and Sharpe (2009)	■ Traditional volunteer management structures may actually hinder volunteer engagement ■ A more vocation-based, networked and collaborative approach which affords greater autonomy to the volunteer can be more effective in managing volunteers

Author/date	Best practice evidence
Allen and Shaw (2009)	■ Volunteers are motivated by doing interesting jobs but also by the social aspects of cooperating with others towards production of an event, sharing and camaraderie important
Cuskelly et al. (2006)	■ The effectiveness of HRM practices to improve retention of volunteers varies across different categories of volunteers.
Weed et al. (2005)	■ Volunteers do not want to be managed, nor in many cases do they wish to be responsible for the management of others ■ While sport largely depends on formal volunteering, volunteers mainly prefer informal volunteering

---

Case 6.4   Your Local Playing Fields Association

Small community events can be very important for local business, children and young people as well as the wider community including the elderly, busy professionals and families. 'Your Local' Playing Fields Association is a small group of volunteers who administer the maintenance and development of the local playing field. This involved a considerable amount of fundraising and small events for several years and the committee was struggling to raise sufficient funds for some much-needed improvements to the 'football hut' and children's play area.

The members of the committee were motivated by their desire to help the community. They were a very informal group whose meetings were held in the local pub. Five members of the group were older, retired members of the community, two people were middle-aged professionals and three people were between the ages of 35 and 40.

A new committee member joined the group, who had previous experience of working on committees and of managing volunteers. It was quickly realised that the members of the committee were not using their time and resources to their maximum advantage. In other words, they were working very hard, organising lots of events but were not yielding large sums of money. The more experienced, new member suggested the committee could be more selective in its fundraising events and make more money with less effort. It was also suggested they should apply for Lottery Funding to improve their facilities.

The new committee member brought new ideas and enthusiasm to the group, but the dynamic of the committee changed. Existing committee members became resentful of the new member and felt that it was being suggested that everything they had done in the past was wrong and a lot of time was being wasted. Some of the committee members, especially the younger members, whilst they still wanted to help their community, felt that the new member was unsettling the group and were questioning their continuing participation in 'Your Local' Playing Fields Association.

Discussion questions

7 Could this situation have been avoided?

8 How would the culture of the committee have been affected by the new member?

9 Why might it be important to be selective in fundraising events?

Strategies and techniques for managing people

Managing people in the context of events management organisations is complicated by the fact that managing volunteers and paid staff must be considered. The recruitment, training and motivation of paid and unpaid staff needs to be different as these two groups of people have different expectations and needs. For guidance on managing paid staff we can consult the literature on human resource management (HRM), but for volunteers, different strategies and techniques may need to be considered. Taylor et al. (2008: 7) defined HRM as: 'the policies, practices, procedures and systems that influence the behaviour, attitudes, values and performance of people who work for the organisation'.

In many commercial companies, formal policies and procedures (an element of 'structure' discussed earlier in this chapter) are in place to help guide employees in their actions. Yet we know from previous research that too much formal guidance to volunteers can affect their levels of satisfaction and their potential to return to their volunteer position.

For paid staff, we can consider that many of the practices espoused by HRM literature can be applied in the context of events management companies. Strategies for managing people have to be considered within the broader strategic priorities of an events management organisation and so, while an event company can have a strategy for the entire organisation, this needs to consider the strategies for HRM, marketing, operations and finance. Figure 6.6 illustrates how this may work in practice.

Managing volunteers is not like managing paid staff – we cannot create a contract which legally and formally prescribes their responsibilities. Research has revealed that where formal contracts can and do not exist, 'psychological' contracts do exist and these apply to both paid and voluntary staff.

The psychological contract was originally defined by Argyris (1960) and is grounded in social exchange theory. 'The psychological contract is a cognitive state that is subjective and interpretative and refers to the development and maintenance of the relationship between the individual and the organisation' (Taylor et al., 2006: 126). It is the perception of an employee or volunteer concerning what their role and responsibilities entail as well as what their employer should provide in terms of rewards and benefits.

There are two main types of psychological contract: transactional and relational. Transactional contracts are those based on the exchange of economic currency, clearly specified and based on mutual and balanced profitability. For example, the event company would provide some guarantee of volunteering opportunity for a specified period of time (e.g. one event lasting two days, two hours per week volunteering) a safe work environment and clear guidance on what experience they are offering (e.g. work in administration), in return for specified skills and duties. Relational contracts are based on socio-emotional currency, and include an individual's perception of job security, commitment of an organisation to the volunteer, training opportunities as well as likelihood of self-actualisation, satisfaction and personal achievement.

In order to ensure that volunteers are given enough time to 'learn' how the organisation plans to run the event, deal with customers, etc. it is crucial that the organisation plans accordingly. Recruitment, in any type of organisation and for both paid and voluntary staff, can be a lengthy process. The organising committee of the Olympic Games in London began the recruitment process for volunteers more than two years before the event was staged. We are not suggesting that all events management companies need to plan this far in advance, but the time required to attract suitably qualified volunteers needs to be taken into consideration.

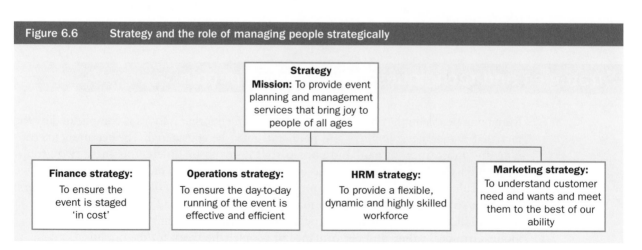

Figure 6.6   Strategy and the role of managing people strategically

Job descriptions and person specifications need to be designed to ensure that the staff recruited, whether on a paid or voluntary basis, will meet the requirements of the organisation (or indeed the event), will know exactly what is expected of them, who they report to (based on management structure) and how long their services would be required. Providing this kind of information to volunteers may impact on their sense of 'belonging' to an organisation or an event and, ultimately, by treating volunteers as if they were paid employees, they are more likely to volunteer at future events thus reducing recruitment and training time.

Tips for success in managing people

1. Listen
2. Be objective
3. Don't get angry
4. Stay positive
5. Consider alternatives
6. Focus on solutions
7. Encourage others to listen
8. Create a structure and culture to facilitate organisational mission
9. Seek ways to develop people, create opportunity in your organisation
10. Lead, be decisive but listen, consider the alternatives and make the rationale for your decisions clear.

Conclusion

The chapter has introduced the reader to some of the key concepts and issues in managing people and the role of volunteers. While the structures and procedures in all organisations have elements of commonality, the way each company is managed is different due to one important feature – the people within it.

The human resources of an organisation are the *most* important aspect of it – staff, whether paid or voluntary, are the 'face of the organisation', dealing with customers, suppliers, the media, sponsors, any individual or company interacting with it. In order to ensure productivity, efficiency and motivation, they need to be managed with respect and understanding, regardless of their role within the organisation.

General discussion questions

10 What is the relationship between the structure and culture of an events management organisation?

11 From your experience can you think of an example where there was a strong culture? Was this a good thing or a bad thing?

12 If you wanted to start your own events management company, what kind of structure and culture would you plan for?

13 Can volunteers make a 'career' of volunteering?

14 How does your job as a manager differ between managing paid staff and managing a temporary volunteer workforce? How do their motivations differ?

15 Do you think people's motivation to work in events management differs from the motivations to work in other industries such as computing, pharmaceuticals or health care?

16 What is the relationship between strategy, structure and employee (or volunteer) motivation?

Guided reading

A useful document to investigate is the Official Report of the Singapore 2010 Youth Olympics, entitled *Blazing the Trail*. It can be found at *http://app1.mcys.gov.sg/Publications/BlazingTheTrailSYOG2010OfficialReport.aspx*

Key journal articles and books in this subject area are:

Carlsen, J. and Andersson, T.D. (2011) Strategic SWOT analysis of public, private and not-for-profit festival organisations. *International Journal of Event and Festival Management*, 2(1), 83–97.

Ensor, J., Robertson, M. and Ali-Knight, J. (2011) Eliciting the dynamics of leading a sustainable event: key informant responses. *Event Management*, 15(4), 315–27.

Maslow, A.H. (1943) A theory of human motivation. *Psychological Review*, 50, 370–96.

Porter, M.E. (2008) The five competitive forces that shape strategy. *Harvard Business Review*, 79, 24–41.

Slack, T. and Parent, M. (2007) *Understanding Sport Organisations: The Application of Organisation Theory*. Champaign, IL: Human Kinetics.

Van der Wagen, L. (2007) *Human Resource Management for Events: Managing the Event Workforce*. Oxford: Butterworth-Heinemann.

Recommended websites

The bigger sports events generally offer comprehensive coverage of volunteering. For example:

The International Olympic Committee: **www.olympic.org**

The Singapore Youth Olympic Games 2010: **www.singapore2010.sg**

London 2012: **www.london2012.com/about-us/volunteers**

The Amadeus website offers a wide range of information from a private sector perspective that is useful: **www.amadeus-holdings.com**

Key words

motivation; organisational culture; volunteer

Bibliography

Allen, J.B. and Shaw, S. (2009) 'Everyone rolls up their sleeves and mucks in': exploring volunteers' motivation and experiences of the motivational climate of a sporting event. *Sport Management Review*, 12(2), 79–90.

Argyris, C. (1960) *Understanding Organisational Behaviour*. Oxford: Dorsey.

Bainbridge, L. (2012) Have we fallen out of love with the great British music festival? *The Guardian*, 31 March. **www.guardian.co.uk/** culture/2012/mar/31/out-love-british-music-festival?newsfeed=true

Barnes, M.L. and Sharpe, E.K. (2009) Looking beyond traditional volunteer management: a case study of an alternative approach to volunteer engagement in parks and recreation. *Voluntas*, 20, 169–87.

Bowes, G. (2012) The best summer music festivals in Europe. *The Guardian*, 20 April. **www.guardian.co.uk/** travel/2012/apr/20/best-summer-music-festivals-europe?newsfeed=true

Cole, Gerald A. (2004) *Management Theory and Practice* (6th edn). London: Cengage Learning EMEA.

Cuskelly, G., Taylor, T., Hoye, R. and Darcy, S. (2006) Volunteer management practices and volunteer retention: a human resource management approach. *Sport Management Review*, 9(2), 141–63.

Drucker, P. (1954) *The Practice of Management* (2nd rev. edn 2007). Oxford: Butterworth-Heinemann.

Drummond, H. (2000) *Introduction to Organisational Behaviour*. Oxford: Oxford University Press.

Ensor, J., Robertson, M. and Ali-Knight, J. (2011) Eliciting the dynamics of leading a sustainable event: key informant responses. *Event Management*, 15(4), 315–27.

Gaskin, K. (2008) *A Winning Team? The Impacts of Volunteers in Sport*. London: The Institute for Volunteering Research and Volunteering England. **www.sportdevelopment.info**

Getz, D. and Andersson, T.D. (2009) Sustainable festivals: On becoming an institution. *Event Management*, 12(1), 1–17.

Herzberg, F. (1968) One more time: how do you motivate employees? *Harvard Business Review*, 46(1), 53–62.

Herzberg, F., Mausner, B. and Synderman, B.B. (1959) *The Motivation To Work*. New York: Wiley.

Hofstede, G. (1980). *Culture's Consequences: International Differences in Work-related Values*. Newbury Park, CA: Sage.

Johnson, G. and Scholes, K. (2002) *Exploring Corporate Strategy: Text and Cases* (6th edn). Harlow: Prentice Hall.

Judge, T., Locke, E.A., Durham, C.C. and Kluger, A.N. (1998) Dispositional effects on job and life satisfaction: the role of core evaluations. *Journal of Applied Psychology*, 83(1), 17–34.

Maslow, A.H. (1943) A theory of human motivation. *Psychological Review*, 50, 370–96.

Media Trust (no date) Inspiring volunteers: a guide to recruitment and communications,

Media Trust. **www.mediatrust.org/uploads/128957702875264/original.pdf**

Misener, K., Doherty, A. and Hamm-Kerwin, S. (2010) Learning from the experiences of older adult volunteers in sport: a serious leisure perspective, *Journal of Leisure Research*, 42(2), 267–89.

Pine, J. and Gilmore, J.H. (1999) *The Experience Economy: Work is Theatre and Every Business a Stage*. Cambridge, MA: Harvard Business School Press.

Ralston, L.S., Ellis, G.D., Compton, D.M. and Lee, J. (2007) Staging memorable events and festivals: an integrated model of service and experience factors. *International Journal of Event Management Research*, 3(2), 24–38.

Sherratt, A., Nicholson, F. and Meek, R. (2009) *Managing Marketing*. Oxford: Butterworth-Heinemann.

Slack, T. and Parent, M. (2006) *Understanding Sport Organisations: The Application of Organisation Theory*. Champaign, IL: Human Kinetics.

Taylor, T., Darcy, S., Hoye, R. and Cuskelly, G. (2006) Using psychological contract theory to explore issues in effective volunteer management. *European Sport Management Quarterly*, 6(2), 123–47.

Taylor, T., Doherty, A. and McGraw, P. (2008) *Managing People in Sport Organisations: A Strategic Human Resource Management Perspective*. Oxford: Butterworth-Heinemann.

Weed, M., Robinson, L., Downward, P., Green, M., Henry, I., Houlihan, B. and Argent, E. (2005) Academic review of the role of voluntary sports clubs, Institute of Sport & Leisure Policy, Loughborough University: Sport England Report. **www.sportandrecreation. uk/sites/sportandrecreation.org.uk/files/ web/documents/word/role_of_voluntary_ sports_clubs.doc**

Chapter 7

Marketing and destination branding

Martina Lettner, FH Kufstein Tirol – University of Applied Sciences, Austria, and
Rick Burton, Syracuse University US

'Two things only the people eagerly desire: bread and the circus games.'

Roman poet Juvenal (40–125 AD)

Learning outcomes

Upon completion of this chapter the reader should be able to:

- understand the importance of accurate strategic marketing in modern **media** society;

- identify the characteristics and challenges of **destination** marketing;

- recognise the sensible interplay of destination **brand** identities and events;

- anticipate risks and chances of using events as a destination marketing tool;

- explain possible impacts of mega sports events on the image of a destination and its brand identity.

Overview

In a world that is moved and motivated by and via communications, it is of the utmost importance to gain the attention of the mass media for a business to be successful. This is valid in general, but is even more important for organisations in competitive industries such as destinations in the tourism industry. Not only do organisations seek the short-term attention of potential customers, but they need to stay in their minds, too. To do so, branding and strategic marketing methods are used.

Events offer a possibility to shape the profile of an organisation or a destination, raise its awareness level and address new target groups – see that the event fits the destination's competitive identity and is well organised.

In its first section, this chapter gives insight into the process and characteristics of destination marketing, beginning with a short introduction to modern media society, marketing and branding (Martina Lettner). The second section focuses on the risks and advantages of using sports events as a destination marketing tool. By discussing mega sports events, possible impacts of large-scale events – or 'circus games' as Juvenal called them – on the image of a destination and its brand identity are explained (Rick Burton).

Theoretical background

■ Modern media society

The German sociologist Richard Münch (1992) states that in a world that is driven by communications, no one can deny the need for gaining public attention: 'Whoever misses that goal is to be forgotten and doomed'. This is not only true for business organisations, but also for political parties, non-governmental organisations (NGOs), non-profit organisations (NPOs) and – now more than ever – destinations. In western societies public attention and interest is generated and gained through the mass media (Saxer, 1998); even the individual's knowledge about society and the social world at large is based on the depictions provided by the mass media (Luhmann, 2004).

Some years ago a number of marketers and communications managers still thought that economic success is almost directly related to the number of advertisements placed and the quantity of information provided – the more, the better. As the market has shifted from a seller's market to a buyer's market, their marketing communications efforts became even pushier: a constant and enormous augmentation, acceleration and agglomeration of public communications were to be seen as well as a loss of the perceived trustworthiness of advertisements (Münch, 1992), creating a credibility gap and thus a negative reaction from consumers (Kroeber-Riel et al., 2009). This led to a rethinking in the conduct of corporate communications (Karl Nessmann quoted in Lettner, 2010): instead of seeking 'shrill' short-term attention and using 'chintzy' sales tricks, integrated marketing communications (including public relations) are now about lasting communications, presenting not only the features of a service or product and its usefulness for the customer, but the corporate values, too. Gaining public trust and, based on that, a positive image is of enormous importance, especially for destinations (Anholt, 2007). A unique brand identity and an integrated marketing strategy have to be implemented to achieve this image. Even short-term marketing goals and the use of marketing tools such as marketing events have to be adapted to fit this strategy (Blakeman, 2009) – this is a challenge especially for tourism destinations and their heterogeneous **stakeholders** (Freyer, 2011), even more so as the tourism industry has become highly competitive (Horne and Manzenreiter, 2006).

■ Marketing

Some may think of marketing as selling and advertising only. But successful marketing is much more. Marketing is an entrepreneurial mindset; it focuses on the analysis, planning, implementation and controlling of all internal and external corporate activities which are suitable for improving corporate performance in terms of improving the customer's benefit and hence improving the market-related business objectives (Bruhn, 2010).

Even though people in 'modern media' societies are somewhat surrounded by commercials and direct mailings, marketing nowadays should not be misunderstood as advertising in order to make a sale. Modern marketing is quite the opposite, as management expert Peter Drucker states: 'The aim of marketing is to make selling unnecessary' (quoted in Kotler and Armstrong, 2010) by developing products that provide superior value at an appropriate price and distributing and promoting them effectively. Kotler and Armstrong add: 'Simply put, marketing is managing profitable customer relations. The aim of marketing is to create value for customers and to capture value from customers in return'. This works for all types of organisations, whether they are manufacturing companies, service companies, destinations, NPOs, NGOs, etc.

In order to provide superior value to their customers, organisations have to be aware of shifts in the market as well as of changes in customers' needs (Bruhn, 2010). Therefore

Kotler's description of the five-step marketing process starts with addressing customers (Kotler and Armstrong, 2010):

1. Understand the market place and the customer needs

Marketing is no longer a one-way route: in the modern market place, it is not only marketers who do marketing, but consumers do marketing, too, as they search the market for suitable products (e.g. by using new media), as they try to get in contact with the companies and as they suggest products interactively to other customers on the web. Marketers need to know the trends in the societies that use their products: the shifts of the market place, the shift of customer needs, and where to place information so that their customers can find them. This is done via market research.

2. Design customer-driven marketing strategies

As the company understands the market, first it has to decide which customers it will serve. This process includes market segmentation – defining a target group and doing target marketing. Secondly it has to decide how to bring the target group the value it desires. The set of benefits a company brings to the customer is summarised in the value proposition (e.g. Finland's cell-phone producer Nokia states this as 'Connecting people'). According to Blakeman (2009) the value proposition gives a first answer to the question that customers ask when deciding to purchase a service or product: 'What's in it for me?' In order to give a more detailed answer, companies develop a marketing strategy. This outlines which customers the organisation will serve, how it will create value for these customers and what kind of philosophy will guide the marketing strategy: is it mostly about the interests of the customers, the interests of the organisation or the interests of society?

The philosophy should match the attitude of the customers.

3. Construct integrated marketing programmes that deliver superior value

The marketing programme turns the marketing strategy into action. The marketing tool set used by firms to implement their strategies is called the marketing mix. Already in the middle of the 20th century Jerome McCarthy (1960) divided the mix into four groups, better known as the four Ps – Product, Price, Place and Promotion (see Table 7.1). Half a century later, the four Ps are still useful in developing marketing programmes. But as the market has become a buyers' market, the marketer's attention has turned to the customer point of view (instead of the provider's point of view): the four Ps have become the four Cs.

As every action set by the firm has to fit the value proposition, the marketing programme has to be an integrated one, i.e. no matter which medium is used for promotion, the core message has to match the value proposition, even though the details of the message and its tone may vary (Blakeman, 2009). Most companies define a corporate identity including, for instance, the corporate mission, corporate values, corporate design, corporate behaviour and corporate communications, which is used as a guideline (Pepels, 2011).

Table 7.1	The 4Ps and the 4Cs of marketing	
The four Ps	**The four Cs**	
Product	Customer	Does the offer satisfy the customer's needs?
Price	Cost	How much must the customer spend to get the product or service?
Place	Convenience	How difficult or convenient is it for the customer to get the service or product?
Promotion	Communication	Does the customer feel like a partner? Does the customer feel fairly treated?

Later on, this chapter focuses on the communication aspect of the four Cs, especially on using events for promotional purposes in destination branding and destination marketing: events are one of the most powerful tools – if used correctly (Hall, 2006).

4. Build profitable customer relationships

Only if the first three steps are done properly can the fourth step be successful: building a relationship with the customers. As in every relationship, it takes some time until the relationship is stable and partners feel something like loyalty. The first three steps of the marketing process help getting to know each other, and therefore the core message should not change too often (Blakeman, 2009). Depending on the nature of the target market, oganisations can build relationships on different levels: firms with many low-margin customers will seek to establish a basic relationship (e.g. via advertising), while firms with just a few high-margin customers will try to establish a full partnership with higher involvement with their key customers (e.g. by personal meetings). There are many more levels of relationship in between those two extremes.

5. Capture value from the customers

Efficient marketing is not only done by building lots of customer relationships and constantly increasing their number (growing share of customers), but it is also about keeping them (customer relationship management or CRM). Today, most leading firms develop customer loyalty and retention programmes. They do so by either offering frequency marketing programmes rewarding those customers who purchase frequently or in a large amount, or implementing club marketing programmes bringing benefits to their members. These programmes are of importance as, in today's buyer's market, it is much cheaper to maintain existing customer relationships than to establish new ones.

The ultimate aim of CRM and marketing in general is to produce higher customer equity. This is 'the total combined customer lifetime values of all of the company's current and potential customers' (Kotler and Armstrong, 2010). But not all customers, not even all loyal customers, are necessarily profitable for the firm. So CRM is not only about managing customer relationships, but managing the right customer relationships (for further information see Peelen and Beltman, 2013).

The marketing process described is mostly based on the providers' point of view. Kotler (1984) suggests five elements that constitute a consumer's evaluation of product choices. They are: product family, product class, product line, product type and product brand. So if two firms provide exactly the same service or product at the same convenience level with the same price, the consumer chooses his or her favourite by the brand: 'The brand is a personality the customer relates to concerning the product. A brand is a promise of something' (Moilanen and Rainisto, 2008).

■ Branding

The American Marketing Association defines a brand as a 'name, term, sign, symbol, or design, or a combination of them, intended to identify the goods and services of one seller or group of sellers and to differentiate them from those of the competition' (Blakeman, 2009). Or, as Roll (2005) points out: 'A strong brand creates a unique set of characteristics and added values that helps a product or service differentiate from the competition and win a preferred space in the mind of the consumer'.

It is evident that a strong brand brings advantages to the firms (Kotler et al., 2011). The process of creating a brand, making it publicly known and raising a positive brand image among customers is called branding. Branding is one of the most powerful tools in the marketing arsenal (Holt, 2003). The term branding is misleading, as it indicates etymologically that a brand can be established easily, like a cow can be branded. Quite the opposite is true: 'A brand is created in a consumer's mind' (Moilanen and Rainisto, 2008).

'The aim of branding is to find a brand idea that will run through all the places and situations where consumers, employees, suppliers and investors experience the brand' (Kotler et al., 2011). This goes along with the first two steps of the marketing process described above. So brand management is a long-term process that not only includes the value proposition of the product, but the customers' mindsets as well. Therefore image and identity are of utmost importance, especially when dealing with complex products or services like events or destinations: 'the methods of creating and maintaining a brand, and the methods of utilising the opportunities created by a strong brand differ, significantly between places and companies' (Moilanen and Rainisto, 2008).

Destination branding and competitive identity

The concept of 'destinations' is used in different fields, e.g. in marketing, sociology and geography. Some treat it as a set of attributes and others treat it as a set of cultural and symbolic meanings (Morgan et al., 2011). According to Bieger (2008), there are different kinds of destinations, like industry destinations versus tourism destinations or sports destinations versus cultural destinations. A destination may be a nation, a region, a city or village or even just a part of a town, or a single hotel complex that is perceived and chosen by the customer. As this chapter concentrates on tourism destinations, it refers to the definition of destination by Buhalis (quoted in Morgan et al., 2011): 'a geographical region which is understood by its visitors as a unique entity, with a political and legislative work for tourism marketing and planning'.

'In order to be successfully promoted in the targeted markets, a destination must be favourably differentiated from its competition, or positively positioned, in the minds of the consumers' (Echtner and Ritchie, 2003). This became even harder as the competitive tourism industry reached a high level of standardisation, with product parity, substitutability and competition. Thus, the destination's 'reputation or brand play a hugely significant role in determining just how successful they are in this competition' (Morgan et al., 2011).

So successful branding and efficient marketing seem to be vital to the well-being of a destination. Nevertheless, academics have argued whether a destination can ever be a brand – according to Morgan et al. (2011) in a strict marketing sense they cannot. This is why some prefer the terms 'place reputation management' and 'competitive identity'. This has to do with the very special circumstances a destination marketer has to face.

In order to create a strong brand identity and a positive reputation, the set of values promised by the (destination) brand has to be authentic, believable and attractive to potential customers; the core message has to be *unique, easy to remember and match the promised values,* which is especially hard for destinations because of their heterogeneous stakeholders.

As described above, a brand is strongly related to the brand identity, which again is related to the corporate identity – which has two sides: the inside view (e.g. how employees see their employer) and the outside view (e.g. how customers perceive the service provider) (Pepels, 2011). In the case of a destination, the term 'corporate identity' seems inappropriate as there might be, and usually are, multiple companies offering their services and products within one destination – which makes it even harder (if not impossible) to shape a single identity fitting the various companies together. In addition, the destination's identity is not only determined by the corporate identities, but especially by the social identity of the locals too. These existing identities as companies, individuals and society cannot be shaped externally (e.g. by a destination management organisation or DMO) and therefore all branding efforts might not lead to the desired results (Anholt, 2007). 'Branding' a destination is finding its public identity and promoting its sunny side.

On top of those internal challenges, there are even more stakeholders (Morgan et al., 2011) like the tourists themselves, politicians and investors who influence the collective identity of a destination, and therefore its image and reputation.

In short, on the one hand there are heterogeneous internal factors, like locals and local firms, who have a certain inside view and who are influencing the destination's identity (unknowingly or on purpose) from within. On the other hand, there is the heterogeneous group of customers, like potential visitors, and investors, who have an external view of a destination's identity, who create a certain image of the destination and who influence the destination's reputation by their actions. In both groups different conflicting interests meet, which inflicts potential damage on the brand. As a brand cannot be generated outside the customer's mind, ambiguous or even opposing messages from different stakeholders concerning the destination will harm its reputation.

An integrated marketing strategy, including the many stakeholders, is one of the biggest challenges a DMO has to face – and it is the best chance of achieving and preserving a positive reputation. Still, a lot of destinations are struggling, as Dinnie (2009) shows using the example of nations:

> Identity refers to what something truly is, its essence, whereas image refers to how something is perceived. Evidently, there is frequently a gap between these two states. The identity-image gap tends to be a negative factor, with many nations struggling with the frustration of not being perceived by the rest of the world for what they truly are.

Anholt (2007), who became famous for his idea of nation branding, abandoned this expression for the reasons mentioned above in favour of the term 'competitive identity':

> Competitive Identity is about government, companies and people learning to channel their behaviour in a common direction that's positive and productive for the country's reputation, so they can start to earn the reputation they need and deserve. It is the creation of a common purpose that leads to enhanced Competitive Identity both at home and abroad.

He devised a simple model to show the different dominant communicating factors of a destination in his 'Hexagon of Competitive Identity' (Anholt, 2011):

- *Tourism*: The tourism promotion activities, as well as the visitors' first-hand experience – this is often the most powerful way of communicating the reputation of a destination.
- *People*: The people of the destination themselves: stars, as well as the population in general; how they behave when abroad and how they treat visitors back home.
- *Culture*: Communication through cultural exchange and activities: e.g. famous musicians and orchestras touring the globe, works of famous authors being presented abroad, national sports teams joining mega sports events.
- *Brands*: The exported products and services can act as ambassadors of their destination.
- *Policy*: Even policy decisions have an impact on the perception of a destination, whether it be foreign policy or domestic policy which gets reported in the international media
- *Investment*: The way the country solicits inward investment.

The ideally unique competitive identity of a destination has to be promoted. This is where destination marketing, including communications and events, comes into play.

■ Destination marketing

The offer of a destination is a bundle of different products and, even more importantly, services. Therefore tourism destination marketing has long been seen as a part of service marketing, although it has some peculiarities (Freyer, 2011): touristic offers are abstract and immaterial; not standardisable, not transportable, not storable, not predictable, and singular as they result from customers' interaction with the destination and its offers. Hence tourism marketing is becoming an independent field of research.

Despite this, components of general marketing can be applied to destinations. Considering the five steps of the marketing process, for DMOs the following can be stated:

1. Understand the market place and the customer needs

Due to social changes in general, the tourism market has become more competitive in recent decades. Freyer (2006) considers the following changes to be relevant for tourism destinations and tourists:

■ change of income and wealth;
■ change of free time and working time;
■ change of values in the western world (e.g. self-actualisation);
■ change of mobility;
■ technological evolution;
■ change of population structure and demographic growth;
■ formation of a tourism industry.

These changes have led to an alteration of tourism patterns. In 1950, almost 90% of international tourists crowded at the top 15 destinations. In 2005, the most popular tourism destinations accounted for less than 60% of the tourist arrivals (this number had risen dramatically in the second half of the 20th century) (Morgan et al., 2011).

As destinations in the highly competitive tourism industry have reached a high level of service and infrastructure, it is hard to define a unique value proposition by concentrating on those hard facts. Possible ways to form a unique value proposition are, for example, finding a niche or referring to the change of values in the western world (Bieger, 2008).

2. Design customer-driven marketing strategies

Before defining a target market, destinations need to know their collective identity and possible benefits. Derived from that, the possible target group and core messages can be defined. Usually destinations have more than just one core benefit. So, unsurprisingly, they should promote more than just one benefit. It is important that the different services and products do not provide different and inconsistent benefits or, even worse, images; the promotion of the various benefits should not be a competition among the benefits of a destination (Bieger, 2008), but more like an orchestra where the different instruments play together and support the 'first violin'. The product with the most attractive unique feature should be this 'first violin'.

This is the ideal. In reality, most stakeholders communicate their values in an uncoordinated way. An inconsistent message is the result, which makes it hard for customers to create a positive, attractive or at least distinct image of a destination (Siller, 2010). Financially more potent destinations have already recognised the need for integrating marketing efforts and trying to orchestrate the different messages and senders (see Anholt's Hexagon of Competitive Identity above).

This effort to integrate all stakeholders and their conflicting interests into the marketing strategy may lead to wishy-washy value propositions, communicated by marketing cliché. They lack uniqueness, prominence or even relevance – they become what Morgan et al. (2011) call 'Any country' (see Exhibit 7.1).

Exhibit 7.1	'Any Country'

Any Country – the land of contrast.

Any Country is everywhere's best kept secret. It's so close to home, yet a world apart. The perfect place to escape the stresses and strains of modern life.

Come and discover *Any Country*'s many secret hidden gems. Step back in time at one of hundreds of heritage attractions and museums. Or just kick off your shoes and relax on one of our award-winning beaches. With more than 1,000 miles of coastline, you're sure to find your perfect spot.

Whatever you're looking for *Any Country* has it all: from mountain biking or walking to surfing and sailing. *Any Country* truly is an adventure playground packed full of fun for all of the family.

After all that activity, what better way to unwind than to savour fresh local food at one of our award-winning restaurants. Whatever your taste, you'll find *Any Country* has the perfect ingredients for a short break or longer holiday, all year round. And wherever you go you're sure of a warm *Any Countryish* welcome.

But don't take our word for it, come and see for yourself. What are you waiting for?

Source: Morgan et al. (2011)

3. Construct integrated marketing programmes that deliver superior value

Research conducted for the World Tourism Organisation in 2009 showed that 82% of DMOs had an official brand strategy, and 80% had a toolkit explaining how to apply the brand; remarkably, over a third had spent money on developing a brand strategy which they had no plans to evaluate, even though 75% thought they had a unique positioning (Morgan et al., 2011).

Not only are the accurate planning of a marketing programme and its implementation vital to the wealth of a destination, the analysis of the competition and the controlling of the specific marketing programme and its impact are important, too – no matter what implementation tactics and media are used.

4. Build profitable customer relationships

Only if the DMOs know about the (possible) impact of their actions, and the needs and wishes of their customers, can they work on the relationships with their visitors.

5. Capture value from the customers

Usually DMOs do not directly profit from tourists, but from the economic well-being of tourism service providers at a destination via indirect returns.

Events and destination marketing

In our entertainment-seeking society (Schulze, 2005), events are an effective way to grab the attention of possible customers. Especially in destination marketing they have assumed a key role (Hall, 2006): 'Nations, regions, cities and corporations have used mega-events to promote a favourable image in the international tourist, migration and business marketplace' (Ritchie and Beliveau quoted in Hall, 2006).

Hall (2006) points out that mega (sports) events emerge as central elements in the place competition in at least three ways:

1. infrastructure required for such events is regarded as integral to further economic development;
2. hosting of events is seen as a contribution to business vitality and economic development;
3. the ability to attract events is regarded as a performance indicator in its own right of the capacity of a city or a region to compete.

Further reasons to host (or risks of hosting) mega events are the legacies – whether they are social, environmental or economic. With today's methodologies, the exact measurement of the impacts and financial indirect returns is not possible. The discussion about positive or negative legacies gets even more complicated when talking about intangible effects – those which cannot be measured in pounds, euros or dollars at all. Some argue that via indirect return (almost) every host destination of mega (sports) events benefits from the global attention, from shift of image and the renewed reputation fostering economic prosperity while others argue that forecasts of the benefits are nearly always wrong (Horne and Manzenreiter, 2006).

Both sides present empirical evidence. Barcelona 1992 is cited as an example of an Olympic Games that attracted public investment to a city and region that needed to be redeveloped. There were improvements in transportation; the coast was opened up to the city in a way that had not occurred before; unemployment rates in Barcelona fell compared with the rest of Spain; and a permanent employment effect of 20,000 extra jobs was estimated. The citizens of Barcelona took advantage of the newly built sports infrastructure. Nevertheless, there has been discussion about the costs and the distribution of the social and economic benefits of hosting the Games (Horne and Manzenreiter, 2006).

Innsbruck, which hosted the Winter Olympic Games in 1964 and 1972, is still suffering from the costs of those events: the infrastructure that was built for the Games still generates costs. The former Olympic Village has become a place of social problems. The Olympia World sports infrastructure poses a dilemma for regional government: either politicians seek a higher degree of utilisation (with extra costs) or the infrastructure is not used – which generates (albeit lower) costs as well. In 2008, the Tyrolean audit court stated that the expenses for the Olympia World had reached almost €25 million within six years. Nevertheless, Innsbruck continues to bid to host sports events in order to maintain its image as a sports city. In 2012, Innsbruck hosted the first Youth Olympic Games, which, again, probably were more expensive than the forecasts predicted. Innsbruck wanted to host another Olympic Winter Games, but the citizens turned those plans down (Fasser, 2010).

In the same way as between events and sponsors, the image transfer theory is valid for destinations and events as well: *the event's image rubs off on the destination's image and vice versa*. The image congruity between the event and the destination significantly moderates the event–destination image transfer model (Deng Qiang, 2011): the better the event's image and the destination's image match, the more both images benefit from the transfer.

The destination's image is dependent on the competitive identity of the destination, which in turn relates to the various individual identities of the destination's stakeholders. If those stakeholders do not agree with the DMOs or the government's plans to host a mega event, the event either is not likely to take place or will not be successfully conducted. Consider the case of Austria's capital, Vienna, wanting to bid to host the Olympic Summer Games. It never got the chance to bid as this fell through following a public opinion poll in spring 2013: the Viennese disliked the idea of hosting the Olympic Games (Gantner, 2013).

Summing up, in our modern entertainment-seeking society, events are an effective way to get attention and influence a destination's image. The larger the event, the higher the possible benefits and risks. Therefore it is of importance to inform and integrate the local individuals and companies as partners quite early in the process of planning a mega event, to calculate the risks and to try to be aware of possible issues and problems.

Implementation experience

The second section of this chapter deals with mega events such as the Olympic Games which grab the attention of millions. If the competitive identity of the destination and the brand of the sports organisation fit, conducting the mega event might help the destination and the sports organisation. The word 'might' was chosen carefully as there are certain risks related to using mega events as a marketing tool for destinations.

Short history of mega sports events and destinations

The idea of combining mega sports events and destinations is quite old. The earliest known example of sport or gaming is possibly Egyptian 'Senet', a marble-type game which dates to 3000 BC. For a book published in the 21st century, that means organised competition has been around for more than 5,000 years. That is a significant length of time and, of course, during those five millennia, sport has evolved in many varied forms and to fit many unique forums.

Interestingly, as was the case in antiquity (and still is today), the most significant sports event has been either the ancient Olympic Games or the modern version of the Olympics – specific sporting events that have traditionally gathered city-states or nations together to compete in a wide range of sports. This creation, the Olympics, by the ancient Greeks, has provided arguably the greatest sports legacy of all time.

We know (with relative certainty) that the ancient Olympic Games can be traced to Olympia, Greece in 776 BC and that this first version of the Olympics would last, in varying formats, until 393 AD. The modern Olympics did not appear for another 1,503 years (not until April 1896) when a French nobleman named Pierre de Coubertin, building on the work of the Greek philanthropist Evangelos Zappas, brought the Olympic movement back to life in Athens, where athletes from 14 countries competed in nine different sports. At roughly the same time (23 June 1894), de Coubertin created the umbrella brand for this sporting institution and named it the International Olympic Committee: a non-governmental international body that would supervise quadrennial gatherings of international athletes.

Mega sports events and destinations

Combining the interests of sports organisations and destinations suggests itself as both have parallel interests.

Destination-branding consultancy TSE Consulting (2009) suggests that sport organisations develop into brands by combining three core elements: the organisation, the sport form and the product the sport organisation offers. In this way, sport organisations, be they committees (like the IOC), leagues (like the NFL or La Liga), teams (e.g. Manchester United), host city organising committees (such as those at Sochi or Rio), sport federations (like FIFA) or events (e.g. the Formula 1 race at Monaco), consistently seek 'to become relevant to members and other stakeholders [by] building and promoting a brand which is constantly nurtured and developed'. These sport organisations, sometimes incorporating only one sport (e.g. football) and sometimes involving multiple sports (e.g. The Olympics, Asian Games or Commonwealth Games), must 'view external partners as an integral part of its activities' (TSE Consulting, 2009).

DMOs too have to view external partners as an integral part of their activities. DMOs and sport organisations need another partner to achieve their main goal of improving customer relationships: sport organisations need a hosting destination for their sports events; DMOs need unique services to get the attention of possible visitors.

Tied to the interests of the sport organisation and the destination management organisation are what might be identified as the five elements which Kotler (1984) suggests constitute a consumer's evaluation of product choices (see Table 7.2):

The consumers must decide if they are interested in sport, which class (or type) of sport they might follow or invest in, which teams or athletes from that specific sport are most compelling, and which events they might wish to attend or watch via TV or online. The same continuum of choices is valid for destinations and their potential customers.

Table 7.2	Applying Kotler's five elements	
Kotler's five elements	**From a DMO's perspective**	**From an SO's perspective**
Product family	Destination	Sports (rather than music, films or museums)
Product class	Tourism destination	Internationally competed sport competitions held every four years such as the Olympics, FIFA World Cup or Rugby World Cup
Product line	City	The Summer Olympics (or Winter Olympics)
Product type	Trip in a South American city with special offers in mega sports events	The contested sports of the Summer Olympics such as swimming, athletics, judo or gymnastics
Product brand	The Rio de Janeiro 2016 Summer Olympics	The Rio de Janeiro 2016 Summer Olympics

Source: Kotler (1984)

For the concept of destination branding to take hold (as in the example in Table 7.2 where Rio de Janeiro sits as the product brand), we will see that thousands of other brands go to work seeking to connect their product or services to the Rio 2016 Games. This can include countries (e.g. the German Olympic Committee), sports (e.g. the International Equestrian Federation – FEI), athletes, sponsors, advertisers, suppliers and sports marketing agencies. The collision of all of these brands can produce unwanted clutter, but even so the city brand (in this case Rio de Janeiro) hopes to benefit because all of those brands will focus their energies on associating the best attributes of their brands with the best attributes of Rio de Janeiro. Those brands can be split up into major types of consumer-focused (or business-to-business) companies:

Sports properties or entities

These organisations (e.g. FIFA's World Cup) are the essence of sport because they manufacture the organised sport experience for athletes, coaches, suppliers and fans. They are also, in most cases, the owner of the content they produce (which can be sold to broadcast networks, sponsors, licensees, concessionaires and merchandisers). But to survive as a business, they must market to and attract customers – so they have the same main goal as the DMOs.

Companies that make products or equipment for sports entities or athletes

These sporting companies (e.g. Nike or Puma) would not exist without sports events or sports activities and their business is driven by a need for equipment or products beneficial to participating in the sports experience. In this case, we can talk about the manufacturers of balls, sticks, clubs, uniforms, shoes, goals and nets, but we can also refer to stadium architects, stadium operators and concessionaires. These groups must market themselves to sports organisations or athletes in order to survive.

Companies that sponsor sports or use well-known athletes as endorsers to tie in with sports via advertising, sales promotions or employee enhancements

These companies (e.g. Heineken, Visa) are not, in essence, sporting companies but often use an alignment with sport via advertising or sponsorships to help sell more of their products and grow their businesses. Even if they don't need sports per se, they have a vivid interest in supporting mega sports events.

Companies that market sport relationships or work to help bring sports events to countries, regions, provinces, states and cities

These companies (e.g. TSE Consulting) are often identified as sports marketing firms and, like advertising agencies, they seek clients that wish to leverage sport for the benefit of their business model. TSE, for instance, is known for its engagement of cities, states, regions and countries as it seeks to bring global sports events into a fixed location.

Companies that have nothing to do with sport

Sometimes these organisations end up connected to sport when they purchase tickets for their employees or clients, or use values drawn from sport (most notably the concept of 'winning') in their marketing materials. For students who live in competitive capitalistic economies, the concept of growing one's business is often equated with (or compared to) the competitive nature of sports. In many instances, net profitability is equated with victory or winning.

By identifying these five types of company sectors above, it becomes apparent that:

1. sport is a major global business (thought by some estimates to now approach US$300 billion worldwide); and
2. sport, as a vehicle or marketing tactic (or lever), can be used as a foundational aspect of an organisation's strategic orientation, its consumer or business-facing communications, and its revenue-generating positioning strategies.

Reasons for using mega sports events as a destination marketing tool

Sport grabs the attention of millions of people

Mullin et al. (1993) suggest that sport holds 'an almost universal appeal and pervades all elements of life'. It does so geographically (sport is played, in some form, in every nation on the earth), demographically (sport appeals to all ages, races, genders and incomes), and socio-culturally (sport holds notable value as an element of leisure, recreation, physical discipline and mental motivation).

Mullin et al. (1993) then cited Harry Edwards, a sports psychologist, who went so far as to suggest that, from his research of copious media coverage, he had found that sport represents a type of creed because it supplies seven value themes that people generally accept and embrace. To Edwards, sport (as revealed through the media) provides:

- character building;
- discipline;
- competition;
- physical fitness;
- mental fitness;
- religiosity;
- nationalism.

Today, sport is such a defining activity of most international cultures that it is thought that every country in the world incorporates sport (in some fashion) into its national fabric. This was certainly the case in 2008 at the Beijing Summer Olympic Games when 204 nations[1] sent nearly 11,000 athletes to participate in 28 sports (302 events) in China's capital city. Notably, these athletes were followed, it is claimed, by an estimated 4 billion people, roughly two-thirds of the world's population, who viewed or read about some portion of the Olympic Games on a TV, laptop, newspaper, magazine or mobile phone.

The Olympic Games are not the only big sporting circus on this planet; the world's football/soccer federation (FIFA) stages a massive World Cup every four years generating billions of viewers and millions of game attendees. The most recent World Cups were staged in Germany (2006), South Africa (2010) and Brazil (2014). What makes the

---

1 The IOC allows 'nations' such as Hong Kong, Macedonia, Bermuda, Puerto Rico and the British Virgin Islands to compete even though they are not recognised as members of the United Nations. This means disputed areas, protectorates, territories and/or dependencies may field Olympic teams even if the competitors coming from these 'nations' also hold citizenship in another country.

World Cup so amazing is that it is a sporting event that features, in its finals stage, only 32 countries (not 200+) and only two of them make the actual Final. Still, more than 3 billion cumulative viewers (nearly 50% of the world's population) were engaged in watching at least one minute of the 2010 South African World Cup, with an estimated 620 million witnessing Spain's first-ever world championship in Johannesburg (FIFA, 2011). In Spain, it was thought that 86% of that country's population watched the Cup Final, making it the most watched television show ever in Spanish TV history.

Advertisers are interested in the possibility of promoting their offers to millions of people

In another form of football, this time the American version, The National Football League's (NFL) 47th annual Super Bowl, was held on 3 February 2013 in New Orleans and featured a victory by the Baltimore Ravens over the San Francisco 49ers. According to CBS, the official broadcast partner for the NFL, the telecast reached nearly 114 million Americans and became the third-most watched American TV programme ever. Hype surrounding the game made the broadcast so valuable as an advertising platform that a single 30-second commercial on CBS reportedly cost companies like Doritos, Mercedes-Benz, Volkswagen, Coca-Cola and Budweiser in the range of US$3.8 million for the advertising time, and many advertisers spent more than US$2 million to produce each commercial they aired. At nearly $6 million in total to produce and air commercials, advertisers were spending approximately $200,000 per second during the Super Bowl. The biggest ad spender of the Super Bowl was the brewery Anheuser-Busch InBev, which spent US$239.1 million on advertisements from 2002 to 2011 (CNBC, undated).

Destinations are interested in publicity to strengthen their competitive identity

The economic impact for New Orleans, where the big game was played for the 10th time, was estimated to be US$432 million spent by an estimated 150,000 tourists on airfares, hotels, meals, rental cars and souvenirs, and by the more than 71,000 that attended the game.

Beyond the advertisers and city planners, there were also musicians who performed at the Super Bowl and built their brands. Singer Beyoncé played at halftime (re-uniting for part of the show with her old band, Destiny's Child) and experts expected that, like Madonna and the Black Eyed Peas before her, Beyoncé's music catalogue would enjoy a significant increase in purchases via downloads or at retail stores. Similarly, pre-game singers Jennifer Hudson and Alicia Keys were also expected to benefit from the huge visibility associated with performing at this event. Their fame and visibility at the event helps the destination strengthen its competitive image.

The intent in winning the bid to host mega sports events is usually to stimulate a country's economy, often through sustainable tourism, or to bring the world's media and/or opinion leaders to a country or city that they might not normally have visited. Australia's Tourism Board invested heavily in the staging of the Sydney 2000 Summer Games and tried to make sure that the entire country, not just one city, benefited from the winning bid.

In Sochi's case, in 2014, it is believed that the Russian leaders have long wanted to showcase a 'new' Russia and that hosting the Winter Olympics would provide such a global platform.

Table 7.3 lists the hosts selected for the Summer Olympic Games.

■ Risks using mega sports events as a destination marketing tool

Financial risks

In the Olympic world, the production stakes can be even higher than a Super Bowl because instead of staging one game on one day, the IOC must sustain the world's inspection for 17 days, with not only massive opening and closing ceremonies but also multi-sport competition spread across numerous venues for the days in between.

Table 7.3	Cities that have hosted the IOC's modern Summer Olympic Games
1896	Athens, Greece
1900	Paris, France
1904	St Louis, USA
1908	London, England
1912	Stockholm, Sweden
1920	Antwerp, Belgium
1924	Paris, France
1928	Amsterdam, Netherlands
1932	Los Angeles, USA
1936	Berlin, Germany
1948	London, England
1952	Helsinki, Finland
1956	Melbourne, Australia
1960	Rome, Italy
1964	Tokyo, Japan
1968	Mexico City, Mexico
1972	Munich, West Germany
1976	Montreal, Canada
1980	Moscow, Soviet Union
1984	Los Angeles, USA
1988	Seoul, South Korea
1992	Barcelona, Spain
1996	Atlanta, USA
2000	Sydney, Australia
2004	Athens, Greece
2008	Beijing, China
2012	London, England
2016	Rio de Janeiro, Brazil
2020	Tokyo, Japan

Note: London (1908, 1948, 2012) has hosted the greatest number of times with Paris (1900, 1924), Los Angeles (1932, 1984) and Tokyo (1964, 2020) also hosting on multiple occasions. Rio de Janeiro (2016) will be the first time the Olympic Games have been held in South America. They have never been held in Africa or the Middle East; however, a victory by Istanbul in September 2013 (for 2020) would have addressed that omission. The Summer Olympics will be held in Tokyo in 2020.

Building those stadiums and arenas is one thing, but just reaching that point takes an enormous appetite for risk. In fact, the average cost for a city (or country) to bid for the right to host the Olympics now runs into the hundreds of millions. Persistent rumours suggest that Sochi, Russia, may have spent as much as US$500 million just to win the 2014 Olympic Winter Games and the Russian government will spend $60 billion between 2006 and 2014 to stage these Games. In fact, one report by the UK's BBC suggested Sochi would become the most expensive Olympic Games ever staged (exceeding US$50 billion) and cost more than three times what was needed to deliver London 2012.

The financial risks may be a reason why destinations in the western democratic world do not pursue the chances of hosting mega events as much as they used to. In fact, nowadays it is mostly developing societies or authoritarian societies joining the bidding wars to host Olympic Games (Fritsch, 2013).

Bad media coverage

Winning the bid to stage the Olympics ensures a city will become immortalised for hosting all the other nations of the world and staging an event the world will watch and dissect with great scrutiny. Observers all over the world will ask questions like:

Did the host city get things right?

Were their stadiums finished on time?

Were the athletes happy with their living conditions?

Did the media find it easy to report on the events?

Did numerous heads of state attend the opening ceremonies?

Were the non-sports moments entertaining?

Did the athletes generate world record performances?

Did any countries boycott these Games?

Were any activists prompted to disrupt the Games?

Did any terroristic activities take place during the competition?

How much did the host city spend on security? On construction? On making the host city more liveable?

Were any existing citizens (or animals) displaced?

Did the Games generate record revenues, ratings and attendances?

This close observation can lead to bad news coverage, and many of the recent Games have suffered in varying degrees from poor publicity. Table 7.4 outlines some examples of this.

Table 7.4	Examples of poor publicity for recent Olympic Games
Mexico City 1968	Black-gloved salute by two American athletes created political statement related to the treatment of African-Americans in the USA
Munich 1972	Terrorist attack left 11 Israeli athletes dead
Montreal 1976	Poorly conceived plan left city of Montreal with millions in debt that took the city and provincial government 30 years to pay off
Moscow 1980	Boycott initiated by the USA; a total of 65 countries did not participate
Los Angeles 1984	Boycotted by the Soviet Union, joined by 13 other Eastern Bloc countries
Atlanta 1996	Considered by many to be too commercialised and scarred by a terrorist bomb that exploded in Centennial Olympic Park killing two people
Salt Lake City 2002 (Winter Games)	Scandal caused by bribery and voting corruption associated with the host city's bid to win the Games
Athens 2004	Hurt by numerous reports before the Games started that stadia in Athens would not be completed on time
Beijing 2008	Reports surfaced before the Games began that long-time Beijing residents had been displaced in order to claim land to build stadia or roadways to support tourism. Further, numerous reports suggested the air quality in Beijing would not be healthy for world-class athletes to breathe
Vancouver 2010 (Winter Games)	Widely publicised issues included the death of a competitor in practice before the Games began, poor weather conditions for certain outdoor events, and an opening ceremonies malfunction

Conclusion

Mega sporting events have existed in some form since at least 776 BC and have grown from a position of attracting thousands of spectators to grassy hillsides in Olympia, Greece, to today's sport celebrations where billions of people around the world take part via in-person attendance, watching on TV, following online or reading about events in newspapers or magazines. The value of such visibility for the hosting destination is hard to quantify. Hosting a major sports event brings a significant number of benefits, challenges and risks to that locale.

Summing up, in modern entertainment-seeking society, events are an effective way to get attention and influence a destination's image. The larger the event, the higher the possible benefits and risks. Therefore it is important to inform and integrate the local individuals and companies as partners quite early in the process of planning a mega event, calculate the risks and try to be aware of possible issues and problems.

Case 7.1   Selecting the Olympic host city

Every two years, the International Olympic Committee (IOC) convenes its approximately 115 voting members and they make a decision to award the Summer or Winter Olympics to a city that will then host the world at those Olympics seven years later.

The voting is only the final step in a long process. For example, the first thoughts of London bidding to host the Summer Olympics in 2012 go back as far as 1997, and the vote was taken in 2005, giving London seven years to prepare.

The basic timetable in the decision-making process was as follows:

1997	The British Olympic Committee has its first discussions
Dec 2002	UK government holds a short enquiry to decide whether to back a bid
May 2003	UK government decides to back a London bid
Jul 2003	London bid notified to IOC, along with eight other contenders
Jan 2004	London plans revealed
May 2004	London makes shortlist with Paris, Moscow, Madrid and New York
Feb 2005	IOC inspects London
Jul 2005	London bid is selected by IOC voters in Singapore

The process of reaching a successful conclusion in winning the bid can be seen in terms of five consecutive phases:

1. Get government backing.
2. Produce a thorough paper submission to the IOC, making clear where the finance will come from.
3. Get media and public support.
4. Impress the IOC during their inspection.
5. Secure a majority of the voters at the final session with a unique selling proposition (USP).

Discussion questions

1 As the five phases in bidding are proceeded through, how does the nature and extent of the demands on marketers change?
2 If you were an IOC voter, what factors would influence your vote among the cities available to choose from?

Case 7.2   For and against hosting

Cities often bid to host major events like the Olympics or the US National Football League's Super Bowl. The argument in favour of hosting such an event is that awareness of the city will grow, impressions of the city will be positive, and a significant economic impact will be felt by the city's residents. Often

▶

> **Case 7.2** *(continued)*
>
> bidding will be connected to a regeneration programme, and new infrastructure will transform brownfield sites, and provide important new transport links.
>
> But others will argue against such an event because they believe people will be displaced in order to build new stadia, or that money spent on hosting a sporting event could have been spent on community affairs that better served disadvantaged members of the city, on schools or hospitals for example.
>
> **Discussion questions**
>
> **3** Find evidence for both views using a major event of your choice.
>
> **4** What is your position on this topic? Give your reasons.

Guided reading

A useful book specifically on events marketing is:

Jackson, N. (2013) *Promoting and Marketing Events: Theory and Practice*. Oxford: Routledge.

Textbooks specifically on the marketing of sport include:

Beech, J. and Chadwick, S., eds (2006) *The Marketing of Sport*. Harlow: Pearson Education.

Mullin, B., Hardy, S. and Sutton, W. (1993) *Sport Marketing*. Champaign, IL: Human Kinetics.

A very useful book is:

Moilanen, T. and Rainisto, S.K. (2008) *How to Brand Nations, Cities and Destinations*. Basingstoke: Palgrave Macmillan

For destinations and business conferences, the following is recommended:

Davidson, R. and Rogers, T. (2006) *Marketing Destinations and Venues for Conferences, Conventions and Business Events*. Oxford: Butterworth-Heinemann

Recommended websites

The FIFA World Cup: **www.fifa.com/worldcup/index.html**

The IOC Olympic Games website: **www.olympic.org/olympic-games**

Key words

brand; destination; media; stakeholder

Bibliography

Anholt, S. (2007) *Competitive Identity – The New Brand Management for Nations, Cities and Regions*. New York: Palgrave.

Anholt, S. (2011) Competitive identity. In N. Morgan, A. Pritchard and R. Pride (eds), *Destination Brands*. Oxford: Butterworth-Heinemann.

Bieger, T. (2008) *Management von Destinationen*. Munich: Oldenbourg.

Blakeman, R. (2009) *Marketing Communications* (5th edn). Lanham, MD: Rowman & Littlefield.

Bruhn, M. (2010) *Marketing* (10th edn). Wiesbaden: Gabler.

CNBC (undated) The 10 biggest Super Bowl ad spenders. **www.cnbc.com/id/46193625/ page/11**

Deng Qiang, C. (2011) *Leveraging the Mega Event: The Event-Destination Image Transfer Model and the Moderating Effect of Image Congruity*. Hong Kong: Hong Kong Polytechnic University.

Dinnie, K. (2009) Nation branding. In S. Paliwoda (ed.), *Exporting, International and Global Marketing Management: Beyond the Fundamentals,* The Marketing and Management Collection. London: Henry Stewart Talks Ltd.

Echtner, M. and Ritchie, B. (2003) *The Meaning and Measurement of Destination Image*. Calgary: University of Calgary, Canada.

Fasser, M. (2010) Innsbruck: Zweimal Olympia, und was jetzt? *Die Presse,* 13 February. **http://diepresse.com/home/ panorama/oesterreich/539500/Zweimal-Olympia-und-was-jetztInnsbruck_ Zweimal-Olympia-und-was-jetzt**

FIFA (2011) Almost half the world tuned in at home to watch 2010 FIFA World Cup South Africa™. **www.fifa.com/worldcup/ archive/southafrica2010/organisation/ media/newsid=1473143/index.html**

Freyer, W. (2006) *Tourismus: Einführung in die Fremdenverkehrsökonomie*. Munich: Oldenbourg Wissenschaftsverlag GmbH.

Freyer, W. (2011) *Tourismus-Marketing: Marktorientiertes Management im Mikro- und Makrobereich der Tourismuswirtschaft*. Munich: Oldenbourg Wissenschaftsverlag GmbH.

Fritsch, O. (2013) Olympische Spiele, bloß nicht! *Die Zeit*. **www.zeit.de/sport/ 2013-03/olympia-ioc-graubuenden-bach**

Gantner, M. (2013) Wiener durchkreuzen rot-grüne Pläne. *Kurier,* 12 March. **http:// kurier.at/chronik/wien/volksbefragung-in-wien-klares-nein-zu-olympia/4.695.888**

Hall, C.M. (2006) Urban entrepreneurship, corporate interests and sports mega events: the thin policies of competitiveness within the hard outcomes of neoliberalism.

In J. Horne and W. Manzenreiter (eds), *Sports Mega-Events: Social Scientific Analyses of a Global Phenomenon.* Oxford: Blackwell Publishing.

Holt, D. (2003) *Brands and Branding.* Boston MA: Harvard Business School.

Horne, J. and Manzenreiter, W. (2006) *Sports Mega-Events: Social Scientific Analyses of a Global Phenomenon*. Oxford: Blackwell Publishing.

Kotler, P. (1984) *Marketing Management* (5th edn). Englewood Cliffs, NJ: Prentice Hall.

Kotler, P. and Armstrong, G. (2010) *Principles of Marketing* (13th edn). Upper Saddle River, NJ: Pearson.

Kotler, P., Armstrong, G., Wong, V. and Saunders, J. (2011) *Grundlagen des Marketing* (5th edn). Munich: Pearson Studium.

Kroeber-Riel, W., Weinberg, P. and Gröppel-Klein, A. (2009) *Konsumentenverhalten* (9th edn). Munich: Vahlen.

Lettner, M. (2010) *TV-Duelle*. Vienna: University of Vienna.

Luhmann, N. (2004) *Die Realität der Massenmedien* (3rd edn). Wiesbaden: VS Verlag.

McCarthy, J.E. (1960) *Basic Marketing: A Managerial Approach*. Homewood, IL: Richard D. Irwin.

Moilanen, T. and Rainisto, S.K. (2008) *How to Brand Nations, Cities and Destinations*. Basingstoke: Palgrave Macmillan.

Morgan, N., Pritchard, A. and Pride, R. (2011) Tourism places, brands, and reputation management. In N. Morgan, A. Pritchard and R. Pride (eds), *Destination Brands*. Oxford: Butterworth-Heinemann.

Mullin, B., Hardy, S. and Sutton, W. (1993) *Sport Marketing*. Champaign, IL: Human Kinetics.

Münch, R. (1992) *Dialektik der Kommunikationsgesellschaft* (2nd edn). Frankfurt am Main: Suhrkamp.

Peelen, E. and Beltman, R. (2013) *Customer Relationship Management*. Harlow: Pearson Education.

Pepels, W. (2011) *Marketing-Kommunikation* (2nd edn). Munich: UVK.

Roll, M. (2005) *Asian Brand Strategy: How Asia Builds Strong Brands*. Basingstoke: Palgrave Macmillan.

Saxer, U. (1998) Mediengesellschaft: Verständnisse und Missverständnisse. In U. Sarcinelli (ed.), *Politikvermittung und Demokratie in der Mediengesellschaft*. Bonn: Bundeszentrale für politische Bildung.

Schulze, G. (2005) *Die Erlebnisgesellschaft: Kultursoziologie der Gegenwart* (2nd edn). Frankfurt am Main: Campus.

Siller, L. (2010) *Strategisches Management alpiner Destinationen*. Berlin: Erich Schmidt Verlag.

TSE Consulting (2009) *The New Sports Organisation: Eight Essentials for Renewing the Management of Sport*. Switzerland: TSE Consulting Publishing.

Chapter 8

Financing events

Martin Schnitzer, University of Innsbruck, Austria

Learning outcomes

Upon completion of this chapter the reader should be able to:

- identify the features of financial operations that are specific to managing events;

- understand the difference between right-holder events and non-right-holder events and their implications (e.g. **bidding costs**);

- differentiate between the main cost drivers and revenues of an event organisation and the peculiarities of financing events (e.g. non-organiser-related costs);

- identify tools for measuring the financial impact of events;

- understand the basic principles of **management accounting**;

- conduct a **break-even analysis** and appraise a **business plan**;

- provide a basic analysis of financial statements.

Overview

There is a lot of discussion about financing events. Very often event costs increase dramatically; especially in sports events, cost overruns seem to be one of the biggest issues on the agenda of event organisers. Therefore, it is important to have a good overview of the costs of an event and the potential benefits event organisers face.

The main goal of this chapter is to give the reader a comprehensive understanding of how events can be financed, what the main cost drivers are and how the financing of events differs from other areas. In particular, the unique features of (sporting) events show how difficult it is to manage events where their financing is concerned.

An important part of the chapter looks at the 'event's financing frame', which will show firstly the characteristics of major events and what these mean for the financing of an event. The event specifics will make clear to the reader that event budgeting and controlling is not an easy task and also includes costs and benefits which are not only linked to the organisers (e.g. bidding costs, non-event-related costs and benefits).

Financing events is also about understanding the most important cost drivers. Finally, the reader will see shortly how the accounting for an event can be managed. Applied accounting practices (e.g. break-even analysis, development of business plans, financial statement reading) will be explained. The chapter will conclude by highlighting the critical success factors of event financing.

A number of case studies will underline the theoretical framework and will illustrate core aspects of the financing of events.

Introduction

The financing side of events is one of the most difficult aspects of preparing and delivering events. Why? Because events have quite a few characteristics which may have an impact on financing them. Preuss and Schnitzer (2013) have noted that scholarly research very often debates the economic impacts of major events (e.g. Baade and Matheson, 2004; Matheson, 2009; Preuss, 2009) and that 'it is often a debate over the forecasts of economic effects, in particular when studies are commissioned by event organisers in an attempt to justify the use of taxpayers' money for the bidding process, the organisation of the event or capital investments'.

Apart from the discussion on events potentially boosting a (regional) economy, many 'scholars agree that events may also create intangible effects, such as for instance an improvement in the event host's image in terms of place marketing, or the non-use values

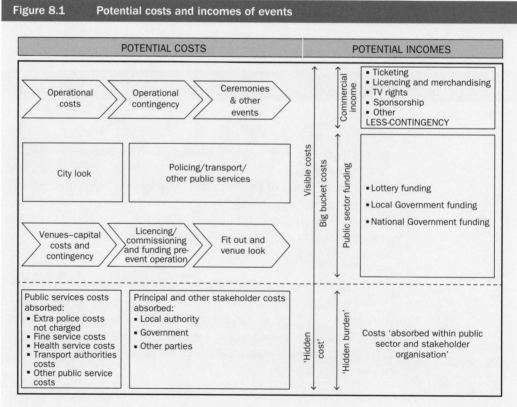

Figure 8.1   Potential costs and incomes of events

Source: Own illustration adapted from Games Legacy (2002: 26)

such as the populations' happiness and national pride' (Preuss and Schnitzer, 2013). Less research has been conducted in the past into organising committee budgets; a first attempt to approach this issue was made by Preuss and Schnitzer (2013) by comparing the FIFA World Cup budgets during the bidding stage.

Where the potential costs and incomes of an event organiser are concerned, the Manchester 2002 Commonwealth Games Organising Committee gave in its debriefing documents (Games Legacy, 2002) an overview of the financial aspects of managing a multi-sport event. Figure 8.1 gives a generalised overview.

Features unique to events and their impact on event financing

Kaspar and Schnitzer (2011) worked out nine typical characteristics of major events, which also pose evident challenges for the financing of events:

1. Major events are proper projects with clearly defined goals; there is a complex environment with a lot of stakeholders; there is a timeframe; and there is no predefined way the project goals need to be achieved.

    In terms of financing an event this means that there is no way of planning, organising and implementing the event. Events differ from each other and therefore they are often not comparable to each other, which makes benchmarking them quite challenging at a financial level.

2. Very often an event owner (for example, an International Sports Federation) owns the rights to host the event. The event owner usually organises a tendering (bidding process) and after that the event organiser has rights, but also duties when delivering the event.

    In terms of financing an event this means understanding bidding procedures, the costs of these procedures, timeframes, requirements and most importantly the financial impact of operating the event.

3. Major events are typical service goods; there is no possibility to stock; the consumption and production of the event occurs at the same time; the quality of the events may differ a lot.

    Where the financing aspect is concerned there is demand for considerable flexibility by the event organisers; in scenario techniques, contingency planning is also requested by the financial operations, and especially financial control mechanisms are required.

4. Major events are defined by many possible negative and positive impacts for the host city depending on size, time and the people involved.

    The larger the event and the more the event is directed to a wider audience, the bigger the positive and negative impacts may be. Where the financing of the event is concerned, organisers should be aware that staging an event may influence many stakeholders such as inhabitants of a city or a complete industry positively or negatively.

5. Major events may create high media attention attracting celebrities, politicians and the world of business.

    In terms of financing an event, high media attention may also create large revenues due to commercial TV rights. These revenues have become the most important area of financing events, especially events with global impact such as the Olympic

Games, the FIFA World Cup or other (mostly sporting) events with a worldwide reputation.

6. Since a high number of organisational issues need to be solved in a short time period, a large number of human and financial resources are always required.

    After a long preparation phase, events are typically delivered within one day or a maximum of a few weeks (e.g. tournament). Where managing an event is concerned, many tasks need to be carried out at the same time. This also impacts on the financing as financial control and expenditure become crucial, but also revenues (e.g. cashing entry fees) need to be dealt with within short periods.

7. Mental and physical pressure on event organisers and stakeholders is also typical for events. Everything needs to be ready at the same time and so-called peaking of tasks is the outcome.

    Peaking is typical for events. A crucial financial aspect, therefore, is that the liquidity of an event organiser is granted. As, typically, 75% of all invoices from organisers need to be paid no later than two months prior and two months after an event, cashflow needs to be planned carefully to ensure permanent clients (e.g. staff, office rental) and event suppliers are paid.

8. Major events are often publicly funded and create legacies for the host city. These legacies, which may also be negative, need to be considered when bidding for an event.

    Especially cultural events, but also increasingly sports events, are dependent on funding from public institutions. This is because events may have long-term benefits, which may positively influence the host city. But also, non-event-related costs, like investments made specifically for an event (e.g. Olympic villages, new transport system) can be a financial burden for a city.

9. The hosting of a major event requires venues subject to the requirements of the event owner. Required venues may already exist, be upgraded, built completely from scratch or be a temporary construction.

    In any case, it is of paramount importance that the post-use of the infrastructure, especially for the wider public, is considered early in the planning stage. But also re-investing and operating venues which have been created for an event may have financial implications – for example, venue owners may estimate that operating the venue for 20 years would cost the same as building it.

Introducing a frame for financing events

The reader should gain a systematic view of the complexity of financing events by taking into account the characteristics of events combined with the experiences of the Manchester 2002 Commonwealth Games Organising Committee, which is representative of many other events. To this end, a generic frame for financing events is introduced below. The frame includes different phases (e.g. bidding for the event, delivering the event), different types of costs and benefits of an event (e.g. direct vs indirect costs/benefits) and also considerations, such as costs and benefits related to the organiser and not related to the organiser (e.g. economic impacts).

When following the frame for financing events, different steps/questions should be raised in order to understand what financing an event really means.

Finding the right event (search costs)

Events are becoming increasingly complex and have many unknowns (Horne, 2007). It is impossible to have an overview of the event market. Sportcal's calendar (Sportcal, 2013), which provides an online database of sporting events across 140 sports up to the year 2022, lists 32,000 events every year. Due to possibly huge impacts and the high level of financial resources required, finding the right event(s) for a venue has become a challenge. Being permanently updated on what is going on in the event industry is difficult. In the sports industry, therefore, the annual Sportaccord Congress (Sportaccord, 2013) helps potential hosts, but also event owners, to understand where major sporting events are taking place in the world. Before even bidding for an event, the venue, the national sports organisation and professional event organisers need to understand what is going on in the market by filtering: the right event for a particular venue is linked to search costs. These search costs are typically linked by running an (event) office, having travelling expenses, costs related to fairs and congresses and for promotion. For instance, in Denmark, Sport Event Denmark (2013) tries to attract events to Denmark; other examples may be found in the USA, Australia or the UK (e.g. Event Scotland).

The search costs also include mostly time costs such as internal decision-making processes within a destination or costs related to countrywide tendering processes (e.g. national bid campaign) or quite simply long discussions amongst different stakeholders (e.g. referendum to run for a bid or not in a local community in Switzerland).

Event ownership

Is it possible that a city may organise Olympic Games independently of the regular Olympic Games being staged in London, Sochi or Rio de Janeiro? Definitely not, as the International Olympic Committee is the event owner of the Olympic Games and, on the basis of well-defined regulations, it is the only entity allowed to award the Olympic Games to a host city and its National Olympic Committee. In sports, most of today's prestigious events are owned by someone (e.g. International Federation or, to give another example, the X-Games are owned by the TV company ESPN).

For this reason, when financing an event, one of the first questions to ask is whether someone owns the rights for hosting the event in question!

Situation 1 – there is an event owner

Usually a standardised candidate procedure, supervised by the event owner, helps to select the best candidate, especially by checking the bid cities' potential to host the event. Therefore, the event owner has a mandatory list detailing all requirements for the organisation of the events, which is binding for the event organisers on signing the hosting agreement (host city contract). Before starting the official tendering process, bidders are given information packs to ensure they fully understand the requirements. By referring to the list of 'essentials', the candidate is able to understand the requirements in terms of accommodation, transport, venues, etc. Having established these organisational requirements, the potential host is able to study how many resources (especially financial and human resources) will be needed in order to satisfy the event owner's needs (Schnitzer and Redl, 2011).

Situation 2 – there is not an event owner

Figure 8.2 also shows that it may not be possible to have an event owner or that an event is being staged for the first time and is thus completely new. This situation has the big advantage of not having any bidding process and that basically the event can be introduced from one day to the next. The disadvantage is that a new event incurs invention costs, which can be described as the cost of putting the event on the market. These

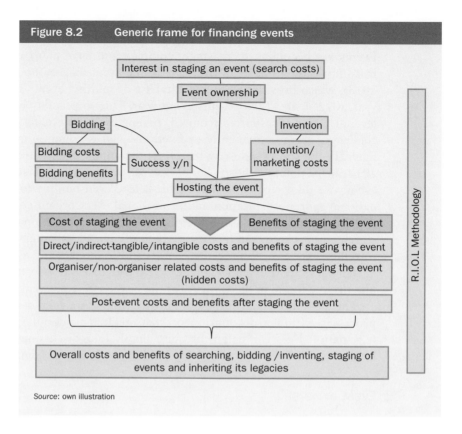

Figure 8.2   Generic frame for financing events

Source: own illustration

costs, therefore, include the cost of studying the feasibility, the cost of funding the event in terms of finding investors, who believe in its potential success, as well as the actors (e.g. sportsmen, artists, etc.) and an interested target group (e.g. on-site spectators, interested media). There are a few examples of completely new events such as the X-Games, which were mainly driven by ESPN, the Air&Style contest in Innsbruck, Austria or fun events such as the 'Wok-World Championship' invented by Stefan Raab, an entertainer working for the German TV station PRO7.

After their successful introduction, newly created events develop into events with ownerships and protected rights; after absorbing the invention costs, a successfully launched event may, therefore, also sell rights and run bidding procedures to find new event sites and hosts.

Exhibit 8.1   RIOL model

When bidding for an event the RIOL model can be used as a major guideline. The RIOL stands for requirements–input–output–legacies and describes the four steps of understanding and assessing required resources and impacts of hosting major (sports) events.

First of all, there is the need to understand R = requirements (step 1) for delivering the event. Secondly, event organisers should know about I = inputs (step 2) or the amount of resources (e.g. financial resources, human resources) required to operate an event. While the O = outputs (step 3) are impacts occurring when delivering the event and having an immediate effect on the host city, spectators and other stakeholders (e.g. overnight stays due to the event), the L = legacies (step 4) are long-term impacts for the stakeholders involved in the event (e.g. image – branding of host cities, infrastructure).

Seven criteria (sports, economy, society, ecology, infrastructure, tourism and media) are described by 55 sub-criteria such as sports campaign, consumer behaviour, volunteerism, permanent venues, crowding-out effects and media coverage.

The main difficulty before delivering and even bidding for an event lies in understanding the specific in- and outputs and operationalising the criteria and sub-criteria.

Bidding versus invention costs

Where the costs of an event are concerned, the two situations explained above show that part of the costs of staging an event is incurred either through bidding or, in the case of a new event, as invention costs.

Costs for bidding for major events can often be found in the bid documents themselves. In 2008, Sport Business evaluated different bids and identified that London 2012's bid budget was £29 million (Sport Business, 2013). Sochi is said to have spent $60 million on its successful 2014 campaign and the Winter Youth Olympic Games Innsbruck 2012 cost €0.36 million (Innsbruck 2012, 2008). Typically a bid to host the FIS Alpine Ski World Championships such as Cortina 2015 or 2017 costs around €0.75 million (see Case 8.1). Also, unsuccessful bids may lead to benefits, because many feasibility studies are carried out in the process and benefits arise as a result, such as urban planning, promotion of the candidate city; the case of Leipzig 2012 shows that projects were realised regardless of the result of the bid.

Where the invention costs of an event are concerned, situation 2 (no event owner) clearly shows that an event creator either has investors behind him/her or the power and endurance to develop and sustain the event. In many cases, events start as niche products and then continue to grow. Lamprecht and Stamm (2002) discuss the life cycle in sports and Kaspar (2006) examines the life cycle approach in the context of events and highlights the fact that events also need to go through a kind of life process from their invention/bidding to their positioning in the market and their contribution to the local community (see Case 8.1). Table 8.1 setsout the budget proposed for Cortina's bid for the 2014 World Cup.

Case 8.1   Bidding by Cortina d'Ampezzo

The Italian Winter Ski resort Cortina d'Ampezzo hosted the Winter Olympic Games 1956. The ski resort in the Dolomites gained a good reputation and, since the 1980s, Cortina d'Ampezzo has regularly hosted the World Cup competition, but also other (winter) sport events.

Table 8.1   Budget of the bidding committee Cortina d'Ampezzo 2017

Area – sub-area	in EUR
GMG (general management)	
Event owner (candidature fee)	150,000
Meetings with event owner, travel expenses	15,000
Further obligations (training camp) from event owner	15,000
Administration/office 2017/project management	35,000
Final presentation and congress	45,000
R&R (resources and relations)	
Paid staff/contractors	175,000
Volunteers	5,000
Education programme (internships, study groups)	15,000
Research projects	5,000
Legal, accounting, taxes, bank	7,500
SPT (sport) and operations	
Feasibility studies (slopes, roads, venues)	50,000
M&E (marketing and events)	
Sponsorships and hospitality	20,000
Media	5,000

▶

Case 8.1 *(continued)*

Table 8.1 *(continued)*

Area – sub-area	in EUR
Side events World Cup	80,000
Own events	30,000
Artwork, graphics	15,000
Printing	25,000
Internet and publications	10,000
Corporate identity	5,000
Contingency	50,000
Total	**757,500**

Source: www.cortina2019.it

Over the years, a lot of moss has grown over Cortina's Olympic rings and unsuccessful bids for the Winter Olympic Games in 1988 and 1992 also expressed Cortina d'Ampezzo's mood. The famous and prestigious 'Queen of the Dolomites' had become a bit long in the tooth – hotels and services were no longer state of the art.

In 2007, the Alpine Ski World Committee and the municipality decided to bid to host the FIS Alpine Ski World Championships and, after three unsuccessful attempts for 2013, 2015 and 2017, is currently running again to host the event in 2019.

Of course, after losing the previous candidacies and spending a lot of money on feasibility studies, promotion, experts and staff, etc., a discussion was sparked about the sense of making unsuccessful bids and about actually learning lessons from these attempts.

Looking into the details of the bids, following the strategy of 'winning, even if you lose' and specifically referring to Cortina's bid as the reason for applying for funding, the municipality obtained guarantees for €250 million in investments through 'investment programmes' funded by the Veneto region and the central government for infrastructure measures such as roads, parking, ski lifts and venues in the town. It is a matter of course that these investments will help to boost the town.

Furthermore, the bid campaign for Cortina d'Ampezzo received high media attention, with talk of the bid and the need to (re)develop the area of Cortina promoting this tourist hot spot for a few years. Finally, the bid also contributed to social cohesion, as many of the young generation are now involved in the bid with a view to shaping the future of Cortina d'Ampezzo together.

Discussion questions

1 Why should a town bid to host events?

2 What are the differences between bidding costs and invention costs?

Costs and benefits of hosting events

After a successful bid or invention of an event, the planning and preparation phase begins and is the driver for delivering a successful event. Understanding the real costs of an event during the bidding phase is very difficult, especially due to long-term budget forecasts in the bidding stage, due to the lack of reliable data for bidding committees, but also because of other circumstances such as inflation rates or currency exchange rates (Preuss and Schnitzer, 2013).

Preuss (2004) has studied the economics of staging the Olympics in the period from 1972 to 2008 and outlines the different stages at which an Olympic Games host has its expenditure. He makes a distinction between pre-Olympic activities, Olympic activities (with primary and secondary economic effects) and post-Olympic Games (Preuss, 2004). Preuss also identifies different examples (from Montreal 1976 to Beijing 2008) and examines the cost of staging the Olympic Games. Interestingly, depending on the time and the location, the costs were shouldered by the public and/or private sectors to varying degrees, with everything from 90% of costs being covered by the public sector (e.g. Montreal 1976) to 90% of costs being borne by the private sector (e.g. Los Angeles 1984).

Understanding the costs of events is therefore related to the place and cultural background of the host city and requires knowledge within many management disciplines, especially project management skills. Also experience through testing is crucial to delivering a successful event and its financial impact. Furthermore, the involvement of stakeholders is indispensable when hosting an event. For event organisers relying on third parties, this also means establishing good cooperation and relationships. Where the financial side is concerned, it becomes more and more difficult to retain a good overview of costs and therefore costs need to be determined and limits set.

■ Direct and indirect costs/benefits of events – tangibility of costs/benefits

It is crucial to understand not only the event's direct costs and benefits (balance of accounts), but also the costs/benefits that are not related to the event organisers. These costs are often defined as tangible and intangible costs/benefits. Tangible costs/benefits monetarily impact on stakeholder groups pertaining to the event organisers, while intangible costs/benefits are difficult to quantify in monetary terms.

Scholars discuss these types of costs in different ways; Heinemann (1995) distinguishes between macroeconomic and microeconomic impacts and divides the microeconomic impacts into direct (costs/benefits of the event organisers) and indirect ones (monetary/non-monetary costs/benefits). Maennig (1998) uses the term pecuniary costs/benefits when quantifying these types of costs. Preuss (2004) also illustrated tangible and intangible costs/benefits in relation to time and gives some examples as shown in Figure 8.3.

Where the measurement of costs and benefits apart from the direct costs and benefits is concerned (**see also expenses/revenues in this chapter**) scholars have introduced different methods for measuring the economic impacts of events. Taking a scientific approach, cost–benefit analysis (Hanusch, 1994), as well as other instruments (e.g. input–output charts, measurement of multiplier effects), helps organisers to understand the costs and benefits as well as the impacts of events. Event managers should be aware of these types of costs and benefits as they have a significant impact not only on the event organisers, but also on the stakeholders, especially the local community. Crompton (1995) highlights potential mistakes and sources of misinterpretations when using these tools. The sense and 'non-sense' of staging events is discussed controversially in academic literature, leading to the growing significance of these impact measuring tools, as shown in Case 8.2.

■ Organiser-related costs versus non-organiser-related costs (hidden costs)

The organisation of a major event not only creates costs for the organisers, but also for the host city, which can be of a very different nature as shown in Figure 8.1. There are event-related costs and non-event-related costs. Event-related costs are caused by the organisation of the event and potentially have multiplier effects and usually long-term effects. Non-event-related costs may occur specifically as a result of the event, but would have been incurred anyway. This typically encompasses the cost of major infrastructure projects. Both cost areas need resources and can be listed in all public-financed projects. The key question when assessing the input of the costs related to the event is: 'What input is required to achieve the minimum requirements for a successful event?'

While academic literature on the impacts of events is plentiful (e.g. Ritchie, 1984; Hall, 1992; Getz, 1994; Jeanrenaud, 1999; Jefferson-Lenskyi, 2002; Cashman, 2006; Gratton and Preuss, 2008; Preuss, 2009) there is little information on and research into the real cost of events (the budgets of organising committees plus public costs for staging the event). This is probably due to the fact that real costs are often hidden and that host

Figure 8.3   Tangibility of costs/benefits

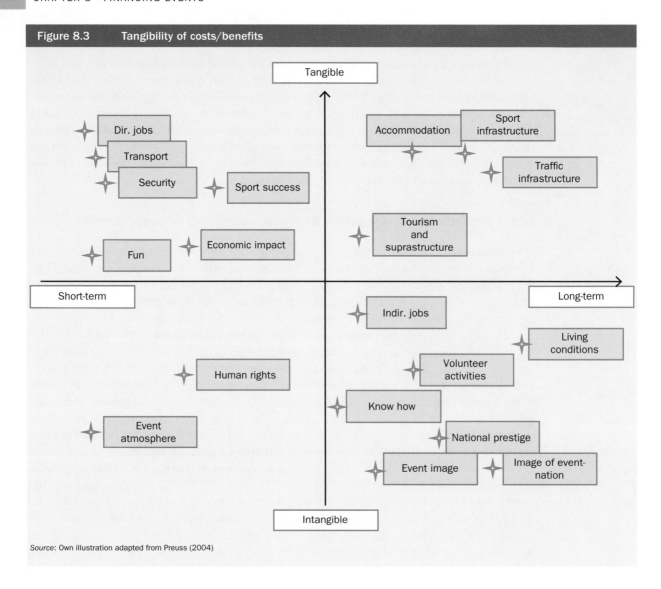

Source: Own illustration adapted from Preuss (2004)

Case 8.2   The eventIMPACTS Toolkit

The eventIMPACTS Toolkit has been developed by UK Sport, Visit Britain, Event Scotland, the London Development Agency, the North West Development Agency, Yorkshire Forward and Glasgow City Marketing Bureau. It comprises some key guidance and good practice principles for evaluating the social, economic, environmental and media-related impacts associated with staging major sporting and cultural events.

The toolkit assesses economic and media-related impacts, but also social and environmental impacts. For instance, eventIMPACTS highlights that there is a variety of established approaches to quantifying the media impact of events, including the benefits of place marketing. Because methods of measuring and reporting on impacts can be inconsistent, event organisers have sometimes struggled to understand which methods will best suit their needs. In these respects, therefore, the purpose of eventIMPACTS is to provide organisers with templates for carrying out, or commissioning, such studies which are based on some central principles and which will facilitate comparison across events.

A relatively new agenda, for which there is little supporting evidence, is that major events can deliver directly, or act as catalysts for, wider social impacts such as the development of the community and development of skills. Furthermore, as environmental issues become increasingly significant, event organisers

Case 8.2 *(continued)*

should be mindful of the potentially adverse environmental impacts of events. In these respects, event-IMPACTS is designed to help event organisers move towards more developed approaches to measuring, monitoring and managing the social and environmental impacts of their events.

Source: eventIMPACTS Toolkit

Discussion questions

After consulting the eventIMPACTS website:

3 What type of impacts may occur when hosting an event?

4 How can impacts of events be measured?

5 What might the major difficulties in measuring impacts of events be?

cities frequently absorb costs (see Figure 8.1). Furthermore, after the event, people rarely ask how much public money was spent on staging it. Figure 8.1 shows these visible costs and 'hidden costs'.

Organiser-related costs are visible costs and comprise operational costs. Other visible costs include the city's appearance, policing, transport, other public services, venues (capital costs and contingency), licensing/commissioning and funding pre-event operations as well as fitting and decking out the venue. 'Hidden costs' are services absorbed by public institutions (local authorities, government). Examples include extra policing, where the costs are not passed on, as well as costs for the fire service, health service, public transport and other public services (Games Legacy, 2002).

Exhibit 8.2   Overall costs and benefits of events

Stages	Type of cost	Example	RIOL phase
A	*Search costs*	Finding the event, e.g. running an event agency, event commission	Requirement
+	Bidding/invention costs	Costs for running a bid or marketing costs for creating/inventing an event	Input
−	Bidding	Benefits of bidding (e.g. promotion, feasibility studies)	
B	*Costs before staging an event*		
+	Direct/indirect costs	Direct/indirect costs of staging an event	Input
−	Direct/indirect benefits	Direct/indirect benefits of staging an event	Output
+	Tangible/intangible costs	Tangible/intangible costs of staging an event	Input
−	Tangible/intangible benefits	Tangible/intangible benefits of staging an event	Output
+	Hidden costs	Health service costs, transport authorities costs, public service costs	Input
C	*Event input-output (during)*	Total event costs and benefits (when preparing and delivering events)	Input/output
+	Long-term impacts	Long-term positive/negative impacts	Legacies
D	*Event result*	Total event costs–benefits incl. legacies (e.g. white elephants, destination branding)	

Source: Author's own illustration

Revenues and expenses of an event

As noted above, it is crucial to differentiate between the business view and the economic view of an event. While the economic view is larger, involves stakeholders, a local, regional or even a national economy and potentially macroeconomic dimensions, a business-orientated view basically looks at the operating result (profit/loss) on an expense–revenue basis. As already shown in the section on tangible costs and benefits, the economic view may reveal costs that need to be quantified through different mechanisms (e.g. potential tax-payer interest in investing in an event through a contingent-valuation method).

Where revenue is concerned, an event owner such as the International Olympic Committee differentiates between the following revenues:

- event owner funding (e.g. accommodation contribution, contribution for TV production or TV/marketing rights);
- sponsorships (local, national, global);
- suppliers (typically value-in-kind sponsorships);
- ticket sales;
- licensing (e.g. merchandising, coin programmes, philately);
- lotteries;
- donations;
- disposal of assets (e.g. furniture, garage sales);
- subsidies (local, regional, national government);
- special programmes (e.g. EU funding programmes, national grants);
- contribution from tourism organisations/boards (mostly public);
- commission (through: overnight stays, meals, venue entrances).

Other events also include income through participation fees (such as a popular sporting event like a running competition) or VIP hospitality packages, tournament registrations, selling of advertising space, parking or other fees (such as broadcasting fees).

The expenses incurred by an event organiser are manifold and are shown in Table 8.2. A distinction is made between costs/expenses related to the venue, to the operations of the event, to the promotion and presentation of the event and to the guests at the event. Many costs are also related to the main players, who may be sportsmen or artists performing at the event. Table 8.2 can be used as a guideline for identifying the costs/expenses of an event.

Table 8.2	Costs/expenses of events
Macro area	**Examples of costs/expenses**
Examples of sports event facility costs	Rent of facility and furniture (chair and table rentals)
	Construction staff
	Front-of-house staff (ushers, ticket takers, security)
	Tradespeople (electricians, carpenters) and other staff such as cleaners, scoreboard operators
	Group sales and other sales commissions, credit card commissions
	Crowd control equipment (e.g. barricades, ropes and stanchions)
	Pipe and drape dividers
Examples of game- and player-related costs	Accommodation, player guest expenses, meals and per diems
	Appearance fees, prize money and recognition

Macro area	Examples of costs/expenses
Examples of sports events operations costs	Equipment managers and trainers, locker room supplies
	Medical staff, EMTs, ambulance
	Playing surface preparation and maintenance
	Timing equipment and score clocks, coaches' fee and equipment
	Transportation, inbound/outbound (to/from home airport, airfares) and local
	Uniforms, including numbering and lettering
	Accounting services, payroll services
	Computers and printers, copiers, facsimile machines
	Credentials or ID cards
	Insurance, legal services
	Mobile communications equipment (e.g. walkie-talkies, cell phones), telephone and high-speed data
	Office space, hotel meeting rooms, and/or office trailers, office supplies
	Power and generators, power distribution (the labour required to bring power where it is needed)
	Shipping, trucking and overnight couriers
	Software (existing applications and custom programming)
	Staff and volunteer expenses (meals or per diems, transportation, parking)
	Storage and warehousing
	Temporary staff, including event specialists, freelancers and interns
	Volunteer programme expenses (e.g. recognition, food and beverages, parking)
Typical sports event marketing and promotion expenses	Advertising agency expenses (copying, postage, press kits) and fees (creative charges), logo
	Internet website development
	Kickoff or announcing press conference or event
	Media accreditation and hospitality, press conference area
	Media centre expenses (rental of furnishings, draping, and meals, refreshments and snacks)
	Outdoor advertising (creative, production and rental of billboards and street banners)
	Pre-event promotional giveaway items
	Print advertising creation and space
	Public relations agency expenses and fees
	Radio advertising production (i.e. costs of creating a commercial) and advertising time
	Staff photographer and videographer
	Statistician(s)
	Television advertising production and advertising time
Typical sports event guest management and hospitality expenses	Custom ticket printing
	Directional signage
	Gifts, welcome baskets and room amenity drops
	Guest transportation (e.g. airport pickups, shuttle transportation to event)
	Hospitality suites, parties and receptions

Table 8.2	(continued)
Macro area	**Examples of costs/expenses**
Typical sports event presentation expenses	Hotel accommodation, hotel attrition and cancellation penalties
	Information kiosks and printed information guides
	Invitation design, printing and postage
	Electricians and technical staff
	Flags, banners and bunting, riggers
	Lighting (e.g. follow spots, computerised lighting, television lighting), music and voice recording
	Production staff (as required, see text for more details) and stagehands
	Set design and construction
	Sound (e.g. playback equipment, public address system, microphones, mixer)
	Special effects (e.g. pyrotechnics, lasers, flame effects, confetti cannons, etc.)
	Video production, video screens, matrix board, camera package and playback equipment

Source: Adapted from Supovitz (2005)

Case 8.3   The Südtirol Classic Festival – Music Weeks Merano

Everything began 27 years ago in the Stadttheater of Merano in Italy. That is where the first Merano Music Festival was inaugurated in 1986 as a contribution to the 150th anniversary of the health resort. The president of the Music Festival Society and the artistic director, both of whom have been connected to the festival since its very beginning, very quickly gained the confidence of the general public. The fact that the 400 seats of the Art Nouveau building would not be sufficient was obvious by 1987. Even the spacious St Nikolaus parish church could not accommodate all those wishing to attend a concert by I Solisti Veneti. Since the very beginning, the festival has settled for only the highest musical quality. Guests of the second festival season included the 12 cellists of the Berlin Philharmonic, the Emerson String Quartet and the Orpheus Chamber Orchestra of New York – top ensembles that are otherwise only to be heard in the major music metropolises of the world.

The desire to procure only the best artists in the city was also defined by the programme offering of the Merano Music Festival after moving into the restored Kursaal in the autumn of 1989. The fact that the courage to take risks can pay off is shown by a musical event in 1994. At that time, the London Symphony Orchestra, whose appearance in Verona had surprisingly been cancelled, was 'spontaneously' booked for two evenings in Merano. Both concerts were sold out, and the Music Festival once again achieved a new audience record. In subsequent years, the Kursaal stage was regularly host to some of the world's best classical groups, including the City of Birmingham Orchestra, the Russian National Orchestra and the Israel Philharmonic Orchestra.

Since 1990, the Night Concert has been a fixed institution of the Music Festival. Night Concerts have presented such varied artists as the 'King of Klezmer' Giora Feidman, jazz legend Joe Zawinul, violinist Gidon Kremer, the eccentric Friedrich Gulda, or vocal wonder Bobby McFerrin. Along with the successful 'additional series' of Colours of Music and Matinée Classique, the Night Concerts also show that the Merano Music Festival is more than just a classical festival which only attracts friends of symphonic music. In Merano, both jazz fans and lovers of chamber music will have a great time again and again.

The annual budget is around €1 million and 20 concerts with 12,000 spectators take place during a period of six weeks. Almost 80% of the budget is spent on the artists. 50% of the revenue comes from the public and 50% from the private sector via ticketing, sponsors and foundations (see Table 8.3).

Case 8.3	*(continued)*	

Table 8.3   Distribution of revenues and expenses for Südtirol Classic Festival

Revenues	%	Expenses	%
Ticketing	28	Artists (incl. taxes, travel and accommodation)	79
Subsidies from regional government	37	Advertising and printing	8
Municipality	13	Administration and organisation	8
Foundations	11	Venue rental	3
Sponsors	11	Staff	2
	100		*100*

Sources: Cappello (2011); *www.meranofestival.com*

Discussion questions

6 What makes a cultural event different from other types of events (e.g. sporting event)?

7 Why should public money be invested in (cultural) events?

Techniques applied to financial operations

A short overview of some of the principles and techniques applied to financial operations will give the reader an understanding of management accounting, break-even analysis, financial statement analysis and the development of a business plan.

Principles of management accounting

Event organisers provide mainly services and need to understand how much the production of these services is costing them. Furthermore, they need to control these costs, which are often not as evident as they would be in a production plant. Management needs to be in a position to determine financial costs, to plan and measure performance in order to compare results easily. The organisation's accounting data needs to be gathered and compared on a periodical basis. For the American Accounting Association (2013) 'management accounting includes the methods and concepts necessary for effective planning, for choosing among alternative business performances'. To sum up, management accounting contains the areas of budgeting and forecasting, general (financial) and cost accounting, cost control procedures, statistics and audits, taxation and legal provisions.

Data modification, analysis and interpretation of data and facilitating management controlling as well as the formulation of business budgets can be named as the main functions of management accounting. Compared to financial accountancy, management accounting is mainly forward looking, model based, confidential and therefore for internal use, and computed with reference to the managers' needs.

Therefore, for event managers' particular interest, management accounting covers the areas of strategic management (in terms of broader decisions), performance management (in terms of decisions about single services/products) and risk management (in terms of identifying, measuring, managing and reporting risks to the achievement of the organisation's objectives).

Applied tools in management accounting include the Grenzplankostenrechnung (GPK – marginal planned cost accounting), lean accounting, resource consumption accounting, standard costing, throughput accounting and transfer pricing.

■ **Break-even analysis**

For event managers, the break-even analysis (BEA) is probably the most important tool in cost accounting. The BEA identifies the break-even point (BEP), which is the point where costs or expenses and revenue are equal. Doing this analysis is crucial for planning any event and it is based on a simple question: 'How many tickets do I need to sell in order to cover my costs?'

To conduct a BEA, it is necessary to have all fixed costs (costs not directly related to the volume of production) and all variable costs of production (costs that change when production output changes). By determining the BEP, which can be calculated in units, e.g. tickets or revenues, and shows the point at which neither a profit nor a loss is made, the event organisers know how realistic their business goal is. This can be shown in a simple example.

A theatre manager has a hall with a maximum capacity of 1,200 seats and needs to decide whether to book a performer. The manager calculates the fixed costs of the performance (costs related to performer, such as his remuneration, accommodation, agency costs, travel expenses, costs related to the venue such as lighting, heating, etc.) as well as variable costs (e.g. food and beverages for spectators). By calculating the total costs, the theatre manager arrives at an estimated figure of €30,000. The theatre manager knows his clients quite well and knows that the pain barrier for paying a ticket is around €50. The BEP in this case lies at 600 sold tickets, which means that by selling only 500 tickets the theatre would make a loss of €5,000 and by selling 750 tickets the theatre would make a profit of €7,500 (see Figure 8.4). Ways of shifting the BEP include reducing the costs (e.g. reducing services) or selling other types of tickets (e.g. VIP tickets for the first 5 rows).

In reality, identifying the BEP is less easy than described above as other types of costs such as semi-variable costs also exist. Semi-variable costs are partly fixed costs and partly variable costs. In the case of the theatre, the number of spectators also impacts the number of staff. Working to capacity or selling only 40% of tickets means having more/fewer ushers, security staff, cleaning hours, etc.

Whalley (2011) explains the ways in which the BEP can be calculated:

BEP (for output) = fixed costs/contribution per unit (p.u.)

Contribution (p.u) = selling price (p.u.) – variable costs (p.u.)

BEP (for sales) = fixed costs/contribution (p.u.) x selling price (p.u.)

BEP = total fixed costs/contribution (p.u.) – average variable costs

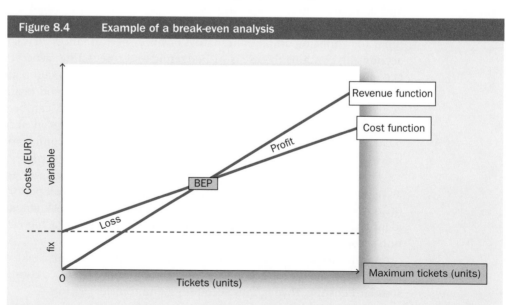

Figure 8.4   Example of a break-even analysis

Whalley (2011) also refers to the margin of safety (MOS) and defines the MOS as 'the excess of budgeted or actual sales of the BEP of sales. It states the amount by which sales can drop before losses begin to be incurred. The higher the margin of safety, the lower the risk of not breaking even'.

Margin of safety (money or units) = total budgeted or actual sales − break-even sales

Margin of safety ratio = (expected sales − break-even sales)/break-even sales

Limitations of the BEA are that:

- the BEA tells you nothing about what sales are actually likely to be achieved for the product at these various prices;
- fixed costs are assumed to be constant whilst the average variable costs are likewise constant per unit of output (e.g. linearity);
- in complex organisations, such as an event could be, it assumes that the relative proportions of each product sold and produced are constant.

Basic analysis of financial statements

Conducting a financial statement analysis (FSA) is an integrative part of managing and financing events. As events usually involve many stakeholders, it is crucial to understand the profitability and/or risks related to the activities. Normally, the FSA is provided on a regular basis (annual, quarterly reports) and contains financial information of various types. The first part of the FSA is typically the reformulation of the financial information. Commonly the income statement is divided into recurring (normal) items and non-recurring (special) items. Earnings can, therefore, be separated between core and transitory earnings, which is important for valuations and predictions. Furthermore, earnings should be divided into net operational profit after taxes and net financial costs. Usually, the balance sheet is finally grouped into net operating assets, net financial debt and equity. It is also important to analyse and adjust measurement errors related to the reported accounting numbers.

Finally, a financial ratio analysis (FRA) is used to analyse risks on the one hand and profitability on the other. The risk analysis consists of a liquidity (e.g. cash flow analysis) and solvency analysis (i.e. would the organisation recover from losses or a period of losses?). The profitability analysis relates to the analysis of the return on capital – for example, return on equity (ROE), defined as earnings divided by average equity.

As far as the FSA of an event organiser is concerned, many of the explained peculiarities of an event need to be taken into consideration. Especially due to the high demand for resources in just a short space of time, a cash flow analysis is essential, as delivering an event also means having enough 'change' as many uncertainties may occur when delivering the event.

Business plan

Having a business plan is also essential for event organisers. When bidding to host an event, the bid documents are very often already a kind of business plan, as they contain answers to questions and goals linked to the events, as well as promotional aspects, financial aspects and information on how the event should be operated. But also newly created events need to think about the four P's (product, price, place and promotion) in order to win over financial supporters or public investors such as a municipality.

Typically, the business plan is between 10 and 50 pages long. Apart from measures to be taken in order to enter into the market, strategic and operative goals need to be defined. Furthermore, an internal and external analysis needs to be executed. Very often a SWOT analysis (strengths and weaknesses – internal view, opportunities and threats – external view) is carried out in order to identify the organisation's core competences/unique selling proposition (USP).

Part of the business plan is a marketing plan, procurement plan, production plan, HR and, of course, a financial plan as stated before. Again, the peculiarities of events need to be taken into consideration, such as working with many volunteers, having goals that often differ from those of public decision makers, or the need to involve stakeholders in different planning phases.

Critical success factors for financing events

As the reader will have noticed and as experience has shown, it is difficult to budget and control the finances of an event. The complexity of an event as outlined earlier in this chapter is often under-estimated. Preuss and Schnitzer (2013) highlighted the fact that, in the planning phase, many mistakes can be made including errors with respect to analysing the situation (especially the requirements), forecasting errors (e.g. expectations regarding financial support, changes in the currency value, interest rates and inflation) as well as errors arising from a lack of information (insufficient experience in hosting certain types of events). In the realisation phase, Preuss and Schnitzer (2013) see internal aspects (e.g. long decision-making processes), issues concerning government support (e.g. political instability; changed decision competencies), intentional mistakes (e.g. showing a weak financial situation to signal the need for financial support) and external aspects (e.g. weather conditions, strikes, oil/steel/financial crises) as issues to be considered when budgeting for an event. The million dollar question is therefore: how can an event manager be successful where finance is concerned? Or, in other words, what are the critical success factors when financing events?

1. *The dynamics of budgets,* especially in the bidding stages (inflation, exchange rates) need to be understood, tracked, continuously evaluated and discussed within the organisation delivering the event. Thinking through different scenarios and playing through different situations helps to avoid making big financial mistakes.

2. *Contingency planning* is crucial – some event owners ask the organiser to add 10% of all costs to the ordinary budget as a reserve. First of all, events have many, mainly negative surprises, where finances are concerned. Secondly, showing the stakeholders that the organiser is aware of potential surprises and has allowed for a reserve is also a sign of professionalism. The major guideline for budgeting is: be very careful, moderate and pessimistic rather than optimistic when budgeting. Also think about who would cover an economic shortfall; always think it could be yourself.

3. Very often *'big bucket' costs are not quantifiable* and need to be borne by third parties, mainly the public. Be honest with public funders and make them understand that variability of costs is part of managing expectations. Especially working in a political context involves being very clear about the financial implications of the event. Discussing and pointing fingers after the event and explaining to politicians why the costs were overrun is always an unpleasant experience.

4. The costs and also potential revenues greatly depend on situations that cannot be influenced. The *unpredictability of the results of a sports event* can have massive impacts. For example, the success of the host team during a tournament may create historic moments for a country for generations (e.g. Springbock's victory at the Rugby World Cup 1995 in South Africa). Such implications may also have impacts on the consumer behaviour of event tourists, positively in the case of sporting success and negatively in the case of unsuccessful sporting outcomes. These situations need to be considered and may be part of an overall risk management strategy.

5. The *principles of good governance* (transparency, accountability, democracy, responsibility, equity, effectiveness, efficiency) may also be used as guiding principles for financing events. For example, transparent decision-making policies within the event organisation may prevent conflicts within the team.

6. *Planning liquidity* is also crucial to success. Event budgets 'explode' just before and right after the event and high amounts of financial resources are required during this peak period. It is crucial to guarantee good planning with regard to who will be paid during these hectic phases, whilst spreading pay deadlines with service providers over longer periods before and after the event. The organiser must also talk to the bank about having a sufficient chart of accounts.

7. *Written agreements* have not always been part of the agenda in the event business and many organisers have had to learn from bad experiences. Where financial management is concerned, a contracting service provider also means that there is a clear understanding of the costs, fewer problems and fewer misunderstandings while a legal framework also helps handle potential conflict.

8. *Empowerment* on a financial level leads to increased motivation among employees. Also, giving financial responsibility to the team members leads to increased commitment. Nevertheless, a clear frame and power limitations as well as control are crucial if unpleasant surprises are to be avoided after the event.

9. *Setting priorities* in terms of understanding the essentials and the desirables when budgeting and decision making is necessary. In the event planning phase, internal (between the different functions) and external forces (from stakeholders) must try to bind as many economic resources as possible. Clear strategies and shared goals help distinguish between the desirables (e.g. fancy opening ceremony) and the essentials (e.g. security measures required by the authorities).

10. The importance of *value-in-kind sponsorships (VIK)* is often under-estimated. Very often sponsorships are related only to cash income in an organisation, but for many sponsors, providing their products (e.g. cars, food, drinks, IT solutions) is cheaper; the products can be tested on potential clients and gain increased visibility among potential consumers. For the organisers, VIK helps obtain services which would otherwise have been bought which, in turn, helps save money; a typical win–win situation, which in practice often does not receive enough attention.

11. Having the *knowledge* of how to organise the event is essential, but often financial aspects and areas linked to these aspects are neglected. Discussions regarding tax systems and specific legal and contractual questions require time, consultation and very often some issues need to be gone over twice. Apart from this very specific knowledge, a basic understanding of financial management tools (e.g. break-even analysis) and logic (e.g. what are variable and what are fixed costs and how do certain decisions impact on them) is also necessary. Where knowledge is concerned, its transfer is an important part that avoids reinventing the wheel. It is crucial for an organiser to understand any mistakes made and to avoid making them again; also the ability to apply the knowledge in different environments needs to be considered (e.g. transferability of knowledge).

12. Budgeting and control is a very important discipline in events management. Get the *right people* for this job who are prepared to be the 'bad cops' and to say 'no' more often than 'yes'. These people need to have a certain amount of experience and be completely opposed to a laissez-faire style. Finally, it is very common to contract sponsors and providers at the very last minute, just before the event starts, so negotiating until the end to gain resources also requires a lot of energy and stamina.

See Case 8.4 to learn about the financial experiences of an organising committee delivering a major sporting event.

Case 8.4	Successful financial management of the Winter Universiade Innsbruck/ Seefeld 2005

The 22nd edition of the World University Winter Games (Winter Universiade) in 2005 took place in Innsbruck and Seefeld, Austria: 2,223 participants (1,449 athletes and 774 officials) participated from 50 different countries in 69 medal events; 85,000 on-site spectators, 34,000 overnight stays, 801 volunteers (14,000 man days of work), 480 hours TV coverage worldwide and an overall organising budget of €7.94 million was required to organise this elite athlete student sporting event. Untypically for these types of events, with financial TV and media rights income, the organisers managed to have a surplus of almost €0.5 million. In their Final Report (2006), the organisers themselves referred to the following key lessons where the financing of the Winter Universiade 2005 was concerned:

1. Consistent cost monitoring and re-budgeting where required is only possible if all planning data is recorded in the project cost centres on an ongoing basis and as accurately as possible.

2. The regular monitoring of the different budgets together with the project managers contributed to the further contextual development of the individual projects, and brought to light the interdependence between projects.

3. The financial consequences of different scenarios can quickly be simulated through the central logging of such variables as the number of participants and the US dollar and euro exchange rates.

4. The structuring of the exchange of services and its detailed calculation as a basis for written agreements are accepted by project partners following initial scepticism, not least because it makes possible hidden costs in their area transparent.

5. If no real financial implications or other consequences are stipulated, entries from participating countries tend to be late and incorrect, which dramatically raises organisational and financial risk.

6. Sponsorship and TV rights as part of the commercial income also create production costs for organising the deliverables (e.g. media coverage). Public sector funding partners demand tangible results which, in the ideal case, are aligned with commercial sponsors' interests but can sometimes conflict with them. Sponsors and sponsorship revenue goals should therefore be carefully chosen.

7. Whenever possible greater buying power of organising committee members should be facilitated. Most often public procurement regulations will apply for organising committees in any case.

Source: Final Report (2006)

Discussion questions

8 What benefits may central cost centres and regular budget monitoring have?
9 Why is budgeting in scenarios so important?
10 What role do written agreements play in financial issues?

Conclusion

Financing events is a very exciting topic as it covers all areas that an event organiser has to face and deals with most stakeholders. It is interesting to note that other areas of event planning and organisation (e.g. volunteer management) are covered much better in the academic literature than the financing of events. The only areas that are quite well-developed are the studies commissioned by event owners, public authorities or the event organisers themselves in order to justify the money spent on the event. Very often, the legacies of events are barely visible and therefore the event very soon becomes history. It is, therefore, crucial that the event owner, the event organiser and their stakeholders succeed in creating exciting events and working in clear economic settings and frameworks.

General discussion questions

11 What elements are specific to an event and what impact do these features have on the financing of such an event?

12 What are the differences between right-holder events and non-right-holder events and what are their implications in terms of costs/benefits?

13 What are the main cost drivers and revenues for an event organisation?

14 Which tools can be used to measure the financial impact of events?

15 What are the basic principles of management accounting and how does a BEA work?

16 What should the single chapters of a business plan contain?

Guided reading

The bibliography contains many useful sources for the student. See, in particular:

Crompton, J.L. (1995) Economic impact analysis of sports facilities and events: eleven sources of misapplication. *Journal of Sport Management*, 9(1), 14–35.

Getz, D. (1994) Event tourism: evaluating the impacts. In J.R.B. Ritchie and C.R. Goeldner (eds), *Travel, Tourism and Hospitality Research: A Handbook for Managers and Researchers*. New York: John Wiley.

Gratton, C. and Preuss, H. (2008) Maximising Olympic impacts by building up legacies. *The International Journal of the History of Sport*, 25(14), 1971–87.

Preuss, H. (2004) *The Economics of Staging the Olympics. A Comparison of the Games 1972–2008*. Cheltenham: Edward Elgar.

Recommended websites

American Accounting Association: **http://aaahq.org**

EventIMPACTS: **www.eventimpacts.com**

Event-Scorecard: **www.event-scorecard.ch** (in German only)

EventScotland: **www.eventscotland.org**

SENTEDALPS: **www.alpine-space.org/temp-results1385254.html?&L=93837%22%20onfocus%3D%22blurLink%28this%29%3B#1395**

Sportaccord: **www.sportaccord.com**

Sport business: **www.sportbusiness.com**

Sportca:l **www.sportcal.com**

Sport Event Denmark: **http://sporteventdenmark.com/da.aspx?sc_lang=en**

Key words

bidding costs; break-even analysis; business plan; management accounting

Bibliography

American Accounting Association (2013) **http://aaahq.org**

Baade, R. and Matheson, V. (2004) The quest for the cup: assessing the economic impact of the World Cup. *Regional Studies,* 38(4), 343–54.

Cashman, R. (2006) *The Bitter-Sweet Awakening – The Legacy of the Sydney 2000 Olympic Games*. Sydney: Walla Walla Press.

Cappello, A. (2011) Interview with the Artistic Director of the Südtirol Classical Festival Weeks Merano, 30 November.

Crompton, J.L. (1995) Economic impact analysis of sports facilities and events: eleven sources of misapplication. *Journal of Sport Management,* 9(1), 14–35.

Event Scotland (2012) **www.eventscotland.org**

Final Report (2006) Final Report of the Winter Universiade Innsbruck/Seefeld 2005.

Games Legacy (2002) Lessons learnt: review of the 2002 Commonwealth Games in Manchester for DCMS, Sport England and Manchester City Council – Final Report, December 2002. **www.gameslegacy.co.uk/files/cglessons.pdf**

Getz, D. (1994) Event tourism: evaluating the impacts. In J.R.B. Ritchie and C.R. Goeldner (eds.), *Travel, Tourism and Hospitality Research: A Handbook for Managers and Researchers*. New York: John Wiley.

Gratton, C. and Preuss, H. (2008) Maximising Olympic impacts by building up legacies. *The International Journal of the History of Sport,* 25 (14), 1971–87.

Hall, C.M. (1992) *Hallmark Tourist Events. Impacts, Management and Planning*. London: Belhaven Press.

Hanusch, H. (1994) *Nutzen-Kosten-Analyse*. Munich: Vahlen.

Heinemann, K. (1995) *Einführung in die Ökonomie des Sports – ein Handbuch*. Schorndorf: Hoffmann Verlag.

Horne, J. (2007) The four 'knowns' of sports mega-events. *Leisure Studies* 26(1), 81–96.

Innsbruck 2012 (2008) Candidature file of the candidate city for the Winter Youth Olympic Games 2012.

Jeanrenaud, C. (1999) *The Economic Impact of Sport Events*. Neuchâtel: Editions CIES.

Jefferson-Lenskyi, H. (2002) *Best Olympics Ever? The Social Impacts of Sydney 2000*. Albany, NY: State University of New York Press.

Kaspar, R. (2006) The event life cycle approach – the long marathon from bidding to hosting and finally positioning the host city on the world destination map. In *Valencia Summit 2006: Major Sports Events as Opportunity for Development: The International Promotion of the City,* Noos Institute, Spain, 112–19.

Kaspar, R. and Schnitzer, M. (2011) Recurring vs. hallmark events. In L. Swayne and M. Dodds (eds), *Encyclopedia of Sports Management and Marketing*. Thousand Oaks, CA: Sage Publications.

Lamprecht, M. and Stamm, H. (2002) *Sport zwischen Kultur, Kult und Kommerz*. Zürich: Seismo-Verlag.

Maennig, W. (1998) Möglichkeiten und Grenzen von Kosten-Nutzen-Analysen im Sport [Scope and limits of cost benefit analysis in sport]. *Sportwissenschaft,* 28(3), 311–27.

Matheson, V. (2009) Economic multipliers and mega-event analysis. *International Journal of Sport Finance,* 4(1), 63–70.

Preuss, H. (2004) *The Economics of Staging the Olympics. A Comparison of the Games 1972–2008*. Cheltenham: Edward Elgar.

Preuss, H. (2009) Opportunity costs and efficiency of investments in mega sport events. *Journal of Policy Research in Tourism, Leisure and Events,* 1(2), 131–40.

Preuss, H. and Schnitzer, M. (2013) Organization costs for a FIFA World Cup and their significance during a bid. *Event Management* (in print).

Preuss, H., Kurscheidt, M. and Schütte, N. (2009) *Ökonomie des Tourismus bei Sportgroßveranstaltungen. Eine empirische Analyse zur Fußball-Weltmeisterschaft 2006*. Wiesbaden: Gabler.

Ritchie, R.J.R. (1984) Assessing the impact of hallmark events: conceptual and research issues. *Journal of Travel Research*, 23(1), 2–11.

Schnitzer, M. and Redl, M (2011) Price to host events. In L. Swayne and M. Dodds (eds.), *Encyclopedia of Sports Management and Marketing*. Thousand Oaks, CA: Sage Publications, 1170–1.

Supovitz, F. (2005) *The Sport Event Management and Marketing Playbook*. Hoboken, NJ: John Wiley and Sons.

Sportaccord (2013) **www.sportaccord.com**

Sport Business (2013) **www.sportbusiness.com**

Sportcal (2013) **www.sportcal.com**

Sport Event Denmark (2013) **http:// sporteventdenmark.com**]

Whalley, A.J. (2011) Break-even analysis. In L. Swayne and M. Dodds (eds), *Encyclopedia of Sports Management and Marketing*. Thousand Oaks, CA: Sage Publications, 169–71.

Chapter 9

Event planning and strategy

Scott McRoberts, University of Toronto Scarborough, Canada, with additions from **Chris Charlebois** and **Clay Melnike**

Learning outcomes

Upon completion of this chapter the reader should be able to:

- understand the structures of the markets in which events operate;
- conduct SWOT and PEST analyses and demonstrate their use;
- demonstrate how other business functions must be integrated into strategic planning;
- understand the **event planning** process;
- understand the importance of an audit in the event/strategic planning process;
- evaluate a **strategic plan** for an event.

Overview

Event planning is one of, if not the most, critical components of events management. Effective planning allows event managers to optimise their success. Unfortunately, the reality for practitioners is that you can never be 100% prepared for everything related to your event. Excellent event managers ensure that they invest the time and resources into planning so that when issues arise at their event, they have the appropriate protocols, communication procedures and personnel in place to respond. The goal is that those participating or attending do not have the ability to perceive that there was any problem at the event. Furthermore, effective event planning will allow event managers to achieve the goals and objectives that are developed in the strategic plan of their event, organisation or company.

Understanding the event market place

Before an event manager begins the strategic or event planning process, a great degree of research must be undertaken in order to understand how to most successfully host an event. This chapter will allow you to better understand the current market place and trends of events and better prepare you to effectively plan and strategise for the staging of your next event.

Events can fit into a number of categories given the differences in the design and programme of various events. Some events are developed for the public (often celebrations geared towards building social cohesion) and others are created for purposes such as entertainment, business or competition. Figure 9.1 demonstrates the categories of events that are common today.

In 2005, the City of Burlington, Ontario, Canada categorised its festivals and events into three sections:

- *Tourism events*: These events are large and compelling to a major market with potential for high expenditures. They have the potential for mass international exposure and the ability to encourage multi-day visits:
  - *hallmark events*: recurring event possessing significance in terms of tradition, publicity or image so as to provide a destination with a competitive advantage (for example, Mardis Gras in New Orleans, USA).
  - *mega events*: through either size or significance. These events yield high levels of tourism, media coverage, **economic impact,** or prestige for the destination (for example, the Olympic Games).
  - *blockbuster event*: a one-time, large-scale event with enough significance to provide the host community with a competitive advantage. For example, Red Bull Crashed Ice.
- *Growing and emerging events*: These events have the potential to become tourism events (for example, a children's festival).
- *Community-based events*: These events have a community focus and impact as opposed to a tourism focus and impact (for example, a food festival).

It is imperative to understand that there are different scales and types of events that exist in the market place. Alternatively, some researchers have begun to argue that a number of small-scale events can have the same (and in some cases greater) impact on a host in order to achieve strategic goals. Small-scale events have the potential to result in more positive effects for host communities or organisations as they usually operate within existing infrastructure, are manageable in terms of crowd congestion and public services, and require nominal investment of funds (Higham, 1999).

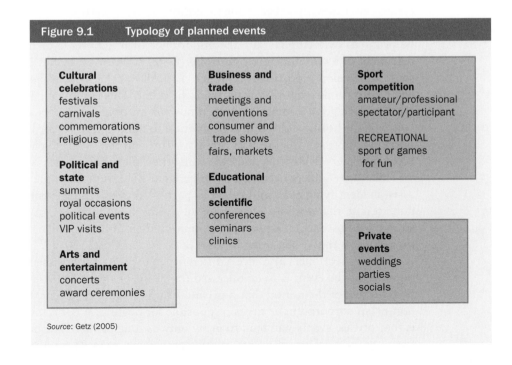

Figure 9.1   Typology of planned events

Cultural celebrations
festivals
carnivals
commemorations
religious events

Political and state
summits
royal occasions
political events
VIP visits

Arts and entertainment
concerts
award ceremonies

Business and trade
meetings and
 conventions
consumer and
 trade shows
fairs, markets

Educational and scientific
conferences
seminars
clinics

Sport competition
amateur/professional
spectator/participant

RECREATIONAL
sport or games
 for fun

Private events
weddings
parties
socials

Source: Getz (2005)

For a number of years, the tourism industry was not considered to be a key player in events management. It was not until recently that the term '**event tourism**' was accepted to be inclusive of all planned events (Getz, 2008). Event tourism is defined as 'a systematic planning, development, and marketing of festivals and special events as tourist attractions, image-makers, catalysts for infrastructure and economic growth, and animators of built attraction' (Ghazali, in Collins and Minnis, 2007). Due to the increasing popularity of event tourism, event managers have had a tendency to take a more holistic and integrated approach in marketing their events in partnership with cities and/or destination marketing organisations (DMOs).

Further to this, because there can be clutter created within a destination as a result of a number of events occurring throughout the year, there has been an emergence of cultural events being attached to those that occur or are being staged within a city (Richards and Wilson, 2004). According to Zukin (1995), 'culture' can cover all of the amenities within a city, and, further, culture can be broken into two categories: 'high' culture (attractions such as classical music concerts, museums, theatre) and 'popular' culture (sport, pop music, fashion). As such, many event organisers and/or destinations are starting to create events that have a diverse offering to participants or attendees. An example of how a city may integrate a cultural component could be an international sporting event incorporating an opening ceremony that includes songs and dances that represent the various countries participating in their event.

Understanding that there are a number of vested stakeholders involved in the event planning process (politicians, tourism, culture, businesses, etc.) as well as types and scales of events, the opportunity emerges for event planners to strategically create an **event portfolio**. An event portfolio is a series of events that take place at different times of the year and that appeal to multiple consumers across a range of psychographic profiles to which an event or destination seeks to appeal (Ziakas and Costa, 2011). Destinations and events management companies have been more willing to strategically create a portfolio of events because it allows these practitioners to identify ways in which they can strategically share resources (volunteers, financial resources or facilities, for example), appeal to different markets, as well as foster collaboration and coordination among the involved stakeholders. By creating these types of relationships amongst multiple industries, event managers can foster synergies among event(s) based on the ability to share resources and create better developed event augmentations (Green, 2001).

When developing event strategies, events management companies, cities or DMOs can be prone to over-emphasising the importance of mega events or hallmark events to the detriment of a more balanced portfolio (Getz, 2008). As a result, it can ultimately make sense to develop a portfolio approach as it allows the various stakeholders in the host city to determine what they want from the event. This could include positively impacting on the destination's image, raising funds for an organisation or cause, building social cohesion, or health and wellness promotion to name a few. According to Getz (2008) the portfolio approach (Figure 9.2) can assist through the strategic planning process, aiding event managers in creating and evaluating their plans for event hosting.

Since stakeholders need to determine what they want from the event(s), this tool can assist in identifying goals and values as part of an overarching event portfolio. It is important to note that without identifying an overarching portfolio, or even individual event strategy, a host faces the prospect of limiting their ability to fully exploit the potential of the resources that it has at its disposal (Ziakas and Costa, 2011).

Event practitioners also face a difference in capacity for hosting their event, depending on whether the event is to be operated for-profit or on a not-for-profit basis. This could be reflective of the notion that a private firm is staging the event, for example, or that a non-profit corporation or city is responsible for hosting. What is important to understand is that private events will tend to grow only as long as there is a positive impact on profitability. Not-for-profit events are not necessarily focused on a profit motive and may

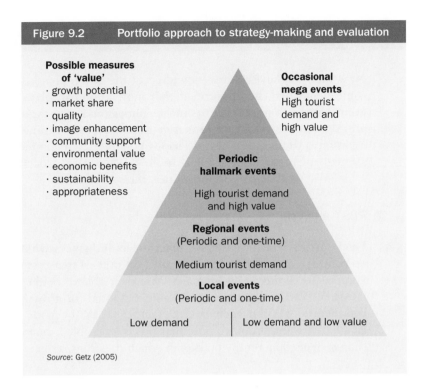

Figure 9.2   Portfolio approach to strategy-making and evaluation

Possible measures of 'value'
· growth potential
· market share
· quality
· image enhancement
· community support
· environmental value
· economic benefits
· sustainability
· appropriateness

Occasional mega events
High tourist demand and high value

Periodic hallmark events
High tourist demand and high value

Regional events
(Periodic and one-time)
Medium tourist demand

Local events
(Periodic and one-time)
Low demand   Low demand and low value

Source: Getz (2005)

seek to continually grow; however, they often face the challenge of staying within budget constraints (Anderson and Getz, 2009). This ultimately means that those staging events in the not-for-profit sector can become beholden to political support, grant programmes or the amount of taxpayer monies available to support the event. In a study conducted by Anderson and Getz (2009) it was determined that the event market place was largely dominated by public or not-for-profit entities (59% in the UK). Although public entities have traditionally dominated the event landscape, the competition for resources, and similar market segments could lead to an increase in the number of public–private partnerships. From an event planning process, it can certainly make sense to develop these types of partnerships as each group can bring a level of expertise to the staging of an event. Further to this, in instances where the two companies are competing for a similar market segment, the event experience could potentially be enhanced as both organisations could more effectively market to their targeted **demographics**.

Understanding motivation

Understanding the motivation of participants and attendees at your event is critical to ensure its success. In a study conducted by Woo et al. (2011) it was suggested that five of the most popular motivators for attending an event are: socialisation, excitement, event novelty, family togetherness and escape. The study further revealed that although there are commonalities in motivation for event participants and attendees, there is a significant difference in motivators depending on the festival product being offered (Woo et al., 2011). As such, it is imperative that event managers and marketers truly understand the audience they will be serving. By understanding important demographic information (such as age, annual income, ethnic background), event managers are better equipped to develop successful event and festival product offerings. Understanding the target market will also assist event managers in developing their overall plan, as this type of information will often influence the goals and objectives that are identified in the strategy.

Determining the viability of your event

Now that you have an understanding of the general landscape in which events operate, some trends and the importance that motivation can play in developing your strategic/event plan, it is important to further understand the market place in which your event will operate. By taking a proactive approach to planning, event managers can equip themselves to make the best decisions possible. Two common tools that are used within strategic planning are the PEST (political, economic, social, technological) and SWOT (strengths, weaknesses, opportunities, threats) analyses.

PEST analysis

PEST factors refer to external, macro-level influences which we generally have little to no control over. This tool is generally best utilised to assess the market place in which an event will operate. Event managers are then able to better understand the 'fit' for their festival or event offering, as well as its potential for growth. Table 9.1 lists some of the considerations within each external factor that can be made when developing your strategic plan. It is important to note that this is a flexible framework and that influencers can change depending on the market in which the event is operating.

Table 9.1	PEST factors

Political	**Economic**
■ Ecological/environmental issues	■ Home economy situation
■ Current legislation home market	■ Home economy trends
■ Future legislation	■ Overseas economies and trends
■ International legislation	■ General taxation issues
■ Regulatory bodies and processes	■ Taxation specific to product/services
■ Government policies	■ Seasonality/weather issues
■ Government term and change	■ Market and trade cycles
■ Trading policies	■ Specific industry factors
■ Funding, grants and initiatives	■ Market routes and distribution trends
■ Home market lobbying/pressure groups	■ Customer/end-user drivers
■ International pressure groups	■ Interest and exchange rates
■ Wars and conflicts	■ International trade/monetary issues

Social	**Technological**
■ Lifestyle trends	■ Competing technology development
■ Demographics	■ Research funding
■ Consumer attitudes and opinions	■ Associated/dependent technologies
■ Media views	■ Replacement technology/solutions
■ Law changes affecting social factors	■ Maturity of technology
■ Brand, company, technology image	■ Manufacturing maturity and capacity
■ Consumer buying patterns	■ Information and communications
■ Fashion and role models	■ Consumer buying mechanisms and technology
■ Major events and influences	■ Technology legislation
■ Buying access and trends	■ Innovation potential
■ ethnic/religious factors	■ Technology access, licensing, patents
■ Advertising and publicity	■ Intellectual property issues
■ Ethical issues	■ Global communications

■ SWOT analysis

A SWOT analysis is a detailed examination of internal factors of your organisation or event and external variables that may affect your success (Graham et al., 1995). Prior to completing a SWOT analysis, you must be familiar with the details about your event, including personnel, time, date, location, target audience, population of the host community and capacity of infrastructure and public services, to name a few. A SWOT analysis is used on a more granular level as it assesses a product or service rather than a market. Table 9.2 gives a sample of questions and considerations to make when completing a SWOT analysis.

Table 9.2	SWOT factors
Strengths	**Weaknesses**
■ Advantages of proposition? ■ Personnel capacity and capability? ■ Competitive advantages? ■ USPs (unique selling points)? ■ Resources, assets, people? ■ Experience, knowledge, data? ■ Financial capacity? ■ Marketing reach, distribution, awareness? ■ Innovative aspects? ■ Location and geographical? ■ Price, value, quality? ■ Accreditations, qualifications, certifications? ■ Processes, systems, IT, communications? ■ Cultural, attitudinal, behavioural?	■ Disadvantages of proposition? ■ Gaps in capabilities? ■ Lack of competitive strength? ■ Reputation, presence and reach? ■ Financials? ■ Own known vulnerabilities? ■ Timescales, deadlines and pressures? ■ Cashflow, start-up, cash-drain? ■ Infrastructure and capacity of host community? ■ Morale, commitment, leadership? ■ Consumer awareness? ■ Cultural barriers? ■ Communication barriers?
Opportunities	**Threats**
■ Market developments? ■ Competitors' vulnerabilities? ■ Industry or lifestyle trends? ■ Technology development and innovation? ■ Global influences? ■ New markets? ■ Niche target markets? ■ Geographical? ■ Major contracts, suppliers, sponsors? ■ Business and product development? ■ Information and research? ■ Partnerships, agencies? ■ Seasonal, weather influences?	■ Political effects? ■ Legislative effects? ■ Environmental effects? ■ IT developments? ■ Competitor intentions? ■ Market demand? ■ New technologies, services, ideas? ■ Vital contracts and partners? ■ Obstacles faced? ■ Insurmountable weaknesses? ■ Employment market? ■ Financial and credit pressures? ■ Economy – home, abroad? ■ Seasonal weather effects?

■ PEST vs. SWOT

While PEST and SWOT analyses complement each other with respect to strategic planning, PEST allows you to understand the external and macro-level factors that can impact the market place in which you will be operating. A SWOT analysis, on the other hand, further allows you to understand the product or service which you will be offering as well as the external factors that could affect its success or failure at a micro-level. Planning is not a precise science. As such, using a PEST analysis instead of a SWOT analysis is neither right nor wrong; in fact the two can be integrated into one tool in some cases. What is important to note is that PEST becomes more useful when the event proposition is on a larger scale. However, smaller events can also benefit from conducting a PEST analysis, as it is likely to identify at least a few issues within the market place that may not otherwise have been thought of.

Case 9.1   Cross-Border Marathon

The Cross-Border Marathon (CBM) has been running for 20 years. The organisation has five paid staff members in the following roles: Managing Director, Meet Director, Volunteer Coordinator, Special Events Coordinator and Operations Coordinator. The CBM has a dedicated and trained volunteer group of approximately 300 people. The event starts in the City of Apathaca, Montanaco, crosses the border and finishes in the City of Beladrus, Finnacky. The 2012 race was the largest yet with over 2,500 racers participating.

During the winter planning season, the Managing Director has learnt that international laws require all participants to carry a passport to cross the border between Apathaca and Finnacky. Further to this, new sanctions have been imposed by border security on bus travel groups which requires transportation manifests to be provided two months in advance of an event date. Moreover, each traveller is required to carry a letter from the event organiser symbolising that they are an event participant.

The majority of CBM's participants has an average income of $80,000+ per year and they are typically Caucasian. Sixty per cent of participants are male and 40% are female. Seventy per cent of participants travel from outside of a 100-mile radius, and approximately 45% of participants stay overnight. Beladrus is a historic and iconic international destination with a number of attractions and activities that are suitable for people of all ages.

During the winter planning season, the Managing Director also learnt that a local government authority approved road use for a major cycling event to occur during the same weekend as the CBM. The CBM Board of Directors has set three priority goals for the CBM this year:

- to increase participation;
- to increase exposure of the event;
- to increase profitability.

Discussion questions

1 Using the information provided, conduct both PEST and SWOT analyses of the CBM.
2 Based on your assessment, do you think that the CBM will have a successful year? Why or why not?
3 Based on your assessment, how would you suggest that the Managing Director achieve the goals as identified by the Board of Directors?

The event planning process

Too many organisations and professionals spend an enormous amount of time developing plans which are then filed away and rarely looked at. Successful events have a very detailed plan that is used by all levels of staff and volunteers as a critical tool for building success. Often during the planning process, a strategy or strategic plan is developed and should align with the mission, vision and goals of the host committee or organisation, creating synergy between each level of detail. The event planning process is arguably one of the most important aspects but can also be the most time-consuming and frustrating. It is often referred to as 'peeling back the onion'. An onion has many layers and as one layer is peeled back, there is another waiting beneath the surface. The same holds true for the event planning process. With so much detail and consideration when planning an event, there are often multiple layers and various processes that one must go through in order to capture all details including high-level and those that seem obvious, as well as those that may be minuscule on paper but critical to the overall plan. For instance, transportation for an event may be obvious; you need a vehicle, driver, pick-up and drop-off points. However, there are about 30–40 details surrounding transportation in order to make the pick-up and drop-off happen seamlessly, which is conducted during the planning process. For an event manager alone to think of everything is impossible. The goal of the process is to plan, organise, communicate and implement all aspects as part of the planning process to ensure 99.9% of all details have been thought through. A good mechanism or tool to organise your thoughts around each section appears in Figure 9.3. This is an example of how 'the wheel' can be an effective planning tool early on in the process, using transportation as an example.

For those factors that were missed, **contingency plans** and personnel, including proper means of communication, are integral for an effective response. The following provides some detail surrounding different stages and situations involved in the event planning process, as well as how five key business functions – legal, finance, human resources, marketing and guest services – should be integrated into the overall event plan or strategy.

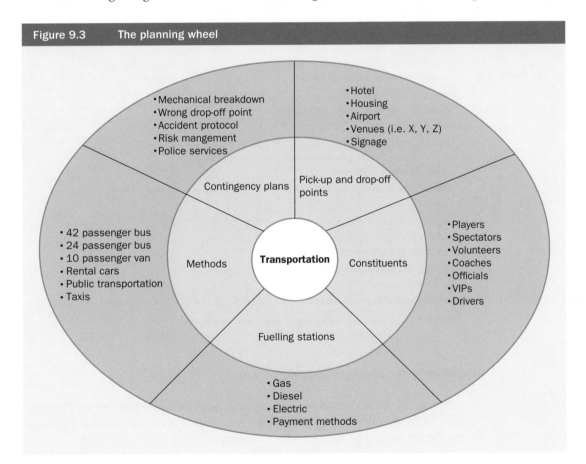

Figure 9.3   The planning wheel

■ Working backwards

The initial step in the planning process often involves working backwards. Compilation of a critical dates calendar from *end* to *start* can help the organiser establish essential benchmarks and priorities that must be reached. At this time, all the critical parts required to stage the event can be laid out, which can also be part of a strategic planning process. This establishes an efficient way of organising all the functions in chronological order and begins to define the critical path of work, tasks and sub-tasks as well as potential issues and challenges early in the process. Work tools such as Microsoft Excel or Gantt charts are great, cost-effective project management tools to help you stay organised, on task and on time. Table 9.3 identifies another method for organising your thoughts and data, a simple task list that can be used for pre-planning or smaller events.

Table 9.3 Task list			
Task/action: Sponsorship and fundraising:	**Who**	**When**	**Status**
Prepare general sponsorship package and determine appropriate sponsorship levels and servicing requirements		Bid phase	✓
Identify potential event sponsors and forward proposal – potential supporters and/or sponsor categories include:	Charlie, Kendra	Ongoing	
■ water company	Brian, Adam	Jan/Feb	
■ tournament awards (MVP, All Stars, Team Awards)	Ross, Wanda	May	
■ food and hospitality room	Nancy/Facility	February	
■ product for athlete registration packages	All	Jan	
■ host hotel	Wanda	Jan	
■ transportation, vehicles and fuel	Adam	Jan	
■ contact City Tourism	Nancy		
■ Hershey (Sergio is contact)	Wanda		
Provide appropriate sponsor servicing and ensure sponsors receive all promised benefits – signage, websites, print material, etc. – create system to monitor	Charlie		
Consider inviting key sponsors to awards banquet and championship game with possible involvement in award presentations/ceremonies.	Charlie		
Acquire all sponsor logos in suitable format (jpeg and eps/bw and colour)	Charlie		
Thank all sponsors with a sponsorship recognition gift and ensure appropriate recognition on event websites, in Newsletters and Annual Reports	Charlie		
Investigate sale of tournament items (t-shirts, hats, etc.)	Wanda	May	
Determine structure for gate admission (by donation/ free of charge/weekend passes)	Nancy		

Note: all sponsor contracts must be approved by event organiser and facility.

■ Defining the decision-making process

Defining the decision-making process and responsibilities early can prevent larger issues from unfolding or coming to the forefront during a critical period. At times this process can be controversial, but having an effective board or management team with the right expertise can provide guidance to the process and help determine the right organisational structure or organisational chart as it is commonly referred to. Please refer to Figure 9.4, which represents a sample overview of a top-down hierarchal organisational chart for a mid-sized event.

As well as finding the best people to fill the roles within the board, it is critical in the early stages to recruit the right people at the staff level. The assistance of a human resource manager can be beneficial during this process.

Once the company/organisation has determined the structure that it would like to have in place, it can be beneficial to ensure that legal advice is sought to ensure proper protocols and control mechanisms are in place to protect the event organiser.

Figure 9.4	Organisational chart

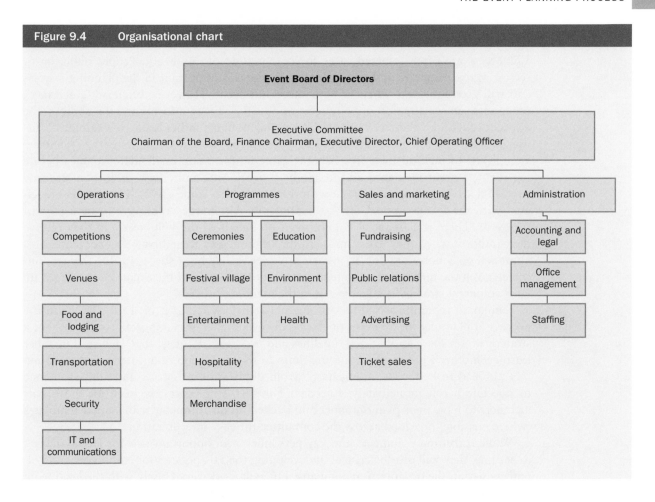

Legal

One of the first things that any event manager should consider obtaining is insurance for their event. Insurance can play a critical role in the policies and procedures that you will have to develop in your event planning process. Depending on the event, you may be required to post certain signs in visible areas, develop training protocols or hire professionally certified staff (such as physicians or unionised employees) to complete due diligence in protecting your event. Consultation with your insurance provider will allow you to better understand what protocols or other services you will have to include in the planning process.

When a corporation (non-profit or for-profit) is staging an event, it is also important to have a legal adviser who can develop terms of reference and bylaw documents that will detail who within the organisation can make certain decisions and how much can be spent without board approval, and define roles of the board/committee members and volunteers who comprise a part of your organisations structure. Having these types of documents in place will certainly assist not only in the planning process, but also in the development of the overall strategic plan. Furthermore, the legal team can also advise staff/volunteers of any other legal protocols they may want to undertake. For example, if you are registering for an event which has associated risks (for example, injury or possible death), it is crucial to ensure that you have taken the necessary legal precautions to inform participants of this risk and that they acknowledge and are educated that there could be negative consequences associated with their participation. (For a more detailed discussion of legal aspects, see Chapter 11.)

■ **Human resources (HR)**

Volunteers are often referred to as the cornerstone of any event. Proper planning to recruit, train, recognise and retain these individuals is important in the planning process and will go a long way in ensuring a successful event. However, often on 'game day', organisers can see attrition of volunteers of 20–30%. Free uniforms and the ability to be a spectator with a volunteer credential is enticing to many individuals. An example of this was in 2007 at a North American professional league All-Star Game festivity. Volunteers were asked to pick up their free All-Star game uniform and credential five days before the event, a great memento and keepsake! On All-Star game day, the organisers saw over 45% of its volunteers not show up for their shift. Some events, often those associated with the Professional Golf Association (PGA), charge volunteers to be a part of the event. There is a financial commitment on behalf of the volunteer and they receive their uniform when they arrive prior to the beginning of their first volunteer shift. This approach does not work for all events; however, it has been successful for this circumstance given the number of volunteers *wanting* to be a part of the event. How you set up your volunteer strategy is a key factor in the planning process.

Similar to retention is the loss of key personnel. Whether it be a job change in the process of planning for an event or during the event itself, it is important to implement a strategy of job share and written timelines and processes. Request that each staff member learn each other's jobs and set specific times to share and communicate their role. Often this can lead to better communication, avoid duplication of efforts and allow someone to step into a role immediately if needed. This also emphasises the need for those staff members to have their plan on paper and backed up on computer with similar templates (where possible) provided across the committee for easy interpretation.

While recruiting volunteers and key personnel is an important role for HR managers to assume, they will also be critical in developing the HR policies for employees and volunteers within the organisation/company. HR will work very closely with the legal team or advisor to ensure that standards of employment law are being followed and maintained. They will draft contracts for paid staff and volunteers (when necessary). They must also work closely with the legal department to ensure that policy handbooks are in place for their organisation (for example, staff code of conduct). The HR team will work either independently or with key decision makers to evaluate performance of individuals within the organisation as well. (**For a deeper discussion of human resource management see Chapter 6.**)

■ **Finance**

Identifying budget and revenue streams early on is essential for an event to break even or produce some sort of revenue. At the same time, events can operate at a budget deficit so long as there is a contingency plan to pick up a loss should one occur. This often happens with a large event that has a considerable amount of economic impact and social and political benefit, which far outweighs a potential loss of the event budget. When conducting an analysis to determine if an event is worth staging when there is a loss, it is important to consider that some event organisers will over-estimate the true value of the event because these individuals who provide the data are also those favouring the staging of the event (Kasimati, 2003).

As part of the planning process and strategy, it is important to identify a timetable for costs, similar to what was mentioned earlier in identifying critical dates and tasks. Expenses can begin to accumulate the moment the budget is approved, if not some time before, so it is important to have some money on hand for start-up/operational costs in the early stages. Determining the expenses and revenue needs often ties into the early stages of your strategy by identifying objectives, timelines and scope of work. Often in large-scale events such as the Olympic Games, the initial budget approved is rarely what the end budget looks like. Cost overruns and increases in necessary expenses through a 5–7-year planning process can prove difficult and therefore flexibility is needed (Black, 2012).

Potential revenue streams differ from event to event, and often depend on the venue, type of event, location and its objectives. A proper assessment of potential revenue streams is important and an effective board can be integral in this process. Figure 9.5 offers some examples of revenue streams that can be common across different events.

Further to this, the finance team, or in some cases a senior manager, will monitor and approve all expenses and work with the human resource department to ensure that staff are paid at the appropriate times, in accordance with employment law. As such, the individual(s) in charge of managing the finances must keep a detailed record of accounts payable and receivable. All of these documents need to have the utmost detail, as generally an auditor will review these documents at a pre-determined fiscal year-end. (Chapter 8 offers a more detailed approach to finance.)

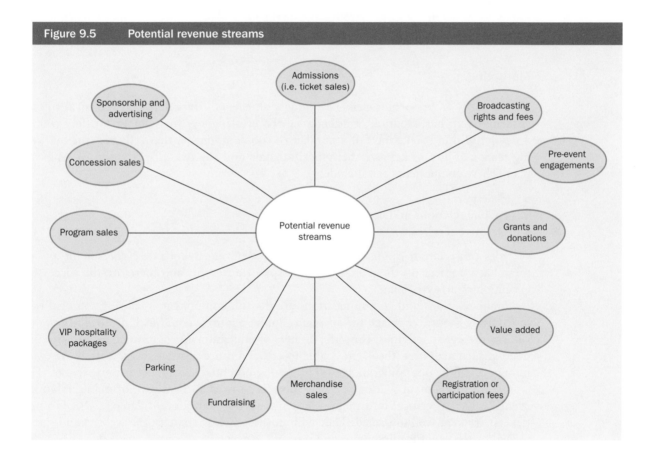

Figure 9.5   Potential revenue streams

■ Contingency planning

Despite hours upon hours spent planning, there are certain acts of God or other unplanned scenarios that may occur that are out of your control. With proper planning and communication protocols in place, you will be able to handle these situations as they develop with minimal impact, awareness and concern of your guests and event. These are called contingency plans and situations often involve human resources or weather, for example.

■ **Weather**

On an annual basis, the weather system continues to be unpredictable. Hurricanes, violent thunder and lightning storms, snow and flooding often create havoc and can also pose a significant **risk management** issue at the same time. Advance planning is important in handling such crises, including cancellation insurance, to protect your investment where and when possible. A related example is an event that required no rain and a totally dry surface in order for the event to successfully commence and avoid significant risk management issues. Although a contingency plan was put on the table, a historical analysis over 99 years of precipitation during this particular week of the year resulted in a total accumulation of 2mm of rain. Essentially there was a better chance of being hit by lightning than for it to rain. Although a loose contingency plan was eventually discussed, four hours prior to the start of the event saw 3mm of rain fall. That was 1mm greater than the total rain accumulated during that week in the past 99 years!

As you can see, it is essential to consistently play the 'what if' game without reaching a level of paranoia. Playing this game and having a contingency strategy in place can go a long way in helping you prepare for the unexpected. (The subject of risk management is returned to in greater detail in Chapter 11.)

■ **Marketing**

Marketing is an important element amongst all events. Marketers play a critical role in ensuring event participation or attendance and creating a positive image for the event as a whole. Within marketing fall a number of sub-components that influence the marketing team's ability to achieve their specific goals and the overall execution of an event plan. These components can include:

- sales;
- public relations and communication;
- creative services.

Sales can relate to sponsorship, advertising or event ticket sales. The sale of any of these has an effect on the overall profitability of an event, and therefore the successful execution of an event plan.

Public relations and communications are the sub-components that play a crucial role in fostering a positive image for an event. Public relations could include ancillary events such as pre-event activities, concerts, dinners or educational/promotional events. By conducting such activities, the event is able to create a more positive image within the community it will be operating in, as well as among potential spectators or participants. The communications team will ensure that those who need to be aware of public relations events as well as critical information (e.g. registration dates, event date(s), where to buy tickets) are kept well informed. They will most likely also manage the website and social media for the event leading up to and during the event.

Creative services works with the entire marketing team to assist in providing them the tools needed to accomplish their goals. This could include the development of a website, event flyers and posters, signage, sales sheets, logos or tickets. All of these items also have an influence on the execution of the event, as they not only allow different team members to achieve their goals within a strategic plan, but can also positively or negatively contribute to the participant/attendee experience.

You can then imagine how important each of these sub-components is to effectively marketing an event. Depending on financial resources available as well as the strategic goals of the event, event managers may want to have their marketing services provided internally, or look to external agencies to assist them with all or some of their marketing initiatives. Depending on the scale of the event, all of these sub-components could also play into video or TV production which could be used in different phases of the event planning process (for example, promotional video, live feed during event day). (Marketing is covered more deeply in Chapter 7, and sponsorship is addressed in greater depth in Chapter 20.)

■ Guest services

Almost every event has some aspect of guest services associated with it. For mass participation events, this could include involving hotels and restaurateurs, VIP areas, ticketing issues and participant questions/complaints, to name a few. For smaller events, this could include setting up an information booth with knowledgeable volunteers to direct attendees and answer any questions they may have.

However, regardless of the size of the event, guest services will always play a vital role in maintaining the positive image and professionalism of your event. It is imperative to have guest service areas staffed with trained and knowledgeable personnel who have excellent customer service skills. A guest services agent has the ability to positively or negatively affect the perception of your event, and thus its ability to attract future participants/attendees.

■ Knowing your clientele and engaging the community

From the outset of planning, it is important to determine your clientele – spectators, participants, officials and even volunteers – and understand their needs and expectations. It is imperative that you continue to assess this area and keep this in mind in all stages of planning and as you continue towards event day. At the same time, depending on your event, a critical assessment of how to engage the community should be addressed in the early process and may even warrant a member of the community or city government as part of your board or management team to fill vital roles in the overall committee structure. Engaging the community is often mistakenly overlooked early in the planning stages, and when it becomes a necessity, it can sometimes be too late. Access to volunteers, police, ambulance and fire services as well as facilities and materials are all key factors in the event planning process. At the same time, events can often draw community concerns, and at times obstacles can be put in the path of staging a well-conceived event. By having an engaged community early on in the process, the organising committee can identify key concerns before they surface. With the right engagement strategy, the community is often a key asset in delivering a successful event rather than a hindrance.

It is important for event managers to understand how each of these common business functions must operate in an integrated manner to achieve goals and objectives as set out by a strategic/event plan. No department can operate in a 'silo' and communication at planning meetings as well as continuous monitoring of tasks and results will help in ensuring that everyone within the event is moving in the same direction.

Going through a planning process similar to the one outlined above is critical to the overall success of an event. The time and attention to details is critical, including having the right people around the table that can best advise you, and who are experts in the field. Although it may seem daunting, this process will help you establish protocol and contingency plans for various elements of the event while staying on budget and on time. A well-thought-out plan will capture the majority of details, and for those surprises on event day, protocol and processes established during the planning process will allow your team to handle any situation as it arises subtly, professionally and in an efficient manner without posing risk to individuals or the event. Risk management is an ongoing factor in all levels of planning and needs to be carefully recognised and discussed with the right individuals every step of the way. It is important to acknowledge that each event is completely different and therefore requires a separate strategic plan; however, a practical approach to each planning process will help streamline the course of action.

Appraising a strategic plan and auditing the planning process

It is important for a strategic auditor to be concerned with not only a strategic plan or document, but also with the planning process. Therefore, building a strategic plan can be very similar to constructing a house. Both endeavours can be very expensive to undertake. In a case where we seek a near-optimal result, we hire expensive specialists such as architects and contractors. A great amount of our own time is consumed in this process, which factors into opportunity cost.

Building a house poorly – and in our case a strategic event plan – can be very costly. If we are unhappy with the building plan, we have wasted our time, and are obliged to redevelop the plan – and in our case set new objectives and goals. Furthermore, the earlier you determine an oversight in the building plan, the easier it is to fix. If oversights and mistakes are not identified until late in the building process, the cost of fixing the problems will multiply. The key to construction and events management is catching oversights and mistakes early and fixing them immediately. Having an independent audit/assessment can save headaches and money later in the project.

Mellalieu (1992) suggests that a strategic auditor can apply lessons from the building industry to the strategic planning process. An internal auditor (homeowner) should apply their own auditing skills at a number of places in the strategic planning cycle:

- *Research*: before the commencement of the strategic planning exercise.
- *Planning*: immediately after the plan has been documented.
- *Implementation*: soon after the plan has begun to be implemented.
- *Evaluation*: a long time after the plan has been implemented.

A strategic plan should be a document that is ever-changing – updated on an annual, or more frequent basis by the senior management team and/or board of directors. As such, it is important to note the importance of auditing a strategic plan within different phases as mentioned above. In order to audit the effectiveness of a strategic plan, event organisers must ensure that there are control mechanisms in place to monitor the plan throughout its entire cycle. As such, there are different considerations at each stage of the planning process that the auditor needs to consider.

■ Stage 1 – Prior to planning exercise

In order to begin to develop a strategic plan, an auditor must be certain that those who are responsible for planning have a thorough understanding of the event. There is no limitation to the amount of information that can be made available to form the foundation of your strategic plan. However, Mellalieu (1992) suggests that one of the most traditional tools in preparing the development of a plan is the SWOT analysis, as discussed earlier in this chapter.

Another factor to consider prior to planning is the need/desire to hire expert strategic planners. Although it is not mandatory to hire expert help, specialist planners can be of benefit in two specific ways (Mellalieu, 1992):

- *Facilitating*: asking strategic questions and not moving on until there is a degree of satisfaction with the answer.
- *Investigating*: obtaining information needed to answer strategic questions.

The decision to hire a planner will most likely be determined upon an organisation's financial capacity, amount of time available and willingness to complete planning activities and the amount of expertise readily available within the organisation. Before investing in a project manager, the organisation responsible for the event must be accountable and undertake some form of planning audit assessment. A third party audit would be the most effective, but unfortunately it is also the most costly. As part of the recommended events management process we have created a 'no cost' self-assessment planning audit that can be used to give your event organisers a snapshot of the effectiveness of the planning completed to date. Based on the results of this snapshot, a decision can be made to either hire a project manager, specialised part-time staff, or, if the planning audit score is sufficiently high, continue with existing staff and/or volunteers. Below is an overview of the six-step planning audit process, but also see Appendix A for the complete Self-Assessment Event Planning Audit Tool.

The planning audit process includes the following six elements:

1. research and market place planning;
2. strategic planning framework;
3. human resources planning;
4. marketing planning;
5. financial, legal and insurance planning;
6. operational planning and evaluation.

■ Stage 2 – Auditing results of planning process

According to Mellalieu (1992), there are at least two results that should come out of strategic planning: (1) a planning document and (2) a stronger appreciation of the organisation (strengths, weaknesses, vision, mission, etc.). This planning document may contain measurable objectives, but oftentimes will have a short-term focus as the objectives may be immediate priorities. The planning document may not contain information about every aspect of the organisation – for example, financial statements. One reason for this omission is that this information is only meant for key decision makers, and the strategic event plan is meant for all within the organisation to see. As an alternative, general financial projections may be included, but full details are not included because each department of the event has its own budget to adhere to. The Event Planning Audit Assessment Tool (Appendix A) will provide you with a list of questions that you may consider utilising when auditing the planning process. Have key assumptions upon which the plan is based been recognised and documented?

It is imperative for the auditor to understand if the key assumptions upon which the plan is based have been recognised and documented. These assumptions could be based on market growth, resource availability or current market conditions, for example. Ensuring that this data is correct is important, as Johnson and Scholes (1989) argue that assumptions that are built into a plan can become fact and therefore unquestioned. This means that certain areas of the plan could be disguised and the reasons for any shortcomings may not be recognised.

A strategic auditor therefore plays an important role in assessing the validity of information presented within a strategic planning document and, therefore, the overall success of the plan in achieving its goals.

■ Step 3 – Implementation of the plan

According to Mellalieu (1992) it is possible to begin auditing the implementation of the plan within three to six months after the planning document was produced. Some key questions that auditors may want to consider at this stage include:

■ Is there a list that assigns people to key responsibilities?
■ Have all (or any) of the top priority tasks been completed?
■ What control systems or processes have been put in place?

Since the auditor is working with a strategic plan rather than an operational plan, it is important to note that at this phase it can be difficult to have measurable results (for example, financial data, market analysis, etc.). The rationale behind conducting an early audit following the development of the strategic planning document is to ensure that all members of the organisation are staying on-task with target dates and tasks.

■ Step 4 – Auditing over the long term

Auditing over the long term (12 months to three years) consists of two approaches: strategic evaluation and strategic control (Sharplin, 1987).

The evaluation component is concerned simply with measuring strategic performance. One aspect of this will certainly be financial evaluation, but could also include performance measures such as sales, profits, increased participation, training protocols or policy development/changes.

The control component is concerned with comparing data produced during the evaluation process, and analysing the differences between targets and results. In events management, this could involve comparing profitability year-over-year, attendance numbers, sponsorship sales, number of volunteers recruited or number of media impressions over following years.

■ Why is it important to audit the strategic plan?

By following the steps previously identified, event managers can ensure that their strategic plan is executed, and targets are achieved to the best of the organisation's abilities. By conducting the audit in different steps of the planning process, event managers and auditors also allow themselves the flexibility to change the strategic plan if needed. Deviation from the strategic plan could come as a result of a change of personnel that are executing tasks within the plan, or alternatively a change in the targets and outcomes of the plan (this could be for a number of reasons including organisational capacity, lack of resources, changes in market place, etc.). By continually auditing the performance of a strategic plan, organisations further allow themselves to be flexible and responsive to an ever-changing event market place.

Case 9.2   Auditing a strategic event plan

Below is a sample of an event strategy document. Please read the strategic document and, using the tool provided (Appendix A), conduct an evaluation of the plan and answer the discussion questions.

The country of Ardistan has funded a non-profit national basketball programme through its Ministry of Sport. As a means of generating sustainable revenue for the organisation, Ardistan Basketball has decided to run a national basketball championship. Understanding that effective planning will be critical to the success of the tournament, Ardistan Basketball developed the following strategic planning document to guide its efforts:

Environmental scan

Ardistan Basketball (AB) has conducted a SWOT (strengths, weaknesses, opportunities, threats) analysis to understand the landscape for basketball in the country.

Strengths:
    Support of national government
    Dedicated volunteers
    Strong support from business community (sponsorship)
    Large pool of athletes to draw on (10,000 members)

Case 9.2 (*continued*)

Weaknesses:
- Have never hosted a tournament of this magnitude
- AB does not have a staff member dedicated to communications
- AB is responsible for all financial commitments (financial risk)

Opportunities:
- Can up-sell current sponsors on event (generate more revenue)
- Creates a new revenue stream for AB
- Video streaming or television coverage of event
- Through online surveys of AB's membership, it was determined that 83% (8,300) members would support the creation of a national championship event

Threats:
- Conflicting needs for gym space
- For-profit sport and recreation companies
- Member clubs hosting tournaments through their provincial association

Vision

To be the premier basketball event in the country of Ardistan

Mission

To grow, sustain, celebrate and promote the sport of basketball in Ardistan

Values

- Keep it fun
- Fair play
- Respect
- Cooperation and collaboration
- Teamwork

Objectives

- Develop a sustainable source of revenue for AB
- Grow the number of citizens participating in basketball
- Celebrate the accomplishments of our nation's athletes

Key strategies

- Identify a unique host city with the capacity to host a tournament of this magnitude
- Create and develop an awards banquet as a part of the overall event
- Secure major sponsorship
- Form an organising committee responsible for the execution of the event and planning process
- Further develop officiating and volunteer training programme across Ardistan

Major goals

- Achieve a minimum profit of $5,000 in year one, increasing profitability by 20% annually
- Secure a minimum of $35,000 in sponsorship
- Grow AB's membership by 15% over three years
- Secure a broadcast/media partner(s)
- Develop policy and procedural handbook for volunteers, officials, coaches and athletes
- Develop training manual for AB volunteers

Strategic action programme

- CEO: Prepare sponsorship package and asset inventory
- CEO: Work with political agencies to apply for grants/additional funding
- CEO: Seek assistance from current media partner to identify broadcast options
- Director, operations: Develop operational plan
- Director, operations: Create bid document to be distributed to member clubs
- Coordinator, development: Create training manuals and handbooks based on AB's established guidelines

▶

Case 9.2	*(continued)*

Discussion questions

4 Are there any elements that could be added to strengthen Ardistan's strategic plan?

5 Do you think that Ardistan should have conducted a PEST analysis? Why or why not?

6 Do you think that Ardistan Basketball could develop an event portfolio? How might the 'portfolio' be different if this organisation runs both programmes and events?

Case 9.2 illustrates well the close link between, on the one hand, the higher level of 'strategy' and, on the other, the more hands-on practitioner approach of 'planning'. We return to the subject of 'planning' in greater detail in Chapter 12, which covers 'Event Operations and Project Management', and gives details of the relevant tools which enable a manager to ensure that strategic objectives are actually met. The reader is advised to refer to this chapter, and also to consider the strategic implications which arise from the design of an event, the topic of Chapter 18.

Conclusion

Effective planning plays a critical role in the successful execution of any event. It is arguably the most important component of events management, as good planning and strategy development encompasses all other departments and business functions of the events management process. Planning and strategy development are the most time-consuming tasks to undertake; however, you will always receive a return on the investment made in planning. Those that execute efficient and effective planning and strategy development are the most successful event organisers.

Given the diversity and competition that exists within the event market place, practitioners will inevitably need to continue to identify creative and innovative ways to execute their events. This could be through the creation of public–private partnerships, hiring of private events management firms or by contracting sub-components of your event to industry experts (not-for-profit or service agencies, for example). Additionally, event managers will need to concern themselves with funding mechanisms. Given the global economic climate, many cities and government-funded programmes are experiencing higher demands for funding requests. As such, they are unable to fund all events, or they are eliminating funding programmes. It will be critical for event managers to consider non-conventional methods, as well as synergistic and mutually beneficial partnerships to access the resources that will make their event(s) sustainable. Engaging in effective planning practices should assist the event manager in ensuring their event's success.

General discussion questions

7 Compile a calendar of critical dates for a high school reunion. Create an organisation chart and job descriptions for key roles that individuals will need to play in order to manage and execute the event properly.

8 You have been asked to organise a youth hockey tournament and have been given $2,500 in starting capital to develop the event and recruit participants. Your facility costs are all offset by the city. How will you use your $2,500 to generate enough revenue for an event you estimate will ultimately cost $10,000?

9 Using Figure 9.3 (the Planning Wheel), select a particular area within an event (e.g. accommodation, transportation, food and beverage, venues, etc.) and place it in the centre of the wheel. Then begin to add details around the wheel and expand out. Have fun peeling back the onion!

10 You are an employee of the City of Zukai. Since 2000, the city has staged a summer food festival that attracts approximately 20,000 people. Throughout the rest of the year, the city also stages the following events: Brazilian Jujitsu Tournament (500 participants), a mass participation obstacle challenge (25,000 participants) and a music festival (1,000 attendees). Briefly outline the common resources and markets that each event would target and summarise how the City of Zukai could potentially develop an event portfolio.

Guided reading

A useful source for studying current strategic issues is the *Sport Business Journal*.

For deeper insight into events strategy, the following are recommended:

Leopkey, B., Mutter, O. and Parent, M.M. (2010) Barriers and facilitators when hosting sporting events: exploring the Canadian and Swiss sport event hosting policies. *International Journal of Sport Policy*, 2(2), 113–34.

Skoultsos, S. and Tsimitakis, E. (2009) Event tourism: statements and questions about its impact on rural areas. University of the Aegean, Interdepartmental Program of Postgraduate Studies in Tourism, Planning, Management and Policy, Research Paper.

Taks, M. et al. (2009) Factors affecting repeat visitation and flow-on tourism as sources of event strategy and sustainability. *Journal of Sport and Tourism*, 14(2–3), 121–42.

More general sources on the strategy process which are recommended are:

Johnson, G., Scholes, K. and Whittington, R. (2008) *Exploring Corporate Strategy* (8th edn). Harlow: Pearson Education.

Tapinos, E., Dyson, R. and Meadows, M. (2011) Does the balanced scorecard make a difference to the strategy development process? *Journal of Operational Research Society*, 62, 888–99.

Recommended websites

Business Development Bank of Canada: **www.bdc.ca/en/advice_centre/articles/Pages/strategic_planning.aspx#.US7n8zApySp**

Canadian Sport Tourism Alliance: **http://canadiansporttourism.com**

Newfoundland and Labrador Strategic Planning Facilitation Guide: **www.ibrd.gov.nl.ca/regionaldev/StratPlanGuide.pdf**

Timeline for Events: **www.timelineforevents.co.uk**

Key words

contingency plan; demographics; economic impact; event portfolio; event tourism; event planning; risk management; strategic plan

Bibliography

Anderson, T. and Getz, D. (2009) Tourism as a mixed industry: differences between private, public and not-for-profit festivals. *Tourism Management,* 30, 847–56.

Black, M. (2012) Winners curse? The economics of hosting the Olympic Games. *CBC News,* 18 July. **www.cbc.ca/news/canada/story/2012//07/18/f-olympic-host-city-economy.html**

Collins, T. and Minnis, R. (2007) Perceived community impacts of event tourism: case study of the 2006 'Hot Wheels Event' hosted in Speed, Kansas. Report, Docking Institute of Public Affairs.

Getz, D. (2005) *Event Management and Event Tourism* (2nd edn). New York: Cognizant Communications Corporation.

Getz, D. (2008) Event tourism: definition, evolution and research. *Tourism Management,* 29, 403–28.

Graham, S., Goldblatt, J. and Delpy, L. (1995) *Ultimate Guide to Sport Event Management and Marketing.* Chicago, IL: Irwin.

Green, B. (2001) Leveraging subculture and identity to promote sport events. *Sport Management Review,* 4(1), 1–19.

Higham, J. (1999) Commentary – sport as an avenue of tourism development: an analysis of the positive and negative impacts of sport tourism. *Current Issues in Tourism,* 2(1), 82–90.

Johnson, H. and Scholes, K. (1989) *Exploring Corporate Strategy.* Englewood Cliffs, NJ: Prentice-Hall.

Kasimati, E. (2003) Economic aspects and the Summer Olympics: a review of related research. *International Journal of Tourism Research,* 3, 433–44.

Mellalieu, P. (1992) Auditing the strategic plan. *Managerial Auditing Journal,* 7(1), 11–16.

Richards, G. and Wilson, J. (2004) The impact of cultural events on city image: Rotterdam, Cultural Capital of Europe 2001. *Urban Studies,* 41(10), 1931–51.

Sharplin, A. (1989) *Strategic Management.* New York: McGraw Hill.

Woo, E. et al. (2011) A Comparative Study of Motivation across Different Festival Products. Report, Pamplin College of Business.

Ziakas, V. and Costa, C. (2011) The use of an event portfolio in regional community and tourism development: creating synergy between sport and cultural events. *Journal of Sport and Tourism,* 16(2), 149–75.

Zukin, S. (1995) *The Culture of Cities.* Oxford: Blackwell.

Appendix A Self-assessment tool

Events management – planning audit

The following is a planning audit assessment that will be used to evaluate the event planning of an organisation. There are six sets of questions that will be evaluated based on a five-point Likert scale. The values on the planning based Likert scale are as follows:

0. Not appropriate
1. Not considered
2. Limited discussion
3. Some discussion and commitment
4. Strong planning commitment
5. Very strong planning commitment

The highest score possible will be 280 points. Any score above 200 is considered an acceptable score and the organisation should be congratulated on a quality event planning effort! Any individual question scores of '#1' should be a concern to the organisation. The organisation needs to spend more time reviewing the impact of the question. Furthermore, if any of the individual six elements scores less than 50%, the organisation should be concerned.

Please read the following statements and write in the most appropriate rating score based on your perception of the organisation's event planning. This planning audit will help assess the state of the organisation's event planning. The overall objective of the audit is to help you and your organisation plan an event that will be as effective as possible.

The planning audit process includes the following six elements:

1. Research and market place planning
2. Strategic planning framework
3. Human resources planning
4. Marketing planning
5. Financial, legal and insurance planning
6. Operational planning and evaluation

Element #1 – Research and market place planning

The organisation has:
1. collected research on similar events prior to selecting the event? ___
2. reviewed local and regional government planning, past events and census documents to assist with the selection and planning of the event ___
3. collected demographic data on your customers/members that will attend the event (e.g. education or age) ___
4. researched psychographic attitudes of the customers and/or members that will attend the event – e.g. attitude or lifestyle ___
5. estimated the event's economic opportunity/capacity in the community and region ___

6. completed a PEST (political, economic, social and technological) analysis to review and segment the market for the event ___
7. defined a set of specific target markets based on criteria like: sizeable, meaningful and reachable ___

Total is out of a possible 35 points _____

Element #2 – Strategic planning framework

The organisation has:

8. completed internal research to assess the capability and unique abilities of the event __
9. discussed and completed a SWOT (strengths, weaknesses, opportunities and treats) analysis for the event ___
10. determined, in detail, the measurable criteria that will be used to determine the success of the event ___
11. completed a strategic plan that includes a 'mission and vision' statement ___
12. determined a set of values that will guide organisational behaviour and decision making __
13. established priorities and short/long-term action plan ___
14. established the necessary governance documents (i.e. conflict of interest guidelines) to effectively plan and manage the event ___
15. established an organisational culture that encourages innovation and new ideas ___

Total is out of a possible 40 points _____

Element #3 – Human resource planning

The organisation has:

16. designed the event's organisational structure based on the research and the strategic planning of the organisation ___
17. established control measures that have been put in place to ensure operations and decision making will be implemented effectively ___
18. identified a champion that provides the necessary leadership and motivation to be successful ___
19. provided all committees with clear terms of reference ___
20. meetings that have an agenda, minutes/action items and start and finish on time ___
21. established all the necessary risk management systems, policies and procedures, ensuring the event will be safe and sustainable ___
22. created job descriptions for all staff and volunteers ___
23. all the necessary policies and procedures to guide the event planning and operation ___
24. a customer/membership strategy to effectively communicate the benefits and opportunities of the event ___
25. established goals and measureable objectives that are communicated to staff and volunteers ___

Total is out of a possible 50 points _____

Element #4 – Marketing planning

The organisation has:

26. taken the time to assess ALL possible revenue generating opportunities for the event ___

27. researched and formally contacted all suppliers that could have a stake in the event ___
28. identified a series of target markets identified for the marketing and sales of the event – i.e. tickets or programmes ___
29. developed a polished sponsorship presentation and a comprehensive list of possible businesses that may want to sponsor the event ___
30. developed a detailed sales strategy to maximise all potential revenue generating opportunities ___
31. identified new partners and stakeholders that might be interested in the event ___
32. positioned the event effectively with the community, region and the industry ___
33. an event pricing strategy that includes a series of incentives and discounts ___
34 a customer service, coaching and training programme for all staff and volunteers ___
35. established an effective promotional strategy that includes: media, brand development, a website and a social media strategy ___

Total is out of a possible 50 points _____

Element #5 – Financial, legal and insurance planning

The organisation has:
36. developed a realistic operational budget that is reviewed regularly ___
37. reviewed its insurance needs and has at least adequate insurance for the event ___
38. managed the assets of the organisation and the event as effectively as possible ___
39. developed an effective cash management system ___
40. a comprehensive capital budget process that includes post-event plans ___
41. been financially responsible by maximising event profit margins wherever possible ___
42. reviewed all the legal issues and developed a plan of action (i.e. commercial and sponsorship rights and tax planning) ___
43. established an event Balance Sheet and Income Statement that is clear, simple and has been updated regularly ___
44. used financial ratios in an effort to understand the financial impact of organisational decision making (i.e. profit margins on sales and inventory turnover)

Total is out of a possible 45 points _____

Element #6 – Operational planning and evaluation

The organisation has:
45. a written event operational plan that had been updated recently ___
46. planned the event with environmental sensitivity (e.g. food hygiene, waste collection) ___
47. a strategy to ensure security and maintenance are well planned and budgeted ___
48. planned for the 'extra touch' – atmosphere, fan/customer involvement, personal service, etc. ___
49. a detailed communication plan that includes effective signage __
50. customer service policies that include a specific complaint procedure ___
51. events management policies and procedures that contain a full range of emergencies including: major injury, fire, bomb threat ___
52. plans to collect data from customers at the event to improve future events ___
53. established a contingency plan for the event challenges and obstacles ___
54. determined a method to measure event success – i.e. success indicators ___
55. complied with all environmental compliance issues in the area ___
56. an economic impact formula to measure the impact of the event ___

Total is out of a possible 60 points _____

Business planning audit assessment summary

Six elements		Total score is out of	Total score (over 200 is acceptable)	Listing of all #1 answers
1	#1 Research and market place	35 points		
2	#2 Strategic planning	40 points		
3	#3 Human resources	50 points		
4	#4 Marketing planning	50 points		
5	#5 Finance planning	45 points		
6	#6 Operations and evaluation	60 points		
	Overall totals	280 points		

General comments and recommendations

(*Note*: Any score less than 50% for any of the six elements needs to be explained)

_____

_____

_____

_____

Organisational decision-making criteria

Low score – Need to commit to significant planning and consider hiring a project manager

Medium score – More planning is required, specialised part-time support staff may need to be hired

High score – Congratulations! You are doing an excellent job of planning and may have the opportunity to manage the event internally

Action plan moving forward

_____

_____

_____

_____

_____

_____

Guideline answers

Guiding answer to Question 1:
- Table 9.3 should be considered for use
- Figure 9.4 should be considered to create an organisational chart

Guiding answer to Question 2:
- Answers could consist of:
    - Registrations
    - Sponsorships
    - Advertising
    - Hotel commissions
    - Spectator fees

Guiding answer to Question 3:
Answers will vary based on area of responsibility selected. Respondents should have three tiers of answers:

- Tier 1:
    - Area of responsibility, e.g. food and beverage
- Tier 2:
    - Stakeholders, procedures, processes involved, e.g. suppliers, deliveries
- Tier 3:
    - Specific tasks, e.g. pick up Styrofoam cups

Guiding answer to Question 4:

- Common resources could include:
    - Sponsors
    - Media
    - City staff:
        - communications
        - parks and recreation
        - tourism
        - economic development
    - Service organisations:
        - destination marketing organisation
        - volunteer agencies
    - Fencing
    - Free-standing temporary toilets and sanitation
    - Staging
    - Transportation
    - Marketing mechanisms
        - TV, radio
        - magazines

- Common target markets might include:
  - Male 18–35
  - Female 18–35
- Some ways to create an event portfolio:
  - Combine events into same week(end)
  - Create a summer music series (new concerts attach themselves to existing events)
  - Combine all events under one event 'umbrella': for example, Zukai Summer Fest
  - Allow the city to organise and source each event's logistics (bulk buy discounts)

Part 3
Management issues specific to the events sector

Chapter 10

Sustainable events management

Cheryl Mallen and Chris Chard, Brock University, Canada

Learning outcomes

Upon completion of this chapter the reader should be able to:

- identify key forms of interaction in event environmental, economic and socio-cultural spheres of sustainability and key members in event **sustainability citizenship**;

- apply the key forms of sustainability to events management using the resource-based view, the behavioural-based view and **appreciative theory**;

- explain the contemporary environmental situation, the impact of events on the natural environment and the subsequent consequences;

- outline management techniques for measuring impacts of events;

- critically examine event sustainability cases and develop strategies for arising issues and advances in sustainability.

Overview

This chapter begins with a brief introduction to sustainability before diverse meanings within the concept of sustainability are discussed. This is followed by a definition specifically for sustainable events management and a discussion on the resource-based and behavioural-based theoretical lens in events management sustainability. Next, a discussion is provided on sustainable citizenship in events management that includes an adaptation of the United Nations guiding principles to guide managers when applying sustainability. Further, a section on measuring sustainability is outlined, including an overview of seven types of measurement strategies, including the corporate environmental management (CEM) model, the triple bottom line (TBL), the triple top line (TTL), the balanced scorecard (BSC), life cycle assessment (LCA), carbon footprint method and the sport event environmental performance measure (SE-EPM). Finally, a short discussion on case studies pertaining to managing events for sustainability is offered. This discussion includes the application of appreciative theory and the case discussion framework that includes Kallio and Nordberg's (2006) fundamental questions. These questions concern what is being done for event sustainability, if the actions are correct to generate sustainable events management, where the barriers exist and what can be done to overcome the barriers. Four case studies are outlined to illustrate key issues concerning offsetting the impacts of events towards sustainability prior to the conclusions.

There are four case studies outlined in this chapter and each offers questions to guide a discussion. These questions have been framed with an adaptation of Kallio and Nordberg's (2006) fundamental questions on sustainability. These questions are offered to extend the discussions and include:

- What are we doing in events management with respect to sustainability?
- Are we doing things correctly to generate sustainable events management?
- Where are the barriers when attempting to generate sustainable events management?
- What can be done in the future to hurdle over these barriers towards sustainability?

In addition, the case studies are also framed with appreciative theory or 'a paradigm of thought and understanding that holds organisations to be affirmative systems created by humankind as solutions to problems' (Watkins and Cooperrider, 2000: 6). This means that a positive lens is promoted (Cooperrider, 1986, 2008) or the concept of a 'glass half full' is used in discussions that can lead to an exploration of possibilities and potential actions instead of focusing on the negative aspects (van Buskirk, 2002; Grant and Humphries, 2006). In events management, this lens is a tool for evaluating the environmental, social and financial constructs of event sustainability that can emphasise the identification of strengths and can encourage the building of conceptual ideas for advancing event sustainability (Koster and Lemelin, 2009).

It is our belief that there is a paradigm shift occurring in events management whereby sustainability is being implemented. However, the case studies provided indicate that this shift has not been easy, as sustainability is challenging and complex (Heugens, 2006; DeTombe, 2008). There are plenty of emerging issues in the implementation of sustainability strategies. The case studies are offered to illustrate the complexity and difficulties in instituting sustainability in events management and to encourage debate on conceptual directions that can be generated for sustainability within the events management industry.

Introduction to sustainability

It has been noted that 'environmental concerns have now moved from being a fringe issue to becoming a major socio-economic issue' (Sandhu et al., 2010: 356). Further, a movement for sustainability has been promoted in the authoritative 2007 United Nations Environment Programme (UNEP) report called the *Global Environment Outlook 4: Summary for Decision Makers* which states that we are on a path of unsustainable land, forest and water use and the production of pollution that impacts on world societies, including the multiple cultures and their financial stability. In addition, a need for sustainability is promoted by the authoritative Intergovernmental Panel on Climate Change (IPCC, 2007) that outlines the progression of climate change, the way humans degrade the Earth and the subsequent impacts.

No field of endeavour is immune from affecting the environment. This means that events management impacts on the Earth. The impacts stem from activities such as the use of non-renewable energy at event conference centres, the overuse of paper and packaging, the impact of travel and more. Those in events management need to understand sustainability, including defining the concept and the application of theory to practice. Further, it is important to understand that sustainability encompasses multiple integrated components, spheres or dimensions that include the environment, economics and socio-cultural issues (GEO4, 2007). These three conceptual spheres require 'learning to think in new ways, generating a mindset that thrives in uncertain and complex conditions' (Mitchell and Saren, 2008: 408). Indeed, this complexity makes sustainability difficult to put into practice due to the breadth and depth of the topic. This difficulty begins in the definition stage as a comprehensive definition needs to be generated for every field, including events management. A discussion on defining events management sustainability is offered next.

Defining sustainability for events management

Sustainability can be a vague term to understand as it has multiple meanings and degrees of complexity depending on the context in which it is used. A standard definition of sustainability, used throughout the world, has been established by the United Nations (UN) Brundtland Report (1987: 1). This report posits that sustainability involves the overall capacity of an organisation to 'meet the needs of the present generation without compromising the ability of the future generations to meet their own needs'. It has been found, however, that the definition of sustainability continues to require clarity concerning understandings of the application of the term. In an effort to provide some clarity, Peattie (1999: 133) indicates that sustainability encompasses two principles:

First, only using the earth's resources at a rate which allows them to be regenerated, or (in the case of non-renewable resources) which allow sustainable substitutes to be developed. Secondly, it involves creating waste at a rate that can be assimilated by the environment, without impairing it.

Clearly, sustainability encompasses multiple stages of environmental protection and stewardship; this includes the extent of resource utilisation, resource regeneration and, ultimately, the capacity and capability to manage the waste generated by modern society. Indeed, Iles (2008) indicates that sustainability involves three categories: production conditions; product characteristics and performance; and exposures and risks. The first category, *production conditions,* involves how a product is made and if this process is sustainable for the natural environment. The second category, *product characteristics and performance,* concerns the constituent elements used to create a product and the resultant impacts of this creation on the natural environment; this category also concerns the role that this product fulfils. Finally, the third category, *exposures and risks,* is concerned with the pathways, or supply chains, of particular products and the fact they could expose humans to chemical risks through production, transportation and consumption. These three categories encompass a myriad of components that apply to events management and indicate that sustainable events management involves consideration of the spectrum of potential environmental impacts that need to be managed in order to safeguard the natural environment. Standards for environmental sustainability in events management, however, have not been formalised or legally enacted. Consequently, environmental sustainability is a fluid process.

Further, events management needs to expand the definition for sustainability to include both socio-cultural and financial/economic impacts of environmental activities. The practices employed to reduce or offset an event's impacts thus must consider the current needs and how they can be met without restricting the opportunities of future event managers or producers, cultures, societies and their economies. As such, a suitable definition of events management sustainability needs to be multi-dimensional.

In this text, sustainability for events management is defined utilising an adaptation of Kaspar's (1998) multi-dimensional definition. Events management sustainability is the capacity of an event to provide 'economic development that serves current needs without having a negative impact on future generations. In other words, it reflects an improvement of the quality of life within the capacity of an ecosystem. It comprises economic, social [cultural] and environmental dimensions' (Kaspar, 1998: 67).

Consequently, those managing an event must determine how to specifically apply a definition of sustainability to their situation. It is also necessary to determine the threats and opportunities that could arise from this particular selected engagement with sustainability.

Theories provide different lenses through which to view definitions that can aid in answering questions; in this case, the definition and questions concern interpretations of sustainability. This means that framing a definition or different questions with various theories can present different answers. The differing answers can be used to generate multiple insights for formulating a definition, providing an answer or choosing a solution to a problem. Two theories will be used as examples in this chapter: the resource-based view and the behavioural-based view.

Case 10.1 The International Children's Games water bottle programme

The 42nd International Children's Games (ICG) were held in 2008 in San Francisco, California, USA. The 1,200 male and female elite athletes, aged 12 to 15 years, represented six continents from around the world.

The ICG was determined to eliminate the use of disposable water bottles at the Games. Each participant was given a refillable water bottle upon arrival and refill stations were plentiful throughout the multiple venues used for the Games. The refillable water bottle programme was outlined in the written material provided to each participant and announced at the opening ceremonies.

On the first day, a large number of youth participants, and their accompanying adult supervisors, forgot to bring their refillable water bottles. The ICG ran out and purchased small paper cups that were placed at the water stations so the participants would learn to utilise the refillable water programme. These cups resulted in water spills throughout the venues and at the outdoor sites the cups were blown around by the wind, adding to the spillage. Announcements were made for participants to remember to bring their refillable bottles. The interpreters assigned to the various groups of participants were asked to make announcements in multiple languages to encourage participants to remember to carry their refillable water bottles with them. The next day was hot and sunny, and again, many of the youth participants and their adult supervisors did not bring their refillable water bottles. The ICG purchased disposable water bottles for distribution at the venues and again reminded participants to refill these bottles for the day only and to bring their refillable water bottles in the future. A trend began whereby the participants now expected to be provided with a disposable water bottle. Further, participants began to pester the catering services staff to put out disposable water bottles that the participants could take with them after each meal. After numerous more announcements and reminders (in a variety of languages), the catering staff was instructed to put out the disposable water bottles.

Despite considerable efforts, the elimination of disposable water bottles was not fully successful.

Discussion questions

1 What are the benefits of a refillable water bottle programme and should efforts be made to encourage participants to utilise refillable water bottles?

2 What part do various countries' cultural and/or societal norms play in the participation in a refillable water bottle programme?

3 How would you design a future response to this water distribution situation in order to encourage participants to utilise the refillable water bottles?

Resource-based theory and sustainability in events management

In events management, the resource-based theoretical view is concerned with generating a 'persistent superior . . . performance using . . . resources as a unit of analysis' (Barney and Arikan, 2001: 134). This means that sustainability is linked to the resources available, how the resources are utilised, if an advantage can be achieved based on how each resource is managed and if a superior economic performance can be obtained with the manner in which the resources are being utilised. This theory makes the assumption that the management of resources is fundamental to achieving sustainability. Determining how to specifically apply a selected definition of sustainability would, therefore, focus on the management of an event's resources.

Behavioural-based theory and sustainability in events management

In events management, the behavioural-based theoretical view is concerned with an event's 'goals, expectations and choice' (Bowen, 2007: 98). This means that event managers must pay attention to the issue of sustainability based on the resources that are available to manage the issue (Bowen, 2007). Consequently, event managers have the discretion to define sustainability and to determine how to apply the definition to a particular event. Further, event managers and their management team or board of directors need to be aware of the politics or pressures within the event organisation when determining how social, financial and environmental sustainability will be viewed and applied to the event, taking into consideration the event's objectives. Indeed, the introduction of sustainability objectives may establish priorities which conflict with other event objectives. Differing objectives compete for time, attention, resources and create a difficult managerial challenge. Research indicates that when managers face multiple priorities (in this case events management objectives as well as sustainability objectives) they tend to concentrate on 'day-to-day objectives like efficiency and effectiveness, at the expense of the longer term gain' (Ghobadian et al., 2001: 384). The **behavioural-based theory** perspective indicates that event managers can use personal and organisational choice or decision making concerning what they aspire to achieve and what needs to be sacrificed in the process of striving to achieve successful social, financial and environmental sustainability.

It is also necessary to review how the events management leaders are involved in the decision making regarding sustainable events management.

Case 10.2	The 2010 Vancouver Olympic Games and the snow conditions

The 2010 Vancouver-Whistler Games Bid Book submitted in 2001 outlined the Games' environmental sustainability commitments and the subsequent environmental decisions made at the Games.

The Vancouver Organizing Committee for the 2010 Olympic and Paralympic Winter Games (VANOC), indicated that the 2010 Games would be conducted using resource conservation, pollution prevention, natural system protection and enhancement, waste management and greenhouse gas management.

The 2010 Games joined the International Olympic Committee's (IOC) Global Impact Project. This Project was initiated in 2003 and aimed to measure and report on Olympic Games environmental protection commitments. This programme comprised a number of elements, including monitoring air and water quality, and was expected to be an undertaking of over 10 years of measurement assessments. This marked a substantial movement towards ensuring that an environmental commitment was enacted.

The weather at the Games did not cooperate. The year after the Olympics, the Nordic ski area saw record snowfalls; however, in 2010, the snow did not fall as hoped. What snow did fall, along with the

Case 10.2	*(continued)*

warm weather, was not conducive to excellent Nordic race conditions. The snow was wet and tended to stick to the bottom of the skis, slowing the racers. To improve snow conditions, the organisers decided to spread tonnes of fertiliser. The fertiliser made the snow harder and more in line with the Games' race condition requirements (Robinson, 2010).

The use of fertiliser proved to be a misstep in terms of environmental sustainability as it generated biodiversity challenges. This area was an old growth forest with wetlands, a series of ponds with rare frogs and a bear habitat. During the snow melt, the fertiliser entered the water system and had 'a negative effect on wetlands, particularly ponds where it accumulates and contributes to algae growth . . . killing the pond, harming mammals . . . and contaminating drinking water' (Robinson, 2010: para. 19). Further, the fertiliser encouraged meadow growth creating excellent conditions for bears – whereby spring skiers and bear contact should be expected (Robinson, 2010).

Nevertheless, VANOC quickly determined that the condition of the snow was not conducive to support Olympic and world records. Although there were commitments to safeguard the natural environment, fertilisers were utilised to improve snow conditions.

Discussion questions

4 Under what circumstances should Olympic Games organisers disregard environmental commitments for the sake of athlete competition conditions? If there is a hierarchical order for event objectives is the environment secondary?

5 Can the competition conditions and environmental sustainability go hand-in-hand? What solutions could be generated that satisfy both?

6 Apply the resource-based theoretical view and then the behavioural-based theoretical view to generate different options to solve this case issue.

Sustainable citizenship in events management

Bateman and Organ (1983) presented the term 'organisational citizenship' to apply to individual citizens, and/or groups made up of individual citizens, who use discretionary behaviours to positively impact their organisation beyond the specific requirements of their job. So . . . who are the citizens promoting sustainability in events management? In the context of the current discussion, 'sustainable citizenship' would likewise apply to individuals or groups of individuals who contribute positively to environmental, economic and socio-cultural organisational initiatives. Therefore, it is argued that the term 'sustainable event citizenship' might logically be coined to describe any person involved in the events industry who exhibits care, concern and actions – beyond the minimum requirements – for event sustainability. An implication is that 'sustainable event citizenship' embodies the full spectrum of those involved in events, including facility staff, event production staff and volunteers, the consumers of events, the media, government partners, sponsors and other event stakeholders. Further, 'sustainable event citizenship' can come from any of the multiple sectors within the industry, such as marketing, human resources, accounting and legal. These sustainable event citizens are responsible for creating, performing, monitoring and managing the policies and directions taken by the event.

To help guide sustainable event citizens in their role, the United Nations' principles for sustainability education were adapted to generate six guiding principles for events management, including:

> **Principle 1:** To generate a high level of value for the concept of sustainability in all sectors of the events management field. This includes valuing and working towards instituting sustainability in events management.

Principle 2: To be concerned with the application of the international sustainability initiatives outlined in the United Nations Global Compact within the field of events management. These initiatives can be found at *www.unglobalcompact.org* under the icon: Blueprint for Corporate Sustainability Leadership.

Principle 3: To be involved in the development of educational frameworks and the necessary supporting materials to generate sustainability leadership, new thinking and a mindset for sustainability in events management.

Principle 4: To advance research that aids in understanding the need, the impact and the directions taken for sustainable environmental, economic and social-cultural value in events management.

Principle 5: To develop partnerships to aid in meeting the arising challenges of sustainable events management.

Principle 6: To generate dialogue and debate concerning definitions of sustainability, sustainable event citizenship and how to move the agenda forward in sustainable events management.

With respect to this final principle, it is important to note that 'sustainable event citizenship' has not yet been fully reflected upon and debated. We would certainly encourage debate on this concept including discussion on such questions as:

1. How do the multiple sectors in the events management industry relate to sustainable event citizenship?
2. What role does each sector play in sustainable event citizenship?
3. What role could one personally play in advancing sustainable event citizenship?

It is evident that the relatively embryonic stage of event sustainability, and the acknowledged vagueness of the concept, gives rise to much discussion on creating sustainable events. This discussion is a necessity if event sustainability is to be developed further and, in so doing, the ability to *measure* sustainability is generated which can then be utilised to create benchmarks and set goals for future improvements in event sustainability. Accordingly, a discussion on measuring sustainability follows.

Case 10.3   Sustainable event volunteer education

The Festival of Recording Artists Together (FRAT) is a conceptual case that considers the education and training of volunteers for their roles at a forthcoming large-scale event.

FRAT was established by a group of successful recording artists and an events management student, Mark Robertson, as a means of 'giving back' to the music industry. FRAT, a charitable organisation that is run by Robertson, operates one concert each year to achieve its strategic objectives including: (1) raising funds for developing musicians; (2) promoting new musical artists; and (3) promoting a passion for the earth and its people through the love of music.

On an annual basis, FRAT produces a concert to meet the strategic objectives of the organisation. The concert is nomadic in that it takes place at a new site – all over the United States – each year in order to enhance the breadth of organisational touch-points with fans, musicians and corporate America. The festival is a one-day event and always occurs on Memorial Day in May. Typically, the event attracts in excess of 50,000 people. Wherever possible the charity is interested in enhancing operations to become more efficient while maintaining the strategic objectives of the organisation.

Robertson is charged with managing the annual festival with a full-time staff of three individuals and five contract employees. Given the size of the event, there is an obvious need for human resource assistance; in 2009 there were 600 accredited volunteers. Historically, the budget for training volunteers has been significant – over $10,000 – and relatively inefficient. The model for volunteer training over the past decade has been to gather the volunteers at off-site venues (often hotel conference rooms), for a one-day training session approximately two weeks prior to the event. The five contract staff members

▶

Case 10.3 *(continued)*

operate one training venue each, broken into geographical segments to make it easy for volunteers to attend one of the sessions. Essentially, one staff member operates a downtown (central) volunteer training session while the other four staff members manage a location to the north, south, east and west of the central location. Some training venues may attract as few as 50 volunteers while some will have in excess of 150, making planning a challenge. Predominantly, the training session involves a PowerPoint presentation with additional video footage to augment the presentation. Attendance at one of the training sessions is mandatory. Individuals who do not attend a volunteer training session are not given accreditation to work at the FRAT concert. Once the individuals receive their accreditation at the end of the one-day training session, they are given a FRAT Volunteer shirt that they will be required to wear at the Memorial Day event.

One of the FRAT staff members has recently approached Robertson with a proposal to change the volunteer training model. It is the belief of this individual that everything that is covered at the five separate training sites could be included in an e-learning module. The e-learning module would cost approximately $10,000 to develop but would remove the need for on-site training venues.

Robertson is intrigued by the idea of implementing an e-learning volunteer training model but needs to weigh the pros and cons of altering a system of volunteer training that has served the FRAT organisation well over the past 10 years. Some logistical considerations are weighing on his mind as he contemplates this organisational shift (i.e. logistics of volunteer uniform dissemination). Consider the benefits and drawbacks of the case at hand.

Discussion questions

7 List the potential benefits of implementing an e-learning volunteer training programme and the potential impact on the event environmental sustainability training.

8 What are some of the drawbacks of this type of learning programme?

9 Are there other viable volunteer training options (aside from the e-learning or existing model) you can think of that would be viable?

Measuring sustainability

Peter Drucker (1999) is credited with the old management adage that states: 'If you do not measure it, you cannot manage it?' Adopting this maxim and applying it to the concept of 'sustainable event citizenship' provides an excellent starting place for understanding the current state of sustainability, and the future advances that are needed for sustainable events management. A number of methods for measuring sustainability are available to event managers and have been outlined in previous research. These sustainability measuring strategies include: the corporate environmental management (CEM) model; the triple bottom line (TBL); the triple top line (TTL); the balanced scorecard (BSC); life cycle assessment (LCA); the carbon footprint method; the licence model of environmental performance; and the sport event-environmental performance measure (SE-EPM). Each of these sustainability measuring strategies is outlined below.

1 The corporate environmental management (CEM) model

The corporate environmental management (CEM) model by Raufflet (2006) guides organisations to rate their sustainability efforts. The evaluation is based on three interconnected paradigms: *incremental, adaptive* and *radical*. According to Raufflet, if an organisation is at the *incremental* level of sustainability then the organisation exhibits a low-level approach to reducing environmental impacts. If an organisation is at the *adaptive* level, then the organisation reflects a medium-level approach to reducing environmental impacts, involving rethinking their practices to align an organisation with its natural environment. If an organisation is at the *radical* level of sustainability then the organisational management team has completed a high level of transformation within the production and consumption systems in order to synchronise its functions to safeguard the natural environment. Paquette et al. (2011) expanded upon these three categories and stated that if an organisation is at the *detrimental paradigm* then it has shown a disregard for the safeguarding of the natural environment and can be rated as being harmful with respect to sustainability.

When making a decision concerning which paradigm an organisation is at with respect to sustainability, Raufflet suggested the use of five questions that can be asked. The combined answers to these questions help to generate a decision on the paradigm – incremental, adaptive, radical or detrimental – that the organisation has achieved. These five questions have been adapted for events management as follows:

1. How does the organisation frame the sustainability issue in its correspondence or communications – does it meet the incremental, adaptive, radical or detrimental paradigms?
2. What are the organisational assumptions used in their sustainability actions – do they meet the incremental, adaptive, radical or detrimental paradigms?
3. What are the sustainability expectations that result from the assumptions – which paradigm do they fall within?
4. Does the organisation consider the natural environment as a source of supplies, as a dumping ground or as an overall living habitat?
5. What organisational examples can be found that illustrate the incremental, adaptive, radical or detrimental paradigms?

■ 2 The triple bottom line (TBL)

In business, the 'bottom line' has long been regarded as the litmus test for organisational success or failure. 'What's the bottom line?' asks management to communicate whether organisational efforts have succeeded in producing an excess of revenues over expenses on the Income Statement. It is a financially motivated metric. The TBL adapts and expands upon this financial metric to include social and environmental measures in the analysis framework, creating 'a new measurement of corporate performance' (McDonough and Braungart, 2002: 251). Essentially, the TBL prescribes that organisations must recognise and manage all of the costs associated with their activities, including social, environmental and financial. Stated more succinctly, the TBL encourages organisations to track and account for the 3P's: people, the planet and profits.

■ 3 The triple top line (TTL)

The triple top line (TTL) was designed to expand upon the traditional measurement and reporting frameworks to include a more holistic view of organisational effectiveness and expand upon the work of the TBL. The point of departure from the TBL is that the TTL moves 'accountability to the beginning of the design process' (McDonough and Braungart, 2002: 252). Managers utilising a TTL approach hope to integrate sustainability into every facet of planning for product or service development. For event managers, this could include site location selection, transportation decisions, seasonal hosting decisions, payment and registration options, or any other 'up-front' determinations.

■ 4 The balanced scorecard (BSC)

The balanced scorecard (BSC) was initially designed by Kaplan and Norton (1996) as a management reporting tool and developed into a 'strategic management system that aims to clarify strategy and to translate it into action (Braam and Nijssen, 2004: 335).

The foundational concept guiding the BSC is that managers cannot adopt an unwavering focus on an organisation's financial considerations at the expense of other detriments of success. In the BSC intangible assets such as processes, customer loyalty and organisational learning are of equal importance to financial outcomes.

A distinct benefit of the BSC is its functionality and adaptability to organisations of any size, geographic location, industry sector, profit motive or strategic desire. Considering the last point, having the flexibility to design a balanced scorecard that factors environmental sustainability in the metrics of measurement makes this tool one of great utility. Indeed, Epstein and Wisner (2001) argued that environmental factors can be built into any one of the four BSC areas, or integrated as a fifth stand-alone category. Figge et al. (2002), as well as Moller and Schaltegger (2008), offer similar perspectives suggesting the creation of a sustainability BSC.

Clearly, there is a growing desire and capability to integrate sustainability metrics into existing management measurement systems. For event managers, the BSC offers the flexibility to create sustainable initiatives within the assessment of an event thereby providing knowledge of best practices for use by future event managers.

5 Life cycle assessment (LCA)

In the life cycle assessment (LCA) process, a full and accurate accounting of the environmental impact of a service or product is calculated (Glavič and Luckman, 2007). The assessment is concerned with the whole lifecycle from the 'natural resource extraction through manufacturing, distribution use, and disposal' (Suzuki, 2010: 3). This assessment aids in advancing awareness of the current impact of an event or service on sustainability and in generating understanding of the options to improve the sustainability of the service or product. The calculations begin in the design and development stages and include the use of elements such as the raw materials, energy and the generation of by-products, including waste and emissions. Also, the calculations include the impact of the by-products on societies (for example, does the waste get dumped in a developing world site?). Next, the LCA continues through the packaging and transportation stage, if applicable. Finally, the LCA assesses the end stage of the service or product. The LCA regards all the stages as being interdependent – each stage impacts on the sustainability of the service or product and the leadership at each stage generates a portion of the environmental impact. The consideration of the whole life of a service or product has been considered the 'cradle to grave' cycle; however, recently, this has been adapted to a 'cradle to cradle' cycle – showing an openness to the process in nature whereby by-products are re-purposed. The LCA provides an opportunity to learn about the current process of production and to determine options for adapting methods to ensure the advance of sustainability.

6 Carbon footprint method

'With growing awareness of elevated carbon dioxide levels and climate change, attention is turning to individual behaviour' (Padgett et al., 2008: 106) or to the behaviours of groups of individuals, as is the case with events. The principle underlying the carbon footprint method is that emissions produced by an individual or event can be calculated. Subsequently, offsets can be purchased to mitigate the effects of one's carbon footprint to create a system of environmental balance or neutrality. Indeed, today, 'carbon neutrality is in, and is being advertised worldwide as an effective means for consumers to take action on global warming' (Trexler and Kosloff, 2006: 34). Examples of event managers adopting footprint analyses and instigating offset initiatives are growing, including tree planting efforts by Super Bowl committees (Babiak and Wolfe, 2006; Falt,

2006), investment in hydro-electric plants by an NBA team (Fenton, 2010), Olympic committees' utilisation of low or no emission vehicles (Roper, 2006) or simply instituting price increases to offset carbon emissions (Laing and Frost, 2010).

The carbon footprint method of measuring sustainability is not without its challenges as the consistency and transparency of the myriad of calculators available in the market place is wanting (Padgett et al., 2008). However, the benefit of measuring organisational footprints is invaluable 'for estimating CO_2 emissions and for providing information that can lead to behavioural and policy changes' (Padgett et al., 2008: 113) to enhance the sustainability of events.

7 The sport event-environmental performance measure (SE-EPM)

The sport event environmental performance measurement (SE-EPM) model by Mallen et al. (2010) provides a comprehensive framework for evaluating a sport event's environmental performance. The model is significant because it offers a comprehensive measure based on both the environmental management performance and the environmental operational performance themes and subsequent sub-themes. Specifically, the SE-EPM involves an easy-to-use and inexpensive process whereby a self-rating or third-party rating of the sport event is based on a five-point Likert scale (1 as low and 5 as high). A rating out of five is generated for each of the sub-themes. First, the environmental management performance is evaluated and the coding sub-themes include how the event defines environmental sustainability, the environmental organisational system (including environmental policies and organisational structure), stakeholder environmental disclosure and relationships and operational countermeasures. In addition, the SE-EPM includes the coding theme of environmental operational performance. A rating for this second theme is generated by rating the following sub-themes: environmental tracking (including elements such as energy use, waste, water drainage, air and water pollution, greenhouse gases and compliance) and measuring of environmental inputs (such as the usage of oil, gas, electricity, water, paper, chemicals) along with environmental outputs (tonnage of general waste, carbon dioxide emissions, sulphur oxide emissions, water drainage and chemical waste). Importantly, the items being rated must be described in terms of how they were measured and what was measured so that there is a record for future comparison. Then the rating numbers for the environmental organisational system are tallied. Next the rating numbers for the environmental operational performance sub-themes are tallied and the average score out of five for both themes provides a measure of the sport event's environmental performance. The aim is to provide feedback concerning where an organisation is doing well with respect to sustainability and where further work needs to be completed.

Case 10.4 **Capital planning for sustainable event managers**

This case considers the role of a conceptual capital investment and the necessary decision making on such expenditure for a sustainable event manager.

Peter Collins is a sustainable event consultant with his own business – Evergreen Events Management (EEM) – that is dedicated to helping event managers implement sustainable event practices. Typically, the working engagements for EEM focus on operational augmentations (improving efficiencies and reducing waste) to improve event sustainability. However, recently Collins was approached with an interesting assignment. The President of SportzRinkz Ltd, Ken Douglas, wants Collins to assess the merits of a capital improvement project that, if completed, would enable SportzRinkz Ltd to host the Amateur Sports Association's (ASA) Summer Hockey National Championships (SHNC).

SportzRinkz Ltd is a company that specialises in ice hockey arena operations. The company is based in Basingtown, with a population of 180,000 people. SportzRinkz Ltd has been in operation for over 20 years. For the first decade of the company's existence there were no competitors offering a similar

Case 10.4 *(continued)*

service; however, the most recent decade has seen a proliferation of arena operators descend on the city, building state-of-the-art facilities.

ASA is a not-for-profit organisation that operates the annual championship event and held the inaugural SHNC at SportzRinkz, 20 years ago. The organisation is committed to promoting environmentally sustainable events. Annually, ASA puts out a 'request for proposals' (RFP) to organisations interested in hosting the SHNC. Environmental considerations, including waste disposal, sustainable operational practices and energy efficiency, are paramount in the site selection. For the coming year, ASA has committed to hosting the event in Basingtown; selection of the venue has not been determined but the sentimental choice is to return to SportzRinkz. In fact, it is widely known that the event will be awarded to SportzRinkz if the company complies with all the requirements outlined in the RFP.

Douglas and the management team at SportzRinkz Ltd are very interested in hosting the SHNC event; however, the energy efficiencies in the 20-year-old building fall below the standards required and outlined in the SHNC bid book. In order to comply with the ASA/SHNC energy policy, SportzRinkz Ltd must make capital improvements to the existing facility. Two competitors of SportzRinkz Ltd are also interested in hosting the event and already meet all of the stipulations outlined in the RFP.

Important considerations for Collins to take into account in his assessment of the proposed capital project include the following:

- Capital improvement costs to meet the required energy standards will total $50,000 for SportzRinkz Ltd.
- SportzRinkz Ltd will receive revenue from ASA for hosting the SHNC totalling $25,000.
- Hydro savings for SportzRinkz Ltd will total $2,000 per year* for a 10-year period as a result of the enhanced energy efficiencies in the facility due to the capital improvements.
- After 10 years the capital improvements will be obsolete and need to be replaced.
- The capital improvements will provide significant environmental benefits through enhanced energy usage.
- The capital improvements will make the venue more enjoyable for spectators and athletes for the SHNC and subsequent games for the next decade.
- The government of Basingtown is encouraging all businesses to become eco-friendly, although no financial support for doing so is available.

Collins quickly determines that the economic merits of pursuing the SHNC do not make sense for SportzRinkz Ltd. However, Collins is an advocate of the triple bottom line and recognises that there are other factors influencing this decision beyond the purely financial considerations. For Collins, generating a SWOT (strengths, weaknesses, opportunities, threats) analysis of the potential impacts the capital improvement may have on people, the planet and profits helps to structure his analysis.

*For the purpose of this case, the time value of money will not be considered.

Discussion questions

10 What are the potential triple bottom line benefits of embarking on the capital improvement for people, the planet and profits? Why?

11 What are the potential triple bottom line pitfalls of embarking on the capital improvement for people, the planet and profits? Why?

12 Based on your knowledge of the case, what recommendation should Collins make to SportzRinkz President, Ken Douglas?

Conclusion

This chapter indicated that the concept of sustainability has been defined in vague terms and is complex and difficult to enact. This text posits Kaspar's (1998: 67) definition for sustainability as the capacity of an event to provide 'economic development that serves current needs without having a negative impact on future generations. In other words, it reflects an improvement of the quality of life within the capacity of an ecosystem. It comprises economic, social [cultural] and environmental dimensions'. Although six guiding principles were provided in this chapter, a set of complete guiding instructions for enacting sustainability in events management has not yet been fully debated and determined. Also, elements emphasised when working to achieve sustainability can change based on the perspective utilised, such as the resource-based or behavioural-based theoretical perspectives. However, a starting point for event managers to increase event sustainability centres on the measurement of current environmental practices. Within this chapter a number of sustainability measuring strategies were introduced, including the corporate environmental management (CEM) model; the triple bottom line (TBL); the triple top line (TTL); the balanced scorecard (BSC); life cycle assessment (LCA); the carbon footprint method; the license model of environmental performance; and the sport event-environmental performance measure (SE-EPM). While unique in their approach to event sustainability measurement, each of the strategies can be applied by event managers depending on managers' preference or comfort; indeed, there is no 'right' method to measuring sustainability. However, utilisation of *one* of the measurement methods is valuable for creating benchmarks and instigating management action to address areas of shortfall in sustainability performance; 'if you do not measure it you cannot manage it!'

Considering sustainability measurement, and subsequent management, through the lens of appreciative theory allows managers to focus on the 'possible' and 'doable' rather than being encumbered by thoughts of the 'impossible'. Indeed, coupling sustainability measuring strategies with constructive leadership and managerial action should continue to produce positive advances in sustainable event citizenship.

In sum, it is evident that sustainability has risen to be a contemporary issue in events management. This means that event managers must lead the way in determining the multiple elements for sustainability within each event hosted, measure the current state of sustainability, establish strategies for advancing sustainability and manage the implementation of these strategies. This is a difficult contemporary challenge but one that has been given to this generation to solve.

General discussion questions

13 How do you define sustainability in events management? What are the principles included within your definition and how do the economic, social (cultural) and environmental dimensions impact on your definition?

14 How should sustainability be enacted within events management and what are the barriers to this enactment?

15 Select a local event and measure the sustainability – including the environmental, financial and socio-cultural sustainability – with one of the seven measuring methods provided in the chapter.

16 Who are the members within sustainable citizenship in your local events? How do the citizens change from local to international events?

Guided reading

Collins, A., Flynn, A., Munday, M. and Roberts, A. (2007) Assessing the environmental consequences of major sporting events: the 2003–04 FA Cup Final. *Urban Studies*, 44(3), 457–76.

This article provides an overview of the footprint method for determining environmental impacts of major events.

Ghobadian, A., Viney, H. and Holt, D. (2001) Seeking congruence in implementing corporate environmental strategy. *International Journal of Environmental Technology and Management,* 1(4), 384–401.

This article discusses the need for congruence in successful sustainability. The emphasis is on consistency from sustainability strategy formulation through until the completion of implementation of each strategy.

Hubbard, G. (2009). Measuring organisational performance: beyond the triple bottom line. *Business Strategy and the Environment,* 18, 177–91.

This article provides an overview of the triple bottom line concept – emphasising the social, financial and environmental elements of sustainability.

Mallen, C. and Chard, C. (2011) A framework for debating the future of environmental sustainability in the sport academy. *Sport Management Review,* 14, 424–33.

This article frames a debate on how the natural environment is impacting on sport; however, the debate elements can be applied to any major event. The debate encompasses setting directions for meeting the challenges by the year 2050.

Paquette, J., Stevens, J. and Mallen. C. (2011) The IOC: an interpretation of environmental sustainability, 1994–2008. *Sport in Society,* 14(3), 355–69.

This article outlines Raufflet's paradigm to develop understanding concerning how the IOC and the Olympic Games have defined environmental sustainability over the last two decades.

Recommended websites

GEO-4: Summary for Decision Makers by the United Nations Environmental Programme: **http://hqueb.unep.org/geo/geo4/media/GEO4%20SDM_launch.pdf**

Intergovernmental Panel on Climate Change: **www.ipcc.ch/publicaitons_and_data/publicaitons_and_data.shtml**

United Nations Brundtland Report (1987). 96th Plenary meeting, UN General Assembly Report to the World Commission on the environment and development: **www.on.org/documents/ga/res/42/ares/42-197.htm**

United Nations Educational, Scientific and Cultural Organization (UNESCO). (2005). *UNESCO and Sustainable Development*: **http://unesdoc.unesco.org/images/0013/001393/139369e.pdf**

United Nations Global Compact: **www.unglobalcompact.org** (under the icon: Blueprint for Corporate Sustainability Leadership).

Key words

appreciative theory; behavioural-based theory; resource-based theory; sustainability citizenship

Bibliography

Babiak, K. and Wolfe, R. (2006) More than just a game? Corporate social responsibility and Super Bowl XL. *Sport Marketing Quarterly,* 15, 214–22.

Barney, J. and Arikan, A. (2001) The resource-based view: origins and implications. In M. Hitt, R. Freeman and J. Harrison (eds), *The Blackwell*

Handbook of Strategic Management. Oxford: Blackwell.

Bateman, T.S. and Organ, D.W. (1983) Job satisfaction and the good soldier: The relationship between affect and employee 'citizenship'. *Academy of Management Journal,* 26(4), 587–95.

Bowen, F. (2007) Corporate social strategy: competing views from two theories of the firm. *Journal of Business Ethics,* 75, 97–113.

Braam, G. and Nijssen, E. (2004) Performance effects of using the balanced scorecard: a note on the Dutch sustainability management to business strategy. *Business Strategy and the Environment,* 11(5), 269–84.

Cooperrider, D. (1986) Appreciative inquiry: toward a methodology for understanding and enhancing organizational innovation. Unpublished doctoral dissertation, Case Western Reserve University, Ohio, USA.

Cooperrider, D. (2008) Current commentary on AI and positive change: going green maximum velocity through Al's sustainable design factory. **http://apreciativeinquiry. case.edu/intro/commentMar08.cfm**

DeTombe, D. (2008) Towards sustainable development: a complex process. *International Journal of Environment and Sustainable Development,* 7(1), 49–62.

Drucker, P. (1999) *Management Tasks, Responsibilities, Practices.* Oxford: Butterworth-Heinemann.

Epstein, M. and Wisner, P. (2001) Using a balanced scorecard to implement sustainability. *Environmental Quality Management,* 11(2), 1–10.

Falt, E. (2006) Sport and the environment. *Environmental Health Perspectives,* 114, A268–9.

Fenton, W. (2010) Using sponsorship to drive environmental awareness and change. *Journal of Sponsorship,* 3(2), 124–9.

Figge, F., Hahn, T., Schaltegger, S. and Wagner, M. (2002) The sustainability balanced scorecard: linking sustainability management to business strategy. *Business Strategy and the Environment,* 11(5), 269–84.

Ghobadian, A., Viney, H. and Holt, D. (2001) Seeking congruence in implementing corporate environmental strategy. *International Journal*

Environmental Technology and Management, 1(4), 384–401.

Glavič, P. and Luckman, R. (2007) Review of sustainability terms and their definitions. *Journal of Cleaner Production,* 15, 1875–85.

GEO4 (2007) GEO4: Environment for development. United Nations Environmental Programme (UNEP). **www.unep.org/geo/geo4.asp**

Grant, S. and Humphries, M. (2006) Critical evaluation of appreciative inquiry. *Action Research,* 4(4), 401–18.

Heugens, P. (2006) Environmental issue management: towards a multi-level theory of environmental management competence. *Business Strategy and the Environment,* 15(6), 363–76.

Iles, A. (2008) Shifting to green chemistry: the need for innovations in sustainability marketing. *Business Strategy and the Environment,* 1, 524–35.

IPCC (2007) Climate change 2007. World Meteorological Organisation, Geneva, Switzerland. **www.ipcc.ch**

Kallio, T. and Nordberg, P. (2006) The evolution of organizations and natural environment discourse: Some critical remarks. *Organization and Environment,* 19(4), 439–57.

Kaspar, R. (1998) Sport, environment and culture. *Olympic Review,* XXVI(20), 67–70.

Kaplan, R. and Norton, D. (1996) *The Balanced Scorecard: Translating Strategy into Action.* Boston, MA: Harvard Business School Press.

Koster, R. and Lemelin, R. (2009) Appreciative inquiry and rural tourism: a case from Canada. *Tourism Geographies,* 11(2), 256–69.

Laing, J. and Frost, W. (2010) How green was my festival: exploring challenges and opportunities associated with staging green events. *International Journal of Hospitality Management,* 29(2), 261–67.

Mallen, C., Stevens, J., Adams, L. and McRoberts, S. (2010) An assessment of the environmental performance of an international multi-sport event: understanding the organisational barriers to event sustainability. *European Sport Management Quarterly,* 10(1), 97–122.

McDonough, W. and Braungart, M. (2002) Design for the triple top line: new tools for sustainable commerce. *Corporate Environmental Strategy,* 9, 251–8.

Mitchell, K. and Saren, M. (2008) The living product – using the creative nature of metaphors in the search for sustainable marketing. *Business Strategy and the Environment,* 17, 398–410.

Möller, A. and Schaltegger, S. (2008) The sustainability balanced scorecard as a framework for eco-efficiency analysis. *Journal of Industrial Ecology,* 9(4), 73–83.

Padgett, P., Steinemann, A., Clarke, J. and Vandenbergh, M. (2008) A comparison of carbon calculators. *Environmental Impact Assessment Review,* 28, 106–15.

Paquette, J., Stevens, J. and Mallen, C. (2011) The interpretation of environmental sustainability by the International Olympic Committee and Organising Committees of the Olympic Games from 1994 to 2008. *Sport in Society,* 14(3), 355–69.

Peattie, K. (1999) Trappings versus substance in the greening of marketing planning. *Journal of Strategic Marketing,* 7(2), 131–48.

Raufflet, E. (2006) Re-mapping corporate environmental management paradigms. *International Studies of Management,* 36(2), 54–72.

Robinson, L. (2010). The Vancouver Olympics: A critical retrospect, 24 August. **www. playthegame.org**

Roper, T. (2006) Producing environmentally sustainable Olympic Games and 'greening' major public events. *Global Urban Development Magazine,* 2(1). **www. globalurban.org/GUDMag06Vol2Iss1/ Roper.htm**

Sandhu, S., Ozanne, L., Smallman, C. and Cullen, R. (2010) Consumer driven corporate environmentalism: fact or fiction? *Business Strategy and the Environment,* 19, 356–66.

Suzuki, D. (2010) *Solutions in Nature: The Lifecycle of a Product.* Ottawa, Ontario: Terrachoice Group Inc.

Trexler, M. and Kosloff, L. (2006) Selling carbon neutrality. *The Environmental Forum,* March–April, 34–9.

United Nations (UN) Brundtland Report (1987) *96th Plenary Meeting, United Nations General Assembly Report to the World Commission on the Environment and Development.* **www.on.org/ documents/ga/res/42/ares/42-187.htm**

Van Buskirk, W. (2002) Appreciating appreciative inquiry in the Catholic school. In R. Fry, F. Barrett, J. Seiling and D. Whitney (eds), *Appreciative Inquiry and Organizational Transformation: Reports from the Field.* Westport, CT: Quorum.

Watkins, J. and Cooperrider, D. (2000) Appreciative inquiry: a transformative paradigm. *Journal of Organization Development Network,* 32, 6–12.

Chapter 11

Events, the law and risk management

Dominik Kocholl, University of Innsbruck, Austria

Learning outcomes

Upon completion of this chapter the reader should be able to:

- define risk and construct a risk management plan;

- understand the role of risk management in the events management process, the influence of the event context and the role of risk communication;

- think through the multiple tangible and intangible factors that can go wrong separately and together (interactions between hazards);

- identify the necessary **contracts** for events and their components;

- understand the variety of rules and regulations governing events;

- know how to gain **insurance** (and its limitations);

- understand the importance of undertaking a systematic approach to risk management;

- explain what legal **liability** is and how event organisations can protect themselves from its consequences;

- understand that 'Murphy's law' is not real law, and recognise the necessity to approach a specialised attorney-at-law at an early stage to discuss your plans.

Overview

This chapter is about risk management and legal aspects concerning various different events. Legal-based risk management tries to combine both of these major topics to be discussed in this chapter. Many of your actions, measures and omissions as an event manager will be dealt with by authorities, stakeholders and courts in a legal way – especially if things go wrong, but also if harm and damages occurred on your side.

Whatever you are managing, bear in mind that when transferring your ideas and objectives to real life you will need law, e.g. contracts, structures, companies or associations. Therefore try to make sure that law is – and can be – your friend. Law is about chances as much as it is about risks. When identifying and later managing risks, consider their potential impact on your goodwill, your purse and your legal situation. Use both common sense and your improving basic legal knowledge, plus your knowledge on how to deal with hazards and risks, to have a lasting effect and fun as a successful event manager.

Introduction and disclaimer

Events produce both positive and negative impacts. No risk – no fun. Chinese language uses the same word for risks and chances. Risk is not necessarily bad. Risk management and a certain legal knowledge are very important to act successfully in the event and festival business. Predominantly this chapter refers to European Union law and the legal systems in England and Wales, Germany and Austria. Although legal systems and precedents vary, fundamental legal principles are more or less the same. Please remember that this chapter must not be treated as a source of definite legal advice and does not take the place of consulting with an attorney-at-law who is knowledgeable of the parts of event law you need and licensed to practise in your jurisdiction/state. The author, the editors and the publisher do not accept responsibility for any advice inferred.

Event risk management

Due to their nature events have the potential to generate risks and crises. What *can* go wrong, *will* go wrong ('Murphy's law'). Potential risks vary to a great extent depending on the type of event, but several risks appear on a regular basis. Festival crises and failures do happen quite often as risks were not managed appropriately. In the event context, risk can be defined as the likelihood of an event not fulfilling its objectives (Allen et al., 2005: 346) because of uncertainty. However, risk is also the basis of the entrepreneur's advantage, and good risk management can be an effective way to reduce costs. The goal is more fun, less risk. Minimise risks and maximise opportunities.

Risk management is the practice of identifying, anticipating, assessing and prioritising risks, and appraising and controlling them. It assists event organisers in trying to prevent or minimise costs, losses or problems, and to protect assets. Risk management assists event organisations in planning and conducting events in the safest possible (and affordable) manner. Risks can be defined in different ways, but most definitions include uncertainty (probability of occurrence) and the potential magnitude of damage (Brühwiler, 2011: 28). Such damage may include deaths, injuries, cancellation of the event, pollution, damage to property, legal liability claims, costly lawsuits, negative public image or financial loss. Risk affects the event organisers as well as event stakeholders.

On the one hand, there is increasing social pressure to perform risk management practices. On the other hand, event risk management becomes a silent marketing tool (Tarlow, 2002: 209, 210). A full risk assessment should be carried out for all events during their whole event life cycle and become an integral and strategic part of organisational processes and decision making (Ferdinand and Kitchin, 2012: 155).

■ Identifying and characterising the hazards/threats

A hazard is something with the potential to cause harm. All hazards should be identified by understanding the environment or the context in which the event takes place. Clearly the structure, resources and legal aspects of the event host organisation also need to be considered. Understanding the type and nature of an event is going to indicate possible hazards and risks it will be exposed to. Additionally event organisers will have to analyse the capability of the organisation to tolerate risks, and whether individuals in the team organising the event plan to live off anticipated profits (Ferdinand and Kitchin, 2012: 157).

A comprehensive identification of risks is necessary. To identify risks and hidden dangers the following techniques might help:

■ Work breakdown structure (WBS, a decomposition of a project into smaller components);

- scenario development (what-if modelling);
- brainstorming (cf. Brühwiler, 2011: 160);
- fault diagrams;
- statistical methods;
- testing a range of scenarios of potential risks and their effects;
- incident reports of similar events or different events at the same venue;
- and, of course, consultation (see Bowdin et al., 2006: 321).

While working on the identification of specific hazards and risks, integrate intuitive knowledge, list your event risk management assumptions and evaluate them (Tarlow, 2002: 32). Try to work on a 'Credible-Worst-Case-Scenario' with a matrix (Brühwiler, 2011: 164) or a 'Critical Incidents Reporting System' (Brühwiler, 2011: 173) and try to use 'Value at Risk' as a risk measure, which can be used in non-financial applications as well.

The Olympic Games, a very large international event, uses test events a year before the actual Games take place. In Weymouth, where the sailing disciplines had their venue during the 2012 London Olympic Games, a similar competition was held in the same waters a year before by the same staff and race officials who would be on duty when it really counted in 2012.

Risk identification should be practical, anticipatory, realistic and, of course, systematic. Hazards and risks not discovered are 'unknown unknowns' and potentially highly dangerous. It does make sense to have the whole team involved in identifying the hazards/risks. However, 'prophets of doom' can bring in an overly pessimistic approach to the planning process and are therefore a threat in themselves (Bowdin et al., 2006: 323).

Risk communication

Improve collective and individual decision making by communicating cooperatively and proactively with stakeholders. There are internal (managers, paid staff and volunteers) and external stakeholders to consult. In doing this, seek the advice of an attorney-at-law who works for the events management business on a regular basis, talk to the police, sponsors, media (build up good contacts and understanding) and the emergency services. Ask health or weather agencies and government authorities as they have much more data than is otherwise available.

Open communication channels – especially during the event it is necessary to encourage suppliers, staff and volunteers to report problems, or that a task has not been completed. Bear in mind that there are formal and informal methods of communication and that both can help.

Areas to consider

Risk is the likelihood of harm arising from the hazard. During the process of identifying risks, the following areas (including several examples) might be useful to consider in a meaningful assessment:

Environmental risk – weather – acts of God

First, analyse the physical location and site area conditions. Secondly, especially regarding outdoor events, it is very clear that bad weather can lead to an event's failure. Note that weather insurances exist. Due to global warming winter tourism has become vulnerable; a possible climatic change bears the risk of having serious impact on the winter recreation sector. During summer events think of heat-related risks. Thirdly, pollution should also be regarded as an environmental risk. Establish provisions for sufficient waste management. Damage that occurs as a result of such events as earthquakes, avalanches, floods, lightning, storms, hurricanes, tornadoes and other natural disasters is seen as the result of 'acts of God' as they cannot reasonably be foreseen or prevented. If performance of the contract becomes impossible in such situations, the parties have no legal responsibility to continue performance of the contract.

In 1998, during an exceptionally strong storm, five yachts sank and six sailors died while participating in the famous Sydney-to-Hobart yacht race. Of the 115 boats that started, only 44 made it to Hobart. As a consequence, a coroner's enquiry took place to check the safety measures and the rules the race management had provided. As a result of the coroner's findings, the organising club's race director resigned his position.

Fire

Fire safety is a major task to be considered. Nevertheless, important parts of these risks often remain more or less unconsidered. Apart from obvious threats and general fire precautions, do think of electrically induced fires, lightning, hot surfaces, pyrotechnics, naked flames, smokers materials, etc. Think of sources of ignition, sources of fuel and sources of oxygen.

Health and safety risks, alcohol and drugs

For bigger events, emergency medical services and ambulance cars should be available at the venue. Consider participants' exhaustion, food safety and drinking water quality, injuries to people, good lighting, stage safety (stage construction is a form of light construction), pyrotechnic safety and communicable diseases like the SARS outbreak or the influenza virus. Event organisers are legally responsible to provide a safe working environment for their workers and volunteers. Stay away from bulk distribution of alcohol (Tarlow, 2002: 73) and do provide non-alcoholic drinks. What do you think about an alcohol-free and glass-free event? Prevent drug consumption.

Human error and crowd management

Human error proves to be a frequent cause when various types of risk are investigated. Crimes happen (fraud, theft, terrorism, vandalism, mischief, etc.). Events are no safe harbour. Think of additional security and clean-up costs, of noise control, etc.

In crowds high density levels may lead to panic. In 1989 the disastrous death of 96 people at Sheffield's Hillsborough Stadium is an example of what can happen and shows that crowd control and crowd safety might have required different measures. In 2010 a tragic stampede at the Love Parade electronic dance music festival in Duisburg, Germany, caused the death of 21 people.

After the death of six spectators at the end of the Air & Style snowboard event held in Innsbruck in 1999 the annual Bergsilvester event held on New Year's Eve makes sure that similar tragedies do not occur again.

(Electrical) power

Smaller indoor venues and several outdoor events have power requirements (e.g. for sound systems and for lighting) that exceed the power available, especially the maximum amount of power deliverable at any one time. Generators plus the fuel for them might be expensive. Have a backup power plan.

Financial risk

Default risk, market risk, currency exchange rate changes, decreasing cash flow, the unsatisfactory financial state of sponsors – to name but a few – can possibly jeopardise the sound financial footing of an event organisation. For example, if the successful organisation of an event is heavily reliant on ticket sales for revenue and it is an outdoor event, check the weather forecast, noting any bad weather forecast.

Risk to your communication system

Voice communication, etc. can be endangered if the mobile phone networks break down. For this reason make sure you have walkie-talkies or radio sets available!

Reputation risk

Adverse media coverage, bribery and corruption, losing key personnel, accusations of child abuse, allegation of safety deficiencies all pose a massive threat to the reputation of both the event and the event organising company. Extensive damage to organisational reputation has to be avoided. One incident can put an event organiser out of business for the rest of his life.

Legal risk – litigation

Most books and articles on risk management do not refer to legal risks for one reason: they are not written by lawyers. Legal risk is risk which lawyers can help to identify or mitigate. The approach of consulting an attorney-at-law only when things have all gone terribly wrong is certainly not a good idea. Underpinning all aspects of an event are the complex legal issues involved. Legal risks can be found both internally and externally. Legal liability is becoming a major risk for event managers. Negligence in identifying and preventing hazards and risks shows not only a problem in your risk management, but can cause litigation itself.

Compile records which are suitable and sufficient to demonstrate, should the need arise, how you complied with all the necessities of risk management and with legal obligations. Please refer to the legal-based risk management section and the topics on law below.

Religious, moral and ethical questions

Consider religious, moral and ethical issues as potential risks. In 2012 the death of Nick Zoricic during a ski-cross event led the event organisers to cancel their event whereas earlier in 2012, the accident and death of freestyle skier Sarah Burke did not stop the Winter X-Games in Aspen happening shortly after that incident as all parties wanted to profit from that event. Although professionals build such slopes/pistes they are to be considered dangerous and athletes do face risks which officials try to minimise.

Local event law in Carinthia, Austria, has allowed a Euro-Challenge ice-hockey match between Austria and Belarus to take place, but forced it to take place without any spectators because the event date fell on Good Friday, a religious holiday observed primarily by Christians. As the flights of the Belarus team were already scheduled, the date could not be changed once the organisers finally discovered the problem.

Terrorism

During the 1972 Summer Olympic Games in Munich members of the Israeli Olympic team were taken hostage and eventually killed, and several more died during a failed rescue attempt. However, terrorism could not halt the Games. During the 2012 Olympic Games the author visited London as well as Weymouth/Portland, where the Olympic Sailing Event took place in or near a former naval base and was protected by warships and up to 1,000 policemen. Full security cannot be guaranteed as the explosions during the Boston marathon 2013 have shown; anyway the event will be held once again in 2014.

Psychology – the risky fear

Better information through the internet, etc. potentially increases anxiety among the public. Fear of risk may create a whole new set of risks. Partial knowledge, as opposed to full knowledge, may produce the risk of public anxiety and even panic (Tarlow, 2002: 209).

■ Developing a risk management matrix

Assess the vulnerability of the event and evaluate the risk

Identified risks need to be analysed and evaluated as regards their probability of occurrence (on a scale of 'rare' to 'likely') and the severity of the consequences/impact ('insignificant' to 'catastrophic') on the event's goals, stakeholders and resources. In fact, the potential severity of impact can be multiplied by the probability of occurrence. A comprehensive stakeholder analysis is a prerequisite for thorough risk management. Determine whether any of the stakeholders are highly risk averse.

A risk management matrix will not only clarify your thinking on the concrete risks the event may face, but also give you a guideline to work from in managing or mitigating risks. Think of the interactions between hazards/risks and find out which risks are acceptable. Consider individual psychological factors, personal attributes and socio-cultural norms.

The matrix will assist a systematic and structured approach. Make sure to take into account human factors, and that your matrix is based on the best information available, and capable of continual improvement and enhancement. Constantly monitor the ever-changing conditions and risks – have a live risk register (Bowdin et al., 2006: 344) – plus the effectiveness of your measures. Keep risk management plans up to date and gain important knowledge for the future. Standards help to provide a consistent approach. Have a look at the standard ISO 31000 of the International Organization of Standardization.

Risk treatment and control

After one understands what might happen, the risk can be managed in a number of ways. These ways have in common the transfer of the risks to those who have the resources (including skill, knowledge, experience or deep pockets) to handle it. Accepting the risk is another way of dealing with risks – called risk retention – but risks should be evaluated before they are accepted.

Avoid or prevent certain risks which are not worth it. Reduce the vulnerability of the event (cancel a part of it or change the location/venue or have many sponsors in case several pull out). Reduce the dependencies – have work done in-house and avoid outsourcing important tasks.

Reduce the impact of potential damage by selecting the least damaging option and documenting the steps considered and taken whereby the risk is diminished. Do have your documents up to date, notably operational plans, an emergency evacuation plan, a crowd management and control plan, a crisis communication plan, incident reports, etc. Do have backups and alternatives. Spread out potential risk by storing essential equipment at different locations.

Transfer risk to another company contracted to perform certain tasks and responsibilities (e.g. private security companies). Choose only collaborators with a good reputation and considerable experience. Transfer risk to (liability) insurance companies. The measures listed above are those risk managers most often refer to. Communicate actual risks or incidents as soon as they appear. Deferment (adopting a 'wait and see' approach) and cancelling or postponing the event should also be considered.

Try to avoid incidents as a result of risks. If incidents do occur, prevent them from becoming crises. If a crisis occurs, minimise the impact on the event, the event organisation and the stakeholders. Establish a crisis management team (Brühwiler, 2011: 229–33).

Risk management does face difficulties in allocating resources. All risks can never be fully avoided or mitigated. Money spent on risk management and resources/measures taken could have been spent on more profitable activities (e.g. opportunity costs). To be in a position to spend money/resources to mitigate risk, create a valuable event with reliable revenue.

Summing up, strategies to manage risk might include transferring the risk to another party, reducing the negative effect or probability of the risk, avoiding the risk or accepting a particular risk (risk retention). Another additional strategy is to take legal precautions through legal-based risk management and compliance.

Legal-based risk management – limiting liability

Whether we like it or not, we live in a highly litigious, interdependent society. Therefore legal issues are becoming increasingly important and can be found in almost any aspect of an event. Legal duties have to be considered, including their nature and to whom they are owed (O'Dowd, 2008: 1151). They amount to legal risks which do not stop at just being financial. Think of grievous bodily harm or imprisonment. All too often this legal risk is ignored because managers are weak in identification ability. Legal risks cannot be discovered easily by those not trained sufficiently in the (practical) field of law. What should you know about the legal system?

First of all, the structure of your event organisation is highly important to reach your goals and avoid incidents, crises, (reputation) losses and liabilities.

Secondly, tailored advice on contract formation and terms is important to ensure that they are binding and legally enforceable. Does the contract provide the level of protection intended by the contractors? Further, get advice on liability issues.

Thirdly, anticipate changes in the law. Legislative changes are more comprehensive than most practitioners can imagine. New precedents are given by the courts on an almost daily basis.

Fourthly, bear in mind that various differences exist between legal systems – for example common law systems differ considerably from civil law systems. Which law will apply in international disputes? Access to courts and dispute resolution mechanisms may vary.

To reduce liability, put yourself in the shoes of others, review the waivers you are asking for and your event's signage from a jurisprudential point of view, and resist accepting responsibility for the actions of another person unless you are in control of what they do or are responsible for because of a statute's provision. Provide – at the formation of the contract – for liquidated damages/penal damages (penal/supra-compensatory ones are rarely enforceable in count) payable if your (key) suppliers do not perform or if artists, musicians or DJs do not show up, because without those it will be difficult to prove the damage sustained. Additionally such clauses in a contract encourage appearing and performing.

■ Legal compliance

Legal compliance is the process of ensuring that an organisation follows all relevant laws, regulations and standards. Through legal compliance there is the potential to systematically manage/minimise liability risks, to prevent the cancellation of the event on legal grounds and to avoid criminal or non-criminal fines. Thinking about how to comply with (local) government permits, sanctions and regulations, with licences, forthcoming legislation, police acts and insurance requirements regularly is a wise idea.

■ Contract management

Event management organisations need a far-reaching range of contracts to facilitate their operation. Contract management is a process of efficiently and systematically managing contract creation, execution and analysis to maximise operational and financial performance and minimise liability/legal risk. This process is sometimes known as contract life cycle management (CLM). Whatever name is chosen, it is clear that event contracts need to be reviewed again and again – whenever the conditions change, contracts should also change, especially insurance contracts.

Typical contracts are those with the owner of the venue. Once multiple locations are used, the event management has to deal with many venue owners (often public authorities, or via obtaining multiple short-term licences from a series of land owners), and may share the use of the ground with others or have exclusive rights (O'Dowd, 2008: 1129, 1135, 1141).

Negotiating contracts

Be prepared when entering any negotiation and know your goals. Develop a game plan of the outcomes sought. Learn as much as possible about the other side's position and their bargaining leverage.

Do learn the basic elements of contract law. Who will be the contracting parties? This chapter can just act as a starting point. Contracts should be specific and reflect the total negotiation between the parties. Be thorough and do not assume anything. Have alternatives to boost your bargaining leverage. Never sign a contract in which major items are left to further negotiation.

Pre-contractual liability in the bargaining period

The parties to a contract must act in good faith. A party should not pretend to represent others unless duly authorised to do so. Additionally it should not create the other party's reliance on the (future) conclusion of a contract. Any negligent violation of a pre-contractual duty might result in having to pay damages for the reliance interest of the other party.

Drafting agreements

In drafting agreements a lawyer has to work precisely, otherwise there may be scope for ambiguity in the course of interpreting the intended meaning of the terms of the agreement. This in turn can lead to subsequent dispute between the parties to an agreement. Therefore, as an example, clarify the responsibility/liability of the facility hosting the event in the contract with the facility's organisation. Think about the implications of terminating the contract when entering it, regulate the issue in the contract, and prevent lawsuits for wrongful termination.

The law and event law

■ The ever-changing law

Event businesses operate within certain legal parameters. Law underlies our society as it establishes a framework for the conduct of almost every activity. Law strives to ensure justice, promote freedom, economy and risks, but also security. It imposes duties on each of us but also protects our rights. When thinking of your fundamental rights, start with the constitution (if your country has one), the European Convention on Human Rights (and Fundamental Freedoms; ECHR) and the Charter of Fundamental Rights of the European Union.

When societies change, public policies and the law have to change too. Law changes to reflect changes in society (cf. Kocholl, 2008: 398). But how does law change? In continental Europe, parliaments have to be mentioned first when discussing the process of law making. The legislative process is backed up with case law where judges support the development of law by composing convincing precedents. Jurisprudence has a significant indirect influence on law making and implementation. Nevertheless, in a democratic country law has to follow public opinion, as acceptance of the law is important for the functioning of the whole legal system.

The attitude of society to risk is changing with people's perceptions of an acceptable level of risk being revised downwards. The law of obligations commonly deals with issues on who has to bear the risk(s).

◼ Legal systems and sources of law

The relationships between statutes and judicial decisions can be complex. In theory at least there is a huge contrast between regions where the legal system is based on common law (as used, for example, in England and Wales, Northern Ireland, Canada (excluding Quebec), the USA (excluding Louisiana), Australia and New Zealand) and those where it is based on civil law (as practised, for example, in most of middle and South America, China, Japan and South Korea). Scots law shares elements of both systems, but it also has its own sources and institutions combining both systems. At the end of the day those differences are not that big and are beginning to harmonise because of various influences like European Union law.

In a civil law country the main source of law is the comprehensive compendium of codifications/statutory law, and the decisions of the supreme courts act as an important guideline (persuasive precedent) for the application of the law. Writings of law professors are given significant weight by courts.

In common law countries the main source of law is the decisions in cases by judges – often called 'case law'. The doctrine of *stare decisis* or (binding) precedent by courts is the major difference to codified civil law systems. Abstract principles of law which have led to the decision (*ratio decidendi*) are searched for in the decision and transferred to other cases with similar deciding facts. The Court of Justice of the European Union takes an approach mixing both the civil and common law systems. For the purpose of a basic introduction to event law, I will take a similar approach.

In both systems, public law rules the relations between a private person/legal entity and an official/state entity or between two official/state entities. The constitution, administrative law, criminal law, procedural law, taxation and revenue laws are typical parts of public law.

In criminal procedure law significant differences between the civil law and common law criminal procedure still exist; however, they can no longer be deemed either inquisitorial or adversarial. Relevant persons are the public prosecutor, the accused defendant with her/his counsel for the defence and the victim(s) (and intervenor).

International law can be divided into public international law and private international law. Public international law governs the relationship between nations and international organisations, etc. For example, have a look on the United Nations Convention on the Law of the Sea. Private international law (conflict of laws) decides on the law which has to be applied to resolve a private law dispute between individuals (once the question of **jurisdiction** has been solved).

European Union law is a system of treaties and legislation such as Regulations and Directives which have a direct or indirect effect on the laws of European Union member states. It is supranational law. The Court of Justice of the European Union is the highest court to interpret European Union law. In *Costa v ENEL* (1964) ECR 585 the Court of Justice of the European Union held that in situations of conflict between the laws of a member state and European Union law, European Union law prevails (principle of supremacy). Accepted general principles of European Union law include fundamental human rights, proportionality, legal certainty, equality before the law and subsidiarity.

◼ Administrative regulations, licences and permits

A long list of regulations, licences and permits need to be satisfied when staging an event. These can include local noise regulations, traffic regulations, liquor law and other health and safety regulations, etc. Carry out careful research on what is necessary for your event and act in time, bearing in mind that governments can take a long time to respond to requests. A worst case scenario could be, for example, the police stopping your event from taking place while the featured (or headline) entertainer/artist performs.

It is always the responsibility of an event organiser to find out and comply with all the pertinent Acts, rules, regulations and licensing requirements (Bowdin et al., 2006: 342).

Civil procedure

Civil law courts provide a forum for deciding disputes involving private law to right a wrong, honour an agreement or settle a dispute. Most cases settle before actually going to trial. Good litigators nevertheless 'think trial' and prepare the case in the long term on the premise that the case *will* go to trial. The specific procedure, rules of court and degree of formality expected of an attorney-at-law/advocate may vary depending on which legal jurisdiction is involved.

Generally, the parties control the lawsuit. It is the claimant who files the claim/ complaint, which together with the defendant's response defines the subject matter and the topics. A properly filed suit interrupts the period of limitation. The parties can end proceedings at any time, for example through settlement of the case. The Austrian Civil Procedure Code, as an example, regulates five types of evidence: documents, witnesses, court-appointed experts, judicial (on-site) inspection and the testimony of the parties. The burden of proof requires the claimant to convince the judge of the claimant's entitlement to the relief sought. As a result s/he must prove each element of the claim or cause of action in order to be successful.

Within certain limits, either party may request a review of a court decision by a higher court. A timely appeal suspends the legal validity and generally speaking the enforceability of the judgment. In review proceedings no new evidence, no new allegations of facts, claims or defences, may be introduced.

The term 'civil procedure' encompasses a variety of procedures conducted in civil courts. Usually the first stages lead to a final decision (a judgment) by the court which will have to be enforced by a court (the second stage), if the debtor does not voluntarily comply with the final judgment. There are various forms of special civil procedures – for example, commercial jurisdiction, labour and social security jurisdiction and insolvency procedures. In the international event business context, recognition and enforcement of foreign judgments and arbitrational awards should be seen as an important part of civil procedural law.

Nowadays most states recognise the private settlement of certain disputes by arbitration tribunals outside the state's court systems. Provided minimum procedural standards are observed, the courts will enforce an arbitral award as long as their *ordre public* (public policy doctrine) is not threatened. The important New York Convention on the Recognition and Enforcement of Foreign Arbitral Awards obliges the contracting states to recognise foreign awards and to enforce them in their territory.

Injunctions are court orders requiring a party to do or refrain from doing something. Injunction applications are almost invariably of an urgent nature.

Private law

Private law is a branch of law dealing with relations between individuals or organisations (as opposed to public or criminal law). Sometimes it will also be called 'civil law', but then with a different word-meaning from when talking about 'civil law systems'. The main branches of private law are the law of obligations (as it is called in civil law systems) or contract and tort law (as it is called in common law systems), consumer law, property law, succession and family law; generally speaking, commercial law/business law (which covers also corporate law) and labour law are also to be considered as private law. An obligation is a legal bond between two or more persons, by which one person, the debtor for example, is held liable to another, the creditor, to perform an act or omission/default when non-performance leads to legal sanctions. An obligation contains the duty of the debtor and the corresponding right of the creditor.

■ Contract law

Contract law is concerned with legal rights and remedies resulting from an agreement entered into between individuals and/or companies. Terms of an agreement may be expressed (oral or written) or implied. An implied term is one which is necessary or obvious, custom and practice. The usual remedy the court may order for breach of contract is damages.

Freedom of contracts (the freedom of the parties to shape their agreements) is limited by statutory provisions (if *ius cogens*) and public morals. A contract is created by the mutual consent of both parties. Both parts of a contract – offer and acceptance – can take place via a declaration of intention. A contract need not be called a contract but can be referred to as an agreement; most types of contracts do not have to be in writing. However, do bear in mind that form requirements exist for certain contracts. Remember that it is the content that counts, not the title of a document. Generally speaking each contract is a specific and individual one.

The essential elements of a contract are offer, acceptance of that offer and the intention to create legal relations (in some jurisdictions such as the UK additional consideration is necessary). An invitation to treat is not a binding offer but is seen as an offer to receive an offer, therefore price labels in shops, price lists and catalogues are considered to be only invitations to treat and not offers to sell. A mistake with the price on a price tag is thus not legally binding.

It is advisable to specify a binding/validity period in your offer. Offers can only be revoked prior to acceptance; even in this case damages might have to be paid if the offeree has commenced the task. A rejection of the offer by the offeree or a counter-offer terminates the original offer. In order for an offer to be accepted, the acceptance must be unequivocal and in the same terms as the offer. Any deviation is just another (counter-)offer. Usually mere silence will not be regarded as an acceptance. Often when two companies deal with each other in the course of their business they use standard form contracts. The conflict of these terms is called a 'battle of forms'.

Once valid acceptance takes place a binding contract is formed. Therefore it is important to know what constitutes a valid acceptance in order to establish if the parties are bound by the agreement. Three main rules relate to acceptance:

1. The acceptance must be communicated to the offeree and received by her/him. Make sure you understand which circumstances are necessary for a message to be deemed to have been received in your jurisdiction.
2. The terms of the acceptance must exactly match the terms of the offer.
3. The agreement must be certain.

Capacity to contract is the legal competence to enter into and be bound by the terms of a contract. Minors (people who are 'under age' in the particular jurisdiction) possess a limited capacity to contract. Contracts entered into under the influence of alcohol or drugs, depending on the degree of incapacity, may be voidable. Other important questions to ask are the following:

■ Do the signatories have the right to sign on behalf of the contracting parties?
■ Will that party be bound by that signature?

Nowadays especially consumer protection laws and labour law frequently protect the weaker party in a (typical) situation of imbalance of economic (bargaining) power. The EU Unfair Contract Terms Directive (93/13/EEC) prevents significant imbalances in the rights and obligations of consumers on the one hand and sellers and suppliers on the other as unfair standard contract terms and other terms of a contract would be found not binding for the consumers. Commercial codes applicable to business-to-business (B2B) contracts do not contain a broad range of protection provisions. The German civil code

(BGB) provides in Article 242 that 'the debtor is bound to perform according to the requirement of good faith, ordinary usage being taken into account'.

When interpreting a contract becomes necessary, research takes place as regards the 'true intention' of the parties – what could the addressee have recognised as being the intention of the person making the declaration, the customary meaning of a declaration as well as standard practices in a certain profession? Many contracts contain clauses which specify that the written document contains the entire agreement and supersedes all previous and oral (spoken) agreements, and that changes to that written contract are only valid in written form.

■ Tort law – the duty of care

Basically tort is a civil wrong and the remedy is damages (to put the claimant back in the position s/he would have been if the tort had not been committed). For the tort of negligence the claimant must establish that there was a duty of care, a breach of that duty, and some damage caused directly by that breach of that duty. One of the fundamental concepts common to all countries is the 'duty of care'. Exercising a duty of care means taking all reasonable care to avoid acts or omissions that could injure a 'neighbour'. As often there is no contract, the concept of negligence is covered by tort law. The usual remedies are damages (most likely in the form of compensation). To be held liable, the risk for the damage must have been foreseeable and the duty reasonably practicable. There are different standards of care. A defendant should be able to give evidence that s/he has taken reasonable precautions and have exercised due diligence. 'Neighbours' (see *Donoghue v Stevenson* (1932) AC 562) could be performers, event staff, volunteers (see Andreff, 2006: 219–24; Kocholl, 2012 *passim*), guests, members of the audience or the public in surrounding areas. Occupiers' liability deals with the duty of care which can be expected of the operator (O'Dowd, 2008: 1129).

Actual harm or damage is needed – no harm, no foul. The breach of duty has to be the proximate cause of the harm, or, in other words, there has to be a reasonably close/direct causal relationship between the breach and the harm. The 'reasonable person' test means that in the absence of other (soft) law your standard of care would be based upon what someone with the same level of training and experience would have done under similar circumstances. There is a distinction here between a breach of duty owed to people and imposed or recognised by law and a breach of duty arising from a contract: a contract should be regarded as a special law only in force between the parties to that contract (*lex contractus*).

■ The owner of the event

Who 'owns' an event? First of all the legal owner – a legal entity (natural or legal person(ality)) – has to be defined. Being the owner is not just an honour but entails legal responsibility and therefore liability. Often each member of an organising committee can be held jointly and severally liable. A legal person could be a corporation, company or an association. Establishing an appropriate legal structure for an events management organisation reduces potential liability. Each structure has different liability risks and funding opportunities/possibilities for buying a credit. With respect to a particular event, get advice!

■ Associations, partnerships and corporations

Event organisations regularly consist of more than one person. Whereas an association has to pursue the realisation of an ideal, in partnerships persons agree to unite their services or their property for common benefit/profit. There are various types of partnership:

an unlimited/general partnership (in German, 'Offene Gesellschaft') is a business in which the partners jointly share their management, risks and profits and are personally liable for the debts. A limited partnership ('Kommanditgesellschaft') has the liability of some of the partners limited to the fixed capital contributions that they have granted the business. There has to be a least one general partner who runs the business and is fully liable for all the obligations of the partnership. Examples for corporations are:

- company with limited liability (GmbH);
- joint stock company (Aktiengesellschaft);
- and the Societas Europea.

Service contractors and their responsibilities

Often (independent) service contracts (contracts of service) are distinguished from contracts for service/work. A person undertakes to provide services for an employer for a certain period of time, owes an effort (he sells his labour but does not guarantee successful performance) but uses the resources of the employer, whereas the contractor for service/work uses their own resources and bears the entrepreneurial risk. S/he guarantees a specific successful performance (and end product of the labour) and is under no obligation to do the work personally (unless stipulated otherwise).

Most events include lots of service contractors such as electrical companies, models and hostesses, florists, transportation services, security staff, riggers, providers of sound and audio-visual equipment and services, sales, lawyers, etc.

General service contractors (GSC) are responsible for providing the material, labour, equipment and services necessary for the event. Often a broad range of events management services is provided by the GSC and it can be great just to have to deal with one opponent (or sue only one company) if something goes wrong. On the other hand, speciality service contractors only deal with a specific area of the event. Examples are catering, freight, drayage (the transport of goods over a short distance), security and cleaning services.

Agency

An agency contract obliges an agent to perform legal transactions for the account of the principal who usually has also given the authority – the legal power of the agent to act in the name of the principal and bind the principal directly by those legal transactions.

Legal liability – some details

Understanding liability and negligence will help with your risk analysis efforts. Society has become increasingly risk averse and freedom is under attack. We live in a society that tends to relieve individuals of responsibility for any risk they might be exposed to. Technical and legal measures are applied regularly. As society re-evaluates what are 'acceptable risks', it seems we increasingly assume that somebody else is to blame when an accident occurs. The 'culture of "an accident equals blame, then claim" is completely contrary to the ethos of personal responsibility and self reliance that would seem to be normal characteristics of a healthy society' (Macnae, 2006).

The continental European Civil Code's systems of liability in tort and contract are essentially based on the defendant's fault (negligence or intent). The standard of fault is subjective, and therefore based on personal ability; a person is considered to be at fault if he or she was able to act voluntarily, if he or she *should* have acted differently, and if he himself or she herself – and not the ideal person in his or her situation – *could* have acted differently. An objective standard is applied with regard to the degree of the tortfeasor's (wrongdoer's) attention and diligence.

Commercially organised fun outdoor sports events, for example, enlarge the zone where there is almost zero tolerance of accidents. When incidents happen, victims think of legal claims. More and more cases are filed with the courts. The smaller the amount of self-responsibility that is left with the customers of your event, the more risk management duties are put in the charge of the event organiser and their staff, including volunteers. The concern of liability risks for these people rises proportionally to their charges. The more they invest in security and safety, and the more marketing instruments are involved in promoting their high safety standards, the higher the justified expectations of the customers will become. Especially in contractual relationships between the parties, these justified expectations are becoming more important than ever. So far the floodgates against the litigious trend mentioned – where risk awareness has turned into compensation awareness – are only leaking.

A (potential) claimant is required to mitigate his or her loss. Therefore he or she has to take all reasonable steps to reduce or obviate the loss sustained. Furthermore, liability/compensation is reduced to the extent the court considers the claimant was personally to blame for his or her loss.

Information, informed consent – assumption of risk

The duty to inform the other party is a collateral duty often implied to a contract. This duty aims at the protection of the partner in contract, whereas more often providing information is a reasonable measure to boost self-responsibility (of your customers) and to establish informed consent. As a result of information duties, event managers should inform the customer about the special risk inherent in an (outdoor) activity and the current danger level. If clients are suitably experienced they should even be involved in the decision-making process. Clients should be briefed carefully on the limits of support that guides and leaders can reasonably provide. However, an experienced client would find it hard to show that s/he is unaware of the normal risks associated with outdoor recreation.

Volenti non fit iniuria (i.e. a willing person cannot be injured in law) is a very old legal principle. If somebody has accepted a voluntarily assumed risk and was fully aware of the dangers involved in their chosen activity then that person could be in a weak position to sue (see Kocholl, 2008: 403).

Contractual waivers or releases

Contractual waivers or releases in which customers acknowledge that they are aware of and accept the risk inherent in the activity, participate voluntarily and agree not to bring any claim against the event organisation/staff/volunteers, etc. might be useful. Consider that under Austria's Consumer Protection Act or similar statutory provisions of your country, terms of a contract with a consumer excluding liability for personal injury are invalid (Art. 6 (1) 9 KSchG).

Misrepresentation

Be aware of false statements to the other party – e.g. where material promoting the event gives a wrong idea of a material fact. Any behaviour by words or conduct is sufficient to be a misrepresentation if it is such as to mislead the other party (*Curtis v Chemical Cleaning and Dyeing* [1951] 1 KB 805). Exaggerations could be seen as misrepresentation and allow the other party a remedy of rescission (unwinding of the transaction), and damages.

◼ Vicarious liability

Vicarious liability means the liability of one person for the wrongdoing committed by someone else, especially the liability of an employer for the acts committed by an employee in the course of their work. Event organisers should be aware of the concept of vicarious liability for auxiliary persons – including independent entrepreneurs – who assist in the performance of contractual obligations. The principal is liable for those persons' fault as if it was his or her own (Kocholl, 2006:185).

Insurance

You should have noted so far that, in order to minimise liability, obtaining the correct insurance is of paramount importance. Insurance is a means of risk management and is mainly used to hedge against the risk of a contingent uncertain loss. The insured receives a contract, called an insurance policy. It deals with the conditions and circumstances under which the insured will be compensated financially by the insurer.

Helpful suggestions regarding insurance include the following:

- Have your risk management matrix ready.
- Give the insurance broker all the relevant information.
- Buy the relevant insurance policies, but be ware not to buy too many as premiums (what you have to pay to get the insurance) have risen and will rise again.

However, premiums give you a figure to calculate and build your management and business administration upon.

Event managers are increasingly obligated to produce risk management plans to gain insurance cover at acceptable premium levels. They could consider third party/public liability insurance, insurances for professional liabilities, directors' and officers' liability insurance (D&O – protects an organisation from costs associated with litigation resulting from errors made by directors or officers for which they are liable; it may provide some coverage including defence costs), an employer's liability insurance, a business interruption insurance and a legal expenses/protection insurance (usually covers potential costs of legal action). A contingency insurance can include, for example, cover against adverse weather conditions.

◼ Legal principles of insurance

The main principles of insurance are utmost good faith (duty of the insured to act in good faith (§ 242 BGB) and to disclose all material (relevant) facts to the risk being covered at any time), indemnity, subrogation, contribution (insurers which have similar obligations contribute to indemnify the insured), insurable interest, mitigation and proximate cause (the cause of loss must be covered under the insurance agreement).

- *Indemnification:* The insurance policy obliges the insurer to make whole again – to reinstate to the position that one was in prior to the happening of a specified peril or event.
- *Insurable interest:* The insured must have an interest in the subject matter of his or her policy; otherwise the policy would be void and unenforceable.
- *Mitigation:* In case of any loss or casualty, the asset owner must attempt to keep the loss to a minimum. The insurance cannot be called upon to pay for avoidable losses.

Intentional torts are not covered, and public policy does not allow them to be covered, by any insurance.

■ Lower the premiums you are paying to your insurance company

An insurance company is afraid that the people and organisations it insures may not be as risk averse as they might otherwise be, because they bear in mind that they have transferred the risk (moral hazard). Insurers attempt to address carelessness through policy provisions requiring certain types of maintenance, through inspections and offering discounts on premiums or other benefits for risk and loss mitigation efforts.

■ Claims and loss handling

On the one hand, there are the contractual relationships between those insured and the insurance company, where the claims are adjusted on the basis of contract law, customer satisfaction, administrative handling expenses and the prevention of fraudulent or bad faith practices; on the other hand – especially in the area of liability insurance – third parties are involved. A potential claimant is under no contractual obligation to cooperate with the insurer, and the insurers will often (have to) appoint an attorney-at-law for the insured to protect their legal position.

Labour law

Be mindful of law and statutes that have an impact on the employer–employee relationship, such as occupational health and safety, salaries/wages, wrongful/unfair dismissal, discrimination and other working conditions. Volunteers might be entitled to damages if negligence can be shown.

Data protection, personality rights and security

Privacy concerns exist wherever personally identifiable information is collected, stored or processed. The EU Directive on Data Protection and national legislation in the member states protect these fundamental rights, and legal compliance with data privacy rules has become an essential business practice.

Further, be aware that personality/publicity rights and privacy rights exist when considering texts and photographs to be published. They protect against economic exploitation or humiliation, and ensure, for example, the right to one's own picture/name/likeness, human dignity and the right to free development of the personality.

Intellectual property and broadcast contracts

There are four legal categories of intellectual property:

- copyrights;
- patents;
- trademarks;
- and trade secrets.

Copyright is an area of huge importance to events because copyright is granted for almost all texts, websites, filming, theme songs, sound recording and broadcasts. Broadcast contracts can be very complex. Trademarks, logos, event symbols, database rights, designs, Olympic symbols, acquired goodwill, trade/company secrets have to be protected against ambush marketing, 'passing off' and other adverse effects. Get in touch with collection societies, which monitor intellectual property (IP) rights and collect royalties on behalf of their members (authors, music composers, publishers, etc.)

Sports law and the Olympic Games

Sporting event organisers should examine their relationship to sports organisations and the linkages and dependencies within those. Self-regulatory bodies that govern sports have the capacity to act in a 'quasi-governmental' manner while still possessing the legal structures of private bodies. Their advantages are expertise and efficiency (Gardiner et al., 2012: 90). As a sporting event organiser be aware of the internal regulations of the specific sport associations. These sport codes not only influence the contracts necessary for the event, but also establish standards of care (Heermann, 2008: 59, 157). As an example, the International Ski Competition Rules of the International Ski Federation (603.7.2) regulate the Alpine skiing disciplines and state, for example, that the course setter has to respect the rules, the existing safety measures and course preparation. Furthermore s/he must take speed control into consideration. Summing up, in extreme or risk sports, not only risk management is required but additionally the sporting bodies have to oversee sporting codes to provide a fair and safe working environment for the athletes. Be aware, sports litigation is growing.

The Olympic Games are the pinnacle of all sport events, the exclusive property of the International Olympic Committee (IOC) and, at the same time, mega events. The IOC is the owner of the global broadcasting rights for the Olympic Games; agreements to use those rights are the principal driver of the funding of the Olympic Movement and the Olympic Games (cf. regarding their economic effects for a host city: Preuss, 2006: 183–196). These Games are governed by the Olympic Charter, the Host City Contract, together with strict by-laws, the rules of national or international sports federations (IFs), and National Olympic Committees (NOCs). The Olympic regulations prevent the athlete's personal or 'home' sponsors from receiving any exposure during the time of the Olympics. Only specific advertising is allowed (e.g. manufacturer's identification). Frequently even venues must be renamed during the Olympics. The IOC goes so far that it asks hosting states to pass new legislation and the hosting city to accept the Host City Contract. The Olympic Partner (TOP) Programme for sponsors, the IOC and the Organising Committee do their utmost to prevent ambush marketing (see Rules 2 and 50 of the Olympic Charter – *www.olympic.org*).

Sponsorship contracts

Sponsorships often help to ensure profitable success for an event by providing funds or value-in-kind. Bear in mind that sponsorships usually are a marketing tool, not just a charitable endeavour for a company. According to the Code of Sponsorship of the International Chamber of Commerce (ICC – *www.iccwbo.org*) a sponsorship agreement is:

> any commercial agreement by which a sponsor, for the mutual benefit of the sponsor and sponsored party, contractually provides financing or other support in order to establish an association between the sponsor's image, brands or products and a sponsorship property in return for right to promote this association and/or for granting of certain agreed direct or indirect benefits.

Most sponsorship contracts are complex, long-term and strictly confidential. These agreements need to be drafted very carefully to ensure that there is no ambiguity and confusion later on. They should not interrupt or disturb the event. Sponsors want quality representation and often additional hospitality rights. Their contracts might specify in which position their logo has to be shown, and its size. Be aware of the exclusivity rights granted to sponsors and the scope of the brand sectors they want to protect. Whereas the sponsors do want the brand sectors to be wide, the event organisers will try to keep them as narrow as possible. Sponsors do want media coverage – can you really ensure that they will get it? Do not be too specific in the contract as, generally speaking, media coverage will not be guaranteed by media companies.

Value-in-kind – not just cash – clauses need to be very clear (for example, who pays extra expenses and running and maintenance costs of supplied goods and services such as cars, mobile phones and photocopiers)? Furthermore, the good-will of the event brand and the sponsor should be protected via termination clauses and other contract clauses like penalty clauses (cf. DiMatteo, 2010: 193, 200–2). Some sponsorship contracts have similarities with licensing because the main object of the contract is an intellectual property right. For instance, TOP and NOC contracts are based on the value of (the image of) the Olympic rings (Jagodic, 2011: 532).

International business

In the field of law substantial differences exist from country to country and state to state. Laws are often similar, but never the same. When doing business abroad in *any* foreign jurisdiction (or with somebody located in a foreign jurisdiction) you should ensure that your contract includes favourable and valid choices of law and place of jurisdiction clauses. Otherwise even just establishing these starting points for any legal dispute resolution could become time-consuming and costly.

Providing for dispute resolution by way of international arbitration in your contract is an important part of risk management (cf. Adolphsen, 2012: 257–262). In the event of a dispute, an effective arbitration clause can limit your company's exposure to foreign courts and the intricacies of foreign jurisdictions and facilitate the enforcement of your arbitral award. Sporting event contracts could be dealt with at the Court of Arbitration for Sports (CAS) in Lausanne, Switzerland. An example of a case regarding advertising was *Fédération Française de Gymnastique v Sydney Organising Committee for the Olympic Games (SOCOG) (CAS OG 2000/014)* – at the medal ceremonies a logo had to be concealed to the detriment of the commercial sponsor of the French team.

Conclusion

Use common sense! Take into account all risks. Gain (legal) knowledge (Tarlow, 2002: 67). (Legal-based) risk management is a task for the top management of an event and neither should nor can be delegated (Brühwiler, 2011: 46). It is a 'must' for leaders and the many others assisting them. Think of risk management assessment as a living tool.

Case 11.1 Youth Olympic Winter Games 2012 in Innsbruck

The 1st Winter Youth Olympic Games, a new event of the International Olympic Committee, has been staged successfully in Innsbruck, Austria, and neighbouring villages up to more than half an hour's drive away. It was an international multi-sport event for young people, and took place from 13 to 22 January 2012. Innsbruck had hosted the Winter Olympic Games twice before, in 1964 and again in 1976. It was the second ever Youth Olympic Games, following the Youth Olympic Summer Games held in Singapore in 2010.

In December 2008 the bid committee was transferred into the Innsbruck Youth Olympic Games Organising Committee (IYOCOG), a limited liability company. The organisers were bound by the Host City Contract and the Manuals of the IOC; sustainable Games were to be held on a limited budget (€23.7 million). Only official IOC Worldwide Olympic Partner sponsors, plus 15 specially selected sponsors, were allowed. A torch relay was held. The event took place over 10 days starting, with an Opening Ceremony and ending with a Closing Ceremony. Away from the sports competitions, special culture and education programmes were held.

Throughout all functional areas, strong partners like a local insurance broker were supported by the IYOCOG in designing a claims model incorporating risk analysis. One was selected after three insurance brokers had been invited to tender. A special insurance package was composed largely of event liability insurance and health and accident insurance for the Games. Instead of acquiring legal resources within the Organising Committee, it was decided to conclude a contract with a local law firm involving several attorneys-at-law who covered a wide range of legal areas. The large number of experts available ensured the high level of flexibility required by a large-scale event of this kind. Again, three law firms were invited to tender. Much of the legal advice provided dealt with calls for tender (2,250 tenders were received) and the drawing up of sponsorship agreements.

Local security agencies provided security services and oversaw security services within each venue. This in-venue security was assured by a professional security agency assisted by specially trained volunteers.

The process of analysing risk management issues by the heads of the management and all units started in September 2010, when a claims model was designed incorporating risk analysis. In the next steps the management assessed those risks. Table 11.1 shows the risk ratings that were assessed. This phase took until February 2011 when the contract with the insurance broker was concluded and he got involved in the risk management of the event. In March and April 2011 the management and insurance/risk management specialists assessed and calculated those risks. This process was documented.

Their risk management analysis identified 144 risks. In the end they were covered by insurance and contingency plans. An impact–probability of occurrence matrix was developed beforehand (See Figure 11.1). In March 2011 the insurance contracts were tendered, renegotiated and finally concluded. The IYOGOC decided that no directors' and officers' liability insurance (see above) and no legal expenses insurance for criminal cases were needed. There was no need to insure the cars provided as the car manufacturer had them insured. All other insurance policies/contracts were scrutinised thoroughly. April 2011 saw a seminar on risk assessment and in July a risk management report. During the next three months guidelines/instructions and flowcharts were drafted and feedback given by the insurance company. In November 2011 – less than two month before the Opening Ceremony – the report, the emergency and contingency plans, a crisis management plan and a crisis communication plan were updated or drafted.

For the Youth Olympic Winter Games special general terms and conditions were created. They were designed to facilitate the conclusions of all the necessary contracts with service contractors. Contracts should be concluded in writing only. Preventive aspects of legal work were emphasised well in advance, building upon the experience and expert knowledge of the attorneys-at-law involved. Of course, those lawyers had a look over contracts while the events management team negotiated them.

Table 11.1 Risk ratings

Rating Criterion	1 Extreme	2 High	3 Moderate	4 Low
Financial (in €)	More than €5m	From €250k up to €5m	From €10k up to €250k	From €1k up to €10k
Human	Death of several persons	Death of a person	Many severe injuries	Severe injuries
Reputation	Worldwide negative headlines	Regional negative headlines	Extensive national negative headlines	Several national negative headlines
Interruption of the YOG	Cancellation of the event	Parts of the event cancelled	Substantial delay	Delay

Case 11.1   (continued)

Figure 11.1   Handling, mitigating and reducing specific risks

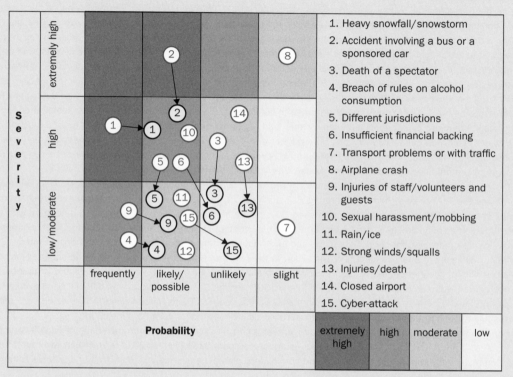

Sources: Schnitzer and Bayer (2012); IYOGOC (2012)

Discussion questions

1   What were the unique features of this event, and how did they contribute to the management of risk?

2   Can you identify areas where legal-based risk management is applied?

3   What were the risks in relation to approximately 1,400 volunteers, considering the Innsbruck 2012 Volunteer Agreement stipulated that 'This agreement is an understanding based on mutual trust; there is no legal basis and substantive law shall not apply'? What does this clause mean?

4   Who was responsible for risk management? Which risks are involved in Table 11.1 and Figure 11.1, and which other (unmentioned) risks can you suggest? Why have such risks not been mentioned in the matrix?

5   Who were the event owners, the organisers, the stakeholders and others involved in the Youth Olympic Winter Games (and thus those who were bearing any relevant risks)?

Case 11.2   Glastonbury Festival 2011

Make a quick investigation using internet sources into the 2011 Glastonbury Festival, where not only U2, Radiohead, Beyoncé, Coldplay and many more acts were performing, but where torrential rain, along with knee-deep mud and burning, dehydrating sun during the last day created serious problems.

Then, have a look into the safety management and legal-based risk management for a similar event in the future in approximately that area. Having learnt lessons from the past, assess the risks involved and draw your own risk management matrix.

Rethink and discuss your findings in groups or in class!

> **Case 11.2** *(continued)*
>
> **Discussion questions**
>
> **6** How can event organisers deal with weather risks and natural hazards?
>
> **7** What types of events are similar and which are considerably different from a risk manager's or a lawyer's point of view?

General discussion questions

8 How do you define legal-based risk management? What is ambush-marketing? What are the boundaries of personality rights?

9 Select a local event and think about all the contracts you need to be concluded and the risks of those relationships.

10 List the areas covered by a sponsorship contract between the event organisers and the sponsor.

11 How can you minimise liability for an event you are planning?

Guided reading

Read the book by Paul Slovic; the bibliography contains many useful sources for the interested student.

Slovic, P. (2000) *The Perception of Risk*. London: Earthscan.

The following books are also recommended:

Beech, J. and Chadwick, S. (eds) (2012) *The Business of Sport Management* (2nd edn). Harlow: Pearson Education.

Fenich, G. (2008) *Meetings, Expositions, Events and Conventions: An Introduction to the Industry*. Harlow: Pearson Education.

Ferrand, A. with Chanavat, N., et al. (2006) *Guide Book for the Management of Sport Event Volunteers*. Chavannes-Lausanne: Sentedalps.

Funke, E. and Müller, G. (2000) *Handbuch zum Eventrecht*. Cologne: Schmidt.

Holzbaur, U., Jettinger, E., Knauss, B., Moser, R. and Zeller, M. (2010) *Eventmanagement* (4th edn). Heidelberg: Springer.

Lewis, A. and Taylor, J. (eds) (2008) *Sport: Law and Practice* (2nd edn). London: Tottel Publishing.

Nafziger, J. and Ross, S. (2011) *Handbook on International Sports Law*. Cheltenham: Edward Elgar.

Petsche, A. and Mair, K. (eds) (2011) *Handbuch Compliance*. Vienna: LexisNexis.

Risch-Kerst, M. and Kerst, A. (2011) *Eventrecht kompakt*. Heidelberg: Springer.

Rosner, S. and Shropshire, K. (eds) (2004) *The Business of Sports*. Boston, MA: Jones and Bartlett.

Torggler, U. (ed.) (2012) *Rechtsprobleme von Sportveranstaltungen*. Vienna: Verlag Österreich.

Vögl, K.C. (ed.) (2012) *Praxishandbuch Veranstaltungsrecht* (4th edn). Vienna: LexisNexis.

Also recommended:

Kocholl, D. (2012) Discussion of Austrian Supreme Court Decision 6 Ob 122/11a – Haftung des Veranstalters nach einem Inline-Skate-Unfall während der Veranstaltung 'Wörthersee-Autofrei 2008' – ÖJZ 2012, pp. 1012–14. Vienna: Manz.

Kocholl, D. (2012) Olympic values, Olympic media and arbitration – awards in Olympic sailing events and to safeguard IF's sport formats, Book of Abstracts, 5th International Sport Business Symposium during the Olympic Games in London 2012 at Birkbeck University of London.

Recommended websites

The official account of the Glastonbury Festival 2011 can be found at **www.glastonburyfestivals.co.uk/history/2011**

The UK government's Health and Safety Executive provides a useful portal on risk assessment issues at **www.hse.gov.uk/risk/index.htm**

The Federation of European Risk Management Associations has a comprehensive website at **www.ferma.eu/risk-management**

Key words

contract; insurance; jurisdiction; liability

Bibliography

Adolphsen, J., (2012) Schiedsgerichtsbarkeit – Internationales Sportrecht. In Adolphsen, J., Nolte, M., Lehner, M. and Gerlinger, M. (eds) *Sportrecht in der Praxis,* pp. 247–318. Stuttgart: Kohlhammer.

Allen, J., O'Toole, W., McDonnel, I. and Harris, R. (2005) *Festival and Special Event Management* (3rd edn). Milton, QLD: John Wiley & Sons.

Andreff, W. (2006) Voluntary work in sport, in Andreff, W. and Szymanski, S. (eds), *Handbook on the Economics of Sport*, pp. 219–24, Cheltenham: Edward Elgar.

Bowdin, G., Allen, J., O'Toole, W., Harris, R. and McDonnel, I. (2006) *Events Management* (2nd edn). Amsterdam: Elsevier.

Brühwiler, B. (2011) *Risikomanagement als Führungsaufgabe* (3rd edn). Bern: Haupt-Verlag,

DiMatteo, L. (2010) Enforcement of Penalty Clauses: A Civil-Common Law Comparison, IHR 2010, pp. 193–202; *Internationales Handelsrecht*, vol. 10, issue 5, pp. 193–202. Munich: Sellier, de Gryter.

Ferdinand, N. and Kitchin, P. (2012) *Events Management – An International Approach*. London: Sage.

Gardiner, S., O'Leary, J., Welch, R., Boyes, S. and Naidoo, U. (2012) *Sports Law* (4th edn). Oxford: Routledge.

Heermann, P. (2008) *Haftung im Sport*. Stuttgart: Boorberg.

IYOGOC (2012) *Be Part of It: Official Report of the Innsbruck 2012 Winter Youth Olympic Games*. **www.innsbruck2012.com/newsroom/the_official_report**

Jagodic, T. (2011) Legal aspects of international event sponsorship. In J. Nafziger and S. Ross (eds), *Handbook on International Sports Law*, pp. 518–544. Cheltenham: Edward Elgar.

Kocholl, D. (2006) Organisationsverschulden bei Alpinveranstaltern im Rechtsvergleich. In Österreichisches Kuratorium für Alpine Sicherheit, Jahrbuch 2006: *Sicherheit im Bergland*, pp. 184–201. Innsbruck: Kuratorium für Alpine Sicherheit.

Kocholl, D. (2008) Mountain sports law in multiple changed adventure tourism – consumer desire and global warming. In A. Borsdorf, J. Stötter and E. Veulliet (eds), *Managing Alpine Future, Proceedings of the Innsbruck Conference 2007*, pp. 397–408. Vienna: Austrian Academy of Science.

Kocholl, D. (2012) Volunteers bei Sportveranstaltungen – ihre Rechtsposition und das Risiko der Freiwilligkeit. In U. Torggler (ed.), *Rechtsprobleme von Sportveranstaltungen am Beispiel der Olympischen Jugend-Winterspiele*, pp. 93–133. Vienna: Verlag Österreich.

Macnae, A. (2006) Risk, freedom and the law. **www.thebmc.co.uk/modules/article.aspx?id=1544**

O'Dowd, P. (2008) Venues and Event Management. In A. Lewis and J. Taylor (eds), *Sport: Law and Practice* (2nd edn), pp. 1128–52. London: Tottel Publishing.

Preuss, H., The Olympics, in Andreff, W. and Szymanski, S. (eds) (2006), *Handbook*

on the Economics of Sport, pp. 183–96, Edward Elgar, Cheltenham.

Schnitzer, M. and Bayer, P. (2012) Risikomanagement bei Sportgroß veranstaltungen am Beispiel der Olympischen Jugendwinterspiele Innsbruck 2012. In U. Torggler (ed.), *Rechtsprobleme von Sportveranstaltungen am Beispiel der Olympischen Jugend-Winterspiele,* pp. 135–52. Vienna: Verlag Österreich.

Tarlow, P. (2002) *Event Risk Management and Safety.* New York: John Wiley & Sons.

Chapter 12

Event operations and project management

Martin Egger, FH Kufstein Tirol – University of Applied Sciences, Austria, and
Helmut Lux, kpp consulting gmbh, Austria

Learning outcomes

Upon completion of this chapter the reader should be able to:

- defend the use of project management tools in events management;
- explain the characteristics of project management for events;
- distinguish categories of events and their challenges;
- create your own structure and phases of the events management process.

Overview

The application of project management techniques and treatment of events as **projects** has become standard practice for professional event agencies worldwide in recent years. This chapter is intended to clarify some fundamental issues surrounding the topics of **project management** and event operations, and to provide the student with preliminary insight into the use and value of project management and its tools as applied to events. In particular the focus is on introducing useful methods.

Examples of such application are presented in the case studies. In addition, the subject areas of quality and crisis management are treated – based on the categorisation of an event as a project with an anticipated **project crisis**.

An overview of the characteristics of project management for events and events operations is given in Figure 12.1.

Why use project management (when organising an event)?

When looking into the past, and in particular at outstanding cultural achievements, in architecture for example, many questions remain unanswered when it comes to understanding the underlying management techniques. Of course in retrospect the construction of immense structures such as the pyramids in ancient Egypt, the Coliseum, or the palaces and sacred buildings of eastern cultures (e.g. Angkor Wat, Mahabodhi Temple) is almost inconceivable without 'project management' of some sort. Large-scale celebrations or public events were also being organised as far back in time as the ancient world – just

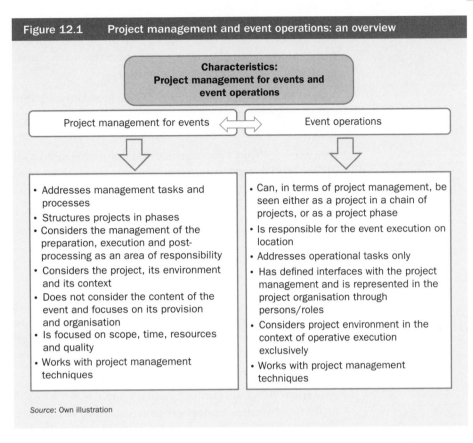

Figure 12.1   Project management and event operations: an overview

Source: Own illustration

think of recurring ceremonies like the Saturnalia festival in ancient Rome, the ancient Olympic Games or the religious ceremonies of pre-Columbian cultures, or think of singular events like the triumphal processions of the Caesars (as, for instance, described in the literary works of Gaius Suetonius Tranquillus). It is hard to imagine that they could have been organised without resorting to rather sophisticated management techniques. Much of it still remains in the dark, awaiting a closer look from historians.

Project management as a tool of modern management didn't emerge until the middle of the 20th century and was initially limited to military usage (e.g. the Manhattan Project). Starting from there, project management increasingly caught on in business, and over time developed into one of the most significant and most commonly used management tools as well as a business philosophy in itself (management by projects). The main reason for this development is that project management (project management methods) first made it possible to cope with the increasing pressure to plan more precisely, complete and implement developments faster and control costs more efficiently.

Use of the term 'project' has become rather inflated in recent years. There are 'projects' everywhere and for any occasion, in private as well as professional contexts, and they all need to be managed. In order to do so, 'project management' has been employed and – partly for that reason – the term has started to irritate many managers recently, being but a buzz word. There was also generally no check on whether a development proposal deserved to be called a project. The fact that some project managers introduce and conduct project management without the necessary intuitive feel for it (i.e. completely method-based) has also contributed to this development. The assertions listed below may help in understanding project management and how it may be 'correctly' applied:

Assertion 0: Not everything that seems a project at first glance really is a project.

Assertion 1: Project management takes place implicitly (the only question is how efficiently and effectively).

Assertion 2: 'Good' project management is teamwork. Even the most capable project leaders need a team that understands them and works with them. Project management always takes place in a social context, and the quality of the output also always depends on the quality of cooperation.

Assertion 4: Project management is never exactly the same. Different challenges need different tools and different efforts (tools and techniques have to be adapted to the purpose).

Assertion 5: Project management (and the associated tools) generates added value for all concerned, especially when it comes to complex projects such as events, because the degree of 'uncertainty' about the development and result decreases continuously if the right tools are used in the right way.

Assertion 6: The use of tools requires an associated know-how. At least some basic knowledge (as well as relevant practical experience) of how project management works (correctly) is needed for the correct application of project management tools.

Assertion 7: Project management is process management. The progress of each project is determined by the processes (starting/planning the project, controlling/coordination, monitoring, marketing, concluding the project). The process of cycle planning–executing–monitoring–controlling forms an iterative part of a project from start to finish.

Assertion 8: 'Bad' project management wastes resources (manpower, money), neglects or ignores important spheres of activity, creates murky scenarios (or even chaos), loses track of goals, and thereby results in dissatisfaction among stakeholders and less than satisfactory results for the client(s) or contracting body.

Assertion 9: 'Good' project management creates structure and thereby allows for:

- a clear overview of all relevant issues (integral approach);
- optimisation of resources employed (efficiency);
- achievement of the goals set (effectiveness);
- minimisation of deviations of the current actual situation from the scheduled target situation;
- flexible adaptation of project content and work stages within the project in order to reach goals in an optimal manner.

Who and what basics: explanation of terminology

What is an event? It is not so easy to answer this question and at times the word is given a 'positivist' definition: an event is what we perceive to be an event. The definition we use is in the glossary.

Events can be divided into many different categories. For practical reasons we will only present a few ways of dividing which are particularly relevant to an overview of our subject area.

1. *Large, medium and small events* (distinction criteria: budget for the event, size of the project team and number of participants).
2. *Customer events and own events* (distinction criteria: external vs internal project owner).
3. *Outdoor and indoor events* (distinction criteria: essential parts of the event are taking place out of doors).
4. *Singular* and *recurring events* (distinction criteria: uniqueness).

About the relevance of the criteria (why these distinctions are made)

Small events naturally need less planning. Even a birthday party can be regarded as an event. In that case it will not be necessary to marshal the whole armoury of project management tools in order to organise a successful event. Possibly the team is quite small and coordination can take place rather informally. Nevertheless it remains important to think within the structures of project management (scope, time limits, resources) because that will ensure that the guests, the birthday boy or girl and the birthday cake get together on the right day at the right place.

Medium events (with a budget starting at approx. €10,000.00, a project team with more than two members, and/or at least 50 guests) need a higher level of structure and planning. In these cases there should definitely be a project assignment, a work breakdown structure, a budget plan and the planning of **milestones**. Other project management tools can be introduced/used as needed if they add noticeable value to the project.

Large events (with a budget starting at approx. €100,000.00, a project team with more than five members and/or at least 300 guests) definitely require professional planning, preparation and follow-ups. In addition to the tools which are used for medium-sized events, large ones certainly need detailed risk management, comprehensive project controlling, project meetings at regular intervals, well-defined roles and communication structures, work package specifications and generally (depending on requirements) sophisticated project marketing.

When it comes to *events which are commissioned as a project*, recourse to project management (involving drawing up and signing a project contract, for example) can by now be regarded as standard and is usually demanded by the owner of the project. This, however, is often not the case with projects of a similar size which are planned and carried out without any specialised advice. Sometimes the consequences are dramatic because in practice it is often seen that

- Roles (leadership and control function!), responsibilities and competences are specified with less precision (if at all).
- Budgets are planned vaguely and project controlling is done with less rigour.
- Planning of the project only takes place in bits and pieces and sporadically (as the need arises).
- There is no communication or it is for a specific reason only.

All in all, this causes the project to run poorly on the whole, which results in economic and social problems that could have been avoided.

The budget, i.e. budget planning, also makes for a significant financial difference between commissioned and self-run projects because necessary (additional) funds for important tasks first have to be approved/released by the project owner.

Outdoor events pose a particular challenge in regions where the climate is such that medium term weather forecasts are generally unreliable. Infrastructure (planning of the infrastructure), scheduling, financial planning and risk management are critical. Major risk factors have to be analysed in the areas of infrastructure (technical input), safety/security (dangerous situations for visitors/participants/crew) and business management (number of visitors).

Recurring events are usually easier to organise because experience (from previous events), structures (experienced team, partners) and documentation is readily available. While the emphasis is on successful completion in the case of singular events, the focus should be on optimisation and quality management in the case of recurring events.

Defining quality in events management

The concept of 'quality' can be viewed from various perspectives. This is especially so when the result of a project is intangible, i.e. there is no end product. Therefore the concept of quality is easier to apply to a physical product, because some of the characteristics are measurable (some easily, some less so) and can thus be objectified. In the case of an event, the result for the customer (participant or 'consumer' of the event) is the subjective experience – and in addition the anticipation and then the memories of the experience – which is shaped by many subjective factors (atmosphere, basic human needs, the company of other participants, attitude towards content on offer, experiences during the event, etc.).

We can infer that the assessment of the quality of event projects is always complex. As Patzak and Rattay (1998) note rather succinctly, 'Quality is meeting the customer's wishes'.

Therefore we consciously take a step back and start with a simple attempt at a definition:

Quality (including that of events) can be recognised when the customer (or the large majority of customers) is satisfied with the product and/or rates it positively.

Consistent with this approach, the two central customer groups (the public at one's own project, the public and ownership of a commissioned project) have to be considered separately.

The notion of the content quality of a project is quite difficult to make into an operationally applicable concept. At best the reaction (satisfaction) of the public can be measured and usually there is congruence of perception between the two groups mentioned above: if the public is happy, the project owner will be happy. In a broader approach focusing on the implementation process there are, however, some factors relevant to event projects (especially customer projects) which are of decisive importance (Figure 12.2).

The quality of the execution of an event can be viewed and evaluated from three distinct aspects as illustrated below. The three levels suggested here are *result* (quality of the result equals goal achievement, *procedures* (technical quality of execution – technology and techniques) and *management* (quality of the management process).

Although the factors influence and depend on each other they are not on an equal footing. But it has to be noted that the quality of the management process has a very immediate effect on the quality as viewed from the other aspects.

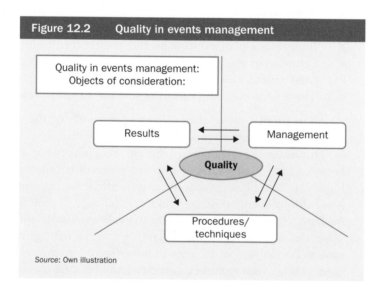

Figure 12.2   Quality in events management

Quality in events management:
Objects of consideration:

Results

Management

Quality

Procedures/
techniques

Source: Own illustration

Points to consider when assessing the quality of an event project in the *ex post* evaluation

■ goal achievement;
■ quality of planning;
■ use of resources;
■ customer satisfaction;
■ procedure and use of technology;

- compliance;
- safety/security;
- sustainability;
- total impact;
- relationship management.

Goal achievement (effectiveness)

Question: Were the goals that were set for the event during the planning stage achieved/to what extent were they achieved?

Sign of quality: Goals were fully achieved or exceeded (operative and strategic level of goals); if it seems likely that goals may not be achieved as determined, this is communicated in time, and goals are adjusted in consultation with the project owner.

Quality of planning/adherence to plans

Question: Were the goals achieved with the means and resources that had been planned for the purpose?

Sign of quality: Minor or no discrepancies between planning and execution, in terms of time (adherence to schedules) as well as resources and results.

Use of resources (efficiency)

Questions: Were the resources that were planned/used for the execution employed in the right way? Were they employed in accordance with the principle of economy? Was the input of resources appropriate for the extent of goal achievement?

Signs of quality: Resources were used with no or minor deviation from the plan. Lower deviation of benchmarks of comparable (own/external) events.

Customer satisfaction

Questions: Were the customers (event consumers) satisfied with the service and what was the extent of such satisfaction? Were the project owners (internal and external) satisfied with the service and what was the extent of such satisfaction?

Signs of quality: High degree of (measured) customer satisfaction. Commissioning of subsequent projects.

Procedure and use of technology

Questions: Were the correct technical tools/aids used for management, infrastructure and staging and were technical alternatives sufficiently considered and evaluated? Were adequate processes chosen for dealing with the various tasks?

Signs of quality: Extensive research and documentation; analysis of best practice examples; tender management and comparison of quotes; thorough planning of processes and sequence; expert discussions; capturing feedback and careful evaluation of all comments.

Compliance

Question: Were legal/statutory provisions, requirements set by the authorities and instructions by major partners adhered to during implementation?

Sign of quality: Proof of compliance with all provisions/requirements/agreements; no complaints from authorities, no complaints from partners.

Safety/security

Questions: Did any situations arise at the event which posed a danger to participants, protagonists, crew? Were there adequate planning and resources in the area of safety/security? How was the interaction with external services (police, ambulance, fire brigade, etc.) organised?

Signs of quality: All potential dangers were identified in advance, correctly assessed and 'diffused' as far as possible. No dangerous situation arose. There was no shortage of resources for safety/security; there were always sufficient resources for dealing with potentially dangerous situations. Cooperation with external organisations/service providers was smooth.

Sustainability

Questions: Were the major environmental factors (regarding the host or the location, for example) surveyed and taken into consideration? Were measures for the protection of the environment (waste, noise, protection of sensitive areas, etc.) planned and implemented? Were resources (water, energy, air) used in an environmentally friendly manner? Were the special requirements of individual groups of visitors appropriately taken into consideration (e.g. accessibility)? Were the requirements of crucial stakeholders (the public at the event, residents, crew) included in the planning and taken into account with appropriate measures?

Signs of quality: Screening the local surroundings for potentially controversial issues (e.g. is the event in keeping with the location/image of a proposed site? What kind of negative repercussions might be expected?). Taking nature and environmental protection into account by involving experts in the planning, documentation and evaluation of measures. Using eco-friendly materials and technologies, developing a plan for mobility and waste management. Definition, implementation and evaluation of measures per target group: information, property protection for residents; service and safety for the visitors; coaching and planning tasks for the crew; accessibility.

Total impact

Questions: Did the event exceed the customers' expectations/is it rated above the benchmarks of comparable projects? Have relevant public communities outside the circle of visitors been reached with the project?

Signs of quality: Above-average positive customer feedback; top position in rankings, awards. Above-average, detailed and positive reporting (word of mouth, media); 'copycat projects'.

Relationship management

Question: How have relations to the project's essential stakeholders (owner, suppliers, team, authorities, etc.) changed?

Sign of quality: Existing (positive) communication; intent to work together again; positive feedback from stakeholders

Usually the *quality of the management process* can only be assessed by the members of the project organisation. Naturally the views of the project owner may differ from those of the contractor (as may also those of the project/operations manager from those of the project team/the crew). Even for this reason alone it is extremely important that project controlling takes place continuously, and that work done is extensively documented.

When assessing the quality of the management process, 'factual' and social aspects have to be evaluated separately. A central aspect of evaluation is the analysis of communication within the project, especially the question of whether the owner of the project was continuously kept informed and consulted.

The *quality of the result* (in terms of the consumers) can usually be assessed reliably with the help of various methods drawn from market research. Naturally the most significant feedback comes from the internal or external owner of the project. Such feedback is often subjective because it is likely to be based on personal perceptions, personal values and experiences.

The *quality of the processes* also has to be analysed and scrutinised as part of the project review. Were the means, methods/techniques and processes that were chosen for the project adequate and, in their respective roles, did they support or rather hamper achievement of goals (for example, managing access to mega events)?

Project: event

In some respects there are huge differences between event projects and projects of other kinds (e.g. investment, development of organisation or IT projects). One of the major distinguishing features is the division into three distinctly separate phases: *preparation, implementation* and *follow-up*. Allocation of resources and even more so the duration of the three phases is another characteristic.

The preparation and follow-up phases are usually much longer than the implementation phase itself. Furthermore, in the majority of cases the follow-up phase uses far less resources than the preparation phase (although there are exceptions). This is another reason why the preparation phase is subjected to a further sub-division for practical purposes. There are several approaches to that and we will explain the approach that we have chosen and give the reasons for our choice.

■ The phase-orientated approach to an event project

The consideration and structuring of the project phases is an important step on the way to successfully implementing an event (see Figure 12.3):

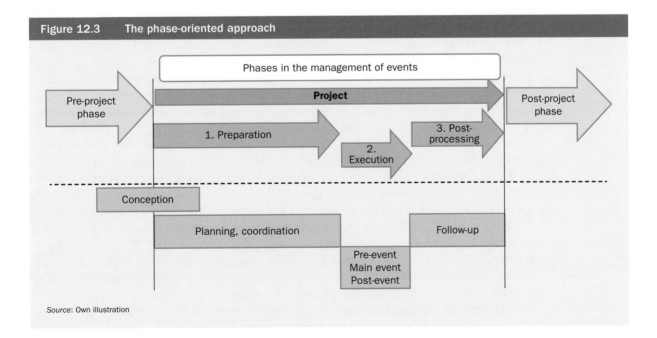

Figure 12.3   The phase-oriented approach

Source: Own illustration

Setting project limits with regard to both time and content

Even during preparation for the project, limits are set for the pre-project phase, the project itself and the post-project phase. The assignment of a project divides the pre-project phase from the project, while project approval divides the project and post-project phases. Divisions of project content are defined in accordance with project objectives, non-objectives, project scope and the budget. Considerations about phases, or the content of an individual phase, also depend on the perspective, i.e. the role, of the observer. The team implementing an event may also see an event as a chain of projects to be organised (e.g. a procurement project, marketing project, implementation project, follow-up). From the owner's point of view an event project may also be part of a programme (company marketing).

Pre-project phase

Preparation of event projects is characterised by the necessity to compile a draft plan as the basis for all subsequent steps. The starting point of the draft plan is a briefing (internally or externally). In the case of new projects the draft plan is preceded by brainstorming. The practicability of the idea is analysed by means of a feasibility study (Getz, 2005, points out that a pre-feasibility study may be advisable for major projects). Holzbauer et al. (2005) calls the subsequent decision-making process (go/no go decisions) as the project's first milestone (M1). The conclusion of this phase is characterised by the milestone 'contract granted' – 'M2' or 'go on/stop decision' according to Holzbauer et al. (2005).

Note: In the majority of cases the draft plan stage does not form parts of the actual project. It may happen, however, that the concept for the project (commissioned event projects) is part of the project. It follows that compiling a draft plan is then also part of the project.

The preparation phase is sub-divided into planning and coordination. The planning sub-phase is for the most part characterised by a follow-up briefing from the project owner (team) on the basis of the order, so-called 'moving' (adaptations to the concept) and the subsequent milestone of freezing. This means that content details, including the budget, are approved by the project owner, creating the basis for a binding agreement. The coordination phase involves preparation for the event on the basis of the agreement made. Cancellation or postponement is no longer possible after the coordination phase. Holzbauer et al. (2005) call this milestone 'M3' or the 'point of no return'.

Execution of the event (operations)

Thomas et al. (2004) understand execution as the actual implementation of the event. They sub-divide this phase into pre-event, main event and post-event. Following the preparation phase the event is 'started up'. The pre-event includes any necessary setting up on-site, plus any preparatory measures contained in the operating plan. These include installation of equipment by all technical crews, the arrival of all involved/staff as well as briefing and supporting them, merging and motivating staff, and continuous controlling of processes by those responsible. This sub-phase ends with the milestone denoted 'M4' or official opening of the event (doors open) by Holzbauer et al. (2005). Doors open is the start of the main event phase which ends with the official closing (doors closed).

This active phase of the event is the core phase. All planning and preparation is geared to it. After the official conclusion of the event, all installations, technical equipment, the stage and other structures are dismantled and removed and finally the site is returned (Holzbauer et al., 2005, milestone 6: end of all activities connected with the event).

After the event the question of how successful it was arises. Were all objectives achieved? Was it a success financially? What kinds of lessons were learnt? These and other questions are dealt with in the follow-up phase. Several tasks fall within the scope of this phase, depending on the type and size of the event. As the significance of event marketing is increasing, reporting and following up on it are becoming a particularly important task. The final accounts and the documentation of the project are equally important. The project only wraps up after the final documentation of the event, disbanding of the project team and acceptance by the owner of the project. Holzbauer et al. (2005) call this milestone 'M7' or 'end of project'.

Characteristics of event projects

If project management of an event is viewed in its entirety it can also be defined as a *project with an anticipated crisis* from the project management point of view, because the implementation of an event is generally characterised by the unpredictability of processes (e.g. protagonists dropping out, unexpected visitor activity, a sudden change in the weather or a technical breakdown) and the fact that possibilities for resolving the crisis are restricted by time and resources.

Project crises are best prevented or overcome by appropriate risk management, which therefore is an important issue to be examined in the context of projects (see Meredith and Mantel, 2010). Conventional strategies for dealing with project crises (interrupting or stopping the project or starting over) are not an option for event projects for fundamental reasons (exception: elementary event). **For more in-depth explanations please see Chapter 11.**

Methodical problems in project controlling are another characteristic of event projects. In particular it is more difficult to design a progress report for event projects, even more so if progress categories are expected in percentages. Instead (although relatively uninformative) categorisations like 'started', 'in progress' and 'finished' can be used in controlling to maintain a coarse overview concerning the project's progress. Working to deadlines which are set when each work package is to be completed is relevant and tested in practice.

Blending project management with the implementation of an event is also characteristic of event projects, though not exclusively so. Raising awareness of that is one of the tasks of the current chapter. It is, for example, typical to assign project management as well as project implementation to one person (in a company). A strict separation of the function/roles is imperative especially with regard to the processes of supervision and controlling.

■ Project management processes

Managing a project

Project management is a method, or management model, aimed at structuring a project in order to manage it effectively and efficiently. Project management is dynamic, views matters in their full context, employs various tools and methods and also takes the project's environment into account.

Project management is the task of the project leader (who consults and liaises with the project owner, a steering committee where applicable, and the project team). The name of the project leader is already included in the project assignment form. He or she should have sufficient project management know-how or relevant experience and (in the case of major projects) deal solely with the processes of project management. In practice roles tend to overlap because the project leader is often operationally responsible for implementing the event as well, or is forced into this role by circumstances. The scope of his or her tasks and duties is ideally put down in writing in the job specifications, which also helps to identify potential role conflicts. As for smaller projects, it is probably unavoidable that the project leader also deals with tasks which have to do with content or operations. Social competence is one of the key factors for a project leader's success.

Planning a project

Project planning examines the content (scope, qualities), schedules and resources (staff, budgets) and demarcates them. This is done with standard tools (project scoping and context analysis, milestone plan, work breakdown structure, bar chart, cost plan, risk analysis, etc.). The choice and employment of tools depends on the size and scope of the project, and should be selected with intuition.

For a project leader, assigned for the execution of an event, project planning will include the capturing and processing of information on the envisaged course of the project. The steps below should definitely be taken into account in the planning phase.

■ *Define the project/set the scope*: Description of the project (the big picture), including a formal description of the owner's desires. This document is more than a briefing – it is a 'statement of understanding', intended to create a joint understanding of the envisaged project (transfer of pre-project knowledge into the project phase).

■ *Decide on project management instruments and methods*: The most important tools for controlling, supervising and managing the project are chosen. The tools should be continuously updated during the entire course of the project. For example: project structure plan (PSP), communication plan, Gantt chart, schedule, projection of costs, project manual, etc.

■ *Conduct eco-analysis for the project*: Examine relevant environments based on selected dimensions, examine risks and chances.

Project plans are continuously refined. As mentioned above, parts of the planning process will possibly be shifted to the pre-project phase. Defining goals is one of the most important steps in the planning process. Operational goals especially should be defined the SMART way so that afterwards the project's success can in fact be measured and evaluated. Exhibit 12.1 illustrates a helpful definition of SMART goals.

Exhibit 12.1   Definition of goals

Definition of goals: 'If you don't know where you want to go you mustn't be surprised if you end up in a totally different place' (attributed to Mark Twain).

It is imperative to define project goals the SMART way or else the processes of supervision and controlling become needlessly complicated.

Goals must be:

S = Specific, M = Measurable, A = Attainable, R = Relevant, T = Time-based

---

Content/services are deduced from the goals and recorded in a phase/structure plan which highlights the main tasks in the project. Milestones (important events within the project) are assigned to the phases, including an initial schedule of time limits which will be subsequently refined with a Gantt chart/network plan or similar tools. Resources are also recorded, presented and budgeted with the help of tools.

Coordinating a project

Next to planning and controlling, coordinating is the project manager's most important task during the ongoing project.

Project coordination is one of the project manager's continuous activities. Communication between the players follows the rules which were stipulated in the project-start process (personal discussion, telephone, email, video conferences). The project leader also keeps in touch with the project owner. Communication is supported by project management tools/methods (e.g. one-on-one talks, team meetings, to-do lists, protocols, etc.). Managing the environment of the project and the project's stakeholders is an essential task which tends to be neglected, however. Project marketing is often seen as a process in its own right, but in the case of event projects it can be regarded as a project coordination task of minor importance because the stakeholders as well as most of the team members rarely differentiate between the project and the event.

Project controlling

Project controlling is a project management process to discover deviations of the actual situation from the planned situation. Most of the impulses for the controlling process emerge from project monitoring. The elements of execution, monitoring, controlling and implementation go through an iterative process. Its purpose is to ensure goal achievement in all dimensions even when instructions/circumstances have changed. Various tools are available for controlling a project.

Project controlling uses many tools which are also employed in project planning because they provide important reference points for the target/actual comparison. Project controlling is the responsibility of the project leader and the project team since deviations from plans first come to awareness in the course of their work. Functioning communications structures and a ready schedule of measures in controlling are important here. Crucial issues in controlling are deliverables (quality), schedules and resources, and also the risks inherent to the project. The progress report is a central tool. Crucial results are documented in the project manual. Adjustment of plans (services/objectives) in consultation with the owner (team) is particularly important in project controlling.

The tasks/areas of event controlling in each phase are set out in Exhibit 12.2.

Exhibit 12.2   Tasks/areas of event controlling in each phase

In the planning phase: Re-examining the definition of the objectives, concept of the event (quality briefing), planning schedules and time limits, planning resources, budget planning (first draft budget = pre-calculation; continuous revision of the budgets = fine-tuned budget and permanent target/actual comparison)

In the implementation phase: Checklists, production plan, troubleshooting, feedback (area manager, visitors, customer), event concept (target/actual comparison). Quality controlling can also be seen as objective controlling. The focus is mainly on whether the goals that have been set are still achievable and whether the quality standard defined can be maintained. However, a planned objective which cannot be reached does not necessarily cause the project to fail. Objectives can be adjusted. Consulting with the stakeholders concerned and with the project owner, of course, is also important in that case.

In the final phase: Post-calculation (financial success; turnover, yield, marginal return for the agency), quality check (degree of goal achievement, e.g. number of participants, turnover, awareness, image, visitor satisfaction, feedback from staff, visitors, customer, service providers; assessed from the feedback are, for example, process quality, internal communication, professionalism), project manual (lessons learnt).

■ Project management methods and tools

This section discusses the following methods and tools of project management:

1. setting project scope and context analysis (environmental analysis, risk analysis);
2. project assignment;
3. project structure plan, work package specification and to-do list;
4. scheduling (milestone plan, schedule);
5. planning of resources (budget planning, staff deployment planning);
6. project organisation chart, diagram of functions, role descriptions, project rules;
7. controlling (progress report, risk management, quality controlling);
8. aids for executing the event (checklists, freight list, production plan).

Project boundaries and context analysis

The planning process always starts with defining the boundaries for the project and an analysis of the project context. It has proved useful to follow certain schemata, for example, by defining boundaries and conducting the analysis in different dimensions. Sterrer and Winkler (2006) suggest examination of the dimensions of time, content and 'social matters'. Another dimension could be added to this model: financial aspects. This is generally viewed as part of the content dimension. The *environmental analysis* (project context social) is an important tool in project management. Projects do not exist in a vacuum. The surrounding environment always affects practicability, the sequence of contents and the success of a project. Particular attention has to be paid to inter-personal aspects which can have a massive impact on the project.

Project assignment

The project assignment should mark the start of any project (commissioned projects and own projects). Schedules, roles, objectives, costs and income, risks and content are roughly outlined in the project assignment. It is thus a roadmap for the (further) course of the project.

The important and decisive first step in project management is the assignment itself. According to Gareis (2005), the assignment contains the objectives which have been jointly agreed between the project owner and the project team in the start process. The assignment always has to be confirmed in writing. A signed document may help to avoid complications later on and is therefore indispensable. The project assignment may replace a traditional confirmation letter, or both may be used. In general, the project assignment is seen as legally binding, and is thus a contract. For this reason alone ample time should be taken for drawing up the assignment and checking it before it is signed.

Exhibit 12.3 provides an example of a project assignment:

Exhibit 12.3   Example of project assignment

Project assignment

Project start event:	Project start date and time:
Project end event:	Project end date and time:
Project rationale/initial situation:	

Intended benefit:

Overall project objectives:	Non-content:
Measurable project objectives and deliverables:	

Main tasks/project phases:	Milestones:
	■ <milestone + planned date>

Project owner:	Project leader:
Member of the project team:	■ Others involved (e.g. in the company):
Project risks:	Project costs/resources:
<e.g. quality, schedule, team, acceptance, cost, technical risks, etc.>	<incl. rough estimate of hours or days by members of the project team>
<Date>, signature project manager	<Date>, signature owner

Work breakdown structure (WBS) and work package specification

The work breakdown structure (WBS)/phase plan is the 'Swiss penknife' among project management tools and the backbone of project planning/controlling/monitoring. The WBS provides an outline of tasks, interdependencies of content, processes and priorities.

A project structure plan breaks the global goals down into operational tasks and generally presents the main tasks/phases and work packages of a project. The task structure of the whole project is analysed and presented as a top-down procedure. A distinction can be made between project structure plans which are object-orientated, function-orientated, mixed-orientated or phase-orientated. A phase-orientated project WBS for organising events is presented in Exhibit 12.4. The complexity and the level of detail depend on the size and complexity of the event.

Exhibit 12.4	A phase-orientated project work breakdown structure					

Work breakdown structure

1. Conception	2. Planning	3. Coordination	4. Pre-event	5. Main event	6. Post-event	7. Follow-up
1.1 Receive briefing	2.1 Realise re-briefing	3.1 Agree PSP with area director	4.1 Realise locally area director meeting	5.1 Realise team briefing	6.1 Realise acknowledgment to the team	7.1 Be in charge of the customers and the employees
1.2 Realise brainstorming	2.2 Realise brainstorming (moving)	3.2 Brief project employees	4.2 Survey event location	5.2 Realise current coordination	6.2 Realise meeting destruction team	7.2 Realise billing of personnel
1.3 M0: event idea	2.3 Revise pre-calculation	3.3 Determine schedule	4.3 Realise check event setup	5.3 Realise reflection of customers and employees	6.3 Coordinate the removal of the event infrastructure	7.3 Conclude project documentation
1.4 Realise pre-calculation	2.4 Presentation for principal	3.4 Coordinate suppliers	4.4 Realise acceptance of areas (incl. official inspection)	5.4 M5: event formally closed (doors closed)	6.4 Return event-areas/ M6: end of work associated with the event site	7.4 Cash up project (post-calculation)
1.5 Analyse feasibility	2.5 Detail concept with substance determined (freezing)	3.5 Check authorisations	4.5 Realise final rehearsal			7.5 Establish internal project closure (dissipate project team)
1.6 M1: go/ no go	2.6 Project team determined	3.6 Agree plans	4.6 M4: event formally opened (doors open)			7.6 Realise project closure with principal/ customer
1.7 Submit an offer	2.7 Compile accurate budget	3.7 Develop Event scenarios				7.7 M7: project end
1.8 Order placed M2: go on/stop	2.8 Draft action plan and schedule	3.8 Realise closing meeting about all areas				
	2.9 Contract/ agreement signed (M3: point of no return)					
Booster phase		Preparation phase		Execution phase		Conclusion phase

Work package specification

The work package describes a task, or bundle of tasks, and explains what has to be done. The work package specification provides details on the various tasks (description of actions and results) and facilitates implementation of the work package as well as controlling it.

A work package describes a cohesive task within the project. It is a basic building block, handled by one member of the team or a group of the project team. The project manager defines the expenditure of time, the results and costs. Processes may arise within a work package which the project manager does not have to keep track of, as there is a person responsible for each of the work packages.

Scheduling

Milestone plan

Phases and milestones help to structure the project with regard to time and content. Milestone planning provides an overview of important events in the project, and forms an important starting point for project controlling.

In events management it is advisable to time projects with the help of phases (Holzbauer et al., 2005). By using phases the project can be realised in a structured and comprehensible manner. The course of the project is divided into time (phases) and organisational units, and milestones are defined for each phase.

Holzbauer et al. (2005) define the significance of milestones as follows (see Figure 12.4):

M0: Idea for the event.

M1: Those responsible decide whether the event will take place or not (basic go/no-go decision).

M2: At the end of the start phase a decision is taken whether to begin with the preparations for the event (opportunity to abort: go on/stop decision).

M3: After the preparation phase the event is initiated. Cancellation or changing the date is in general impossible after that (point of no return).

M4: Official opening of the event (doors open).

M5: Official end of the event and start of dismantling work.

M6: End of all activities connected to the event.

M7: End of the project.

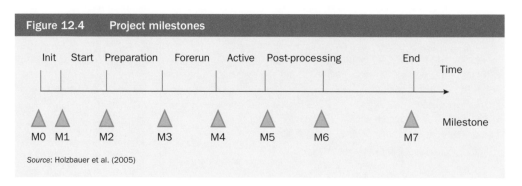

Figure 12.4   Project milestones

Source: Holzbauer et al. (2005)

Gantt chart

The Gantt chart tool is used for the graphic illustration of processes through time (and their interdependencies) in the project. The illustration is based on the main tasks and the milestones in the project.

The Gantt chart (also known as the bar chart) is probably the most widely used planning instrument for the illustration of project processes. A time limit is allocated to each process (Schreiter, 2009). In order to be able to depict correlation clearly it is necessary to illustrate it graphically as well.

In a Gantt chart individual processes are sorted according to their earliest launch date. The chronological structuring can also be presented with a project timetable (Wedekind and Harries, 2006). A timetable helps to structure the various project phases in a meaningful way.

Planning of resources (budget planning)

Planning of resources/estimation of outlay

Planning of resources is a complex task for which a number of tools are available. Staff, budget and infrastructure are important issues for consideration.

The following schema for estimating outlay is by Holzbauer et al. (2005):

1. Goal of the project, specifying the planned event.
2. Divide the whole project into manageable work packages based on the project structure plan.
3. Record the most important influencing factors:
   a. volume/number of visitors;
   b. complexity/size of the event;
   c. number of staff;
   d. duration of the project.
4. Look for similar projects/events with comparable influencing factors. Determine outlay by analogy (adjust according to the differences between cost drivers).
5. Determine outlay for the work packages, including estimate of possible deviations. Determine outlay by adding up outlays for all work packages.
6. Control through comparison of results.

The total outlay for the project is the sum of all partial outlays. Wherever possible, one should draw on experience and expert knowledge in order to make at least a rough estimate of the volume.

Budget planning

Budget planning shows what can be done and what has to be dropped. It is essential for planning and completing the project successfully, and it is one of the most important instruments of control.

Sound calculation of costs is the basis for any event's success. According to Wedekind and Harries (2006), many of the best and most creative ideas for events have to be abandoned in the end due to high costs.

The distinction between between different calculation phases

Pre-calculation (rough calculation)

Pre-calculation is done internally to determine the anticipated costs of a project and externally to determine the quotation price. In most cases, the costs are just estimated roughly – the event manager draws on experience or desk research. If similar events have been implemented in the past, their costs, according to Wedekind and Harries (2006), can serve as a guide. This first outline of costs is preliminary and non-binding. A precise definition of the costs has to be ready before the start of the project. The cost estimation has to be updated continuously and is reflected in the interim calculation.

Interim calculation

According to Wedekind and Harries (2006), this calculation phase requires a lot more effort than pre-calculation and the level of detail is much higher. Concrete determination of price is done after the decision to go ahead with the project has been taken. Quotes from service providers are compared and possibly renegotiated. Step by step the cost estimate of the pre-calculation is defined more precisely by the quotes obtained. This process ends with the freezing of the plan and thus fixing of the budget by the owner. After that, changes to the budget require supplementary budgets and follow-up billing.

Final costing

According to Wedekind and Harries (2006), the final costs can only be certain once the event has ended and all invoices have been received. Bills are compared to the estimates on which the interim calculation was based, and only then does it become apparent whether cost controlling was implemented successfully. Since in practice transactions and billing for events largely take the form of package deals, the deviations which become apparent through final costing are also decisive for the financial success of the organiser.

Case 12.1   Quoting for a staff party

An Austrian mobile phone company arranges a staff party once a year. Apart from being a relaxing get-together, it also provides a platform for intensive communication between management and staff. The agency's briefing is that an extensive programme of extra activities is desired, with several of a join-in nature (e.g. slot car race track, DJ workshop, Segway course or human soccer table). The highlight of the programme is an address by management followed by a buffet. It is to be a one-day event, preferably at a location with good public transport connections, and not too far from the company in order to boost the staff's willingness to attend. Based on previous experience, some 700 participants can be expected. Catering is a particular challenge in adhering to the budget because all drinks are to be included. This results in the biggest element of uncertainty when it comes to estimating the budget. Three agencies have been asked to submit a quote for this project. Based on a preliminary concept the budget estimate is as follows:

No.	Description	Quantity	Units/days/hours	Unit price	Total
A.	ADVERTISING MATERIAL/GRAPHICS/COMMUNICATION				
A1	Presentation preparation and production	-	-	-	300.00
A2	Signage, branding, graphics layouts	-	-	-	2,500.00
A3	Signage, branding, graphics production	-	-	-	2,300.00
A4	Texts, invitation procedure, internet	-	-	-	1,200.00
A5	Programming internet	-	-	-	0.00
A6	Balloons incl. helium and fastening	1400	-	-	950.00
A7	Packing balloons	(included in A6)	-	-	620.00
A8	Invitation cards	(included in A3)	-	-	540.00
A9	TPE ribbons incl. imprinting	1500	-	-	1,350.00
A10	Area plan and nameplate	1100	-	-	870.00
B.	HOTEL/LOCATION/INFRASTRUCTURE				
B1	Location rent	-	-	-	4,000.00
B2	Beach chairs	20	1	25.00	500.00
B3	Pillows	50	1	2.00	100.00
B4	Palms, big	10	1	50.00	500.00
B5	Palms, small	20	1	10.00	200.00
B6	Blanket	20	1	5.00	100.00
B7	Tables	20	1	5.00	100.00
C	PERSONAL				
C1	Taskmaster	1	6	550.00	3,300.00

Case 12.1   (*continued*)

No.	Description	Quantity	Units/ days/ hours	Unit price	Total
C2	Hostesses and hosts invitation and reminder	6	1.5	190.00	1,710.00
C3	Hostesses care action area	21	1.5	190.00	5,985.00
C4	Hostesses reception	3	2	190.00	1,140.00
C5	Logistician	5	3	190.00	2,850.00
C6	Moderation	1	1.5	700.00	1,050.00
C7	Photographer	1	1	650.00	650.00
C8	Technician	2	3	450.00	2,700.00
C9	Wardrobe	2	1	190.00	380.00
C9	Bus shuttle	1	0.5	190.00	95.00
C9	Security	3	1	190.00	570.00
C10	Expenses	-	81.5	15.00	1,222.50
D	CATERING				
D1	Catering dishes and drinks	-	-	-	66,000.00
E	SIDE EVENTS				
E1	Slot car train	1	-	-	1,500.00
E2	Goal wall	2	-	-	600.00
E3	Playstation park	3	-	-	450.00
E4	Aerotrimm incl. delivery	-	-	-	1,500.00
E5	DJ workshop and DJs	3	-	-	1,500.00
E6	Zorb	1	-	-	2,000.00
E7	Boule	5	-	-	750.00
E8	Neck-massage pillow	10	-	-	640.00
E9	Foot-jacuzzi bath	10	-	-	100.00
E10	Seven-league boots	5	-	-	500.00
E11	Basketball hoop	1	-	-	430.00
E12	Human table soccer	1	-	-	650.00
E13	Segway	5	-	-	1,150.00
E13	Stylist	1	-	-	0.00
E13	Bungeerampoline	5	-	-	1,150.00
F	TECHNICAL				
F1	AV, light and sound technology stage (incl. setup and removal)	-	-	-	9,200.00
F2	Delivery, transport	-	-	-	850.00
F3	Electricity incl. survey	-	-	-	600.00
G	OTHER ITEMS				
G1	Delivery, transport	-	-	-	500.00
G2	Videoteaser and videodocumentation	-	-	-	4,500.00
G7	Costumes and make-up artist for video	-	-	-	800.00
G3	Overnight stay	-	-	-	960.00
G4	Shuttle service	-	-	-	1,100.00
G5	Stamp for pointcard	-	-	-	380.00
G6	Decoration	-	-	-	500.00
G8	Crew clothes	-	-	-	850.00
G9	Other expenses	-	-	-	900.00

▶

Case 12.1 *(continued)*

No.	Description	Quantity	Units/ days/ hours	Unit price	Total
G10	Incidentals	-	-	-	600.00
G11	Event insurance	-	-	-	350.00
H	AGENCY				
H1	Fees, daily rate for visits/planning	-	-	-	12,500.00
H2	Phone costs	-	-	-	350.00
				Total	151,643.00

Source: MK Marketing GmbH (2011)

Based on its previous experience and enquiries to potential suppliers, the agency submits a first budget proposal amounting to €151,643.00. Total expenditure on the event after final costing is €150,268.00 excluding VAT, a result well within the original quote.

Discussion questions

1 What data and research are used as basis for the pre-calculation, interim calculation and final costing?

2 Discuss advantages and disadvantages of package deals for events from the project owners' point of view.

Project organisation chart, job description, staffing, diagram of functions, project rules

Project organisation chart

The project organisation chart is a tool for presenting the main features of project organisation. The chart displays responsibilities and powers as well as organisational relationships.

The more people are involved in a project, the more important it is to have a clear depiction of the structure of decision making and responsibility. The project organisation chart has proven to be a suitable method. It shows in a visual way the people involved in the project and their interconnectedness. It also illustrates the distribution of decision-making authority and specialist responsibilities. In a straightforward project organisation, according to Schreiter (2009), the project leader has full authority to give any instructions and make decisions, and thus bears overall responsibility for the project.

Case 12.2 Project organisation chart for a mega event

The Surf World Cup in Austria is one of the largest windsurfing events in the world. More than 100 competitors display their breath-taking freestyle skills at Lake Neusiedl. As the metropolitan areas of Vienna (Austria) and Bratislava (Slovakia) are not far away, the event attracts impressive numbers of spectators every year – some 100,000 visitors turn the 'Sea of the Viennese' into the hub of the international surfing world for a few days. A staff of more than 350 is on site to ensure smooth realisation of the event. A project organisation chart presents a clear division of the project into different sections, the transparent assignment of responsibilities within each section, and their competencies.

Discussion questions

3 What forms of project organisation charts are you familiar with?

4 Can team members be involved in several sub-teams? If so, under what conditions?

Case 12.2   (continued)

Project leadership
Kloibhofer Georg
DMG

Event location — Kloibhofer Georg / DMG
- Submission-documents / Egger Martin / lautstark
- Contract negotiation / Polak Gerhard / DMG

Frontoffice — Fröhlich Lisa / DMG
- Administration info booth / Fröhlich Lisa / DMG
- Personal info booth / Fröhlich Lisa / DMG
- Info cash desk, 09.05. / Fröhlich Lisa / DMG
- Office equipment / Fröhlich Lisa / DMG
- Preparation accreditation / Fröhlich Lisa / DMG
- Admission controll / Security / Doc X
- EDV System Akk. / Lehner Ralf / Fröhlich Lisa / RDL / DMG
- DMG office / Lehner Sabine / DMG
- Concept admission controll / Polak Gerhard / DMG
- Security / Schemann Florian / Doc X
- Infra. support / Berger Bernd / bb-support

Communication — Martin Egger / lautstark
- Concept of communication / Egger Martin / lautstark
- PR budget / Kloibhofer Georg / DMG
- Press accreditation / Egger Martin / lautstark
- Class. media relations / Egger Martin / lautstark
- Sport media relations / Egger Martin / lautstark
- Concert media relations / Egger Martin / lautstark
- Party media relations / Egger Martin / lautstark
- Graphic / ? / ?
- Photodesk / Patrick / Lackner / Pranger Solutions / DMG
- TV production / Zartl Chris. / TC / xxx / DMG
- Press office / ?

Sponsoring — Paul Marlene / DMG
- Concept of sponsoring / Polak Gerhard / DMG
- Accreditation section / Paul Gerhard / DMG
- Bannering plan / Polak Gerhard / DMG
- Zipfer / Zauner Bernhard / TC / Brau Union / DMG
- Pepsi / Sto Claudia / LP / Vöslauer / DMG
- Bacardi / Schwarz Alex / MP / Bacardi / DMG
- ATV / Höllmüller Gertraud / TC / ATV / DMG
- DOTZ / Mittenhofer Cornelia / LP / DOTZ / DMG
- LG / Takvorian / MP / LG / DMG
- Colgate / Takvorian / MP / Colgate / DMG
- Hawaiian Tropic / Takvorian / MP / HAT / DMG
- Bezirksblätter / Müller Sabrina / TC / BB / DMG

Organisation — Kloibhofer Georg / DMG
- Approvals / Kloibhofer Georg / DMG
- Insurances / Kloibhofer Georg / DMG
- Meeting coordination / Kloibhofer Georg / DMG
- Accommodation / Dunst Claudia / CCM incoming
- Event cash desk / Kloibhofer Georg / DMG
- Contracts for work / Kloibhofer Georg / DMG
- Total budget / Kloibhofer Georg / DMG
- Personal / Kloibhofer Georg / DMG

Infrastructure — Paul Elisabeth / DMG
- Infra. support / Berger Bernd / bb-support
- Infra. plan / Kloibhofer Georg / DMG
- Tents / Heinz / Sakelit
- Electricity / Kohl Andreas / Event Elektrik
- Area service / Trummer Christian / Sicherheitsdienst
- Approvals / Berger Bernd / bb-support
- Tent-backplane / Berger Bernd / bb-support
- Store and transport / Berger Bernd / bb-support
- Emergency medial services day / Trumer Christian / Sicherheitsdienst
- Decoration / Berger Bernd / bb-support
- Water/sanitary / Berger Bernd / bb-support
- Controlling / Kloibhofer Georg / DMG

VIP — Paul Marlene / DMG
- VIP support / 1,5 and 8,5 / Paul Marlene
- Facility & decoration / Paul Marlene / DMG
- VIP boat / Paul Marlene / DMG
- Security / Schemann Florian
- Dance lounge / Paul Marlene / DMG
- Cleaning VIP area / Clemens / Gebäudereinigung
- Infra. support / Berger Bernd / bb-support
- VIP boat/Judge boat / Harasser Toni / Mariakeller

PWA / EFPT Contest — Polak Gerhard sen.
- Organizer / Polak Gerhard jun. / DMG
- Registration / Verhung Martin / DMG
- Driver-support / DMG
- Airport shuttle / DMG
- PWA / Page Richard / PW
- EFPT / Schaffrian Harald / EFP
- Medical support / Dr. Kristen Karl-Heinz
- Competition crew / Polak Gerhard sen. / DMG
- Approvals BH / Polak Gerhard sen. / DMG
- Boat jetski / Verhung Martin / DMG
- Race-grid printings / Polak Gerhard jun. / DMG

Sport side events — Lach Mario / DMG
- Trend sports / Lach Mario / DMG
- Surf-kite programm / Lach Mario / DMG
- Surf exhibition / Lach Mario / DMG
- Driver's area - Pit Walk / Lach Mario / DMG
- Gambling hall / Lach Mario / DMG
- Pepsi playground / Lach Mario / DMG
- Infra. support / Berger Bernd / bb-support
- Programm planing / Dalinger Matthias / bb-support

Program — Dalinger Matthias / DMG
- Programmplaning / Trachta Carina / DMG
- Program on site / Dalinger Matthias / DMG
- Direction on site / Lach Mario / DMG
- Surf moderation / Hofmann Roberto
- Main moderation / ?
- Music day / ?
- Inh. sport side events / Lach Mario / DMG
- Ing. sponsor ingside events / Paul Marlene / DMG
- Inh. PWA contest / Polak Gerhard jun. / DMG
- Technical support / Groiss Reini / Light & Sound

Gastronomy — Kattier Lisi / DMG
- Cash desk / Guggenbichler Andreas / DMG
- FM sun deck / Wagner Sylvie / DMG
- FM Pepsi Playground / Paul + Nicky / Boardriders Club + U4
- FM DanceLounge / Club Fusion
- FM disco tent / Wendl Dina / Paul Lisi / DMG
- FM Royal captains / Plechura Mike / DMG
- Police / Kloibhofer Georg / DMG
- Emergency medial services night / Samariterbund
- Fire brigade
- Security / Trummer Christian / Schicherheitsakademie
- AKM / Polak Gerhard / DMG

Seaside festival — Trachta Carina / DMG
- Backstage area / Trachta Carina / DMG
- Sondchecks / Trachta Carina / DMG
- Band support / Trachta Carina / DMG
- Show crew technique / Backstage
- Accreditation section / Trachta Carian / DMG
- Cotrolling / Trachta Carina / DMG
- Accomodation artists / Dunst Claudia / CCM incoming
- Stage opening 30.4. / Dalinger Matthias / DMG
- Booking / Trachta Carina / DMG
- Infra. bachstage / Berger Bernd / bb-support
- Backstage catering / Kreiml Adiran / Kreiml bros.

▶

Case 12.2 (continued)

Organisation chart boxes:

- Parking area management / Trummer Christian / Sicherheitsdienst
- Tickets lido / Waller Gisch / PTF

- Assistance on site / ? / ?
- Media cooperation / Egger Martin / lautstark
- TV spot / Egger Martin / lautstark
- Radio spot / Egger Martin / lautstark
- HP: surfworldcup.at / Lackner Theresia / DMG
- HP: summeropening.at / TC / DMG
- HP: partyweek.at / Lackner Theresia / DMG
- Crises PR / Egger Martin / lautstark
- Printing products / Kloibhofer Georg / DMG
- Photographer day / night / Trachta Carina / DMG
- Photographer sport EFPT / Singer / Trachter / DMG
- Photographer sport PWA / ?? / Trachta Carina / D/G
- Controlling / Trachta Carina / DMG
- Infra. support / Berger Bernd / bb - support

- Red Bull / Schmid Werner / MP / Red Bull / DMG
- Persil / LP / Selina / DMG
- Ö3 / TC / DMG
- Zigaretten / Scheuchner Alex / KG / GWS / DMG
- Booths left / Lach Mario / DMG
- Exhibitor centre right / Paul Marlene / DMG
- Sponsor production / Paul Marlene / DMG
- Bannering / Berger Bernd / bb-support
- Infra. support / Berger Bernd / bb-support

- Sound & music sundeck / Groiss Reini / Light & Sound
- Sound & music dance lounge / Spitz Ivo / Spitz Ivo
- Sound & music disco tent / Heimo / Heimo
- Community achievements / Berger Bernd / bb-support
- Container / Kloibhofer Georg / DMG
- VIP restrooms / Luely / Luely
- Cleaning / Clemens / Gebäudereinigung
- Rental-furniture / Haburka / Schönbrunn Verleih
- Rental-bars / Johannes / Groove Prod.
- Plants / Eibinger / Eibinger Graz
- Rental-elements / Pesi / MAPE

- Surf moderation / Hofmann Roberto
- Security driver'sarea / Trummer Christian / Sicherheitsdienst Trummer
- Infra. support / Berger Bernd / bb-support
- Driver's area / Lach Mario / DMG

- Video & photo / Patrick TM
- Sound/light sun deck / Groiss Reini / Light & Sound
- PWA program point / Poiak Gerhard / DMG

Source: DMG Marketing GmbH (2009)

Job description

Job/role descriptions are a tool used in recruiting members for the project team. They facilitate the selection of team members and provide clarity about duties, roles, responsibilities, interfaces and necessary qualifications.

Staffing schedule

The staffing schedule is a tool for planning the use of human resources. It helps to determine requirements and reveals overlapping and wastage. It is also an important risk management tool.

Diagram of project functions

The diagram of project functions presents tasks and responsibilities. Roles are shown in a structured manner. The diagram of functions is an important tool in project controlling.

Establishing a project culture/setting project rules

Project rules generate and define the project culture, boost work efficiency and can significantly reduce the amount of work in a project. Project rules apply to different sections of a project, facilitate or make possible the integration of different personalities/work cultures, contribute to avoidance of conflicts and support project marketing.

An example is shown in Exhibit 12.5.

Exhibit 12.5   Example of project rules

Conduct in a project
Punctuality
No phone calls during project meetings
Those present have a say in decisions
Joint responsibility for results
No side discussions during project meetings

Project documentation
All data is centrally saved on the server drive xxxxx
The project number is added to the title block of all correspondence
Templates filed at/on xxxxx are to be used

Project marketing
In external discussions the project is always mentioned in a positive way, problems are dealt with and solved internally

---

Controlling (progress report, meeting controlling, project manual, protocols)

The progress report shows whether the project is on track. Apart from progress and the use of resources, the report also records social parameters such as the atmosphere in the team.

One precondition for successful event controlling (Holzbauer et al., 2005) is meaningful, comprehensive and timely reporting which provides information on whether the objectives for deliverables and costs are being achieved. Reporting should also be the basis for reaching agreement on goals and for controlling compliance with agreements.

According to Holzbauer et al. (2005), the following questions have to be answered to establish successful reporting:

- Who is responsible for compiling reports?
- To what level of detail/summarisation level should the data be recorded?
- What type of calculations have to be made?

- Should comparisons be included and what data should be compared?
- What reporting cycle should be used?
- What type of (software) assistance is needed?
- What is the purpose of the report (documentation, analysis, evaluation)?

The *progress report* is the most important instrument for keeping all persons and interest groups involved in the project, and especially the project leader, informed about the project's current status. The report is a tool for deadline controlling. Most importantly: information is provided to superiors to monitor whether implementation is progressing according to plan.

Another tool for controlling is the *meeting on controlling* where schedules, costs and services are dealt with using the tools employed in the planning phase. To conclude the meeting, results are recorded and measures are deduced or specified. Important issues to examine in a meeting on controlling are the milestone plan and the Gantt chart (or other instrument chosen for time planning), the costs projection, the finance plan (if available) and the staffing schedule. The WBS and the work package specifications complement the issues to be considered.

Project documentation

The most important tool for project documentation is the 'project manual' (for our purposes this is a generic term for various forms of written documentation). The manual addresses the important issues of the project assignment, the progress report and all other tools which are relevant to planning. It illustrates the major content of the project and related activities. Software tools are increasingly employed for the purposes of documenting a project. An extensive range is already available. Alternatively, 'home-made' templates based on spreadsheet software, for example, are also excellently suited for this purpose. Furthermore, 'cloud' project platforms have existed for some time now which can be used to document and discuss (by video conference or chat) a project's progress and allow a selected group of people access to the results.

Project documentation is an important prerequisite for efficient project management because it reflects everything connected to the project (Schreiter, 2009). In order to ensure that this is indeed the case, documentation needs to be complete, up-to-date and structured. Project documentation is based (Schreiter, 2009) on all information, both internal and external, within the project and on the subject of project. According to Schreiter (2009), *protocols* are an important building block for documentation and detailed guidelines are needed. Protocols record the status quo of the project, and often very concretely determine the further course of action. Therefore it is necessary that all relevant persons are verifiably made aware of them. Ideally, protocols are addressed in the project manual.

Aids for executing an event (checklists, supplies lists, production plan)

When events are staged one takes whatever help is available, i.e. not only the classic methods, techniques and tools of project management. Creativity and flexibility are permitted and even to be encouraged. Complementary techniques support the realisation of the main processes and contribute to ensuring/increasing quality.

Checklists

Checklists help to make complex project work easier (Holzbauer et al., 2005). Advantages of using checklists:

- They ensure that all the important points which are necessary for the successful realisation of a project are taken into consideration and dealt with.
- Checklists can be used for precise definitions of areas of responsibility.
- Processed checklists show procedures and decisions and thereby ensure control and traceability.

When checklists are compiled it needs to be kept in mind (Holzbauer et al., 2005) that it is impossible to record every single partial task which is necessary to complete the main task in a checklist. This would only lead to confusion and unnecessary inflation of project administration.

Holzbauer et al. (2005) recommend giving a name to each checklist. In order to work effectively with checklists, it is necessary that uniform standards are applied to their compilation and volume of information. Each individual cell refers to one item, object, task or decision that needs to be dealt with. Following the style of Holzbauer et al. (2005), they should be structured as follows:

- *Status*: in process, dormant, completed.
- *Subject*: individual task.
- *Result*: catchword illustrating the result.
- *Who*: person who dealt with this.
- *When*: date of dealing with this.

Holzbauer et al. (2005) provide a more detailed discussion on the subject of checklists and illustrated examples of different checklists.

List of names

It often happens that many of the staff involved in an event meet one another for the first time just before the start of the event. The list of names is a document which contains all relevant contact persons, not only internal staff, but also all the suppliers and service providers (Wedekind and Harries, 2006). Apart from company names and contact details, it is important to also include the contact persons on site, their role and telephone number. This list is handed out to all members of staff and the service providers at the event.

Production plan

The production plan presents the course of the event. It ensures (Wedekind and Harries, 2006) that every service provider and staff member knows the place and time where they have to render their service. It rarely happens, however, that everything goes according to plan – in practice it is therefore clear that changes to the plan have to be expected in the course of the event, and often at very short notice. The project leader is responsible for keeping track in this situation, for continuously updating the production plan and coordinating the players in question according to the changed requirements.

Supplies list

The supplies list or packing list is continuously updated and contains all the equipment required on-site, plus the logistics requirements (who delivers what, when, in which quantity and where). The importance of this tool increases with the size and complexity of an event. A checklist of the necessary equipment is usually sufficient for smaller functions. Exhibit 12.6 provides an example.

Conclusion

Anyone in events management who believes they can get by without project management has only themselves to blame for the consequences. Project management (and its associated tools) facilitates planning, implementation, controlling and the evaluation of event projects. Project management tools should be employed according to requirements, and with a sure intuition. Event projects have some peculiarities/characteristics which set them apart from other types of projects. The presence and involvement of the public, for example, is a major challenge which always brings a dynamic into the project, because the behaviour and expectations of people can only be anticipated or manipulated to a

Exhibit 12.6   Example of supplies list

cargo list

item	purpose	total	supplier	transport	state	car	delivery	collection
Nokia charger	–	1	lautstark	lautstark		Voyager	18.08.2008	
scored card smart on boat	accreditation	100	lautstark	lautstark				
announcement list DVD dispatch KBFilm	accreditation	1	lautstark	lautstark				
announcement slip TN	accreditation	1600	lautstark	lautstark		Jumper	19.08.2008	
car flag	accreditation	1000	Proad					
autograph card "ShySays"	accreditation							
batteries (Digicam Nikon)	accreditation	2	lautstark	lautstark		Voyager	18.08.2008	
bar B-kit, 5 pieces	accreditation	1	smart Stuttgart	delivery lounge-furnitures		Voyager	20.08.2008	
office box	accreditation	1	lautstark	lautstark		Voyager	18.08.2008	
digicam (Nikon) + electric cable, main cable	accreditation	1	lautstark	lautstark		Voyager	18.08.2008	
DVD dummies for showcase	accreditation	6	lautstark					
felt pen for autograph session	accreditation	10						
flipchart + pens (whiteboard)	accreditation	1	lautstark			Jumper	19.08.2008	
flyer A6 for distribution Stadtfest	accreditation	1500	digit-aldruck.at			Jumper	19.08.2008	
guest list MBÖ-dinner Steigenberger	accreditation	1	MBÖ	BAP				
guest list MBÖ-lunch Areitalm	accreditation	1	MBÖ	BAP				
guest list Ö3 winner	accreditation	1	Ö3	BAP				
mobile phone for accreditation Nokia - 0699 11114040	accreditation	1	lautstark					
hostesse's suitcase (make up, plastes, medication)	accreditation	1	NIC			Jumper	19.08.2008	

cargo list

item	purpose	total	supplier	transport	state	car	delivery	collection
hotel list	accreditation							
info package	accreditation	5	lautstark	BAP				
Kahla showcase with decoration / "Mallvitrinen" showcase 4 (Kahla) with 3 shelfs	accreditation	1	smart GmbH DE/ Klartext Gmbh				20.08.2008	
folding monotube frame A4	accreditation	1	lautstark			Jumper	19.08.2008	
Laptop Sony Vaio (reparation)	accreditation	1	lautstark			Jumper	19.08.2008	
list of members smarttimes.at	accreditation	4	lautstark	BAP				
dust bin (caterer on site)	accreditation	2		on site				
Pago sponsorware 0,33l squirted and Guave)	accreditation	2000	Pago	on site				
paper	accreditation	10 Pack.	lautstark	lautstark		Jumper /1 Pack Voyager	19.08.2008/ 18.08.2008	
staff planning list	accreditation		lautstark					

limited extent. At the same time, a particular perception of the event, or attitude towards it, is a central goal of event projects.

In practice the boundaries between project management and operational management become hazy at times – if the event project is awarded to a general contractor, for example – because the designated project manager (often an external service provider) is at the same time in charge of the event and its realisation. As a result, several views on setting the scope of the project, on objectives, output and the use of resources may exist in parallel and have to be brought into alignment. Quality (and its management) and risk (and its management) are particularly delicate issues in project management for events. Particularly in the case of outdoor events, risk increases exponentially. Corresponding analysis and appropriate management tools help to assess the impact and to cope with blatant project crises. The project leader has the most important role in the project team, and in addition to experience and know-how s/he should have a stable, communicative personality. The project assignment document is an indispensable project tool, also for events, because it ensures the players perform a minimum of planning activity, which at least outlines the most important deadlines, the timeframe, the costs and the responsibilities congruently (agreement between project owner and project team). Implementation takes on a central role when the characteristic phases of an event project are examined. Due to the high risk potential which is associated with this usually very brief phase, event projects may be defined as 'projects with an anticipated project crisis' – it can be overcome, however, with the strategies customary in project management (discontinuation, postponement, etc.).

General discussion questions

5 Discuss the term 'quality' in an events management context.

6 Describe the usefulness of the project assignment and specify the information it should contain at a minimum.

7 Specify the significant risks with which project managers have to deal when organising events, and cite methods of risk assessment and risk analysis.

8 Specify methods of structuring event project tasks time-wise, and address the advantages and disadvantages of these methods.

9 List the differences between project management and event operations.

Guided reading

An extensive literature on project management now exists. See especially:

Gareis, R. (2005) *Happy Projects* (English edn). Vienna: Manz.

The author offers a system-orientated approach to project management which also fits in well with the concrete subject.

Also see:

De Bono, E. (1971) *The Use of Lateral Thinking*. London: Jonathan Cape.

Kerzner, H.R. (2009) *Project Management, A Systems Approach to Planning, Scheduling and Controlling*. Hoboken, NJ: John Wiley & Sons.

Mehltretter, R. (2006) *Eventmanagement im Sport – Planung, Durchführung und Kontrolle*. Saarbrücken: VDM Verlag Dr Müller.

There is a wealth of information in:

Getz, D. (2005) *Event Management and Event Tourism* (2nd edn). Putnam Valley, NY: Cognizant Communication Corp.

There are also numerous blogs on project management; some of the more useful ones are given below under 'Recommended websites'.

Recommended websites

Fear No Project: **http://fearnoproject.com**

PMI: **www.pmi.org/**

Project Management blog: **http://projectmanagementblog.com**

Project management:

Top 25 Project Management Blogs: **www.odesk.com/blog/2009÷05/top-25-project-management-blogs**

Top 50 Project Management Blogs: **mastersinprojectmanagement.org/top-50-project-management-blogs.html**

Key words

milestone; project; project crisis; project management; project planning

Bibliography

Gareis, R. (2005) Happy Projects (English edn). Vienna: Manz.

Getz, D. (2005) *Event Management and Event Tourism* (2nd edn). Putnam Valley, NY: Cognizant Communications Corporation.

Holzbauer, U., Jettinger, E., Knauss, B., Moser, R. and Zeller, M. (2005) *Eventmanagement – Veranstaltungen professionell zum Erfolg führen*. Heidelberg: Springer.

Meredith, J. and Mantel, S. (2010) *Project Management, A Managerial Approach*. Hoboken, NJ: John Wiley & Sons.

Patzak, G. and Rattay, G. (1998) *Project Management*. Vienna: Linde Verlag.

Schreiter, D. (2009) *Der Event als Projekt – Ein Leitfaden zur Anwendung von Projektmanagement*. Wilhemshaven: Academic Transfer.

Sterrer, C. and Winkler G. (2006) *Let Your Projects Fly*. Vienna: Goldegg Verlag.

Thomas, O., Kaffai, B. and Loos, P. (2004) *Referenzmodellbasiertes Event-Management mit ergebnisgesteuerten Prozessketten*. Saarbrücken: Institut für Wirtschaftsinformatik.

Wedekind, J. and Harries, J.W. (2006) *Der Eventmanager – Das Handbuch aus der Agenturpraxis*. Münster: LIT Verlag.

Chapter 13

Events and new media technologies

Lukas Rössler, Fosbury e.U., Austria

Learning outcomes

Upon completion of this chapter the reader should be able to:

- describe **new media** and explain how they can be categorised;
- explain how you can use new media for events management;
- identify which theoretical principles are crucial for the development of **events 2.0**;
- discuss how important new media are and what kind of position they have in regard to events management of today and of the future.

Overview

Figure 13.1
QR code to
access case
studies

This chapter on Events and New Media Technologies introduces the current trend of combining offline events with online components in a convergent way. The seven pillars of the underlying theoretical concepts will be illustrated, followed by an overview of the specific possibilities for event managers in the area of new media technologies. In addition to **social media**, which are utilised as an interactive expansion of events, **interactive event tools** will be presented that allow the instant transfer of the event participants' emotions into the online world. The last section of the chapter is dedicated to a new event type, called 'events 2.0', which emerged from new media technologies.

This chapter features regular best practice examples by innovative agencies and renowned companies so that readers can get to know the mentioned technical possibilities with their practical implementation. In order for the chapter to live up to its name, the case studies (videos of the mentioned examples) can also be directly accessed with a smart phone via QR codes. In order to do so, you need to own a smart phone with an integrated camera, download a QR reader app for free (e.g. i-nigma), open the app and scan the QR code (see Figure 13.1).

Introduction

The event industry is rapidly changing. Trends appear, are reflected in events and disappear quickly again. Some trends manifest themselves, become a part of mainstream usage and begin to grow unstoppably. Therefore, in addition to the know-how illustrated in this book, event managers should acquire knowledge of new media and mobile technologies. This is more necessary than ever. According to the IBM 5-in-5 Research Study (IBM, 2011), 80% of the world population will own mobile devices in 2016 – which offers completely new possibilities for international events management. If one takes into consideration that, in the UK, already more than 50% of mobile access minutes fall upon social networks (The Guardian, 2010) and the Facebook app alone is utilised by 250 million smart phone users (Grabs and Bannour, 2012: 397), it is clear where this road is leading.

The fact that new media trends have led into their own convergent event niches, and that their monetarisation is well underway, is further proof that now is the time to contribute a chapter entitled 'Events and New Media Technologies' to this book.

Events 2.0 – the convergent combination of offline events with the online world

The strength of real-life events mainly lies in the transfer of information. But even more so, their power is the transfer of emotions through the directorial and dramatic act per se. People encounter each other, interchange and have a multi-faceted experience designed by the event manager that circulates between the five sub-processes of emotion, the senso-motoric system, imagination, linguistics and communication (Frank, 2012).

The strengths of the online world mainly lie in pushing the locally given boundaries of the event location, in providing the emotional as well as informative processes with viral effects and, thus, spreading the message. As a result, the publicity of the event can be increased significantly (Amiando, 2011).

In order to use and promote these effects in event planning, a mix of the following seven pillars between the poles of offline events and new media technologies has to be given:

- media convergence;
- interactivity;
- digital storytelling;
- collaborative media usage;
- participative media production;
- game theory, ludology and the playful usage of media;
- gamification.

Seven pillars between the poles of offline events and new media technologies

The basics of the above-mentioned success factors are seven theoretical concepts that have their origins in the scientific areas of psychology, media science and interactive entertainment.

■ Media convergence

According to Latzer (1999: 31), the term 'media convergence' describes the merging of the different types of media – telecommunications, television, computer, radio broadcasting, print and internet – on a technical and functional as well as on a content-wise level. Thereby, the internet is the integrating medium of all 'old' media as it technically combines telecommunicative media (e.g. Skype telephony), audio-visual media (e.g. live streaming, Video on Demand or YouTube) and auditory media (e.g. radio live streaming or iTunes) as well as print media (e.g. *The Guardian* or *Frankfurter Allgemeine Zeitung* online). But websites, social media, blogs, etc. are also structured on a content-wise level in such a way that usually more than two of the above-mentioned media can be found on modern websites.

The consequences of this concept determine the following trends:

■ The internet in combination with modern, high-performance smart phones leads straight to the replacement of traditional media – and, in any case, to their mobile integration.

■ The concepts of what is 'real' and what is 'virtual' are blurring more and more (e.g. smart phone apps: Runtastic, eCaddy, Wikitude, etc.).

■ A trend towards activating the user with the help of mobile internet/smart phone as a 'lean forward medium'. The user becomes the director and designer of their own media use.

■ Each one of us becomes a medium. Through Twitter, Facebook and others, every recipient is also a transmitter. One-way communication is broken through. Everybody has the possibility of running their own medium with the help of status updates, blogs, links and the like (one-to-many, many-to-many).

■ Interactivity

'*Inter*' means 'between' and implies an exchange of at least two parties – a dialogue. '*Activity*' implies an active relationship between two parties. Interactivity is one of the most-used terms in the area of events. Thereby, the goal is to involve the guests in what is happening at the event through personal activity with the content of the event. Miller (2008: 54 et seq.) distinguishes between the following interactivity types:

■ *Sensormotoric system*: the perception of the stimulus through the sensory organ and the motoric behaviour are directly related. These processes take place simultaneously, for example between eye, ear and the targeted control of arm and foot movements when driving a car. The sensormotoric system combines the sensory system with the motoric system. At events, the guest is activated sensorimotorically by certain *sensible* items on the programme such as walking, running as well as moving the arms and legs.

■ *Emotion*: is a psychophysiological process that is triggered by conscious and/or unconscious perception and interpretation of an object or a situation. It goes hand in hand with physiological changes, specific cognitions, subjective experience of feelings and a change in behavioural willingness. The event participant is emotionally charged through sensory inputs. The aim is the emotional engagement with the topic of the event.

■ *Cognition*: the cognitive capabilities of a person include, for example, attentiveness, memory, learning, creativity, planning, orientation, imagination, argumentation, introspection, will, beliefs and quite a few more. With the help of deliberately staged intervention possibilities within the story (e.g. 'Do I get information B before A?' or 'Do I decide on path A or B?'), the event designer gives the guest the possibility of directing and influencing the individual event experience through their own cognitive capabilities.

Interactivity is only one of two possibilities of reacting to narrative content. The other possibility is passive consuming. Interactive content turns the participant into an active user. Interactive content should be designed in a *multi-sensory* way.

◼ Digital storytelling

Two old forms of social interaction are the big predecessors to digital storytelling: rituals and games. Despite the long time span between 'back then' and 'today' and the technical possibilities available to us nowadays, rituals and games help us to define the critical components of digital storytelling.

But, first, let us take a look at the characteristics of traditional storytelling:

- ◼ Stories are pre-constructed. Elements of the story cannot be changed.
- ◼ Stories have a linear narrative form (the plot).
- ◼ The author/writer is the sole creator of the story.
- ◼ Stories are experienced in a passive way.
- ◼ Stories have an unalterable ending.

Now we compare them with the possibilities of digital storytelling:

- ◼ *Interactivity*: the user controls, or at least influences, the exact course of the story.
- ◼ *Non-linearity*: scenes or sub-events do not necessarily need to take place in a set order. Characters do not necessarily need to appear at set places and times.
- ◼ *Strongly involving*: the story involves the event participant due to their activity. Their experience is absorbed with all senses. The participant thereby becomes the co-author of the story.
- ◼ *Self-navigation*: the event participant looks for their own path through the story.
- ◼ *Breaking through the 'fourth wall'*: the participant can communicate with the characters of the event. They behave like real persons.
- ◼ *Blurring of reality and fiction.*
- ◼ *Different perspectives*: many digital storytelling events offer the participants the possibility of taking different perspectives and/or being different characters within a story (e.g. interactive movie *Heavy Rain*).
- ◼ *Different endings are possible.*
- ◼ *Designed for the collective memory*: participants can share information and, thus, help each other.

Event designers can use these digital storytelling possibilities to create and bring to life completely new perspectives within the staging of events, thus enabling a range of new experiences. Devices such as smart phones, tablets and interactive tools are the realisation tools for this interactive staging (Miller, 2008: 19 et seq. and 59 et seq.).

◼ Collaborative media usage

Collaborative media usage is a theoretical concept describing the fact that people preferably use media together. In the primeval times of analogue media, people would gather at the village square in order to read the new announcements on a bulletin board or listen to them being read from the village stage and then discuss the issues (e.g. 1517: Martin Luther's 95 theses on the main door of the Castle Church in Wittenberg). Later on, people would gather around the radio and television set for important events. The collective experience of the cinema is still popular. And also new media depict this human need with the largest collaborative websites Wikipedia and Facebook (Rössler, 2009: 151 et seq.)

■ Participative media production

Participative media production is the result of collaborative media usage and one of the most-discussed buzz words in the entertainment industry. Thereby, the task is to try to satisfy the needs of the shared media experience with the help of interactive exertion of influence on the events. The staging of the participative media production can take place in three different ways:

- *Technical design:* Technical aids are supposed to help turn the passive viewer into an interactive part of the event. Examples therefore are TED (televoting) or SMS voting in game or casting shows. But also newer technical tools such as augmented reality (more on that topic further below) are used for the interactive integration of participants.
- *Emotional design:* A story is embedded in a cross-medial way in people's minds with the help of *brainscripts*. This story, supported by the actual event, triggers a great extent of involvement. An example therefore is the FIFA World Cup, where the following brainscript can be triggered within football enthusiasts: 'If I had started playing football earlier and had more talent, I would have been transferred from my village football club to the national team. If I would have been born in the country of the champions, I would be playing in the world cup final now'. Due to this brainscript, every person is theoretically a part of the final event of the FIFA World Cup, which therefore triggers such strong emotions.
- *Hybrid model of technical-emotional design:* Emotional brainscripts are triggered with the help of technical tools. Their goal is to lead the participant into a convergent event world where the boundaries between reality and virtual fiction blur. An example for this is the online sports event *Ski Challenge* that is referred to as the world's biggest ski race. Parallel to the Ski World Cup, 3.5 million participants race on the 'real' ski runs in order to win the virtual title (Rössler, 2009: 152 et seq.).

■ Game theory, ludology and the playful usage of media

Game theory is the science of playing and describes a still young, transdisciplinary branch of research. It deals with the aesthetic, cultural, communicative, technical and structural aspects of the game phenomenon, where cultural and structural sciences meet. The main focus lies on history, development, analysis and the theory of play. The focus of ludology, however, is primarily on digital games. Digital games have become a mass-cultural phenomenon, with the computer considered a universal medium. This way, not only can any kind of traditional game be implemented, simulated or played with computer assistance, but also a whole range of new games or events is only possible with the computer – partly in combination with content and techniques of other media forms (e.g. literature and film). This convergence development makes digital games ideal study objects in order to acquire general knowledge on playing (Tadelis, 2013: 5 et seq.).

■ Gamification

According to Stampfl (2012), gamification is the approach to applying the concept of playing to situations that actually do not have anything to do with real games. The aim is to make these situations as interesting, entertaining and motivating as 'real' playing is. A few simple examples are points that can be earned and goals that are given with the help of Nike+ or Runtastic. This motivates the user to more effort and enables winning points due to their own performance. These points can then be used to enable new features.

Therefore, gamification means the transfer of elements from computer games into real life, away from the television set or the monitor. In particular, it also means to keep users loyal to a product or a brand and to confront them with it again and again. Already in 2008, there were critical lectures on the combination of real actions with game mechanics – but hardly anyone was interested in these theories on the 'transparent gamer' until Foursquare got millions of people to document their daily life on the Web 2.0 by distributing colourful pictures. The rest of the trend is history and future at the same time.

Social media

Take a look at the following video (Figure 13.2) as an introduction to the topic.

**Figure 13.2
QR code for
*The Social
Media
Revolution***

*Source: www.
youtube.com/
watch?v=ZQzsQkMFgHE*

Here are some of the most important statements from the video *The Social Media Revolution*.

- '96% of the people born after 1980 are members of a social network.'
- 'Every fourth search result for the global top 20 brands leads to user-generated content.'
- '78% of the users trust recommendations from their network – only 14% trust advertisements.'

Social media networks change the business and private worlds. With more than a billion Facebook users, the same amount of YouTube users as well as 200 million Twitter enthusiasts one has to acknowledge that the critical mass in social media has been reached. We can no longer talk about a trend, we have to talk about a communication revolution. With its countless interaction possibilities, Web 2.0 has created new feedback channels for the consumer and, of course, for the event participant. The historically developed one-way communication of old media such as TV, radio, print, etc. has evolved into multi-way communication. This particularly means that the event participant gains more power over the design process of events and – due to an average of 305 Facebook friends or 208 Twitter followers – becomes a (reactive) medium.

Social media are predestined to create virality with snowball effects. This means nothing else than that – with a competently designed **social media marketing** strategy – it is possible to reach an extremely high media penetration through recommending and sharing. These viral effects can be catalysed by integrated features. On Facebook, for example, event invitations can be made, friends can be tagged or marked on photographs and videos, location information or status updates. There are also location-based services such as Facebook Places or by third-party suppliers such as Foursquare via the open interface Facebook Connect. A viral strategy is usually supported by advertisements in social networks, videos posted on YouTube as well as service companies such as seeding agencies that are supposed to spread the message in Web 2.0 with the help of opinion leaders.

But social media is not only suitable for the promotion of events. In the sense of the events 2.0 philosophy, it also can be utilised to transfer emotions from real events directly into the virtual world and to conceptualise event stagings in a convergent and cross-media way. Furthermore, the staging that is locally limited, because it takes place on-site, and the corporate claim can be transferred across these boundaries within a split second – with the help of Facebook, YouTube and Twitter. Smart phones and tablets play an important part as interactive transmission media in the present and the future.

It is recommended to take the following *five virtual rules* into consideration when it comes to event staging with the help of social media marketing:

- With social media marketing campaigns you have to be willing to cede the control over the message.
- If you are *transparent, open and communicative,* you have nothing to fear!

- Don't ask what you gain with social media marketing. Rather ask yourself what you and your expertise can contribute. *Create respect and trust!*
- Respond to positive as well as negative criticism immediately.
- Be part of the community – it is only then you will come across as authentic.

To summarise, these are the principal reasons why a social media strategy makes sense for events:

- Generating valuable linking leads to better search engine rankings of the event website with the search algorithms by Google.
- Social media increases the planning capabilities and offers an opinion research tool relating to content for event managers.
- Feedback can be directly obtained from the guests.
- Questions can be answered and interactively communicated immediately with the help of event tools such as social media walls.
- Social media – in terms of integrated brand communication – can serve as a worldwide carrier of the message and the staging of the locally limited media penetration.
- Emotions can be shared and spread via smart phones and tablets immediately within social networks.
- Thanks to innovative approaches, a modern image is communicated (Weinberg, 2012: 60 et seq.).

Interactive new media tools for events management

Two interactive new media tools have evolved that can be brought into action to build a bridge between the virtual and real level in events management. They therefore ensure interactivity.

Invitation management 2.0

Invitation management 2.0 means the use of websites and database systems that are especially programmed for the needs of event managers when it comes to event invitations. They can be administrated easily, offer numerous graphic possibilities to illustrate online registration as well as the perfect content-wise connection to the event itself.

Application possibilities in events management

- Email invitation with a personal code and an individually brandable and personal microsite is possible, including programme information, directions, etc.
- It is possible to send the invitation by QR code as an MMS to the smart phone of the guest.
- Ascertain all necessary information (rooms, smoker, vegetarian, etc.).
- Real-time overview of the registered participants. A personalised email can be sent at the touch of a button – e.g. to all guests who have not yet registered.
- On-site registration: barcode on smart phone or a print of the email. Display: '*Welcome, Ms XYZ*'.
- Side events: ID with barcode lanyards (e.g. lotteries, photo allocation).
- Follow-up on personalised microsite (e.g. photos, videos, questionnaire).

Voting tools 2.0

Voting tools were already used in the TV shows of the 1990s, from which we remember the large and heavy TED boxes (televoting). In the last few years, several technology systems were developed that offer voting tools in credit card size and weight, as well as implementing them on an app basis. These applications function with a very low failure rate and can be directly integrated live and interactively into the presentation of the lecturer (e.g. as a PowerPoint Chart). However, there are also creative application possibilities that are available to the event manager.

Application possibilities in events management

- Voting analysis in real time. Complete integration into the PowerPoint presentation of the lecturer is possible.
- Anonymous or personalised queries of the event participants are possible via input options on the smart phone. The lecturer can immediately react to these questions that are loaded onto his or her monitor.
- Increased sustainability of event goals through the active involvement of the participants.
- Integration of additional information in the app menu (e.g. agenda, lecturer profile, product information).
- Installation of photos or video clips is possible.
- Short-term intervention of the operator into the content before and during the event (e.g. shifting programme parts, times for breaks).
- Web-enabled with WiFi.

Interactive multi-touch applications

These represent media that enable users to experience digital content extensively. Interactive, playful elements can visualise even complex data or processes in a descriptive, comprehensible and especially playful way. Visualisation is possible on almost any surface, whether the multi-touch tables, walls, phones or floors. Thereby, unique communication environments are created that can be adjusted quickly and inexpensively to the various locations and therefore allow for the utmost flexibility. Tracking technologies replace human interface devices such as mouse and keyboard by human gestures and movements, gaming pieces, infrared pens, multi-touch applications or wireless headphones. Thereby, several event participants can access information at the same time. This democratic participation significantly increases the level of attention: the participants absorb content more intensively and for a longer time.

Application possibilities in events management

- *Multi-touch tables* have a large screen as the table surface as well as an invisible integrated computer. Usage is via the touch-sensitive screen. If this touch screen can distinguish several touching fingers or objects at the same time, it is called a multi-touch screen.
- *Multi-touch floors:* the projection is directed towards the floor. The users interact with their feet. The size of the projection is variable. Multi-touch floors can be operated easily and in a playful way. They are extremely effective and therefore especially interesting for exhibition stands and product presentations. As orientation and navigation systems for museums or exhibition halls they provide visitors with multimedia edited information on the current position in the location.
- *Multi-touch walls* help users to experience digital content intuitively. The user interaction takes place through laser or gesture-supported multi-touch technology. It doesn't matter what kind of texture the wall has: it can be made of wood, glass, stone or a different material and, before you know it, turns into an interactive multi-touch screen of any size. This can always be used when complex content requires descriptive and interactive illustration: for product presentations, lectures, infotainment, event introductions, etc.

**Figure 13.3
QR code for
video on
applications
of multi-touch
systems (This.
Play Showreel
2012)**

Source: *http://vimeo.
com/58150713*

■ *Interactive phones* are wireless headphones that have an integrated laser beam. This way, users can navigate through different audio-visual content on a projection surface. The selection is made by a long glance. The deposited picture, sound or video files are then activated and shown. This leads to extended interaction possibilities with the event environment.

■ Case multi-touch systems

Use your mobile device and watch the following video (Figure 13.3). It will show you the possible applications of multi-touch systems.

■ Social media wall

This is an interactively projected and easy-to-handle discussion surface for events. It is used by the event audience directly on their smart phones via the below-mentioned social network apps Facebook, Twitter and Foursquare. The social media wall combines Facebook postings by users, tweets on Twitter, check-ins on Foursquare and photos in a stream. Additionally, if so wished, email messages can also be included.

This is depicted on a web browser that can also be integrated on the Facebook fanpage for a limited amount of time. An administration tool is also used which enables an administrator to approve of the content before publishing it or to block unwanted content. Additionally, an SMS service can be enabled via a free or value-added number from which also text messages can be sent to the social media wall.

**Figure 13.4
LeWall@
LeWeb '10**

Source: *www.
youtube.com/
watch?v=0ZyKj7UJ9Sg*

Case 13.1	Social media wall Le Web '10

The social media wall was put to use with great success at the Le Web '10 exhibition.

Use your mobile device and watch the following video (Figure 13.4). It will show you the use of a social media wall at Le Web '10:

Discussion questions

1 What social media can be integrated in a social media wall and what makes sense?
2 What are the advantages and drawbacks of a social media wall?

Mobile tools for smart phones and tablets

According to Wikipedia, *mobile marketing* describes all kinds of communicative business activities that involve the provider establishing services on the basis of mobile devices (smart phones, tablet PCs) such as digital content (games, songs, videos, etc.), information (news, alerts, product information) and/or transactions such as shopping, video streaming, payments, etc. – and catch the attention of potential consumers. This ideally leads to a sale.

The relevant and most effective forms of mobile marketing for event managers are described below. These are apps, mobile tagging, mobile augmented reality, RFID as well as Bluetooth marketing.

Krum (2012: 32) confirms that mobile marketing is especially useful for events that take place in real time, such as sports events, concerts, conferences, festivals or conventions. It is important to know which content and what type of interaction the guests expect. Mobile marketing can help to cause interaction, to give information at the relevant time, to generate customer data and to link the real event world with the online world. The 'always on' mentality of mobile users allows the recipients to be reached in any situation with their personal devices.

▣ Smart phones and tablets (mobile media)

According to the 2011 IBM study 5-in-5, 80% of the world population will own mobile devices in 2016. The possibilities that will arise from the expansion of the mobile broadband standard LTE seem to be huge. The following list of smart phone and tablet PC functions is intended to increase comprehensibility and relevance for events management:

- broadband internet access;
- integration of software applications;
- GPS positioning;
- compass function;
- proximity sensor;
- acceleration sensor;
- microphone;
- Bluetooth;
- near-field communications (NFC);
- camera;
- touch screen;
- audio rendition;
- high-resolution graphic display;
- telephony;
- SMS.

According to Mayer (2012: 26), the biggest advantages of mobile media are the following:

- Permanently carried: mobile web is always accessible as the necessary terminal device is pocket-sized and can be carried around everywhere.
- Always online: mobile web is accessible anywhere anytime. The technical infrastructure and flat-rate models will make this possible very soon.
- Available at creative impulse: the mobile web can be used spontaneously and impulsively any time.

The two most important negative factors in 2013 seem to be the topic of data security as well as the still insufficient battery service life, especially when the devices are used a lot with 3G, WiFi and GPS.

Apps

Ten years ago, having their own website was of high importance for an event organiser. Today, its equivalent is a mobile app. Many organisers ask themselves if it makes sense to have a mobile app programmed. Today, its equivalent is a mobile app, and many organisers are asking themselves if there is a case for having a mobile app programmed from the point of view of either customer value or commercial interests. It is not only tablet hype that has brought mobile apps and the mobile web increasing attention from the prosumer crowd.

According to Bernoff (2010: 91), modern and successful apps for events feature three factors of success:

- immediateness;
- simplicity;
- context.

Immediateness means that the guest is provided with something that is needed in just that instant. A crucial factor is *simplicity* – one or two clicks have to be enough to reach the desired purpose. The *context* increases the utility of the app – as, with the help of GPS, smart phones know where the customer is, who their contacts are and what has just been photographed.

■ Mobile tagging

QR codes are the best-known type of mobile tagging technology. They are highly popular in Japan and have been expanding from Asia to Europe and the USA since 2007. The background and overriding objective of all applications is the vision of *media convergence*. Mobile tagging combines static, analogue information carriers with the internet and, furthermore, encourages the consumer to *act interactively* (Winter, 2011: 11 et. seq.)

The process of mobile tagging

- *Coding*: website addresses, text, SMS, contacts (free service *http://goqr.me*).
- *Decoding*: smart phones with camera and scanning software (e.g. free app *i-nigma*).

Application possibilities in events management

- *Extended information*: Give your event a secret theme which only guests can activate and which thereby focuses increased attention on the product.
- *Direct download*: give away ring tones, videos and singles at music festivals with the help of smartly placed QR codes.
- *Convergent combination of online and offline*: provide flyers, posters or texts with additional information, e.g. YouTube videos or raffles.
- *Branding*: design the QR code with the logo of the event or replace the black dots with contrasting colourful dots. Background information: up to 30% of the codes can be hidden or not legible.
- *Digital business card*: offer this service at networking events, for example, as a new form of contact exchange. At exhibition appearances, you can also scan the guests' QR codes instead of collecting conventional business cards.
- *Selling device mobile/online*: in real stagings, lead your guests to the online shop via the mobile device without them having to memorise complicated URLs.

**Figure 13.5
The QR job
application**

Source: *www.
youtube.com/
watch?v=acnLepjWe8E*

Case 13.2   Mobile tagging

In order to show you an in-practice example, an idea of how to use QR codes for your own application in a creative way has been mapped out for you.

Use your mobile device and take a look at the following video matching this case (Figure 13.5).

Discussion question

3 New media technologies can be used in several creative ways. What would be your idea of implementing QR codes in your life as an event manager?

Mobile augmented reality

Mobile augmented reality is computer-supported expansion of the perception of reality. This information can address all human senses. Often, however, augmented reality is only understood as the visual illustration of information. It is the addition of pictures or videos with computer-generated supplementary information or virtual objects with blending-in/overlaying.

The user requires a smart phone with an integrated camera and augmented reality software (e.g. Wikitude). The app thereby uses the position of the user generated from the GPS and compass data.

Application possibilities in events management

- Virtual objects at events, in museums, at exhibitions, e.g. display of photos and videos that were made at a special location.
- Navigation and routeing through the event area – facilitates finding stages, catering, ATMs or the own tent at a festival.
- Image detection: this means that – analogous to the QR code – each event flyer or event poster can generate added value with the 'scanning' of a photo by smart phone. Possibilities range from reduced entry fees to additional information on the event, etc.

Figure 13.6
Google Project Glass

Source: *www.youtube. com/watch?v= 9c6W4CCU9M4*

Case 13.3	Augmented reality

For a few years now, mobile augmented reality techniques have been tested that do not run on smart phones or tablets. Google, for example, announced in 2013 that it was putting augmented reality glasses called *Google Glass* on the market. This means a further development step towards complete convergence. Use your mobile device and take a look at the following video matching this case (Figure 13.6).

Discussion questions

4 What does a technology such as the Google Glass mean to you in terms of interactive event staging?

5 How could this technology be used in real event cases?

6 What does media convergence in this case mean to you?

Bluetooth marketing

Bluetooth – well-tested over several years – offers a reliable possibility to transmit information with creative staging tools. Mobile phones in the nearer proximity are addressed by the Bluetooth Trigger Server. The three steps on how Bluetooth marketing works are:

- *Device detection*: devices with Bluetooth switched on are searched within a radius of 1 to 100 metres from the Bluetooth Station.
- *Permission request*: the user is asked for permission to receive data. If the answer is positive, content upload starts. If it is negative, the device ID is put on a black list in order to prevent another permission request.
- *Content upload or activation*: after approval by the user, the content is transmitted to the mobile phone or activated free of charge.

Application possibilities in events management

- De-escalation management at mega events in order to reach participants in critical areas, even if the mobile network does not work, e.g. due to overload.
- Locating pre-installed material on the mobile phone for paper chases or quizzes (e.g. videos).

- Locating websites (streaming).
- Handing out mobile coupons (e.g. at the entrance).
- Event agenda/guide with map.
- Product information.
- Audio samples (e.g. at concerts).
- Preliminary results, results (e.g. football, tennis).

■ RFID

Radio-frequency identification, normally referred to as *RFID* enables the automatic iden-tification and localisation of objects and living creatures and therefore considerably facili-tates the acquisition of data.

The advantages of this technique result from the combination of the *small size*, the *low key selection possibility* in a distance of a few centimetres to 10 metres (e.g. ski lift tickets, swimming pool chips) and the *small price* of the transponder (often only a few cents).

Application possibilities in events management

- Anonymised route analyses, e.g. at exhibitions and conventions.
- Admission control and statistical acquisition of attendance figures.
- Triggering function for media, e.g. when somebody approaches a welcome screen, a video is played. The registered ID can then, for example, be linked to the name of the participant.
- Time registration at running events.

New interactive ways of event staging – Events 2.0

With new media, brand staging is developing fast. A big shift in the perception of such stagings could be observed in the last few years. All signs indicate that event manag-ers will no longer get along with knowledge of classic storytelling, staging and dram-aturgy. They will have to become familiar with (cross-)media literacy in the areas of interactivity, online, social media, mobile, film, literature, IT, user campaigning, with how mass media works, with parlour games and theme park staging in order to be able to cope with tomorrow's challenges.

New forms of staging have developed due to the above-mentioned influencing fac-tors. Their aim is to *combine the best of the real world with the best of the virtual world in order to create a convergent event experience world.*

The participants should be integrated to an extent that they themselves become the act of the evening. This means that the participant slips from the approaching passive viewer role into the role of the active participant.

In the early years of this millennium, marketing events especially began the develop-ment of this trend. The aim of a brand is to obtain sympathy and loyalty to the brand with the help of an active occupation in an attractive environment.

During the planning phases for customer loyalty events (e.g. top customer events or incentives) or classical marketing events placed within the marketing mix (e.g. product presentations, jubilee gala, opening events), it was always the following questions that were posed by marketing experts:

- Which possibilities do I have to promote my product in an innovative way?
- How can I reach as many people from my target group as possible?
- How can I offer my customers something new that they have never experienced before?
- How can I make my brand come alive in an interactive way?

For marketing and event managers, new perspectives have opened up due to trends and developments in the areas of cross-media, viral marketing, online marketing, social media marketing and mobile marketing.

Social media events

**Figure 13.7
Coca Cola
Village 2010**

*Source: www.youtube.
com/watch?v=
SSZ9v8oUaRY*

Social media events frame the combination of *social media content* with *real event worlds*. Traditionally, this type of event is staged and realised in a cross-media way. Sometimes this type of event is also called *Real Life – Social*. In any case, it is about a convergent event design between the poles of social media and real life.

Social media events are therefore the next step when it comes to transferring Web 2.0 into real life. The convergent transfer of social media into 'real life' is the next step when it comes to Web 2.0 – for reasons of simultaneous realisation and for branding-policy reasons.

**Figure 13.8
Heineken case
study**

*Source: www.
youtube.com/
watch?v=tEqJV1acgN4*

**Figure 13.9
Hyundai i40 –
Light reveal**

*Source: www.youtube.
com/watch?v=
xp4TOE8UP58*

Case 13.4	Dramaturgy and staging of a social media event

On a dramaturgical and technical level, the following types of characteristics can be observed in the area of social media events. Thereby, often the characteristics and cases mentioned below overlap:

Staging with the help of transmission media such as RFID, NFC or Bluetooth in combination with social media such as Facebook. Find the video on the *Coca Cola Village 2010* case (Figure 13.7).

Cross-media staging with the help of TV or web streaming, social media and event storytelling. Find the video on the *Champions League Match vs Classical Concert* Heineken case study (Figure 13.8).

The usage of interactive virtual social media applications for smart phones or PCs in combination with the realisation of real life events. Find the video on the *Hyundai i40 light reveal* case, a convergent car presentation (Figure 13.9).

Discussion questions

7 What are the challenges of staging social media events?

8 What do you think are the factors of success of social media events?

Pervasive entertainment

> Pervasive entertainment – entertainment that is all around you, 24 hours a day, persistent – probably location based – possibly merged with real world – driven by devices that are mobile, always on & location aware
>
> Gary Hayes (Transmedia expert)

Pervasive entertainment formats use smart phones and tablets as playing devices and enhancement of the virtual dimension. Thereby, apps and interactive websites are used that are especially programmed for use with smart phones and tablets. These interactive technologies turn participants into the main character of their very own event.

Pervasive entertainment formats can be played and experienced outdoors as well as indoors. They usually work location-independent and are embedded into the 'real world' with GPS, NFC or augmented reality. A customised storyline fuels the course of the game, offers new mysteries and gives hints to reaching the goal. The players interact with the story through virtual as well as real world experiences. Reality and fiction merge. The reality perception of event experience can be intensified by including videos, augmented reality applications as well as real actors.

■ **Dramaturgy and staging of a pervasive entertainment format:**

- Application of *localisation technologies* such as GPS, Bluetooth as well as augmented reality.
- Pervasive entertainment formats can be played indoors as well as outdoors. Most of them can be used independently from the location and are embedded into *location-based maps* such as Google Maps or OpenStreetMap.
- *Smart phones* are used as playing devices and as enhancement of the virtual dimension. Often, *apps* and *responsive websites* are used that are programmed especially for the use of smart phones and tablets.
- Some pervasive entertainment formats can be played in a certain *time window*; others can be played at any time.
- *Storytelling elements* become more and more important when it comes to the development of pervasive entertainment formats, as they fuel the course of the game and activate new riddles. Thereby, so-called '*locative media*' (also widgets or gadgets) come into action. This term describes digital media (usually as an illustration on the game map on the smart phone) referring to the real location with the help of localisation technologies. The usage of these locative media leads to events in the real game world.

**Figure 13.10
The Witness**

Source: *www.
youtube.com/
watch?v=Yis6is8v9jA*

Case 13.5   **An outernet movie:** *The Witness*

As *best practice example,* please watch the movie, *The Witness – The first movie in the outernet* (2011), a real-life social thriller in Berlin (Figure 13.10).

Discussion questions

9 How can pervasive entertainment formats change the way of thinking in the process of event staging?

10 Which professionals are needed when drafting a pervasive entertainment format?

Conclusion

New media can do important things for events management: involve people, create interaction and fascination, transfer brand messages in an innovative, direct and social way as well as make events virally known across the local borders. The goal of this chapter was to provide you with an overview of the available new media technologies and to show you their importance with the help of the examples. The young discipline of events 2.0 should give event managers new tools so that they – with new convergent ideas – can offer the event sector exciting content and stagings. As the sector has just begun turning to the creative use of new media technologies, all doors are open to use these wow-effects for events.

Guided reading

The combination of events and new media technology is a relatively new field. As a result very little literature on this general topic can be found. However, there is a lot of special literature dealing with social media marketing (e.g. Weinberg) and mobile marketing (e.g. Krum) issues. Additionally if you like to be aware of the future trends and state-of-the-art in this topic you have to read online blogs, watch YouTube videos and attend conferences.

Krum, C. (2012) *Mobile Marketing*. Munich: Addison-Wesley.

Weinberg, T. (2012) Social Media Marketing – *Strategien für Twitter, Facebook & Co.* Cologne: O'Reilly.

Recommended websites

A newsblog related to this rapidly moving topic: **www.facebook.com/events20**

Key words

events 2.0; interactive event tools; social media; social media marketing

Bibliography

Amiando (2011) Social Media und Events Report 2011. **www.amiando.com**

Bernoff, J. (2010) *Empowered*. Munich: Carl Hanser Verlag.

Frank, G. (2012) *The Experience Science*. Vienna: Lit.

Grabs, A. and Bannour, K.-P. (2012) *'Follow Me!'*. Bonn: Galileo Press.

IBM (2011) **http://ibmresearchnews.blogspot. co.at/2011//12/ibm-5-in-5-mobile-is-closing-digital.html**

Krum, C. (2012) *Mobile Marketing*. Munich: Addison-Wesley.

Latzer, M. (1999) *Die Zukunft der Kommunikation*. Innsbruch/Vienna: Studienverlag.

Mayer, A. (2012) *App-Economy*. Munich: mi Wirtschaftsbuch.

Miller, C.H. (2008) *Digital Storytelling*. Burlington, MA: Focal Press Verlag.

Rössler, L. (2009) *Massenphänomen Online-Sport-Events: Am Beispiel der Ski Challenge*. Munich: Grin Verlag.

Stampfl, N. (2012) *Die verspielte Gesellschaft: Gamification oder Leben im Zeitalter des Computerspiels*. Hanover: Heise.

Tadelis, S. (2013) *An Introduction to Game Studies: Games in Culture*. Princeton, NJ: Princeton University Press.

The Guardian (2010) **www.guardian.co.uk/ media/pda/2010/feb/08/facebook-rise-mobile-web-use**

Weinberg, T. (2012) *Social Media Marketing – Strategien für Twitter, Facebook & Co.* Cologne: O'Reilly.

Winter, M. (2011) *Scan Me – Everybody's Guide to the Magical World of QR Codes*. Napa Valley, CA: Sustainable Living.

Chapter 14

The event life cycle

Robert Kaspar,[1] FH Kufstein Tirol – University of Applied Sciences, Austria

> ## Learning outcomes
>
> Upon completion of this chapter the reader should be able to:
>
> - analyse the long-term perspective for bidding and hosting mobile events;
> - understand the **event life cycle**;
> - differentiate between the stages of the event life cycle;
> - explain the importance of the event life cycle for the host destination;
> - give advice how to develop a long-term destination strategy through an event.

Overview

Most events follow similar patterns from the idea, the hosting to the post-event perspectives. Especially for mega events, the long-term impacts can only be evaluated years after the event. In the following chapter, the event life cycle and its significance for a long-term destination development perspective will be discussed. From the idea to the feasibility study, the stages of planning and organising an event are described. A special emphasis is put on the venue and general infrastructure master planning and the destination branding process. The chapter concludes with the view on the long-term destination positioning, tourism product development and venue management. A case study on the Ramsau Nordic Ski World Championships and the Sochi Olympic Winter Games complements the chapter.

Introduction

As discussed in Chapter 2, events can be characterised by different dimensions, e.g. size (micro, macro, mega events), event content (culture, sport, business and society), origin of active participants (regional, national and international). Regardless of what kind of event it might be, it has a local, national or even international impact. Hence all political, economic, social, technological, legal or environmental (PESTEL) aspects must be taken into account during the planning of short- and long-term impacts of an event. The event life cycle gives an overview of all the stages of an event which must be considered. Events

---

1 The author would like to acknowledge the support of Julia Schwarzmayr and Felicia Kerschbaum.

need precise planning through all stages in order to finally reach the predefined objectives. The key issue is that the post-event development needs to be carefully considered even in the earliest stages of the event life cycle.

The event as product – the product life cycle

Polli and Cook (1969) interpret the product life cycle (PLC) as a time-dependent model of sales. The PLC model says that sales follow a consistent sequence of stages, beginning with introduction and proceeding to growth, then to maturity, and afterwards into decline. In the beginning, a product finds initial resistance and is purchased by only a limited segment of the buying population. Later, as the product's performance and value are known and communicated to a greater part of the buying population, a larger segment of buyers adopt it, and sales begin to increase faster. As the proportion of adopters gets closer to a maximum, so the rate of growth decreases. At this stage many sales represent repeat purchases. From this point on, the rate of adoption remains more or less constant throughout the maturity phase and diminishes in the decline phase (Figure 14.1) (see Polli and Cook, 1969: 386–390). PLC theory concludes that all products go through these four basic stages: (1) introduction, (2) growth, (3) maturity and (4) decline (Kozak and Martin, 2012: 189).

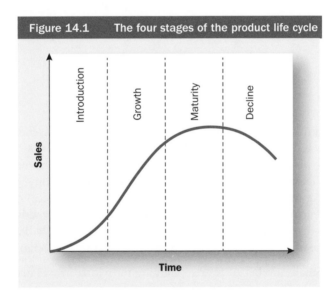

| Figure 14.1 | The four stages of the product life cycle |

The destination as product – the destination life cycle

'Tourism area life cycle (TALC) is one of the most cited and contentious areas of tourism knowledge' (Hall, 2006: xv) As Hinch and Higham (2011: 190 f.) state, 'destination and product life cycles are dominant features of tourism . . . Various implications emerge from these cycles, with the most obvious being that management intervention is needed to sustain tourism resources if the destination's life span is to be extended'. The tourist area life cycle model describes – in analogy to the PLC model – the stages of a destination's progression from (1) exploration, (2) involvement, (3) development, (4) consolidation, (5) stagnation, to (6a) rejuvenation or (6b) decline (Cole, 2012: 1128).

The destination life cycle model is based on the product life cycle concept. Visitors will come to an area in small numbers initially, restricted by lack of access, facilities and

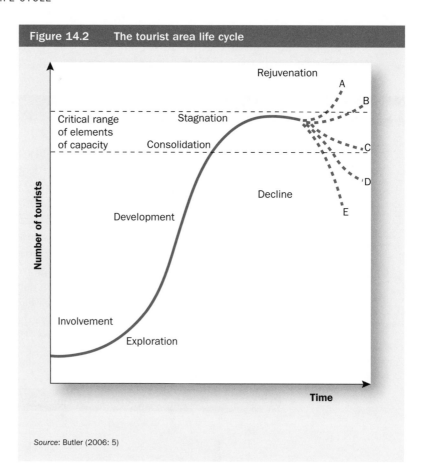

Figure 14.2   The tourist area life cycle

Source: Butler (2006: 5)

local knowledge. As facilities are provided and awareness grows, visitor numbers will increase. With marketing and additional facility provision, the area's popularity will grow rapidly. However, the rate of increase in visitor numbers will decline. This may be because of environmental factors (e.g. land scarcity, water quality, air quality), limitations in capacity (e.g. transportation, accommodation, other services) or social factors (e.g. crowding, resentment by the local population). As the area's attractiveness declines relative to other areas, the actual number of visitors may also eventually decline (Figure 14.2).

The tourist area life cycle model and its stages are characterised as follows:

1.   Small number of tourists making individual travel arrangements:
     ■   no specific facilities for visitors;
     ■   high level of contact with local population and extent of use of local facilities;
     ■   arrival and departure of tourists has little to no impact on local community; the social milieu or the physical fabric of area;
     ■   emphasis on natural and cultural-historical features of area.
2.   Involvement:
     ■   number of tourists increases, tourist season emerges, involvement with local population remains high;
     ■   start of provision of specific facilities for visitors;
     ■   advertising in a basic initial market, destination awareness increases (see Kozak and Martin, 2012: 189);
     ■   first pressure on the area's government to develop better transport, facilities, etc.
3.   Development:
     ■   well-defined tourist market area, shaped in part by heavy advertising in main markets; during peak periods number of visitors will equal/extend number of local population;

- local involvement and control will decline rapidly;
- local facilities start to be replaced by larger, more up-to-date facilities by non-locals, especially visitor accommodation; changes in physical appearance of the area are obvious;
- attractions, both natural and cultural, are developed and marketed; man-made attractions are invented;
- during peak periods imported labour will be utilised;
- market extension, type of tourist will change.

4. Consolidation:
    - total numbers of visitors will increase but rate of increase will decline;
    - great part of the area's economy will be tied to tourism;
    - greater extent of marketing and advertising;
    - extension of tourist season and market reach;
    - local population, especially those not involved in tourism, will try to develop restriction mechanisms to tourism.

5. Stagnation:
    - peak numbers of visitors reached;
    - environmental, social, economic problems;
    - well-established image, but no longer an 'in-destination';
    - heavy reliance on repeat visitation and conferences, etc.;
    - surplus bed capacity;
    - resort image is no longer connected to geographic environment;
    - frequent changes in ownership (e.g. accommodation);
    - organised mass tourism.

6a. Rejuvenation:
    - through a change of tourist attractions (man-made attractions are added or previously untapped natural attractions marketed);
    - reorientation of the area.

6b. Decline:
    - destination no longer competitive, therefore declining market (spatial and numerical);
    - increase in weekend and daytrips;
    - high property turnover (e.g. accommodation);
    - tourist facilities start to be replaced by other businesses;
    - involvement of population increases (purchase of facilities);
    - decrease in/losing of tourist function (see Butler, 2006: 4–8);
    - survive by creating a unique niche (see Kozak and Martin, 2012: 189).

Tourist destinations tend to follow this development pattern. The aim is to prevent visitor decline. Therefore tourism managers and policy makers try to reposition their destinations and market them to more tourist segments (see Kozak and Martin, 2012: 188). Research findings put emphasis on the importance of synergies between activities at a destination. Tourism managers and planners try to enhance these synergies from small ways (such as consistent signage) to total concept design (such as an all-inclusive holiday resort like Club-Med) (Cole, 2012: 1139).

The event life cycle

As tourist destinations can have a desperate need to constantly rejuvenate not only their image, they increasingly start to develop event concepts. Getz, who had already started developing an 'event life cycle' concept during the 1980s, states that 'events are an important motivator of tourism, and figure prominently in the development and marketing plans of most destinations. The roles and impacts of planned events within tourism have been well documented, and are of increasing importance for destination competitiveness' (Getz,

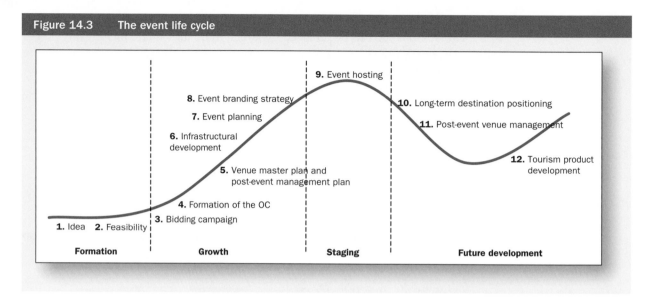

Figure 14.3 The event life cycle

2008: 403). Within a portfolio approach tourism managers have to think about the image and freshness of events invented for and thought to attract those specific market segments, and the attractiveness of the overall mix of events (Getz, 2008: 418).

Based on theories of the destination and the product life cycle, the author defines the following stages for an event with a focus on mobile and especially mega events (see Figure 14.3):

1. idea;
2. feasibility study;
3. bidding campaign;
4. formation of the organising committee (OC);
5. venue master plan and post-event management plan;
6. infrastructural development;
7. event planning;
8. event branding strategy;
9. event hosting;
10. long-term destination positioning;
11. post-event venue management;
12. tourism product development.

The 12 stages can be attributed to four different categories, which resemble those of the product life cycle with the difference that events should be planned for a long-term perspective keeping **sustainability** in mind. Therefore, the aim is to avert degeneration and to convert it into growth (future development).

The following sections give a detailed analysis of the 12 stages, their planning and the long-term effects on the hosting destination.

Formation

From idea to feasibility

Olympic Games, Expos, European Capitals of Culture, the Football World Cup and other culture or sport mega events are highly sought-after mobile events. Destinations expect various dimensions from hosting the event. The idea for bidding is based on the expected

Figure 14.4   Stakeholders

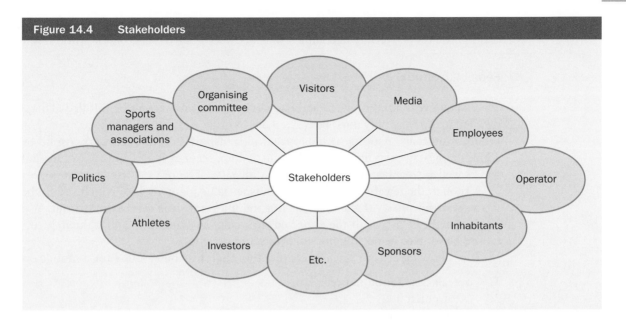

international media coverage, the development of infrastructure and tourism, the formation of jobs, or the creation of an image for the host destination. The impacts of events, which can also serve as reasons for bidding for an event, can be categorised according to the PESTEL principle (Kotler et al., 2007). The abbreviation stands for political, economic, social, technological, ecological and legal aspects which have impacts on an event and are supported by different stakeholders to a certain extent (see Figure 14.4).

The idea of bidding for a mega event typically originates from different stakeholders, ranging from politicians to business people and including core stakeholders from sports or culture.

The idea may arise from one of the following stakeholders:

- sports (federations, clubs, athletes);
- culture (venues, existing festivals, cultural groups);
- business (venues, companies, business development agencies);
- politics (all levels of government).

The underlying risk in this stage is that the idea is often developed by a certain group of stakeholders having their key target groups in mind. This may result in the idea:

- to bid for a sports event being launched by politicians;
- to bid for a cultural event by local tourism stakeholders; and
- to bid for a business event by the venue event owner or marketers.

At this very early but crucial stage an alignment of the singular event idea and an integrated event strategy/event portfolio needs to be examined. While one single mobile event may make sense for some of the stakeholders, it should be taken into consideration whether a long-term event strategy may sensibly follow fully from the single event. Another question of paramount importance is the issue of infrastructure, which will be discussed in the following section on feasibility. Generally it needs to be analysed whether the event fits the destination image at all and what the overall strategy of the host is.

Lillehammer hosted the Olympic Winter Games 1994 very successfully and will host the second edition of the Winter Youth Olympic Games in 2016. While considered to be the last benchmark for a small Olympic Games with a very strong sporting spirit, the idea was generated by seven local business people. The reason for Lillehammer to bid for the Olympic Winter Games in 1994 was that economic stagnation had been impacting the region since the 1980s. New growth potential was necessary in order to revitalise the economy and to strengthen regional tourism (Montville, 1994). The Olympic Games were managed by a successful business personality and left a strong and very positive image in the world of sports.

Feasibility study

To host an event a full range of stakeholder expectations need to be fulfilled. Therefore a detailed feasibility study must be carried out in order to analyse all expectations, potential benefits and risks. Aspects such as logistics (transport, accommodation), a solid budget, a long-term usage plan for the newly built venues, security issues and environmental matters as well as the integration of all stakeholders (see Figure 14.4) are of great importance.

Although the feasibility study is an indispensable planning tool which should be used in the start-up phase of the idea for hosting an event, it is rarely carried out. A consequence might be a lack of the expected (touristic) sustainability and ultimately an event failure because of neglecting possible risks and deficits.

The following are the key aspects of a thorough feasibility study for a mobile event:

1. overall destination master plan;
2. event portfolio;
3. destination and event image goals;
4. budget and financial risks;
5. city infrastructure;
6. venues;
7. accommodation;
8. transport;
9. rotation and event strategy.

The overall destination master plan should be either developed or cross-checked with the needs and benefits of the event. A city may strive to develop certain underdeveloped parts or aim for a regeneration of, most often, former industrial sites (also known as brownfield sites). Another dimension is the plans for extending train/metro networks and urban developments such as conference centres, stadia developments and other major infrastructural issues such as inner city redevelopments.

The event should also be integrated into a wider event portfolio; consequently the planned place and mobile events as well as potential complementary and succeeding events need to be listed in order to get an understanding whether the event fits the overall long-term event perspective.

A destination may have decided to position itself as a sports, cultural or business destination, and consequently it bids for a designated portfolio of events. It may also be the case that a city wants to rebrand itself utilising the power of the event and its image boost.

Destination brand and destination image

A brand is an impression perceived in a client's mind of a product or a service. It is the sum of all tangible and intangible elements, which makes the selection unique.... There are three essential concepts . . . that are related to brands: identity; image; and communication. The identity of the brand is defined by the sender itself, whereas a brand image is the real image developed in the receiver's mind. Brand identity means how the owner of the brand wants it to be experienced. On the other hand, brand image refers to how the brand is being experienced in reality.

(Moilanen and Rainisto, 2009: 6f.).

Therefore it is understandable that place branding is considered to be an extremely complex and highly political activity that is able to enhance a nation's economy, national self-image and identity. Hence different organisations and groups pursue different interests in the promotion of specific identities, which may be in direct conflict with the interests of others (Morgan et al., 2004: 14).

London, Venice, Rome and many other great cities were marketed informally over the centuries. They were known around the world from the accounts of travellers as well as from the efforts of these cities themselves to attract tourists, skilled workers, investors and buyers of their products and services (Kotler, 2009: viii). But nowadays cities are in direct competition with one another, and so one of the biggest problems in place marketing is that the marketed place can be easily replicated by others. Destinations are striving to apply different branding methods to differentiate themselves from other destinations and to emphasise their uniqueness (Moilanen and Rainisto, 2009: 3). Professional destination management is therefore essential in order

Table 14.1	Destination image formation			
Personal factors	→	**Destination image**	←	**Stimulus factors**
Psychological factors		**Perceptual or cognitive**		**Information sources**
Values		Affective		Amount
Motivations		Global		Type
Personality				
Social factors				**Previous experience**
Age				**Distribution**
Education				
Marital status				
Others				

Source: Baloglu and McCleary (1999: 870)

Case 14.1   The Sochi Olympic Games and their brand potential

Sochi was awarded the right to host the 2014 Olympic Winter Games in 2007, seven years before the event. Sochi is renowned as a subtropical summer destination and very popular amongst Russian and international tourists. In the preparations for the Olympic Winter Games the existing skiing resorts in the Krasnaya Polyana mountain village were greatly expanded and upgraded to international standards. Additional Olympic snow sports venues and training centres were built for ski and snowboard, cross-country, biathlon and ski jumping. Hosting the Olympic Winter Games creates international television and media exposure, from the test events to the Olympic events on a worldwide level, while most interest will be created in the countries interested in winter sports and thus the generators of potential future winter sports tourists to Sochi. The challenge for Sochi and its mountain stakeholders has been to decide whether to use Sochi as the key brand for the international marketing of its resorts, or to keep the village/mountain range name of Krasnaya Polyana as the main association with the ski area. The ski areas are currently still marketed as separate resorts, namely Gazprom, Rosa Khutor and Carousel. It remains a challenge for all stakeholders involved to focus on a strategic mountain marketing campaign in order not to leave the brand opportunity under-exploited.

Discussion questions

1 Should the mountain resorts use the Sochi brand in their post-event destination marketing strategies?

2 How long does an Olympic host city benefit from its image boost?

to accomplish the goal of branding a destination. It has very much to do with building partnerships and collaboration within the destination; and it also means protecting the destination, which is the actual product, and developing sustainable policies (Davidson and Rogers, 2006: 35).

Research from the last two decades makes clear that image is a valuable concept in understanding the destination selection process of tourists, and that image is mainly caused, influenced or formed by two major forces: stimulus factors and personal factors (Baloglu and McCleary, 1999: 868 ff.).

Within the feasibility study the current brand and the desired brand development need to be discussed within the framework of desired images. Furthermore, it should be noted which key target groups (leisure, city, sports, cultural or business tourist) and markets (global, continental, regional) are in focus.

A core issue is event ownership and consequently the funding of the event. All options need a clear analysis in order to scope the responsibilities of all layers of government and the private sector. The shareholders of the event and the potential split of ownership of the event need a clear focus, especially regarding funding, assumption of a potential deficit and the redistribution of a potential financial surplus. Even the bidding budget should be defined and benchmarked with the bidding campaigns of the same event format. A careful description of the main event risks is necessary (**as discussed in Chapter 11 on risk management**).

The city infrastructure and venues are the area with the highest risks for failure, and can often be a financial burden in the post-event daily operational management. On the other hand, a renewed venue infrastructure for the residents may yield the widest positive impact for the coming generation.

Within the framework of a feasibility study, all potential city infrastructure potentials should be listed, such as airports, train stations, new roads, telecommunications infrastructure and city beautification programmes. As an event may require a certain dimension of city infrastructure, it might serve as a tool to draw national subsidies into the destination that would otherwise be invested in different regions of a country. The venues, whether for sports, culture or business, are a further key issue to be reviewed. A city/nation may in any case want to create sports venues for its elite athletes or the wider general public, and the event year may be the incubator for the timely construction of the venue. Most European Capitals of Culture have developed new cultural infrastructure for the event, such as a new opera house or museum. In this section of the feasibility study a focus should be on the event venue requirements in relation to the city's requirements in the long term bearing in mind the venue ownership, venue marketing and venue utilisation. Any surplus venues (needed for the event, but not financially viable or necessary for the city) should be planned as temporary venues, or alternative locations in neighbouring regions should be considered.

Accommodation is of obvious importance to an event, and a first review needs to contrast the event requirements with the existing accommodation potentials. Again, temporary solutions (e.g. accommodation on cruise ships, camping sites) may serve to provide accommodation without a long-term financial burden on the destination. A similar perspective applies to the transport dimension in order to develop an understanding of the potential strategic investments in the enhancement of transport infrastructure with a long-term benefit for the local population in mind.

Rotation is a key issue before launching a bid for a mobile event. Global events naturally rotate between continents and thus a certain continent assumes the right to host the event only after a certain cycle. If the continent just recently hosted the event, a potential bid should only be launched if a long-term strategy (i.e. bidding for consecutive bids) is financially secured and backed by the key stakeholders of the bid.

Growth

■ Bidding campaign

The decision for or against bidding for an event should be made on the basis of the feasibility study. There exists a precise bidding procedure for hosting a mobile event in sports (e.g. Olympic Games, many World and European Championships), in culture (e.g. European Capital of Culture) and business (e.g. EXPO).

The event ownership is held by the global federations and institutions, resulting in a strong power situation dominating the preconditions for the bidding city/nation.

While conceptualising the event, the bidding committee needs to follow precise requirements for a bid, as defined in the appropriate bidding guidelines. In many federations and institutions, the bidding process has similar elements. First of all, an overall bid concept has to be presented to an event's rights holder, endorsed by politicians and the local and national stakeholders. An evaluation commission typically assesses the proposal on its technical merits and moves the particular bidder forward to the final stage of bidding. The host city/nation is ultimately selected by either the association members or an executive council/board. Naturally, lobbying the decision makers is of utmost importance in order to secure the event. Lobbying encompasses winning the hearts and minds of the decision makers based on a proposal that fits well into the institution's strategic directions for the event.

In the case of the Olympic Games, the International Olympic Committee (IOC) pays attention to the following key topics:

- support of politicians and the public;
- infrastructure;
- sports venues;
- Olympic village;
- environmental issues and impacts;
- accommodation;
- transport;
- security issues;
- know-how from previous sports events;
- financial and overall concept.

Whereas the IOC tries to downsize the venue requirements, the International Ice Hockey Federation (IIHF) and the International Skating Union (ISU) provide a statement of requirements according to the minimum size of their sports venues at the Olympic Winter Games. Many international sports federations in principle follow the bidding process of the IOC. The European Commission has just recently changed the selection procedure for European Capitals of Culture, bringing a more international focus into the host city selection process. Given the fact that the European Union has 28 member states (as of 1 June 2013), two cities are selected each year, resulting in each member state receiving this status every 14 years. Typically, a larger nation co-hosts the event together with a smaller nation.

The Bureau Internationale des Expositions in Paris, as owner of the rights to the world and international as well as the horticultural EXPO, has its own bidding and selection process.

In the field of business events, there is an enormous market of conferences and congresses that can be bid for by host cities, and many tourism boards have formed their own convention bureaux in order to facilitate the bidding for a business event.

It is often discussed whether the bid for an event itself draws benefits, and this is a controversial topic. The marketing value depends on the global or continental interest in the decision, but media coverage can be expected for the world's mobile events bidding processes. Additionally, bidding cities can exploit the benefits of being branded 'candidate city' for the time period of the bid.

The key date for a bidding city/nation is the date of the announcement of the host city leading either to the next steps as discussed in the event life cycle, or into the discussion of whether a consecutive bid will be envisaged. That relates strongly to the bidding strategy. If plans have been elaborated for the case of not being selected, a repeat bid can be started quickly giving the bidder a competitive advantage at the start line.

Event bidding strategies are complex, but a long-term striving for an event portfolio with various scenarios proves to be the most logical. Most often, failed bids unfortunately result in political frustration and no further event bid is pursued.

From the formation of the organising committee (OC) to the event branding strategy

Once the hosting contract is signed between the event's rights holder and the local organising committee, a number of key decisions have to be taken in order to guarantee the event's success. Failures at this stage may be very costly for the event's planning and cause major delays.

The human resource management and political dimensions are the first ones to be tackled. An executive board with its *chair* needs to be defined by the event shareholders. This process tends to be very political as the positions bring with them media exposure and prestige once the event is delivered successfully. After the completion of the institutional setting the general manager/general secretary/CEO has to be searched for and selected. It has proved beneficial to involve executive search firms to find the ideal candidate to plan and deliver the event. Sports and business events are very different in this context to cultural events. Whereas sports events are driven and governed by rules and the framework of the international sports federations, and business events are driven by the companies and institutions involved, cultural events require both an executive and an artistic management. Consequently, often two leaders selected for both areas can be a source of conflict about who ultimately is the key decision maker. As a final stage in the organisational build-up, the departments have to be staffed (**as discussed in Chapter 6 on human resource management**).

Branding is an early issue in the event planning phase, and should ideally be in line with that of the destination management organisation so that the event brand and the tourism brand find a common denomination. Often a destination chooses to position itself as a sports or cultural or business destination, and naturally it yields positive benefits if the event and the destination work jointly on the branding and ultimately on their marketing and communication campaigns.

The creation, planning and execution of the event programme and organising of television and radio host broadcasting and global transmission are key tasks of the organising committee. The host broadcasting is usually assigned to a host broadcasting company (national state or private television channel, international broadcasting companies) which delivers the signals to the designated broadcasting rights holders. In the field of sports, core tasks of the organising committee are the coordination of the sports competition schedule, accommodation and transport of athletes, media, officials and visitors and ceremonies. Key support functions to be delivered are transport, communication and community relations and security.

The progress is often monitored by the event owner by sending coordination commissions to the host city in order to inspect the progress, and to advise on best practices and the execution of the overall event master plan, often supported by sophisticated transfer of knowledge programmes and former event host debriefing meetings.

An essential aspect which needs close consideration during the planning phase is venue development. The following questions are of paramount concern, and have a major financial impact:

- Should venues be temporary or permanent?
- Who are the future operators and users of the venues, and therefore which aspects need to be considered in the planning and construction phase?
- Can a multifunctional venue be constructed?
- Who are the investors and will the venue have private or public owners?

The discussion of the above questions is important in order not to develop 'white elephants' whose maintenance will cost more than they can generate. Ultimately a long-term management concept for all venues needs to be defined and budgeted for, as will become clear in the final stages of the event life cycle.

The OC of the Lillehammer Games had already considered the long-term usage of the sports venues in the planning phase. The organisation of the post-Olympic usage of the venues was distributed to the five host communities. This strategy meant not only that the budget of one city was debited but that the responsibility and coordination of the long-term strategy for the venues was divided. The post-Olympic plan succeeded, and today the venues are used for tourism, businesses or schools, offices, university buildings or student apartments (Montville, 1994).

An issue that has emerged, mainly in sports events, causing a financial burden, is the security costs governed by the requirements of the event owner and participating athletes. While often not accounted for in the organisers' budgets, the workload for military and police forces may be enormous.

This planning stage should be governed by an overall events master plan driven by a strict project management team with key milestones; however, the organising committee is often governed by institutional requirements, e.g. by a Host City Contract or the requirements of the stakeholders, and therefore cannot always decide autonomously on long-term plans.

Staging

Event hosting

The actual event hosting is the moment when visitors, participants, the media and all other stakeholders are most involved. The foremost goal is the successful delivery of the event based on the operational plans. Any major problems occurring at the event need to be tackled at the lowest level possible and a main operation centre typically manages any changes to the event programme. In sports, very often live television and radio coverage enhance the complexity of the event delivery. The media are the key stakeholders for the perceived image of the event, especially by those who have not visited the event on site. Transport and security are further key issues for the event being perceived as successful. An often neglected part of the image building is the audience, and how positively the residents and visitors are perceived by the media.

Future development

■ **Long-term destination positioning, post-event venue management and tourism product development**

> The key to success (or otherwise) of hosting major events such as the Olympics is largely dependent on the ability of the city to leverage off the images and perfections created during the event itself and to continue delivering on the dream long after the circus has left town.
>
> (Hinch and Higham, 2011)

The staging of a mobile event can have great potential for the host destination, especially regarding the international attention due to media coverage. A mega event is a one-time opportunity to design or boost the image of the destination and to promote it world-wide. The strengthening or changing of the image can help the city to approach tourists, investors and inhabitants by giving new (touristic) growth potential. But in order to uti-lise the event as an image carrier, the OC needs to cleverly integrate the unique selling propositions (USPs) of the hosting destination into all marketing campaigns.

Once the organising committee has successfully delivered the event, it is often dissolved and the remaining infrastructure is handed over to the venue owners. If venue ownership has been decided on early enough in the event life cycle, the post-event venue owners will have already developed the venue business and marketing plans, and the venue will be utilised by the population, visitors, tourists or athletes. Even if the post-event venue management has been cleverly set up, political interests may still inter-fere in the clashes of interest between business and society (e.g. whether a swimming venue is to be made available to the wider general public or purely for athletes, and at what cost).

A successful venue may yield great benefits to the tourism stakeholders. In sports, it may be of interest to athletes as well as local residents and the tourist.

Case 14.2	The 1999 Nordic Ski World Championships in Ramsau/Dachstein (Austria) and its post-event sports tourism legacy

Ramsau/Dachstein hosted the 1999 FIS Nordic Ski World Championships comprising ski jumping, Nordic combined and cross-country events. While Ramsau was already an established Nordic winter tourism destination, it needed to create sports infrastructure in order to offer the athletes world-class facilities. The management and sports director decided to use an existing ski-jumping hill in nearby Bischofshofen in order to only have to build a smaller one with a post-use for both winter and summer training in mind. The cross-country trails were developed in such a way that they created an attractive sports event venue, and are now still used 100% for winter sports tourists. In the meantime, the tracks are also used in summer time as a running circuit. In order to complement the sports infrastructure, a high-performance training centre was built for the benefit of elite athletes as well as the sports tour-ist. After having hosted the mobile event in 1999, Ramsau has annually hosted a FIS world cup event in order to keep its positioning as a world class Nordic destination.

Discussion questions

3 What are key challenges after having hosted a mobile sports event?

4 How can sports tourism benefit from hosting a sports event?

Cultural events may be the incubator for building new cultural venues such as opera houses, theatres and museums that will contribute to the cultural tourism product of a destination. Business events such as the World Expo leave a series of business venues that can either stand empty and develop into a burden for the city or kick off the development of a vibrant trade fair location.

Conclusion

The event life cycle clearly demonstrates that in order to optimise the long-term benefits of hosting a mobile event, all stages need to be well planned. Ideally, the long-term vision is formulated by the key shareholders at a very early stage, and supported by all stakeholders involved throughout the planning and hosting stages. Once the event is successfully delivered, the challenge is to keep the destination brand alive, and to develop a long-term events portfolio to draw continuous media attention. Investments in the enhancement of the venue infrastructure and the development of clever tourism products may contribute to a positive trend of the event life cycle, even years after the event took place.

General discussion questions

5 Why are destination image and destination branding considered such important factors in an area's success as a tourist destination?

6 During which stage of the destination life cycle would you implement an event? Give your reasons.

7 In your opinion, which factors influence destination image most, when considering Moilanen and Rainisto (2009), who say that image is how the brand is experienced in reality?

Guided reading

The following books are useful for developing the appropriate themes:

Butler, R., ed. (2006) *The Tourism Area Life Cycle: Applications and Modifications*, Vol. 1. Clevedon: Channel View Publications.

Getz, D. (2007) *Event Studies, Theory, Research and Policy for Planned Events*. Oxford: Butterworth-Heinemann.

Kotler, P. and Armstrong, G. (2010) *Principles of Marketing* (13th edn). Harlow: Pearson Education.

Morgan, N., Pritchard, A. and Pride, R., eds (2012) *Destination Brands, Managing Place Reputation* (3rd edn). Oxford: Butterworth-Heinemann.

Recommended websites

European Capitals of Culture: **http://ec.europa.eu/culture/our-programmes-and-actions/capitals/european-capitals-of-culture_en.htm**

Official Site of the Bureau International des Expositions: **www.bie-paris.org/site/en/expos.html**

The official website of the Olympic Movement: **www.olympic.org**

Key words

event life cycle, sustainability

Bibliography

Baloglu, S. and McCleary, K. (1999) A model of destination image formation. *Annals of Tourism Research*, 26(4), 868–97.

Butler, R. (2006) The concept of a tourist area cycle of evolution: implications for the management of resources. In R. Butler (ed.), *The Tourism Area Life Cycle: Applications and Modifications*, Vol. 1. Clevedon: Channel View Publications.

Cole, S. (2012) Synergy and congestion in the tourist destination life cycle. *Tourism Management*, 33, 1128–40.

Davidson, R. and Rogers, T. (2006) *Marketing Destinations and Venues for Conferences, Conventions and Business Events*. Oxford: Butterworth-Heinemann.

Getz, D. (2008) Event tourism: definition, evolution and research. *Tourism Management*, 28, 403–28.

Hall, C. (2006) Introduction. In R. Butler (ed.), *The Tourism Area Life Cycle: Applications and Modifications*, Vol. 1. Clevedon: Channel View Publications.

Hinch, T. and Higham, J. (2011) *Sport Tourism Development* (2nd edn). Bristol: Channel View Publications.

Kotler, P. (2009) Introduction. In T. Moilanen and S. Rainisto (eds), *How To Brand Nations, Cities and Destinations, A Planning Book for Place Branding*. Basingstoke: Palgrave.

Kotler, P., Armstrong, G., Saunders, J. and Wong, V. (2007) *Grundlagen des Marketing*. Munich: Pearson Studium.

Kozak, M. and Martin, D. (2012) Tourism life cycle and sustainability analysis: profit-focussed strategies for mature destinations. *Tourism Management*, 33, 188–94.

Moilanen, T. and Rainisto, S. (2009) *How To Brand Nations, Cities and Destinations, A Planning Book for Place Branding*. Basingstoke: Palgrave.

Montville, L. (1994) Once upon a time . . . the Lillehammer Games, says the disbelieving author, were simply too good to be true. *Sports Illustrated*, 7 March, p. 90.

Morgan, N., Pritchard, A. and Pride, R. (eds) (2004) *Destination Branding: Creating the Unique Destination Proposition* (2nd edn). Oxford: Butterworth-Heinemann.

Polli, R. and Cook, V. (1969) Validity of the product life cycle. *The Journal of Business*, 42(4), 385–400.

Chapter 15

The role of sports and event venues

Louise Bielzer, Karlshochschule International University, Germany

Learning outcomes

Upon successful completion of this chapter the student will be able to:

- explain the historic development of sports and event venues and compare it to the current situation of event venues;

- understand key issues in planning and designing an event venue;

- indicate key success factors in the management of sports and event venues;

- appraise the interdependencies between event venue construction and event venue operations as well as the relationship between venue operators and event organisers;

- evaluate the risks and opportunities of multifunctional event venues.

Overview

Event venues as 'built setting' contribute to a large extent to the success or failure of an event. Nevertheless, the role of sports and event venues is often under-estimated when discussing current trends, challenges, risks and opportunities in events management. This chapter therefore reviews the major issues relating to that part of the events industry which still lacks comprehensive consideration in research and publications.

The chapter starts with a historical outline of the development of sports and event venues. Accordingly, by comparison with the past, the reader should develop an understanding of the characteristics of modern sports and event venues.

After that, four common dimensions of sports and event venues are introduced: the architectural dimension, the programme dimension, the organisational dimension and the economic dimension. Besides a general explanation, the focus will be on the interdependencies of those four dimensions.

Based on the **life cycle model** of a sport or event venue, the discussion first addresses key issues in planning and designing an event venue. Major issues include initial situations and stakeholder considerations when thinking about a new sport or event venue and necessary steps when conducting a **feasibility study**.

Furthermore, this part of the chapter is dedicated to the interdependencies between event venue construction and event venue operations, also referring to the role of venue operators and permanent tenants such as professional sports teams.

Two case studies are included to illustrate key issues of event venue development and management. Relevant learning points are reinforced by review questions at the end of the chapter which have bearing upon the issues raised in the text or in the case material.

Due to the limited space, the chapter is written from the perspective of a city which intends to have a new sports/event venue. According to this perspective, the requirements and procedures of planning and operating a sports or event venue may differ (for instance a private investor may have a different perspective in terms of effectiveness, return on investment, etc. than a city or a local authority which will focus rather on issues such as legacy in terms of urban development or an increase in the city's prestige).

Historic development of sports and event venues

As well as events themselves, sports and events venues have a history of more than 2,000 years. Already during ancient times, cultural or political gatherings, religious celebrations and sports competitions were staged in built venues. Similar to today, events in ancient times often had a political function. Sometimes, different types of events such as the Roman 'circenses' combined social events with political purposes or – as in case of the Ancient Olympic Games – included sports competitions and religious ceremonies (see Fried, 2010). There are often interdependencies between the locations of those events, the use of natural or built infrastructure, and the type of event taking place. Accordingly, the historic development of sports and event venues is strongly influenced by the development of the types of events themselves.

As selected examples, the historic development of sports stadia, trade fair centres and conference centres will now be described and evaluated.

Looking at ancient stadia, for instance the Circus Maximus or the Coliseum in Rome, it can be stated that they were already multi-purpose buildings, planned not only to host sports events but also religious ceremonies or entertainment events such as nautical competitions (see Fried, 2010). Accordingly, multifunctionality, which is often a highly discussed topic for today's event locations, arenas and stadia, is nothing new. The most important differences between ancient stadia and contemporary sports stadia infrastructures are reflected by the use of building materials and technology which, centuries ago, were not that technically complex.

The Middle Ages were not a particularly important time for the development of sports stadia since – due to the power of the Church but also due to other factors such as the class structure of society – sports as an activity was generally less common and organised.

Finally, Frank and Steets (2010) indicate that the Arena on the March Field in Paris, which was built by the end of the 19th century for several hundred thousand spectators, is the direct predecessor of our contemporary sports stadia. Indeed, the 19th and 20th centuries were crucial for the development of modern sports stadia. New types of sports and sports trends impacted on the construction of sport stadia infrastructure. Especially in the USA the so-called 'intercollegiate sport', sports competitions between colleges, also boosted the development of built sports events infrastructure (see Fried, 2010).

Generally, almost everywhere hallmark events such as the Olympic Games boost the development of new sports and related event facilities.

Similar to sports events, trade fairs and exhibitions also have a long history. Already in the Middle Ages a public market to exchange goods, the so-called 'missa profana' which took place after the 'missa sacra' was held in the church, was common (see Rodekamp,

2005). Accordingly, the first built infrastructure to host trade fairs and exhibitions were market places and church squares.

During the period of industrialisation, manufacturers of goods became initiators and key players with respect to trade fairs. Since the 1850s, World Exhibitions have been established to display new products and innovations not only to experts but also to the general public. Again, the host cities took advantage of this opportunity to present themselves in an international context and to further develop their image by offering unique exhibition venues such as the Crystal Palace in Hyde Park, London, during the World Exhibition in 1851. As a consequence of the World Exhibitions many cities enlarged their exhibition and event venues. In the case of London, new exhibition halls and venues, for example the Royal Agricultural Hall, Alexandra Palace and Earls Court, were built in the decades following the Great Exhibition of 1851 (see Leapman, 2002; Bowdin et al., 2006),

In the 20th century the further development of already existing exhibition sites and the building of new sites continued. Even though ownership structures and management structures differ from country to country, it can be said that exhibition venues play an important role in the built event infrastructure in many European countries. Our current built exhibition infrastructure represents multimedia exhibition venues which are often directly connected with convention facilities. Although exhibition business and sites, for example in Asian countries, have started to become more and more important, the European exhibition industry and especially Germany is still seen as a 'pacesetter' which sets standards in terms of competitive exhibition venues and know-how (see AUMA, 2011).

Comparing with historic development, it can be said that modern sports stadia infrastructure has a great deal more in common with its ancient predecessors than exhibition venues do, the latter having somewhat different design and layout characteristics compared to their counterparts in the past.

Looking at convention centres or conference facilities as the third selected category of event venues, we can note that there is a wide variety of historic predecessors – that is, buildings which were used for political, ecclesiastical (such as councils) or scientific gatherings. For instance, in ancient times the Roman Senate already used a purpose-built facility for its meetings: the 'Curia Hostilia' (see Richardson, 2005). Political gatherings often took place in castles; those of an ecclesiastical nature were held in monasteries and specific churches such as the Sistine Chapel ('Capella Sistina') in Rome or Council buildings such as for example in Constance.

Already in mediaeval times, mainly in Italy and Great Britain, scientists from all over Europe met to discuss ideas and innovations at university sites such as Bologna, Padova, Oxford or Cambridge; a pattern which became increasingly important from the beginning of the 19th century. Today universities still play an important role in the convention industry. Due to their layout, equipment and their reputation as locations for science and as think tanks, they can be regarded as a serious competitor to private convention centres, hotels or publicly managed conference facilities.

Furthermore, so-called special event locations, for example old industrial sites (conversion projects), corporate conference facilities or branded spaces, or even cruise ships, can be seen as new and important competitors in the field of built convention infrastructure today (see also Lawson, 2001).

To sum up this historic overview, it may be stated that all venue types have historic predecessors, which still have an influence on at least some of the current-day functions and features of those venue types. Basic structures of sports and event venues – for example the building layout, tribunes, stages and backstage areas, access to the building, limited access to special building areas such as suites or VIP areas, entry systems and even catering areas – still hark back to their historic predecessors.

Furthermore, the involvement of public authorities in terms of planning, financing and operating the sports and event venues is also similar. Public authorities and politics still have a comparable interest in offering event venues as part of public infrastructure in order to benefit from the social and political functions events may fulfil.

Nevertheless, not only the venues themselves but also the user structures have changed in relation to earlier times. Currently, the access to sports and event venues is not usually linked to any social class or gender. In terms of technical equipment and operational procedures the venues have become far more complex. This has a direct impact not only on the initial building costs but also in the maintenance and operating costs of the venues.

If sport and event venues are to remain competitive and to retain a successful position in the market, they will need to continue to adapt to social trends and developments, such as an ageing society or new requirements regarding economically, ecologically and socially sustainable operations.

Sports and event venues in a complex environment: four dimensions and their interdependencies

Sport and event venues are influenced by many different factors, such as the general economic situation, market trends or the concrete requirement of the multiple stakeholders and users of the facilities.

When planning a new venue or analysing the current and future market position of an already existing one, it therefore might be useful to first carry out an environmental analysis – for example by conducting a so-called PESTEL analysis (see, for example, Gillespie, 2007). PESTEL is an acronym which stands for the following categories of influencing factors and might be adopted for every sports or event venue:

- political influencing factors (often interfaces with legal impacting factors, for example as regards laws or regulations);
- economic influencing factors (e.g. spending capacity of users);
- social influencing factors (e.g. demographic development, trends in spending and leisure time);
- technological influencing factors (e.g. new technologies, use of social media);
- environmental influencing factors (e.g. standards and/or requirements in terms of sustainability);
- legal influencing factors (e.g. fire safety regulations, venue regulations).

In practice, the factors often overlap and influence each other interdependently.

In addition to this, you could define the specific environment which a sports or event venue will have to face later by applying, for example, Porter's Five Forces Model (see e.g. Porter, 1980, 2008), adjusted for the case of an event venue.

What all sports and event venues have in common are four interrelated dimensions at least: an architectural dimension, a programme dimension, an organisational dimension and an economic dimension, which may be further distinguished into a primary and a secondary economic dimension.

Figure 15.1 shows the impacting factors, the dimensions of a sports or event venue and their interdependencies in a stakeholder-driven environment.

The architectural dimension includes the design, the room layout and the functional concept of the sports or event venue, but also the life cycle with its different stages. Based on a market analysis (including an evaluation of demand and competition situation), an adequate room and functional layout has to be developed which is able to meet the requirements of different user groups and other stakeholders. The architectural dimension not only has an impact on the other three dimensions of the venue but also on the marketing opportunities. Especially if the sports or event venue is a landmark due to its

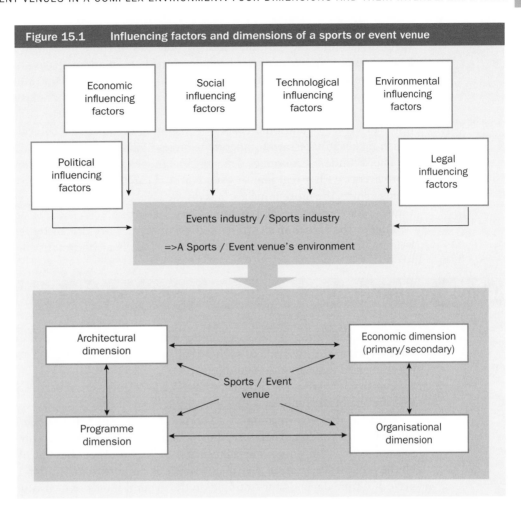

Figure 15.1   Influencing factors and dimensions of a sports or event venue

unique architecture (for example the Bird's Nest in Beijing, China, or the Sydney Opera House in Australia), it may well be used for general destination marketing of the city since there are many marketing opportunities for the building beyond the purpose of hosting events (see e.g. Davidson and Rogers, 2006).

The programme dimension covers elements such as the **utilisation concept** of the sports or event venue, different user groups and the event programme. It will also take into account the role of home teams or other permanent tenants and their impact on the venue. When planning a new sport or event facility, it is vital to forecast the number of events and visitors per year in order to estimate future economic dimension in later operations (=> business planning).

The architectural dimension and the programme dimension are directly dependent on each other. This means, for example, that the more multi-purpose an event venue is, the more different types of events may be hosted in the venue. On the other hand, multifunctionality often causes complex building structures and also compromises in operations.

The organisational dimension comprises the legal structure, ownership and governance structures and the overall operational concept (structural and process organisation). Depending on how many supplementary services a sports or event venue plans to provide, the managing company may be a full service provider or fulfil the role of a landlord that rents the venue and outsources the most possible services to third parties.

Finally, the economic dimension has to be expanded upon, which includes primary and secondary economics of the venue – that is, the question of profitability or loss but also possible secondary economic benefits. The primary economics depend not only on the programme dimension but also on the architectural and organisational dimension, again underlining the multiple interdependencies of the dimensions. If an event venue is a very complex building or has been developed on an ad hoc basis – that is, where newer parts were added over the decades and event operations weren't in focus when planning the venue – it is quite probable that the staging of events is more expensive. Furthermore, the cutting of architectural features and cost savings during the construction stage may result in higher operational costs (for example, because of technical equipment missing which makes it necessary to operate tribunes by hand, or similar).

The secondary economics depend to a large extent on the programme dimension: the more events with a regional or even national catchment area are hosted in the sports or events centre, the more impact it has on the level of publicity and the more important the venue is for tourism development and city marketing.

Due to the fact that all sports and event venues are driven by many different stakeholders, strategic management of those properties is a continuous challenge.

Key issues in planning and designing a sports or event venue

Before discussing key issues in planning and designing a sports or event venue, we will have a look at the life cycle of such a facility in order to distinguish the different stages of planning and managing the building.

Figure 15.2 shows the different phases and the connection between the intensity of use and the age of the building.

Usually, after the opening of a sports or event venue, the venue first has to be established on the market. Therefore, the number of events is continuously increasing (start-up phase). If the event venue is in full use and well established then the number of events will be the highest. Presuming that maintenance is done regularly, after 15 or 20 years – the period of time depends for example on the general intensity of use and the marketability of the venue – the question then is about re-investment in order to keep to the standards the different user groups demand.

From the very beginning, the sports or event venue is impacted by other similar facilities and has to be positioned successfully in an often strongly competitive market. Therefore it is important to carefully plan the building for sustainable use and to always have a mid- and long-term perspective in mind when deciding about the concept of the venue.

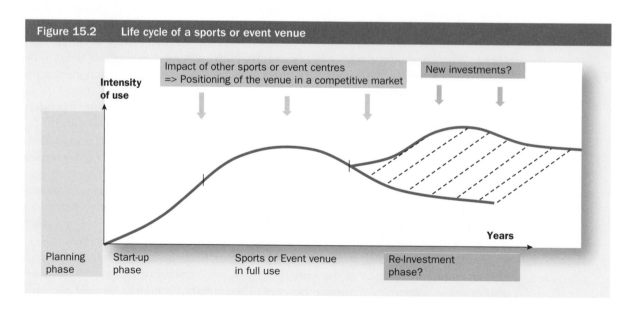

| Figure 15.2 | Life cycle of a sports or event venue |

When starting to think about a new sports or event venue, theoretically there are three initial situations possible:

1. the idea of a sports or event venue exists, but location, financing/capital providers are still undecided;
2. a location exists, but the idea of use or type of event venue and financing/capital providers are still undecided;
3. financing/capital providers exist, but the idea of use and the location are still unknown (rather unusual).

When planning and developing a new sports or event centre, different parties contribute to the project: project corporations, investors, building companies or contracting businesses, architects, consultants and technical advisers, and – in the case of a formerly existing sports or events facility which will have to be replaced – sometimes even an operating company.

As Figure 15.3 shows, an event venue has multiple stakeholders who all have different and specific requirements towards the venue.

There are stakeholders who have a clear economic interest in the new facility, such as investors, event managers/event agencies and artists and – at least in case of private sports and event venues – the owners and operators. Others have rather a political interest and regard the project as part of trade and industry or tourism promotion. This is often the case for politicians or local municipalities.

Stakeholders, like event visitors, simply want to be entertained or educated. Locals – who of course may also be employees or visitors and therefore overlap with other groups of stakeholders – may focus on smooth operation procedures and don't want to be negatively impacted by noise or traffic.

Bearing in mind both the different types of party contributing to the project's realisation and the multiple stakeholders involved, the complexity of such a project is clear. Accordingly, a clear and focused marketing and communication concept is necessary from the very beginning.

When planning to build a new sports or event facility, it is imperative to first carry out a feasibility study (see also Peterson, 2001). Generally, the feasibility study confirms the feasibility and cost-effectiveness of the project.

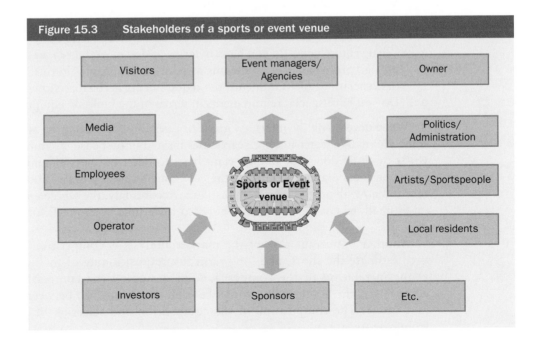

Figure 15.3   Stakeholders of a sports or event venue

Important elements of a feasibility study for a sports or event venue are:

- description of idea and scope of the project;
- market and demand analysis;
- utilisation concept;
- room and functional concept;
- locational analysis;
- impact analysis;
- operational concept;
- financial concept/cost estimation/business planning;
- constraints of the project.

A detailed market and demand analysis is vital in order to know about the general market situation, the competition and the concrete requirements of potential future users (event organisers, home teams, visitors, etc.).

During the market analysis stage, it may be helpful to first sum up all possible stakeholders and users of the new sports or event venue. Furthermore, you should research current market trends and carry out some expert interviews to find out possible future trends and developments of the market to be expected. Usually, the market analysis includes both primary and secondary data collection, the former carried out by asking experts, future users and other potential stakeholders and the latter by researching information in specific journals or studies carried out at universities, etc.

A more complex part of market analysis is the primary data collection for the purpose of analysing needs or demand. In order to get reliable results, it is important to define possible demand clusters first. Secondly, you should fix both the inquiry period and the number of respondents of each demand cluster. Consider the seasonality of the events industry. It probably won't be easy to get answers from event organisers during peak times. After having decided on the interview technique (personal interviews, telephone interviews, use of an interview guide, documentation etc.), you have to define and structure the questions you'd like to ask.

Important questions to ask as part of the demand analysis may cover the following areas:

- What number of events do you plan to organise in the new sports and events venue?
- What types of events do you plan?
- What would the appropriate capacities be for you?
- Do you have special requirements in terms of multifunctionality of the new venue?
- What requirements do you have in terms of design of the venue? (This is vital in case of, e.g., professional sports teams as permanent tenants! In this case, sports leagues or associations often influence the requirements in the direction of sports facilities.)
- Do you have special requirements in terms of the building equipment?

When developing the interview guide or questionnaire, it may be appropriate to define some alternative scenarios, e.g. 'capacities needed in best case' v. 'minimum capacities in worst case'. By doing so, an important basis for later business planning is given. In view of the business planning – that is, the economic feasibility evaluation – it is also important to know about the long-term demand. Accordingly, the whole analysis should focus on estimations not only for today but also for a time horizon of, for example, the next 10 years.

Another important part of the market analysis is competition analysis. The aim is to estimate the short- and long-term future positioning of the new sports or event venue in relation to the competition. In designing the competition analysis and, accordingly, the benchmarks, it may be useful to distinguish between local sites for the new venue. The composition of the competition and selection of competitors varies from case to case.

After having decided on the competitors to analyse, the following issues may be assessed:

- How old is the respective venue and when was it last modernised? How about the current status of the building?
- What capacities, equipment, etc. are available?
- What are the USPs of the venue?
- Which events portfolio is realised in the venue? What are the main target groups?

The results of the analysis should be counterchecked with current and predictable future market standards, and user requirements, for instance in terms of the facilities' multifunctionality or building equipment and market trends.

It is then necessary to base the development of a general utilisation and **room concept** on the results of the market and demand analysis. It may be useful to distinguish between elements and features related to the room layout such as capacities, room disposal, visitors' circulation, equipment, level of comfort of the venue, technique, etc., on the one hand, and functional areas of the event venue, on the other – for example, functional areas for main and supplementary use, such as the main hall or grand hall, restaurants, as well as side rooms, foyers, lounges, other visitor areas, backstage areas, supply areas, etc.

Both parts have a direct impact on construction costs and operations and – as already stated above – are often interdependent.

The utilisation and room concept will also be an important element for the later tendering process.

As soon as the general outline of the planned sports or event venue is clear, a locational analysis should be conducted. It has to be decided if the new sports or event venue should be built outside the city or in the city centre. There are different impacting factors to consider when deciding on the right choice of location. For example:

- Match of the location with the general objectives of the city (e.g. urban development, integration into existing urban structures).
- Legal requirements, e.g. in terms of noise or traffic => foreseeable utilisation conflicts.
- Ability to compete with any other venue at the selected location and to market the venue successfully => venue as a landmark.
- General conditions of the site, ownership, previous use.
- Already existing infrastructure, accessibility, interdependences of venue and environment (e.g. hotels).

An economic feasibility study or profitability analysis gives some indication as regards the future economic situation of the venue, expectable revenues and costs.

In view of successfully managing a sports and event venue later, it is important to appraise the interdependencies between the venue's construction and the venue's operations. The building itself has various impacts on later operations. First of all, a modern, state-of-the-art venue allows the venue operator to easily attract sponsors, event organisers and event visitors – three very important target groups. By doing so, direct monetary (marketing revenue, room rentals, ticket sales, etc.) and non-monetary (image, reputation, attractive events portfolio, etc.) impacts emerge. Secondly, the more multifunctional and expensive a sports or event venue is, the higher follow-up costs will be as well. On the other hand, multi-purpose sports or event venues which are suitable for hosting different types of events have a higher occupancy rate, a more diverse events portfolio and therefore more options to attract new events and sponsors.

Finally, potential constraints of the project have to be discussed and a risk analysis has to be carried out. The planning parameters, basic assumptions of the forecasts (e.g. events and visitor numbers' forecasts, business planning, etc.), scheduling, but also financing, costs, permissions, licences, etc. have to be analysed in terms of potential risks and the probability that they will occur.

Architectural competition and the bidding process

If the feasibility study showed a positive result, the next step usually consists of carrying out an architectural competition in order either to obtain a design solution in line with the city's requirements or to directly select an architect. The former case can be seen as a competition of ideas where the realisation of the project is not necessarily intended. Consequently, it is traditional that the efforts of architects in such circumstances are compensated by prize money.

Generally, there is a broad variety of competitions. A competition can be run as an open competition, a limited competition or an invited competition, or a combination. Participants of limited competitions are often decided by lot. In the case of two-phase competitions, the first phase may be open and the second one limited. Alternatively, there are also so-called two-tiered competitions in which the task is executed in two different stages by all participants. Furthermore, there are other types of competitions, such as cooperative competitions, which are not so common when tendering for a sports or event venue.

Usually, a tendering process includes the invitation to bid, instructions and bid form and a list of specifications and blueprints, for example in terms of the required room layout, capacities, etc.

After the advertising, architects may submit their proposals and drafts. These proposals are then opened and reviewed by an independent jury which usually consists of representatives of the awarding authority, technical jurors and client and local community jurors. Whereas legal conditions may vary from country to country, anonymity and equivalent opportunities for all participants in competition have to be guaranteed.

If public awarding authorities tender the competition, proceedings are usually regulated by public procurement law, which differs from country to country.

In terms of tendering processes and general proceedings, a useful source of information might be the governmental building engineering institutions or the Chambers of Architects of the relevant countries.

In the best case scenario, when reviewing the architects' drafts, the potential future operator of the venue or experts on event venues operations are also integrated in the team of reviewers in order to make sure that the drafts are appropriate for later operations and don't cause disproportionally high follow-up costs.

The next step then is to develop a design and building brief and to advertise the project for bids in order to attract contractors committed to building the venue (see further, e.g., Westerbeek et al., 2006; Mull et al., 2009).

Financing of a sports or event venue

Today, hallmark events such as the Olympic Games, World Championships or European Championships often stimulate the development of sports and event venues. Host cities invest huge amounts of money in the conceptualisation and realisation of new facilities to host those events. This again clearly shows the interrelations between politics, staging of events, commercial or economic interests and the impact on tourism and the image of the respective destination. Frank and Steets underline this interrelationship by saying: 'Since the late twentieth century, against a background of worldwide interurban competition, stadia increasingly serve as location-supporting, urban representative buildings and as driving forces for urban development' (Frank and Steets, 2010: 5). Nevertheless in today's context of less availability of public money, commercial interests are playing an increasingly important role.

When developing a suitable financing concept for the construction of a sports or event venue, it has to be considered first that there are interrelationships between what should be financed on the one hand and the appropriateness of a financing model on the other hand. Sports and event venues are special properties which – for several reasons – are often difficult to finance. Four main issues may impact on financing decisions of potential investors:

■ First, it is fairly difficult to forecast trends in the sports and events industry and therefore long-term usage of the venues. Hence, from a possible investor's perspective it is relatively risky to invest in a sports or event venue.

■ Secondly, fluctuations of the market are comparatively strong and sports types or event types have relatively short life cycles. Again, this results in an insecure environment for investments.

■ Thirdly, in case of a failure of the originally planned use concept, such venues do not have a high adaptability for use by third parties. If sports or event venues will no longer be used for their original purpose(s) (for example in Germany many tennis courts built in the 1980s), it is fairly difficult to convert them for a different use.

■ Finally, sport and event venues often require high costs for continuous maintenance and reinvestments. Actually, looking at the life cycle of a sports or event venue, it can be said that often only between 20% and 30% of the total costs may be allocated to the construction stage, whereas the remaining, by far bigger, share of the total costs occurs during operations (Meinel, 2001; Bielzer and Wadsack, 2011).

All in all, there are high uncertainties and risks for investors, which often make it difficult to find private investors in this sector of the economy. In the case of sports venues hosting permanent tenants such as premier league sports teams and therefore 'guaranteeing' a certain occupancy of the venue, it might be easier to find private investors than in the case of event venues with a broad variety of events and seldom with permanent tenants.

Especially for large-scale projects such as soccer stadia, there is a trend towards structured finance. Developers try to share the various risks by integrating several project partners and combining different financial instruments with diverse risk-return profiles.

In this case the foundation of a legally independent project company is usually the first step. The project company is then the body responsible both for the development of the project and for financing. Shareholders of the project company are often planners, contracting businesses involved in construction, facility management companies, if applicable, the future operator of the venue, etc. The more monetary and non-monetary benefits may be expected, the more options for future development of the location may be given and, where a good local infrastructure exists, the easier it is to find private investors for the project.

Traditionally, event or sports venues were publicly financed. Especially for smaller event venues, this is still the commonest option. From the perspective of a community, an important advantage of a fully publicly financed sports and event venue project lies in the control of the utilisation concept and the integration and reconcilement with other public projects and urban infrastructure. On the other hand, negative aspects such as high maintenance costs and often an operational loss have to be considered. In this context, Schwarz et al. (2010) point out that up to 90% of a sports venue's lifetime costs may be determined by decisions made during the construction stage or during the first years of operation.

For decades, there has been no need for municipalities to refinance investments in event properties. Public authorities argued that it is part of the public task to provide infrastructure of that kind. Today, in times of scarce public funds, more and more event and sports venues are privately financed. But, to some extent, in supposedly private projects there is still public participation in investment, e.g. by providing credit, subsidies,

---

Case 15.1   Festspielhaus Baden-Baden

The Festspielhaus Baden-Baden opened on 18 April 1998 after approximately two years' construction time. With construction costs of about €60 million, the Festspielhaus integrated the former central train station of Baden-Baden with a newly constructed building. All in all, the venue offers a capacity of about 2,500 seats and is one of the biggest opera houses in Europe.

In the first years of operation, management failures and overpriced tickets resulted in negative financial results, and the Festspielhaus Baden-Baden faced insolvency. From March 2000, responsibility for the concert house's management has been in the hands of the private Festspielhaus Baden-Baden Cultural Foundation. The foundation consists of 20 members and had raised about €20 million by the 2007/2008 season.

As well as the Cultural Foundation there is the not-for-profit Friends of the Festspielhaus society, which supports the artistic programme of the Festspielhaus through the contributions of its members. The annual subscription for individuals is €520, for couples €780 and for companies €1,500. In return, the society's members receive, for example, privileged ticket booking rights.

Companies which are part of the so-called Business Pool, paying €5,000 per year, get, for example, access to the business club lounge, invitations to special events and ticket offers for their employees.

By the 2007/2008 season the budget of the Festspielhaus was approximately €24 million, with one-third coming from donors, founders and sponsors, and two-thirds from ticket sales.

Today, the Festspielhaus is well established and hosts more than 300 events per year, amongst others the traditional Herbert von Karajan Whitsun Festival with artists such as Anne-Sophie Mutter and the Russian conductor Valery Gergiev.

Sources: www.festspielhaus.de/en/architecture/history-development and www.festspielhaus.de/en/sponsors

Discussion question

1   Use the information above as a basis for discussing the risks and opportunities of a privately funded cultural event venue such as the Festspielhaus Baden-Baden.

---

absorption of infrastructural costs or similar. Alternatively, a project might be supported by the assumption of guarantees towards creditors by public authorities.

As regards the financing of operations, public subsidies are still an important issue in the sports and events industry. But alternative sources of finances, such as selling naming rights for the venue, the acquisition of sponsors, e.g. for VIP suites, or other revenues from marketing activities also become increasingly important and contribute to financing the running costs of the venues.

Ownership structures and operational concept for a sports or event venue

Generally, there are many different types of ownership and governance structures. In order to simplify the multitude of ownership and management options for sports and event venues, the following constellations are most common:

- Publicly owned venues (single-unit property or multi-unit properties) which may be either managed by a public authority (in different forms of legal organisation) or by a private company such as professional management companies, hotels or restaurant keepers.
- Privately owned venues (single-unit property or multi-unit properties), which are usually managed by a private company or a not-for-profit private body.

It is still very common that public authorities are involved in construction and operations of sports and event venues. One reason is that municipalities in some countries have a public remit to provide sports and event infrastructure for their citizens. Furthermore, sports and events are an important aspect of a location's economic promotion in competition and therefore communities want to have direct access and control of those facilities. In the past public authorities often showed a lack of specific knowledge of the sports and events industry and the requirements of the professional users. Accordingly, many communities established independent boards or even private management companies to operate the venues. Nevertheless, they also have to report back to the municipal authorities and depend on the strategic decisions, investment plans, etc. of the public owners.

The two most common private ownership and government structures are commercially orientated private corporations or not-for-profit private bodies such as sports associations or clubs. An advantage of private investors and management companies specialising in sports and event venues, such as Reed Exhibitions, Anschutz Entertainment Group or SMG Group, is their professionalism and knowledge of the markets and their mechanisms.

Commercial private bodies usually have no interest in investing without getting a ROI. Some rare exceptions, such as the SAP Arena in Germany, can be seen as patronage and are not based on a direct commercial interest of the investor.

In contrast, the involvement of not-for-profit private bodies is normally voluntary in nature and has no primary commercial interest. The services offered in those cases are usually tax-exempt.

Since it is very difficult to generate an operating profit by running a sports or event facility, **public–private partnership projects**, especially the constellation of a private owner – having to target to get an adequate ROI – and a public authority as operator of the venue is very rare.

Important issues to think about when deciding on favoured ownership and management structures are liabilities, responsibility, decision-making processes, control, risks, etc.

It is important to know that ownership and governance structures also have several impacts on the venue's operations, such as the general focus and positioning of the event location, the marketing concept and rent policy, the events portfolio, maybe even the human resources strategy and others.

As regards the general focus and positioning of the event location and the corresponding marketing concept, the following list of questions should make the different options and perspectives of public and private operators clear:

- Which target groups does the operator actively address? Are they 'economically interesting'? Do the target groups match the general objectives of the host city (share of local clubs, associations, etc.)?
- What types of events are targeted by the operator? What are the decision criteria to host an event (commercial targets? image creation?)?
- How will the operator deal with 'economically uninteresting' events (e.g. events of sports clubs, carnival associations, etc. which don't generate profit but are important for social life in a city)?
- How will the venue be marketed? Is there any link with the city's marketing?

No matter who operates the venue, it is crucial to have a comprehensive and in-depth knowledge of the events industry, its key players and networks, current issues and trends.

Generally, when developing an operating concept for a sports or event venue, facility management and operations management have to be considered. Facility management and operations management often overlap and are equally important to running the venue successfully.

Besides general operations, a special focus has to be on maintenance issues such as grounds, housekeeping, plumbing, electrical, heating, ventilation, air-conditioning and sound and lighting systems. In order to keep the venue marketable, market standards and the requirements of event organisers, visitors and other stakeholders have to be continuously taken into account.

In terms of non-technical operations (see for example Lawson, 2001; Westerbeek et al., 2006; Schwarz et al., 2010) many different aspects have to be considered such as:

- human resources management (job design, staff recruitment, orientation, development, training, performance evaluation, etc.);
- marketing and sales (facilities marketing, services marketing, relationship management – B2B customers, permanent tenants, sponsors, visitors, spectators, etc.);
- purchasing (including supply chain management, service provider pools, etc.);
- events management department (planning, implementation and evaluation of own events, staging of guest events; including technical support);
- food and beverage/catering;
- security (access control, crowd management, contingency plans, etc.);
- cleaning;
- financial management (financial statements, accounting, budgeting, financial performance evaluation, key performance indicators – KPIs, etc.);
- risk management;
- quality management.

Legal aspects are also important to consider. Generally, there is a multitude of laws and regulations impacting on sports and event venues. In operations, contract law, marketing-related issues such as trademark law or intellectual property rights have to be taken into account but also laws and regulations in terms of human resources management, financial management, risk management, etc. Once again, these legal issues differ from country to country, or even from federal state to federal state.

When developing an operational concept for a sports or event venue, it also has to be decided which functions will be outsourced and which will be organised by the relevant departments. Whereas outsourcing of services might be cheaper for the event venue, it might also have the negative impact of not continuously providing the same service quality and loyalty of employees towards the event venue. In case of a decision to keep the responsibilities internal, the line departments and – on the other hand – staff departments which provide technical and supportive assistance to the line decision makers have to be set.

Every option of ownership and governance structures has its own advantages and disadvantages. From the perspective of a community, the decision on ownership and governance structures finally always depends on the individual purpose of the sports or events venue in the context of urban development and maybe inter-urban competition and on the respective financial situation. Notwithstanding the above, the overall target must be to run the sports and event facilities in an economically, environmentally and socially sustainable way (see Bielzer, 2010).

Case 15.2   The Allianz Arena

The Allianz Arena in Munich opened in May 2005 and provides a total capacity of 69,901 seats, including 2,200 business seats, and 106 VIP boxes which can accommodate a total of 1,374 guests. The venue is home to both major Munich soccer clubs, FC Bayern Munich and TSV 1860 Munich, both of which have their home matches in the stadium.

The construction of the arena was the result of a two-stage architectural competition which started with a bidding process in July 2001. First, eight of 28 bidding consortiums made a short-list. They were selected to elaborate a draft for a football stadium based on a fixed sum by November 2001. Two consortia were then selected to once again review their drafts before the final decision in favour of the Swiss architects Herzog & DeMeuron and the Alpine Bau Deutschland GmbH construction company was made in February 2002.

On 30 April 2005 Alpine Bau GmbH officially handed over the venue to the new owners, Allianz Arena Munich Stadion GmbH. Construction costs of the arena were about €340 million. It is said that in

> **Case 15.2** (*continued*)
>
> addition to that, the city of Munich and the Bavarian State incurred costs of more than €210 million for area development and infrastructure improvements such as an underground line.
>
> Originally, the two soccer clubs, FC Bayern Munich and TSV 1860 Munich, both had a share of 50% in the holding company, Allianz Arena Munich Stadion GmbH. By 27 April 2006, FC Bayern Munich had purchased TSV 1860 Munich's 50% share for €11 million, after the TSV 1860 Munich club management had been charged with corruption and the club had come into financial difficulty. TSV 1860 had the right to repurchase their shares until June 2010. After they rescinded their right in April 2008, FC Bayern Munich AG became the Allianz Arena's only stockholder.
>
> Arena One GmbH is Allianz Arena's hospitality partner, rents the rooms, VIP areas and 'behind the scenes' areas on days without soccer matches, and provides catering both for soccer events and non-sport events. Amongst others, Arena One GmbH is also responsible for the venue's marketing and guided tours.
>
> Sources: www.allianz-arena.de/en/fakten/allgemeine-informationen and www.arena-one.com/arenaone/ebook/en/index.html#/34

> **Discussion question**
>
> **2** Using the information above as a basis, discuss ownership and management structures and the resulting challenges to running a soccer stadium.

Conclusion: key success factors in planning and managing sports and event venues

As the chapter has pointed out, modern sports and event venues have various predecessors throughout history and even though sports and event venues today are technically very sophisticated buildings, offering a stage for unique experiences for spectators and other users, they still show elements of traditional venues used for gatherings and physical education.

Sports and event venues also entail a lot of different challenges both in construction and in operations. Although there is a multitude of sports and event venues, the two categories of special properties often overlap in terms of their utilisation concepts and show similar management challenges. Success will be determined to a large extent by the consideration of the complex stakeholder environment and the awareness of the interdependencies between event venue construction and event venue operations.

As the chapter has shown, a lot of different skills and qualifications are required to plan, design and operate such a complex building as a sports or event venue. It has to be stated that careful planning impacts considerably on the opportunities to successfully operate these venues later. When planning and designing the facilities, the requirements of the various stakeholders have to be considered as well as market standards and forecasts of future market development. Meanwhile, one of the issues that has been discussed in the events and sports industry for many years is **sustainable event venue management**.

Very often a **sustainable event venue** is seen as a building that is planned, built and operated in an environmentally friendly way. But this is too narrow a focus. Following the United Nations' definition of sustainability, environmental, economic and social criteria have to be combined if an event venue wants to be perceived as 'sustainable'. Even though many venues underline their commitment to sustainability by certifications such as Leadership in Energy and Environmental Design (LEED) (see US Green Building Council, 2011), ISO 14001 or similar, there is as yet no commonly defined worldwide and comprehensive standard. Therefore, one of the remaining major challenges is to reach one common sustainability standard for sport and event venues, which is comprehensible and comparatively evaluable for event organisers and might also be experienced by visitors and other users of the buildings.

But sustainability is not only an issue for external communication. In this context, again, the interrelationships between the construction and operation of an event venue become apparent. For example, the use of environmentally friendly, natural, local and recyclable material, the integration of daylight and natural ventilation, the use of solar energy, or the integration of plants and water into building structures have a direct impact on the working conditions of the employees, their productivity and motivation and finally also on the operating costs of the venue.

To conclude, it has to be underlined that an important factor for the success of a sports or event venue is the definition of a clear vision and mission and the implementation of appropriate strategies in order to realise that vision. On the one hand, market requirements and user expectations are constantly changing and, on the other hand, competition from other sports or event venues (e.g. due to new locations, innovative special event locations, etc.) and 'internal' pressure in terms of financing and the economic benefit of the venues are continuously increasing. Therefore, it is crucial for a sports or event venue's operator to actively and strategically manage the venue.

Coulter (2008) sums up the following steps of strategic management:

- analysis of current situation of the event venue, market trends, competition, expectations of stakeholders, etc. (e.g. SWOT analysis);
- development of appropriate strategies based on the results of the analysis;
- implementation of those strategies;
- evaluation of the strategies put into action;
- modification or change of the strategies as needed.

Thus, applying this to a sports or event venue and strategically managing the facility helps to coordinate and focus various business activities towards achieving the overall goals as stated in the vision and mission statement. It contributes to achieving competitive advantages and to effectively and successfully coping with the fast-changing conditions in a complex and demanding external environment.

General discussion questions

3 Describe both the similarities and differences between modern sport and event venues and their historic predecessors.

4 What are the key issues in planning an event venue?

5 In which ways does the construction of an event venue impact on later operations?

6 What are the advantages and disadvantages of multi-purpose sport or event venues compared to single-purpose venues?

Guided reading

In terms of the history of trade fairs in Europe and the development of built exhibition infrastructure there are several publications such as:

Rodekamp, V. (2005) On the history of trade fairs in Germany and Europa. In M. Kirchgeorg, W.M. Dornscheidt, W. Giese and N. Stoeck (eds), *Trade Show Management: Planning, Implementing and Controlling of Trade Shows, Conventions and Events*. Wiesbaden: Gabler, 5–13.

Kaufhold, K.H. (1996) Messen und Wirtschaftsausstellungen von 1650 bis 1914. In P. Johanek and H. Stoob (eds), *Europäische Messen und Märktesysteme im Mittelalter* (Köln, Weimar and Wien: Städteforschung A/39), 239–94.

A comprehensive examination of the planning requirements and procedures, the design and the management challenges of convention and exhibition facilities is offered by:

Lawson, F.R. (2001) *Congress, Convention and Exhibition Facilities: Planning, Design and Management,* Oxford: Architectural Press.

Especially when dealing with congress facilities, hotels resp. the hospitality industry might also be of interest. Even though the focus is more on facility management than on planning, the following might be mentioned as an example:

Jones, T.J.A. and Zemke, D.M. (2010) *Managing the Built Environment for Hospitality Facilities.* Upper Saddle River, NJ: Pearson Prentice Hall.

The development and management of sports venues in a broader sense is covered by various publications such as:

Mull, R.F., Beggs, B.A. and Renneisen, M. (2009) *Recreation Facility Management. Design, Development, Operations and Utilisation.* Champaign, IL: Human Kinetics.

Sawyer, T.H. (2005) *Facility Design and Management: for Health, Fitness, Physical Activity, Recreation, and Sports Facility Management* (11th edn). Champaign, IL: Sagamore.

An in-depth discussion of different issues of sports facility management can also be found in:

Schwarz, E.C., Hall, S.A. and Shibli, S. (2010) *Sport Facility Operations Management: A Global Perspective.* London: Routledge.

For theatre venues see:

Strong, J. (ed.) (2010) *Theatre Buildings: A Design Guide.* Abingdon: Routledge.

Management issues for operas are covered for example by:

Agid, P. and Tarondeau, J.-C. (2010) *The Management of Opera: An International Comparative Study.* Basingstoke: Palgrave Macmillan.

Recommended websites

Various issues of event venue management are discussed on the website of the 'International Association of Venue Managers': **www.iavm.org**

For information on convention centres as a specific event venue type you may browse the website of the International Association of Congress Centres: **www.aipc.org**

Detailed information on current issues and trends in general facility management is provided by the website of the International Facility Management Association: **www.ifma.org**

In order to find general information on current issues and trends of the event industry you may visit the websites of the various professional associations, for example that of the Global Association of the Exhibition Industry (**www.ufi.org**) or of the International Congress and Convention Association (**www.iccaworld.com**)

Key words

architectural competition; feasibility study; life-cycle model; public–private partnership project; room concept; sustainable event venue management; utilisation concept

Bibliography

AUMA (ed.) (2011) *German Trade Fair Industry, Review 2010*. Berlin: AUMA.

Bielzer, L. (2010) Sustainable development of event venues – selected international examples in facts and figures. In S. Kaiser, R. Kaspar and G. Wolfram (eds), *Sustainable Event Management, Lessons Learnt and Prospects. Kufstein Congress on Sports and Culture 2009, Conference Proceedings*. Norderstedt Books on Demand.

Bielzer, L. and Wadsack, R. (2011) Betriebswirtschaftliche Herausforderungen des Managements von Sport- und Veranstaltungsimmobilien. In L. Bielzer and R. Wadsack (eds), *Betrieb von Sport- und Veranstaltungsimmobilien. Managementherausforderungen und Handlungsoptionen*. Frankfurt am Main: Peter-Lang-Verlag.

Bowdin, G.A.J., O'Toole, W., Harris, R. and McDonnell, I. (2006) *Event Management* (2nd edn). Oxford: Elsevier.

Coulter, M. (2008) *Strategic Management in Action* (4th edn). Upper Saddle River, NJ: Pearson/Prentice Hall.

Davidson, R. and Rogers, T. (2006) *Marketing Destinations and Venues for Conferences, Conventions and Business Events*. Oxford: Elsevier

Frank, S. and Steetsm, S. (2010) Introduction, In S. Frank and S. Steets (eds), *Stadium Worlds. Football, Space and the Built Environment*. London: Taylor & Francis.

Fried, G. (2010) *Managing Sport Facilities* (2nd edn). Champaign, IL: Human Kinetics.

Gillespie, A. (2007) PESTEL analysis of the macro-environment. **www.oup.com/uk/orc/bin/9780199296378/01student/additional/page_12.htm**

Lawson, F.R. (2001) *Congress, Convention and Exhibition Facilities: Planning, Design and Management*. Oxford: Architectural Press.

Leapman, M. (2002) *The World for a Shilling: How the Great Exhibition of 1851 Shaped a Nation*. London: Headline Review.

Meinel, K. (2001) Sustainability: management issues for the design. The involvement of the future manager of a new competition facility during the planning and design phase. An indispensable prerequisite for sustainability. Conference documentation 'Olympic Games and Architecture – The Future for Host Cities', Joint Conference IOC/IUA, May 2001.

Mull, R.F., Beggs, B.A. and Renneisen, M. (2009) *Recreation Facility Management. Design, Development, Operations and Utilisation*. Champaign, IL: Human Kinetics.

Peterson, D. (2001) *Developing Sports, Convention, and Performing Arts Centres* (3rd edn). Washington, DC: Urban Land Institute.

Porter, M.E. (1980) *Competitive Strategy*. New York: Free Press.

Porter, M.E. (2008) The five competitive forces that shape strategy. *Harvard Business Review,* 86(1), 78–93.

Richardson, L. (2005) Curia hostilia. **http://dlib.etc.ucla.edu/projects/Forum/resources/Richardson/Curia_Hostilia**

Rodekamp, V. (2005) On the history of trade fairs in Germany and Europe. In M. Kirchgeorg, W.M. Dornscheidt, W. Giese and N. Stoeck (eds), *Trade Show Management: Planning, Implementing and Controlling of Trade Shows, Conventions and Events*. Wiesbaden: Betriebswirtschaftlicher Verlag Gabler.

Schwarz, E.C., Hall, S.A. and Shibli, S. (2010) *Sport Facility Operations Management: A Global Perspective*. London: Routledge.

US Green Building Council (2011) An Introduction to LEED. **www.usgbc.org/DisplayPage.aspx?CategoryID=19**

Westerbeek, H., Smith, A., Turner, P., Emery, P., Green, C. and van Leeuwen, L. (2006) *Managing Sport Facilities and Major Events*. London: Routledge.

Chapter 16

Economic impact evaluation of events

Norbert Schütte, Johannes Gutenberg University, Germany

Learning outcomes

Upon completion of this chapter the reader should be able to:

- understand the relevance of **economic impact study** of sport events especially for a sport or a cultural manager;

- explain 'impact analysis' and 'cost benefit analysis';

- describe and discuss general methodological approaches to adequately assess the economic impact of an event (*ex ante* v. *ex post*, 'bottom down' v. 'bottom up', with or without qualitative aspects);

- assess in detail the costs and the benefits of an event.

Overview

The chapter starts with the reason why sport managers should know about the method of **cost–benefit analysis** and impact analysis. Basic definitions are introduced and problems of the methods described – for example opportunity costs or the uncertainty of data. Two main approaches are identified. Costs and benefits during the three phases of an event are mentioned. Instruction is given on how to compute the tangible cost and benefits. Two case studies are included. The chapter is completed by a conclusion and some questions to enhance learning.

Introduction

The question is whether to bid or not to bid for an event. Is it worth spending a lot of money – especially public money? Is there a scientific tool to help to decide whether to bid or not to bid? Cost–benefit analysis or impact studies are useful tools in helping make the decision. In Germany any huge public investment – like an airport – has to prove its benefit through a cost–benefit analysis (Rahmann et al., 1998: 85). Typically this kind of analysis is a macroeconomic study. But for several reasons event managers have to know more about the topic:

1. Some sport or cultural event managers work for councils or in other positions within the bureaucratic system of the state. When it comes to making the decision of whether public money should or should not be spent on an event, they have to prove whether it is worth investing the money or not. In this case they have to know what the benefits of an event are. Often the promoters of an event will themselves produce a cost–benefit analysis or an impact study. They should thus be able to validate and interpret it.

2. Some sport or cultural event managers work for agencies or consulting firms that promote an event for their customers. They have to know all about the potential benefits of an event in order to advertise it.

3. Last but not least, it is very useful for an event manager to know the factors that determine the size of the benefits. If the factors can be engineered, it is possible to maximise the benefit. This method is called 'leverage management' (Chalip, 2004; Chalip and Costa, 2005).

This chapter deals with the method of cost–benefit analysis and impact analysis. Even though cost–benefit analysis is a statistical tool and seems to be a mathematical solution to a decision problem, it is more a kind of art due to numerous problems that might be missed at first sight.

Basic definitions and problems

The difference between a cost–benefit analysis and an economic impact analysis is that impact analysis only scopes the economic benefit of the event or the project, and does not include the costs or social effects. There is no consistent terminology to define cost–benefit analysis or economic impact (Rahmann et al., 1998: 86 f.). For example, the OECD Glossary of Statistical Terms gives the following definitions:

> Cost Benefit Analysis is a technique for deciding whether to make a change. As its name suggests, it compares the values of all benefits from the action under consideration and the costs associated with it.
>
> (OECD, 2005)

Knowing the costs and the benefits one can subtract the costs from the benefits. If the result is positive, the project – in our case an event – should proceed. Unfortunately, for a lot of reasons, it is not that easy.

The first reason to be mentioned is the problem of opportunity costs. In real life one can seldom choose simply between going or not going for a specific project. In most cases there are alternative projects that also have to be considered. You can spend money only once. If you spend it on holding one event, you cannot spend it on holding a different event. This effect is referred to as 'opportunity cost' (Buchanan, 1977). Huge projects normally attract opposition. It is very easy to argue unfairly with the concept of opportunity costs. Opponents like to compare the spending of public money for an event with the alternative of spending on a hospital or a kindergarten. But these are not comparable, because a hospital or a kindergarten is an essential for a state whereas events are a kind of luxury. If one holds back from spending on an event, the money would not necessarily be used to invest in a hospital. But there is still the problem of opportunity cost with respect to comparable projects. The good news is that cost–benefit analysis is an instrument to decide between two projects by a clear mathematical approach. It calculates only the benefit and the cost of the two projects, and then the one with the return should be chosen.

This leads directly to the next problem. What are costs and what are benefits? Rahmann et al. (1998: 95) define cost and benefit according to a goal. They see every contribution to the goal as benefit and any damage to the goal as cost. Even though it is a clear concept, in some cases it is hard to measure. One can say that the spending on a new stadium is a cost because of the money needed to build it. Alternatively, one can argue that it is a benefit because a new stadium can be used now and the sport will benefit by it. Preuß (2003d: 19) suggested a macroeconomic solution. Money that enters an economy due to the event is a benefit and money that leaves has to be seen as a cost. Money that circulates inside the economy due to the event can be considered as neutral. This concept is based on Keynesian economics (Keynes, 1936). More money spent in an economy will create jobs and will raise the income of the state through taxes. This leads to higher economic growth. Major events require investment in building and other infrastructure such as roads or hotels. In the case of sports, typically new stadia have to be built, and in the case of culture, exhibition halls have at least to be upgraded. This creates jobs for the local economy. These extra jobs help create a positive multiplier effect throughout the local economy.

The amount of the effect will differ depending on the chosen economy. Even though the national economy is normally under consideration (e.g. Preuß and Weiss, 2003), sometimes a regional economy or the economy of an individual city – e.g. the case of the German Bundesland Rheinland Pfalz and the case of the City Kaiserslautern (Preuß et al., 2010) – is chosen.

Money that enters an economy induces a multiplier effect (Keynes, 1936). Any consumption will create income that again will create further consumption. Money circulates in the economy until it leaves the economy, mostly due to imports. The prime impact of a sport event will induce a multiplier effect so that the real impact will be greater than the prime impact.

Some investments due to the event will not only be used for and by the event. Especially in the case of new infrastructure (roads, railways, etc.), there will be a lot of other users. This type of cost is called 'joint cost'. There is no theoretically correct basis for allocating the costs to the different users of the investment. The only way to cope with this problem is by making a reasonable estimation (McHugh, 2006: 11). For example, the stadia for the Football World Cup 2006 in Germany are all used, with the exception of Leipzig, by clubs in the first division of the League in Germany. Most of them would have been built even without the World Cup. Some of them might have been built later, but it was necessary to have more and better stadia in Germany. So the question is to whom does this cost 'belong'?

The next problem is that not all costs and benefits can be measured in terms of units. These types of cost and benefits are called intangible (Preuss and Heisey, 2012: 307f). It is easy to tell how many units of beer were sold at the event venue, but it is not possible to do the same for an important effect like the boosting of the image of the host nation. This leads to maybe the most important problem of cost–benefit analysis: very important (maybe the main) effects are intangible like a better image of the host nation. To cope with this problem, the cost–benefit analysis has to be extended with a qualitative part that all intangible effects describe (Hanusch et al., 2011).

Another problem is the uncertainty of data: no one knows in advance how many event visitors will come to the event. Even the price of the new infrastructure is vague. Dealing with cost–benefit analysis is always dealing with uncertainty. A cost–benefit analysis has to cope with this problem. A way to do this is to deal with data conservatively. Always tend to *under*-estimate the benefit, and always tend to *over*-estimate the cost. Another way is more deliberate but much more work: set up different scenarios like the 'worst case' and the 'best case'; sometimes even a 'most likely' case is used (Sherman et al., 2010). Another technique to cope with uncertainty is sensitivity analysis. This is an identification, in a mathematical model, of the variables with the strongest impact in a cost–benefit analysis (Schütte, 2003).

Methodological approaches

There are a lot of methodological approaches that can be used, but two main approaches can be identified: the 'bottom down' and the 'bottom up' approach. Both are, in a way, problematic – both can only be done empirically *after* the event has happened and not before. But *ex ante* analysis is necessary for the decision to bid or not to bid. That is why most studies are *ex ante* (literally, 'from before') and only a few are '**ex post**' analyses. But in order to build an *ex ante* **study** you have to have a reference event that was empirically analysed. The more we know about the economy of sport events, the better we can estimate the economic impact of a forthcoming event.

The bottom down approach tries to detect the economic impact of an event in the gross product of the economy. The strength of this approach is that the gross product is easy to get for national economies because it is already computed for statistical reasons. But the weakness of this approach is that only very large effects like economic stimulus packages are able to be detected in the macro data of the economy. Even one of the biggest events in the world like the FIFA Football World Cup 2006 in Germany could not be detected in the gross product (Brenke and Wagner, 2007). This does not mean that the World Cup did not have any effect, but it is below the detectable line by this method.

The bottom up approach tries to compute the impact by using empirical data that stems directly from the event visitors and the data of the organising committee. All consumption due to the event has to be collected. After that it has to be decided whether a consumption is a benefit, neutral or a cost. Only costs and benefits count. Using this method Preuß et al. (2009) found that the FIFA Football World Cup 2006 in Germany had an economic impact through the event tourist, that is 0.13% of the gross product. So the effect was so small that it could be hardly detected in the macro data of an economy.

Costs and benefits of an event

Which consumptions and which effects can be seen as costs and benefits of an event? For a better answer to this question it is useful to differentiate the event into three phases: the pre-event, the event itself and the post-event phase.

Pre-event phase

Cost and benefits are generated long before an event starts. The bidding process can lead to a lot of expenditure. Planning, advertising and promoting the event are the main activities of a bidding process. A part of the money will leave the economy because things have to be imported or the event bid has to be promoted outside the economy. But there is some intangible benefit as well. The bid itself has a signalling effect and can shift the image of the host and even the public administration may get an impulse to work better and harder due to an interesting and desirable goal like a sport or cultural event (Preuß, 2003a: 179f).

If the bid is won then the event has to be prepared for. Small events will normally use available infrastructure. But for major events, stadia or exhibition halls, streets and railways have to be built or renovated. To shift the image effect of an event, landmark buildings have to be built. A good example is the Bird's Nest stadium of the Beijing Olympic Summer Games 2008 or the Eiffel Tower of the Exposition Universelle of 1889. Large expenditure is always a big push for the economy. The question is how much of the investment stays in the host economy and how much leaves. Everything that has to be imported is a cost and will stimulate the economies outside. Another question is where the money comes from? Any money coming from a different economy will be a benefit. This happens when money comes from the state to the host city and the reference economy is the economy of the host city. Usually the money will come out of the host economy from normal budgets or has to be lent (Preuß, 2003b: 127ff).

Before the event starts there is some tourism due to athletes with their staff testing the climate and the sporting facilities, or of artists testing, for example, the acoustics of a venue, and journalists reporting on the coming event. They would not have come without the event so they are a benefit because they bring money to the economy (Preuß, 2003c: 153ff).

Event phase

During the event phase, even more athletes or artists and journalists arrive and spending money. But more important are the event spectators when bigger events were examined. Major events can attract thousands of people who will pay for entrance, food and drinks. The biggest art exhibition *Documenta 12* attracted 754,301 event visitors (Hellstern et al., 2002). Some of them will have gone shopping or bought merchandise. Some will have stayed overnight in hotels and a lot of them will have used public transportation. It follows that a lot of money will have been injected into the economy. But unfortunately it is not that easy. Not all people that attend an event are of the same kind. Applying the framework of Preuß (2003d: 55ff), different types of people have to be differentiated due to their economic impact (see Figure 16.1):

- **Type A. Event visitors:** Persons who travel from their home which is in a different economy to the host city because of the event and would not have come to the city if the event had not happened. So all of their spending is a benefit for the host economy.
- **Type B. Casuals:** Tourists who would have visited the city, region or nation even without the event. For example, German tourists who take their holidays in Austria every year and went to the Euro 2008 football championships to watch some games. As they would have visited anyway, their money cannot be counted as a benefit attributable to the event. Only the extra spending for entrance and merchandise can be counted as benefits (Preuß et al., 2009: 180).
- **Type C. Extensioners:** Tourists who would have come anyway but stay longer because of the event. The *extension* of their journey is a benefit.
- **Type D. Home stayers:** These persons opt to stay in the city and spend their money at home rather than on a holiday out of the region at some other time in the year. Due to the event their money stays in the economy and it is a benefit.
- **Type E. Runaways:** Residents who leave the city due to the event and take a holiday out of the reference economy. Without the event they would not have left the reference economy. Their money leaves the economy so their consumption during the extra holiday is lost and has to be considered as a cost.
- **Type F. Changers:** Residents who leave the reference economy and take their holidays at the time of the event rather than at some other time in the year. Their money would have left the economy even without the event. The only difference is the point of time. Their consumption has to be considered as neutral.
- **Type G. Avoiders:** Tourists who stay away but would have come if the event had not been taking place. This is a crowding out effect by the event. Two kinds of avoiders have to be differentiated, with different economic effects:

- **G1. Cancellers:** Tourists who totally cancelled their trip, so they will not consume anything due to the event. These are costs of the event that are very difficult to calculate.
- **G2. Pre/post-switchers:** Tourists who will come later or earlier so their consumption is not lost and their consumption has to be considered as neutral. Not all crowding out leads to a loss of consumption!

- **Type H. Time switchers:** Tourists who wanted to travel to the city, region or nation but at another time. They switch to the time of the event. They have to be counted like casuals.
- **Type I. Residents:** Persons who would have been in the reference economy without the event. Their consumption is neutral.

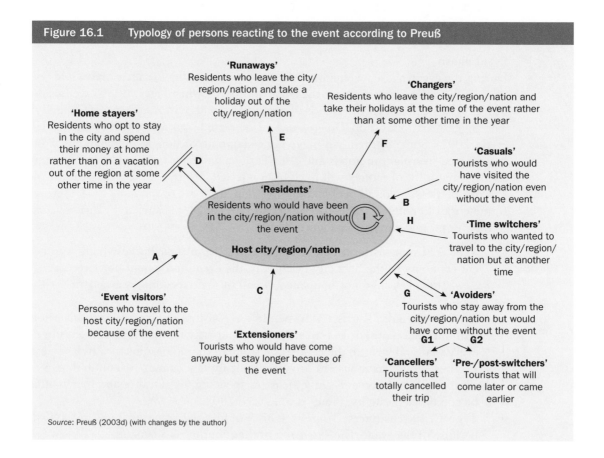

Figure 16.1   Typology of persons reacting to the event according to Preuß

Source: Preuß (2003d) (with changes by the author)

The money coming to the reference economy through entrance fees, media rights and advertising is a benefit, if it stays in the economy. In some cases it leaves the economy directly, because the money belongs to an organisation, such as an international federation, based in another economy. This was the case at the EURO 2008. UEFA owned the ticket money. The entrance fees for games held in Austria thus left the Austrian economy and went to Switzerland, where UEFA has its headquarters; much of it was then redistributed to the members of UEFA (Preuss et al., 2010: 36).

There is also spending in conducting the events. Sometimes the rooms or facilities have to be rented. Staff have to be taken on and paid. If the money leaves the economy, because for example specialists from outside the economy are hired to work at the event, it has to be considered as a cost (Preuß, 2003e: 108ff).

Case 16.1   Types of event visitors

The types of event visitors can differ a lot. In the case of the UEFA Euro 2008 (Austrian part) and of the FIFA World Cup 2006 in Germany, we can find different patterns of visitor types, with different economic consequences:

	Euro 2008	World Cup 2006
Residents	27.0%	38.3%
Home stayers	5%	6.7%
Residents who time switch their vacation	2.0%	9.3%
Event tourists	37.0%	26.6%
Casuals	23.1%	8.3%
Time switcher	5.9%	10.7%
N =	3,472	4,355

Sources: Preuß et al. (2009); Preuss et al. (2010)

The biggest difference is between the casuals. Casuals are visitors who would have come even without the event. They might have made their journey to visit a relative or for business reasons. They do not bring extra money to the economy with the exception of the purchase of merchandise and tickets for the event.

The difference can be explained by the fact that Austria is a major tourist destination. In particular, a lot of German tourists visit Austria every year. Many Germans who were visiting Austria for other reasons simply took the opportunity to attend the Euro events in which Germany were playing and to watch some international football.

Discussion questions

1 Using the figures above as a benchmark, what sort of percentages might you have expected for Euro 2012, held jointly by Poland and Ukraine? Give reasons for your answers.

2 Similarly, what percentages would you forecast for the FIFA World Cup to be held in Qatar in 2022? Again, give your reasons

After the event

The benefits after the event are called the legacy of the event. This term finds its origin in Olympic studies, and it has never found a universally agreed definition (Cashman, 2005: 15). A lot of effects can be included in this concept and most of them are more a possibility than proven knowledge. This is due to the fact that most of them are of an intangible nature. In this chapter only a few will be mentioned.

In some cases post-event tourism has been detected. In particular Australia used the 2000 Olympic Games in Sydney to promote tourism with a lot of success (Chalip, 2002). Tourism always means that money comes to the host economy and has to be considered as a benefit.

Gaining a better image and being recognised in the world is another main legacy of events. Despite the fact that this topic seem to be self-explanatory, research to date into this topic has been insufficient to make good predictions. Research after Euro 2000 found that there was a shift in the image of the hosts Belgium and the Netherlands only in France, which was the winner of the Championship (Oldenbloom, 2006). There is also a difference between cities that were quite well known in the world and those that were not. For example, the two most important exhibitions of modern art in the world are the *Biennale,* which is held in Venice, and the *Documenta,* which is held in Kassel. In fact, Venice is one of the best-known cities in the world, but the small city of Kassel in Germany would not be known by so many people outside Germany without the *Documenta.*

Case 16.2   Olympic legacy of London 2012 for East London

The legacy effect of major sport events is often used to legitimise the investment of public money in the hope of city regeneration and development. The Olympic Summer Games in London 2012 was no exception. For example, David Cameron set out his hopes in his first major speech as Prime Minister: 'Make sure the Olympics legacy lifts East London from being one of the poorest parts of the country to one that shares fully in the capital's growth and prosperity' (www.communities.gov.uk/regeneration/olympicslegacy).

It is an official aim to use the investment required for the Olympic Games to help expand and acceler-ate the renewal of East London. This renewal takes three forms:

- creating a new, successful and growing business economy;
- environmental renewal to improve the quality of East London as a place to live and work;
- a renewed commitment from the mayor and the East London Boroughs to tackle social problems like low educational attainment and life expectancy.

The Games were intended to transform polluted, low-grade industrial land into a modern city land-scape. New infrastructure such as a modern local rail network, new sport facilities and a spectacular new waterside park were built as a result of the Games.

The Olympic and Paralympic Games have been used to provide training for local people, and pro-grammes such as the Local Employment Skills and Training programme (LEST). In addition, local bor-oughs, the mayor and other agencies are working together more closely, with government support, on programmes to address the deep-seated social disadvantages experienced by much of the local popula-tion. Educational attainment, skills, worklessness, crime levels, health disparities and life expectancy are all being targeted (www.communities.gov.uk/regeneration/olympicslegacy/olympiclegacyeastlondon; more on the economics of the London 2012 Games can be found in Blake, 2005).

Discussion questions

3 To what extent do you think these various projects would have taken place without London hosting the Olympic Games in 2012?

4 How easy is it to evaluate the economic benefit of 'legacy'? Give examples to illustrate your answer.

Exports can grow as a result of holding a mega event, because the host will more often be recognised by a potential purchaser when it comes to a buying decision (Preuß, 2003c: 153).

National pride and more integration of the host are often mentioned as part of legacy. A good example is the 1992 Olympic Games held in Barcelona that led to a better inte-gration of the Catalan Region into Spain (Garcia Ferrando and Hargreaves, 2001).

Only one cost after the event is often cited: the cost of running and maintaining facili-ties after the event. Especially highly specialised facilities like the bicycle racing stadium in Berlin are difficult to operate at full capacity. There is a solution to the problem that has been used more and more in recent years – by building temporary infrastructure, no long-term costs such as those for maintenance will be incurred (Preuß, 2003b).

How to compute tangible costs and benefits of an event

After identifying the relevant tangible costs and benefits, the collection of the data can start. Some data can be collected by the organisation committees of the event. In some cases there is a bidding process before the event starts and bid books, containing detailed planned budgets, are available. The cost of building facilities and infrastructure in partic-ular can be found in this way. Another important data source is the published statistical analysis of municipal or national agencies.

It may be necessary to collect the data by interviewing event visitors. Reliable con-sumer patterns of event visitors can only be received in this way. The consumer pattern of an ordinary tourist is different from an event tourist. They pay entrance fees, buy mer-chandise and like to spend more money on food and drink because they are participat-ing in a 'once in a lifetime' experience at the event. Furthermore, the socio-demographic structure of event tourists can be different to that of ordinary tourists. The data from mega sport events like the FIFA World Cup of 2006 (Preuß et al., 2009) and the Euro 2006 Championships (Preuß et al., 2010), in particular, show that these events were visited by more highly educated and richer people compared to ordinary football games. This effect may differ by the event. This kind of data collection is of course only possible after the event has taken place. *Ex ante* analysis, such as this, has to find reference events and use their data carefully, and should use techniques to reduce uncertainty, as mentioned above.

A special and as yet only partly solved problem is that of crowding out. Every impact through event tourism has to deal with the problem that people stay away who, if the event had not been taking place, would have come to the host city. It is not easy to assess their numbers because some are just time switching and will come earlier or later, but in some cases they don't come at all. A new approach to deal with the problem is offered by Preuß (2011).

After receiving all the necessary data, a mathematical model of the event has to be built. The monetary benefits will come mostly from event visitors, public financial support and sponsorship, if they come from outside the chosen economy. After a mega event has happened, there may be a higher level of tourism, which can be a very big effect after Olympic Games (Preuß, 2003c). For every incidence of incoming money, it is necessary to establish how much of it comes from inside the economy and how much comes from outside. In some cases it is hard to determine the origin of the money. In this case it has to be carefully estimated. Investments and other spending for the event also have to be examined to determine how much of it is going out of the economy because it is imported.

A key problem of any cost–benefit or impact analysis is the over-estimation of incoming money and the under-estimation of the money spent. Often important costs are forgotten. Often neglected are security costs and the cost of the investments in the long term (Blake, 2005: 19).

When all monies are included in the model with their real net impact, it is possible to compute the prime impact of the event. In some cases more money leaves the economy than comes into it. So it will make a loss. The prime impact will induce a secondary effect due to the multiplier effect (Keynes, 1936). This effect should be included in the calculations.

Knowing how much is really spent item by item makes it possible to calculate how many taxes and how many jobs were created temporarily. For most economies there is an economic model of the whole economy that is called the 'input–output table'. To calculate taxes and jobs we need to know the amount of money spent and the part of the economy where it was spent. Different parts of the economy, like the hospitality or construction industries, have different patterns that lead to different amounts of jobs and taxes. For example, the German Inforge Modell that was used to calculate the economic impact of the FIFA Football World Cup 2006 has 43 different sectors to fill in (Preuß et al., 2009).

Conclusion

Cost–benefit analysis and impact studies can be used to help in making the decision whether to bid or not to bid for an event. A good ratio of costs and benefits will legitimise the investment in an event. If the analysis is done carefully and honestly, it is a very strong instrument to help decision making, but is very easy to manipulate the results when it is done dishonestly. Therefore it is very important to document the way it is done. And due to the complexity of the calculations, some PowerPoint slides or a small booklet are not enough! It has to be a complete overview so that the results can be considered as proven.

Another important point is that these techniques can help with the decision but, even though they have a mathematical foundation, it is not possible to determine the decision by the technique. It provides good arguments but no final decision. This always has to be in the hands of human beings.

General discussion questions

5   What can be done to maximise the economic impact induced by event visitors?

6   Should mega events be used as economic stimulus packages?

7   Why is the bottom down approach weak as a means of detecting the economic impact of a sport event?

8   Why is cost–benefit analysis always in danger of being manipulated?

9   Economic impact studies always end up with an amount of money. Can different economic impact studies be compared directly?

10   Imagine you were the mayor of a big city and you were in charge of deciding whether to give public money to a sport event. What would be your criteria?

11   Gaining a better image is often stated to be part of the legacy of a mega sport event. Can this be improved by management? Does a better image arise automatically? What circumstances might lead to a loss of image?

12   What can be done if the planning data is vague?

Guided reading

The key texts to read are:

Blake, A. (2005) The economic Impact of the London 2012 Olympics. Discussion Paper. Tourism and Travel Research Institute. Nottingham University Business School. *http://bournemouth.academia.edu/AdamBlake/Papers/345890/Economic_Impact_of_the_London_2012_Olympics*

Preuß, H., Könecke, T. and Schütte, N. (2010) Calculating the primary economic impact of a sports club's regular season competition: a first model, *Journal of Sport Science and Physical Education*, 60, 17–22.

Recommended websites

eventIMPACTS: **www.eventimpacts.com/project/resources/?filter=Economic**

Higher Education Academy: **www.heacademy.ac.uk/assets/hlst/documents/resource_guides/the_impact_of_events.pdf**

UK Sports: **www.uksport.gov.uk/news/1848** and **www.uksport.gov.uk/docLib/Publications/Measuring-Success-2.pdf**

Key words

cost–benefit analysis; economic impact study; ex ante study; ex post study

Bibliography

Blake, A. (2005) The Economic Impact of the London 2012 Olympics. Discussion Paper. Tourism and Travel Research Institute. Nottingham University Business School, **http://bournemouth.academia.edu/**

AdamBlake/Papers/345890/Economic_Impact_of_the_London_2012_Olympics

Brenke, K. and Wagner, G.G. (2007) Zum volkswirtschaftlichen Wert der Fussball-Weltmeisterschaft 2006 in Deutschland.

In *Research Notes 19*. Berlin: Deutsches Institut für Wirtschaftsforschung

Buchanan, J.M. (1977) *Cost and Choice*. Chicago, IL: University of Chicago Press.

Cashman, R. (2005) *The Bitter-Sweet Awakening. The Legacy of the Sydney 2000 Olympic Games*. Sydney: Walla Walla Press.

Chalip, L. (2002) Using the Olympics to optimise tourism benefits: university lecture on the Olympics, Barcelona, Centre d'Estudis Olímpics (UAB), International Chair in Olympism (IOC-UAB). **http://olympicstudies.uab.es/lectures/web/pdf/chalip.pdf**

Chalip, L. (2004) Beyond impact: a general model for sport event leverage. In J.R.B. Ritchie and D. Adair (eds), *Sport Tourism: Interrelationships, Impacts and Issues*. Clevedon: Channel View Publications.

Chalip, L. and Costa, C.A. (2005) Sport event tourism and destination brand: towards a general theory. *Sport in Society,* 8(2), 218–37.

Garcia Ferrando, M. and Hargreaves, J. (2001) Das Olympische Paradox und Nationalismus. Der Fall der Olympischen Spiele in Barcelona. In K. Heinemann and M. Schubert (eds), *Sport und Gesellschaften*. Schorndorf: Hofmann.

Hanusch, H., Ilg, G. and Jung, M. (2011) *Nutzen-Kosten-Analyse*. Munich: Beck.

Hellstern, G.-M., Freitag, C. and Bracht, O. (2002) *Tabellenband und Auswertung zur Documenta11*. Kassel.

Keynes, J.M. (1936) *The General Theory of Employment, Interest and Money*. London: Macmillan and Co.

McHugh, D. (2006) A cost–benefit analysis of an Olympic Games, Queen's Economics Department Working Paper No. 1097.

OECD (2005) OECD glossary of statistical terms: cost/benefit analysis. **http://stats.oecd.org/glossary/detail.asp?ID=6377**

Oldenbloom, E. (2006) *Costs and Benefits of Major Sport Events*. Amsterdam: MeerWarde Onderzoeksadvies.

Preuß, H. (2003a) Erfassen der intangible Kosten und Nutzen. In H. Preuß and H.-J. Weiss, (eds), *Torchholder Value Added – Frankfurt RheinMain 2012*. Eschborn: AWV-Verlag.

Preuß, H. (2003b) Erfassen der tangiblen Kosten und Nutzen – Primäreffekt durch Investition. In H. Preuß and H.-J. Weiss (eds), *Torchholder Value Added – Frankfurt RheinMain 2012*. Eschborn: AWV-Verlag.

Preuß, H. (2003c) Erfassen der tangiblen Kosten und Nutzen – Exporte und Tourismus. In H. Preuß and H.-J. Weiss (eds), *Torchholder Value Added – Frankfurt RheinMain 2012*. Eschborn: AWV-Verlag.

Preuß, H. (2003d) Methodische Grundlagen. In H. Preuß and H.-J. Weiss (eds), *Torchholder Value Added – Frankfurt RheinMain 2012*. Eschborn: AWV-Verlag.

Preuß, H. (2003e) Erfassen der tangiblen Kosten und Nutzen – Primäreffekt durch FOCOG. In H. Preuß and H.-J. Weiss (eds), *Torchholder Value Added – Frankfurt RheinMain 2012*. Eschborn: AWV-Verlag.

Preuss, H. (2011) A method for calculating the crowding-out effect in sport mega-event impact studies: the 2010 FIFA World Cup. *Development Southern Africa,* 28(3), 367–85.

Preuss, H. and Heisey, K. (2012) Macroeconomics of international sport. In M. Li, E.W. MacIntosh and G.A. Bravo (eds), *International Sport Management*. Champaigne, IL: Human Kinetics.

Preuß, H. and Weiss, H.-J. (2003) *Torchholder Value Added – Frankfurt RheinMain 2012*. Eschborn: AWV-Verlag.

Preuß, H., Kurscheidt, M. and Schütte, N. (2009) *Ökonomie des Tourismus von Sportgroßveranstaltungen. Eine empirische Analyse zurFußball-Weltmeisterschaft 2006*. Wiesbaden: Gabler.

Preuss, H., Könecke, T. and Schütte, N. (2010) Calculating the primary economic impact of a sports club's regular season competition: a first model. *Journal of Sport Science and Physical Education,* 60, 17–22.

Preuß, H., Siller, H., Zehrer, A., Schütte, N. and Stickdorn, M. (2010) *Regionale ökonomische Auswirkungen der EURO 2008 für Österreich*. Wiesbaden: Gabler.

Rahmann, B., Weber, W., Groening, Y., Kurscheidt, M., Napp, H.-G. and Pauli, M. (1998) *Sozio-ökonomische Analyse der Fußball-Weltmeisterschaft*

2006 in Deutschland: Gesellschaftliche Wirkungen, Kosten-Nutzen-Analyse und Finanzierungsmodelle einer Sportgroßveranstaltung. Cologne: Sport und Buch Strauß.

Schütte, N. (2003) Sensitivitätsanlayse. In H. Preuß and H.-J. Weiss (eds), *Torchholder Value Added – Frankfurt RheinMain 2012*. Eschborn: AWV-Verlag.

Sherman, G. et al. (2010) Scenario analysis, decision trees and simulation for cost benefit analysis of cargo screening processes, The International Workshop on Applied Modelling and Simulation: WAMS, Buizos, 2010. COPPE/UFRJ, Rio de Janeiro, 287–95.

Chapter 17

Events management and the hospitality industry

Stefan Walzel, German Sport University, Cologne, Germany

Learning outcomes

Upon completion of this chapter the reader should be able to:

- define the terms hospitality and **corporate hospitality**, and appreciate the nature of these activities;
- explain the significance of hospitality in the overall event experience;
- understand corporate hospitality as a **business-to-business communication tool** and its effects;
- describe the different opportunities for corporate hospitality activities;
- understand the market size, current development, market players and challenges in terms of hospitality.

Overview

While the following remarks make particular reference to sporting events, they may be equally applied to cultural or other events. First, two different fields of hospitality will be introduced and a distinction made between them from the perspective of the sporting event organiser. Subsequently, the significance of hospitality for various target groups in the overall context of a sporting event will be explained and its consequences demonstrated in a case study. Later in this chapter, the term 'corporate hospitality' will be discussed and its role as a corporate communication tool explored. The fourth and last section will be dedicated to the sports hospitality market. The size of the market as well as current developments and challenges will be described.

Introduction

As early as in ancient Greek and Roman times, athletic competitions were accompanied by celebrations before their official start, during games and after award ceremonies. Athletes sometimes travelled long distances to participate in the contests. Some were accompanied by friends, family members and other persons supporting them and/or simply wanting to observe the games. In hosting cities and towns, athletes and their companions relied on accommodation, food and drink being provided by locals (Mechikoff, 2010). Athletic competitions can therefore be said to be closely linked with hospitality – in ancient times and to this day.

Even then, arenas were fitted with special seats and VIP boxes for selected guests where food and drinks were served during events (Guttmann, 1981, 1986). This phenomenon could also be observed at knights' tournaments and 19th century horse races (Veblen, 2006) and remains common practice at today's sporting events. This particular form of hospitality, better known as corporate hospitality (Bennett, 2003), has diversified increasingly over the past years and is an important refinancing tool for organisers of sporting events (Walzel, 2011).

The term 'hospitality' generally refers to the hotel, restaurant and entertainment industry (Kotler et al., 2006). At the same time, the term is designed to emphasise the industry's traditional idea of providing services and thus convey an image which places the guest's satisfaction at the focus of all activities (Lockwood, 2000). In relation to sport, 'hospitality' can generally be understood to include any products and services offered to visitors of a sporting event. This comprises, in particular, overnight stays, food and drinks as well as other entertainment services provided before, during and after a sporting event.

This contribution aims at describing in more detail hospitality as a sub-field of events management and analysing its significance for the hosting of sporting events. In this context, two manifestations must be distinguished from the perspective of the organiser of sporting events. On the one hand, there is hospitality for end consumers ('business-to-consumer hospitality'), in particular products and services offered to private individuals, such as food and drinks sold to spectators in a sports arena. On the other hand, hospitality services at sporting events are used by companies. As mentioned above, this is referred to as 'corporate hospitality' ('business-to-business hospitality'). An example would be booking a box in a sports arena. Both hospitality sub-fields are of utmost importance to organisers of sporting events.

Significance of hospitality at sporting events

Sporting events can be regarded as a service package made up of various individual services (including the competition, security checks, hospitality, etc.). From the perspective of the sporting event organiser, achieving the best possible service quality is at the focus of all activities (Getz, 2005; Riedmüller, 2011). In principle, the rule is: the higher the quality of services, the higher the customer's satisfaction. Customer satisfaction helps increase customer loyalty, thus often leading to higher turnover and customer profitability (Hennig-Thurau and Klee, 1997; Anderson, 1998; Szymanski and Henard, 2001). Customer retention is an important performance indicator, in particular for organisers of recurring sporting events, such as football league games or sporting events repeated on a regular basis. Retained customers share their positive experience at the sporting event with third parties and recommend it (Anderson, 1998; Szymanski and Henard, 2001). In addition, evidence has been found to sustain the fact that communication costs are lower if customers return (Hadwich, 2003). For example, loyal spectators of sporting events need not be actively informed of the time and schedule of the event. As a rule, they will retrieve the required information themselves, for example from the provider's website, so that costs to advertise the event can be reduced.

According to Riedmüller (2011), the success of professional sporting events depends on three success factors: (a) athletic performance, (b) attendance and (c) economic success. All of these influence one another, both in a positive and in a negative way. The terms used to describe this are 'spiral of success' and 'spiral of failure', respectively. This means that, the better the athletic performances, the more enthusiastic the spectators, and this, in turn, is also reflected in the economic success of the sporting event. This then provides more resources to increase the athletic performance, thus attracting even more spectators, etc. However, the spiral of success has an upper ceiling and will meet its limits at a certain point, for example in terms of capacity limits for spectators.

Hospitality is part of a complete service package labelled 'sporting event', thus contributing to the satisfaction and, ultimately, the retention or non-retention of participants and visitors of the sporting event. From the perspective of the organiser of sporting events, five target groups of hospitality can substantially be identified: (1) athletes, coaches, supporting staff, referees and officials; (2) media representatives; (3) spectators; (4) staff and volunteers; as well as (5) guests of honour (Graham et al., 2001). All of these groups are at the same time co-producers of the complete service package 'sporting event'. Each group, according to its ability, has a share in the success or failure of the event, so each of the target groups has a special significance in terms of hospitality as well.

The first target group, among others the *athletes,* plays a pivotal role as regards the quality of the service package 'sporting event'. It is thus understandable that athletes can only deliver top performance if the quality of board and lodging is good. This is equally true for the other persons in this target group. At international sporting events, the food menu should cater for cultural particularities. For example, Muslims do not eat pork, Hindus do not eat beef. In this context, the preparation and storage of food and drinks also play an important role. Depending on the country of origin, individuals' digestive systems may be particularly sensitive to certain foods. From time to time, these individuals may suffer from diarrhoea, in particular during sporting events of longer duration. This is one of the reasons why some national football teams travel with their own chef during major tournaments in order to reduce the chance of players being unavailable for selection due to digestion problems.

In the past, individual cases of contaminated food came to light, with athletes being tested positive during doping tests. In some cases, deliberate action by the opponent in order to weaken their competitor or to have him or her disqualified cannot be excluded. Other cases, however, may have occurred without foul play. During sporting competitions in China and Mexico, individual athletes were tested positive for anabolic drugs and/or clenbuterol. These substances are on the Prohibited List of the World Anti-Doping Agency (WADA) and were primarily used to enhance more rapid muscle building for sporting purposes. The athletes concerned, however, were unaware of taking the respective substance. It entered their bodies through the food chain, as these countries use anabolic drugs and/or clenbuterol in pig and cattle breeding, and was absorbed by consuming the meat (see Case 17.1). As a response to this problem the world governing body for swimming (FINA), for example, together with the Chinese and Shanghai governments, initiated additional food protection measures for the 2011 World Swimming Championships to ensure the success of this sporting event. This case study emphasises the importance and delicacy of hospitality, in particular for athletes, and demonstrates that high diligence and excellent quality management are required on the part of the sporting event organiser – from buying to serving food and drinks.

Media representatives are another important target group of hospitality. From the sporting event organiser's perspective, they are crucial multipliers and contribute a great deal to the perception of and opinion making in relation to the sporting event by the public (Masterman and Wood, 2006; Nicholson, 2007; Bowdin et al., 2011). Especially during major international sporting events, such as the Olympic Games, media representatives are often out and about every day from early in the morning until late in the evening for two to three weeks at a time to report on the sporting competitions. This often leaves little time for food intake. To prevent them from reporting in a state of hunger or thirst, it has become common practice during most major sporting events to offer a small selection of complimentary food and drinks to this group in the vicinity of their workplaces (Masterman and Wood, 2006; Nicholson, 2007). Coffee, tea and non-alcoholic drinks are standard. These are often complemented by fruit, sandwiches or hot snacks.

Case 17.1   Clenbuterol warning for Mexico

The problem of clenbuterol-contaminated food seems to be expanding. A recent study of the Manfred Donike Institute and the Centre for Preventive Doping Research at the German Sport University of Cologne has shown an increased risk of unintentional doping with the prohibited substance clenbuterol in Mexico, too.

NADA Germany therefore recommends, similarly to travelling to China, to be highly cautious with victuals in these countries. On Thursday representatives of NADA Germany and the German Anti-Doping Laboratories will deliberate in Paris about further recommendations for athletes.

The study report shows significantly increased values in the urine samples of two travellers who returned in March 2011 after a three-day trip to Mexico. The urine samples were taken on the first day after their return. The concentrations of clenbuterol were around 115 pg/ml and 90 pg/ml. Urine samples taken before the trip to Mexico were clenbuterol-free. These values were even higher than samples analysed of travellers from China, which had led to a warning by the laboratory in Cologne and NADA Germany in mid-February.

So far, there is no threshold level for clenbuterol in the anti-doping-regulations: thus, the concentrations found in the study would result in an adverse analytical finding. As a general rule, athletes are responsible for themselves and should be extremely cautious about any substances which could cause a positive result.

NADA Germany recommends particular vigilance with food when travelling to Mexico or China. As far as possible the consumption of meat products should be omitted. For proposals on alternative protein sources other than meat, please refer to the nutritionists of the Olympic Training Centres, in accordance with the German Olympic Sports Federation recommendation.

The abusive use of clenbuterol as a growth mediator might be the reason for contaminated food in China and Mexico. Due to strict legal requirements in Europe and North America meat products are considered as safe.

For further information on protection measures during the 2011 World Swimming Championship please refer to www.fina.org/H2O/index.php?option=com_content&view=article&id=2054&Itemid=896 and www.youtube.com/watch?v=ARx51CCHtCQ

Source: www.nada-bonn.de/fileadmin/user_upload/nada/News-Bilder/110405_Clenbuterol_Warning_for_Mexico1.pdf

Discussion questions

1 What actions can be undertaken by the event organiser to prevent food contamination at the event itself?

2 What can international sporting federations do in order to avoid such cases of contaminated food?

3 Are the World Anti-Doping Agency (WADA) and/or National Anti-Doping Agency (NADA) responsible for checking such causes before publishing a positive doping test result? Please, justify your answer.

It should be ensured that the consumption of food can be quick and uncomplicated, as media representatives are under constant time pressure. In addition, especially during sporting events of longer duration, the food offered should provide some variety.

Compared with the two target groups mentioned above, *spectators* play a special role. The turnover from this group has a direct impact on the financial outcome of the sporting event. Hosting international sporting events often comes with the expectation that these events will contribute to the long-term economic development of the respective region. In this context, the impact on tourism is of particular interest. According to Hall (1989), sporting events can in principle lead to higher visitor numbers staying at the event venue location for a longer period of time than the average tourist, which is, ultimately, reflected in higher turnover and tax revenue. For the sporting event organiser, hospitality spending by sporting event spectators at the sports facilities is an important source of income for funding the sporting event. Furthermore, additional hospitality spending by spectators outside sports facilities is an important criterion for the economic evaluation of sporting events at national level, which is often done using cost–benefit analyses (Gratton et al., 2005; Preuß, 2006, 2007).

Shortly before and during a sporting event, the *staff* and *volunteers* of the sporting event organiser are at times exposed to extreme stress. Often, they will have worked a large number of hours even before the sporting event officially starts and often go to the limit of their capacity. Lack of sleep, psychological pressure, stress, lack of time and unexpected difficulties are only some of the factors that play a part (Cuskelly et al., 2006). It is all the more important that staff and volunteers are well catered for during the event in order to avoid understaffing and ultimately ensure smooth progress of the event. Hospitality products and services offered must be adapted to the requirements of individual workplaces. While staff working outside at 35 degrees centigrade in the shade should primarily be provided with sufficient amounts of liquid and consume meals in a cooled room if possible, hot drinks are particularly important for persons working at winter sporting events. Again, it should be ensured that food and drinks are of good quality and made available in sufficient quantities. The commitment and motivation in particular of the volunteers, but also of the paid staff, should be maintained at a high level and not destroyed by offering cold food, for example. At the end of a working day or shift, small gestures such as treating staff to a round of beer can improve morale and motivation and also contribute to better solidarity within the team. At major sporting events it is common practice to host a small reception or party to thank staff and volunteers for their effort. This is all the more important if the event will be repeated, as staff will be needed again. Recruitment efforts could be reduced by using experienced staff. Unsatisfied staff and volunteers, however, will probably not be available again and may also discourage friends and acquaintances from working at the event.

Inviting and **catering** for *guests of honour* as part of sporting events is to be considered from the view of strategic relationship marketing (Graham et al., 2001; Masterman and Wood, 2006). Organisers of sporting events rely on the support of a large number of stakeholders, who have a major influence on the success or failure of the respective event (Masterman, 2004; Bowdin et al., 2011). This is not limited to that particular event, but often has a bearing on future events as well. Therefore, the best seats at sports facilities are reserved for and an appropriate food and drinks selection offered to important decision makers (such as sponsors, important suppliers, partners, politicians, etc.). On the one hand, this is to thank them for their usually good cooperation, and, on the other hand, it is to use the opportunity to improve or expand the quality of relations with stakeholders in a casual atmosphere (Bennett, 2003; Walzel, 2011).

Corporate hospitality as a business-to-business communication tool

Building on the same approach that organisers employ, namely to use events also for business relationship management, companies discovered and have for several years been increasing the use of top-level sporting events as a form of business-to-business communication, in particular with their clients.[1] This form of relationship marketing is referred to as 'corporate hospitality'. More precisely, corporate hospitality is 'an independent instrument of dialogical communication with the help of which the quality of the relations to

---

1 At many sporting events, it is possible not only for companies but also for individuals to buy tickets for VIP boxes or business seat areas. Whenever an individual books corporate hospitality activities, this can be considered rather as a 'ticket with extras' and is therefore part of ticketing. While an individual does this mostly for prestigious reasons, a company can usually be assumed to have a strategic intention, as it uses a corporate hospitality activity to attain company goals. This intention distinguishes the activity not only from activities hosted by individuals but also from a so-called 'jolly', which refers to amusement at the company's expense without pursuing corporate objectives (Church, 2003; Kolah, 2004; Masterman and Wood, 2006). This contribution looks exclusively at companies as users of corporate hospitality.

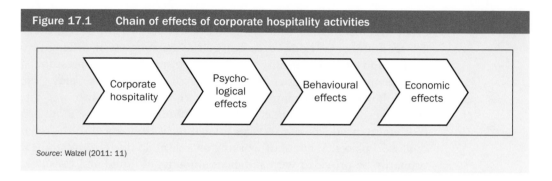

Figure 17.1   Chain of effects of corporate hospitality activities

Source: Walzel (2011: 11)

different stakeholders of an organisation can be improved by jointly experiencing special sporting events in a pleasant atmosphere' (Walzel, 2011: 24). Possible causes for the positive development of corporate hospitality in recent years have been identified as saturated markets, increasingly homogeneous products and services, information overload and a declining interest in traditional communication tools in conjunction with an increasing interest in dialogue and relationships (Davidson and Cope, 2003; Bruhn, 2005).

The focus of corporate hospitality activities is not on generating business or negotiating a contract extension, but on high-quality relations between stakeholders (Walzel, 2011). Against the background of a shift in values towards leisure-, pleasure- and theme-orientated offerings (Kroeber-Riel and Weinberg, 2003), exclusive and unique experiences are intended to contribute to each individual stakeholder's loyalty to the company to secure the company's future success (Key Note, 2007). The focus of corporate hospitality is thus first and foremost on psychological aspects which can be considered prerequisites to achieving desired behavioural effects (see Figure 17.1) and therefore ultimately contribute to the attainment of a company's economic goals (Walzel, 2011).

Psychological effects can be further divided into cognitive and affective effects. Cognitive effects refer to the knowledge about a matter and help assess to what extent information has been absorbed, processed and stored. Therefore, cognitive objectives primarily refer to 'the perception, knowledge, recollection and understanding of offerings and/or services' (Bruhn, 2007: 172). In relation to corporate hospitality activities, this mainly includes sales promotion objectives (MSI, 2002; Davidson and Cope, 2003; Masterman and Wood, 2006; Sportfive, 2009). In particular, it is possible, for example, to increase the perception of products or services, impart information on know-how and performance or even introduce new products and/or services (Church, 2003).

Based on cognitive effects, affective (emotional) effects aim at attitudes, preferences and images. Specific emotions and affections associated with a brand or a company are to be provoked. At the same time, dissociation from other products and/or companies must take place (Bruhn, 2007). Corporate hospitality activities can help achieve affective objectives such as lobbying and image building and/or development (MSI, 2002; Davidson and Cope, 2003; Masterman and Wood, 2006; Voeth et al., 2006; Sportfive, 2009) and initiate new business relations (MSI, 2002; Church, 2003; Masteralexis et al., 2005; Masterman and Wood, 2006; Allen et al., 2008; Sportfive, 2009). Loyalty of clients and business partners, but also employees, is named as another important affective target value (MSI, 2002; Church, 2003; Kolah, 2004; Dann and Dann, 2005; Masteralexis et al., 2005; Gardiner et al., 2006; Masterman and Wood, 2006; Voeth et al., 2006; Mullin et al., 2007; Allen et al., 2008; Sportfive, 2009). Establishing and defending a competitive edge vis-à-vis rivals is also named as an objective (BSML, 1990; Church, 2003).

Conative objectives and/or behavioural objectives mostly refer to the buying pattern(s) of the target group(s), which is reflected in sales by samples, brand switching or additional sales (Bruhn, 2007). While affective effects reflect the inner state of a person and are difficult to observe or quantify, conative effects can be observed and quantified on the basis of the behaviour of an individual, for example in the form of the quantity purchased or the purchase price. Conative objectives are downstream compared with affective objectives. The level of intensity of the affective effects has an impact on the conative effects. The studies identified do not explicitly refer to conative objectives, because in relation-orientated business relations they can almost exclusively be achieved through affective objectives.

The studies by Sportfive (2009) and Walzel (2010) clearly show that corporate hospitality activities are primarily used to achieve affective and conative objectives. In comparison, surveyed companies attributed lower priority to cognitive objectives, although these are often an important precursor for achieving affective objectives. Both studies reveal that a stronger attachment of the client to the inviting company is the most frequently named objective of corporate hospitality activities.

In practice, opportunities for corporate hospitality are often part of sponsoring agreements and present an important argument for purchasing sponsoring packages and/or initiating sponsoring engagements (Kolah, 2004; Mullin et al., 2007; Allen et al., 2008; Bühler and Nufer, 2010; Burton et al., 2011;). Due to limited options at individual sporting events, sponsors on such occasions even obtain exclusive rights to official corporate hospitality.

According to a study by Sportfive (2009), clients, sales and cooperation partners as well as employees are the three most important *target groups* for corporate hospitality activities. These results largely correspond with the results reported by Voeth et al. (2006). In addition to these three target groups, representatives from the media, politics and other important decision makers may be part of the target group of the acceptance market, and bank representatives, owners and shareholders may be part of the target group of the financial market (Davidson and Cope, 2003). When (potential) new clients are invited, the literature does not agree whether corporate hospitality is suitable or not. While many British companies are very critical of it as they consider this form of customer approach too aggressive and as, at the same time, there could be an impression of bribery (BSML, 1990), Davidson and Cope (2003), in fact, regard corporate hospitality activities as particularly suited to win over new clients.

A differentiation between active and passive corporate hospitality activities can be made according to the level of integration of the guests into the sporting event. While the passive form is most common in sport, active corporate hospitality activities have become more numerous in recent years (Kolah, 2004). Compared with the passive form, where the guest witnesses the sporting competition without any own active involvement, active corporate hospitality activities integrate the guest into the sporting event. One of the most popular active forms is golf tournaments with invited stakeholders of a company (Kolah, 2004). In practice, mixed forms may also occur. There, invited guests will start by observing the golf tournament and will later, for example the next day, play a separate tournament with the golf players who participated in the competition.

Passive corporate hospitality activities can be further divided into two characteristic forms: (a) premium seats and (b) VIP boxes (Graham et al., 2001; Church, 2003; Davidson and Cope, 2003; Kolah, 2004; Masteralexis et al., 2005; John et al., 2007; Lawrence and Moberg, 2009;). *Premium seats,* also referred to as 'business seats', are seats which are usually among the best seats in the stadium or arena, from where the sporting competition can be followed best. Furthermore, these seats are often more comfortable than standard seats, for example upholstered leather seats. Additional services, such as woollen blankets for low temperatures or food and drinks served at each seat, are offered free of charge depending on the sporting event. The ticket for such a premium seat is usually linked with access to a 'backstage area', where food and drinks are offered which are included in the premium ticket price (see Case 17.2). This form of corporate hospitality is used mainly by small companies which invite and cater for only a few guests at sporting events.

Case 17.2   Prices of and services offered with premium seats and VIP boxes at sporting events

Hospitality package for a *business seat* at the FIFA World Cup 2010 in South Africa:

- Category 1 match ticket,
- shared hospitality experience with a casual ambiance in outside temporary facilities within stadium perimeters,
- buffet catering before and after the match and bar service,
- casual décor,
- hostess services,
- parking facilities,
- access to MATCH Hospitality Domestic Travel Services.

Price per person for the semi-final 1 at Cape Town Green Point Stadium: 4,000 USD.
Hospitality package for a *suite* at the FIFA World Cup 2010 in South Africa:

- exclusivity for 4 persons or more in a luxurious ambiance,
- adjacent seats with a perfect view of the pitch,
- a world-class hospitality service with a main course, a half-time snack, pre- and post-match entrées, hors d'oeuvres and dessert buffet along with an open bar with fine beverages (this service is uninterrupted throughout the match),
- stylish décor and interior design concept,
- dedicated hostesses,
- match programme,
- exclusive commemorative gift,
- preferential parking.

Price per person for the semi-final 1 at Cape Town Green Point Stadium: 5,500 USD.

Source: Sales prospect of Match Hospitality, FIFA's worldwide exclusive rights holder of the Official Hospitality Programme for the 2010 FIFA World Cup South Africa™

Discussion questions

4 What arguments can be considered in order to justify the higher price for a suite in comparison to a business seat?

5 Which other costs need to be taken into account when a company is thinking of booking corporate hospitality tickets?

6 What are the pros and cons of booking 'normal' tickets and offering hospitality services before and after the event outside of the venue?

Companies which regularly invite a larger group of people to a sporting event often rent a *VIP box*. VIP boxes are often closed-off rooms with a glass front with a view into the sports facility as well as seats in and/or directly outside the VIP box. Guests in the VIP box are also offered food and drinks before, during and after the sporting event. A separate bar, kitchen, coat area and toilet for each VIP box increase convenience. Compared with premium seats, VIP boxes offer a more private atmosphere (see Case 17.2). Companies usually hire VIP boxes for several years and can often design them to their liking, for example in accordance with their corporate design. In some stadia and arenas, VIP boxes may also be used for other purposes than sporting events, for example for company parties or meetings. In addition, many sporting event organisers offer advertising space to their VIP box renters which is located directly above or below the box within the stadium or arena. In addition, users of premium seats and VIP boxes may usually use car parks located in the immediate vicinity to ensure short access routes and stress-free arrivals and departures.

In summary, corporate hospitality is a significant and efficient tool for business-to-business communication for companies as users while, at the same time, providing an important source of income for the sporting event organiser, as will become clear below.

Sport hospitality industry

Having made a distinction between the general term 'hospitality' and the specific term 'corporate hospitality' as well as their significance, the following passages will describe the size of the 'sports hospitality' market, introduce its players and their interrelationships and illustrate current developments and problems.

■ Market size

In one of the most comprehensive studies on the consumption behaviour of spectators of sporting events during the 2006 Football World Cup in Germany, Preuß et al. (2009) came to the following conclusions: Stadium visitors with overnight stays ($n = 1,921$) spent an average €46.97 for food and drinks while day visitors ($n = 1,665$) spent an average €25.62. Accommodation amounted to an average €273.00 per person per night ($n = 1,704$). In this context, the consumption expenditure of public viewing visitors is of particular interest. Public viewing visitors are a target group of sporting events which has not yet been researched in depth. However, the following data illustrates that hospitality proceeds can be further increased by offering public viewing. Public viewing visitors with overnight stays ($n = 1,154$) spent a total average of €46.72 on food and drinks while those without overnight stays ($n = 1,592$) spent a total average of €25.17 on food and drinks, which is only slightly less than the actual stadium visitors (Preuß et al., 2009).[2] If adequately extrapolated, these figures illustrate that sporting events can increase turnover from tourism on the one hand and hospitality on the other, but are also an important contributor to refinancing sporting events.

The entire corporate hospitality market in the UK was calculated to have generated a turnover of £676 million in 2001 (Mintel, 2002). At 18%, spectator sports had the highest turnover growth rate between 2000 and 2003 (Key Note, 2000). Turnover for 2006 was projected at £793 million (Mintel, 2002). Unfortunately, there are no precise figures for the German corporate hospitality market. However, a corresponding development can be identified on the basis of corporate hospitality turnover as well as the number of business seats and boxes in German stadia. The average ratio of corporate hospitality seats to the overall spectator capacity in the German football *Bundesliga* increased from 0.7% in the 1994/95 season to 5.3% in the 2008/09 season and is projected at 6.9% for the 2012/13 season (Schulte, 2008). This development is also reflected in the proceeds of football clubs in the *Bundesliga*. In the 2008/09 season, proceeds from corporate hospitality were 35% of match day proceeds and 8% of total annual proceeds (Schulte, 2008). Considering the fact that 5% of seats account for 35% of match day proceeds of *Bundesliga* clubs (Schulte, 2008), corporate hospitality has become an important funding tool for football clubs in the league. Proceeds from sales of corporate hospitality seats are an equally important source of funding at other national and international sporting events (Wiedmann et al., 2007; Ludwig and Jacobi, 2009). The fact that 18,000 guests of honour participated in the Football World Championship final in Berlin in 2006, which accounted for a quarter of the total number of spectators, is considered by Digel and

---

2 Consumption expenditure is stated in average values which do not take differentiations, such as according to country of origin, into account.

Fahrner (2008b: 6) a 'mass phenomenon of high economic significance and great marketing potential'. Corporate hospitality has developed into an independent product with high profitability for organisers of sporting events.

British companies spend about 5% of their total annual marketing budget on corporate hospitality activities (Key Note, 2000) while German companies spend 8% on average (Becker, 2008). In practice, it has proven difficult to quantify investment in corporate hospitality, as this is often included in the sponsorship expenses. Mullin et al. (2007) estimate that around 25% of sponsoring payments in Europe can be attributed to corporate hospitality activities. In view of a sports sponsoring volume of €2.6 billion in Germany in 2010 (pilot, 2010), this corresponds to a marketing investment in this tool of €650 million.

The economic significance of corporate hospitality in sport can be further substantiated by two other factors: firstly, the infrastructure in sports arenas and, secondly, prices. A thus far unpublished study by the Institute of Sport Economics and Sport Management of the German Sport University Cologne found that, in the 2008/09 season, clubs of the German football *Bundesliga* had an average of 1,972 business seats and 42 boxes, with 97% of business seats and 98% of boxes sold on average. The average price for one season was €3,807 per business seat, €54,000 per box for 10 people and €163,500 per box for over 30 people. The total proceeds of *Bundesliga* clubs in the 2008/09 season amounted to €199.7 million, €142.4 million of which came from sales of business seat tickets and €57.3 million from box rentals.

In their study, Digel and Fahrner (2008a) compared prices for corporate hospitality tickets at different sporting events. Table 17.1 makes plain that the prices vary considerably according to sport and/or event. Causes of these considerable differences may be a limited offer of corporate hospitality options, high demand, as well as the prestige of the sport and/or the event.

Table 17.1	Prices for corporate hospitality tickets at different sporting and cultural events						
	Tennis[1]	Golf[1]	Rugby[1]	Formula 1[1]	Football[1]	Concert[2]	Culture[3]
Event	Wimbledon	Ryder Cup	World Cup	Silverstone	FIFA World Cup	Coldplay	Vienna opera Ball
Hospitality product	Keith Prowse Gatsby Club Debenture Centre Court	Champions Club Table for 10 people	Final Super Series Premium	Formula one Paddock Club	Sky Box Berlin	Diamond Club package	Hospitality package incl. seat at the table
Price per person per day in euros	4,016	827	1,933	2,000	2,800	612 (+VAT)	1,340

Sources:
1 Digel and Fahrner (2008a: 45)
2 Keith Prowse (2012)
3 Ticket & Tours (2012)

■ Market players and their interrelationships

Due to the increased economic importance of hospitality services at sporting events, companies have in recent years specialised in this field, some working globally. Today it is common practice for organisers of professional sporting events to outsource catering at sporting facilities and hire a specialised company for this purpose (Graham et al., 2001). At a large number of national and international sporting events, companies such as ARAMARK or Sodexo are in charge of catering services.

Additional specialised service providers have established themselves in the corporate hospitality field. Agencies such as EB Corporate (an Earthbound, Inc. company), Jet Set Sports, VIP Sportstravel (a joint venture of Sportfive and Zächel AG), Match Services, Infront Sports and Media or THG have specialised in selling corporate hospitality options for professional sporting events, some of them offering a complete management package for rights owners. Digel and Fahrner (2008a) have analysed the players on the corporate hospitality market. There are essentially four players on the corporate hospitality market (see Figure 17.2). The hospitality right owner is usually the organiser of the sporting event, who sells the rights for the corporate hospitality activities during a sporting event to a specialised agency ('hospitality agency') for an agreed fee. Both the sale of the hospitality tickets and the operational implementation of the corporate hospitality activities are then the agency's responsibility. In this way, the organiser of the sporting event can focus on its actual core business while shifting the risk of possible hospitality losses to the agency. The hospitality agency then contacts interested companies ('hospitality customer') to sell the boxes and business seats to them. On successful conclusion of a contract, the hospitality customer then invites his clients and business partners to the sporting event, who are referred to as 'hospitality recipients' here and are the end users of the hospitality activity.

The operational implementation is often carried out with the help of yet more specialised agencies (demand-orientated 'operative service providers'), for example when it comes to decorating, additional entertainment or chauffeur services for guests. Service providers may use additional market players, for example for selling their corporate hospitality packages globally. At major international sporting events, such as the FIFA World Championship, sales licences are sold only per individual continent. The marketing/sponsoring departments of international associations may act as 'mediators' in this market,

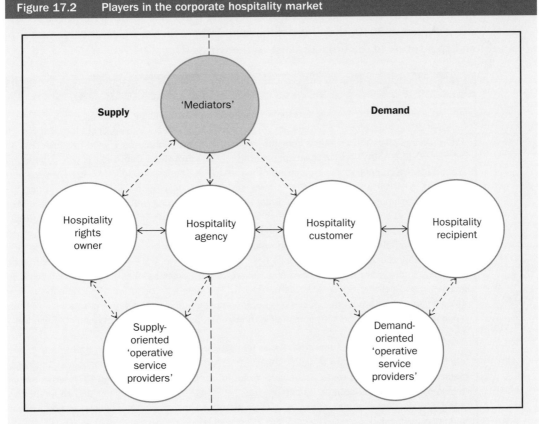

| Figure 17.2 | Players in the corporate hospitality market |

Source: Digel and Fahrner (2008a: 19)

who often warrant corporate hospitality rights to their sponsors and supporters by contract, and then want to ensure that their partners actually receive the agreed services.

Current developments and challenges

The increasing significance of proceeds from hospitality for refinancing sporting events has brought about a number of changes in recent years. To boost hospitality sales, spectators are increasingly offered drinks, ice cream, cold snacks and sweets at their seats during sporting competitions. Furthermore, the food and drink offer at sporting facilities is becoming more diverse. A good example is the Lanxess Arena in Cologne, Germany (*www.lanxess-arena.de/english.html*). In addition to various beer bars, the Piacetto Coffee Bar or the Funny Frisch Crisp Corner, there are offers specifically for women, e.g. the Fürst von Metternich Champagne Lounge. This provides especially manufacturers with an opportunity, in addition to simply selling their products, to position brands in a highly emotional context. Furthermore, electronic payment systems are increasingly available in European sporting facilities. Spectators can use a special chip card for payment at all sales booths in the sports arena, so that waiting times can be cut and amounts of cash carried minimised.

To increase the appeal of booking corporate hospitality activities at sporting events, the sport marketing agency Sportfive in the 2011/12 season created a new offer for matches of the two *Bundesliga* clubs HSV Hamburg and Hertha BSC Berlin. In a dedicated box, the two star-winning chefs Tim Mälzer (Hamburg) and Tim Raue (Berlin) prepare food for guests, intending to create a more special experience for them (Eberle, 2011).

First and foremost, the corporate hospitality field is facing a problem of criminal law, which is gaining significance in more and more countries. Existing and/or tightened anti-corruption laws have an undesired impact on corporate hospitality activities in sports. The issue first attracted international attention before the 2006 FIFA World Championship in Germany, as Case 17.3 illustrates. There are fears also in the UK, where a Bribery Act was adopted in 2010, that this will have an impact on the fields of corporate hospitality and sponsoring in the broader sense of the words (Day, 2011).

Case 17.3   Legal situation of corporate hospitality

The accused was the managing director of Energie Baden-Württemberg AG energy group (EnBW). Before he even started this work, EnBW had purchased sponsoring and advertising rights for the 2006 Football World Championship in Germany from the Fédération Internationale de Football Association (FIFA) in February 2002. EnBW was the main sponsor of the 2006 FIFA World Cup, and the only national sponsor from Baden-Württemberg. Joint initiatives of the state, i.e. the *Bundesland*[3] of Baden-Württemberg, and businesses, which also involved the Federal Government, developed into close cooperation between EnBW and, primarily, the *Bundesland* of Baden-Württemberg. During talks with the Bundesland Marketing Department of the State Ministry, it was agreed to compare invitation lists for the Football World Championship to avoid duplicating invitations.

The marketing department of EnBW developed a sponsoring concept. This included an idea for distributing the approximately 14,000 entrance tickets that EnBW had at its disposal. This invitation concept provided, among other things, that 'a small share of the tickets be used for business, social, cultural, academic and political representatives in order to give guests an opportunity to present and represent their organisations while, at the same time, emphasising and advertising the role of EnBW as main sponsor of the Football World Championship through the public appearance of respected and well-known individuals' (Court decision: 11).

On 20 December 2005, the accused, in his capacity as managing director and in the presence of his personal advisor and two assistants, signed around 700 Christmas greeting cards. The cards were addressed to individuals whose data were stored in a VIP file in the accused's possession and maintained by EnBW. 'Whether or not (a person) was included in the VIP file was decided on the basis of personal acquaintance with the managing director as well as the value of the contact in terms of protocol, but not a business relation to the company' (Court decision: 13).

---

3 *Bundesland = Federal State*

Case 17.3 *(continued)*

The accused inserted by hand the name of the respective addressee, including the salutation, and his own signature, in some cases even some personal words, on the pre-formulated greeting cards. In about half of the cases, the three employees made suggestions for gifts to the addressees. The suggestions were made on the basis of a gift list which had been compiled by the employees together with the EnBW Head of Protocol. The gifts included vouchers for box seats at a Football World Championship match in Stuttgart or Berlin which bore the official World Cup sponsor's logo of EnBW. Due to conditions imposed by the organiser, it was not possible at that time to send the physical tickets. According to the Regional Court, the vouchers were 'personalised and non-transferable' (Court decision: 13, 15). The plan was for the Head of Protocol of EnBW to coordinate and carry out the ticket distribution. The accused agreed to all of the suggestions made by the employees on the basis of the gift list.

In the described manner, the accused had World Cup vouchers sent to 36 persons together with the Christmas greeting cards. Among these were the seven cases that were the subject matter of the legal proceedings: the Prime Minister and five ministers of the *Bundesland* of Baden-Württemberg (two tickets each) as well as the State Secretary of the Federal Ministry for the Environment, Nature Conservation and Nuclear Safety, Mr M., who has permanent civil servant status (one ticket). Five vouchers were issued for Stuttgart as a venue, two for Berlin. As detailed in the court sentence, the state ministers and their ministries were officially in charge of matters which were of considerable importance for the business policy and economic success of EnBW or the accused personally. The same was true for the Federal Environment Ministry. The accused was aware of these relationships – even if not in detail. The greeting card to Federal Environment Minister G. bore the handwritten addition 'Thank you very much for your always excellent cooperation'. At the point in time where the accused wrote these words, however, he did not yet know – according to the findings of the Regional Court – whether the Environment Minister would receive a gift and, if so, what.

The accused was conscious of the (then still open) sponsoring and invitation concept of EnBW, which gave him as the managing director a certain amount of discretion. It was known to him that the seven recipients who were the subject matter of the proceedings were among the circle of high-ranking representatives to be invited.

After the press had reported about the sending of the vouchers and the Karlsruhe Public Prosecutor had instituted a preliminary investigation of the accused in mid-February 2006, the Prime Minister of Baden-Württemberg, in a letter dated 2 March 2006, declined the invitations on behalf of the members of government. On the advice of the counsel for the accused, EnBW refrained both from inviting the other members of government and from matching the invitation lists with those of the *Bundesland,* in spite of the sponsoring concept providing otherwise. State Secretary M. withdrew his initial acceptance, also on 2 March 2006.

All members of the *Bundesland* government and their accompanying guests had free access to all World Cup matches, at least in Stuttgart, through other channels. They had at their disposal seats both in the box shared by the *Bundesland* and the company Daimler-Chrysler and in the FIFA VIP lounge.

On 31 May 2005, the ministers of the *Bundesland* of Baden-Württemberg in the Council of Ministers had passed a resolution on the acceptance of gifts by members of government. Item 4 of the record stated the following: 'Complimentary tickets for events the attendance of which forms part of the representational duties of a member of government, are not to be considered gifts and are therefore not subject to authorisation.'

The Regional Court acquitted the accused 'in fact and in law'.

The acquittal in law was based on the fact that the Regional Court did not consider the tickets an advantage as defined by section 333 para. 1 German Criminal Code (StGB). As far as the six deeds for the benefit of the members of the *Bundesland* government are concerned, the Court furthermore considered the resolution previously passed by the Council of Ministers an authorisation as defined by section 333 para. 3 of the German Criminal Code. As this justification was legally recognised, according to the Court, it led to exemption from punishment. The acquittal in fact, however, was based on the fact that the Court was not convinced that 'a wrongful agreement required (under section 333 para. 1 of the German Criminal Code) for the deed to constitute an offence' had been concluded (Court decision: 51).

Source: German Federal Court of Justice (BGH), sentence of 14 October 2008 1StR 260/08, Karlsruhe Regional Court

Discussion questions

7 What were the consequences for event organisers, hosts and venue owners if the court had found Mr Claassen guilty?

8 What can the hosts of corporate hospitality activities do in order to prevent corporate hospitality being seen as a bribery?

9 How can research in this area help to legitimise corporate hospitality?

Organisers of sporting events have also been observing an increasing use of **ambush marketing** activities in relation to corporate hospitality. As a response to the criminal law issues, but also the high prices, some companies now increasingly opt for taking their clients or business partners out for a fancy dinner before or after a sporting event and experiencing the sporting event together as 'ordinary' spectators (Karle, 2009). Burton and Chadwick (2008) define ambush marketing as a form of strategic marketing using the fame and attention of the sporting event for business objectives without being an official supporter of the event. If a company booked an official corporate hospitality package, this would be considerably more expensive than the total costs for food and tickets together. Therefore, these cases may be referred to as a special form of ambush marketing.

Conclusion

The significance of hospitality in a sporting event setting has been illustrated above. Hospitality was identified, on the one hand, as an essential factor for the service quality and ultimately the success of the event and, on the other hand, as an important source of funding for sporting event organisers. From a financial point of view, the sale of corporate hospitality rights to companies is particularly lucrative. From the perspective of the companies, corporate hospitality activities present an efficient instrument of business-to-business communication, which helps to underline and/or intensify the quality of relationships with important clients and business partners in a casual and highly emotional atmosphere.

Despite positive developments in recent years, the criminal law situation poses a serious challenge for companies and organisers of sporting events. There seems to be no prospect of clear and unambiguous legal regulation on handling corporate hospitality invitations. Furthermore, organisers of sporting events, in cooperation with specialised agencies, try to maintain the appeal of corporate hospitality at a continuously high level and tap new target groups, if applicable. With respect to general hospitality products and services, organisers are keen to expand their offer in quantity and quality and provide stronger customer orientation, so that turnover is increasingly boosted.

In summary, it can be said that the fields of hospitality and corporate hospitality alike belong to the thus far little-researched areas of events management. Further research with regard to consumption expenditure in event settings, analyses of links between turnover and service orientation, contributions to the overall funding of an event as well as effects of corporate hospitality on the success of an event is of particular interest. The findings resulting from such research will contribute to an increase in service quality of sporting events as a complete package.

General discussion questions

10 Discuss how an increasing number of corporate hospitality guests influence the event itself.

11 Discuss how different cultural backgrounds might influence the overall hospitality experience.

12 Discuss what an event organiser can do in order to avoid ambush marketing activities when it comes to corporate hospitality.

Guided reading

There is a plethora of scientific studies and publications on the general subject of hospitality. However, relatively little has thus far been published in relation to sporting events. Individual publications can be found primarily in the following academic journals: *International Journal of Contemporary Hospitality Management*; *International Journal of Sport Management, Recreation and Tourism*; *Journal of Sport and Tourism*; *Journal of*

Hospitality Marketing and Management; *Journal of Hospitality and Tourism Research*; *International Journal of Hospitality Management and Tourism Review*.

As yet, there are very few academic publications on the subject of corporate hospitality. The company Mintel offers regular market reports on the subject for the UK. A good guide and valuable reference for practical corporate hospitality management is:

Kolah, A. (2004) *Maximising the Value of Hospitality*. London: Sportbusiness Group.

A more in-depth analysis of the corporate hospitality market is provided in:

Digel, H. and Fahrner, M. (2008) The international Sports Hospitality Market, Final Report. Research Project Conducted on Behalf of the FIFA. Unpublished research report. Tübingen: University of Tübingen.

Apart from these publications, the corporate hospitality field is only mentioned in the (sporting) event context in some textbooks. Worth mentioning in this respect are:

Davidson, R. and Cope, B. (2003) *Business Travel. Conferences, Incentive Travel, Exhibitions, Corporate Hospitality and Corporate Travel*. Harlow: Pearson.

Graham, S., Neirotti, L.D. and Goldblatt, J.J. (2001) *The Ultimate Guide to Sports Marketing*. New York: McGraw-Hill.

Masterman, G. and Wood, E. (2006) *Innovative Marketing Communications*. Amsterdam: Elsevier Butterworth-Heinemann.

Recommended websites

EB Corporate: **www.ebcorporate.com**

Eventmasters: **www.eventmasters.co.uk**

HospitalityFinder: **www.corporatehospitality.com**

IMG Hospitality: **www.imghospitality.ch/e_index.php**

Infront Sports and Media: **www.infrontsports.com**

Jet Set Sports: **www.jetsetsports.com**

Keith Prowse: **www.keithprowse.co.uk**

Proske Sports: **www.proske.com/sports**

THG Sports: **www.thgsports.com**

VIP Sportstravel: **www.vip-sportstravel.com**

World Anti-Doping Agency: **www.wada-ama.org**

Key words

ambush marketing; business-to-business communication; catering; corporate hospitality

Bibliography

Allen, J., O'Toole, W., Harris, R. and McDonnel, I. (2008) *Festival and Special Event Management*. Milton, QLD: John Wiley & Sons.

Anderson, E. (1998) Customer satisfaction and word of mouth. *Journal of Service Research*, 1(1), 5–17.

Becker, C. (2008) Attraktivität von Corporate Hospitality Maßnahmen bei den Olympischen & Paralympischen Spielen 2008 in Peking für deutsche Unternehmen. Unpublished diploma thesis, Cologne: German Sport University.

Bennett, R. (2003) Corporate hospitality: executive indulgence or vital corporate communications weapon? *Corporate Communications: An International Journal,* 8(4), 229–40.

Bowdin, G., Allen, J., O'Toole, W., Harris, R. and McDonnell, I. (2011) *Events Management* (3rd edn). Oxford: Butterworth-Heinemann.

Bruhn, M. (2005) *Unternehmens- und Marketingkommunikation: Handbuch für ein integriertes Kommunikations-management.* Munich: Vahlen.

Bruhn, M. (2007) *Kommunikationspolitik. Systematischer Einsatz der Kommunikation für Unternehmen* (4th edn). Munich: Vahlen.

BSML (1990) *The Effectiveness of Corporate Hospitality. An Objective, Independent Analysis of the Corporate Hospitality Industry.* London: BSML.

Bühler, A. and Nufer, G. (2010) *Relationship Marketing in Sports.* Oxford: Butterworth-Heinemann.

Burton, N. and Chadwick, S. (2008) Ambush marketing in sport: an assessment of implications and management strategies. CIBS Working Paper Series, No. 3. **www.coventry.ac.uk/researchnet/d/691**

Burton, R., Tripodi, J., Owen, S. and Kahle, L.R. (2011) Hospitality – a key sponsorship service in sport marketing. In L.R. Kahle and A.G. Close (eds), *Consumer Behaviour Knowledge for Effective Sports and Event Marketing.* New York: Routledge.

Church, R. (2003) *Bidding and Hosting. The Guide to Successful Sporting Events.* London: Sportcal Global Communications.

Cuskelly, G., Hoye, R. and Auld, C. (2006) *Working with Volunteers in Sport.* London: Routledge.

Dann, S. and Dann, S. (2005) Australian corporate hospitality in review. Paper presented at the 2nd Australasian Nonprofit and Social Marketing Conference (22–23 September 2005), Melbourne, Australia.

Davidson, R. and Cope, B. (2003) *Business Travel. Conferences, Incentive Travel, Exhibitions, Corporate Hospitality and Corporate Travel.* Harlow: Pearson.

Day, H. (2011) How to avoid sponsorship and hospitality becoming forms of bribery. *Journal of Sponsorship,* 4(2), 100–4.

Digel, H. and Fahrner, M. (2008a) The International Sports Hospitality Market, unpublished research report. Tübingen.

Digel, H. and Fahrner, M. (2008b) Hospitality Marketing im Sport. In G. Nufer and A. Bühler (eds), *Management und Marketing im Sport: Betriebswirtschaftliche Grundlagen und Anwendungen der Sportökonomie.* Berlin: Erich Schmidt.

Eberle, L. (2011) DJ und Sternekoch. *Der Spiegel,* 38/2011, 132.

Gardiner, S., James, M. and O'Leary, J. (2006) *Sports Law* (3rd edn). London: Cavendish.

Getz, D. (2005) *Event Management and Event Tourism* (2nd edn). New York: Cognizant Communications Corporations.

Graham, S., Neirotti, L.D. and Goldblatt, J.J. (2001) *The Ultimate Guide to Sports Marketing.* New York: McGraw-Hill.

Gratton, C., Shibli, S. and Coleman, R. (2005) The economics of sport tourism at major sports events. In J. Higham (ed.), *Sport Tourism Destinations. Issues, Opportunities and Analysis.* Amsterdam: Elsevier.

Guttmann, A. (1981) Sport spectators from Antiquity to the Renaissance. *Journal of Sport History,* 8(2), 5–27.

Guttmann, A. (1986) *Sports Spectators.* New York: Columbia University Press.

Hadwich, K. (2003) *Beziehungsqualität im Relationship Marketing. Konzeption und empirische Analyse eines Wirkungsmodells.* Wiesbaden: Gabler.

Hall, C.M. (1989) Hallmark Events and the Planning Process. In G.J. Syme, B.J. Shaw, D.M. Fenton and W.S. Mueller (eds), *The Planning and Evaluation of Hallmark Events.* Aldershot: Avebury.

Hennig-Thurau, T. and Klee, A. (1997) The impact of customer satisfaction and relationship quality on customer retention. A critical assessment and model development. *Psychology and Marketing,* 14(8), 737–64.

John, G., Sheard, R. and Vickery, B. (2007) *Stadia – A Design and Development Guide* (4th edn). Amsterdam: Elsevier.

Karle, R. (2009) Unternehmer bitten zum Ball. *Handelsblatt,* 4 February, 20.

Keith Prowse (2012) Coldplay concert hospitality. **www.keithprowse.co.uk/ concerts_coldplay-concert-hospitality.aspx**

Key Note (2000) *Corporate Hospitality. Market Report 2000.* Hampton: Key Note Ltd.

Key Note (2007) *Corporate Hospitality. Market Report 2007.* Hampton: Key Note Ltd.

Kolah, A. (2004) *Maximising the Value of Hospitality.* London: Sportbusiness Group.

Kotler, P., Bowen, J.T. and Makens, J.C. (2006) *Marketing for Hospitality and Tourism* (4th edn). Upper Saddle River, NJ: Pearson.

Kroeber-Riel, W. and Weinberg, P. (2003) *Konsumentenverhalten* (8th edn). Munich: Vahlen.

Lawrence, H.J. and Moberg, C.R. (2009) Luxury Suites and Team Selling in Professional Sport, *Team Performance Management,* 15(3/4), 185–201.

Lockwood, A. (2000) Hospitality. In J. Jafari (ed.), *Encyclopaedia of Tourism.* London: Routledge.

Ludwig, S. and Jacobi, N. (2009) Hospitality im Compliance-Umfeld. In FASPO (ed.), *Jahrbuch Sponsoring 2009.* Hamburg: New Business.

Masteralexis, L., Barr, C. and Hums, M. (2005) *Principles and Practice of Sport Management.* Boston, MA: Jones and Bartlett.

Masterman, G. (2004) *Strategic Sports Event Management. An International Approach.* Amsterdam: Elsevier Butterworth-Heinemann.

Masterman, G. and Wood, E. (2006) *Innovative Marketing Communications.* Amsterdam: Elsevier Butterworth-Heinemann.

Mechikoff, R. (2010) *A History and Philosophy of Sport and Physical Education. From Ancient Civilisations to the Modern World* (5th edn). Boston, MA: McGraw-Hill.

Mintel (2002). Corporate Hospitality (Industrial Report) – UK, London.

MSI Marketing Research for Industry Ltd (2002) *Corporate Hospitality UK.* Chester: MSI.

Mullin, B., Hardy, S. and Sutton, W. (2007) *Sport Marketing* (3rd edn). Champaign, IL: Human Kinetics.

Nicholson, M. (2007). *Sport and the Media.* Oxford: Butterworth-Heinemann.

pilot checkpoint Gmbh (2010) Sponsor Visions 2010. Hamburg.

Preuß, H. (2006) *The Economics of Staging the Olympics.* Cheltenham: Edward Elgar.

Preuß, H. (2007) Impact and evaluation of major sporting events. In H. Preuß (ed.), *The Impact and Evaluation of Major Sporting Events.* London: Routledge.

Preuß, H., Kurscheidt, M. and Schütte, N. (2009) *Ökonomie des Tourismus durch Sportgroßveranstaltungen. Eine Empirische Analyse zur Fußball-Weltmeisterschaft 2006.* Wiesbaden: Gabler.

Riedmueller, F. (2011) Service quality perceived by fans at professional sporting events. In L. Kalhe and A. Close (eds), *Consumer Behaviour Knowledge for Effective Sports and Event Marketing.* London: Routledge.

Schulte, P. (2008) Planung und Bewertung von Hospitality-Maßnahmen. Paper presented at the 6th German Conference for Sport Economics and Sport Management (19–21 November 2008). Cologne, Germany.

Sportfive (2009) *Hospitality. Als Gastgeber zu Gast.* Hamburg: Sportfive.

Szymanski, D. and Henard, D. (2001) Customer Satisfaction: A Meta-Analysis of the Empirical Evidence, *Journal of the Academy of Marketing Science,* 29(1), 16–35.

Ticket & Tours (2012) Wiener Opernball 07.02.2013. **www.ttours.de/de/wiener-opernball/950/wiener-opernball.htm**

Veblen, T. (2006) *The Theory of the Leisure Class.* Whitefish, MT: Kessinger.

Voeth, M., Niederauer, C. and Schwartz, M. (2006) Hospitality Maßnahmen als Kommunikationsinstrument für Industriegüterunternehmen. Hohenheimer Arbeits- und Projektberichte zum Marketing, No. 14. Hohenheim:

Förderverein für Marketing e.V. an der Universität Hohenheim.

Walzel, S. (2010) Emotionales Kunden-Commitment: Corporate Hospitality im Sport. *Marketing Review St Gallen,* 3/2010, 50–4.

Walzel, S. (2011) *Corporate Hospitality bei Sportevents – Konzeption eines Wirkungsmodells.* Wiesbaden: Gabler.

Wiedmann, K.-P., Bachmann, F. and Durst, T. (2007) *Erfolgsfaktoren von Hospitality im Bereich des Sports – Ergebnisse einer empirischen Untersuchung.* Hannover: Schriftenreihe Marketing Management der Leibnitz Universität Hanover.

Chapter 18

Creating and designing events

Hilary S. Carty, Co-Creatives Consulting Ltd, UK

Learning outcomes

Upon completion of this chapter the reader should be able to:

- describe the process of creating and designing an event and develop key outcome appraisal tools;
- assess the key metrics of event creation and design and adapt these to a range of environments;
- understand the basis of **stakeholder** relationships and develop approaches to build alignment around shared aspirations;
- develop basic concept design processes for a range of events.

Overview

The business of creating an event matches **creative origination** with design processes and strategy. This chapter places a spotlight on the key elements of form, content and function that underpin the development of events. The approach supports the testing of the creative viability of an idea through the use of a 'creative lens' and the structured assessment of design viability through application of a 'design lens'. The process will, necessarily, involve an element of fluidity as the event originator tests ideas, concepts and approaches as a means of strengthening and consolidating the original proposition.

The creative lens prioritises a review of purpose, success factors and concept testing in order to arrive at a consolidation of the theme. The design lens places the spotlight on a review of stakeholders, logistics and finance as key stages in route to a viable event concept. This two-pronged approach matches elements from existing literature with experience gained in the field, to sharpen the focus on idea generation and concept viability, phases that occur at the earliest points of the events management process.

The creative and design lens framework combines systematic procedures with essential flexibility, in an iterative process that builds rigour through revisiting, reviewing and refreshing ideas until the final concept is secure. It asks key questions to test the creative and practical viability of ideas, enabling the best propositions to be sifted from among the many that will inevitably arise. Finally, it offers a holistic and iterative approach to event creation and design that, practised over time, builds familiarity, knowledge and expertise. In turn, this expertise enables the event designer to move through Maslow's 'Four Stages of Learning' process and achieve a secure level of conscious competence in this field.

Introduction

The business of creating an event matches artistic origination with design processes and strategy. The process will, of necessity, be fluid and iterative as the event originator tests ideas, motifs and approaches en route to consolidating fully developed design concepts. Flexibility is important. Societal, economic and financial uncertainty, along with change, are persistent features of modern society and the advice to 'get comfortable with uncertainty' is repeatedly aired and shared in the events management arena. Acknowledging the persistence of environmental uncertainty, two responses form valuable parts of the event manager's toolkit. First is the adoption of formal systems that bring methodical approaches to event creation and design; Shone and Parry (2006) stipulate that 'there is a need for a systematic approach . . . Being systematic helps us in situations where we have limited expertise' and, indeed, provides a basis for gaining that expertise. Second is remaining flexible. These apparent contradictions in fact combine to build capacity and resilience. Flexibility enables initial ideas to be reviewed and aligned in an iterative cycle as viability is tested. Good ideas explored through this process need not be totally discarded but may be held in reserve, forming the basis of a **Plan B** – an alternative approach that can readily be adopted if, by some act of force majeure, the original proposition cannot be implemented. The development of a 'Plan B' could save critical time and resources and bring a speedy response to challenge or adjustment.

The impetus for an event

The impetus for an event can come in several guises. Three common examples are considered below:

An original idea: introducing something new into the field or market that is not already in existence, or that will complement or build upon existing events. Howkins (2007) identifies originality as offering something 'totally new in time and space' or introducing a 'new association for existing ideas or concepts'. Original ideas might include: a new festival or celebration; a seminar that highlights an emergent theme or issue; or a regional sports event that introduces a new competitive layer, e.g. for local clubs.

A specific request or commission: responding to a prescribed brief to deliver a set event with a given theme or at a particular time. Commissioned events might include the delivery of an opening ceremony, the planning of a named tournament or the management of a centenary celebration.

A regular calendar event that needs a fresh approach: taking on the delivery of a regular festival; refreshing a recurrent sports competition; or organising the annual conference for a federation or network.

Yeoman et al. (2004) note that the idea for an event can be generated by the event organiser, but can equally come from an external 'catalyst' including the public sector, such as 'government, local authority or (regional) agency; private sector (corporation, firm or individual) or voluntary sector'.' Whilst the catalyst may have impact as a key stakeholder and potential provider of resources, the process of actually creating and designing the event is separate to the idea origination. By working through a structured process, a methodology is developed for testing and refining the idea from concept to delivery.

The creative lens

In an interview in 2011 Ian Ritchie, Director of the City of London Festival, describes the need for two creative programming elements – 'origination' and 'conversation'.

> The best creations are compounds of ideas, rather than single elements, and therefore need 'chemistry' to take place between them. A claim of sole ownership is as unhelpful as it is untrue. So you may well have the 'original idea', but as the originator you also have to be prepared to cede power as the idea is shared and stakeholders, partners and/or collaborators add their input.

Whatever and wherever the impetus or catalyst, the process of creating the event will include a response to a range of key factors. These create a filter or lens through which ideas can be viewed, tested and developed. In Figure 18.1 three key elements form the creative lens: purpose, success factors, and concept testing.

■ Purpose

What is the rationale for the event?

A majority of organisations now boldly stipulate their mission and vision statements as a core element of marketing and promotion. This enables the organisation to develop a short but effective communication of the organisation's higher level and longer term aspirations to the world at large. Richards and Palmer (2010) note: 'A program vision is a statement of the central idea behind the programme of activities for an event'. It also provides a shorthand for harnessing energy and enthusiasm: 'A coherent mission statement

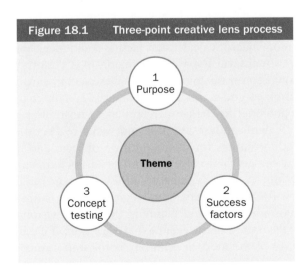

Figure 18.1   Three-point creative lens process

can be an invaluable tool for establishing a common direction in a team and promoting unity among its members' (Bowdin et al., 2011).

In the context of a single event, the more pragmatic articulation of 'purpose' – the reason for which something is delivered or created – provides a direct, and perhaps more specific, focus to drive development: 'At a minimum, a clear statement of purpose and vision should underpin every event' (Bowdin, 2007).

The actual description of purpose can be quite succinct, e.g. 'to raise the profile of local arts and artists', or structured to include sub-levels of objectives. However defined, the purpose should be clear, concise and written down. Articulating the purpose provides a starting point for the development of ideas and the central pivot for testing viability. 'Does this approach serve/support our stated purpose?' is a useful question when faced with challenge or options in the creation or design process.

If taking forward an original idea, the core purpose could be the act of innovation – to introduce a new development or prospect. In responding to a commission, or developing a fresh approach to a regular calendar event, there will be some creative and design parameters already set within the **commissioning brief**. These parameters, which bring constraints to the creative development process, might include a prescribed date, time, overarching theme or target audience. In this case the area for creativity lies in developing or weaving an interesting and credible treatment that delivers well in line with the prescribed parameters.

Success factors

What would success look like?

Having defined the purpose, a useful exercise is to envisage the end of the journey and describe the 'success factors' – the key elements or outcomes that will bring expected benefits to the commissioner, or simply result in the a sense of a 'job well done'. 'What would success look like?' Asking this question at the outset is effective because it provides an important checklist to feed into the creation and design process, to respond to the articulated purpose and ensure specific outcomes.

Getz (2005) notes that 'Historically, festivals and fairs performed important roles that were not discussed or planned, they just happened because they were needed . . . But for the most part that era has passed and most events are planned to meet numerous specific economic, business, social, cultural and other policy aims'. Yeoman et al. (2004) describe a range of potential success factors at the micro level which focus on the profile of a location when the commissioner is a public body or part of the governmental infrastructure – the ambition to 'increase awareness of a venue, occasion, tradition, or sociocultural value, increase civic pride, heighten an area's profile, satisfy the needs of special interest groups or conserve local heritage'.

On a more macro scale, success factors could focus around profile-raising on a national or international level for a city, a region or a country, where the success factors may include longer term outcomes such as increased inward investment or additional exports of local artefacts and wares. Foley et al. (2012) write that 'Mega events have been credited with the potential to change perceptions of host cities and nations, generate significant economic value, catalyse physical and social regeneration, reposition a destination and provide opportunities for the celebration of local and national identities'. Looking specifically at success factors for eventful cities, Richards and Palmer (2010) outline six key areas for impact and assessment: culture (content); place (context); power (leadership, political will); relationships (involvement, partnerships, autonomy); resources (funding and human resources); and planning (long-term vision, clear objectives). In many such instances the nature of the event experience is itself a major factor of success: 'One of the key features of the modern economy is the importance of "experiences". . . consumers are increasingly looking for experiences in addition to services' (Richards and Palmer, 2010). Building on this, Shone and Parry (2006) highlight the importance of providing mementos to capture and stimulate the memory of an event – 'a programme, a guest list, postcards, small wrapped and named chocolates . . . efforts to make the experience of the event more tangible; a memento that the experience happened'. Mementos help in sharing the value and nature of the experience beyond those who actually attended, and in so doing, the practical function of building awareness, civic pride or raised profile is additionally achieved.

Other success factors might include reaching specific delegate, participant or attendance numbers; securing a set number of 'sign-ups' to a particular endeavour; or reaching key demographic targets (young people, the unemployed, women or people from specific ethnic groups). Quantitative targets may also include reaching the financial break-even point; gaining a specific percentage of box office, or achieving a prescribed level of profit. But it is also important to consider the inclusion of qualitative success factors such as the nature of the debate, the 'look and feel' of the venue, the quality of the audience experience; or the quality and level of cross-fertilisation or networking. At an even deeper level, success factors may include audience/attendee engagement with priority issues; or the influence on changing perspectives or behaviours, for example, as a result of an issue-based seminar or conference. Whilst the quantitative factors will arise from basic data collection and review, the qualitative factors can only be assessed with attention paid to more sophisticated monitoring and evaluation methods, ideally established to assess views at appropriate points pre-/post- and during the event itself.

Concept testing

Is this idea 'fit-for-purpose'?

The testing of concepts as an early part of the creative lens affords the timely opportunity for external input, feedback, creative collaboration, development and/or consolidation. Critically, it also enables ideas that are tested and found lacking to be rejected and/or improved prior to the investment of significant resources.

Nevertheless, concept testing can be a sensitive area, fraught with concerns. While some fear their original ideas may be appropriated or hijacked, others seek to hone and refine ideas to absolute perfection prior to any sharing or request for feedback. In either case, careful thought must be given to the execution of concept testing and any parameters that might properly constrain the exercise in order to address potential areas of concern while gaining optimal feedback. The decision as to whether and how to conduct concept testing will lie with the idea originator and s/he will determine the best group to consult. In cases where originality, confidentiality or surprise are important, then the testing group will necessarily be small, and verbal or contractual confidentiality agreements might provide additional reassurance.

A range of questions can help to focus the concept testing process, including considerations of originality, authenticity or uniqueness. Bowdin et al. (2011) pose the value of providing 'an experience outside the normal range of choices or beyond everyday experience'. Is this event really introducing something special and new, or has the same idea been presented in another location or at another time? Consideration should also be given to notions of effectiveness, expectedness and appropriateness – does the event meet the articulated and aspirational needs of the brief? This is of particular importance when a range of stakeholders have commissioned the event and need to be convinced that their particular aspirations and requirements have been understood, met or, at least, addressed.

Other considerations include deliverability, inclusivity and appeal – will the event reach its target group and serve its purpose? Where new or diverse audiences are being sought, for instance, special consideration will need to be given to the extent of direct appeal encapsulated in the creative proposition – from the perspective of the audience rather than the originator. In such cases, it will be imperative to ensure that the concept testing group includes responses from the discrete audience/target group and their early feedback on appeal and inclusivity informs the design process.

It will be important to include general financial considerations at this stage. While the formal budgeting will be addressed as part of the next stage, the design lens, the desired level of financial return should impact on the concept testing phase, particularly where finance-based success factors have been stipulated. If financial outcomes are important then the question of compromise has often to be faced – the challenge of providing original, innovative but perhaps costly events against the prospect of 'playing it safe' with more tried and tested approaches that contain less creative risk, but also less potential for financial slippage.

Richards and Palmer (2010) note that 'Events can be viewed as repetitive structures. An international arts festival, a cultural Olympiad, a parade or world music weekends often follow similar patterns'. So it is additionally useful to set the creative idea in the wider context of what has worked previously, and whether it is optimal to build on that past practice or to chart new pathways. This is most critical in the context of an annual event, where the new incumbent will need to learn and fully appreciate what has been delivered in previous years, in order to develop strong creative concepts that are truly original to both the individual and the event over a long-term perspective.

Finally, consideration of the wider context should certainly include the assessment of any other events that compete in either time or space. A proposal for new Christmas or Easter celebrations needs essential cognisance of what else may be happening at these crowded times of the year; otherwise there is the risk of 'splitting the market', i.e. forcing your audience to choose one event over another when, differently timed, they may deem it valuable to attend both. Similarly, events occurring within close proximity need careful attention to detail otherwise they appear as a clash or duplication to the core audience, again resulting in a split.

■ Theme

The process of reviewing purpose, success factors and concept testing affords a dynamic scoping of the creative idea and brings into play some key factors from the wider external environment. The originator can then proceed with greater confidence to consolidate and articulate his/her theme, bringing a clear and robust proposition to the design stage. While the design stage remains critical and could, legitimately, cause a review of the creative concept, the potential is significantly reduced as the core contingencies that might impact on the theme have previously been assessed. The creative lens, therefore, affords an enhanced level of confidence in confirming the theme as a viable proposition.

Case 18.1   City of London Festival, London, UK

The City of London Festival (COLF) is an annual Summer Festival which seeks to bring the city's unique buildings and outdoor spaces to life with an extensive artistic programme of music, visual arts, film, walks and talks, much of it free to the public. The Festival exists to entertain and refresh the city's workers, residents and visitors with special events and world-class artists in beautiful surroundings. Festival performances range from large-scale orchestral concerts in St Paul's Cathedral to intimate chamber recitals in the city's beautiful but hidden livery halls, and from innovative aerial acrobatics to jazz bands in the Guildhall Yard. Inaugurated in 1962 to revitalise the cultural life of the city, COLF has established itself as one of the UK's leading arts events.

Ian Ritchie, Festival Director, describes the parallel existence of a set methodology in delivering an annual event and the essential imperative to create something different each year. For COLF this is manifested through the presence of an overarching and contextualising theme of 'Trading Places', stimulated

Case 18.1   (continued)

by London's historic and current role as a centre for international trade and exchange. Working within that banner, the Festival then explores a range of changing concepts, and focal points to stimulate the artistic programming, venue selection and marketing focus each year.

Looking back three years, the Trading Places theme has enabled the Festival to explore its creative connections with a wide-ranging selection of cities and cultures:

- In 2009 the international spotlight followed the latitude of 60°N, connecting the Northern Isles of Scotland to the Baltic shores of Russia, via Kirkwall, Oslo, Stockholm, Helsinki, Tallinn and St Petersburg as historic maritime trading places.
- In 2010 the concept was delivered through a spotlight on Portugal and the Portuguese-speaking world, celebrating the rich cultural diversity found within and between these countries.
- The 2011 Festival featured an unprecedented array of music from Australia, New Zealand and the South Pacific.

This approach enables a layering of ideas and multiple levels of creative possibilities. Ritchie sees the power of ideas as a key leverage for the Festival: 'By having a concept, ideas come alive with better chances to survive and thrive. Be not afraid to have plenty!'

Acknowledging the International Year of Biodiversity in 2010, COLF additionally combined its artistic concept with an environmental theme, to shape aspects of the Festival programme. Again this approach was delivered through an overarching theme and annual creative concepts: Bees in 2010, Birds in 2011 and Flowers in 2012.

Source: Interview with Ian Ritchie, Director, City of London Festival 2011

Discussion questions

1 What are some of the challenges of maintaining interest in an annual event?
2 How does the existence of an overarching theme aid the development of fresh concepts for an annual festival?

The design lens

With a robust and tested theme as a starting point for the design stage, a clear rationale can be developed and articulated to outline the purpose of the event, its critical success factors, its originality, audience appeal and potential impact in relation to competitor events. That forms Stage One of the creating and design process.

The old adage 'Form Follows Content' very much applies and Bowdin et al. (2011) provide certainty on the hierarchy of elements: 'Whatever the nature of the event, once the theme is established, the elements of the event must be designed to fit in with the theme'. Stage Two looks then at the specific issue of 'design' – the precise form and format of the event that will enable the purpose and objectives to be delivered; specific audiences to be reached; and the event to stand out amongst the dynamic array of alternative options.

Paying proper attention to design reaps significant rewards in the events management process as time spent effectively resourcing this early stage of development will provide a more secure platform on which to build and deliver. 'Understanding and embracing the core design principles of an event gives that event a clear direction that is easily marketed and easily understood by all those involved, whether internal or external to the organisation' (Bowdin et al., 2011). Taking this a step further, Yeoman et al. (2004) rue the absence of the specific 'design' component from the typical event manager profile: 'Design is essential to an event's success because it leads to improvement of the event on every level'.

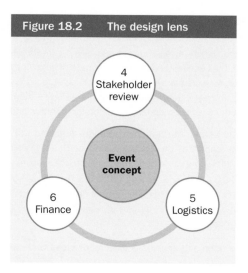

Figure 18.2 The design lens

Therefore, the articulation of a clear and effective design development process serves well the ambitions of good events management, and the design lens shown in Figure 18.2 provides a series of key filters that support the journey from creative idea to a concrete event rationale.

Stakeholder review

Which key relationships impact this event?

Bowdin et al. (2011) identify a diverse range of potential stakeholders including 'client organisations, the local community, government at various levels, potential attendees and participants, sponsors and volunteers'. This diverse group possesses an eclectic range of 'stakes' that pin down their engagement and interaction with the event. Richards and Palmer (2010) note that 'differing stakeholder roles also imply different degrees of power. Those funding the event, providing the cultural content or the audience will likely have most power'. It is critical that each stakeholder is acknowledged and responded to as appropriate to the level and nature of their investment (human as well as financial), and building medium- to long-term 'relationships' with stakeholders is important to gaining a better understanding and developing better dialogue and mutual interest. If there is a range of stakeholders, including representation from all the groups Bowdin describes, then a strategy for managing these relationships across a team will bring distinct advantages.

Conducting a stakeholder map is a first stage and this could take the form of a simple list; a grid referencing a range of data including their level of investment; a flow chart; or a 2-by-2 box diagram capturing their level of interest, influence and/or engagement. The more information and clarity gained about the nature of the stakeholder's interaction with the event, the better the ability to respond directly to their needs. This becomes more critical if the stakeholder is a commissioner or sponsor, but a rounded view of all stakeholders can provide both insight and foresight regarding potential or likely reactions to creative propositions or innovations in content or delivery: 'We also have to examine meanings from different perspectives. Each stakeholder in the process wants, expects and receives potentially different perspectives and attaches potentially different meanings to the event' (Getz, 2005).

Richards and Palmer (2010) stipulate that 'clear communication with stakeholders is therefore crucial to ensure that these diverse groups feel included in the process of event development'. So engaging priority stakeholders with the event theme at the earliest feasible stage is an important action that allows them to comment and respond. This, in turn, enables the event manager to test the level of stakeholder alignment with the theme and adjust if and where possible. If adjustments cannot or will not be made, then dialogue with the stakeholder is yet more imperative as it enables open discussion and agreement on a way forward.

■ Logistics

What are the practical considerations?

The consideration of design logistics provides some of the most critical pragmatic considerations and includes its size or scale, location, timing and preparation. While this is not an exhaustive list and other logistical elements may impact, these four remain critical in supporting a deep rationalisation of the creative idea.

The *scale* of the event will be driven significantly by the parameters necessary to fulfil the theme (which, using the creative lens, has already been mediated to ensure a good fit with the articulated purpose). A variety of other considerations also impact on the scale of an event, including stakeholder aspirations; the necessity for and extent of profile raising required to meet local, national or international ambitions; the potential to attract appropriate audience numbers; the budget available; and the technical capabilities obtainable for the event. Getz (2005) notes that 'built attractions and facilities have everywhere realised the advantages of 'animation'' – the process of programming interpretive features and/or special events which make the place come alive with sensory stimulation and appealing atmosphere. Hence the increased evidence of medium-to large-scale events that are now regularly used to bolster civic pride and create a sense of 'place'.

In a similar vein, consideration of the *most appropriate location or venue* is critical and a key concern must be whether and how well the venue is in congruence with the theme. For example, city centre conference facilities are well located for transport and other connections, but may not offer a conducive atmosphere for an intensive conference of two or more days when an additional benefit will be the sense of space, air and green scenery that a semi-rural or rural venue might offer. In addition, it is important to gather some knowledge of the range of activities typically programmed into a venue, as that will determine how it is viewed by its core audiences. Whilst large-scale 'arena' venues are succeeding in programming an eclectic range of sports, classical and contemporary arts programmes to a diverse range of audiences, this is not easily achieved on the small scale, where there is less flexibility to reconfigure seating and atmosphere to accommodate the 'look and feel' expectations of an eclectic range of audiences. In addition, these venues would normally lack the financial resources to conduct diverse and targeted marketing campaigns to reach different audiences. The smaller-scale venue, therefore, is more likely to have audience/spectators for a dedicated and more restricted programme.

On a purely pragmatic level, thought must also be given to the nature of the dialogue or *relationship with the venue* and the level of priority they will afford your event. Are venue contacts supportive, flexible, adaptive and positive? Having invested energy, commitment and resources in developing the creative idea and meeting the needs of key stakeholders, it will be imperative to ensure that this hard work is not undermined by unsupportive staff within the venue itself.

A review of *access requirements* and the adoption of any necessary adjustments is an imperative logistical consideration. In the UK, for instance, the Disability Discrimination Act 1995 and later amendments introduce measures aimed at ending discrimination and giving rights to people with disabilities, for instance requiring service providers to assess obstacles and make reasonable adjustments to the physical features of their premises to overcome physical barriers to access. Goldblatt (2010) notes: 'The design phase enables the Event Leader to work closely with the disabled community to determine the services and accommodations that must be implemented to ensure the comfort and satisfaction of all guests'. Different disabilities need specific adjustments and it is always advisable to get appropriate and detailed advice as early as possible in the process.

The consideration of '*timing*' takes many forms in the design process. First and foremost there is timing in terms of the calendar year – are there weather considerations that would make one part of the year more or less favourable than others? Certain sports disciplines, for example, have a set calendar and working around key pressure points is essential. Similarly, outdoor events require much careful planning regarding the time of year (and, at least in the UK, inclement weather can be expected at any time!). The other aspect of timing is the schedule of the event itself. Silvers (2004) states that 'an event experience must be choreographed and blocked out as carefully as any dance or play'. So consideration must be given to the flow of the event – how will participants encounter and explore the theme? This is important for a sporting event, but perhaps even more so for a cultural or training event where participants will significantly value some reasonable time to meet, exchange information, swap contacts and expand their network. Issues of content, pace, breaks and the crucially important time for offline networking all need to be factored in.

The final element of timing is the 'time-line' which links to preparing for the event. The time-line should note key dates and times for both macro and micro activities leading up to the event, including, but not limited to:

- dress rehearsal;
- technical rehearsal;
- venue get-in;
- contracts signed and returned;
- rehearsal dates;
- venue confirmation;
- key artist/sports persons/speaker confirmation;
- headline production staff secured;
- finances secured.

Allen (2009) notes:

> In deciding the amount of planning time required, list everything that you will need and assign a time frame to each of them. Begin with the end in mind. What needs to be done for your event to be a success? Work backwards with your calendar and start to pencil in the proposed schedule of events. Remember to build in some buffer. Take the time to research in order to determine realistic timelines.

Time-lines are most useful when developed as visual maps that include priorities for the event as a whole and show the activities and deadlines for all aspects of event delivery. A detailed milestone chart is a useful mechanism which allows checks on the progress of production and promotion priorities. But it is also important to see the 'bigger picture' and gain a summative high-level understanding at a glance. **Gantt charts** and other project management software provide extremely useful tools and applications to support this process.

Logistics form a critical aspect of the design lens, aiding the review and rationalisation of the theme to ensure the event is both realistic and deliverable within time, location, personnel and delivery constraints.

Case 18.2   **World Class Performance Conference 2011, UK Sport,[1] London, UK**

The World Class Performance Conference is UK Sport's annual conference for key staff working in high-performance sports. The conference provides a multidisciplinary forum to meet, debate and share best practice across key themes influencing athletes' performances. The aim is to equip coaches, practitioners and leaders with the skills and knowledge to make sustainable changes to their World Class Performance Programme. The best national and international speakers are sought to present the most up-to-date and cutting-edge information to delegates.

Each conference has a common theme that runs throughout all workshops and presentations as, for UK Sport, the development of a theme is an important first stage in the detailed design process, informing not simply the content but the structure itself. With the 2012 Olympic Games and Paralympic Games in London as an immediate performance arena, Sam Whale, UK Sport's Coaching Coordinator and conference organiser, felt it imperative to include elements that made the learning 'live' so that the coaches attending could make direct connections to their key workloads and priorities. So the theme for the November 2011 conference was 'Aspiration' – an aspiration for immediate success in 2012, but also the aspiration to generate a high-performance legacy that would go far beyond the impending milestone of London 2012.

The design of the conference, across the three days, therefore, took participants on an exploratory journey voyaging through *Hindsight* – the ability to reflect; *Insight* – consideration of the present; and *Foresight* – an opportunity to look beyond.

Stakeholders for the conference included, UK Sport, the coaches and the event sponsor. All confirmed that the theme and the approach delivered well against its stated purpose, optimising the small window of opportunity for learning and consolidation remaining prior to London 2012.

Location formed a critical design factor and the selection of the ExCeL Centre, overlooking the Olympic Park was a deliberate reference back to both the theme and the context. The Excel Centre London 2012 Games venue, was set to stage seven Olympic and six Paralympic events. The prospect that conference delegates would return to coach the UK's leading athletes through the most important competition of their lives brought congruence with the conference theme and enabled a direct emotional, motivational and immediate connection between their workload, the conference and the wider sporting context.

In terms of logistics, a 'walk-through' of the entire conference from the perspective of the delegate enabled assessment of the 'flow' and 'energy' of the event from moment to moment; activity to activity. The business of entering the experience and mindset of a delegate was critical to assessing not just the core content packages, but the breaks, the moments for pause, reflection, consolidation and networking – all critical to the flow of the event as a whole.

Source: Interview with Sam Whale, Coaching Coordinator, UK Sport

---

Discussion questions

3   What aspects of the event might be important to the key stakeholders?

4   How could the choice of venue impact positively or negatively on the World Class Performance Conference?

Finance

Is there enough money?

At the design stage, the financial resources necessary to deliver the event may be pre-determined, open to negotiation or need securing. Where the available amount is determined in advance, it becomes critical to produce a framework budget that captures the key expenditure and income areas and tests the feasibility of delivering the creative theme in line with stakeholder expectations; at the scale and location that logistics demand; and within the sums available. The event manager must take responsibility for this area (as it is mission-critical), even if the financial project management is delegated or delivered elsewhere.

---

1 UK Sport is the nation's high performance sports agency responsible for investing over £100 million per year in the UK's best Olympic and Paralympic athletes.

If there are insufficient resources to deliver the event then options need to be explored, including seeking additional resources from the project commissioner, raising additional funds through sponsorship/ fund-raising and/or reducing costs within the budget itself. Of course, the ultimate sanction is to cancel or postpone the event, which is why a review of finances at the design stage is critical.

Where the sum required for the event is open to negotiation or needs to be secured, it is imperative to develop a budget that captures all the key income and expenditure areas relevant to the project. The process of building the budget for a new event can be challenging as costs are, necessarily, estimates – 'there is no set formula or format' (Allen, 2009). It is useful to start, where possible, with reference to a budget from a previous event of similar scale and content. This will cluster key elements and highlight the main cost centres for activities and income. The budget will need to be tested, however, and this can be done by seeking quotes from suppliers of particular services or equipment. Placed on a spreadsheet, the individual items can then be adjusted and manipulated while keeping track of the likely impact on the financial bottom line.

Having created a comprehensive budget for the event, the size and scale of the costs of designing and delivering the project are now more transparent and can be used as part of a process to reduce or moderate ideas, should resources be limited. This chapter does not seek to provide the 'definite' answer to event finance (which is covered elsewhere); it seeks instead to highlight the impact of finance as a key metric in both the creative and design lens processes.

Event concept

The final outcome of the design lens is the consolidation of the key elements described above into a final event concept (see Figure 18.3). Reflecting the creative idea, rationalised through both the creative and design lenses, the event concept then forms the basis of dialogue with potential partners, collaborators and other parties necessary to effect the delivery of the project.

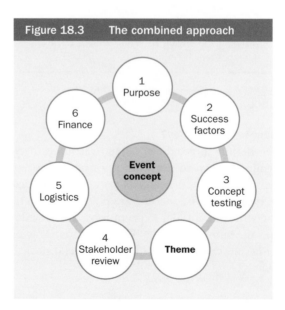

Figure 18.3   The combined approach

Conclusion

This process of creating and designing an event sees an iterative journey from initial thoughts, or a commissioning brief, through to a fully developed event concept. The process is not linear and the rationalisation of certain aspects may highlight the necessity for adjustments or alterations in areas previously considered to be consolidated. The review of logistics, for example, might indicate the need for adjustments to the preferred scale of the event; that, in turn, could affect the priorities of stakeholders and the delivery against success factors. It is, therefore, important to maintain as much flexibility as possible whilst the filters of the creative and design lenses are applied, adjusted and consolidated:

The creative lens

1. Purpose
2. Success factors
3. Concept testing

Theme

The design lens

4. Stakeholder review
5. Logistics
6. Finance

Event concept

Collectively, these six filters form a development and review regime that allows the event designer to work steadily and consistently through the creative design process, building capacity and expertise through repetition of the methodology in different contexts. Over time, preferred ways of working are developed and the designer uses that familiarity to move steadily through Maslow's Four Stages of Learning model (Watson and Gallagher, 2005):

1. Unconscious incompetence
The individual does not understand or know how to do something, does not recognise the deficit, and has no desire to address it.

2. Conscious incompetence
Though the individual does not understand or know how to do something, he or she does recognise the deficit, without yet addressing it.

3. Conscious competence
The individual understands or knows how to do something. However, demonstrating the skill or knowledge requires a great deal of consciousness or concentration.

4. Unconscious competence
The individual has had so much practice with a skill that it has become 'second nature' and can be performed easily (often without concentrating too deeply).

At Stage 1, unconscious incompetence, the event designer is at the earliest encounter with event design, perhaps through witnessing or working alongside an event. Initial experience of event delivery, or engagement with design theories shapes the move to Stage 2, conscious incompetence, where both the knowledge and experiential gaps become evident and there is an increasing awareness that progression will require specific actions to address both skills and knowledge deficits. Stage 3, conscious competence, sees direct action to gain experience in the field, combined with formal or informal learning to bring rigour to the fore. A structured process – as proposed with the filters of the creative and design lenses – enables a structured proficiency to develop, alongside confidence and the marshalling of technical skills. Stage 4, the state of unconscious competence, aligns with the development of a creative instinct – the honing of a distinct style combined with an innate appreciation of what may or may not be feasible, based on past practice. While this cannot become a substitute for the formal process, it does bring about an adeptness with the stages of review that affords both speed and efficiency as well as an increased ability to discern the viable from the non-viable with a few key questions.

General discussion questions

5 What are the pros and cons of having a high level of flexibility in the creation and design process?

6 Name the key individuals that might form part of the concept-testing group for (i) a local rugby tournament; (ii) a training seminar; (iii) the visit of an international theatre production to a specific regional location.

7 What mechanisms or approaches could be used to build good relationships with key stakeholders?

8 What are the dangers of leaving insufficient gaps in activity within a milestone chart?

9 If building an event budget from scratch, how could you test its feasibility and the viability of the cost centres and amounts determined?

Guided reading

For a comprehensive overview of creativity and the context in which creative ideas are nurtured and flourish see:

Howkins J. (2007) *The Creative Economy – How People Make Money From Ideas*. London: Penguin Books.

For an accessible and comprehensive account of key elements of the event design process with a focus on tools, tips and practical guidance to support a range of event types see:

Allen, J. (2009) *Event Planning: The Ultimate Guide to Successful Meetings, Corporate Events, Fundraising Galas, Conventions, Conferences, Incentives and Other Special Events* (2nd edn). Toronto: John Wiley and Sons Canada Ltd.

For extensive frameworks on the management of events and significant detail on aspects of the design lens: stakeholder review, logistics and finance see:

Bowdin, G. et al., eds (2011) *Events Management* (3rd edn). Oxford: Elsevier Butterworth-Heinemann.

Shone, A. and Parry B. (2006) *Successful Event Management. A Practical Handbook* (2nd edn). London: Thomson Learning.

Bowdin also contains many recent case studies and examples to bring a contemporary immediacy to the areas highlighted.

For those new to the field and the industry jargon or vocabulary, providing in one place a key reference for both common and less common terms used across the events management sector see:

Goldblatt, J. and Nelson, K., eds (2001) *The International Dictionary of Event Management* (2nd edn). Hoboken, NJ: John Wiley & Sons.

Foley et al. use a significant range of recent examples to highlight the increased adoption of events by local and central governments and other voluntary and private sector agencies as a strategic driver for political, economic, social and cultural change:

Foley, M., McGillivray, D. and McPherson, G. (2012) *Event Policy. From Theory to Strategy*. London: Routledge.

For a comprehensive and detailed overview of technical terms and resources to underpin 'advanced core knowledge' for the event producer see:

Matthews, D. (2008) *Special Event Production: The Resources*. Oxford: Elsevier.

Recommended websites

City of London Festival: **www.colf.org**

European Capital of Culture: **http://ec.europa.eu/culture/our-programmes-and-actions/doc413_en.htm**

London 2012 Festival: **http://festival.london2012.com**

Sydney Festival: **www.sydneyfestival.org.au**

Key words

commissioning brief; creative origination; Gantt chart; plan B; stakeholder

Bibliography

Allen, J. (2009) *Event Planning: The Ultimate Guide to Successful Meetings, Corporate Events, Fundraising Galas, Conventions, Conferences, Incentives and Other Special Events* (2nd edn). Toronto: John Wiley and Sons Canada Ltd.

Bowdin, G. et al., eds (2011) *Events Management* (3rd edn). Oxford: Elsevier Butterworth-Heinemann.

Foley, M., McGillivray, D. and McPherson G. (2012) *Event Policy. From Theory to Strategy*. London: Routledge.

Getz, D. (2005) *Event Management and Event Tourism* (2nd edn). New York: Cognizant Communications Corporation.

Goldblatt, J. (2010) *Special Events, The Next Frontier for a New Generation* (6th edn). New York: John Wiley & Sons.

Howkins, J. (2007) *The Creative Economy – How People Make Money from Ideas*. London: Penguin Books.

Richards, G. and Palmer, R. (2010) *Eventful Cities: Cultural Management and Urban Revitalization*. Oxford: Elsevier.

Silvers, J. (2004) *Professional Event Coordination*. Hoboken, NJ: John Wiley & Sons Inc.

Shone, A. and Parry, B. (2006) *Successful Event Management. A Practical Handbook* (2nd edn). London: Thomson Learning.

Watson, G. and Gallagher, K. (2005) *Managing for Results* (2nd edn). London: Chartered Institute of Personnel and Development.

Yeoman, I., et al., eds (2004) *Festival and Events Management, An International Arts and Culture Perspective*. Oxford: Elsevier Butterworth-Heinemann.

Chapter 19

Events in public spaces

Gernot Wolfram and **Claire Burnill**, FH Kufstein Tirol – University of Applied Sciences, Austria

'Yet it is necessary to notice that the space which today appears to form the horizon of our concerns, our theory, our systems, is not an innovation; space itself has a history in Western experience, and it is not possible to disregard the fatal intersection of time with space.'

(Michel Foucault)

Learning outcomes

Upon successful completion of this chapter the student will be able to:

- be aware of the historical significance, theoretical approaches to, and definitions of the term 'space';
- recognise and understand the particular benefits of events held in public spaces;
- understand how to organise **sustainable cultural events** in this field;
- identify the stakeholders involved when planning a cultural event in public spaces.

Overview

The chapter begins with a definition and explanation of the terms *space* and *public events* within the field of cultural events. The term *cultural events* is used in this context due to the strong connections and complex relationships between public spaces and the historical and cultural development of cities and their visible and invisible heritage.

Public spaces are strongly connected to the history and cultural identity of nations, and are becoming increasingly important to local regional, city, district and neighbourhood identities. Cultural events delivered in public spaces enjoy numerous advantages over conventional event venues and provide a wealth of opportunities for improving public participation. Use of these spaces enables cultural events to be opened up to a broad spectrum of society and diverse social groups. Use of public space allows for rich diversity and a reaches a range of social groups, in a way that conventional spaces may not. Cultural events in public spaces provide an opportunity to reach new audiences, especially young people, who are, broadly, more sceptical of traditional cultural institutions.

The chapter will illustrate how the term *participation* in the context of society is key to understanding that conventional barriers to cultural events can be reduced by using public spaces. Many theories emphasise that cultural events as social highlights have the capacity to gather different sectors of societies in a new way. Furthermore, they can improve the interconnections between different societal groups, thus building stronger civil participation and engagement. Additionally, issues of integration and communication will be discussed in this context. The chapter will examine some of the organisational aspects of planning cultural events in public spaces. Who are the potential stakeholders? What are the special features of the planning processes in this area? And how are aspects of sustainability integratable? Furthermore, the chapter discusses the role of partners and media partnerships. The chapter will be completed by three case studies.

Public festivals, concerts, theatre and dance performances as well as city festivals and commercial events touch and draw upon elements of historical traditions and benefit from a shared, implicit knowledge that public events are, especially in modern democratic systems, unable to exclude people from the event on the grounds of social or ethnic background. It is precisely this that makes events in the public sphere so exciting and successful. In order to manage the successful organisation of events in public spaces, it is important to understand the following aspects, which we will expand upon throughout the chapter.

1. Cultural events in the public realm reveal particular interactions between citizens, visitors, real topographies of cities/regions and the virtual appearances of these spaces via media channels.
2. Cultural events in public space are much less affected by conventional barriers of events.
3. The democratic character of public space delivers a unique set of characteristics which collectively improve **access** for a range of societal groups (for example of minority groups)
4. Public spaces reveal social changes and stimulate stronger citizenship participation, in part as a result of the recognition of their right to be there.
5. The success and sustainability of cultural events in public spaces is always connected with the grade of accessibility and working in partnership with local people.

What do we mean by 'space'?

Within the field of cultural history and sociology the debate surrounding space has a long and complex tradition. Since the time of Antiquity, and through the Middle Ages, the central places of villages formed meeting places for society. The concept of the Greek *agora* remains an important idea, whereby citizens and strangers can exchange not only tradable goods and services, but also ideas and artistic expression. 'Speakers' corners can be found in the public parks of many global cities. Here people are given a platform to express ideas with impunity. 'Events' held in these spaces, throughout their history, have been commonly accepted rituals and celebrations with strong political, social and religious meaning (see Sennett, 1996). They make a symbolic difference to the culture of everyday life and the self-assurance of a society within the event. Even today, this tradition is an important basis for understanding the implied meanings of events in the public sphere.

Over a long period of time the term *space* was academically under-estimated in comparison to the terms *time* and *action*. As Talcott Parsons stated in the 1960s, 'While the phenomena of action are inherently temporal . . . they are not in the same sense spatial' (Parsons 1967: 46). Frequently, spaces were seen as the static and less dynamic fields of everyday life. Moreover, the political debate about the role of space, especially in the time of World War II, was a further problematic reason for many sociologists viewing reflections of space sceptically. With the rapid development of new media, changes within conventional media, and the virtual presence of international events in cinemas, on TV programmes and later over the internet, a new consciousness regarding the role of space in modern media societies has arisen. These new media have produced new virtual spaces and places – on various levels, that is, within new public spaces themselves (cinemas for example) as well as via virtual worlds. The experience gained through witnessing events, either live or recorded, that are located in one space but viewed in another space, allows the viewer to identify with and experience a place in which they are not physically located via virtual means. Without these public spaces many internationally renowned events wouldn't have gained their fame and popularity. The presence of virtual spaces is also a special part of the public realm – the practical implications of which we will examine later with regard to events such as 'flash mobs'. The early Michel Foucault described so-called 'heterotopias' (Foucault, 1980) to make clear that it is necessary to understand the multi-dimensional factors of the term space:

> Utopias are sites with no real place. They are sites that have a general relation of direct or inverted analogy with the real space of society. They present society itself in a perfected form, or else society turned upside down, but in any case these utopias are fundamentally unreal spaces.
>
> (Foucault, 1980: 18)

Cultural spaces are important to our sense of identity. They can include the place in which we grew up, or the place we currently identify as our 'home' – however, this doesn't necessarily refer to the physical buildings we occupy, but the cultural meanings that are created in these places. We ascribe strong cultural meanings to our sense of place – which then form part of our identity. Our sense of belonging to a particular street, area, town, region or even country distinguishes and shapes us and our relationship with other cultural spaces. This sense of identifying with areas or spaces is clear throughout history and in essence contributes to a sense of nationhood – and further not only to a sense of commonality, but also to conflict as we understand, ascribe meaning and importance to our own unique cultural spaces as distinctly different to those of people occupying an 'other' cultural space.

The ways in which we move through public space can be for us a direct connection with our sense of identity and belonging. As we move in our everyday lives through public spaces, we meet here with history and society. Within these places we form relationships with others and with the place itself. Our everyday lives take us necessarily through the public sphere – our journeys to, and activities in, school, university, work, or in undertaking leisure activity move us through the public sphere and with this a host of interactions, reactions and connections with it, its past and our role in its future are formed.

Definitions of space have become very important for modern academic works. In Richard Florida's *The Rise of the Creative Class* (2002) he categorically refutes the argument that once pervaded modern economics in which it was argued that modern economies would remove people's sense of place – that 'spaces' will simply be filled and utilised according to push and pull factors of the economy. Florida goes on to state that, in reality, there are a number of other underlying factors that dictate people's choice of location – essentially these are the cultural connections that people make with place. Richard Florida's reflection about the 'creative classes' and their preferred spaces within post-industrial cities (Florida, 2002) or the 'third space theory' of Edward Soja (1996) show that spaces always have strong connections in people's minds, to their expectations and associations. Spaces are seen in this concept as a complex mixture of real topographies, of media topographies and of topographies people create in their minds.

> Place and community are more critical factors than ever before. And a good deal of the reason for this is that rather than inhabiting an abstract 'space' as Kelly suggests, the economy itself increasingly takes form around real concentrations of people in real places.
>
> (Florida, 2002: 219)

Florida goes on to add, more critically, that the very specific places where creative economies thrive are those that are diverse, vibrant and welcoming.

Conventional barriers to cultural events

Towards the end of the twentieth century, many conventional cultural venues were (and in some cases continue to be) struggling to find an audience for their exhibits and events. Across much of Europe and North America, attendances in theatres, galleries and museums were falling. Innumerable theories regarding, and research into, modern cultural shifts point to a large and complex range of causes for the reduction in numbers (see Chaney, 2002; Held and Moore, 2008). These theories examine the democratisation of people – changing demographics, a rise in mass culture – fuelled by mass media, shifts in working lives, the availability of time and a wealth of other leisure opportunities to choose from. The research into these cultural events continues and would require a book in itself, but Bunting et al. (2008), for the Arts Council England's research, revealed that the following factors play a significant role in people's propensity to access cultural events/venues:

- level of education (high level of education more likely to attend);
- social status;
- being from a Black ethnic group (less likely to attend);
- gender (females most likely to attend);
- age (older age groups more likely to attend than 16–29 year olds);
- being from an Asian or 'Other' ethnic group (less likely to attend);
- having children aged 0–4 (having young children decreasing attendance);
- health;
- religion;
- income;
- living in social housing;

The report goes on to suggest that there is:

> a strong sense among many members of the public of being excluded from something they would like to be able to access, a belief that certain kinds of arts experiences were not for 'people like me' and a nervousness about stepping outside the comfort zone of their familiar leisure activities. This feeling was found across the sample, even among those who already had some degree of engagement with the arts (Creative Research, 2007).
>
> (Bunting et al., 2008: 66)

These findings are not restricted to English audiences. Birgit Mandel (2008) corroborates this in her work in Germany, stating that people assume that the arts can be too difficult to understand and that they are not suited to their lifestyle, that none of the people they know take part in cultural events and that people are afraid that they will not understand the nature of the event. Research in the USA would seem to suggest similar patterns there (see National Endowment for the Arts, 2009).

The point here is that people value cultural events, but feel somehow disconnected from them. They feel unable to access them. Traditional theatres, opera houses or museums are connected with specific traditions of education and citizenship. These spaces are accepted and well known by majority groups of society (see Bourdieu, 1986) or by those with a particularly high level of education. However, they often exclude the so-called 'silent audiences' – groups who are unfamiliar with the symbolic character of these spaces. Minority groups find themselves unable to connect their everyday lives with the cultural events on offer to them.

The democratic nature of public spaces

In an increasingly globalised world, many global cities are 'micro-globes', that is many different cultural influences, various processes of migration, different religious and social backgrounds are all encountered within different areas of cities and regions. Diversity abounds. Such diversity brings with it a set of wonderful opportunities, but it is also flashpoint for conflict. As illustrated in the previous section, traditional cultural events have tended to passively exclude large sections of the diverse demographic in which they operate. The traditional dichotomous conflicts between young and old, rich and poor are joined by struggles and tensions between different ethnic groups, nationalities and political ideologies. This leads to a particular problem for the organisation of events – cultural managers strive to engage 'target groups' and build specific niche markets in order to make a name for themselves.

Traditionally arts were the mark of the elite, patronised and used as a justification for their rule. The arts set the 'cultured elite' apart from the 'masses'. However, the arts have also been used as a tool by the elite in attempts to 'civilise' the masses. Chaney (2002: 129–30) points out that war memorials, great public buildings, statues to national heroes and even parks have been used as a means of 'national integration' in order to produce a 'public culture'. This argument then would suggest that traditional public art has a distinctly 'nationalistic' nature. When we consider the role of national museums and galleries, there has traditionally been an institutional agenda laid out, one that celebrates the successes and victories of one group, often to the detriment of another. National museums, for example, display and exhibit artefacts 'won' from battle, a visible artefact depicting the victory of one nation over another. In this regard, traditional venues serve to perpetuate **cultural imperialism** and notions of power and elitism. It is no great surprise then, that those from disadvantaged backgrounds, or minority ethnic groups, find little relevance in these cultural events.

The advantages of holding events in public space then are abundantly clear. Public spaces are those spaces which all sections of society can access and find relevant to their own lives. Streets, squares and parks are by their very nature designed to be accessed.

The British Joseph Rowntree Foundation describes these advantages thus:

> Public spaces (including high streets, street markets, shopping precincts, community centres, parks, playgrounds, and neighbourhood spaces in residential areas) play a vital role in the social life of communities. They act as a 'self-organising public service', a shared resource in which experiences and value are created.
>
> (Rowntree Foundation, 2011: 2)

The Rowntree Foundation supports a number of practical and research projects which reveal the tremendous power of events in public spaces because of their integrative capabilities. Very important in this is context the self-organising character of these events. 'People make places, more than places make people' (Rowntree Foundation, 2011). This motto shows that event managers in this context should be careful with fixed project plans and prefigured project structures.

Public space: living museum, gallery and stage

Throughout the mid-to-late twentieth century and beyond, the growth of the mass media has fuelled mass and popular culture. Music, fashion and art have become increasingly accessible and can be cheaply reproduced. The proponents of the Frankfurt School are critical of mass and popular culture, suggesting that mass culture is a 'dumbing down' of high culture, and it dilutes the worth of original art and is cheapened via mass reproduction. However, postmodernists argue that popular and mass cultures are authentic in their own right.

Increasing urbanisation and immigration has resulted in the creation of 'global diasporas' (Cohen, 2008) whereby we witness, for example, reggae music being reproduced outside the Caribbean, by non-Afro-Caribbean musicians. This phenomenon is illustrative of how cultures are being fused and interwoven to become hybrids; we are becoming 'glocalised' citizens (Robertson, in Bennet, 2000: 138). The works that are produced in this context are representative of modern lives. Through events such as Mardi Gras-style carnivals or reggae festivals we see not only global roots, or a celebration of the 'other', but we witness integration and acceptance as such genres as these have become an entirely unsurprising part of everyday life and no longer seem unfamiliar to us.

What is crucial to understand here is that much of this politicisation of culture is played out in public spaces. When we consider modern, popular culture, it is easy to see that much of this is played out in an urban or 'street' context. Examples of this are numerous. The genres of Hip Hop and Rap, 'musicalised dialogue between the peoples of African origin who collectively make up the African diaspora' (Bennet, 2000), are rooted in American street culture. We also see graffiti art as depicted in (amongst others) the works of Banksy and street performance arts including free running, urban base jumping and urban mountain biking.

The public realm gives the public space to both *play out* culture and *witness it*. Furthermore, new technologies have taken traditional street cultures to new audiences. The use of internet-based technologies, social media and mobile technologies has created a host of new audiences for street performances, and with this new platforms for traditional culture have emerged. Most notably perhaps, the digitalisation of information has led to new artistic concepts and creative strategies.

Alan Brown (Brown et al., 2011), arts management consultant, lists five levels of participation in the arts as follows:

- *Inventive participation* engages the mind, body and spirit in an act of artistic creation that is unique and idiosyncratic, regardless of skill level.
- *Interpretive participation* is a creative act of self-expression that brings alive and adds value to pre-existing works of art, either individually or collaboratively.
- *Curatorial participation* is the creative act of purposefully selecting, organising and collecting art to the satisfaction of one's own artistic sensibility.
- *Observational participation* encompasses arts experiences that you select or consent to have.
- *Ambient participation* involves experiencing art, consciously or unconsciously, that you did not select.

Brown's levels of participation can be used in this context to clearly illustrate how events in the public realm have the capacity to engage the public in all aspects of participation in the arts. Events taking place within the public sphere provide the public with opportunities to engage at the very least at the ambient level, and widens the audience base at the observational level.

New social media allow for both new audiences and new performers to participate in the arts. The use of public space enables greater participation on all levels. New events such as flash mobs have a multiple effect. A flash mob requires a significant number of people to gather in one place and reproduce a cultural, artistic act (seemingly) spontaneously. What is important to consider about flash mobs is that they have the capacity to engage new performers and provide a stage for new performances; they engage the public directly and then are reproduced digitally and distributed via social media. They impact on both the public and the public space. Flash mobs have sound a novel way to gain new audiences for traditional cultural events. The Knight Foundation in the USA is dedicated to funding programmes for the arts that engage new audiences and break down conventional **barriers to access** to the arts. Among their programme of work is their 'Random Acts of Culture' programme, in which traditional high arts are taken into the public sphere and performed. These ideas have been taken not only to bring arts to new audiences but also as marketing tools for conventional art forms. The Philadelphia Opera and the Salzburg Opera are amongst the professional organisations that have chosen to use the 'flash mob' idea for marketing their conventional concerts. Tourism Ireland's St Patrick's Day 'Riverdance' flash mob staged in Sydney Central Station was a creative marketing tool that gave a platform to young performers from inside the community, engaged a broad audience passing through the station and went on to be one of the most viewed advertisements on the internet in the month that followed. The benefits of such events are clear. The rationale for citizenship participation in cultural events, however, goes beyond that of building audiences and marketing. It has been shown that involving communities and engaging them in public events can enable regeneration of communities and help revive neighbourhoods, increase community capacity and can help contribute to a sustainable economy.

Event planning in the public sphere

Public events should use the knowledge of 'daily life experts', a term the innovative German theatre group 'Rimini-Protokoll' uses to describe the people who collect a wealth of valuable experience from their own physical environment.

They should focus on the relationship between spaces and different groups of society: which organisations, associations, political forces and partners from the field of economy are connected with the place where the event is planned?

One thing that is becoming clear regarding the success of any cultural events – but particularly with regard to events in the public realm – is that the key to the success and sustainability of the event relies on the consultation and participation of the wider community. Involving all relevant stakeholders is crucial and requires careful, sensitive, gathering of knowledge about the traditions and peculiarities of the public place where an event will take place. Consultation processes should reflect the local demographic and consider when, how, why and by whom any space is being accessed. Local stakeholders, residents and businesses should be invited to participate in the event. It requires careful planning by event managers and they must learn to trust the voices of the people they consult. All too often consultations ask people what their wishes are, and then choose to ignore them. Listen carefully to the voices of local people and do not under-estimate their creativity and desire for quality events.

Consulting stakeholders and giving them a role in the event develops a sense of ownership, it raises support for the event and encourages wider participation. Without full consultation with local stakeholders, it is very easy for an event to fail. Engaging community groups in the event itself reduces local hostility towards it, and **active participation** is more likely to induce a sense of pride. A sense of ownership and pride in the event amongst local people is likely to ensure its longevity.

Local consultation must acknowledge all those who use the space. Communication with minority groups, particularly those who are marginalised, requires long-term relationship building. Building trust amongst ethnic groups can often only be successful when they are able to represent themselves – this may mean ensuring linguistic translation for non-native speakers, or better still finding a member of the group who is able to bring others on board. **Marginalised groups**, all too often, are forced to operate in a climate of discrimination and isolation. Therefore, event organisers need to ensure that they take time to build trust with various groups and work carefully to understand sensitivities and build meaningful partnerships.

Beyond the consultation phase, event planners need to find opportunities for participation and engagement of stakeholders. This can include simply making the event relevant to them, or giving them space and time to take part in the event itself. Harnessing the creative output of local people can save time and money. The rationale for participation, again, goes beyond that of reaching new audiences, and simply ensuring the success of the event. Participation and engagement in the arts can be used as a tool to build community strength and cohesion in the long term. Even prior to Florida's evaluation in *The Rise of the Creative Class* (2002), research into the role of community participation in cultural events has shown that participation can contribute to the regeneration of deprived areas. Inclusion, consultation and participation all result in capacity building within community groups. Furthermore, research has shown that cultural events increase community cohesion (Matarasso, 1996), provide an increased sense of neighbourhood identity (Lowe, 2000) and can contribute significantly to the economic well-being of a given area. With this in mind, events held in public spaces can have a large number of positive long-term effects if they are well managed.

To implement a successful event within the public realm with the aim of establishing a long-term concept requires the event to reflect the life structures of the area. If the event is not accepted by the local inhabitants then the whole event is likely to collapse. Therefore the organisation must involve local representatives through every step of the planning process (Figure 19.1).

After discussing the event concept with different stakeholders, the organisation should look for financial support by foundations, offices of the creative industry or in the commercial sector. The main focus here should be a logical connection between supporter and event. Seek cooperation with local authorities. There is often public funding available for cultural events. By working in partnership with local authorities and local businesses it may be possible to access financial support for the event.

Events in public spaces are subject to the legal restrictions and regulations of the local authority/state. Public events' licences, public health regulations and highways will all need to be taken into consideration. This knowledge is paramount and varies widely according to national and regional jurisdictions. Appropriate policing, refuse disposal and the consideration of environmental impacts need to carefully considered and planned for.

When planning the event, the timing of event highlights should be carefully considered. The footfall in the space will vary considerably according to the time of day. For example, a busy square at 8 a.m. might be a thoroughfare for business people on their way to work, at midday a bustling lunch venue and by 8 p.m. a space for skateboarders and young people to collect. It is worth considering what the event has to offer at different times of day, and which groups of people are likely to be accessing the event: 'Some

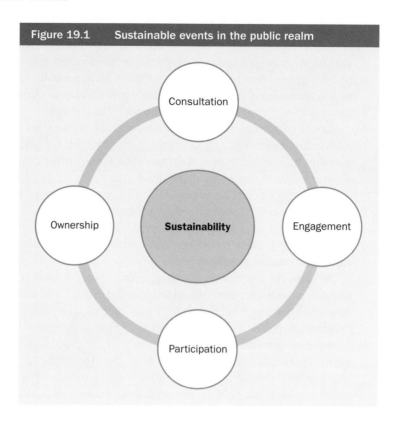

Figure 19.1   Sustainable events in the public realm

groups may be self-segregating in their use of different public spaces at different times, with social norms affecting how and whether people engage with others' (Rowntree Foundation, 2011).

Investigate and pay attention to 'micro spaces' – those small areas with a special social use within public spaces, for example meeting places or 'hang-outs' for young people, street corners or housing estates.

One of the long-term benefits of thorough consultation and the formation of meaningful partnerships with stakeholders in the organisation of an event such as this is that the event is able to maintain its position and success over the long term regardless of the changes that naturally occur across the community. The event relies not on only one particular group, or sponsor, but largely upon the people who help to create the event – the community itself.

Media partnerships can help to raise awareness of events in public spaces – especially initial events and one-off events. Where the intended event is planned to be filmed and posted to social media and media sharing websites, high-quality and well-positioned filming needs to be undertaken. Capturing a high-quality record of the event in this instance is as important as the event itself. Try to think beyond conventional media; while not everyone has the luxury of the 'dream job' that Australia's Queensland had to offer (see http://www.news.com.au/national/power-pom-wins-island-dream-job/story-e6frfkp9-1225710409447), the idea of events being officially blogged in order to create publicity has proven highly successful. Using bloggers for an event, as well as setting up Facebook events and creative use of social media, can open the event to new audiences and create new awareness beyond conventional newspaper, fliers, radio and television marketing. Jennings (2007) states that blogs have the advantage of being 'first person narrative' and having the 'personal touch' thus getting a more direct empathy with readers. Blogs are the equivalent of 'word of mouth' and, whilst the raw numbers may not be high, the quality of the message is. However, Jennings goes on to state that blogs, as with any marketing tool, must be authentic in order to be of value.

Successful events, unavoidably, have an impact on the local environment. Where people collect in large numbers, increases in noise, overcrowding on access routes, increased traffic, demand for public facilities (from refreshments to toilets) all need to be carefully considered. Every attempt should be made to minimise negative impacts of the event. Using local partnerships, making the best use of existing infrastructure and local knowledge can help to reduce environmental damage.

Conclusion

Society's relationship with 'space' has been recognised as being of importance by sociologists and cultural scientists. Our relationship with everyday space is not only physical but also psychological and cultural. Public spaces offer opportunities to stage cultural events that bring new audiences to them. Unlike conventional venues, the public realm has the advantage of being a democratised space which can be reached by everyone. The public realm is already a place in which cultural activities take place. 'Street' culture, including arts and music and sports activities, is increasingly viewed as being of legitimate expression of the public voice. Events in public spaces access a broad spectrum of the public in a way that many conventional events cannot. They offer a wealth of opportunities for engaging audiences beyond a merely observational one. Through active participation in events it is possible to contribute to increased local capacity and cooperation.

When organising events in public it is important to:

- identify and consult local groups;
- reflect local demographics;
- consider timing;
- understand local statutory laws and legislation;
- use media channels creatively;
- minimise environmental damage.

Case 19.1   Berliner Wintersalon – festival in Mongolian yurts

Every year the 'Werbegemeinschaft' (Association of Companies) Sony Centre Berlin organises a literature festival. The festival offers free access for citizens of and visitors to Berlin. A hundred readings (some in English) over four days are held in two Mongolian yurts under the roof of the Sony Centre Berlin at Potsdamer Platz. The juxtaposition between the modern glass architecture of the Sony Centre and the traditional Mongolian yurts creates high visibility for the event. Literature and stories for children and adults, chanson programmes, dramatic readings and non-fiction books are all presented. The yurts stay open until midnight.

The Sony Centre becomes Public Space for four days, presenting the space as a place for listening, contemplation and the art of literature

The passers-by on the Potsdamer Platz and an interested audience gather within the yurts. Thus, a new audience is created with a new awareness of the space, as is a new framework in which to appreciate literature.

Many media partners are involved as well as local radio stations and TV. The concept is sustainable because the event takes place every year in winter time.

The programme for children is particularly successful. Conventional barriers including the conventional 'scholarly' understanding of literature cease to exist.

Every citizen and visitor of Berlin has free access. The representation of the event in the city and in various media channels has much more value than the organisational costs.

Source: www.salonkultur.de

Discussion questions

1 Potsdamer Platz is one of Berlin's busiest and best-known locations. In which ways is the choice of location crucial to the event's success?

2 How is the use of Mongolian yurts relevant to the festival?

Case 19.2   Festival of Britain, Southbank Centre, London, UK

The self-styled 'Arts Quarter' of London's Southbank has become a festival site and important cultural venue for both local people and visitors. The site is made up of the area from Lambeth Bridge along the Thames riverside to Blackfriars Bridge. Whilst the site is home to conventional cultural venues including the National Theatre and the Royal Festival Hall, it has worked hard to use its geographical location to bring a broad range of people from all walks of life to participate in cultural activities. The stretch of London's riverside has in the past 25 years become an example of how public space can be used effectively to attract new audiences and play host to successful cultural events. With a wealth of bars, restaurants and an imaginative repertoire of events along the river bank, the 21-acre area of public space has become acknowledged as a cultural capital that attracts and serves not only tourists, but has at its heart the needs of the community.

The Festival of Britain 2011 was designed to mark the anniversary of the first festival of Britain held in 1951. The festival organisers sought to provide not only ticketed events, but also a wealth of over 400 free events which were attended by more than 100,000 people.

The Southbank site has worked hard to develop an outdoor area that attracts visitors of all backgrounds. The artistic director of the Southbank Centre, Judith Kelly, OBE, has carefully considered the role of the site in history, its importance by the river and acknowledges the role of the graffiti-covered undercroft for skateboarders, parkour and free-runners.

The festival of Britain offered food markets, fun fair attractions, live music, poetry and outdoor installations. There were a series of local community events across the four-month festival. Londoners were requested to adorn their bicycles with flowers and cycle around the Southbank site to recall the 1951 floral parade, and the festival concluded with 'The Big Sing', which invited singers from choirs and the public from across London to join in a riverside chorus of songs.

The Southbank aims to put on annual summer festivals that reach out to, and are relevant for, a broad spectrum local people.

Source: www.southbankcentre.co.uk

Discussion question

3 Are graffiti and urban sports relevant to a cultural event and site?

Case 19.3   Florence Marathon

The very nature of road running is illustrative of how we are able to move freely through public spaces. Runners move daily through urban and rural environments choosing routes and paths through such spaces, both witnessing and contributing to them as they move through.

Road running events in urban spaces such as the one in this case study make interesting use of public space. The space is public and accessible to all – although runners themselves are confined to a designated route; however, over the race course they are given an opportunity to gain an insight into the public spaces of the city.

The Florence Marathon is one of the fastest growing marathons in Europe. A relatively new event, established in the 1980s, it is now Italy's second largest race and boasts over 10,000 participants. The event is organised by a committee and works in partnership with the Florence town council, and Tuscany region. The event boasts a large number of sponsors, including international as well as local businesses.

Events such as this make use of public space in a variety of ways. As with most road running events, it is free for spectators to access. Onlookers, tourists, locals and race supporters are at liberty to watch the race, or have the freedom to simply walk the streets of the city as they please.

Spreading themselves along the length of the standard 42.195 km marathon course, spectators may choose to position themselves in parks or piazzas as they wish, mingling with non-supporters. Those who are in the city on a non-sporting agenda are still able to witness the cultural sites of the city – while being unavoidably caught up in the atmosphere of the race.

For those taking part, the use of public space affords participants the opportunity to marry a cultural exploration with sporting achievement, as the route passes the historic Cathedral Square and over the Ponte Vecchio and into Piazza Santa Croce. At the same time, those tourists who sought a cultural visit to Florence, or everyday locals, may find themselves being engaged in a sports event as they witness the

Case 19.3 (continued)

city – potentially engaging new audiences for sport. Similarly, runners who visit the city to compete on a fast course find themselves engaging in a cultural experience that they may not otherwise have had.

Source: www.firenzemarathon.it

Discussion question

4 Athletes entering the marathon must pay an entry fee to take part in the event. Spectators pay no fee to line the route. Does this have an impact on the democratic nature of the event?

General discussion questions

5 Why is 'space' first of all a sociological term?

6 What is the democratic nature of public spaces and what organisational consequences come from this perspective?

7 What are advantages of events in the public space?

8 How would you explain the term 'public voice' and which economic factors are affected by this term?

Guided reading

Brown, Alan S.. Novak-Leonard, J. and Gilbride, S. (2011) Getting in on the act: how arts groups are creating opportunities for active participation, published in *Focus*: James Irvine Foundation and WolfBrown, *www.irvine.org*

This online publication gives an interesting overview of how and the extent to which people are able to participate in the arts, from the most simple form – observing – to the most engaged form – creating the art itself. Brown explores the idea that audiences are moving from a 'sit back and be told' culture to a 'making and doing culture' and looks at the ways in which institutions should adapt to this.

Howkins, J. (2001) *The Creative Economy: How People Make Money from Ideas*. London: Penguin.

Howkins discusses how individual creativity, creative businesses and creative cities contribute to the global economy.

Jennings, D. (2007) *Net, Blogs and Rock 'n' Roll*. London: Nicholas Brealey Publishing.

This explores how technologies are changing consumer behaviour. New technologies have changed the ways in which consumers and creators of cultural products behave. Consumers are able to make discoveries for themselves as well as publish their own works. The landscape of the cultural consumer is changing.

Martin, J. and Nakayama, T. (2010) *Intercultural Communication in Contexts*. New York: McGraw Hill Higher Education.

This looks at the importance of engaging diversity and understanding some of the social and cultural contexts of human interactions.

Said, Edward W. (1993) *Culture and Imperialism*. New York: Alfred A. Knopf.

Culture and Imperialism examines the idea that Western imperialism has dominated other cultures via use of the written word. Some of the West's most effective tools for oppressing indigenous voices have been the use of the mass media and works of literature. Said goes on to explore the way in which new voices need to be found and heard in order to redress the balance in modern times.

Recommended websites

Random Acts of Culture programme: **www.randomactsofculture.org**

Joseph Rowntree Foundation: **www.jrf.org.uk**

Demos: **www.demos.co.uk**

Wolf Brown: **www.wolfbrown.com**

Rimini Protokoll: **www.rimini-protokoll.de/website/en/about.html**

Key words

active participation; barriers to access; cultural imperialism; marginalised groups; sustainable cultural event

Bibliography

Bennet, A. (2000) *Popular Music and Youth Culture – Music, Identity and Place* London: Palgrave.

Bourdieu, P. (1986) The forms of capital. In J. Richardson (ed.), *Handbook of Theory and Research for the Sociology of Education*. New York: Greenwood, 241–58.

Brown, Alan S., Novak-Leonard, J. and Gilbride, S. (2011) Getting in on the act: how arts groups are creating opportunities for active participation, in *Focus*: James Irvine Foundation & WolfBrown. **www.irvine.org**

Bunting, C., Chan, T.W., Goldthorpe, J., Keaney, E. and Oskala, A. (2008) *From Indifference to Enthusiasm: Patterns of Arts Attendance in England*. London: Arts Council England.

Chaney, D. (2002) *Cultural Change and Everyday Life*. London: Palgrave.

Cohen, R. (2008) *Global Diasporas: An Introduction* (2nd edn). Oxford: Routledge.

Florida, R. (2002) *The Rise of the Creative Class*. New York: Basic Books.

Foucault, M. (1980) *Power, Knowledge. Selected Interviews and Other Writings 1972–1977*. New York: New York University Press.

Held, D. and Moore, H.L. (2008) *Cultural Politics in a Global Age: Uncertainty,*

Solidarity and Innovation. Oxford: Oneworld Publications.

Jennings, D. (2007) *Net, Blogs and Rock 'n' Roll*. London: Nicholas Brealey Publishing.

Lowe, S. (2000) Creating community: art for community development. *Journal of Contemporary Ethnography*, 29(3), 357–86.

Mandel, B. (2008) *Audience Development, Kulturmanagement, Kulturelle Bildung*. Munich: Kopeaed.

Matarasso, F. (1996) *Northern Lights: the social impact of The Fèisean (Gaelic Festivals)*. Stroud: Comedia.

National Endowment for the Arts (2009) *Survey of Public Participation in the Arts 2008*. Washington, DC: NEA.

Parsons, T. (1967) *Sociological Theory and Modern Society*. New York: New York University Press.

Rowntree Foundation (2011) *The Social Value of Public Spaces*. York: Joseph Rowntree Foundation.**www.jrf.org.uk/sites/files/jrf/ 2050-public-space-community.pdf**

Sennett, R. (1996) *Flesh and Stone: The Body and the City in Western Civilization*. New York: Norton.

Soja, Edward (1996) *Thirdspace: Journeys to Los Angeles and Other Real-and-Imagined Places*. Oxford: Wiley-Blackwell.

Chapter 20

Events as sponsorship investment

Ariane Bagusat, Ostfalia University of Applied Sciences, Germany

Learning outcomes

Upon successful completion of this chapter the student should be able to:

- define the expressions **sponsorship** and **event sponsorship**;
- understand the development of sponsoring;
- explain the advantages to both **sponsor** and event organiser;
- identify and understand the different phases of event sponsorship acquisition and management;
- distinguish between successful and unsuccessful **sponsorship** possibilities and the risks of specific sponsorship partnerships.

Overview

The chapter offers an introduction to the sponsorship of events. The chapter's primary goal is to provide some general information rather than investigating all of the theoretical aspects that are connected to events as sponsorship investments. The chapter focuses on the possibilities and benefits through the sponsorship of events.

After defining sponsorship and how events could be a sponsorship investment, the growth and development of sponsoring and sponsorship of events is considered. Subsequently, the chapter examines the advantages and benefits of sponsorship for both sponsors and event organisers. In the main part of the chapter, a detailed insight into the acquisition and management process of event sponsorship are given. Finally, the determining factors for a successful sponsorship, as well as the limitations and risks, will be reviewed.

Introduction

Sponsorship has become one of the major sources of funding for local and international events involving sports, the arts, the environment, media, humanitarian and community projects, education and various other fields. Sponsorship benefits the general public by making possible the staging or broadcasting of events and activities which might not have been feasible otherwise and adding additional benefits to existing events and activities.

Event sponsorship has been long recognised as an effective means through which companies can communicate with target markets and attendees of events. For companies and organisations sponsorship is an important marketing tool to convey a broad message through association with the sponsorship property (e.g. the event, activity, organisation, individual, media or location). On the other hand, sponsorship, provided either as cash or in-kind support like products or services, is central to the revenue and resources of new and continuing events. Event managers are usually actively engaged in tasks such as identifying potential sponsors, preparing sponsorship proposals and managing their ongoing relationships with sponsors, as event sponsorship is a large part of modern events management (ICC, 2003; Bowdin et al., 2011: 441). Nothing has made a greater impact on the events industry than corporate sponsorship, which was responsible for the huge growth of numerous events and has provided start-up funding for many new ones (Skinner and Rukavina, 2003: ix).

Successful sponsorship therefore benefits all the parties concerned, including sponsors, organisers, the media, performers, spectators and the general public.

Defining sponsorships and events as a sponsorship investment

The definition of sponsorship is not easy, because many different concepts and understandings exist in practice and in the academic literature. The American sponsorship consultancy IEG defines sponsorship as 'a cash and/or in-kind fee paid to a property (typically a sport, entertainment, event or organisation) in return for the exploitable commercial potential associated with that property' (Cornwell et al., 2005). The following definition, called the International Code of Sponsorship from the International Chamber of Commerce (ICC), also explains the concept: sponsorship is 'any commercial agreement by which a sponsor, for the mutual benefit of the sponsor and sponsored party, contractually provides financing or other support in order to establish an association between the sponsor's image, brands or products and a sponsorship property in return for rights to promote this association and/or for the granting of certain agreed direct or indirect benefits' (ICC, 2003).

The key elements determining all definitions are the following (ICC, 2003; Hermanns and Marwitz, 2008: 44; Bruhn, 2010: 6):

- *The sponsor*: any corporation or legal person providing financial or other sponsorship support (e.g. products, services, know-how).
- *The sponsored party*: any individual or legal person, profit or non-profit organisation owning the relevant rights in the sponsorship property and receiving direct or indirect support from a sponsor in relation to the sponsorship property.
- *The rights*: any (commercial) rights to promote or communicate this association and/or for the granting of certain agreed direct or indirect benefits.
- *The contract*: the sponsorship should be based on contractual obligations between the sponsor and the sponsored party.

Sponsorship is an integral part of the marketing strategy, but differs from other forms of commercial communications as well as from donation and patronage. The goal of patronage, which is centuries old, is to support the artist as a provider of a cultural product and not to achieve a certain benefit. It determined the artist's social status, constituted a traditional way of financing artists, and glorified the patron. Similarly, sponsorship is not a donation which is altruistic and does not constitute commercial activity. Yet sponsorship is also more than advertising. Advertising is a one-way business street,

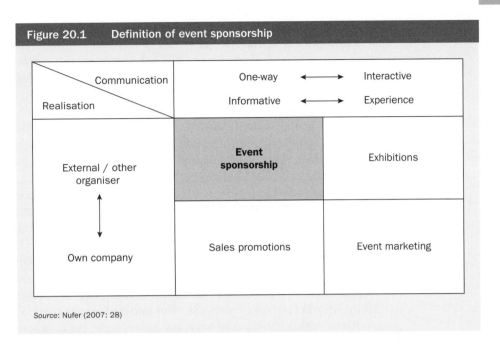

Figure 20.1   Definition of event sponsorship

Source: Nufer (2007: 28)

as products, services and activities are advertised in order to maximise sales and profits. Rather, sponsorship can be defined as (financial) support to cultural activities, with the expectation of a return on the investment (ICC, 2003; Skinner and Rukavina, 2003: 210–11; Hermanns and Marwitz, 2008: 45–6; Bruhn, 2010: 3–6). Sponsoring can be used as a single marketing activity, but will often utilise other marketing skills such as advertising, public relations, events and promotion in order to leverage the sponsorship and increase the impact (ICC, 2003; Hermanns and Lemân, 2010: 17).

Sponsorships are often linked with events because events can be used as an instrument to get in (personal) contact with a special **target group**. Companies have to decide whether they will sponsor an existing event, or whether they will create their own event. In the first case we are speaking about 'event sponsorship', whereas in the second case we are speaking about 'event marketing' or 'events management'. For this chapter, only the first case is relevant. Other forms of a company's communication, like exhibitions, sales promotion or events marketing, are not subsumed under the expression 'event sponsorship' (see Figure 20.1). As the sponsor has to submit to the rules of the event organiser, normally there isn't much freedom for the sponsor to adopt and create special communication or promotion tools. Though event sponsorship is more a one-way than an interactive communication tool, event sponsorship is usually used as an investment by a company and can be seen as a strategic marketing tool.

Development and growth of sponsorship

The first roots of sponsorship can be traced back to the year 4000 BC. Painters and musicians, who showed off their talents at the court of the Egypt's Pharaohs, received glory, food and accommodation. In the years 70–80 BC, the Roman Gaius Clinius Maecenas, who was a friend of the Emperor Augustus, supported poets and artists. Sponsorship in this era was not sponsorship in its modern-day sense, as individuals, and not companies, sponsored artists. Moreover, the 'return on investment' (ROI) was different to today's expectations: they didn't get any commercial potential, rights, etc. Hence this kind of 'sponsorship' is distinguished by calling it 'patronage' (Skinner and Rukavina, 2003: xix).

The first recorded instance of sponsorship that we would recognise as sponsorship was undertaken by the Medici family who ruled Florence from 1434 to 1637. Cosimo the Elder and particularly his grandson Lorenzo the Magnificent sponsored graphic artists, sculptors and poets such as da Vinci, Donatello and Boticelli, who helped Florence to be at the centre of the artistic Renaissance period. It is reasonable to assume that they sponsored these artists for the same reason that Walker Morris sponsored the inaugural exhibition at the Saatchi Gallery in London – to generate goodwill towards themselves from a target market, to generate awareness and acceptance of their business, and to entertain their clients with hospitality centred on these artistic endeavours (Bruhn, 2010: 3–4; Bowdin et al., 2011: 441–2).

The Eveready Hour was the first sponsored radio programme in 1924. Motor sports, golf and tennis were the forerunners of modern-day sponsorships. Cigarette, alcohol and automobile companies became the first to sponsor events. Firestone and Bosch have been sponsors of the Indianapolis 500 since 1911. The Goodyear Tire and Rubber Company developed the Goodyear airship and started using it extensively in 1959 through the vision of the company's Vice President of Public Relations, Bob Lane. In 1956, the Kentucky Derby Festival was the first festival to have a sponsor for one of its events: the Philip Morris Festival of Stars (Skinner and Rukavina, 2003: xx).

Faced with a situation of very few government funding sources, Peter Ueberroth sold more than $400 million-worth of sponsorship for the Los Angeles Olympic Games of 1984, which led to an explosion of sponsorship marketing. Companies found that they could increase sales through sponsorship, and event managers increased their sponsorship levels. At the same time, Lesa Ukman of the International Events Group (IEG) published the first sponsorship newsletter in 1983, which was the beginning of a learning period and academic discussion about this subject (Skinner and Rukavina, 2003: xx–xxi). Today, sponsoring is a central element in the integrated marketing communication mix of many private and public sector organisations. Among the different types of marketing communications, for example, public relations, advertising, personal selling, sales promotions or direct marketing, sponsorship is one of the most powerful instruments used to communicate and form relationships with stakeholders and target markets, especially if it is attached to social causes and broadcast media such as television programmes as well as special events (Grey and Skildum-Reid, 2003; Hermanns and Marwitz, 2008: 40–2; De Pelsmaker et al., 2010: 372–3).

It is difficult to put an accurate value on the total size of the sponsorship market. Globally, sponsorship expenditures reached US$44 billion in 2009, a 2.1% increase from 2008 (IEG, 2010). North America-based companies spent a total of US$16.51 billion on sponsorship, of which US$11.28 billion (68%) was spent with sports properties such as the US Olympic Committee, the (American) National Football League and a multitude of local teams and athletes (IEG, 2010). Overall sponsorship spending in the UK is estimated to be around £934 million, made up of sports (51%), arts and business (18%), broadcasting (20%) and others (10%) (Mermiri and South, 2009). With a volume of about €4,200 million in the year 2010 and an estimated €4,400 million in the year 2012 (Pilot checkpoint and FASPO, 2010: 7), sponsorship has become an important marketing communication instrument in Germany as well: 81.1% of the biggest companies in Germany utilise sport sponsorships as a communication tool, which has been the most used sponsoring type ever, followed by the sponsorship of culture (66.7%), social areas (59.3%), education (51.7%), environment (20.3%) and media (13.4%) (Hermanns and Lemân, 2010: 14). In Asia as well, sports sponsorship has become a multi-billion dollar business with companies becoming global brands and leveraging investment in global sports. Samsung, for example, made a $4.6 million sponsorship investment in a historic, one-day cricket contest between India and Pakistan (Sudhaman, 2004: 28).

Globally, expenditure on events sponsorship has been escalating each year – from £18.1 billion in 2001 to an estimated £29.1 billion in 2005 according to research by consultant SponsorClick (Day, 2002). By 2008, according to Arts & Business, it was estimated to have reached £43.5 billion, although this was a reduction on the previous year due to the global recession (Mermiri and South, 2009). Importantly, most spending estimates only take into account the sponsorship purchase itself, but it is generally accepted that many sponsors will spend a sum at least equal to the cost of the event property itself on leveraging or maximising investment impacts (Meenaghan, 2001a; Bowdin et al., 2011: 442–3).

In 2010, 71.1% of the 2,500 biggest German companies used event sponsorship as communication strategy (Hermanns and Lemân, 2010: 24). While sports have dominated event sponsorships, accounting for 75–80% of sponsorship expenditure (Harrison, 2004), the corporate sector seems to be seeking a greater balance of investment across the arts and sports. Most large brands now use a sponsorship mix within a wide-ranging brand marketing strategy.

Advantages to sponsor and event organiser

Sponsorship is a two-way business activity, mutually beneficial to the sponsor on one hand, and to the event (organiser) on the other. It combines commercial and charitable activity, providing for profit goals and non-profit intentions at the same time. The sponsorship market consists of cultural institutions and events as properties and corporations as providers (Skinner and Rukavina, 2003: 211). Interest in sponsorship as a form of integrated marketing communication originates from a range of socio-cultural and business (including marketing and media) trends.

Firstly, sponsorship seems to be a more effective and efficient promotional method than traditional advertising. Whereas sponsorship is perceived to be a commercial activity with some benefit to society, consumers are more cynical about advertising as being more manipulative, with far less social value (Meenaghan, 2001b). The interest in event sponsorship by marketers is also a result of a number of factors (Bowdin et al., 2011: 446):

- The rising costs of media space and the perceived reduced effectiveness of advertising – many consumers now simultaneously use multiple media, such as television, the internet, mobiles and text messaging (Duncan, 2002).
- A growth in the overall number of media outlets (including pay television channels, radio stations, specialist magazines, direct mail pieces and the internet), with media advertising becoming extremely cluttered (Duncan, 2002; De Pelsmacker et al., 2004).
- The expansion of pay television channels (satellite and cable) and their subsequent need for programme material. Events, especially sports events, have greater potential to be televised, enhancing exposure opportunities available to event sponsors (Lieberman and Esgate, 2002).
- The globalisation and commercialisation of sports (Hinch and Higham, 2004) as both amateur and professional sports offer more opportunities for organisations to engage in sponsorship of events that have huge television audiences.
- A proliferation of brands, products and services offered by fewer manufacturers/providers (Duncan, 2002). Companies, therefore, choose to improve their distributors' relationships with event-related entertainment and hospitality.
- The relative inability of mass media to target a desired particular market segment, making the promotion not as effective as more tightly targeted promotions.

Sponsorship, especially through events, has been able to exploit these trends because it communicates in experiential environments, rather than via static media. Moreover, sponsorship provides the following advantages:

■ Creative sponsorship can reach consumers in non-commercial environments in which they are having a good time and so they are more likely to accept a well-considered marketing message (Blyth, 2003).

■ Event sponsorship offers a higher contact quality than other communication instruments.

■ Committed and loyal fans of a special event (e.g. a music or sports event) will attach themselves to those brands that support their interest. Barclays, Coca-Cola and Vodafone, for example, are companies that have gained significant brand equity from UK sports sponsorships (Bowdin et al., 2011: 444).

■ International companies also view sponsorship as an effective means of connecting to their international markets. For example, renowned British events such as the Open Golf Championship were sponsored in 2012 by Doosan, HSBC, MasterCard, Mercedes-Benz, Nikon, Ralph Lauren and Rolex (see Case 20.1). All these companies must believe that their target market both watches golf and will feel emotionally closer to the product as a result of their sponsorship.

■ Event sponsorship helps to create **brand awareness** in new markets. An example of this is Europe's biggest car manufacturer Volkswagen Group, which decided in 2010 to sponsor the Olympic Winter Games 2014 in Sochi, Russia. The sponsorship of Olympic Games fits with Volkswagen's plan to become one of the leading foreign car manufacturers in the Russian market, and to generate over a certain period of time (2–3 years) nationwide brand awareness and empathy.

New trends in marketing communications media give event sponsors the chance to interact directly with their markets and thus to create a brand relationship. Simultaneous brand exposure can be achieved through a range of on-site communication and alternative media. Sponsors are getting extra exposure, for example, as a result of the live streaming of events on the internet, text messages, sponsorship of live sites away from the event and giant screens at festivals that display text and photo messages from the crowd responding to billboard advertisements (Bowdin et al., 2011: 445–6).

Case 20.1   Mercedes-Benz tee off at the Open Championship

Mercedes-Benz celebrated its 125th anniversary in the year 2011 at the world's oldest golf tournament, the Open Championship at Royal St George's, Sandwich. Having signed a five-year partnership to be an official patron of the Open Championship, Mercedes-Benz will pair its experience as the world's oldest car manufacturer alongside its reputation for innovation, by showcasing the world's first-ever car, the Benz Patent-Motorwagen, alongside its newest addition, the SLS AMG, at the tournament in 2011. Lueder Fromm, Director of Global Marketing Communications for Mercedes-Benz Cars, commented: 'For our brand, this association is not only an excellent platform but also a great honour. With our commitment to this event, we very much look forward to being able to promote the close ties between the sport of golf and Mercedes-Benz.' The agreement in place with the Open adds to the company's current sponsorship portfolio in world golf, which sees it as official partner at the Masters, the PGA Championship and the Ryder Cup 2012.

Throughout the duration of the tournament, which runs in July, all the golfers competing in the prestigious event will be chauffeured to and from the course by a fleet of the latest Mercedes-Benz cars. Former Masters' champion and Mercedes Ambassador Bernhard Langer commented on the deal saying, 'It is an exciting time for Mercedes-Benz to be associated with the world's oldest golf tournament, The Open Championship. Golf is growing in popularity and with the support of brands like Mercedes-Benz, this can only improve year on year.'

Source: Simon May, Sports PR Enquiries, Daimler Communications

Case 20.1   (*continued*)

Discussion questions

1 Why did Mercedes-Benz sign again a five-year contract to sponsor the Open Championship? What are the advantages for Mercedes-Benz?

2 Which other national/international event sponsorships are operated by Mercedes-Benz?

3 In your opinion, which goals/objectives could Mercedes-Benz try to pursue with this event sponsorship?

Event sponsorship acquisition and management

The management of sponsorship depends on several issues, including:

- a clear definition of goals on both sides;
- the seeking and coordination of mutual benefits;
- the formal identification of mutual relationships; and
- the long-term and global nature of business cooperation.

The first condition for sponsorship to be effective is a clear identification of the objectives that both parties wish to achieve. The principal long-term objective of a company is usually to maximise its values and profits, complemented by other factors, such as company development, market and social position, goodwill, image and social accountability. The objectives of an event are establishing brand or company awareness, relationship building, reinforcing event corporate image, and possibly generating sales leads and selling products (see Skinner and Rukavina, 2003: 211; Nufer, 2007: 57–60; Bowdin et al., 2011: 204–6).

Two perspectives have to be distinguished: the perspective of an event manager, who is in the role of attracting sponsors for his/her event, and the perspective of the sponsor, who is looking for the right sponsorship investment. From the point of view of an event manager, the acquisition and management process of potential sponsors could be carried out as illustrated in Figure 20.2.

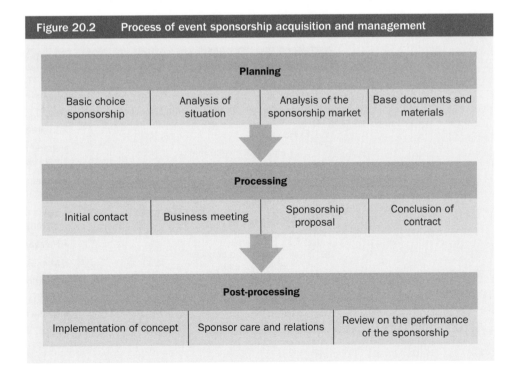

Figure 20.2   Process of event sponsorship acquisition and management

Planning			
Basic choice sponsorship	Analysis of situation	Analysis of the sponsorship market	Base documents and materials

Processing			
Initial contact	Business meeting	Sponsorship proposal	Conclusion of contract

Post-processing		
Implementation of concept	Sponsor care and relations	Review on the performance of the sponsorship

Developing an event sponsorship strategy is a distinct task, which will have an interactive relationship with the event's marketing strategy because the sponsor's brand must be integrated with the event's marketing plans, whether it is venue design, ticketing, integrated marketing communications or even the programme itself (Bowdin et al., 2011: 458). Before planning an event sponsorship strategy, the event manager first has to decide whether sponsorship is the right choice to achieve the event objectives.

Basic choice of sponsorship

Importantly, from point of view of a sponsor, sponsorship is a strategic marketing investment, not a donation (philanthropy) or a grant (a one-off type of assistance). Therefore event managers, who use sponsorship as a purchasing tool, must view sponsorships as working business partnerships. Consequently, event managers must obtain a good understanding of the full suite of potential benefits that a sponsorship will bring to their event, and to their sponsors, so they can customise their strategies. Most sponsors are investors who expect to see a direct impact on their brand equity (enhanced awareness and imagery) as well as the potential for increased sales and profits (Bowdin et al., 2011: 443, 447). Ideally there is some kind of fit between the objectives of the event (manager) and the sponsor (see Figure 20.3).

Before embarking on an event sponsorship strategy, the event manager should consider the benefits of sponsorship for the event, and whether the event is 'sponsorship ready' (Bowdin et al., 2011: 447). Therefore the event manager has to decide if the event is suitable for a corporate sponsorship investment, and if it can provide a communications platform for sponsors (see Bortoluzzi Dubach and Frey, 2011: 23). This involves thinking about the event target group (event visitors) and its fit to the target group of the sponsor/business brands. It also involves thinking about the attributes and values of the event (including relevant factors such as media and location) and companies that might share those values (see Figure 20.4).

From the perspective of an event, sponsorships often represent a significant potential revenue stream, but they can also become business partnerships that offer resources beyond money. Sponsorship brings a valuable opportunity for long-term business

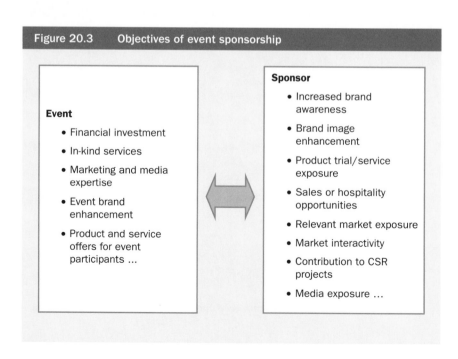

Figure 20.3   Objectives of event sponsorship

Event

- Financial investment
- In-kind services
- Marketing and media expertise
- Event brand enhancement
- Product and service offers for event participants ...

Sponsor

- Increased brand awareness
- Brand image enhancement
- Product trial/service exposure
- Sales or hospitality opportunities
- Relevant market exposure
- Market interactivity
- Contribution to CSR projects
- Media exposure ...

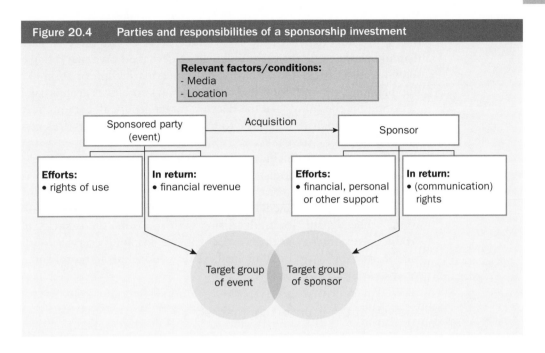

Figure 20.4   Parties and responsibilities of a sponsorship investment

partnerships that assist in growing not only the event but also the audience numbers of a particular art form or sport.

Geldard and Sinclair (2002) identified a number of questions that an event manager should ask before seeking sponsorship as a revenue stream:

- Does the event have sufficient rights or benefits that can be offered to sponsors?
- Are the event's stakeholders likely to approve of commercial sponsorship?
- Is the target market of the event congruent with the target market of the sponsor?
- Are there some companies that are simply not suitable as sponsors?
- Does the event have the resources to market and manage sponsorship?

To succeed in attracting and keeping the sponsorship stakes, event organisers must develop a clear framework for both events and sponsors to decide on the value and sustainability of potential partnerships. Moreover, event managers should keep in mind that the acquisition of potential sponsors requires lots of time, and personal and financial investment (costs for trips, personal meetings, information material), to be successful (see for further details Goldblatt, 2011: 341). Therefore the event manager has to check whether sponsorship is the right financial source in comparison to other fundraising tools like patronage or donation.

Analysis of situation

After the decision has been taken to pursue an event sponsorship strategy, the next steps consist of preliminary research, and SWOT and PEST analyses, including a comprehensive analysis of the event situation and communication potential for potential sponsors. Hence a product portfolio should also be used for describing details and the special features of the event (for further information, see Bortoluzzi Dubach and Frey, 2011: 31).

Again the target markets/groups of the event should be considered by adopting market segmentation strategies in order to have a sound basis for establishing fit between potential sponsors and the consumers who visit the event. Like all forms of integrated marketing communication, event sponsorship is most successful as a marketing medium when there is a solid database that profiles existing visitors and members/subscribers and their preferences. Sponsors will look for a reliable picture (demographics, socioeconomic status, psychographics) of the event audience to ensure there is market congruence and that an investment in the event will help achieve their own marketing objectives efficiently (Bowdin et al., 2011: 459). To obtain detailed market information to assist with sponsorship planning, research tools like on-site surveys and focus groups can be especially useful.

Alongside the analysis of the relevant target group, all communication tools should be listed which a sponsor could use to reach these target groups. Despite the variation in the size and scope of different events, some common assets (defined as benefits that the event can offer the sponsor) include the agreement to purchase product/services from a sponsor (for example, alcohol, transport, food), event **title rights**, exclusivity (the capacity to lock out competition within a brand category), business and sponsor networking opportunities, merchandising rights, media exposure, including advertising opportunities during the event, venue signage, joint advertising with sponsors, the capacity to demonstrate their product or technology at the event, corporate hospitality services and a volume of tickets for the sponsor's use (Bowdin et al., 2011: 460). Furthermore, some tailor-made assets for sponsors can be devised.

Analysis of the sponsorship market

In designing a sponsorship strategy, event managers have to work out how a list of potential sponsors can be established, given the bundles of event assets that are available for purchase. Different strategies could be identified, but there are three basic structural approaches (Geldard and Sinclair, 2002; Solomon, 2002: 67–9; Masterman, 2010: 287–9; Bowdin et al., 2011: 461):

- a sole sponsorship, where only one sponsor is involved with the event;
- tiered structures, where there is more than one, in a hierarchy of sponsors, for example hierarchical packages (e.g. tiers of gold, silver, bronze), a pyramid structure (e.g. full-, main-, co-sponsor), where the quantity of sponsors of each level decreases from the top down, and the amount which each sponsor has to pay increases from the bottom up (see Figure 20.5); and
- flat structures, where all sponsors enjoy the same status, although not necessarily the same types of rights or benefits, and do not always pay the same, such as a level playing field (all sponsors negotiate and leverage their own benefits) or an ad hoc approach.

Although sole sponsorship of an event may have the advantage of 'keeping it simple', the event's survival is threatened if the sole sponsor is lost. For this reason, many events

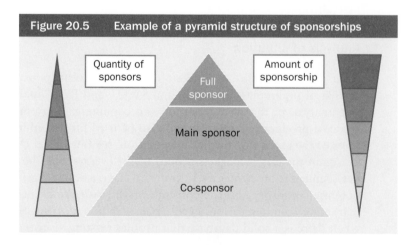

Figure 20.5   Example of a pyramid structure of sponsorships

Quantity of sponsors

Amount of sponsorship

Full sponsor

Main sponsor

Co-sponsor

with a limited number of assets choose a hierarchical or pyramid structure (different levels of investment for set benefit packages). But, as most events 'end up formulating their packages so that all of the levels get access to the best benefits, with the lower levels simply getting less of the supporting benefits' (Grey and Skildum-Reid, 2003: 97), many events now tailor their benefit packages for each sponsor using only broad categories, such as major media, corporate and support sponsors. Using this approach, the sponsors are usually grouped according to their type (e.g. title rights; presenting sponsorship of a section, event, entry, team or particular day; preferred suppliers; etc.) and their exclusivity (among sponsors at any level; among sponsors at or below a given level; as a supplier or seller at the event; or within event-driven marketing collateral). The purchase of other event assets, such as merchandising rights, licences and endorsements, hospitality, signage and database access by sponsors, to name just a few, can serve to further differentiate the event sponsor packages (Solomon, 2002: 68–75; Grey and Skildum-Reid, 2004: 97; Bowdin et al., 2011: 461). Modifying an existing sponsoring structure by adding a new level in a hierarchical or pyramid structure can produce advantages as well as disadvantages.

The use of tailor-made sponsorship packages is recommended for a number of reasons (Bowdin et al., 2011: 461–2):

- Packaged event properties are rarely a perfect fit for potential sponsors – most are either too broad or too narrow in their consumer reach, and the rights available may be either more or less than those the sponsor wants.
- Sponsors are often seeking more control over their sponsorship and its potential leveraging than packaged strategies offer – the simple transactional nature of buyer–seller arrangements is being replaced by partnerships, and, in some cases, the sponsor clearly has leadership in driving the relationship.
- Poor sponsorship packaging by events can lead to a greater instance of **ambush marketing**[1] in certain industry/product categories (for example, banking and finance) or attempts by non-sponsoring companies to capitalise on an event's image and prestige by implying that they are sponsors (for more details, see Sachse and Dregner, 2010).
- Multiple layers of sponsorship introduced by events can cause confusion among audiences and sponsors – as the different sponsorship categories become more prolific, there is more potential for a loss of control by event organisers and sponsor conflicts (Shani and Sandler, 1998).

Once the approach to building a potential sponsorship list is determined, the process of monitoring the sponsor market begins. Criteria to identify suitable sponsors could be:

- fit of event and company;
- fit of target groups (same audience or a significant component of it);
- awareness of the company;
- specific issues, for example, market, image or penetration of a segment, for which event sponsorship may be a solution;
- the motivational criteria each company adopts when assessing a sponsorship investment (for further information see Bortoluzzi and Frey, 2011: 56).

There are various research techniques to identify potential sponsors. By keeping track of business developments through industry associations, business and financial media, and the web, a great deal of information can be gathered on the marketing directions of firms in order to guide sponsorship targeting. Event managers can also obtain insights into potential sponsors by reading their annual reports or viewing their websites. These

---

1 Ambush marketing involves a company seeking to associate with an event without making payment to the event owner; often it places itself in direct conflict with a competitor who is a legitimate and paying sponsor.

sources often provide a good picture of the broad strategies the organisation is pursuing. They also indicate the types of sponsorship they already have in place and whether they have any specific requirements for sponsorships.

Another means of finding potential sponsors is to simply identify who has sponsored similar events in the past. This can be done by examining programmes, promotion material or websites of these other events, or directly contacting the event organisers (many events now see the value in some productive networking and information sharing). Therefore, the existing sponsors of an event can be a very useful source of referral to other potential sponsors. This method of finding sponsors can be highly successful because the existing sponsor is presenting its company as a satisfied partner of the event in 'opening the door' and endorsing the event as a sponsorship property. Once potential sponsors are identified, a more detailed examination of their business and marketing objectives and the types of asset that will meet their needs can be completed (Bowdin et al., 2011: 462–4).

■ Base documents and materials

The last step of the acquisition planning phase consists of formulating a compilation of different materials, like the sponsoring guidelines, the sponsoring concept and information about the event (event concept, booklet, flyer, videos). While the sponsoring guidelines define the goals and principles of the sponsorship (for further information, see Bortoluzzi Dubach and Frey, 2011: 60), the sponsorship concept is the main document for the sponsorship acquisition. The concept should include all results of the analysis of the situation as well as all main data and points of the event and should illustrate the communicative advantages for the sponsor. All the information should be tailored to the objectives and communication goals of the sponsor, as figured out during the analysis of the sponsorship market. At least two main goals should be pointed out for the sponsor:

- image establishment through an intensive and quality contact with the main target group (event visitors), and/or
- brand awareness enhancement through a quantitative contact by broadcasting with the further target group (event watchers).

■ Initial contact

Once the potential sponsors have been listed, the next challenge for the event manager is to determine the marketing or management person who will be the sponsorship decision maker within the targeted company. In small companies, this person is likely to be the chief executive officer or managing director. In companies of moderate size, the marketing or public relations manager may make such decisions, while in large corporations a dedicated sponsorship section could exist within the marketing, public relations or corporate affairs areas (Bowdin et al., 2011: 464–7). All the names, addresses and details should be registered in a special data bank.

The initial contact with the sponsor can be via telephone or post/email, but the telephone call is preferred to find out the right addressee and to get in touch with the sponsor as fast as possible. A telephone guideline based on a straightforward aim like obtaining permission to send the sponsoring concept should be prepared. Before developing any written proposal, it is customary to write a brief introductory letter to profile your event and the sponsorship opportunity. With the aim of getting a personal meeting date, all the advantages and benefits for the sponsor should be pointed out and all information materials should be attached. Some sponsorship managers make direct contact by email or telephone, especially if they have been referred by another sponsor, or have some informal rapport with the company's personnel. But in most cases some follow-up calls could be necessary. However, the ability to personally discuss one's interest in a partnership may depend on the company's policy about written or verbal communication in the first instance.

Business meeting

There are many benefits in becoming acquainted with the company in a personal meeting before preparing a proposal, simply because of the need to fully understand their product/brand attributes, their business objectives, their competition, how they use their current sponsorships, and the ways in which sponsorships proposals need to be structured to satisfy their needs. The most successful sponsorship approach is one where the event manager has put a lot of effort into planning before approaching the sponsor.

There will also be the possibility to argue about the advantages of the event sponsorship through presentation, video or print material, to answer questions, to resolve all doubt and to discuss financial or other support. If it is possible to develop some preliminary rapport with those deciding on the value of the proposed partnership, there will be a better grasp of why the company may be interested in sponsoring the event and how the proposal should be written to attract their investment. Thinking about and exploring how to marry the event with the company's culture could be an innovative way to address the company's marketing objectives before commencing the final proposal (Bowdin et al., 2011: 465). Fixing all appointments and agreements by protocol could be good advice and a basis for the final proposal.

Sponsorship proposal

The sponsorship proposal must be based on the previous analysis and agreements of the business meeting. Besides the benefits and rewards, all rights and financial consequences for the sponsor should be mentioned. In particular, the following main questions should be addressed in a formal, tailored proposal (Geldard and Sinclair, 2002):

- What is the company/organisation being asked to sponsor?
- What will the company/organisation receive for its sponsorship?
- What is it going to cost?

The length and level of detail a proposal uses to answer these questions depends on the value and cost of the sponsor partnership. As a general rule, the proposal should be as short as possible and as long as necessary. If the value of the sponsorship is substantial and the proposal is over five pages, an executive summary should give a snapshot of its key elements along with a contents page. The sponsorship proposal should also include (Bowdin et al., 2011: 465–6):

- an overview of the event (including its mission/goals, history, location, current and past sponsors, programme/duration, staff, past or anticipated level of media coverage, past or predicted attendance levels, and actual or predicted attendee profile);
- the offered sponsorship package and its associated costs (the sponsorship should not cost more than other marketing communication tools, reaching a similar volume of their target market);
- the proposed duration of the sponsorship agreement;
- the strategic fit between the event's and the sponsor's objectives; and
- the event's contact details for the sponsor's response and follow-up negotiations.

Many sponsors, especially big companies, have developed specific proposal guidelines or criteria, which should be addressed to avoid failure. Besides these criteria, event managers should attend to the following attributes for a successful proposal (Bowdin et al., 2011: 466–8):

1. *Sell benefits, not features*: Many proposals describe the features of the event, such as the artistic merit of the festival, rather than the event's marketing assets and sponsor benefits. Sponsors buy marketing communication platforms so that they can reach their stakeholders and market(s) to form relationships or sell products/services.

2. *Address the sponsor's needs, not those of the event*: Many proposals emphasise the event's need for money, rather than the sponsor's needs such as market access, corporate hospitality or a better understanding of a new brand. Remember, event sponsorships should be seen as partnerships, not a means to patch holes in the event budget (Harrison, 2004).

3. *Tailor the proposal to the business category*: As noted, each of the event's benefits will have a different level of importance to each potential sponsor.

4. *Include promotional extensions*: The two major sources of sponsor benefits are addressed here. First, there are the benefits being purchased – for example, identification in marketing material and on-site signage that come with the sponsorship and only require action on the part of the event manager. The second set of benefits emerges from the sponsor's event leveraging – for example, trade, retail and sales extensions. Particular leveraging activities might include competitions, redemption offers (such as free ticket offers for the customer of a sponsor's wholesalers) and hospitality.

5. *Minimise risk*: Risk can be reduced through indicating some guaranteed marketing activities (including media space reach and frequency) in the package, listing reputable co-sponsors and showing the steps that will be taken to minimise the risk of ambush marketing by other companies. A clear indication of how the event will service the sponsorship should also be given prominence in the proposal.

6. *Include added value*: The proposal should be presented in terms of its total impact on achieving results for the sponsor – how the sponsorship will build relationships internally with staff, ways in which it will facilitate networking with other sponsors or potential business partners and how it can build sales among consumer and business audiences.

Commonly, organisations apply a screening process to sponsorship proposals as they seek to determine which relevant benefits are present. An understanding of this screening process (which includes customer audience, exposure potential, distribution channel audience, advantage over competitors, resource investment required, the event's characteristics, the event organisation's reputation and entertainment and hospitality opportunities) is useful to the event manager as it assists in crafting sponsorship proposals (Bowdin et al., 2011: 469).

■ Conclusion of contract

It is standard business practice to commit the sponsorship agreement to paper to avoid misunderstandings about the event assets and benefits being offered, their costs, payment terms and the responsibilities of both parties. Where the contract was once just a reference for event managers and sponsors, in the case of major sponsorship deals the contract now establishes the ground rules for the ongoing working relationship between the sponsorship partners. With large-scale events, a contract is essential to ensure that the obligations of both the event manager and sponsor are met and that category exclusivity for the sponsor is protected to discourage ambushers. Closer event–sponsor relationships may technically be easier to establish in smaller-scale events, but the business practicalities of having a contract (approved by the lawyer of both parties) makes a lot of sense. If a prolonged period of negotiation is needed for a sponsorship (this is usual for a very large event sponsorship property), having a legal letter of agreement to confirm that the sponsorship will go ahead is important (Bowdin et al., 2011: 472).

The contract should include at a minimum the following constituent parts (for details see Solomon, 2002: 83–6):

- name and address of the parties;
- sponsor's efforts or obligations (e.g. financial or other support-like products, service, know-how) and benefits;
- sponsor benefits (equal with the efforts of the sponsored party), generally communication rights at least;
- duration of contract (period of the sponsorship);
- reduction of efforts in case of any abruption;
- guidelines for liability, indemnity and insurance;
- confidentiality;
- a salvatory clause;
- applicable law, contractual language, jurisdiction.

All in all, there are no existing regulations in form or content for a sponsorship contract. Oral agreements are also possible, but not advisable. Fixing at least the main important points is recommended to avoid conflicts afterwards.

Implementation of concept

Once the sponsorship contract has been signed, it is good practice to construct a sponsorship management plan to operationalise the agreement. At its most basic, this plan should identify what objectives the sponsorship will achieve for the sponsor, the benefits that have been promised, costs associated with providing specified benefits, review and evaluation approaches, and the timeline for activities that need to be conducted to deliver on the sponsorship (see Bowdin et al., 2011: 475–8).

Objectives associated with any given event sponsorship will be tailored to the needs of that partnership, but they should be specific to the sponsorship, measurable in that the success or otherwise of the sponsorship can be established, and agreed to by the person responsible for carrying out the plan. While perhaps challenging, the objectives can be achieved under normal circumstances and remain realistic; they should have a time-frame in which the objectives have to be achieved. Stakeholders affected by the sponsorship also need to be addressed in the management plan – these groups would include attendees, members of the broader community in which the event is taking place, staff of the sponsoring organisation and media. All 'benefits and associated actions' need to be clearly identified, along with the target groups to be reached and (financial) costs which are associated with them. These costs might include signage manufacture and erection, supporting advertisements, promotional material, prize money, sponsor hospitality costs, professional fees, labour costs associated with hosting sponsors on-site, tickets, postage and preparation of an evaluation report. A budget needs to present all costs, and show those costs in the context of the overall value of the sponsorship. It should also be remembered that sponsorship (both in-kind and cash) attracts tax, and this tax must be factored into any bottom-line calculations. However, in many cases, particularly smaller events, such as conferences or community festivals, the benefits that accrue to the sponsor cost the event virtually nothing, except for the management time given to ensuring that what was promised is delivered. The sponsor supplies the promotional material, such as banners, signage and artwork for advertisements, and other costs are absorbed into the administration of the event. Nevertheless, it is good practice to isolate costs associated with the sponsorship to establish the net benefit to the event that the sponsorship generates. A list of the 'actions' necessary to fulfil the sponsorship should be made, specifying what is to be done, when it is to be completed and who is responsible. Mapping out all the management and marketing activities on a spreadsheet or other form of graphic display such as a Gantt chart is a useful management aid (Bowdin et al., 2011: 475–6).

Sponsor care and relations

Effective relationships between events and sponsors, like any other relationship, are built on a strong foundation of communication, commitment and trust. For this purpose professionalism and quality in communication is essential:

- *Understand the sponsor*: A method of maintaining harmonious relationships is to get to know the sponsor's organisation, its mission, its staff, its products and its marketing strategies. By doing this, it becomes easier to understand the needs of the sponsor and how those needs can be satisfied.
- *One contact/face to the sponsor*: One person from the event organisation team needs to be appointed as the contact point for the sponsor.
- *Support the sponsor*: Take care of the sponsor at every opportunity – before, during and after the event.

It is important to establish effective communication with sponsors so that they see the event manager as a serious marketer who will look for joint leveraging opportunities. Both the sponsor and the event need to have a reasonably equal input to how the sponsorship can be used to achieve its full potential. If a sponsor believes that its sponsorship has been effective – as defined by achieving the marketing and business objectives of the sponsorship – it's most likely that it will renew the sponsorship for another year. The longer a sponsorship lasts, the better it is for both parties (Bowdin et al., 2011: 473).

Review of the performance of the sponsorship

An 'evaluation and review' process needs to be built into the sponsorship management process, as evaluation is essential for both sponsor and event. The review process should be ongoing for the whole process and act to identify and address any problems that could affect sponsorship outcomes. Evaluation is concerned with providing a clear understanding of how the sponsorship performed against the objectives that were set for it. A shared responsibility of the event manager and sponsor (**corporate social responsibility – CSR**) is the measurement of the overall impact of the partnership.

There are two components to measurement and evaluation: first, the evaluation of the effectiveness of the partnership and how the sponsor and event have contributed to it and, second, the measurement of the consumer-related marketing objectives set by the sponsor.

The first-named evaluation seeks to answer questions like:

- Did the promised media coverage actually happen?
- Did the attendee profile of the event reflect the market profile described in the sponsorship proposal?
- What was the overall quality of the sponsorship's delivery and management?

Of particular importance in sponsorship measurement is the second-named evaluation: the measurement of the consumer-related marketing objectives. For this, audience research is used that measures, for example, unaided and aided recognition of the event sponsor's name (sponsor awareness), attitudes towards the sponsor and any actions/ behaviour that the sponsorship has caused in its target audience (Bowdin et al., 2011: 477–8; Goldblatt, 2011: 346). There could be some factors that complicate the measurement of sponsorship. For example, if brand marketers use a number of media, including sponsorship, to create brand relationships, there will often be carry-over effects of previous media and marketing expenditure on brand awareness and image (for more details, see Castan, 2011).

Evaluation gives the partners the chance to fine-tune the sponsorship arrangements, so that both parties are well placed to renew the partnership in subsequent years. With the review, the event manager establishes a good base for the next event sponsorship planning phase (for further information, see Bortoluzzi Dubach and Frey, 2011: 203 ff.), as the review process is part of the planning and organisation phase of the new sponsoring acquisition process or a foundation for an existing sponsor relationship. The more satisfied a sponsor was with the implementation of the sponsorship agreements and the support, the more likely is further sponsorship in the next year. Therefore it is possible to establish sponsor retention, which is most important with continuous events. With a high sponsor retention rate the costs for acquisition will be reduced, and planning security will be increased. Moreover, there is a lot of potential for synergy (e.g. experience or learning effects), that optimises the instruments of the sponsorship management.

Case 20.2 on the TUI Feuerwerk der Turnkunst points out some aspects of the event sponsorship acquisition and management process in detail to give a practical insight.

Case 20.2   **TUI Feuerwerk der Turnkunst (TUI fireworks of gymnastic arts)**

The Lower Saxony Gymnastics Association is one of Germany's largest federal single-sports associations. Its subsidiary,[2] the TSF GmbH, manages the nationwide annual artistic and acrobatics tour known as 'TUI Feuerwerk der Turnkunst'. Over the past 25 years, this event has developed from a once-a-year show with an audience of 3,000 people in 1988 to a nationwide, annual, four-week tour playing in Germany's biggest event halls with an overall audience of 170,000 people and a seat capacity utilisation of more than 97% in 2012.

Basic choice for sponsorship

The main objectives which should be achieved with the 'TUI Feuerwerk der Turnkunst' are to increase the awareness of gymnastics, to strengthen the collaboration between the different gymnastic associations in Germany and – last but not least – to gain (some) profits with the event. The most important objective is to give the audience an understanding of what gymnastics could be. The audience should be activated to participate in gymnastic groups on site, e.g. gymnastic groups for parents and children or elderly people. The whole family should be involved in this kind of sport. Therefore the TSF GmbH pursues a special event pricing strategy: the ticket prices are significantly lower than the prices of all competitors' with a comparable event quality. This derives directly from the association's mission: offering a wide range of sports and leisure activities that promote a healthy lifestyle with a particular focus on families. Being 'an association for the families', the event is clearly positioned in the market as family-orientated entertainment with family-friendly ticket prices.

While offering a high-quality show remains the event organiser's fundamental objective, increased customer expectations require an enhanced overall event experience. Modern event halls provide easy access to transportation and accessible parking, comfortable seating, easily accessible catering booths, exclusive VIP lounges, etc. . . . and greatly contribute to the overall customer experience. Moreover modern event halls are expensive to rent.

Maintaining stable ticket prices while maximising customer satisfaction is a challenging balance that would not be possible without any sponsorship partners.

▶

---

2 27 million people in Germany (that is, approximately one-third of its overall population) hold a sports club (not health club) membership. The responsibilities of these clubs exceed simple practice sessions. The club system contributes a great deal to various aspects of German society, including, but not limited to, education, healthy lifestyle and the integration of people from various cultural backgrounds. Therefore, the German government provides many legal benefits to sports clubs and associations that register as incorporated non-profit organisations under the German legal term 'eingetragener Verein' abbreviated as 'eV'). Given that legal framework, non-profit clubs and associations are challenged with several management limitations that have a direct impact on their competitiveness in the fast-paced event industry. To meet customers' high expectations and increasingly sophisticated management requirements, professional sports organisations have capitalised on subsidiaries that operate as registered corporations and manage a club's or association's pro teams and events. The benefit of this combination is that it allows the subsidiary to use the infrastructure of the club or association while being a fully fledged player in its respective market(s).

Case 20.2   (*continued*)

Analysis of the sponsorship market

The present sponsoring strategy includes a title rights partner, a presenter, two main sponsors, several media partners and a huge pool of local sponsors and cooperation partners. Touring Germany each year for four weeks gives the possibility and necessity to work together with many local sponsor partners. Thereby, the branch exclusivity for each local sponsor is limited to each playing location.

In 2010 the organisers added 'TUI' as title rights partner on top of the sponsoring pyramid, which generated advantages and disadvantages. Teaming up with a title rights partner is a great opportunity for both the partner and the event organiser, as there is a strong value behind this special long-term relationship. But, when analysing the overall value from an organiser's perspective, some change management issues need to be taken into consideration. For example, adding a title rights partner warrants adding a new top tier to your sponsorship pyramid. As a result, former top-tier sponsors will instantly be demoted to second-tier sponsors.

Depending on the goals of the respective partner, a variety of different marketing activities are exercised throughout the course of the tour. Generally speaking, global partners often prefer sponsorships which give their brand high levels of brand visibility during the event campaign and the actual show while local partners place more emphasis on additional live marketing activities at the event venue which introduce a high-quality brand experience to the audience.

An excellent example of a successful sponsorship which combines both brand visibility and brand experience is shown by the mobility partner and main sponsor, Volkswagen. As a repeated tour sponsor for many years, the Volkswagen logo is prominently displayed on all promotional tour marketing campaign activities. A Volkswagen vehicle fleet is also used for all transportation throughout the tour. Additionally, local Volkswagen dealers capitalise on shows in their local markets to display cars at the event venue and invite top-tier customers to a VIP event experience. This combination of sponsorship activating marketing activities allows Volkswagen to fully exploit its sponsorship investment on both national and local scales. Unprompted sponsorship recollection among show visitors regularly exceeds the 90% mark.

Sponsor care and relations

The event tours every January with a new show and ensemble and continually returns to its established venues. Additionally, one to two new sites/towns are tested each year. As a sports association, there's a necessity to support young athletes. Therefore, one to two local sports clubs will always be invited to perform the opening act in their respective home town. Meeting the stars and performing in front of up to 10,000 people are great motivating factors for young talents as well as for their coaches, who mostly serve their clubs as volunteers. Supporting local sports clubs also benefits local businesses, which pursue locally orientated sponsorship strategies to promote their products or causes. Long-term relationships, not only with customers, but also with local businesses, are established through these localised strategies. Throughout the years, many businesses have become not just partners but fans of the event. A collaborative management approach that is not just based on contractually agreed benefits but also on mutual trust and a thorough understanding of each other's businesses and goals ensures long-term partnerships and, ultimately, maximises ROIs for the sponsors as well as long-term profit and planning reliability for the event organiser.

(With thanks to Marco Müller, Turn- und Sportfördergesellschaft mbH for the information provided; see also *www.tsf-showwelt.de*)

Discussion questions

4 In 2010 the event manager added a title sponsor, adding a new tier to the existing sponsoring pyramid. What does this mean for the event and the then existing sponsor hierarchy? What are the main advantages and disadvantages/risks for the event and sponsor?

5 What happens if the event or sponsor is going to embark on an international strategy approach? What does this mean for the event sponsorship from both points of view?

6 How could the performance of the sponsorship be measured? Describe possibilities for evaluation from the point of view of the event manager and the sponsor.

What makes a sponsorship investment successful?

This chapter has described in detail the process of event sponsorship acquisition and management. The influencing factors, which make an event sponsorship successful, have to be distinguished between the two perspectives of the event manager and the sponsor.

From the point of view of an event manager, event sponsoring could be called successful, when the event manager:

1. is able to attain sponsors. Therefore the event manager has to offer solid and reliable base information about the event (e.g. clear positioning of the event, project plans, statistical reliable data on average visitors and target groups, expected media coverage) as well as solid financial planning, anticipating possible risks and describing alternative settings;
2. could attract sponsors who fit the event (for example there is no fit between a monster truck show and Volkswagen as a potential sponsor), which could result in leverage effects;
3. has the ability to manage the coexistence of different sponsors;
4. runs a reliable project management to keep sponsors constantly up to date;
5. is able to manage the event itself properly with also a focus on the special needs of the sponsors (e.g. VIP access, infrastructure for sponsors, possibility for side-events);
6. delivers reliable documentation of the event (e.g. number of visitors, press coverage); and
7. is able to install and run proper risk management to cope with unexpected and critical incidents (e.g. bad weather conditions, safety arrangements, cancellation of a live act).

From the point of view of a sponsor, an event sponsorship investment could be called successful, if:

1. generally the sponsor's benefits/results are higher than the efforts/costs of the sponsorship investment;
2. the sponsorship has a positive influence in achieving strategic and tactical goals/objectives (e.g. enhancement of brand awareness, sales and market share);
3. the sponsor could benefit positively from the event's image (e.g. a sponsorship investment in sport events improves the sponsor's brand image as young, sporty, dynamic and trendy);
4. the sponsor gets direct access to a special target group for detailed and ongoing communications;
5. the financial value of media coverage (e.g. press articles, TV, social media) is on a value base higher than the sponsorship contribution.

In addition, an effective method of calculating the worth of an event sponsorship is to calculate the cost of communicating with the target market using other media, such as print. For example, if the cost of newspaper advertisements that reach a target market of 10,000 three times is £x, the value of an event sponsorship that reaches the same size target market should not be less than £x, given all the other advantages that come to a sponsor with a good 'fit' with an event (Bowdin et al., 2011: 471–2).

Risks of sponsorship investment

The generally positive effects of sponsorship investments for event managers and sponsors could – of course – turn into negative effects caused by different determining factors for which the event manager, the sponsor, or neither or both is responsible. According to the event manager, the event sponsorship will not be successful, when:

■   the event itself suffers mismanagement, such as unprofessional organisation, inadequate locations, lack of security, inadequate event infrastructure, which – in the worst case – ends in a disaster (e.g. the mass panic of the participants at the Love Parade 2010 in Duisburg, Germany, which resulted in 21 deaths and 510 injuries);
■   events become cluttered with the diverse brands of multiple sponsors – research by MEC MediaLab across 20 countries suggests that over 40% of respondents believed

sports events have become too heavily sponsored (Sudhaman, 2004). In this context, the event manager's task of making strategic decisions about an event's portfolio of sponsors is evident to avoid confusion among audiences and sponsors;

■ the event (organiser) is tainted by scandals, corruption, bribery, misappropriation of funds, etc.

From the perspective of the sponsor, apart from many other less important factors, event sponsorship is unsuccessful, if:

■ the sponsor is tainted with scandals or bad publicity;
■ the sponsor hasn't got enough resources to 'activate' the sponsorship: the amount of money, or its equivalent value, that will be raised in sponsorship should be (at least) double the amount of the costs to get the sponsorship (Harrison, 2004: 8). From this one can derive the following '1:1–2' rule: if you pay €1 for rights and licences, you have to spend at least an additional €1–2 for the 'activation' of your sponsorship (e.g. below-the-line activities, special branded products, special offers in dealerships and points of sale, mentioning the sponsorship in advertising).

Setting aside the points the event manager or sponsor is responsible for, there are also unforeseeable und incalculable risks, which could endanger the success of the event sponsorship, such as:

■ the event itself is instrumentalised by governments or regimes at a national level (e.g. Formula 1 in Bahrain);
■ public awareness and interest is turning from acceptance towards rejection (e.g. during the bidding process of the Olympic Games in Munich 2018 or the planned boycott of the Olympic Games 2012 in London by Indian athletes);
■ the event suffers under bad weather conditions, storms, accidents or natural catastrophes, which cause personal insurance claims;
■ the event is exploited by violent or rowdy groups;
■ the event is the focus of terrorism (e.g. the Olympic Games in Munich in 1972).

Some risks could be also caused by competing companies which undertake ambush marketing activities, such as advertisements that obliquely refer to a major event. These activities, so long as they stop short of trademark infringement or false advertising, are perfectly legal, which has frustrated major sports event managers and sponsors for years. Therefore, in the last decade, major sports event organisers such as the International Olympic Committee and the Fédération Internationale de Football Association have pressured national governments to pass legislation prohibiting ambush marketing as a condition of a successful bid to host an event (Scassa, 2011: 354).

Conclusion

The chapter defined and described event sponsorship as a communication instrument for sponsors and a fundraising instrument for event managers. For the latter, the acquisition and management process to gain a sponsor was described step by step. Ideally, well-organised and managed sponsorships are able to bring benefits for all parties, which is one of the reasons why sponsorship has become an important and powerful instrument in marketing communications.

Event managers have to keep in mind that getting sponsors on board means more than just creating financial and additional support for the event. Having sponsors on board also needs significant management attention (personal, financial and temporal), capacities and resources, which did not originally form part of the event management portfolio. Moreover, the (positive) leverage effect of an event sponsorship could also work in the opposite direction. For example, if the main sponsor struggles for existence or is involved in a scandal, the event and its image could also be damaged.

If event managers keep these potential risks in mind, they will be able to use sponsorship as a powerful instrument.

General discussion questions

7 As an event manager, what would you do to gain a special, big company as a main sponsor for your event?

8 What can you do, from the point of view of an event manager, when a big company would like to sponsor your event, if the company doesn't fit your event's conception and objectives, but would pay a lot of money for a title sponsorship?

Guided reading

Over the past decade, there has been a significant increase in the number of texts offering guidance related to sponsorship and event sponsorship.

Event sponsorship issues may be investigated through a range of sources. There are only a few journals which are specialised in sponsorship/events, like *Sponsors* (a German journal) or *IEG Sponsorship Report*. Nevertheless, event sponsorship is also addressed in mainstream management and marketing journals, for example, *European Journal of Marketing* and *International Journal of Advertising*. As event sponsorship is very popular in the field of sports, a lot of sport-specific academic journals such as *International Journal of Sports Marketing and Sponsorship* also provide a rich source of information.

Apart from academic journals, which deliver the most up-to-date information, a further source of valuable information is specialised books. A basic insight into event sponsorship is provided by:

Bowdin, G., Allen, J., O'Toole, W., Harris, R. and McDonnell, I. (2011) *Events Management* (3rd edn). Oxford: Elsevier. Butterworth-Heinemann, Chapter 13.

Skinner, B.E. and Rukavina, V. (2003) *Event Sponsorship*. Hoboken, NJ: Wiley.

Solomon, J. (2002) *An Insider's Guide to Managing Sporting Events*. Champaign, IL: Human Kinetics.

The measurement of event sponsorships is discussed by:

Jeffries-Fox, B. (2005) *A Guide to Measuring Event Sponsorships*. London: Institute for Public Relations.

Sponsorship of sports events is discussed in:

Amis, J. and Cornwall, T.B. (2005) *Global Sport Sponsorship*. Oxford: Berg.

Graham, S., Neirotti, L.D. and Goldblatt, J.J. (2001) *The Ultimate Guide to Sports Marketing* (2nd edn). New York: McGraw-Hill, Chapters 5 and 9.

Hermanns, A. and Riedmüller, F., eds (2003) *Sponsoring und Events im Sport, Von der Instrumentalbetrachtung zur Kommunikationsplattform*. Munich: Vahlen.

More basic material and specific details on the management of sponsorships in general can be found in:

Bagusat, A., Marwitz, C. and Vogl, M. (2008) *Handbuch Sponsoring, Erfolgreiche Marketing- und Markenkommunikation*. Berlin: esv.

Bruhn, M. (2010): *Sponsoring – Systematische Planung und integrativer Einsatz* (5th edn). Wiesbaden: Gabler.

Geldard, E. and Sinclair, L. (2002) *The Sponsorship Manual: Sponsorship Made Easy* (2nd edn). Victoria (Australia): Sponsorship Unit.

Grey, A.M. and Skildum-Reid, K. (2003) *The Sponsorship Seeker's Toolkit* (2nd edn). Sydney: McGraw Hill.

Hermanns, A. and Marwitz, C. (2008) *Sponsoring, Grundlagen – Wirkungen – Management – Markenführung* (3rd edn). Munich: Vahlen.

Lagae, W. (2005) *Sport Sponsorship and Marketing Communications: A European Perspective*. Harlow: Financial Times Prentice Hall.

You will also find a lot of useful information in single chapters of basic marketing books like:

De Pelsmacker, P., Geuens, M. and Van den Bergh, J. (2010) *Marketing Communications – A European Perspective* (4th edn). Harlow: Financial Times Prentice Hall, Chapter 11.

Recommended websites

International websites (in English):

International Events Group (IEG) of Chicago: **www.sponsorship.com**

Sponsor Tribune: **www.sponsortribune.nl**

German website:

Sponsors, Wissen fürs Sportbusiness: **www.sponsors.de**

Key words

ambush marketing; brand awareness; corporate social responsibility (CSR); event sponsorship; sponsor; sponsorship; target group; title rights

Bibliography

Blyth, A. (2003) Joining the throng, *New Media Age*, July, 31.

Bortoluzzi Dubach, E. and Frey, H. (2011) *Sponsoring – Der Leitfaden für die Praxis* (5th edn). Bern: Haupt.

Bowdin, G., Allen, J., O'Toole, W., Harris, R. and McDonnell, I. (2011) *Events Management* (3rd edn). Oxford: Elsevier Butterworth-Heinemann.

Bruhn, M. (2010) *Sponsoring – Systematische Planung und integrativer Einsatz* (5th edn). Wiesbaden: Gabler.

Castan, B. (2011) *Erfolgskontrolle von Events und Sponsoring, Instrumente für die Evaluation ihrer Werbewirkung*. Berlin: ESV.

Cornwell, T., Weeks, C. and Roy, D. (2005) Sponsorship-linked marketing: opening the black box. *Journal of Advertising*, 34(2), 21–43.

Day, J. (2002) Global sponsorship market soars. *Media Guardian*, 15 January. **www.guardian.co.uk/search?q=event+ sponsorship+expenditure&section=media**

De Pelsmaker, P., Geuens, M. and Van den Bergh, J. (2010) *Marketing Communications – A European Perspective* (4th edn). Harlow: Financial Times Prentice Hall.

Duncan, T. (2002) *IMC: Using Advertising and Promotion to Build Brands*. Boston, MA: McGraw-Hill Irwin.

Geldard, E. and Sinclair, L. (2002) *The Sponsorship Manual: Sponsorship Made Easy* (2nd edn). Victoria (Australia): Sponsorship Unit.

Goldblatt, J.J. (2011) *Special Events, A New Generation and the Next Frontier* (6th edn). Hoboken, NJ: Wiley.

Grey, A.M. and Skildum-Reid, K. (2003) *The Sponsorship Seeker's Toolkit* (2nd edn). Sydney: McGraw Hill.

Harrison, P. (2004) *Sponsorship – Cutting Through the Hype*. New South Wales: The Australian Council for the Arts, February. **www.australiacouncil.gov.au/ resources/reports_and_publications/ subjects/marketing/fund_development/ sponsorship_-_cutting_through_the_hype**

Hermanns, A. and Lemân, F. (2010) Sponsoring Trends 2010, Corporate Social Responsibility und Sponsoring im Fokus, sponsored by BBDO Live, Bonn.

Hermanns, A. and Marwitz, C. (2008) *Sponsoring, Grundlagen – Wirkungen – Management – Markenführung* (3rd edn). Munich: Vahlen.

Hinch, T. and Higham, J. (2004) Sport tourism development. In C. Cooper (ed.), *Aspects of Tourism*. Clevedon: Channel View Publications.

IEG (International Event Group) (2010) Who spent what in '09: IEG's top sponsors list, IEG sponsorship report. Chicago, IL: IEG.

ICC (2003) ICC International Code on Sponsorship, Commission on Marketing and Advertising, 17 September 2003. **www.iccwbo.org/id926/index.html**

Lieberman, A. and Esgate, P. (2002) *The Entertainment Marketing Revolution*. Upper Saddle River, NJ: Financial Times Prentice Hall.

Masterman, G. (2010) *Strategic Sports Event Management: Olympic Edition* (2nd edn). Oxford: Butterworth-Heinemann.

Meenaghan, T. (2001a) Understanding sponsorship effects. *Psychology and Marketing,* 18(2), 95–122.

Meenaghan, T. (2001b) Sponsorship and advertising: a comparison of consumer perceptions. *Psychology and Marketing,* 18(2), 191–215.

Mermiri, T. and South, J. (2009) Private investment in culture 2007–2008, London: Arts and Business. **www.aandb.org.uk/ Central/Research/Other-projects/Private- investment-culture-recession.aspx**

Nufer, G. (2007) *Event-Marketing und - Management: Theorie und Praxis unter besonderer Berücksichtigung von Imagewirkungen* (3rd edn). Wiesbaden: DUV.

Pilot checkpoint and FASPO (2010) Sponsor visions 2010, Hamburg.

Sachse, M. and Dregner, J. (2010) The dark side of sponsoring and ambushing mega sports events: is successful communication hampered by too many, too similar, and too ambiguous stimuli? In C. Zanger (ed.), *Stand und Perspektiven der Eventforschung* (1st edn). Wiesbaden: Gabler.

Scassa, T. (2011) Ambush marketing and the right of association: clamping down on references to that big event with all the athletes in a couple of years. *Journal of Sport Management,* 25, 354–70.

Shani, D. and Sandler, D.M. (1998) Ambush marketing: is confusion to blame for the flickering of the flame? *Psychology & Marketing,* 15(4), 367–83.

Skinner, B.E. and Rukavina, V. (2003) *Event Sponsorship*. Hoboken, NJ: Wiley.

Solomon, J. (2002) *An Insider's Guide to Managing Sporting Events*. Champaign, IL: Human Kinetic.

Sudhaman, A. (2004) Game, set and client match. *Media Asia,* 9 May, 28–9.

Part 4
Conclusions

21. Trends in events management

Chapter 21

Trends in events management

Andreas Reiter, ZTB Zukunftsbüro, Austria

Learning outcomes

Upon completion of this chapter the reader should be able to:

- identify the most relevant forthcoming trends in sports, culture and the meeting industries;
- understand these trends in the context of social and cultural changes;
- appreciate the development of hybrid event formats and cross-events;
- develop innovative event formats in the defined segments.

Overview

This chapter commences with a general introduction about the volatility of markets, the fragmentation of society and the impacts on events, which are that the more fragmented the society is, the more powerful the instruments of (brand) communication are.

The focus of the chapter then turns to trends and issues in sport events. In sport, the polarisation between 'hard' and 'soft' sports, and between 'kicks' and healthy activities, is going to be stronger, all these trends having an impact on the design of sport events. Case studies of **hybrid events** and green sport events are included.

As the second main focus, the **creative economy** is introduced, with new hybrid formats of events, targeting a new generation of urban nomads; a further case study is included. Trends and issues of events in an urban context are presented as well as the creative interventions of landscape and nature.

The chapter concludes with an outlook on the meeting industry, meetings in future being more intensified, with the participants being more interactive and the locations more inspiring.

Introduction

The world is in constant change, the cycles of consumption and innovation ever shorter. The economy and society are re-inventing themselves. In this era of extreme volatility and permanent (personal and collective) updating, a successful future depends on how we manage complexity and on how we act in a proactive rather than merely a reactive way.

To reach this goal it is necessary to identify the weak signals of the key trends coming up in the next years. After all, product development – including that in the event sector – takes place in a framework defined by the big driving forces such as individualisation, sustainability and digital networks. Corporate foresight tools – always trying to learn from the future – are now used to monitor and forecast these and other trends.

Consumer behaviour is changing, as postmodern consumers have a very complex mind set; they are, as the Italian playwright Umberto Eco has called them, 'truffle pigs of excellence' – hybrid people, demanding hybrid leisure products in one package – simultaneously 'kicks' *and* 'chill out', 'move forward' *and* 'lean back'. Consumers are demanding 1:1 customised products and services, authentic ambience, high convenience and, increasingly, sustainability.

Markets are atomised and target groups fragmented. In this era of value communities and affinity groups, traditional tools of communication in traditional channels won't reach lead users (who are important as brand ambassadors); therefore the use of social media is of increasing importance in event planning and communication. At the same time, smaller events for special peer groups have to be developed *complementary* to mass events.

Future events should contain core values such as:

- communication of the brand essence (either of the organising company or destination);
- compatibility with the hybrid values of consumers (boosting the main event with side acts containing elements of entertainment, fun, interactive transfer of know-how etc.);
- sustainability (CO_2 neutrality should be achieved throughout the business process and throughout the event phases, from before the opening of the event through to after-sales).

All these parameters have a strong impact on the event market, on business strategies, and on the development of new event formats. The volatility of markets, as well as the exploding number of lifestyle peers and value-orientated communities, reinforces the existing fragmentation, a factor which makes traditional channels of communication increasingly inefficient. An old saying by Ronald S. Burt is currently more relevant than ever: 'What you cannot manage in fact, you must manage emotionally'. Events, as the most emotional tool of communication, will be even more appreciated in the future.

Trends and issues in sport events

Sport and body design

In an individualistic society – which allows us to be self-reflective and experimental – sport, body design and (holistic) well-being have an increasing importance. Sport provides the ideal stage to shape our body. The human body turns into a blue-chip asset in the market for attention – 40% of Europeans practise sport at least once a week (Eurobarometer, 2010). An attractive body is a sign of social distinction. But sport is not only a tool for self-branding and identity building, it is also a pillar of a healthy lifestyle, which is more and more important in an ageing society, with a growing number of proactive 'Best Agers'. Sport practised in pure nature is the most appreciated symbol of a healthy lifestyle – many outdoor brands have growth rates of 10% per year and more.

As a mirror of our hybrid society, the polarisation between 'hard' and 'soft' sports, and the consumption of 'kicks' and healthy activities is going to be stronger.

Extreme sports

Hardcore sports have been reflecting *one* part of society's and customers' mind set for many years, a mind set focused on fitness, power and speed. Adrenalin-driven sports, such as speed boating, free styling, river bugging and free running, are 'Darwinistic' symbols of our non-stop society, with its culture of 'survival of the fittest'.

Extreme events like the adventure racing *Red Bull X-Alps* reflect our performance-orientated society – the world's best athletes cross the Alps from Austria to France, as quickly as possible, travelling by paraglider or simply on foot. Cross-country events like *X-Alps* or races like *X-Fighters* (a freestyle motocross tour on a global level, featuring the world's best motorbike riders), also organised by Red Bull, contain the brand essence of future events – breathtaking locations and spectacular riders pushing their personal boundaries.

Extreme sports have a lot to do with the main goal of the leisure industry: providing happiness (in case of extreme sports, by boosting one's ego). After all, endorphin-driven sports promise an escape from the daily routine, with a high dose of kicks on demand. Leisure entrepreneurs deal in happiness and have to consider that their clients are 'junkies' – for them, the dose has to be augmented step by step, which is why extreme sports are going to be differentiated and customised.

Hybrid sports

Living in a hybrid society, where the borders are softening in any field and between various branches, we are observing an increasing number of cross-products, especially in sports. Trend sports in general combine aspects of various activities, often paradoxical elements. This is part of their attraction among young people, who expect hip innovations (mostly they are the innovators themselves) and surprising features.

Cross-sports and border-line sports target especially young and 'freaky' consumers, who prefer being beyond the mainstream, and who create fun activities in extraordinary surroundings. Unusual events like the *Wok World Championship* (see Case 21.1) or the *Autoball World Championship* (autoball is a version of football played in cars, using an exercise ball to score goals) are rising steadily as new hybrid events formats in order to

---

Case 21.1   Wok World Championship

Wok racing is a hybrid format, developed by the German TV host and entertainer Stefan Raab. In this crazy 'sport' event, athletes race down bobsled tracks on modified Chinese woks in timed runs. The participants compete in one-person woksleds and four-person woksleds.

The Wok Championship first took place in Winterberg in Germany in 2003, and was then transferred to Innsbruck, Austria. Among the participants are B-stars of the entertainment worlds (music, fashion, TV), as well as famous athletes with ongoing professional careers. One of them, Georg Hackl, famous Olympic luge champion from Germany, won the one-person wok races in the last couple of years. He also holds the speed record for one-person wok (91.70 km/h).

The so-called 'World Wok Racing Championships' are aired as a special edition of Stefan Raab's TV show *TV Total* on the German TV channel ProSieben. As the event is obviously explicitly developed for television (which is not typical for sport events) and because the profits benefit the network directly, it is labelled as an 'infomercial'.

Source: http://tvtotal.prosieben.de/tvtotal/specials/wok_wm2011

Discussion questions

1 What is your opinion about such mergers of sport and entertainment? Are they events symbolic of a fun society, or do they have any additional value?

2 As a destination manager, would you choose such events to promote your location?

attract young visitors. These events are designed to be a strategic mix of sport, fun, entertainment and celebrity shows (as the participants are mostly celebrities from the worlds of sport, fashion, film, etc.) explicitly for TV shows – therefore they are ideal for brand communication with this clearly defined target group.

Cross-events correspond to hybrid values of consumers. Pure sports events will always be attractive, but, nevertheless, special affinity groups are addicted to cross-events combining elements of sport, entertainment, fashion and high tech. One of the most spectacular events in this segment is *Hannibal,* which has taken place since 2001 in the Tyrolean Ötztal. This co-production of the second biggest Austrian destination, Sölden (with more than 2 million overnight stays just in the small village itself), the famous Red Bull brand and Lawine Torrèn (see *www.torren.at/en/lawine-torren/info.html*), is based on a creative script: the historic Alpine crossing of Hannibal is beamed up in the 21st century.

The spectacular scenery of the Rettenbach glacier by night facilitates tremendous illumination and sound effects, with a cast of 500 actors – Hannibal's soldiers are ski runners, mountain climbers, parachutists, skidoo drivers and so on. This event might not be ecologically sound because of its hundreds of high-tech instruments installed in the middle of the glacier, leading to enormous energy consumption, but it communicates the core values of Sölden as a destination hot spot in the Alps – power and energy.

Sport – and this is one of the important characteristics of future activities – will be much more embedded in a different and unexpected context (for example, street sports are practised in nature and vice versa). Street surfing, free running, parcours, cross-golfing, cross-bocia, etc. are examples of these trend sports, practised in an urban context by an increasing number of young people. The public space (cities, landscape, etc.) is turning into a playground and becoming a three-dimensional stage – with events typical for a creative destination.

Other cross-sports like wake boarding, cross-mountain bike, Nordic-cross, snow kajak, stand-up paddling, disc golfing, snow biking and mountain boarding are making leisure locations like sea and mountains much 'cooler' and more attractive to younger people. New event formats like trail running correspond to small peer activities – the runners have to cross the Alps in a tandem team.

▪ Soft sports

Sportive activities have many different aspects and do not only provide adrenalin kicks. Another main aspect is that of fitness and pleasure by soft activity: 57% of Germans like to hike, and the main motive for them is not primarily physical performance but to enjoy nature and landscape (Deutsches Wanderinstitut, 2008). Therefore new trails in the Alps (e.g. in Tyrol) are designed for 'convenience' hikers, who prefer to hike easily through beautiful natural scenery. There are organised walking events for normal people, like the most famous one in the Alps, the fan walk of Hansi Hinterseer, an Austrian pop star, which attracts 12,000 fans to walk with him up into the mountains, singing and praying, each year.

In an ageing society (in all Western industrialised countries, the 45+ generation is the biggest and most attractive target group) the trend towards soft sports is obvious. Pure nature is considered to provide energy, and leisure consumers more and more likely to combine fitness activities with an outdoor feeling. Nature is becoming a 'vitality park', a stage for proactive Best Agers. Nordic sports, hiking, etc. are among the most popular activities, but there are new ones emerging, such as sea walking (a new trend in France, where one walks, in small groups, inside the water along the shore, fighting against the waves).

Finally, sport events don't only provide 'kicks', fitness and community; they can have an added social value as well. An increasing number of young people participate in sport events with a social goal. Competitions like the *youwave Bowlingcup* or *Sailing4Good*

Event combine sportive activities with social engagement, the goal being the support of social projects. As Nelson Mandela said: 'Sport has the power to change the world'. Social sport events as a symbol for personal social responsibility meet the values of a younger generation.

■ Polarisation between mega and peer events

In a postmodern hybrid society not only is the polarisation between hard and soft sports evident, but also the polarisation between mega and micro (peer) events.

The big sport events – a major tool of live communication for companies and destinations – will always play the main role in the event landscape, as they build up a strong *community* feeling and provide a high dose of emotions. But complementary sport events will increasingly have the touch of smaller meetings with peer activities. As the origin of subculture, trend sports build up communities and strengthen peer groups. It is a culture of hidden places and non-habitual locations, from backyards to bridges – this is where youngsters are coming together for their cross-sports.

Sport events, for sure, are instruments of brand communication. Mega events in particular can boost the image of a destination. We are living in an economy of attention. Main sport events, more than any other event (be it cultural, or for entertainment) attract this attention via symbols, heroes and stories. This is why destinations worldwide try to be part of the game and attract famous sport events such as Formula 1 Grand Prix, Champions League, the WTA tournaments, the America's Cup, etc.

In any case, an event should be brand-orientated, and transmit the core values of the brand (the goals, as well as the target groups, should be well-defined, otherwise events can lose money). Many top destinations, for example in the Alps, are organising big sport events such as marathons, triathlons and mountain bike races to attract attention and people. But do these events always communicate the brand values? Do they guarantee any differentiation?

There are, in my professional consulting experience, only a few alpine destinations (even amongst the leading ones) with a precise brand communication via sport events – for example, Austria's Kitzbühel ('the most legendary city of sports', as it brands itself) and St Moritz in Switzerland (where sport events in general follow the branding 'top of the world'). However, the consciousness in tourism destinations is changing, as event planning becomes increasingly professional and measured (from the pre-event stage to the post-event stage) (see Luppold and Rück, 2011: 253), as destination managers increasingly understand the importance of sport events as real-time communication of their brand message.

Sport events are ideal branding tools when sport reflects the key values of the location. For example, Oklahoma City in the USA is the number one destination for rowing, kayaking and other water sports. The Boathouse District surrounding the Oklahoma River is a hot spot for athletes, but also for families practising water sports and for corporate events such as team building by rowing. Races and regattas take place throughout the whole year, and the US Olympic Committee has recognised the Oklahoma River as a location for US Olympic and Paralympic Training. The city underlines its 'water competence' with a highly developed infrastructure.

The city of Klagenfurt, situated on Wörthersee, an Austrian lake, had its best time in the 1960s and 1970s. The lake was, in that era, one of the most popular holiday destinations in Austria during summer time, and the happy few used to socialise there in their chalets and the grand hotels. But with the rise of new sun and beach destinations and a much more complex lifestyle, Wörthersee (like many other lakes in Central Europe) lost its appeal and became – in the eyes of a lifestyle-orientated clientele – boring. The decline of the whole destination was obvious. The lake had to be boosted in a new way to, again, become a trendy spot.

It was in 1997 that the first beach volleyball competition took place, forming a community which slowly grew. The 1990s was the era of beach volleyball all over the world, following its breakthrough in Almeria (Spain) in 1992, as a counterpart to the Olympic Games.

Today, the Beach Volleyball Grand Slam at Klagenfurt is a premium sport event, famous for top athletes, high-end entertainment and an iconic location. Spectacular tournaments with international stars, and side acts such as air shows and pop concerts have pushed forward the whole destination, which is now frequented by frenetic young lifestyle-orientated clients. In 2011 the event had 135,000 visitors. For Wörthersee as a destination brand this festival was better than a dose of Viagra.

Special outdoor arenas like Area 47 in the Tyrolean Ötztal (with facilities such as a rubber tube, climbing area, water ramps, where 'adrenaline junkies' can develop their jumping skills and work on their creative stunts on skis) are ideal venues for trend sport and future holiday destinations, because they provide an all-inclusive adventure.

Green events

Society is facing a change in values focused on the holistic quality of life in economic, ecological and social terms. Lead consumers and early adopters, like the so-called 'Lohas' (Lifestyle of Health and Sustainability), demand sustainable products which are ethically and socially correct, as well as being regional and conveying an authentic spirit.

This new Green Deal of the second decade is reconciling economy with ecology, as well as regional value chains with global competitiveness. It is focusing consumer values as well as a responsible, sustainable management of existing resources. Consumers' eco-awareness is due to external factors (energy costs, climate protection, etc.), but additionally has a lot to do with social aspects (higher level of education, more ethical value orientation, etc.).

Eco-awareness is rising and has a strong impact on the culture of products in nearly every sector, including in the event branches. The 'greening' of tourism is, in the medium term, changing the tourism infrastructure. Sustainable tourism is based on regional value chains (networks of local suppliers, local producers of food, etc.) and is including renewable energy concepts – e-tourism, in the meaning of energy efficiency, electro mobility, etc.).

In the long term, destinations which organise green events will be rewarded by greater public acceptance, as 'the tourism sector has discovered the value of the mega trend "sustainability", but has not at all tapped the full potential' (Willers and Agata Kulik, 2011: 311).

Green leadership cannot be achieved by any destination – a global hot spot with an enormous frequency of guests has a different starting position compared with a small Alpine village, for example – but it is an important factor of differentiation.

Case 21.2	Green Mountain-biking World Cup in Schladming, Austria

Starting with a pilot project 'Green Event' in 2006, Schmalding, a sports destination in the Styrian Alps, was the first among the top Alpine destinations to organise sustainable events. The organisers demonstrated how big events can correspond to social and ecological correctness and be successful in economic terms too.

Main focus:

2006 Pilot project 'Green Event'
2007 CO_2 neutrality
2008 Barrier-free sport events
2009 Climate protection and social media

Case 21.2   *(continued)*

For the organising team of the high-end competition it was a strategic challenge to use the resources in an economic and sustainable way. Key factors were identified: energy efficiency, climate neutrality (the event in total is organised to be CO_2 neutral), smart mobility concepts (reduction of individual traffic, cooperation with public transport – railways, free citybus during event), waste management, regional catering, gender mainstreaming, free entry for handicapped persons, etc., social media marketing and communication.

Key facts:

15–20,000 visitors

11,000 additional overnight stays in the region

Total revenue: +€500,000

Enormous media response: 250 accredited journalists from 19 nations, 20 international TV stations, international coverage (230 hours), new target markets in Central and Eastern Europe

Discussion questions

3 How serious do you consider green sport events to be, when addressed to a mass public?

4 With respect to the 'Green Games' in London 2012, discuss the opportunities of value communication, and the risks of green-washing.

Trends and issues in culture

Creative economy

In a networked information-based society values of creative branches such as creativity, flexibility and self-fulfilment are core. Boundaries between products, services and consumption are softening. In an economy driven by innovation and competition, creativity is the most important competitiveness factor. Creative industries are, with their mostly patchwork-orientated life and project-based work, role models for a new work–life balance.

Creative economy is considered to be – especially in urban agglomerations – a growth market with interesting future prospects. In Vienna, for example, more than 100,000 jobs and 18,000 companies represent the creative sector; in London every third job is in the creative industries. The creative sector can be divided into creative professionals (people working in information-based jobs) and super-creatives (scientists, researchers, technicians, artists, designers, etc.).

Creative excellence is a highly important location factor and has a strong impact on the identity and the well-being of a location. This excellence grows in the context of high-tech labour, cultural and sub-cultural scenes, and in the convergence of campus, media and creative agents.

In the battle for talents every city tries to attract the creative milieu – highly qualified young people with great brain power. These people, mobile and sought on an international level, have special needs and lifestyle values, as far as infrastructure, place of work, amenities (hotels, bars, restaurants) and cultural and social life are concerned. In short, they are the key drivers of improvement of local quality of life. An 'advanced lifestyle' is attractive for creative people.

Considering the rising importance of the creative class, creativity plays an important role in place making and place branding. The vibrancy of culture is one key factor determining a global city brand (Anholt, 2009: 17), and high-performing cities like Copenhagen 'strike a balance between efficiency and creativity' (Moilanen and Rainisto, 2009: 91).

Creative city

The 'creative city' is a new type of city brand, standing for coolness and advanced, future-orientated lifestyles. Cities like London, Amsterdam, Barcelona or Berlin can be considered as prototypes, but also second cities like Liverpool, Antwerp or Helsinki communicate the brand message of being a cultural hot spot with a vibrant, creative scenery.

In this creative place branding, the role of events as communication tools cannot be underlined enough. For example, the Life Ball in Vienna (see *www.lifeball.org/index.php?option=com_content&view=article&id=117&Itemid=80&lang=en*), the (sub-)cultural and creative top event of the Austrian capital, has helped greatly in transforming the city's image from an imperial city to a modern creative metropolis. The Life Ball today is known as one of the most powerful AIDS charity events in the world, creating enormous interest and media attention, especially because of its extraordinary creative performances.

In Berlin, the most vibrant city on the European continent, the Bread & Butter fashion trade show (see *www.breadandbutter.com/winter2012-hifi*), an event for the contemporary clothing sector, is not only a European brand in the textile industry, but it also underlines Berlin's role as a creative city, where talents from all over the world are boosted by the special spirit of the location.

Urban living means complexity, irritation and inspiration, and it guarantees a variety of experiences. The attractions offered have to be adapted to new lifestyle tendencies and the changing mind-set of new 'urbanites'. Cities all over the world have brought to perfection their management of attractions, and their iconic branding, by installing new spaces of experiences, hip locations and cool events. But in a way they all look the same: the same style of brand lands and green towers built by international star architects, urban lounges, waterscapes and city beaches, as well as the same type of events (city marathons, street parades, etc.).

A city brand cannot achieve differentiation via the conventional management of cool spaces alone. A repetitive product semantic has led to many cities being homogenised as far as possible.

Creative tourists

Cities and cultural venues have to meet the needs of a new generation of creative tourists. These lead users have a high level of education and interests beyond the mainstream. Creative tourists would like to experience events and meetings in a new and unusual context, beyond their ordinary everyday lives. 'People nowadays aren't visiting a city for its urban history or cultural specialties, but because of the sensory enhancement, which it promises' (Design2context, 2010: 132).

Modern urban visitors not only want to be surprised – they are searching for the original spirit of a city, an authentic dialogue with locals, the 'live like a local' feeling. Core values for these urban nomads are:

- self experience;
- community;
- authenticity.

Urban culture is slowly but substantially changing as a result of new urban change agents, the creative class. Not only do they demand new forms of amenities (hotels are out, private facilities with contact with locals are in), but also new types of retailing and services such as pop-up stores (fashion brands like Camper are making use of this new type of temporary retailing), guerrilla restaurants (opened only in private apartments for special guests), guerrilla bakeries, etc. You will be informed about new events via flash mobs or a special message through a Facebook group. Interested only in events and locations outside the mainstream, away from the conventional tourist trail and preferring backyards, creative tourists are mainly attracted to 'rough' cities such as Berlin or New York.

Modern urbanites want to interact with public space; movements such as 'Urban Knitting' (telephone boxes, lampposts, etc. are covered – overnight – in knitted wool) demonstrate this attitude. What began in US cities and has now (discreetly) spread over the world does not have much to do with making places prettier; rather, it shows the need of people to shape their city (if only on a very small scale). Be it street art (by now probably recognised as an established art form) or artistic performances like 'skip conversion' (where skips are turned into swimming pools or table tennis tables, for example, by young people), public space is being converted.

Street art and graffiti are symbols of a new dialogue between resident, visitor and public space. Postmodern urbanites want to find unusual areas which they can experience themselves in a new way. If you have ever seen the giant 3D painting by the German artist Edgar Müller (*Turning Riverstreet into a river*, viewable at *www.zimbio.com/ pictures/AQyV5S3lydC/3D+Street+Art+Artist+Edgar+Mueller+Paintings/0m7hixJux6m*, is considered to be, at about 280 square metres, the largest 3D street painting ever done) during the Festival of World Culture in the Irish town of Dun Laoghaire, you will always remember your own sensations and feelings.

◼ Landscape intervention

New creative, interactive experiences might not only take place in urban spaces, but also in landscapes and tourist destinations. One example of landscape intervention can be seen for the period of two years in Vorarlberg, a small region in the western part of Austria: the installation, called Horizon Field (see www.bregenzerwald.at/xxl/en/839987/_articleId/ 1340736/index.html) comprises 100 iron casts of a human body spread over an area of 150 square kilometres in the mountains of the Hinterer Bregenzerwald, the Kleinwalsertal and the Arlberg. This landscape installation in the high Alps, produced by Kunsthaus

---

Case 21.3 The BMW Guggenheim Lab

In a hybrid world, the role of companies and institutions is changing. Future-orientated companies understand themselves as active parts of society and as driving forces of socio-cultural changes. That is why lifestyle brands such as Adidas, BMW, Audi and many others participate in social and cultural projects. These projects and events are not only communication tools, but also part of the inner development of companies, which are trying to learn from consumers and citizens.

One of the most outstanding projects of this type was the BMW Guggenheim Lab, founded in August 2011. This lab was a hybrid form of urban think tank, community centre and public gathering space. Young talents from all over the world, from different disciplines such as architecture, urbanism, art, design, science and technology, discussed issues relevant to better urban living.

The lab was mobile, travelling to the cities of New York, Berlin and Mumbai before culminating with an exhibition at the Guggenheim Museum in New York. Its goal was the exploration of new ideas, experimentation and the creation of innovative solutions for the problems associated with city life. The lab consisted of three distinct mobile structures as well as three distinct thematic cycles. Each structure was designed by a different specialist, for example an artist, an architect or a scientist. In each of the chosen cities, the team convened to develop ideas around the cycle's theme. The BMW Guggenheim Lab communicated issues and projects via its website and social communities. The public was invited to attend and to participate in free programmes and experiments at the lab.

Source: www.guggenheim.org/guggenheim-foundation/collaborations/bmw-guggenheim

---

Discussion questions

5 What are the challenges companies like BMW face in participating in such interactive projects and events?

6 Do such projects have an impact on brand awareness and on the image of the company?

Bregenz together with the British sculptor Antony Gormley, is a highlight in the modern management of nature attractions. Visitors can explore for themselves the landscape in a new and unexpected way. Gormley is also responsible for a similar installation called *Another Place* at Formby in northern England (see *www.sefton.gov.uk/default. aspx?page=6216*).

In South Tyrol, the artist Franz Messner has installed 30 wooden seats on the top of a mountain. It is a 'nature' cinema in the open air, high above the city of Meran. You take a seat and watch the most interesting 'film' you can get – nature and the clouds passing by. The natural scenery is impressive and you have a unique and an interesting experience.

Creative communities

The wind has changed. The cat walk was still predominant in the 2000s, with the orchestration of the public area as a stage, with events such Christopher Street Days (CSD). Nowadays the city area increasingly mutates into a three-dimensional space. Creating a young image and attracting young talents, be it as tourists or residents, can only be achieved with openness towards new trends.

The changing of consumers' behaviour towards making use of one's surroundings is reflected in the variety of urban trend sports. Trend sports such as free running, street bouldering and buildering (also known as urban climbing) are, among others, manifestations of an experimental acquisition of public space by young people. Some climb bridges, others 'house' walls and others jump across garage roofs. These performances are an expression of specific lifestyles (and a great viral marketing tool for the city when communicating over Web 2.0) and belong to what Vejlgaard (2010) has characterised as 'the lifestyle puzzle'.

A famous example is the Eisbach in the centre of Munich. The fast-running river through the Englischer Garten (English Garden) is still good for a unique adrenalin kick, even though by now it is already established as an icon (see *www.360cities.net/image/ surfing-at-eisbach-munich-germany#-61.97,3.26,60.0*). Young surfers made use of a raging point of the Eisbach to surf (illegally, of course) many years ago; the reputation of this hot spot then spread rapidly worldwide among the surfer community, leading to devotees tucking their surfboards under their arms and heading for Munich. In particular, such non-constructed but developed experience spaces are a part of the urban quality of life.

This temporary utilisation, which began a few years ago with the pop-up stores from the fashion industry, picks up an important characteristic from lead users – they make use of the city; they (re)produce public leeway.

The future belongs to those communities where locals and visitors come together for a limited period of time. Visitors and entrepreneurs form a kind of value-orientated community. This is what some boutique hotels have understood, notably the ones frequented by young people. The Hotel Cosmo in Berlin knows that guests and hosts are affinity groups, which have the same spirit and thus choose each other.

COSMO knows the people and places that move and stir Berlin. The COSMO concierge is your connection to the local scene and recommends to you the hottest restaurants, bars and clubs in town. He knows where the avant-garde of Berlin lives art and culture. For the ultimate shopping experience he sends you to the up-and-coming designers of and in Berlin.

(Cosmo, undated, *www.cosmo-hotel.de/en/philosophy*)

The 'cosmos' of the hotel community appears on the hotel's website: a variety of galleries, clubs, boutiques and bars in the hotel's periphery. Same spirit, same venue.

In Berlin **peer events** are very popular, with young people joining together in clubs to watch TV instead of watching television programmes by themselves at home. The value of community in an anonymous city is rising – even lectures and small art performances take place in private apartments.

In Barcelona the young boutique hotel *Chic & Basic* acts in a similar way: when entering your room, you find a brochure 'This is not another guide of Barcelona', but which does include listings of the hot spots and cool amenities of the city. The hotel is a community building, and shows the changing role of providers and their clients within a lifestyle-oriented community.

Outlook on the meeting industry

We are living in an information society; economic performance is mainly based on information and the creative implementation of knowledge. So the meeting industry as a lifetime provider of information (through meetings, conferences, etc.) does play an important role in the value chain of each company. In a global economy, international links are getting stronger, involving the *personal* transfer of know-how, which, despite high-tech communication tools and ubiquitous computing, is going to be intensified in the future. Markets are conversation.

As far as the formats are concerned, we can observe a polarisation, too, between main meetings and smaller, more interactive meetings. Obviously, more and more interactive elements are entering the dramaturgy, the art of dramatic composition and representation, of even big meetings, for example through the use of open spaces, structured working groups, world cafés (small groups with changing participants), etc. Participants are in general more (inter)active – rather than just consuming lectures they want to be an integral part proceedings and appreciated as part of the process of knowledge streaming.

No wonder that formats like BarCamps – a special (and more informal) form of open space conferences – are popular among social media addicts. BarCamps or MiceCamps are international networks of 'non-conferences'. The participants themselves design the programme and the issues of the meeting, everyone can speak, and the programme consists of lectures and sessions. The discussions, and their conclusions, are communicated via social web platforms and/or live streams. Experimental formats like BarCamps are necessary to develop the traditional ones, and to find a fertile symbiosis between organised and informal transfer of know-how.

As well as the format, the duration and the venue are important issues for meeting planners. The duration of conferences is getting shorter, but they are becoming more concentrated. Side acts are increasingly important. It is the whole package that counts, and in particular the balance between know-how and entertainment.

Know-how transfer requires inspiration – and this depends on inspiring venues too. And the traditional four-star hotel as a meeting location? Meeting managers develop more and more unusual venues, conferences taking place on cruise ships, in factories, monasteries (traditional power places), etc.

Last but not least, meetings are going to be greener. The label **green meeting** may sound like green-washing, but a venue without a green certification – for example, the Green Globe certification system (see *http://greenglobe.com*) at an international level – will not be acceptable in the future. Sustainable management of resources throughout the business process is a key factor for success as well as for social responsibility. Areas requiring sustainable management practices include:

- reduction of CO_2;
- energy efficiency;
- regional catering;

- regional supply chain;
- waste management;
- smart mobility (intelligent mix of public and private transport, e-mobility);
- social welfare and gender mainstreaming, etc.

Conclusion

Events are, in a fragmented society, powerful instruments of (brand) communication, if they succeed in communicating the brand essence and the brand values, and if they are addressed to a clearly defined target group.

In sport, the polarisation between extreme and soft sports is going to be stronger. Hardcore sports reflect *one* part of society's and the customer's mind set: fitness, power, speed. Extreme events reflect our performance-orientated society.

Younger consumers are especially attracted to cross-sports, preferring to be beyond the mainstream. Cross-events, such as the Wok Championship, correspond to the hybrid values of consumers. Pure sport events will always be attractive (and an ideal medium for the communication of brand messages), but nevertheless special affinity groups can be addicted to cross-events combining elements of sport, entertainment, fashion and high tech.

Soft sports for Best Agers as well as green events have an increasing importance in the leisure industry.

In an economy driven by innovation, events (like, for example, the Life Ball in Vienna) play an important part in creative place making and place branding. New creative formats of events, targeting urban nomads, are coming up, and public spaces turn into playgrounds for interactive youngsters participating in their trend sports in surprising surroundings. Creative communities, linked by the same lifestyle values and by social media, are attracting both residents and tourists.

The outlook for events in general is absolutely positive. Events are getting greener, more interactive and more inspiring.

Guided reading

Issues and new trends in sport and culture may be investigated through a range of sources. Journals such as, at an academic level, the *Journal of Sport Management* and *European Sport Management Quarterly,* and lifestyle magazines such as *Red Bulletin, Monocle* and *Monopol* provide a rich source of information in either sport or creative industries.

A further source of valuable information is corporate publishing, and in particular the websites of companies that are leaders in their sector, such as Adidas, Nike, Red Bull, BMW and Audi are worth reading. Generally the monitoring of websites is recommended (some of them are listed below).

Recommended websites

Cool Hunting: **www.coolhunting.com**

The Berg: **www.the-berg.de** (in English)

The Cool Hunter: **www.thecoolhunter.net**

Key words

creative economy; cross-sports; green meeting; hybrid events; peer event

Bibliography

Anholt, S. (2009) *European Travel Commission Handbook on Tourism Destination Branding*. Madrid: World Tourism Organisation.

Design2context (2010) *The World's Fairest City – Yours and Mine: Features of Urban Living Quality*. Zurich: Lars Müller Publishers.

Deutsches Wanderinstitut (2008) *Profilstudie Wandern. Das aktuelle Barometer zum neuen Wandermarkt. Repräsentative Befragung von Wanderern. National- und Regionalstudien. Trends und Zielgruppen*. Lohra: Deutsches Wanderinstitut.

Eurobarometer (2010) *Sport and Physical Activity*. Brussels: European Commission.

Luppold, S. and Rück, H. (2011) Event controlling and performance measurement. In R. Conrady and M. Buck (eds), *Trends and Issues in Global Tourism 2011*. Heidelberg: Springer.

Moilanen, T. and Rainisto, S. (2009) *How to Brand Nations, Cities and Destinations. A Planning Book for Place Branding*. Basingstoke: Palgrave Macmillan.

Vejlgaard, H. (2010) *The Lifestyle Puzzle: Who We Are in the 21st Century*. New York: Prometheus.

Willers, C. and Agata Kulik, A. (2011) CSR as Corporate Strategy vs. 'Greenwashing'. In R. Conrady and M. Buck (eds), *Trends and Issues in Global Tourism 2011*. Heidelberg: Springer.

Glossary

active participation: To move away from a state of ambient participation where an event merely 'happens' around you to becoming more engaged in an event.

ambush marketing: A promotional strategy whereby a non-sponsor attempts to capitalise on the popularity or prestige of a property by giving the false impression that it is a sponsor.

appreciative theory: A model of thought that frames each issue with a positive or affirmative perspective and involves an exploration of possibilities and potential actions to move forward.

architectural competition: A selection method to decide on an architect and a building design which best fulfils the investor's requirements.

arts management: A special form of understanding management processes as a tool to create, enable, support and follow developments within arts scenarios with the focus on the different expectations and needs of these scenes in comparison with other economic fields.

audience development: A set of changing tools and instruments to gain new audiences for cultural institutions and an attempt to break down conventional barriers of access to cultural productions.

baby boomers: Those born between 1946 and 1964.

barriers to access: Those barriers, both physical and psychological, that prevent people from participating in societal events.

behavioural-based theory: A model of thought that is concerned with 'goals, expectations and choice'.

bidding costs: The costs which a venue must incur to put forward a bid to host a future event to a franchising organisation such as the IOC or FIFA.

brand: The features and characteristics of any product which, in combination, identify that product as different from its competitors.

brand awareness: Consumers' ability to recall a brand when the competitive landscape in which the brand competes is mentioned.

break-even analysis: The process of calculating the number of units to be sold (e.g. tickets) at which the income exactly balances the costs.

business model: As part of an organisation's business strategy, the business model describes the way it creates, delivers and captures value (economic, social, cultural).

business plan: The statement of the organisation's goals and how it intends to achieve them.

business-to-business communication: Direct communication between two business organisations; frequently abbreviated as B2B communication.

catering: The provision of food on a commercial basis.

commissioning brief: A document that sets out the specific requirements from the perspective of those seeking the event to be delivered. It will include detail on the objectives, any essential requirements or constraints and the budget available.

contingency plan: A course of action to be followed if a preferred plan fails or an existing situation changes.

contract: A legally binding agreement between two or more parties; a promise or set of promises which the law will enforce.

co-opetition: This is a characteristic challenge in event tourism management; compared to other industries, the collaboration of competing suppliers is necessary.

corporate hospitality: The entertainment of business clients in the context of an event.

corporate social responsibility (CSR): A concept which describes the status and activities of an organisation with respect to its perceived societal reputation.

cost–benefit analysis: A standardised system for evaluating the net benefit or cost of a project taking into consideration economic, social and environmental factors.

creative economy: Important pillar of urban economy, focusing on creative and intellectual talents.

creative industries: A perspective to connect different economic fields which deal with creative ideas with the goal of improving the infrastructure of cities and improving awareness for the potential of these scenes beyond the cultural sector.

creative origination: The development of an idea that is new and original in its field.

cross-sports: Sports combining product paradoxities and/or elements of different sports (for example, Nordic cross, cross-golfing, cross-bocia). Embedded in an unexpected context (for example street sports practised in the mountains).

cultural imperialism: The creation and reinforcement of cultural hegemony. The imposition of power of one culture over another through media, education and the assertion of values.

cultural policies: political measurements to structure cultural actions and ideas for society.

demand determinants: Aspects that influence the amount of demand for a good or service.

demographics: Objective statistical characteristics of a particular audience.

destination: In a tourism context, a place (town, city, region or even country) which serves as a focal point for people to visit.

economic impact: A measure of the money that will flow into or out of a region specifically because of the presence of a particular event.

economic impact study: A study in which the possible economic impacts, positive and negative, of a project are evaluated.

event: A singular or recurring planned occasion which is arranged at a certain place. It involves one or more people and is made accessible to an audience (present on site or participating via technical facilities).

event life cycle: This defines the stages of an event from the concept to the hosting of the event, the post-event phase, and subsequent tourism developments.

event planning: Setting goals for the organisation and its members and specifying the activities or programme through which to achieve those goals.

event portfolio: A series of events that take place at different times of the year, which appeal to multiple consumers across a range of psychographic profiles to which an event or destination seeks to appeal.

event sponsorship: Cash and/or in-kind fee paid by the sponsor to an (existing) event in return for access to the exploitable commercial potential associated with the event; based on a mutual exchange between event and sponsor.

event tourism: A systematic planning, development and marketing of festivals and special events as tourist attractions, image makers, catalysts for infrastructure and economic growth, and animators of built attractions.

events 2.0: A new way of interactive event staging. The aim of such events is to combine the best of the real world with the best of the virtual world in order to create a convergent event experience world.

ex-ante **study:** A study which is conducted before an event.

ex-post **study:** A study which is conducted after an event.

feasibility study: An in-depth analysis of the risks, opportunities and feasibility of an idea to be successfully transformed into a business.

Gantt chart: A type of bar chart that illustrates a project schedule. Gantt charts illustrate the start and finish dates of the terminal elements and summary elements of a project. Terminal elements and summary elements comprise the work breakdown structure of the project. Some Gantt charts also show the dependency (that is, the precedence network) relationships between activities.

generation Y: Those born between 1980 and 1999.

grassroots event: An amateur, not-for-profit, community sports event or programme.

green meeting: Meeting organised in a sustainable way all along the value chain.

hybrid events: Events combining elements of sport, entertainment, fashion and high tech.

insurance: Agreement that for regular small payments the insurer's company will pay compensation for loss, damage, injury or death.

interactive event tools: Tools developed for immersively involving the guest in the event. They build a bridge between the virtual and real level in events management.

jurisdiction: The legal power of a court to hear and decide on a case before it (e.g. in a geographical area or subject matter).

knowledge transfer: The process of transferring knowledge from one part of an organisation to another (or all other) part(s) of an organisation.

liability: An obligation or duty imposed by the law – being financially and legally responsible for something. An amount of money being owed to somebody (e.g. damages as a financial compensation awarded by a court for a loss suffered by the claimant in an action for breach of contract or tort).

life cycle model: A model which deals with a facility by considering the entire life of the asset.

management: The organisation and coordination of a company's activities (or alternatively in the context of a planned venture) which are predetermined in order to reach defined targets.

management accounting: The branch of accounting which is concerned with the internal finances of an organisation in order to produce financial data which will be useful to managers for planning purposes.

marginalised groups: Those groups living on the fringe of society as a result of social exclusion brought about via a denial of a range of opportunities and resources.

media: The forms of mass communication; typical examples are newspapers and television, and, increasingly, social media such as Twitter and Facebook.

milestone: This is an occurrence which is important for the content of a project. A milestone is assigned a binding deadline and the completion of a major task.

mobile events: Events that move from place to place in a national, international or global context. In today's competitive world, cities, regions and nations compete in attracting mobile events whose rights are usually held by stakeholders such as international sports federations, political institutions (e.g. the European Commission) or other important stakeholders, such as the Bureau Internationale des Expositions or the European Broadcasting Corporation.

motivation: The reason which drives particular behaviour patterns towards specified goals.

networking: The cultivation of productive personal relationships for employment or business.

operations management: When managing event projects, operations management is the specific part of project management which deals with the actual realisation of an event (i.e. refers to the implementation phase – providing the service).

organisational culture: The collective behaviours and values which are specific to individual organisations.

peer event: Event for special affinity and lifestyle groups.

philosophy of games: A philosophical base for the understanding of the common historical and social source of sports and culture.

place events: Events that happen again and again in the same place and thus the place is associated with the event. The event may have historic origins or have developed as result of a clever event strategy to host the same event in the same place on a very regular basis (most often annually).

plan B: A popular term used to mean a reserved, secondary plan, in case a first plan (a hypothetical 'plan A') fails.

procurement: The acquisition, at the most economical cost, of goods, works or services which are required either as a raw material or for operational purposes for a company.

profession(s): According to functionalist theories of Anglo-American sociology, professions can be defined by means of a list of characteristic features which are applicable, for example, to the legal and medical profession. These are: (1) the existence of a self-governing professional association as well as (2) a code of ethics, (3) a theory-based academic formation, (4) the perception of the occupation as a service for the public good and, last but not least (5) social prestige and reputation.

project: A temporary venture (alternatively: an organisation, a task) for the purpose of achieving a predetermined goal. Projects, in contrast to processes, are non-recurring and have to show a measure of complexity and risk potential in order to be rightfully classed as such.

project crisis: An extreme situation which is characterised by serious deviations of the course of the project from the plan. In the worst case such deviations may put the continuation of the project at risk.

project management: Includes any planning, implementation and controlling activities which are intentionally performed in the course of a project and which contribute to achieving the goal: i.e. starting (planning), coordinating, controlling and concluding projects.

project planning: A structured procedure which comes under the terms of the start process. It includes all the steps which are required at the start and during the project itself in order to depict the project comprehensively and in all its dimensions. Project planning uses various tools for setting the scope of the project (services, schedules, resources, goals, persons involved etc.) and for analysing the project context. A project is usually planned in a workshop, or several workshops, and in consultation with the project owner.

public–private partnership project: An infrastructural project jointly organised by the public and the private sectors whereby the public sector partner transfers investments to the private sector partner.

request for proposal (RFP): A document prepared by event organisers for host cities, facilities and vendors that outlines business requirements for successful selection.

resource-based theory: A model of thought that uses resources as the means to advance performance, including the resources available, how they are utilised, if an advantage can be achieved, including an economic advantage, based on managing the resource.

resource-based view (RBV): RBV sees the organisation's configuration of resources as the basis for entrepreneurial success and the creation of long-term competitive advantage.

risk management: The identification, analysis, assessment, control and avoidance, minimisation or elimination of unacceptable risks.

room concept: The number, capacities, shape, organisation and relationship of an event venue's rooms.

service profit chain (SPC): According to the service profit chain theory there is a direct connection between extraordinary service experiences, customer loyalty and the economic success of a company in terms of profit and growth.

social media: Refers to the means of interactions among people in which they create, share and exchange information and ideas in virtual communities and networks.

social media marketing: A relatively new approach of businesses using new media technologies like the internet, smart phones, RFID, etc. for marketing purposes.

spectator: A person who attends a live event but does not participate.

sponsor: Any corporation or legal person providing financial or other sponsorship support (e.g. products, service, know how) to the sponsored party.

sponsorship: Cash and/or in-kind fee paid to a property in return for access to the exploitable commercial potential associated with the property; based on a mutual exchange between two parties.

stakeholder: A person with an interest or concern in the event.

strategic plan: An organisation's process of defining its strategy or direction, and the making of decisions on allocating its resources to pursue this strategy, be it financial or human resources.

sustainability: In events management this is defined as the 'economic development that serves current needs without having a negative impact on future generations. In other words, it reflects an improvement of the quality of life within the capacity of an ecosystem. It comprises economic, social [cultural] and environmental dimensions'.

sustainability citizenship: The members (individuals and/or groups), in this case members of events, who contribute to achieving sustainability. This can include members such as: events facility staff, event production staff and volunteers, the consumers of events, the media, government partners, sponsors and other event stakeholders. In this text, the members of sustainability citizenship are guided in their role with six guiding principles from the United Nations principles for sustainability education.

sustainable cultural event: A cultural event that has the capacity to endure. This endurance requires a number of factors including demand, economic stability and environmental management.

sustainable event venue management: Running an event facility by taking the three economic, environmental and social sustainability dimensions into consideration, thus, for example, by using energy more efficiently, minimising negative environmental impacts, etc.

target group: A group of people for whom an organisation creates and maintains a marketing mix.

title rights: These rights ensure that the sponsor is named in the title of the event so that all references to the title of the event include the sponsor's corporate, product or brand names as agreed.

utilisation concept: Description of the expected usage of the facility, including, among others, information on potential users of the facility (permanent tenants, event organisers, etc.) and their respective requirements, types, frequency and size of events to be hosted.

value in kind (VIK): Products or services provided to an event instead of cash in exchange for a sponsor relationship or other promotional consideration.

viewer: A person who watches a broadcast of an event, usually, but not necessarily, as the event is taking place.

virtual companies: These are company networks that operate very closely together on the basis of shared resources.

virtual events: An occurrence of people gathering together where some or all of the attendees are not physically in the same location but are connected in a common environment. The common environment is usually enabled through the use of computers and the internet.

volunteer: Person who works without pay, generally for altruistic motives.

Index